CORINTH

———

VOLUME XVIII, PART I

THE SANCTUARY OF DEMETER AND KORE

THE GREEK POTTERY

CORINTH

RESULTS OF EXCAVATIONS

CONDUCTED BY

THE AMERICAN SCHOOL OF CLASSICAL STUDIES

VOLUME XVIII, PART I

THE SANCTUARY OF DEMETER AND KORE

THE GREEK POTTERY

BY

ELIZABETH G. PEMBERTON

WITH A CONTRIBUTION BY

KATHLEEN WARNER SLANE

THE AMERICAN SCHOOL OF CLASSICAL STUDIES AT ATHENS

PRINCETON, NEW JERSEY

1989

19921543 up 7-8-99
9176663 open entry

Library of Congress Cataloging-in-Publication Data

Pemberton, Elizabeth G., 1940–
    The Sanctuary of Demeter and Kore : the Greek pottery / by Elizabeth G. Pemberton with a contribution by Kathleen W. Slane.
        p.   cm. — (Corinth ; v. 18, pt. 1)
    Bibliography: p.
    Includes index.
    ISBN 0-87661-181-1 : $65.00
    1. Pottery, Greek—Greece—Corinth—Catalogs. 2. Pottery—Greece—Corinth—Catalogs. 3. Sanctuary of Demeter and Persephone (Corinth, Greece)—Catalogs. 4. Corinth (Greece)—Antiquities—Catalogs. I. Slane, Kathleen W., 1949– . II. Title. III. Series.
    DF261.C65A6 vol. 18, pt. 1
    938′.7 s—dc20
    [938′.7]   89-15004
                                                     CIP

TYPOGRAPHY BY THE AMERICAN SCHOOL OF CLASSICAL STUDIES PUBLICATIONS OFFICE
C/O INSTITUTE FOR ADVANCED STUDY, PRINCETON, NEW JERSEY
PLATES BY THE MERIDEN-STINEHOUR PRESS, MERIDEN, CONNECTICUT
PRINTED IN THE UNITED STATES OF AMERICA
BY THE TOWN HOUSE PRESS, SPRING VALLEY, NEW YORK

FOREWORD

Volume XVIII of the Corinth series will be devoted to the final publication of the results of the American School excavations in the Sanctuary of Demeter and Kore on Acrocorinth. *Corinth* XVIII, i by E. G. Pemberton is the first in the series to appear and presents the pottery used in the Sanctuary from the Protocorinthian period through 146 B.C. It will be followed by *Corinth* XVIII, ii on the Roman pottery and lamps, by K. W. Slane.

Several aspects of the Sanctuary pottery have been excluded from the present volume. It does not include the Mycenaean pottery from the site, which has been published by J. Rutter in "The Last Mycenaeans at Corinth," *Hesperia* 48, 1979, pp. 348–392. The Protogeometric and Geometric pottery will be the subject of a separate study. Also reserved for publication in other parts of *Corinth* XVIII are the miniature votive likna and offering trays—both of which are more suitably discussed as implements of cult than as pottery—and Greek transport amphoras. Stamped handles from Corinthian type A and B amphoras found in the Sanctuary will be treated by C. G. Koehler in *Corinth* XIX, i.

Other individual volumes are planned. They will present the topography and architecture, *Corinth* XVIII, iii; the terracotta figurines, *Corinth* XVIII, iv; other volumes will publish finds such as the Greek and Roman coins, marble and terracotta sculpture, inscriptions, Greek lamps, animal and human bones, miscellaneous finds (including the model likna and offering trays), etc. Since several scholars with varying outside commitments are participating in the final publication, we have decided to issue the separate parts of *Corinth* XVIII as the individual volumes are completed and not to try to group them thematically.

CHARLES K. WILLIAMS, II

1988

TABLE OF CONTENTS

LIST OF ILLUSTRATIONS

FIGURES IN TEXT

PLATES

BIBLIOGRAPHY AND ABBREVIATIONS

BIBLIOGRAPHY

The Sanctuary of Demeter and Kore on Acrocorinth

Stroud, R. S., "Preliminary Report I: 1961–1962," *Hesperia* 34, 1965, pp. 1–24

———— , "Preliminary Report II: 1964–1965," *Hesperia* 37, 1968, pp. 299–330

Bookidis, N., "Preliminary Report III: 1968," *Hesperia* 38, 1969, pp. 297–310

Bookidis, N. and J. E. Fisher, "Preliminary Report IV: 1969–1970," *Hesperia* 41, 1972, pp. 283–331

———— , "Preliminary Report V: 1971–1973," *Hesperia* 43, 1974, pp. 267–307

Daux, G., "Chroniques des fouilles en 1962," *BCH* 87, 1963, pp. 726–727

———— , "Chroniques des fouilles 1963," *BCH* 88, 1964, pp. 693–697

———— , "Chroniques des fouilles 1964," *BCH* 89, 1965, pp. 756–761

Michaud, J.-P., "Chroniques des fouilles en 1968 et 1969," *BCH* 94, 1970, p. 953

———— , "Chroniques des fouilles en 1970," *BCH* 95, 1971, p. 858

———— , "Chroniques des fouilles en 1971," *BCH* 96, 1972, p. 636

———— , "Chroniques des fouilles en 1972," *BCH* 97, 1973, p. 293

———— , "Chroniques des fouilles en 1973," *BCH* 98, 1974, pp. 600–601

Aupert, P., "Chroniques des fouilles en 1975," *BCH* 100, 1976, pp. 602, 604–606

Pemberton, E. G., "Vase Painting in Ancient Corinth," *Archaeology* 31, November–December 1978, pp. 27–33

Rutter, J. B., "The Last Mycenaeans at Corinth," *Hesperia* 48, 1979, pp. 348–392

General

Amyx, *CorVP* = D. A. Amyx, *Corinthian Vase-Painting of the Archaic Period*, Berkeley/Los Angeles/London 1988

———— . *See also Corinth* VII, ii

Agora XII = B. A. Sparkes and L. Talcott, *The Athenian Agora*, XII, *Black and Plain Pottery of the 6th, 5th and 4th Centuries B.C.*, Princeton 1970

ABV = J. D. Beazley, *Attic Black-Figure Vase-Painters*, London 1956

ARV² = J. D. Beazley, *Attic Red-Figure Vase-Painters*, London 1962

Beazley, J. D. *See ABV, ARV², Paralipomena*

Boardman and Hayes, *Tocra* = J. Boardman and J. Hayes, *Excavations at Tocra, The Archaic Pottery*, London 1966, 1973

Brann, E., "A Well of the 'Corinthian' Period found in Corinth," *Hesperia* 25, 1956, pp. 350–374

Braun, K., "Der Dipylon-Brunnen B1, Die Funde, Part I," *AthMitt* 85, 1970, pp. 129–196

Campbell, M. T., "A Well of the Black-Figured Period at Corinth," *Hesperia* 7, 1938, pp. 557–611

Callipolitis-Feytmans = D. Callipolitis-Feytmans, "Le plat corinthien," *BCH* 86, 1962, pp. 117–164

Coldstream, *Knossos* = N. Coldstream, *The Sanctuary of Demeter and Kore at Knossos*, Oxford 1973

Corinth

VII, i: S. S. Weinberg, *The Geometric and Orientalizing Pottery*, Cambridge, Mass. 1943

VII, ii: D. A. Amyx and P. Lawrence, *Archaic Corinthian Pottery and the Anaploga Well*, Princeton 1975

VII, iii: G. R. Edwards, *Corinthian Hellenistic Pottery*, Princeton 1975

VII, iv: S. Herbert, *The Red-figure Pottery*, Princeton 1977

XII: G. R. Davidson, *The Minor Objects*, Princeton 1952

XIII: C. W. Blegen, H. Palmer, and R. S. Young, *The North Cemetery*, Princeton 1964

XV, ii: A. N. Stillwell, *The Potters' Quarter, The Terracottas*, Princeton 1952

XV, iii: A. N. Stillwell and J. L. Benson, *The Potters' Quarter, The Pottery*, Princeton 1984

XVIII, ii: K. W. Slane, *The Sanctuary of Demeter, Roman Pottery and Lamps*, forthcoming

Délos XXXI = A. Laumonier, *Exploration archéologique de Délos*, XXXI, i, *La céramique hellénistique à reliefs, Ateliers "ioniens"*, Paris 1978

Edwards, C. M., "Corinth 1980: Molded Relief Bowls," *Hesperia* 50, 1981, pp. 189–210

Edwards, G. R. *See Corinth* VII, iii

Iozzo, M., "Corinthian Basins on High Stands," *Hesperia* 56, 1987, pp. 355–416

Lawrence, P. *See Corinth* VII, ii

Miller, Stella G., "Menon's Cistern," *Hesperia* 43, 1974, pp. 194–245

NC = H. Payne, *Necrocorinthia*, London 1931

Olynthus XIII = D. M. Robinson, *Olynthus*, XIII, *Vases Found in 1934 and 1938*, Baltimore 1950

Paralipomena = J. D. Beazley, *Paralipomena*, Oxford 1971

Payne. *See NC, Perachora* I

Pease, M. Z., "A Well of the Late Fifth Century at Corinth," *Hesperia* 6, 1937, pp. 257–316

Pemberton, E. G., "The Attribution of Corinthian Bronzes," *Hesperia* 50, 1981, pp. 101–111

———— , "Ten Hellenistic Graves in Ancient Corinth," *Hesperia* 54, 1985, pp. 271–307

———— , "The Vrysoula Classical Deposit from Ancient Corinth," *Hesperia* 39, 1970, pp. 265–307

———— . *See also above, The Sanctuary of Demeter and Kore*

Perachora I = H. Payne *et al.*, *Perachora, The Sanctuaries of Hera Akraia and Limenia*, Oxford 1930

Perachora II = *Perachora, The Sanctuaries of Hera Akraia and Limenia* II, T. J. Dunbabin, ed., London 1962

Thompson, H. A., "Two Centuries of Hellenistic Pottery," *Hesperia* 3, 1934, pp. 311–480 (repr. in H. A. Thompson, D. B. Thompson, and S. I. Rotroff, *Hellenistic Pottery and Terracottas*, Princeton 1987)

Vanderpool, E., "The Rectangular Rock-cut Shaft," *Hesperia* 7, 1938, pp. 363–411; *Hesperia* 15, 1946, pp. 265–336

———— , "Some Black-Figured Pottery from the Athenian Agora," *Hesperia* 15, 1946, pp. 120–137

Wallenstein, K., *Korinthische Plastik*, Bonn 1971

Weinberg, S. S., "Corinthian Relief Ware: Pre-Hellenistic Period," *Hesperia* 23, 1954, pp. 109–137

———— . *See also Corinth* VII, i

Williams, C. K., II, "Excavations at Corinth, 1968," *Hesperia* 38, 1969, pp. 36–63

Williams, C. K., II and J. E. Fisher, "Corinth, 1971: Forum Area," *Hesperia* 41, 1972, pp. 143–184

———— , "Corinth, 1972: The Forum Area," *Hesperia* 42, 1973, pp. 1–44

Williams, C. K., II, J. MacIntosh, and J. E. Fisher, "Excavations at Corinth, 1973," *Hesperia* 43, 1974, pp. 1–76

Williams, C. K., II and J. E. Fisher, "Corinth, 1975: Forum Southwest," *Hesperia* 45, 1976, pp. 99–162

Williams, C. K., II, "Corinth, 1976: Forum Southwest," *Hesperia* 46, 1977, pp. 40–81

———— , "Corinth, 1977: Forum Southwest," *Hesperia* 47, 1978, pp. 1–39

———— , "Corinth, 1978: Forum Southwest," *Hesperia* 48, 1979, pp. 105–144

———— , "Corinth Excavations, 1979," *Hesperia* 49, 1980, pp. 107–134

Williams, C. K., II and P. Russell, "Corinth: Excavations of 1980," *Hesperia* 50, 1981, pp. 1–44

GENERAL ABBREVIATIONS

D.	= diameter	LPC	= Late Protocorinthian
dim.	= dimension	max.	= maximum
EC	= Early Corinthian	MC	= Middle Corinthian
EPC	= Early Protocorinthian	PC	= Protocorinthian
est.	= estimated	p.	= preserved
f.o.	= filling ornament	rest.	= restored
H.	= height	Th.	= thickness
L.	= length	W.	= width
LC	= Late Corinthian		

ABBREVIATIONS OF PERIODICALS AND SERIES

AJA	= *American Journal of Archaeology*
BCH	= *Bulletin de correspondance hellénique*
CVA	= *Corpus vasorum antiquorum*
GRBS	= *Greek, Roman and Byzantine Studies*
MEFRA	= *Mélanges d'archéologie et d'histoire* (École française de Rome)
SEG	= *Supplementum epigraphicum graecum*

GLOSSARY

The Glossary defines the descriptive terms used in this volume, listed from the bottom of the vase to the top (foot to lip), just as the vases are described. Subdivisions in each area are in alphabetical order.

FOOT

The articulated bottom of the vase. If there is no articulation, as with olpai or phialai, the vase has a *resting surface*.

1. Disk

   Vertical exterior face, flat wide resting surface with little inner articulation. See **50** (Fig. 3).

2. Pedestal

   Conical inner face; exterior face is molded, usually with concave upper face, projecting ledge, convex lower face, narrow resting surface (also known as foot in two degrees). Typical of kantharoi. See **84** (Fig. 10).

3. Ring

   Sloping exterior face, well-articulated inner face. Typical of kotylai. See **3** (Fig. 6).

4. Ring (plate)

   Almost a half-round, often double. Characteristic of the Archaic Corinthian plate. See **238** (Fig. 16).

5. False ring

   Sloping exterior face, little or no articulation of the inner face. Characteristic of some small hydriai. See **138** (Fig. 1).

6. Vertical ring

   Vertical exterior face, articulated inner face, usually vertical, sometimes sloping. Typical of Hellenistic saucers. See **94** (Fig. 15).

7. Stem or conical

   Tall, with widely out-flaring, often concave exterior face, deeply cut out inside, so that the profile resembles a truncated cone. The outer edge of the foot may be heavy or thin. Typical of Attic kylikes. See **318** (Pl. 35). On some saucers, the undersurface becomes so recessed that the inner face of the foot approaches a conical form: hence, *proto-conical*. See **132** (Fig. 15).

8. Torus

   Two changes of direction on exterior face; flat, relatively wide resting surface; sharp articulation of inner face. Typical of skyphoi. See **43** (Fig. 7).

FLOOR

Inner, generally horizontal surface of the vessel, created by the wall.

UNDERSURFACE

Bottom exterior surface of the vessel. It may be *nippled* (central thickening, or even small cone), or *inset* (not continuous with the bottom of the wall, as in some Attic saltcellars). If the vessel has no foot, the undersurface and the resting surface are the same. Often, vases with ring or disk feet have slightly *concave undersurfaces*.

WALL

The part of the vase enclosing the contents.

1. Beveled

   Pronounced outward turn above the foot or resting surface, at the bottom of the wall. Typical of type 3 kalathiskoi. See **35** (Fig. 5).

2. Biconical

   A carinated wall with the lower and upper parts of equal dimensions and equal profile. See **478** (Pl. 48).

3. Carinated

   Wall with offset change of direction, without the continuous profile of the wall with compound curve. See **658** (Fig. 24).

4. Compound curve

   Wall continuously and noticeably convex to concave (or vice-versa). Typical of the later stages of the skyphos. See **115** (Fig. 7).

5. Flaring

    Wall expanding in diameter from the foot or resting surface without any significant turn in. It may be *straight*, *convex*, or *concave* flaring in profile. See, respectively, **13** (Pl. 4), **3** (Fig. 6), and **9** (Pl. 4).

6. Globular

    Convex wall with the maximum diameter in the middle. See **96** (Pl. 13).

7. Ovoid

    Wall with maximum diameter either above the midpoint (*high ovoid*) or below the midpoint (*low ovoid*). See, respectively, **34** (Pl. 6) and **135** (Fig. 18).

8. Vertical

    Wall without change in diameter. Also known as *cylindrical*, when quite tall, as with some lekythoi. See **45** (Pl. 7).

SHOULDER

Characteristic only of closed vessels. Area between wall and neck or rim, enclosing the upper part of the vase.

NECK

Characteristic only of closed vessels. Noticeable stem, of varying heights and widths, between shoulder and rim.

MOUTH

Often used as the term for the upper area of a closed vase, including rim and lip. Not used in this study except for two commonly known terms: *trefoil mouth*, typical of oinochoai, and *cut-away mouth*, for a spout with the upper area open.

RIM

The upper termination of the vessel, clearly offset from the wall or neck. Many vessels have no rim; the wall ends in a lip, without any offsetting. The rim has a lip (the area over which liquid pours); but every lip is not necessarily part of a rim.

1. Beveled

    Outward projection, turning in to the lip. Characteristic of a type of small bowl, so named. See **92** (Fig. 13).

2. Flaring

    Rim projecting outwards, without any thickening or other distinctive quality. See **73** (Fig. 2).

3. Folded

    Rim rectangular in section, with a flat top and vertical face. Found on some kraters, some mortars. See **639** (Fig. 22).

4. Inturned

    Distinctive turn in to the interior of the vessel but without a sharp bevel. Characteristic of echinus bowls and some forms of saltcellars. See **447** (Fig. 12).

5. Outturned or concave

    Concave outer face, flaring out from the wall. Found on some kylikes and krateriskoi. See **508** (Pl. 50).

6. Outturned (bowl)

    Specific form of bowl, known in Athens as rolled rim. The term was used in *Corinth* VII, iii and is retained here for consistency. See **449**, **451** (Fig. 12).

7. Outward thickened

    Turning out from the wall, thicker than the wall below the rim. See **10** (Pl. 4).

8. Overhanging

    Rim with noticeable descent past the line of projection. See **75** (Pl. 10).

9. Triangular

    Outwardly projecting rim, triangular in profile. Typical of many small hydriai. See **182** (Fig. 1).

10. Two degrees

    Rim with two different profiles of the outer face. See **372** (Pl. 44).

Rim (Plate)

Terms used to distinguish the distinctive profiles of plates.

1. Convex

   Rim convex on its upper profile, used for the flaring rim of the 6th- and 5th-century plates. See **27** (Fig. 16).

2. Flat

   Articulated both by change of direction and by grooves or ridges. The rim is nearly horizontal. See **197** (Fig. 16).

3. Offset

   Groove on upper face, marking rim off from the wall; there is little or no articulation between the wall and rim. See **472** (Pl. 48).

Lip

Top edge of vessel over which liquid would flow or on which the drinker's mouth would rest.

1. Flattened

   Flat upper face. See **87** (Fig. 11).

2. Peaked

   Lip rises to a pronounced peak at the top. Often found with the triangular rim. See **35** (Fig. 5).

3. Rounded

   Plain rounded termination of the wall. See **3** (Fig. 6).

4. Tapered

   Rounded as No. 3 but narrower in width than the wall. See **40** (Fig. 6).

Flange

A separate projection or ledge made to receive a lid. On lekanides, the flange is the projecting area with horizontal upper face; the vertical rise is the rim. On lopades, it is the inner diagonal projection. On lids, the flange is the vertical face made to be set on the flange of the bowl; it may be continuous with the lid surface or recessed as on pyxis lids. Flange is also used to describe projecting ledges, as on epichyseis and the perforated cylindrical vessels, although these projections do not receive lids.

Handles

1. Canted

   Set below the lip and tilted up to the line of the lip. See **115** (Fig. 7).

2. Horseshoe

   Round in section, with roots set close to each other, the outer handle flaring out to form a horseshoe in plan. Typical of later skyphoi. See **410** (Fig. 7).

3. Loop

   Round in section, forming an oval in plan and set at the top of the wall; nearly horizontal. See **3** (Fig. 6).

4. Lug

   Solid projecting handle, often diagonal on the outer vertical face. See **21** (Pl. 4).

5. Ninety-degree

   Handle beginning with a horizontal projection, then turning up at a sharp 90° angle at the outer edge. Typical of later hydriai. See **138** (Fig. 1).

6. Reflex

   Curved loop handle with projecting ends. See **536** (Pl. 51).

7. Ring

   Handle in the form of a vertical ring. See **135** (Fig. 18).

8. Strap

   Wide, flat vertical handle. See **1** (Pl. 4).

9. Wishbone

   Round in section, horizontal or slightly diagonal in projection; loop form, but with upward projection at outer edge, thus giving it the name. See **414** (Fig. 8).

PREFACE

Over the years, many scholars have helped immeasurably, by discussion, by letter, and through publications. Accordingly, I wish to thank D. A. Amyx, J. L. Benson, D. von Bothmer, N. Bookidis, H. A. G. Brijder, C. M. Edwards, G. R. Edwards, J. Fisher, R. Guy, S. Herbert, L. Kahil, C. Koehler, P. Lawrence, I. D. McPhee, M. B. Moore, S. I. Rotroff, J. Salmon, L. Siegel, K. W. Slane, E. L. Smithson, R. S. Stroud, H. A. Thompson, and C. K. Williams, II. They are certainly not responsible for any errors or omissions.

For the photographs, I am indebted to J. Heyl and particularly to I. Ioannides and L. Bartzioti; for the profiles and restored drawings, to D. Peck, M. Palaima, and J. Ingram. I am grateful to W. B. Dinsmoor, Jr. for his architectural work in the Sanctuary and to David Peck for his plan, printed here as Plan A. Three fine potmenders have recreated vessels out of displaced small fragments, the labor of many years. S. Bouzaki helped immensely by her fine work of restoration and conservation.

The University of Maryland at College Park was very generous with sabbaticals in 1972 and 1979/1980, and with grants from the General Research Board for the summers of 1970, 1974, and 1978. Without the facilities and the support of the American School of Classical Studies at Athens and the Corinth excavation staff, this volume would never have been possible.

Above all I am indebted to the Corinthians. When I was asked to work on the pottery from the Demeter Sanctuary, I accepted for a number of reasons. First, I knew how varied and important the material was. Moreover, the study would be done in Corinth, a wonderful place to work. And most important, I would be able to collaborate with three scholars and friends, Nancy Bookidis, Ronald Stroud, and Charles K. Williams, II. As a token of thanks for their patience in working with me, for reading countless drafts of the manuscript, and for constant support and advice, I dedicate this volume to them, and to my husband, Ian McPhee, for similar reasons.

ELIZABETH G. PEMBERTON

MELBOURNE, AUSTRALIA
February, 1983

INTRODUCTION

THE SITE

The Sanctuary of Demeter and Kore is located south of the center of the ancient city, on the north slope of Acrocorinth. It was either on or near to a road that led up to the citadel, along which were many other sanctuaries, briefly noted by Pausanias.[1]

In 1961, R. S. Stroud dug for one month in what was to be revealed as part of the Middle Terrace; excavations resumed under his supervision in 1962 and 1964–1965; in 1965 he was joined by Nancy Bookidis, who assumed responsibility for the work in 1968. She continued the excavations each year through 1973, with a final season in 1975.[2] When excavations ceased, the area measured in its maximum dimensions 90 meters east–west and 55 north–south, although not all that area was completely uncovered.

The Sanctuary is organized into three terraces, sloping to the north. The highest one has theatral areas, Roman temples, and other buildings. The Middle Terrace is dominated by a Hellenistic stoa but also contains some of the earliest architecture. The Lower Terrace is covered by dining rooms and preserves evidence for the road, either the one coming directly from the city or a separate road leading to the Sanctuary from the main Acrocorinth thoroughfare. The north–south limits of the Sanctuary appear to have been found, but the dining rooms continue to east and to west. The Sanctuary boundaries on these sides are not known. We believe that all these rooms are still part of the Demeter and Kore complex, not of adjacent sanctuaries, on the basis of the kinds of pottery and figurines found in the rooms (see Plan A).

The first indisputable evidence of a functioning Sanctuary on the site is the 7th-century material of Group 1 (pp. 79–81). There is earlier material from the Mycenaean and Geometric periods, but it seems to be more appropriate for a domestic establishment.[3] The relatively small amount of Protocorinthian material is more difficult to interpret. There are fragments of Protocorinthian in many lots, usually with material of much later date.[4] But a few contexts in grid location O–P:22–23 contain fragments of pottery more chronologically limited. Lot 2235 is the most interesting of these; the pottery from it is very fragmentary, totaling 82 sherds: 8 from oinochoai, 31 kotylai, 5 pyxis-kalathoi, 14 small flaring kalathoi, 1 krater rim, and 23 undeterminable (coarse ware or indistinguishable body fragments). Of the oinochoai, two appear to be from earlier 7th-century conical examples (neck, base); the others are wall sherds, mostly black glazed with added purple and white. The 31 kotylai are comprised of 1 handle fragment, 8 feet, and 22 wall sherds. The feet may be the most diagnostic, although from small kotylai and badly broken. One is probably later 7th century, with a double foot and decoration of coursing hounds; 5 may be EPC or MPC, with the characteristic small neat foot and no color on the undersurface; 1 may be LPC, showing a slightly wider resting surface; 1 is too poorly preserved to attempt to date it. There are also several small wall fragments with linear decoration, made of fine fabric but without sufficient criteria for close dating. Several of the fragmentary kalathoi may belong to the earlier 7th century, decorated with pairs of fine lines, but they too are insufficiently preserved; the shape is notoriously conservative.

Lots 2236 and 2238 from the same grid location also have early material. Lot 2236 has 86 sherds, of which 7 might be Protocorinthian (5 kotylai, 1 oinochoe, 1 cup?). Lot 2238 contains 57 sherds, of which 7 also seem Protocorinthian (3 kotylai, 1 kalathos, 1 vertical handle, 2 wall fragments). Lot 4359, the material found

---

[1] Pausanias, ii.4.6–7; a full account of the topography will appear in the architectural volume of the Sanctuary series.

[2] For excavation reports see Bibliography.

[3] Rutter, *Hesperia* 48, 1979, for the Mycenaean material.

[4] For example, lot 2044 (grid location Q:25–26), with a terminal date in the later 5th century, contains a fragment of a krater wall and horizontal strap handle very similar to C-31-41, of the late 8th century (*Corinth* VII, i, no. 103, p. 35). There are also PC fragments in lots primarily filled with Geometric material, as lot 6941 (grid location H:20), with kotylai wall fragments, a few flaring kalathoi, and a conical oinochoe handle. The Geometric material from the Demeter Sanctuary will be published separately.

below the floor of Pit E (see Group 4, pp. 87–88), consists of 72 sherds, primarily from the 5th century. But there are also 2 Protocorinthian kotyle feet, 6 possible Protocorinthian kotyle walls, 5 flaring kalathos fragments (with pairs of fine lines), 1 early conical oinochoe base, and 1 cup rim fragment.

Other Protocorinthian fragments are scattered throughout the Sanctuary. As will become evident in the next section, few strata in the Sanctuary are "clean", that is, chronologically limited, as is characteristic of a hillside site with a long history of continuous building. I think, however, that it is fair to argue for some activity in the area of grid location O–P:22–23, possibly as early as the early 7th century. One notes that the shapes represented by the Protocorinthian fragments from that grid area are the same as those of Group 1, a votive deposit: kotylai, kalathoi, oinochoai. How extensive this activity was, when it began, and even its precise religious nature cannot be more definitely determined on the basis of the limited and fragmentary pottery evidence.

The period of great growth in the Sanctuary was in the 6th century (see Group 2, pp. 81–84); the dedications and other vessels continue without lessening in quantity throughout the Classical period. The cult apparently flourished even after the destructive earthquakes of the later 4th century (see Group 6, pp. 91–96) and continued until 146 B.C. (Groups 10 and 11, pp. 105–109). The Hellenistic material is scanty in comparison to the great amounts of material from earlier periods. Much of the building and of the cult activity in the Hellenistic period took place on the Lower Terrace (the dining rooms); there the fill is the most shallow in the Sanctuary, and consequently not so much material was retained *in situ*.

The Sanctuary was renewed under the Romans after the restoration of Corinth in 44 B.C.[5] How much activity there was in the so-called interim period of 146–44 is arguable. A few fragments appear to belong to that period, as do some coins.[6] Although there is not nearly the evidence for activity during that period in the Demeter Sanctuary that there is in the Lower City, we ought not to dismiss all such difficult fragments as chance strays. There are also some vessels, notably the large plain kotylai **405–409** and the phialai **675–681**, that cannot be labeled as definitely Greek or Roman. Consequently, distinct horizons for the beginning and end of the Sanctuary in both the Greek and Roman phases are not always clear.

CHRONOLOGY OF THE POTTERY

This volume discusses the pottery of the Sanctuary from the LPC period to 146 B.C., the bulk of which is Corinthian. The reader will quickly be aware that most of this pottery comes not from sealed and limited contexts but from large dumped fills with a long range of dates. This situation reflects the larger problem of the lack of such defined contexts in most periods of Corinth's history. Weinberg's volume of Protocorinthian and Corinthian material, articles by Brann and Campbell, and the recent publication by Lawrence[7] present varied material from the Archaic period, usually dated by the attribution of figured pieces to specific periods, painters, or both; the chronology is based on Payne's framework. Many of the contexts of these vessels have a long range of dates[8] and do not necessarily verify the standard dates first assigned to the different periods of Archaic Corinthian vases by Payne. Payne's dates have been challenged by scholars studying Corinthian material found outside Corinth.[9] Possibly the most accurate way of dating is by shape development, a method which is not as yet as well published for Corinthian pottery as it is for Attic.[10]

---

[5] For the Sanctuary after the Roman renewal, see *Corinth* XVIII, ii by K. W. Slane, forthcoming.

[6] For discussion of the interim period, see below, p. 4.

[7] Weinberg, *Corinth* VII, i; Brann, *Hesperia* 25, 1956; Campbell, *Hesperia* 7, 1938; Lawrence, Anaploga Well in *Corinth* VII, ii.

[8] See the dates of many of the earliest deposits in *Corinth* VII, iii; the contexts of many of the groups in *Corinth* VII, i are not very limited. For example, of the Protocorinthian material, nos. 136–143 came from a well at the northwest corner of the museum (Well Z [well 1931-8], deposit no. 42 in *Corinth* VII, iii). But other material from Well Z goes into the Hellenistic period. It appears to be a dump fill, not a use accumulation.

[9] See the summary in J. N. Coldstream, *Greek Geometric Pottery*, London 1968, Absolute Chronology: Foundation of the Western Colonies, pp. 322–327. There is also a useful table of the literary and archaeological evidence for foundation dates of all the colonies in *Cambridge Ancient History* III, iii, Cambridge 1982, pp. 160–162.

[10] Important discussions of the kotyle foot in Lawrence, *Corinth* VII, ii, figs. 1 and 2, pp. 76–77; skyphos rims (Thapsos class) in

The chronology of 5th-century Corinthian pottery is firmly based on the vases found in a well, published by M. Z. Pease in 1937; Attic imports provided the dating.[11] The North Cemetery graves may not be entirely reliable; some shapes show discrepancies in their development.[12] Graves also often contain heirlooms, so that all the contents in a particular grave may not be of the same date.

Chronological problems become even more apparent in the later 4th century, for many deposits excavated in the Forum, and dated in relationship to the construction of the South Stoa for the League of Corinth, may have to be redated. Briefly, the argument is as follows. In the later 4th century, Corinth was hit by one or two bad earthquakes.[13] The destruction(s) led to filling and rebuilding operations in different parts of the city. The Potters' Quarter, Tile Works, Asklepieion, and other sites were badly damaged; some were abandoned. In the area later occupied by the Roman Forum, there was a large drain running by buildings in the southern sector. A coin in one of the destroyed buildings is dated 339–318 B.C.[14] Sometime in the 20-year period, the drain was filled with discarded pottery when the buildings went out of use. The pottery belongs to the third quarter of the 4th century, most of it late rather than early in that quarter, with strong resemblance to pottery of the same period from the Athenian Agora.[15]

The South Stoa was built over part of those demolished buildings. Possibly the coin could have been minted and discarded in a very short space of time, just before the earthquake (thus 338 or 337 B.C.), but the accumulated evidence suggests that the abandonment of the buildings, causing the filling in of the drain, is closer to 325. Thus it seems inevitable that the South Stoa must be dissociated from Philip and the establishment of the League of Corinth in 337 B.C. The building of the large South Stoa may not have been historically or politically motivated but, rather, provided a necessary replacement for buildings destroyed by the natural catastrophe.

As a result, those deposits in *Corinth* VII, iii listed as relevant for the construction of the South Stoa may have to be down dated.[16] Material published in this volume may be as much as a quarter century later in proposed dates than similar material in *Corinth* VII, iii.[17] This redating does not invalidate the remarkable work of G. Roger Edwards. His relative chronology, as set out in *Corinth* VII, iii, is in most cases supported by subsequent finds; only the absolute dating may have to be revised. A similar situation holds for the pioneer work of H. A. Thompson on the Hellenistic material found in the Athenian Agora, the absolute dates for which have been revised on the basis of the Koroni pottery and the contents of Menon's Cistern.[18]

There are in ancient Corinth as yet virtually no limited sealed deposits from the Hellenistic period. All the South Stoa wells, the more recently discovered Forum wells, and fills in the Demeter Sanctuary[19] show long

---

C. W. Neeft, "Observations on the Thapsos Class," *MEFRA* 93, 1981 (pp. 7–88), fig. 7, p. 29. For later material see especially Edwards, *Corinth* VII, iii (Classical as well as Hellenistic); also Pemberton, banded lekythoi, *Hesperia* 39, 1970, fig. 4, p. 279; and observations by Williams in many Corinth excavation reports, for example *Hesperia* 48, 1979, catalogue entries on pottery from the Punic Amphora Building, pp. 118–124. Koehler's work (forthcoming as *Corinth* XIX, i) on Corinthian transport amphoras is invaluable. It must be noted that a number of Corinthian shapes parallel the development of their Attic counterparts; hence *Agora* XII is of great use.

[11] Pease, *Hesperia* 6, 1937; the publication of the Vrysoula deposit, which is essentially contemporary, is based on the earlier work: Pemberton, *Hesperia* 39, 1970.

[12] Pemberton, *Hesperia* 39, 1970, discussion in note 6, p. 268.

[13] Williams and Fisher, *Hesperia* 45, 1976, pp. 115–116.

[14] Williams and Fisher, *Hesperia* 41, 1972, p. 153; coin no. 185, p. 182, Salamis. See also cistern 1979-1 and its relationship to the South Stoa: Williams, *Hesperia* 49, 1980, pp. 120–121.

[15] See footnote 18 below.

[16] In particular, deposits nos. 79 (well 1937-1), 80 (drain 1937-1), and 90 (pit 1937-1).

[17] This change is based on the chronology of the material from the 1971 Forum drain (Williams and Fisher, *Hesperia* 41, 1972, pp. 155–163; drain 1971-1) and other debris associated with the earthquake. For example, skyphos C-37-2493, no. 328 in *Corinth* VII, iii, p. 70, is dated to the second quarter of the 4th century. A skyphos with similar profile from the 1971-1 drain, C-71-194 (*Hesperia* 41, 1972, no. 28, p. 157), is third quarter.

[18] See H. A. Thompson, D. B. Thompson, and S. I. Rotroff, *Hellenistic Pottery and Terracottas*, Princeton 1987 (reprint of Thompson, *Hesperia* 3, 1934). Rotroff's preface, pp. 1–18, summarizes the chronological problems and the history of scholarship on early Hellenistic dating.

[19] South Stoa wells: *Corinth* VII, iii, deposits nos. 95–118; recent Forum wells: well 1975-1, well 1975-5 (see Index III for references), also Katsoulis well, 1965-3; in the Demeter Sanctuary: Groups 7–11, cistern at N:26 (cistern 1965-1), lots 4478–4482.

ranges of dates, and many (including almost all the South Stoa wells)[20] are filled with unstratified dump from the reconstruction of the city by the Romans after 44 B.C.[21] There are no wells that show a steady un-contaminated use fill. Hellenistic graves are also very sparse; domestic fills are unknown.

In addition, and potentially more important, there is what might be called the "146 dilemma". It is possible that Corinth was not entirely abandoned in the 100 years after Mummius' sack; not only are there imports found that date to the interim period,[22] but also a ceramic industry may have existed during part of the period, although on a much reduced scale.[23]

Excavations in the Forum area have produced many more fragments of Hellenistic pottery datable after 146, particularly significant for certain types of vessels once thought to be chronologically fixed, especially the relief bowls with long petals.[24] The link between 146 and the introduction of the long-petal bowls was made over forty years ago: ". . . in the older part of the Stoa of Attalos . . . 159–138 B.C. . . . there was not a fragment of a bowl with long petals. But a few specimens of this type have been found in Corinth (destroyed in 146 B.C.)."[25] The recent study of C. M. Edwards of relief bowls found in the 1980 excavations of Corinth shows how many long-petal and linear-patterned forms are to be found at Ancient Corinth.[26] There are two possible interpretations. First, long-petal bowls and similar late types may have been introduced considerably earlier than *ca.* 150 at Corinth.[27] Second, a ceramic industry may have existed at Corinth (or Sikyon?) during some of the years after 146 and before 44 B.C., accounting for the numbers of these late Hellenistic forms. The two alternatives are not mutually exclusive. With either alternative (or both), 146 B.C. is no longer a *terminus post et/aut ante quem* for certain ceramic evidence. The consequences of this unreliability must be considered with regard to other material at other sites.

The problem of the interim period does not appear to be so serious for the Demeter Sanctuary as for the Lower City. There are only a few fragments that seem to be *post* 146 and *ante* 44: **191, 462, 463, 472, 473**. It is likely that the Sanctuary was dormant for at least one hundred years; 146 B.C. may be used with caution as *terminus ante quem* for most vessels, but always keeping in mind the evidence from the Lower City.

Although some of the dates in *Corinth* VII, iii may have to be revised, the development of shapes as put forward there is workable for the Demeter Sanctuary material. In arranging a sequence for the Hellenistic pottery in this study, the late third or early fourth quarter of the 4th century and 146 B.C. are the two poles between which the representatives of the shapes are placed. Certain changes in decoration and profile are visible in a number of pottery types; it may be arbitrary to assign examples to dates between the poles, but the alternative is to have no dating at all. One may only hope that the proposed relative chronologies of shapes in *Corinth* VII, iii and in this study will be justified by future finds. A more firmly based absolute chronology for the Hellenistic pottery of Corinth must await the discovery of several chronologically limited and uncontaminated contexts, if they exist.

---

[20] There is also a question as to whether the South Stoa wells were contemporary with the construction of the building or were 3rd-century additions. There was a well in front of the building, well 1971-2, open during much of the 3rd century, seemingly unnecessary if every shop had its own water supply; see Williams and Fisher, *Hesperia* 41, 1972, p. 171.

[21] There is a useful summary of the difficulties in G. Siebert, *Ateliers de bols à reliefs du Péloponnèse* (Bibliothèque des Écoles Françaises 233), Paris 1978, pp. 166–167. See also U. Sinn, *Gnomon* 51, 1979, pp. 269–276, esp. pp. 273–274 (review of *Corinth* VII, iii).

[22] Williams, *Hesperia* 47, 1978, pp. 21–23; J. Wiseman, *Land of the Ancient Corinthians* (*Studies in Mediterranean Archaeology* 50), Göteborg 1978, p. 12, and p. 15, note 25.

[23] Most recently, see Edwards, *Hesperia* 50, 1981, esp. pp. 199 and 205; and Russell in Williams and Russell, *Hesperia* 50, 1981, pp. 42–43, describing lamps possibly made in Corinth after 146 and of the same fabric as that of some moldmade relief bowls (see Edwards, *op. cit.*, p. 189, note 1).

[24] Edwards, *op. cit.*, p. 199 and esp. p. 193.

[25] Thompson, *Hesperia* 3, 1934, pp. 457–458. See the review of this evidence and expression of firm belief in 146 as a *terminus post quem non* for Corinthian ceramics (and long-petal bowls) in F. Kleiner's discussion of New Style Athenian coinage: "The Earliest Athenian New Style Bronze Coins," *Hesperia* 44, 1975 (pp. 302–330), pp. 314, 318.

[26] See footnote 23 above.

[27] And possibly at Athens also; the absence of examples in the fill of the Stoa of Attalos could be fortuitous. See S. I. Rotroff, *The Athenian Agora*, XXII, *Hellenistic Pottery. Athenian and Imported Moldmade Bowls*, Princeton 1982, pp. 35–36.

The catalogue entries and the terminal dates of the lots (contexts) are most often very conservatively dated. Wherever possible, relative chronology is given. Dates are usually by quarter centuries; even vaguer terms such as "late 4th century" or "Archaic" are often employed. Any closer dating for many of the shape examples would be misleading at this point in our study of Corinthian pottery. One can only hope that the relative chronology, based on the work of Payne, Amyx, G. R. Edwards, Williams, and others, will last and that in the future, through the continuing excavations in Ancient Corinth and elsewhere, more precise dating will be possible.

METHODOLOGY AND ORGANIZATION OF THE CATALOGUE

The excavations in the Demeter Sanctuary produced a great amount of pottery; when the thousands of terracotta figurines are added, the quantity is astonishing. The 1964/1965 season alone produced 1,080 baskets of sherds. Most of this pottery is small, votive in nature, rather simply decorated, or completely plain, thus similar to material found in other sanctuaries of Demeter.[28] In addition, there is material used in the dining rooms for cooking and eating; there are also some costlier works, intended as more expensive offerings. A few types must have had cult functions. But it is above all the volume of pottery that impresses one, and what that volume may mean. A large population in Corinth? Use of the Sanctuary by non-Corinthian visitors? Several rituals during the year with visitors offering several vessels on each occasion? Use of vessels only once with immediate discarding of them? Dining rooms functioning not just for cult use but also for tribal or civic associations? These are questions raised by the amount of pottery found, at this moment unanswerable.

The volume of pottery created specific problems of storage, and it was necessary to discard great amounts: irrelevant lots (surface, mixed fills), undatable sherds (large body fragments and the like). Consequently precise statistics of shapes and volume cannot be given. All fragments from any usable or significant context were retained, however, including those from large dump fills (see Group 6); all intrinsically important sherds from insignificant contexts were also kept.

During the summers of 1970 through 1975, all the context pottery was studied, each lot separately, to ascertain upper and lower dates. During this work, all decorated sherds (Corinthian and imported, of all periods) were extracted and examined for joins. Many lots were re-examined as the author became more aware of particular problems. Wherever possible or necessary, material from the same area, excavated at different times, was examined as a unit to ascertain the chronology of that area or building. Even so, given the amount of pottery and the large area from which fragments of the same vessel could come, most of the pottery is still very fragmentary.

This study has three functions: 1) dating of the development of the Sanctuary and its buildings through the chronology of the pottery; 2) study of the cult activities through the types of pottery offered and used in the Sanctuary; 3) publication of intrinsically interesting vessels, whether from important contexts or not. Discussion of the first and second functions will be more fully developed in other volumes of the Demeter Sanctuary concerned with architecture and cult activities. It is beyond the scope of this book to treat exhaustively all three areas; it is hoped that the publication will serve as the groundwork upon which other scholars will build.

The catalogue is divided into two parts, so that the different functions of the study are served. Catalogue I consists of 11 groups of vases, spanning the Greek history of the Sanctuary. The groups not only summarize some of the important architectural developments of the Sanctuary but also present the types of pottery, votive and domestic, found in all periods. These groups also give some indication of cult activities on the site:

[28] Knossos: Coldstream, *Knossos*; Tocra: Boardman and Hayes, *Tocra*. The sanctuary at Cyrene appears to have more imported pottery and certainly more stone sculpture; but the mass of the pottery is votive. See D. White, "Cyrene's Sanctuary of Demeter and Persephone," *AJA* 85, 1981, pp. 13–30; G. Schaus, *The Extramural Sanctuary of Demeter and Persephone at Cyrene, Libya*, II, *East Greek, Island, and Laconian Pottery*, Philadelphia 1985, pp. 94–95.

Groups 4, 5, and 7 present material from votive pits, deposits from contexts with limited material, primarily of cult nature. Groups 1, 3, 8, and 9 are deposits of votive discards, material thrown down at one time, of limited date but not within closed contexts. Groups 2, 6, 10, and 11 are important building fills, from key periods in the history of the Sanctuary, with material that spans a long range of dates. Thus, I have used the term *group*, not *deposit*, for these 11 divisions because not all are from closed contexts (in particular the four building fills).

In the fall of 1979, statistics of weight and number were compiled for the 11 groups. These statistics are not complete: much of the context pottery for some of the groups had already been discarded after preliminary study and notation. This discarded material consisted mostly of undatable body sherds and fragments that were substantially earlier than the bulk of the context and therefore irrelevant for dating (see especially Group 6). All decorated and imported fragments were retained as were any sherds with possible usefulness for dating.[29]

The statistics for the quantity of each shape are based on a minimum count. Normally, feet at least half preserved were counted but in some cases other parts were used (strainer mouths for feeders, rims for lekanai). If an entry lists 8 oinochoai of different types, it is likely that only foot fragments, or part of a ribbed wall, or handles provide the basis of the count. The excavators were extremely careful to keep enough of each vessel to show the types of vases present in each context. The published amount in most of the groups is lower than what was originally found, but the relative statistics are reliable. Hence, changes in popularity of shape, relative amounts of imports, votive nature of the pottery, and amounts of household and cooking wares are revealed by the figures and are trustworthy.

In the second part of the catalogue, the pottery is arranged not by context but by fabric and decoration. Many of these pieces are from surface or mixed fills; the context is irrelevant, but the piece is important. Other vessels are from fills which have chronological value but which contained little that is publishable (poor condition, insufficient size); a group could not be created. The pottery in Catalogue II is subdivided by type: fine and coarse wares, the fine wares further divided by decorative schemes, then by shape, and finally by date. Each entry has its lot and grid reference, with the latest date of the pottery in the lot cited and any much later Byzantine material noted.

This division of the pottery inevitably leads to separation of shapes. To reunite kindred vases and to provide discussions of the types, shape studies with full listing of all examples of each form, in chronological order, precede the catalogue proper. These shape studies provide the means for discussion of chronology. Little of that discussion will be found in the catalogue entries. All examples of decorative schemes (red figure, West Slope, and so forth), divided by the catalogue format, can be found in Index II.

After much debate and reworking, the present division of the material was considered to be the optimum one for publishing the pottery of the Demeter Sanctuary in its three different aspects and uses. For any confusion or exasperation caused by the organization of the catalogue, apologies are offered.

TERMINOLOGY

A glossary of pottery terms is found on pp. xv–xvii. Since no two people seem to agree on specific terms, I have developed my own, loosely based on Corinthian practice, modified to suit special needs. All vases are described from the base or foot, since that is the way that most of the objects were made. Lids are accordingly described from the knob. Corinthian and Attic clays are not described; only those fabrics from other sites are discussed, with Munsell numbers and description of the clay texture. The organization of the shapes in the catalogues follows that of Sparkes and Talcott in *Agora* XII, with some modification necessary for the

[29] The original records of the excavations, noting in great detail the amounts collected before discarding, were lost in the excavation-house fire of July 3, 1972.

peculiarities of the Demeter Sanctuary pottery. The descriptions of decoration may seem long, but they attempt to be complete.

There are generally three measurements. D. is maximum diameter wherever found on the vase; other diameters are specified (D. lip, etc.). H. is always the maximum height without handle; p.H. indicates the maximum preserved height. This maximum height refers to the actual height when measured with correct orientation of the sherd by wheel marks. If a fragment is diagonal when so oriented, only the actual extant height is given, not the height that could be calculated from opposite ends of the fragment. In some cases a maximum dimension is given (max. dim.), especially when the sherd is exceedingly small. Other dimensions are restored (rest.) or estimated (est.). The term "glaze" is retained, although we all recognize that it is a misnomer; "added" is used to designate the matt colors. In descriptions of the decoration, "band" signifies discernible width, "line" is very thin, without appreciable width.

The bold lower-case letters that identify separate non-joining parts of the same vase refer to the catalogue divisions, arranged from the bottom to the top of the vase. They are not necessarily the same as the original Corinth inventory number divisions (using roman lower-case letters). Where the original Corinth inventory letter (a, b, etc.) is the same as the catalogue letter (**a**, **b**, etc.), no clarification is needed. In several cases, however, the letters do not match, and even more troublesome, there are in a few instances several different Corinth inventory numbers for the same vase. To resolve this confusion, the specific catalogue letter is given after the Corinth inventory number, to facilitate citation. See, for example, **221**. Where the original Corinth inventory letter (a) is not the same as the catalogue letter (**a**), the former is placed in parentheses after the latter. See, for example, **287**.

Dates not otherwise specified are B.C.

SHAPE STUDIES

I. AMPHORAS

Corinthian

371	fine ware			pre-Hellenistic
372	fine ware		Pl. 44	pre-Hellenistic
373	imitation Cypriot		Pl. 44	third quarter 4th century

Imported

305	Panathenaic		Pl. 34	after 359 B.C.
306	Panathenaic		Pl. 34	after 359 B.C.
307	Panathenaic		Pl. 34	after 359 B.C.
191	Attic West Slope	Group 11	Pl. 21	146 B.C. or later

The major type of amphora in the Demeter Sanctuary was the Corinthian transport amphora.[1] Fine-ware amphoras, decorated or plain, were not found in any quantity. Excavations in the Forum have produced many examples of imitation Cypriot amphoras, popular in the late 4th century.[2] Yet only one fragment, **373**, was found in the Sanctuary. Nor were many examples imported from elsewhere, even from Athens; only parts of two Panathenaics represent the popular Athenian shape. The entire Hellenistic period is represented by **191**. The functions of the fine-ware amphoras, as with the hydriai, must have been assumed by coarse-ware vessels; or else, and rather incredibly, this shape had no usefulness in cult or dining context. One cannot account for the absence of these shapes by postulating metal examples: there are no extant bronze handles, feet, or rims.[3]

II. HYDRIAI

Corinthian

203	red ground	Pl. 22	LC
286	outline style	Pl. 31	5th century
298	red figure	Pl. 33	early 4th century
374	plain		Archaic
375	plain		6th century
376	plain	Pl. 44	Archaic
377	plain		late 5th century
378	plain		Hellenistic

Imported

308	Attic black figure	Pl. 34	later 6th century
309	Attic black figure	Pl. 34	late 6th century
330	Attic red figure	Pl. 37	third quarter 5th century
331	Attic red figure	Pl. 37	end of 5th or early 4th century
332	Attic red figure	Pl. 37	second quarter 4th century

In Corinth, the fine-ware table hydria never had the popularity that it enjoyed in Athens.[4] Black-figured hydriai are rarities in comparison both to other shapes at home and to the numbers of hydriai made

---

[1] The stamped amphora handles from the Sanctuary will be published by C. Koehler in *Corinth* XIX, forthcoming.

[2] See Williams, *Hesperia* 38, 1969, pp. 57–59; there are also hydriai and other shapes in the distinctive fabric.

[3] See Edwards' remarks on the absence of several important shapes in Hellenistic pottery: *Corinth* VII, iii, pp. 19, 49–50.

[4] See also the lack of amphoras, footnote 3 above.

elsewhere. There are only 16 figured Archaic hydriai in *NC*; in *CorVP* Amyx has added 8 more.[5] It is not surprising, therefore, to have only one fragmentary red-ground shoulder.

Five badly preserved examples of unglazed fine-ware hydriai help to fill the lacunae. Body sherds from similar vessels can be found in the context pottery. All five examples, **374–378**, show decorative motifs that are derived from metal. The first, **374**, with a dipinto giving it to Demeter, is the simplest of the three Archaic examples. **375** is the most elaborate; its thumb-rest, tooling, rosettes, and other features link it to many 6th-century black-figured vases with similar additions. The details of **376** resemble those of **375** which should be close in date. Nothing can be said concerning the development of the shape, for all preserve only the rims.

The fluted handle and heraldic sphinxes at the handle base of **377** resemble details of a large group of Classical metal hydriai.[6] But, as argued elsewhere,[7] these details do not allow attribution of the metal vases to Corinth. The sphinxes as yet have no metal counterparts but can be interpreted as an alternative motif for the frontal siren, used on the metal vases.

If one believes that clay vessels with metal-imitative motifs always took the details directly from contemporary metal models, **378** could become proof that Corinth made metal vases throughout its history.[8] But this also may be an erroneous assumption.[9] The profile of the neck and rim of **378** resembles that of the hydriskoi in Group 9.

These few examples suggest that the undecorated hydria was made continuously in Corinth.[10] Yet, given the numbers of dining rooms in the Sanctuary, filled with table vessels used in the meals, there is still a noticeable scarcity of the shape. Metal vessels were not extensively used; very few feet, handles, or rims survive in the debris. The plain glazed hydria, well known at Athens and other sites, is virtually non-existent in Corinth.[11] It is difficult to account for this absence of what would seem to be a very necessary vessel. Ironically, the small hydriai were very popular as votive offerings in the Sanctuary (see Shape Studies, III).

III. SMALL HYDRIAI (HYDRISKOI)

Corinthian

500		Pl. 50	second half 6th century
47	Group 3	Fig. 1, Pl. 7	first quarter 5th century
501		Pl. 50	first half 5th century
502		Pl. 50	late 5th or early 4th century
503		Pl. 50	early 4th century
138	Group 7	Fig. 1, Pl. 17	mid-4th century

[5] The Anaploga Well contained no black-figured hydriai but did have one banded example, C-62-582 (An 236), and four of coarse ware, C-62-674, C-62-675, C-62-673, C-62-645 (An 289, An 305, An 313, An 315: *Corinth* VII, ii). The author noted, however, that only fine-ware vessels associated with wine were found in the potters' dump of the well (p. 69).

[6] E. Diehl, *Die Hydria*, Mainz am Rhein 1964, nos. B137–172; D. von Bothmer, review of Diehl, *Gnomon* 87, 1965, p. 603. See also **627**, probably a handle attachment but conceivably an appliqué on the rim of a fine-ware hydria or similar vessel.

[7] Pemberton, *Hesperia* 50, 1981, pp. 101–111, esp. p. 104.

[8] There is also a fine unglazed horizontal handle in lot 3222 (3222:2), a Hellenistic and Roman context; a disk around the handle root is decorated with impressed eggs. For the possibility that Corinth did not produce fine metalwork in the Hellenistic period, see Pliny, *NH* xxxiv.6–7.

[9] Pemberton, *Hesperia* 50, 1981, pp. 103–104.

[10] There are a few undecorated hydriai from other Corinthian contexts, as C-75-183, from well 1975-4 (Williams and Fisher, *Hesperia* 45, 1976, p. 119, no. 31, pl. 20), a larger and much more utilitarian example than the hydria from the Sanctuary. A few large handles, probably from similar hydriai, remain in the Sanctuary context pottery, uninventoried because so fragmentary and undatable.

[11] One example came from well 1937-3, C-37-1059 (Campbell, *Hesperia* 7, 1938, p. 582, no. 55, fig. 12). Note the Attic black-glazed example from the same well, C-37-981 (p. 581, no. 48, fig. 9). Very few Attic fragments were found in the Sanctuary. Large black-glazed body fragments found in many strata could derive from Corinthian black-glazed hydriai (or other closed shapes). Nevertheless, the plain and coarse-ware hydriai seem to have been more popular.

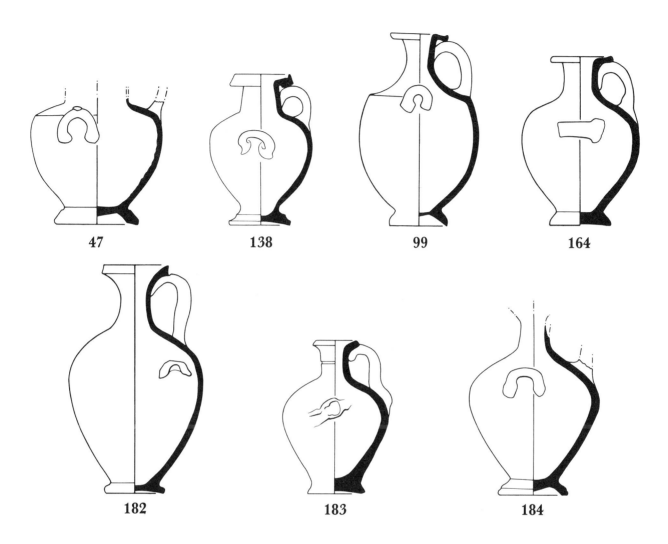

FIG. 1. Small hydriai (hydriskoi). Scale 1:2

504			later 4th century
99	Group 6	Fig. 1, Pl. 13	*ca.* 300 B.C.
505		Pl. 50	late 4th or early 3rd century
163	Group 8	Pl. 18	early 3rd century
164	Group 8	Fig. 1, Pl. 18	mid-3rd century
165	Group 8	Pl. 18	mid-3rd century
182	Group 9	Fig. 1, Pl. 19	second half 3rd century
183	Group 9	Fig. 1, Pl. 19	second half 3rd century
184	Group 9	Fig. 1, Pl. 19	late 3rd century
506		Pl. 50	end of 3rd century (later?)
507		Pl. 50	2nd century

Excluding the cult likna and offering trays, the small hydria (ranging generally from 0.06 to 0.11 m. in height), plain or decorated, is the third most popular votive shape in the Sanctuary, following the kalathiskos and phiale.[12] Many strata have these vessels as the most complete vases for dating; indeed, a few votive contexts consist almost entirely of them (see Group 9). Thus it was necessary to attempt a chronology of the shape.

Almost all the small hydriai have a high ovoid wall: the maximum diameter appears at or just below the shoulder. The important criteria for dating are the ratio of foot diameter to maximum diameter and height; the length of the neck; the type of side handles; the complexity of the rim. Generally, the more contracted the foot, the lighter the rim, the less articulated the handles, then the later the date.

500 represents the 6th century; although there are other examples from the Archaic period, the shape becomes more popular later. The foot of **500** is broad, the wall profile short, the handles are horizontal, the decoration is of conventionalizing form. **47** from Group 3 belongs to the early 5th century and has a taller wall and canted side handles. The shoulder is still well offset and nearly horizontal. The same characteristics appear in the contemporary example, **501**. The end of the 5th century (or slightly later) is represented by **502**, similar to the examples in the Vrysoula deposit.[13] The diameter of the foot is smaller in relation to the height and maximum diameter; the wall merges more continuously with the shoulder; the rim is lighter. These changes become more pronounced in later examples.

503 seems to be early 4th century in date, with a taller neck and more elongated body; the handles turn up but not yet with the ninety-degree form of the later 4th century. **99**, Group 6, shows the late 4th-century profile: narrow foot, elongated body, ninety-degree handles, narrow shoulder, long thin neck, horizontal rim with peaked lip. **505** is similar, probably slightly later. The example from Group 7, **138**, is earlier than **99**, as it retains the shorter neck and less swollen proportions. **504** is approximately contemporary with **138** and is the latest hydria in its lot; uncatalogued examples from the context show an earlier profile.

The hydriskoi from the 3rd-century deposit, Group 8, have varied dates. **163** is closer to **99** of Group 6; the others, **164** and **165**, are later, with narrower feet and less articulation of the side handles.

Group 9 consists mostly of small hydriai and terracotta figurines. All the hydriai have essentially the same profile as the three examples in the Catalogue, **182–184**: elongated profile with the maximum diameter right at the shoulder, tall thin neck, poorly made side handles, poor surface finish. Other vessels in that deposit date the group to the second half of the 3rd century, to which the hydriai also ought to be assigned. The deposit was probably laid down at or near to the end of the century. **184** is the latest and most exaggerated of the hydriai in that group.

The last examples are from Building M:16–17, **506**[14] and **507**, made in the later Hellenistic period. There is no longer any attempt to articulate the side handles, which are now placed on the shoulder; the profile continues the exaggeration of **184**. **507** is probably the later of the two: small, crude, without modeling of the foot, shoulder, or handles, and with the worst finish of all the hydriai.[15]

IV. KRATERS AND LEKANAI

Corinthian

204	figured handle-plate	Pl. 22	MC
205	figured krater	Pl. 22	MC

[12] Hydriai became especially popular as votives in the Hellenistic period. In the Sanctuary of Demeter at Kyparissi in Kos, bothroi filled with terracotta figurines and hydriai were found. These were never published and apparently disappeared in World War II. See R. Kabus-Preisshofen, "Statuettengruppen aus dem Demeterheiligtum," *Antike Plastik* XV, Berlin 1975, p. 32. Two sanctuaries of Demeter in Crete, at Kydonia and Knossos, have also yielded many hydriai. See A. Zois, Ἀνασκαφὴ Βρύσων Κυδώνια, Athens 1976; Coldstream, *Knossos*, especially deposit F (late 3rd—early 2nd century; p. 36, nos. 31–35), deposit G (mid–late 3rd century; p. 37). See also the series from Tocra (Boardman and Hayes, *Tocra* II, nos. 2369, 2370, 2377, 2392, pls. 42, 43).

[13] Pemberton, *Hesperia* 39, 1970, p. 298, nos. 116, 117, pl. 74 (C-64-145, C-64-146).

[14] The context of **506**, lot 3228, appears to end in the late 3rd century, but the hydria may be the latest vessel in that context and bring the date into the early 2nd century.

[15] Similar to **507** is C-28-109, found with a late kalathiskos (C-28-108), a low pyxis bowl (C-28-106; see **179–181**, Group 9), two echinus bowls (C-28-104, C-28-105), the larger of which has a very high profile, and a small West Slope articulated kantharos (C-28-107). The group belongs to the early 2nd century at the earliest, according to the profile of the larger echinus bowl. For the kalathiskos, see also footnote 63 below, p. 25.

206	figured krater		Pl. 22	LC
207	figured krater		Pl. 22	LC
208	figured krater		Pl. 22	LC
209	figured red-ground krater		Pl. 22	LC
192	figured red-ground krater	Group 11	Pl. 21	LC
379	black glazed krater		Pl. 44	LC or later
287	outline style krater		Pl. 31	second quarter 5th century
288	outline style krater		Pl. 31	second quarter 5th century
289	outline style krater		Pl. 32	5th century
290	outline style krater		*Fig. 33, Pl. 32	probably mid-5th century
291	outline style krater		Pl. 32	Classical
299	red-figured bell-krater		Pl. 33	late 5th century
300	red-figured krater		Pl. 33	first quarter 4th century
380	lekane		Pl. 44	Classical
381	lekane		Fig. 2	Classical
382	lekane		Pl. 44	Classical
383	lekane		Pl. 44	4th century ?
75	lekane	Group 6	Pl. 10	earlier 4th century ?

Imported, Attic red figure

334	calyx-krater		Pl. 38	*ca.* 510 B.C.
335	column-krater		Pl. 38	first decade 5th century
336	volute-krater		Pl. 38	mid-5th century
337	krater		Pl. 38	mid-5th century
338	krater		Pl. 38	third quarter 5th century
339	bell-krater		Pl. 38	end of 5th century
340	bell-krater		Pl. 38	end of 5th century
73	bell-krater	Group 6	Fig. 2, Pl. 10	second quarter 4th century
74	bell-krater	Group 6	Pl. 11	mid-4th century

*Decoration only; see catalogue entry.

The inventoried kraters show a variety of styles, shapes, and sizes. It cannot be determined, however, how many of these kraters, Corinthian or Attic, were service vessels in the dining rooms and how many were votives. Fragments of kraters, decorated and plain, were found in Sanctuary strata until the Hellenistic period. It is probable that plain and black-glazed kraters (mostly Corinthian, but a few uninventoried Attic fragments survive) and the banded lekanai served the needs of the diners in the Archaic and Classical Sanctuary. What was used in the Hellenistic period is unclear.[16]

The Archaic Corinthian examples represent the many forms made by the potters of that period. The handle-plate 204 is quite large; several others of equal size, with inferior decoration, remain unpublished. Few of the 6th-century kraters have more than the typical animal frieze; 205 and 206 are typical of the majority of the krater fragments from the site. The cavalry scene on 209 shows the hand of a more ambitious painter. The chain of dancing women on 192 is a motif found on a number of Archaic fragments in different shapes; it may have reference to cult practices. 379 has a handsome maeander in added red and white; the krater was large, finely made, and probably without wall decoration. It represents the most common 6th-century krater, the plain black Corinthian type, attested by many fragments of feet and rims.

In the 5th century a new decorative technique, outline style, was introduced into the Corinthian repertory. The only example with foot and rim preserved, 287, actually shows a skyphos profile, but the restored dimensions are so great that it is more appropriate to call it a krater.[17] A discussion of the technique,

[16] In *Corinth* VII, iii, there are only three examples of Hellenistic kraters; two are fine ware, nos. 188–190, one is of cooking fabric, no. 705. This is another shape not well represented in the later history of Corinthian pottery; see also the hydriai, amphoras, and oinochoai.

[17] Another vase that must also have functioned as a krater is the huge late 4th-century skyphos 80, included under that shape because of the distinctive compound-curve profile (Fig. 7).

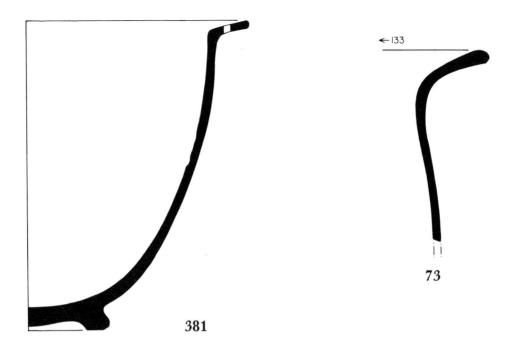

FIG. 2. Lekane and krater. Scale 1:2

painting style, and date is given in the introduction to the examples. It is tempting to believe that these are special vessels for cult purposes, especially since **287** not only may have had a representation of the abduction of Persephone but also was repaired in antiquity, attesting its importance. Whatever the function, this is a special group of vessels, mostly kraters, limited according to present evidence to use in the Demeter Sanctuary, and made in a relatively short span of time. Although most of them are now so fragmentary that the extant painting is usually indecipherable, the vessels in the original state must have been very handsome.

Banded lekanai represented by **380–383** and **75** are popular from the 6th through the 4th centuries; how far into the Hellenistic period they continue is as yet unclear. There are also many coarse-ware body sherds of all periods, coming from large kraters or lekanai.[18]

The imported Attic red-figured kraters present a good cross section in both date and quality. There are a few additional fragments of kraters from the second and third quarters of the 5th century, not inventoried because of the poor state of preservation. Thus the numbers of Attic kraters of fairly good quality exceed what might be expected. Whether the Attic kraters were used in the dining rooms or dedicated as votives cannot be determined.[19] None has a dedicatory graffito.

[18] See the coarse-ware examples **632–634**.

[19] Fragments from the same krater were found all over the Sanctuary. For example, the fine early calyx-krater **334** came mostly from O–P:24–26. But one fragment came from N–O:19–20, another from the Lower Terrace, N:27. The findspots of fragments are not always revealing.

V. OINOCHOAI

Corinthian

1	conical	Group 1	Pl. 4	LPC
2	conical	Group 1	Pl. 4	LPC
210	conical		Pl. 22	LPC
211	conical		*Fig. 26, Pl. 22	EC
212	broad bottomed		Pl. 22	MC
213	broad bottomed		*Fig. 26, Pl. 22	MC?
275	broad bottomed		Pl. 29	first or early second quarter 5th century
384	broad bottomed		Pl. 44	third quarter 5th century
276	broad bottomed		Pl. 29	late third or early fourth quarter 5th century
277	broad bottomed		Pl. 29	fourth quarter 5th century
278	broad bottomed		Pl. 29	second quarter or mid-4th century
279	broad bottomed		Pl. 30	mid-4th century
214	olpe		Pl. 22	MC
33	round mouthed	Group 3	Pl. 6	first quarter 5th century
34	round mouthed	Group 3	Pl. 6	first to second quarter 5th century
76	blister ware	Group 6	Pl. 10	early 4th century
77	blister ware	Group 6	Pl. 10	third quarter 4th century
387	blister ware		Pl. 44	late third to fourth quarter 4th century
388	blister ware		Pl. 44	fourth quarter 4th century
386	chous		Fig. 3, Pl. 44	fourth quarter 4th century
78	beveled (epichysis)	Group 6	Fig. 3, Pl. 10	late 4th century
385	beveled (epichysis)		Pl. 44	late 4th or early 3rd century
389	globular		Fig. 3, Pl. 45	first half 5th century?
154	globular	Group 8	Fig. 3, Pl. 18	later 3rd century
155	globular	Group 8	Pl. 18	3rd century
390	shoulder stop		Fig. 3	early 3rd century?

Imported

310	Attic black figure		Pl. 34	third quarter 6th century
50	Attic black figure	Group 4	Fig. 3, Pl. 8	end of 6th or early 5th century
391	Attic, mug		Pl. 45	second quarter 5th century
79	Attic West Slope	Group 6	Pl. 10	late 4th century
341	Apulian, epichysis		Fig. 3, Pl. 38	late third quarter 4th century

*Decoration only; see catalogue entry.

Oinochoai are not well represented in the Sanctuary catalogue. There are few or no examples of some very common types: Archaic and Classical black-glazed jugs, the Classical and Hellenistic olpe forms, round-mouthed types, and so forth are all absent, or almost so, from the above list. They are not, however, missing in the Sanctuary pottery; rim, wall, and foot fragments from these varieties of oinochoai can be found in many Archaic and Classical strata, but in very small pieces, insufficient for publication. The larger the vessel, the less of it seems to be preserved, when vases are deliberately smashed for burial. Some of the fragments attributed to 6th-century pyxides, a shape more popular at that time for figured decoration among the Sanctuary finds, may be from broad-bottomed oinochoai.[20] Despite these qualifications, it is important to note that there are far more fragments of drinking vessels than fragments of pourers for those vessels. The relative figures for the published fragments for pouring and drinking vessels found at Perachora are much more equal. The numbers of kotylai, skyphoi, and cups in the Demeter Sanctuary fills are staggering. One wonders if a ritual toast was drunk and then the cup discarded.

The problem is compounded by the absence of large Hellenistic fine-ware pouring vessels. This scarcity cannot be blamed on the topography of the slope of the Sanctuary, nor on the specific location of most of the

[20] See *Perachora* II, pp. 205–206, on the difficulties of distinguishing oinochoe shapes, and the oinochoe from the convex pyxis.

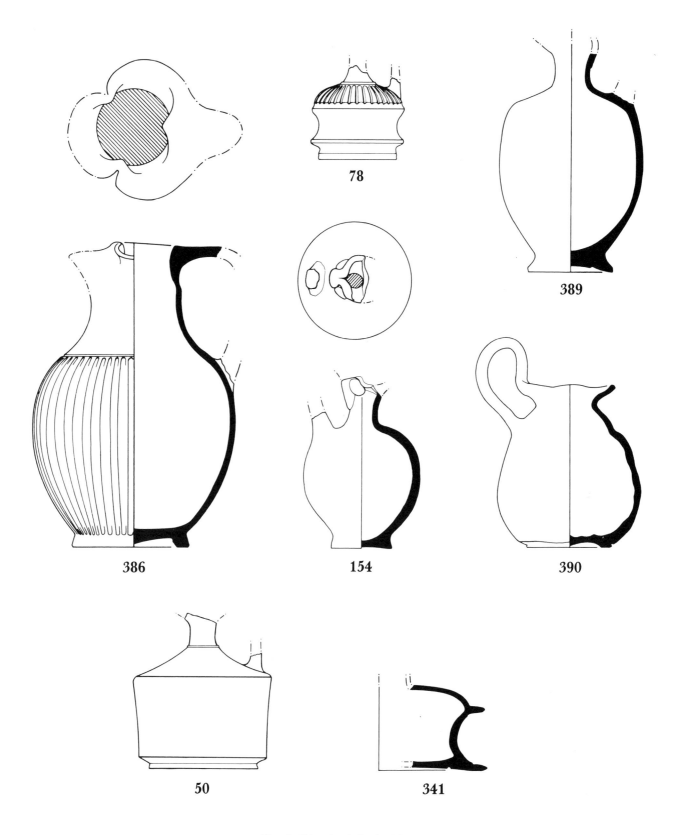

Fɪɢ. 3. Oinochoai. Scale 1:2

Hellenistic strata in the lower terrace where protective fill was lacking. Edwards notes not only the absence in Corinth of decorated wine jugs, in comparison with the contemporary types in Athens, but also ". . . the comparatively inadequate small size of most of the present Hellenistic fine-ware pouring vessels. . . ."[21] The Demeter Sanctuary is even lacking the varieties of decanters, so popular elsewhere at Corinth.[22] Large coarse-ware vessels may have been used, however; fragments were found in almost every area of the Sanctuary.[23] One might tentatively suggest that if some ritual involved the use of wine or water, a few service vessels made of coarse or cooking fabric would have been used repeatedly in each dining room. The drinking vessels may have been discarded after each use.

There are few examples of conical oinochoai. The small LPC examples, **1** and **2**, from the votive deposit Group 1, have many parallels and are useful in substantiating the date of that group. It is strange, however, that two oinochoai appear in the first extant deposit but do not become an important votive type. Two fragmentary decorated necks, **210** and **211**, are later 7th century;[24] the 6th-century form is represented only in uninventoried sherds.

Figured oinochoai of the 6th century are also scarce. **212** and **213** are of different sizes, possibly from the broad-bottomed profile. There are many uninventoried fragments from plain glazed examples. The 6th-century pottery, especially from Room D (R:23–24) is so broken and yet so extensive that it was not logistically possible to spread out all the material from this area for mending into representative shapes. Two very small broad-bottomed examples, **515** and **516**, published with the miniatures, represent these Archaic forms. The Classical broad-bottomed oinochoai are fairly typical, except for the large size and very elaborate decoration on **275** and **276**.[25] There are several examples of oinochoai decorated in the Vrysoula style, **277–279**; the last shows the continuation of the type into the 4th century.

214 is one of the few decorated 6th-century olpai found in the Sanctuary; there are other small fragments attributable to this shape but too tiny for publication. There are many body and neck fragments of the later glazed and plain varieties of olpe, also too battered.[26] Thus the one example of the shape in the catalogue is misleading.

Group 3 contains two examples of the round-mouthed form, **33** and **34**. This shape is not so common as the olpe. If popular more as grave offerings than as service vessels, its absence is understandable.[27] Blister-ware oinochoai are common. It is the most popular shape for this fabric in the Sanctuary, but aryballoi (**97**, **475–478**) and askoi (**98**, **200**) also appear. Blister ware is very fragile, as the state of preservation indicates. All four belong to the 4th century; no 5th-century examples could be inventoried, although small sherds with fine pumpkin ribs do remain in the context pottery. Fragments of this fabric and shape have been found extensively in the Sanctuary strata, very useful for dating.[28]

Three 4th-century oinochoai are Corinthian imitations of two foreign shapes. **386** is a chous; there are few Corinthian versions of this popular Attic shape.[29] **78** and **385** are unusual variants of the epichysis. The Corinthian version is footed, with a flat resting surface under the bevel, in contrast to the South Italian form (**341**). The Corinthian epichysis may be related to the late (4th-century) versions of the concave Vrysoula

---

[21] *Corinth* VII, iii, p. 49.

[22] *Ibid.*, pp. 57–62.

[23] See below, under coarse-ware hydriai (Shape Studies, XXVI).

[24] There are also two very fragmentary oinochoe handles, with subgeometric decoration, from the conical shape: C-62-345 and C-62-346, lot 1982, P:24.

[25] The fragments of **276** came from fill within the Classical Building N–O:22–23, destroyed in the 4th century, with the exception of two fragments, found in M:21, in the foundation trench of wall 36, just to the north of the building. The vessel may have been used in that dining room. **275** came from Building N–O:24–25 (Room L), and so it too may have been a useful item in the dining room.

[26] For olpai, see *Corinth* XIII, p. 133; *Corinth* VII, iii, pp. 50–53.

[27] *Corinth* XIII, p. 134.

[28] Blister-ware shapes and fabrics have been discussed extensively in the following publications: *Corinth* VII, iii, pp. 144–150; *Agora* XII, pp. 207–208; Pemberton, *Hesperia* 39, 1970, pp. 300–301.

[29] Unpublished: C-47-871, from well 1947-2 and C-37-167, from drain 1937-1; both belong to the second quarter of the 4th century. The Corinthian examples do not duplicate the more elongated Attic profile; they are shorter in relation to the maximum diameter and have lower necks.

oinochoe. There are also high-shouldered black oinochoai of the same period.[30] The latter forms and the epichyseis share the profile of foot and lower wall, the neck and handle forms, and the shoulder ribbing. Both epichyseis can be dated only by style; the poor ribbing has parallels in other shapes. They were probably perfume pots.[31]

Four undecorated examples complete the Corinthian series of oinochoai. **389** appears to be early 5th century on the basis of the foot, wall profile, and fine surface finish. The closest parallel for the shape, however, is 6th century. If one attached a foot, narrowed the neck, and eliminated the paint of some trefoil oinochoai with convex walls,[32] one could approximate this shape. I know of no similar jug in Corinth.

390 has already been published in the series of small trefoil oinochoai with shoulder stop.[33] Although this series cannot be traced to a 146 B.C. date, there is another small form that does appear in 3rd- and possibly 2nd-century levels, the globular form of **154** and **155**. These belong to the 3rd century, by comparison of the profiles with hydriai in the same period. **154** and **155** have the foot of the small footed oinochoai with dipped glazing of the 5th and 4th centuries.[34] The body has become more globular, the mouth a cut-away with pellets; the paint has disappeared. But they are of the same size as the earlier variety. It is conceivable that **389** is an ancestor of **154** and **155**.

There are also a few imported oinochoai, all but one of Attic fabric: two decorated in black figure; one 5th-century mug; one neck with West Slope decoration; that is all. The lack of imported examples mirrors the relatively small number of Corinthian oinochoai. The one surprise is the Apulian import, **341**.

VI. MISCELLANEOUS PITCHERS

Corinthian

392	Pitcher with inset rim		Pl. 45	4th century
156	Wide-necked pitcher	Group 8	Fig. 4, Pl. 18	3rd century
393	Narrow-necked pitcher		Pl. 45	Hellenistic

The first example comes from debris on the floor of a dining room of the later 4th century. The shape is very practical: solid ring foot, high ovoid body, tall neck with a carefully made rim to hold a lid. There are three examples from contemporary, datable contexts, all unpublished: C-71-521, C-37-2517, C-40-415.[35] There are a few differences between the examples. **392** and C-40-415 have straighter necks and more sharply articulated rims. Whether these slight changes are indicative of chronological differences in such large vessels is unclear. Also undetermined is the range of the shape. There is a 5th-century version;[36] how far into the Hellenistic period this pourer continues is as yet unknown. It may have been succeeded by one of the two following forms.

156 is an example of a Hellenistic wide-necked pitcher. Two examples were found in South Stoa Well XXX, C-47-130 and C-47-131.[37] Another was found in 1976, C-1976-114.[38] It has a much squatter profile

[30] Unpublished: C-31-129, from well 1931-7 and C-37-2502, from pit 1937-1.

[31] The context of **78** is the fill for the construction of the Trapezoidal Stoa at the very beginning of the 3rd century (Group 6). The fill contains both votive and dining-room debris. The context of **385**, lot 877, contains votive and cult pottery but also has many black-glazed sherds from kotylai and skyphoi, and even some late Corinthian and Attic black-figured fragments. The context of neither epichysis proves votive use; the size may be practical for expensive perfume. Small size does not necessarily mean votive function.

[32] Discussed in *Corinth* VII, iii, pp. 50–53. See especially C-47-750 (no. 199, p. 51, pl. 48), from the mid-6th century (well 1947-5).

[33] C-65-169 (*Corinth* VII, iii, no. 275, p. 55, pl. 48).

[34] Edwards separates the two forms of oinochoai: *Corinth* VII, iii, small trefoil, nos. 245–270, pp. 53–54; small trefoil with shoulder stop, nos. 271–278, pp. 54–55. They may be contemporaneous variants.

[35] C-71-521, from the Forum drain 1971-1; C-37-2517, from pit 1937-1, with second example in the context pottery; C-40-415, from well 1940-1.

[36] In coarse ware, C-34-935 (Pease, *Hesperia* 6, 1937, p. 303, no. 203, fig. 32; well 1934-10) and C-40-67, from well 1940-6, unpublished.

[37] *Corinth* VII, iii, nos. 631, 632, p. 113, pls. 24, 60 (well 1938-1).

[38] From the fill in the basin room, referred to in Williams, *Hesperia* 46, 1977, p. 52 (the underground chamber). The context, lot 1976-101, ranges from the late 4th century to 146 B.C., or later.

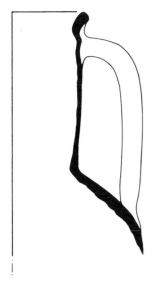

FIG. 4. Wide-necked pitcher **156**.
Scale 1:2

than the earlier, complete example, C-47-130. The shape is also found in Athens, both in the Agora and in the Kerameikos.[39] The two earlier Agora examples show a slight change in profile, with a later example, B 39, exhibiting a squatter profile than A 53. In the Kerameikos series, no. 108 is perhaps closest to Agora B 39. The development appears to be from a heavy, rounded lip to a squared-off form, from a pronounced neck ridge to a vestigial projection or grooved ring, from a slightly articulated to a false ring foot. No. 178 in the Kerameikos sequence, the last of the series in that context, has a neck taller in proportion to the full height. A later example, E 127 from the Agora, shows exaggerations of these profile changes.[40]

The Corinthian examples differ from the Attic in two ways. First, they are made of fine clay, as against the semicoarse fabric of the latter. Second, the few sufficiently preserved examples show a well-formed torus foot. It cannot yet be demonstrated that the Corinthian and Attic examples have parallel developments. **156** from the Sanctuary is incomplete, but its lip profile resembles C-1976-114 more than the South Stoa examples. Only a 3rd-century date may be suggested for **156**, the general date of the context. Firmer dating can be established only when more complete examples of the type are excavated in dated contextual sequences.

The third pitcher, **393**, is a narrow-necked form, a number of which were published by Edwards.[41] The context of **393** is a dumped fill in a cistern of Building M–N:25–26 (cistern 1965-1). The levels in which the fragments of **393** were found seemed to contain mostly 4th-century and early Hellenistic material.[42] But there were joining sherds throughout the levels, with much later Hellenistic pottery and a few intrusive Roman fragments. The cistern also had pre-Hellenistic work. Most of the material was kitchen fabric and was probably deposited in the cistern at one time. Thus the context cannot give firm dating. The profile of **393** is incomplete, but the downturned rim and the handle ridge are not so pronounced as many examples in *Corinth* VII, iii. **393** may well be later Hellenistic, but it cannot be proven.

VII. KALATHOI AND KALATHISKOI

Corinthian
With figure decoration (pyxis-kalathos)

216–219	*Fig. 28, Pl. 23	EC–LC

Flaring, with and without perforations

9–17	Group 1	Pl. 4
63	Group 5	Pl. 9
520–528		Pl. 51

[39] Agora: Thompson, *Hesperia* 3, 1934, p. 324, A 53, fig. 8; p. 343, B 39, fig. 23; p. 417, E 127, fig. 100. Kerameikos: Braun, *AM* 85, 1970, p. 136, no. 23; p. 141, nos. 90–92; p. 143, nos. 108, 109; p. 145, nos. 118, 119; p. 148, no. 139; p. 155, no. 178; comparative photographs pl. 82:2 and 3.

[40] For discussion of the changes, see Braun, *AM* 85, 1970, pp. 165–166. I am grateful to Professor U. Knigge and her staff for access to these pitchers.

[41] *Corinth* VII, iii, nos. 633–642, pp. 113–115, where they are called handle-ridged jugs. Since the type represented by **156** also has a handle ridge, the distinction between the forms is more clearly expressed by the width of the necks. The body profiles are fairly similar.

[42] There is a very fragmentary neck-rim-and-handle fragment, in fine ware, without any decoration, in lot 6722 (6722:2). It has a central neck ridge, from which comes the strap handle. The rim flares slightly but without the heavy downturn of **393** and similar jugs. Lot 6722, a cistern in Building L–M:28, has some Classical material, but the pottery is mostly later 4th century, going into the early 3rd. This fragment could be an earlier or variant form of the narrow-necked pitcher, smaller than the catalogued example.

Kalathiskos, type 1
18, 19	Group 1	Pl. 4
32	Group 2	Fig. 5, Pl. 5
529–532		Pl. 51

Kalathiskos, type 2
55	Group 4	Pl. 8
533–540		Pl. 51

Transitional to type 3
38	Group 3	Fig. 5, Pl. 6
541		Pl. 51

Kalathiskos, type 3
35–37, 39	Group 3	Fig. 5, Pl. 6
56–60	Group 4	Fig. 5, Pl. 8
64–72	Group 5	Fig. 5, Pl. 9
100–102	Group 6	Fig. 5, Pl. 13
542–550		Fig. 5, Pl. 51

Kalathiskos, type 4
103–106	Group 6	Fig. 5, Pl. 13
141–149	Group 7	Fig. 5, Pl. 14
168–171	Group 8	Fig. 5, Pl. 18

With basket handles
551–557		Pl. 51

Handmade of coarse clay
20, 21	Group 1	Pl. 4
558–560		Pl. 51

*See catalogue entry.

There are 100 inventoried examples. That is not an excessive number, for the kalathiskos is the predominant vessel in the Demeter Sanctuary. When work began on the pottery in 1970, an attempt was made to count the kalathiskoi. Before completing study of the pottery excavated in 1961,[43] over 2000 separate kalathiskos bases had been noted. It seemed pointless to continue. The 100 entries give the range of shape and decoration. It is the only vessel that appears in significant numbers in every area and during every period of the Sanctuary. Thus changes in shape are important, since the kalathiskos is very often the only well-preserved vase in a context. It is even found in the shallow fills of the dining rooms on the Lower Terrace, where little pottery of votive nature is found. Simply, there are so many of them that virtually no stratum, no matter how few the sherds, is without at least one fragmentary example.

Most of the inventoried examples are from the 1961 and 1962 excavations, with the major exception of the Group 1 kalathiskoi, found in 1970 (**9–21**). Although kalathiskoi were continually found in subsequent years, it was unnecessary to inventory more. In dating contexts, one may simply note the kalathiskoi that are similar to catalogued examples.

Dunbabin gave "a warning on the difficulty of dating these vases."[44] Yet, for the reasons given above, it was essential to attempt a chronological framework for the shape. The kalathiskos is a votive and thus tends to be conservative in shape. Dating more precisely than by 50-year intervals is difficult, and the chronology is still tentative. The chronological outline was ascertained by comparison of kalathiskoi in different strata in the Demeter Sanctuary with those from fills and deposits elsewhere in Corinth, particularly in the Potters' Quarter, the only other area producing sufficient quantities of the vase for evaluation of shape changes.[45]

The chronology applies only to the small kalathiskos adapted from the concave-sided pyxis, measuring about 0.045 to 0.055 m. in height. Group 3 contains three very large examples of the shape in type 3 profile,

---

[43] One month of excavation, May 23–June 22, produced 31 separate pottery contexts but none so extensive as the fills found in 1962 or in the 1964/1965 season.

[44] *Perachora* II, p. 303, commenting on the kalathiskoi.

[45] For deposits and dates of the Potters' Quarter material, see *Corinth* XV, ii, pp. 21–25; XV, iii, pp. 4–9.

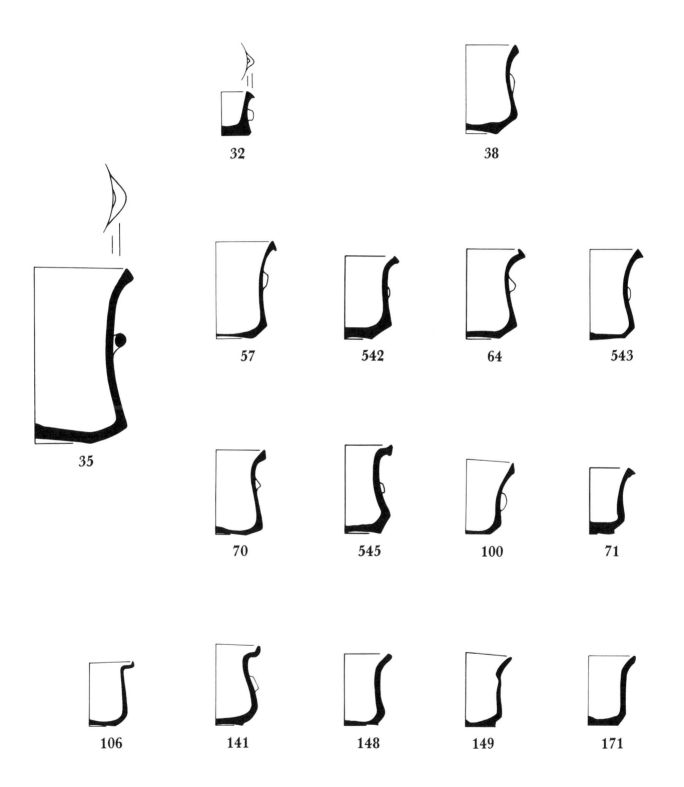

Fɪɢ. 5. Kalathoi and kalathiskoi. Scale 1:2

35–37; they are exceptional and represent only a short-lived experiment when the type 3 form was first introduced.

The earliest form is a flaring flat-based profile; it is very conservative in shape and impossible to arrange into any sort of series, except by changes in decoration.[46] Group 1 contains examples of this form, with only two kalathiskoi from that group representing transitions to the first examples of the concave-sided form (**18, 19**).

The Sanctuary also produced four examples of figured kalathiskoi, **216–219**. The decoration is more ambitious than is usual for the shape. These too are clearly close in shape to the concave-sided pyxis, but the addition of wall handles and heavy rim differentiates them from the true pyxis.[47]

Large flaring perforated kalathoi are very popular in the Archaic Sanctuary. Perhaps the most interesting discovery was that many of these had attached moldmade heads, hitherto thought reserved for convex pyxides (see **521** and the heads **603–620**). It may now be possible to identify other such heads, as for example no. 229 in *Perachora* I, a head attached to a strip of clay apparently with a finished edge: the flaring rim of a kalathos. Such heads may be recognized by the lack of an upper attachment, which the pyxis head always has. The flaring kalathos, with or without perforations, was popular in the 7th and 6th centuries; there is no attempt to formulate any chronology for the type.

Type 1: flat bottomed, concave wall

The concave-sided pyxis is the source for the four types of kalathiskoi to be discussed here. The older flaring form continues well into the 6th century, after type 1 is introduced at some time in the LPC period.[48] The major differences between the concave pyxis and the type 1 kalathiskos are the emphasis on the rim in the latter: flaring, often heavy, set off from the wall (characteristic of the large flaring type also), and a much lower, wider profile of the wall. The type 1 kalathiskos is a horizontal, not vertical, vase.

An important context for the appearance of type 1 is the Aryballos Deposit in the Potters' Quarter, of the later 7th and early 6th centuries. There the most popular form of the kalathiskos is the flaring form, perforated or plain. There are only a few of type 1(KV 372, KV 373), with rounded rims, close to the pyxis prototype. But KV 841, fragmentarily preserved, has the heavier triangular rim.[49] Type 1 kalathiskoi are also numerous in the Sanctuary, appearing with the older flaring form, as in Groups 1, 2, and other lots of Room D (Room R:23–24).

Characteristics of the type are bands inside and out, on wall and floor, and sometimes on the flat resting surface; banding usually neat and controlled; occasional designs in the handle zone, or even above or below the handles; well-articulated handles of loop or lug form. Good added purple is often used in the decoration. Typical designs are groups of S's or Z's, buds or dots, and "worms" alternating with dot rosettes.

Type 2: early beveled

There is no secure evidence for the date of the introduction of this form. It has certainly appeared by the mid-6th century (**533, 537**). In the Trench J deposit of the Potters' Quarter, with a terminal date in the later 6th century, examples of type 2 (KV 555, KV 627, and KV 628) appear with an example of type 1 (KV 551) and also with the older flaring form.[50] Thus the three forms continue to appear together.

Characteristics of the type 2 kalathiskos are wide, open profile (although some taller examples do occur); concave wall rising from a bevel; stressed rim, usually flaring and often well set off from the wall. But there are many variants of type 2; there seems to be no canonical form. These kalathiskoi have a lighter look than type 1; there is a preference for narrow but widely spaced bands of glaze or added colors, or both, inside and

---

[46] Note the Protogeometric example from a grave by the Babbius Monument in the Forum, C-68-58 (C. K. Williams, II, "Corinth, 1969: Forum Area," *Hesperia* 39, 1970 (pp. 1–39), p. 19, no. 27, pl. 9).

[47] See R. Hopper, "Addenda to *Necrocorinthia*," *BSA* 44, 1949 (pp. 162–257), pp. 209–210.

[48] See from Group 1 the transitional examples **18** and **19**. There is an LPC type 1 in the Anaploga Well, C-62-618 (*Corinth* VII, ii, An 239, pl. 72).

[49] For the Aryballos Deposit, see *Corinth* XV, iii, p. 8 (into the MC period). KV 372 and KV 373 are nos. 2080 and 2081 therein; KV 841 is not published.

[50] *Corinth* XV, iii, p. 8 for the date. KV 555 is no. 2084, KV 551 is no. 2085; KV 627 and KV 628 are not published.

out. There is often no handle-zone decoration. Handles are usually of the good lug or loop form, with an occasional pinched-on variant; some have no handles at all. This form is usually banded on the inner wall and floor as type 1 but not on the resting surface. Banding is usually neat; the finish is almost always good. True added purple still appears, although red brown is also used. Typical designs, found in the handle zone, include those cited for type 1 and in addition opposing cones, zigzags, and pomegranate chains.

Type 2 shows experimentation, such as footed examples with loop handles (**535**), looking rather like miniature kraters. Sherds from lot 1985 (Room D) show attempts to combine the perforated form with the profile of type 2: loop handles are placed between the perforations.

The terminal dates of both type 1 and type 2 are as yet unclear. Group 2, which seems to end about 550 B.C., has predominantly flaring and type 1 examples, with only a few of type 2. The Potters' Quarter Stelai Shrine A has one type 1, KP 1329 (unpublished), and examples of both type 2 and type 3. The range of that deposit is too long to be helpful, from the second half of the 6th century to the mid-5th. Tentatively, type 1 seems to disappear after 550, but how soon after is not known. Group 4 has kalathiskoi primarily of type 3, with a few of type 2. Group 3 has fewer of type 2; whereas Group 5, with almost no material before 500 B.C., has no examples of type 2. Lot 898 from Room B (Room P-Q:24), with a lower limit at the end of the 6th century, has kalathiskoi of the flaring form, in part of type 1 but mostly of type 2; it also has one fine example of an early type 3, **542**.

Type 3: black and red, beveled

This form appears at the end of the last quarter of the 6th century, is most popular throughout the 5th, and dies out in the mid-4th. Type 3 has a much darker look than type 2; it is also more uniform in shape and decoration.

The profile has the following form in the early examples: well-finished, often slightly concave resting surface; straight flare from resting surface to sharp bevel; concave wall with minimum diameter at mid-wall; handles usually of pinched-on form at mid-wall; flaring triangular rim. The rim diameter is usually just slightly greater than the bevel diameter. The very large examples in Group 3, **35-37**, show the type at its best. There is a good parallel for the latter examples in the Potters' Quarter Stelai Shrine A, KV 642 (unpublished).

The decorative system usually shows the following: resting surface and bevel reserved; inner wall with a black band just below the lip; circles on the floor and mid-wall of large or early examples; black band on the exterior wall above the bevel; added red below the handle zone, with a glaze line separating the two lower bands (the two colors may be reversed). The handle zone has normally a decorative pattern enclosed by light glaze lines. The upper wall and rim are black, originally in two separate bands; in later examples they merge. True added purple is never used in type 3; the added red or brown is put directly on the clay. Typical designs of the handle zone are S's or Z's, zigzags, and various forms of stopped maeanders (the latter are found only on type 3 kalathiskoi, not on the earlier forms).

The shape begins to degenerate in the later 5th century. Signs of lateness are banding over the bevel; rounded bevel; sharp contraction of the wall or, conversely, loss of concave profile; minimum diameter placed under the rim; loss of offset of rim from wall; poor surface finish; imprecise banding (although this can occur on some early examples). The changes can be followed. The Vrysoula kalathiskos is still good;[51] the contemporary example from well 1934-10 has neat banding and a sharp bevel, but the rim turns in.[52] The Potters' Quarter Circular South Shrine has two examples, KV 379 and KV 1257, with the minimum diameter above mid-wall (although not yet right under the rim). The Potters' Quarter Rectangular South Pit example, KV 376, has banding over the bevel and an exaggeratedly concave wall.[53] The early 4th-century example from Forum drain 1937-1 is not fully preserved, but the banding is very sloppy and the bevel quite rounded.[54]

---

[51] C-64-278 (Pemberton, *Hesperia* 39, 1970, p. 299, no. 124, pl. 74).
[52] C-34-1173 (Pease, *Hesperia* 6, 1937, p. 285, no. 107, fig. 20).
[53] *Corinth* XV, iii: KV 379 is no. 2091, KV 376 is no. 2089; KV 1257 is unpublished.
[54] C-37-196 from drain 1937-1, unpublished.

Two lots in Room D, 1985 and 1991 (Room R:23–24), contain examples of types 1 and 2 and a few examples that appear to be transitional to type 3 (see **541**). The lots appear to span the whole 6th century. They contain no vessels typical of the 5th century. Group 3 has three exceptionally large kalathoi, **35–37**. The group contains pottery of the late 6th into the second quarter of the 5th century, including one perforated kalathiskos wall sherd. Type 2 is not present; there is only one that is transitional to type 3. The latter is overwhelmingly the preferred form. Group 4 shows a similar range in date but with slightly more early material and correspondingly more fragments of type 2. These different contexts support a date of about 500 B.C. for the introduction of the type 3 kalathiskos. Although the shape and decoration have great similarity to 5th-century material introduced in the second quarter of that century,[55] these red-and-black vases must have been made first, 25 to 30 years before the similarly decorated thymiateria, oinochoai, lekythoi, and other shapes.

It is not clear when type 3 disappears in favor of the small undecorated type 4. There is only one poor example of type 3 in the 1937-1 drain,[56] and none in the 1937-1 pit.[57] The latter has a type 4 example, C-37-2648. In the Demeter Sanctuary, lot 878 has two examples of type 3, **546** and **547**, which represent the worst of the series. Unfortunately, the extended date of the context (Classical to early Hellenistic) precludes fixing a precise terminal date for the two examples. The same applies to the two late type 3 kalathiskoi of Group 6, **100** and **101**.

Type 4: small undecorated form

Both Groups 3 and 4 contain very small undecorated kalathiskoi with sharp type 3 profiles. In the later 4th century, the undecorated version is preferred,[58] but it loses its 5th-century articulation. The resting surface is flat, usually with string marks, the bevel rounded, the wall quite straight and merging with a simpler rim. There are often no handles. C-37-2648, from the 1937-1 pit,[59] and the example from the Forum drain 1971-1[60] still have handles; the latter is also well articulated. The former has the looser type 4 shape, as do the examples from the Forum well 1975-4.[61] All three deposits belong to the third quarter of the 4th century.

Groups 6 and 7 contain mostly type 4 kalathiskoi. Uninventoried examples from Group 6 are more varied, including fragments of all the types, but type 4 is overwhelmingly the preferred form. Only the latest type 4 examples are published (**103–106**), as are the late type 3 examples (**100–102**); there are others in the context pottery with sharper, earlier profiles. Group 7 contains type 4 kalathiskoi with and without handles (**141–149**); the profiles, however, are generally similar. **141–143** with slightly heavier rim are probably earlier than **144–149**. The merging of wall and rim may be the most secure criterion for a late date; the absence or presence of handles does not seem to be significant for dating. The latest of the Group 7 kalathiskoi may date to the mid-3rd century. Later Groups 8 and 9, of the Hellenistic period, have similar type 4 vessels (**168–171**). There is no discernible change except a simpler rim and poorer surface finish.

Type 4 probably lasted until 146 B.C., although there are no Sanctuary contexts limited to the last years before Mummius to prove the continuity. In 1928, a group of vases was excavated somewhere in the quarry area running from Temple Hill to the west, past Anaploga.[62] Apparently found together were late echinus

---

[55] See Pemberton, *Hesperia* 39, 1970, pp. 270–271.

[56] See footnote 54 above, p. 23.

[57] The pit is unpublished.

[58] See also the loss of decoration on phialai and hydriai.

[59] See footnote 57 above.

[60] C-71-75, unpublished.

[61] C-75-156, C-75-157, from well 1975-4 (a votive pit). The form has a basket handle (Williams and Fisher, *Hesperia* 45, 1976, p. 123, no. 59, pl. 22).

[62] Corinth notebook no. 100, p. 209, July 18, 1928 (de Waele). The site is not specifically located; it may, according to a later note by H. S. Robinson, be in the field belonging to N. Katsoulis, whose property produced wells with Hellenistic material, excavated in the 1960's. De Waele is not precise about the 1928 excavation: ". . . a heap of sherds . . . all being ware of no high importance . . . it is very probable that we have here a cesspool of vases and sherds. . . ." The material appears to be votive; it may be a votive pit that was excavated. One of the pieces, C-28-110, is a curious cylindrical object, possibly a torch or lamp holder, which also suggests that, before discarding, these vases may have been in a sanctuary.

bowls, an articulated kantharos, a late miniature pyxis bowl, a small hydria comparable to **507**, and a type 4 kalathiskos of the simplest form.[63] This group would seem to date to the early 2nd century, or later, and thus suggests a continuation of the votive to 146 B.C. Surely there would have been need for these most important offerings throughout the Greek period of the Sanctuary.[64]

Basket kalathiskos

The basket form appears to follow the changes of the above types. **551–554** show similarities with type 1, **555** and **556** with type 2, and **557** with the 5th-century form of type 3. No later type 4 examples with basket handles were found in the Sanctuary, although Forum well 1975-4 contained such a vessel.[65]

Handmade kalathiskoi

20 and **21** of Group 1 and **558–560** represent hundreds of similar kalathiskoi, found in both Archaic and Classical strata. They normally show an open flaring profile, with or without handles, usually with pellets decorating the rim. These vessels, of coarse clay with inclusions, seem to disappear in the later 5th century.

VIII. KOTYLAI

Corinthian

3	ray based	Group 1	Fig. 6, Pl. 4	LPC
4	ray based	Group 1	Pl. 4	beginning of EC?
5	ray based	Group 1	Pl. 4	LPC
6	ray based	Group 1	Fig. 6, Pl. 4	LPC
40	ray based	Group 3	Fig. 6, Pl. 6	first to second quarter 5th century
220–233	figured fragments		*Fig. 29, Pls. 23, 24	EC–LC
22	black figured	Group 2	Fig. 6, Pl. 5	LC
23	black figured	Group 2	Pl. 5	LC
41	semiglazed	Group 3	Fig. 6, Pl. 7	second quarter 5th century
42	semiglazed	Group 3	Pl. 7	second quarter 5th century
292	outline style		*Fig. 34, Pl. 32	second quarter 5th century
7	glazed	Group 1	Pl. 4	LPC
8	glazed	Group 1	Fig. 6, Pl. 4	EC?
394	glazed		Pl. 45	late 5th or early 4th century
396	glazed		Pl. 45	mid- or third quarter 4th century
397	glazed		Fig. 6	late 4th century
398	glazed		Pl. 45	late 4th or beginning 3rd century
399	glazed, West Slope		Fig. 6, Pl. 45	mid-3rd century
400	glazed, West Slope			mid-3rd century
401	plain		Pl. 45	later 6th century
113	plain	Group 7	Fig. 6, Pl. 15	end of 4th century
402	plain		Fig. 6	late 4th century
403	plain		Pl. 45	end of 4th or beginning 3rd century
114	plain	Group 7	Fig. 6, Pl. 15	first quarter 3rd century
157	plain	Group 8	Pl. 18	first quarter 3rd century
404	plain		Pl. 45	later 3rd century
405	plain		Fig. 6, Pl. 45	Hellenistic
406	plain		Pl. 45	Hellenistic
407	plain		Pl. 45	Hellenistic

[63] The vases are C-28-104–C-28-109; see footnote 15 above, p. 12.

[64] Group 9, however, contained mostly hydriskoi; in the later Hellenistic period, the latter may have superseded the kalathiskoi as the predominant form of votive.

[65] See footnote 61 above, p. 24.

408	plain	Pl. 46	Hellenistic
409	plain	Pl. 46	Hellenistic
Imported, Attic			
342	red figure	Pl. 39	second quarter 5th century
395	glazed	Fig. 6, Pl. 45	second quarter 4th century

*Decoration only; see catalogue entry.

The kotyle is distinguished from the skyphos by its lighter foot, more convex, thinner wall, and longer history.[66] The different varieties of kotylai in the Sanctuary can be traced from the Late Protocorinthian period (**3–6, 7–8,** Group 1) to the 3rd century (**114, 157, 404**); ray based, figured, black glazed, and semi-glazed are all well represented in Sanctuary strata. Only a few have been catalogued. Since these kotylai are so well known and very carefully documented,[67] there is no need to repeat here the chronological development of the shape. Fragments of these types have been very useful for dating levels of the Archaic and Classical Sanctuary. Two very interesting and rather rare examples are figured works of the 5th century: an Attic red-figured ray-based kotyle (**342**) and a Corinthian outline-style work showing Persephone and running boys (**292**).

The kotyle retains its popularity throughout much of the 5th century, for the conventionalizing and semi-glazed forms normally have the lighter kotyle foot. But in the later 5th century, in the black-glazed forms, the skyphos becomes more popular.[68]

The inventoried examples show the range of the development of the shape in the black-glazed, ovoid form. Only one is Attic, **395**, with crosshatching at the bottom of the wall. Corinthian examples belong to the late 5th and later 4th centuries (**394, 396–398**). In the late stage of the ovoid kotyle, the foot becomes very splayed.[69] Successive profiles can be noted in **397–400**, all from lot 3228. **397** still retains the inner articulation of the foot. With **398** and **399**, the outer foot is virtually horizontal with a conical interior. The wall retains the strong, high ovoid profile, turning in to a rounded lip. But most interesting is the use of West Slope decoration on the last examples, **399** and **400**, related to and possibly influenced by the articulated kantharos.[70]

There is also an unglazed version popular in the Hellenistic period. Undecorated kotylai do appear in the Sanctuary from the late 6th century on, although never in great quantity (see **401**).[71] They are well-made large versions of the ray based or semiglazed. In the 4th century the small plain form becomes more popular and may survive to 146 B.C.[72] It derives from the black-glazed ovoid form, but the profile never shows the extremes of the latest in that type. **113** and **114** (Group 7) show the form in the later 4th and early 3rd centuries: narrow ring foot, convex wall turning in to a rounded lip, small loop handle. **157** has a later profile: lower, wider wall in relation to the foot. The foot has now become a flat, unarticulated resting

[66] This distinction follows Williams in Williams and Fisher, *Hesperia* 41, 1972, p. 155, note 18.

[67] *Corinth* XIII, pp. 127–128; *Agora* XII, pp. 81–83.

[68] An unpublished study by D. Kazazis of the kotylai and skyphoi from well 1937-1 and drain 1937-1 produced the following statistics: the earlier well contained 67 kotylai and 37 skyphoi, the later drain 28 kotylai and 80 skyphoi, thereby showing the change in popularity between the two shapes in the beginning of the 4th century. Demeter context lot 6838 shows an equal number of the two shapes; the date of the context is about 400 B.C., when the two shapes are in the process of changing ratios.

[69] A kotyle in the North Cemetery, T 2451 (*Corinth* XIII, grave 444-2, pl. 71), shows the beginning of the splayed foot and elongated profile. The grave also contained a beveled saucer (T 2453), very nippled, with sharp profile, probably of the third quarter of the 4th century. See also the Etruscan kotyle, C-75-168 (Williams and Fisher, *Hesperia* 45, 1976, p. 120, no. 36, pl. 20; well 1975-4), of the same date. It is obviously imitative of the ovoid form in Athens; the pink bands and use of red clay and lustrous glaze are Attic inspired. But the lip is much heavier and the handles more elongated. The wider splayed foot of this Etruscan import and the Hellenistic forms of Corinthian kotylai in the Demeter Sanctuary is, in fact, more practical than the usual slighter foot for the elongated shape; it could have helped support the exaggerated form of the late kotyle when filled with wine.

[70] For Attic version, see *Agora* XII, p. 83, note 11 and B. Schlörb-Vierneisel, "Eridanos-Nekropole I.," *AM* 81, 1966 (pp. 1–111), grave 158-1, p. 91 (from the Kerameikos), probably early 3rd century, not late 4th as dated therein.

[71] There is a fine large example in lot 4351, Group 4, with a beautifully polished surface.

[72] Pit A, Group 5, contains an exxample (lot 887:5); also lots 2110:2 and 2110:3 of the early 4th century, and lot 6838:2 of the same date. These all appear to be early examples of the form.

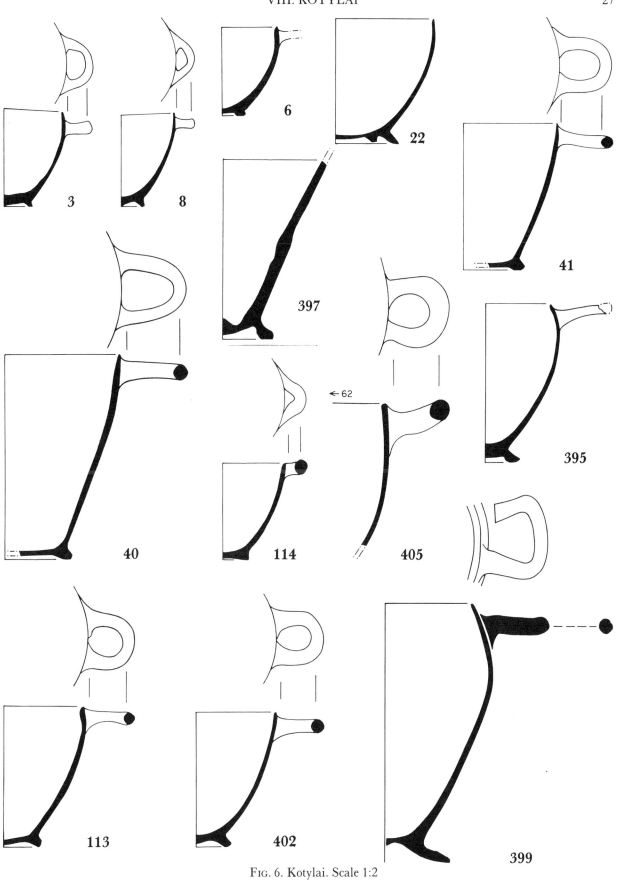

FIG. 6. Kotylai. Scale 1:2

surface; the handles are pinched-on strips of clay. **404** is very similar to an example from Forum well 1975-5.[73]

Whether this small form lasted until 146 is as yet unclear; fragments are found in Mummian debris but not sufficiently well preserved to note changes beyond the *ca.* 200 B.C. shape. The latest examples of that date show a fairly open profile (as compared to the final form of the black ovoid type); the profile in fact resembles the MC kotyle wall.

405–409 are fragments of larger plain kotylai, presumably made in the Hellenistic period; the context, lot 6640, is of Hellenistic and early Roman date. The profiles of foot, wall, and lip resemble the black-glazed kotylai, and thus they are published in this, not the Roman, section. K. Slane and N. Bookidis identified them as Greek.

IX. SKYPHOI

Corinthian

43	ray based	Group 3	Fig. 7, Pl. 7	early 5th century
301	red figure		Pl. 33	*ca.* 420–410 B.C.
302	red figure		Pl. 33	end of 5th century
303	red figure		Pl. 33	end of 5th or beginning of 4th century
304	red figure		Pl. 33	end of 5th or beginning of 4th century
80	glazed	Group 6	Fig. 7, Pl. 12	third quarter 4th century
81	glazed	Group 6	Fig. 7, Pl. 12	third quarter 4th century
410	glazed		Fig. 7, Pl. 46	third or early fourth quarter 4th century
115	glazed	Group 7	Fig. 7, Pl. 15	end of 4th century
158	glazed	Group 8	Fig. 7, Pl. 18	late first or early second quarter 3rd century
412	glazed		Fig. 7, Pl. 46	late first or second quarter 3rd century

Imported

313	Attic black figure		Pl. 34	early 5th century
314	Attic black figure		Pl. 35	early 5th century
315	Attic black figure		Pl. 35	early 5th century
343	Attic glaux		Pl. 39	second quarter 5th century
344	Attic red figure		Pl. 39	second quarter 5th century
345	Attic red figure		Pl. 39	second quarter 5th century
346–349	Attic red figure[74]		Pl. 39	second quarter 5th century
350–353	Attic red figure		Pl. 39	just after mid-5th century
354, 355	Attic red figure		Pl. 40	just after mid-5th century
356	Attic red figure		Pl. 40	mid-5th century
357	Attic red figure		Pl. 41	mid-5th century
358	Attic red figure		Pl. 41	third quarter 5th century
359	Attic red figure		Pl. 41	*ca.* 430–420 B.C.
61	red figure	Group 5	Pl. 9	fourth quarter 5th century
360	Attic red figure		Pl. 41	first or early second quarter 4th century
116	Attic glazed	Group 7	Fig. 7, Pl. 15	late first or second quarter 3rd century
411	Attic glazed		Pl. 46	early 3rd century

Since the skyphos is an Attic invention,[75] it is appropriate that the earliest examples of the shape excavated in the Sanctuary are Attic black figure (**313–315**). They all have parallels in material from the Athenian Agora of the early 5th century, cited under each entry.[76]

[73] C-75-285, of Hellenistic date; the well is mentioned in Williams and Fisher, *Hesperia* 45, 1976, p. 109, note 7.
[74] **346–349**, **350–353**, and **354, 355** represent separate fragments most likely from the same vessels. Because there is no absolute certainty of the connections, I have published the fragments separately in the catalogue, noting the likelihood of attributions.
[75] For the distinction between skyphos and kotyle, see under kotylai (Shape Studies, VIII), p. 26 above.
[76] See the material in Vanderpool, *Hesperia* 15, 1946.

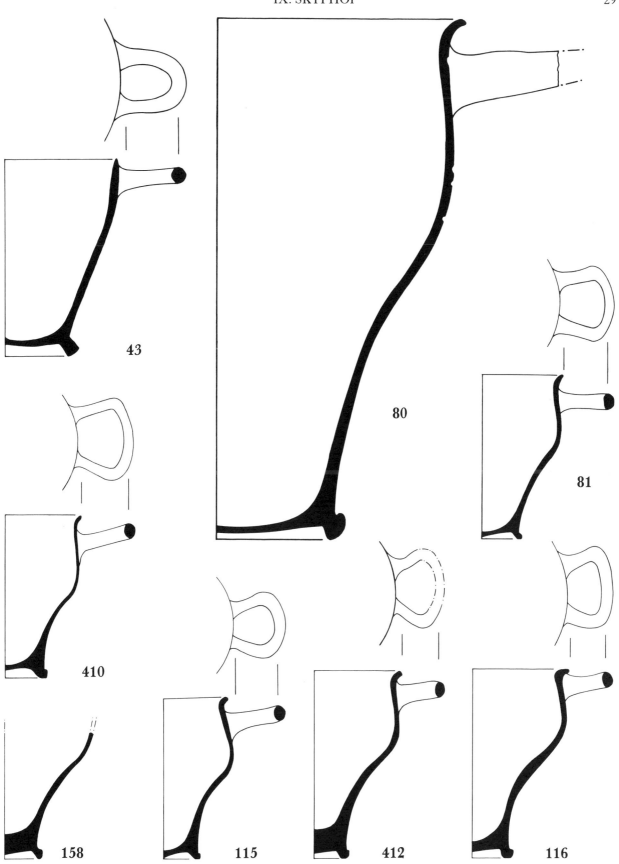

FIG. 7. Skyphoi. Scale 1:2

The series of Corinthian skyphoi begins with **43**, from Group 3, showing the grafting of the torus foot onto the older ray-based kotyle form. The series can be followed into the 3rd century, in both black and figured examples. Since the development of the shape has been thoroughly discussed elsewhere,[77] a summary of Sanctuary skyphoi seems sufficient.

After the introduction of the Attic form into Corinth, many imitations of Attic decoration and glaze were produced. There are numerous fragments of these 5th-century skyphoi from Sanctuary contexts but none adequately preserved for publication.[78] Red-figured Attic examples represent the 5th century, with some fine artists responsible for several fragments (**344**, **345** Penthesilean; **346–349** by the Lewis Painter). By the end of the century, the skyphos begins to acquire a compound curve to the wall, by a concavity below the lip forcing the lip outwards. A curious imported example (**61**) and a Corinthian red-figured fragment (**301**) illustrate this first stage of the change.

For the earlier 4th century, one Attic red-figured skyphos (**360**) shows the compound-curve wall. There are, as with kotylai and other shapes, many well-preserved Corinthian skyphoi of the later 4th century, including an enormous ribbed example, **80**.[79] The shape continues into the 3rd century; **158** and **412** are the latest skyphoi. The shape does not survive the 3rd century.[80] The extremely narrow foot and the expanded wall must have made the vessel, when full of wine, a very hazardous drinking cup.

X. CUPS

Corinthian

413	offset rim		Fig. 8, Pl. 46	EC
24	offset rim	Group 2	Pl. 5	MC or early LC
234	offset rim		Pl. 24	late MC or LC
414	wishbone handles		Fig. 8, Pl. 46	6th century

Imported

318	Attic black figure, Siana		Pl. 35	second quarter 6th century
319	Attic black figure, Siana		Pl. 35	second quarter 6th century
320	Attic black figure, band cup		Pl. 35	mid- or third quarter 6th century
321	Attic black figure, lip cup		Pl. 35	third quarter 6th century
322	Attic black figure, lip cup		Pl. 35	third quarter 6th century
323	black figure		Pl. 35	later 6th century
316, **317**	Attic black figure, deep cup		Pl. 35	late 6th century
159	Attic black figure	Group 8	Pl. 18	early 5th century
361	Attic red figure		Pl. 41	first quarter 5th century
362	Attic red figure		Pl. 41	first quarter 5th century
363	Attic red figure		Pl. 42	first quarter 5th century
364	Attic red figure		Pl. 42	second quarter 5th century
365	red figure		Pl. 43	early 4th century
82	Attic glazed calyx-cup	Group 6	Pl. 12	first quarter 3rd century

All the cups are included in this section, except for the one-handled variety, discussed in Shape Studies, XIII.

---

[77] *Agora* XII, pp. 84–85.

[78] For the 5th-century form in Corinthian fabric, see *Corinth* XIII, p. 124; also C-64-259 (Pemberton, *Hesperia* 39, 1970, p. 297, no. 108, pl. 73). There is also a very large outline-style vessel with a skyphos foot, **287**; but it is published as a skyphoid krater. The shape, decoration, and style are unique.

[79] There is also a very large Attic skyphos (krateroid size) from the Forum drain, 1937-1, C-37-582. See also C-47-858 a and b, C-47-859 (*Corinth* VII, iii, nos. 307–309, p. 69; well 1947-2). See also the late 5th-century skyphos in Basel, painted by an artist in the circle of the Meidias Painter (E. Simon, "Kratos und Bia," *Würzburger Jahrbücher*, n.s. 1, 1975, pp. 177–186).

[80] For the 3rd-century form in Corinth, see E. Pemberton, *Hesperia* 54, 1985, pp. 280–282.

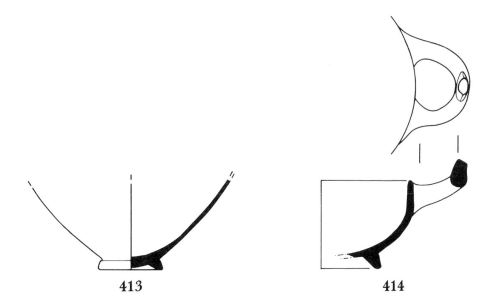

413   **414**

Fig. 8. Cups. Scale 1:2

In the Archaic period, the Corinthian vase painter did not decorate the cup as often as the kotyle, although some very fine cups were produced, especially in the MC period. In the Sanctuary, even the non-figured, black-glazed ones are virtually absent from 6th-century strata. That no gorgoneion cups and no more than a few bird cups (see **234**) were found suggests neither need for nor popularity of the shape.

Only one of the four Corinthian examples is without parallel, **414**; the most important of the four is the deep EC cup with graffito, **413**. The Attic black-figured examples are far more numerous, with a range of cup types, including two fine Siana examples, by the C Painter (**318**) and the Heidelberg Painter (**319**). The most common form found in the late 6th- and early 5th-century levels is the palmette cup, but none mended sufficiently for publication. There are several fine red-figured examples, including one by Makron (**361**), one by a Dourian hand (**363**), and one by the Pistoxenos Painter (**364**). Still, the Attic black- and red-figured skyphoi and glazed forms of the kotylai and skyphoi far outnumber the cups, paralleling the statistics for the same shapes in Corinthian fabric.

Yet, one may note the following: the decorated Attic cups from the Sanctuary, in both red and black figure, are much finer than the figured Corinthian ones. I am unsure whether that has any significance. By the end of the 5th century, imports in the shape virtually cease; there is only one later cup, **82**, a calyx-cup from Athens.

XI. PHIALAI

Corinthian

25	decorated	Group 2	Fig. 9, Pl. 5	before 550 B.C.
415	decorated		Fig. 9, Pl. 46	before 550 B.C.
416	decorated			mid-6th century
417	plain		Pl. 46	mid-6th century
418	decorated			after mid-6th century

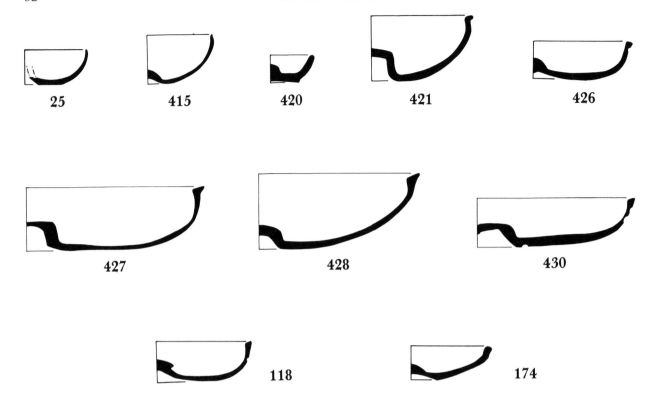

FIG. 9. Phialai. Scale 1:2

419	decorated		Pl. 46	mid- or later 6th century
235	figured		Pl. 24	LC
420	decorated		Fig. 9	end of 6th century, slightly later?
421	decorated		Fig. 9, Pl. 46	end of 6th century
280	figured		*Fig. 32, Pl. 30	third quarter 5th century
281	figured		Pl. 30	later 5th century
424	decorated		Pl. 46	later 5th century
425	decorated		Pl. 46	5th century?
426	plain		Fig. 9	first half 4th century
427	plain		Fig. 9, Pl. 46	third quarter 4th century
428	plain		Fig. 9	third quarter 4th century
429	plain			third quarter 4th century
430	plain		Fig. 9, Pl. 46	third quarter 4th century
431	plain			late 4th century
173	plain	Group 9	Pl. 19	late 4th or early 3rd century
117	plain	Group 7	Pl. 15	end of 4th century
432	plain		Pl. 46	early 3rd century
118	plain	Group 7	Fig. 9, Pl. 15	early 3rd century
119	plain	Group 7	Pl. 15	early 3rd century
175	plain	Group 9	Pl. 19	mid-3rd century
174	plain	Group 9	Fig. 9, Pl. 19	later 3rd century
Imported				
422	Attic decorated			early 5th century
423	Attic decorated		Pl. 46	early 5th century

*Decoration only; see catalogue entry.

Phialai are found in every area and in most periods of the Sanctuary. They surely were important in rituals, both of cult and of building construction (see **427–430**). Although many of the examples are very small, possibly functioning as miniatures for votive purposes, all are included here and are published with the regular wares, not with miniatures. It is impossible to determine at what diameter or height a phiale becomes a miniature. Presumably, a small drop of liquid in a tiny phiale might suffice for the requisite ritual.

Analysis of the shape shows gradual changes in profile but without the more obvious distinctions found in other vessels. One assumes that cult and votive vessels change little, or at least exhibit less of the experimentation in shape change of everyday fine wares. Nevertheless, there are continuous alterations of the profile. The means of isolating the changes was by examination of material from contexts in Corinth other than those of the Sanctuary for comparison with the Sanctuary phialai.

The 6th-century phiale has a wide resting surface, good central depression (unless of very small size), high convex flaring wall terminating in a simple rounded lip, an omphalos variously formed but usually rounded and rising continuously from the floor; the floor and wall are also continuous, not offset from each other. The vessel is often decorated, usually with bands, sometimes with floral or figure designs. Group 2 contains the first example, **25**; lot 1985, also from Room D (Room R:23–24), has similar phialai, decorated and plain (**415–417**). These date to the mid-6th century. **418** and **419** have rounded omphaloi and date to the middle of the century or slightly later, on the basis of context. A phiale decorated in silhouette style, **235**, retains the rounded (earlier) lip, but another phiale from the same lot (1988), **420**, has a heavier rim, thus introducing a characteristic popular in the 5th century.[81]

421 shows the 5th-century profile. The wall is still high and flaring in convex form, but it terminates in a heavier projecting rim. The omphalos is more offset from the floor and has a level top.[82] Some 5th-century phialai are decorated. The Sanctuary yielded two Attic polychrome examples, **422** and **423**. The 5th-century profile is confirmed by **280**, with Vrysoula animals and palmettes, and by **281**, probably related to the Sam Wide group of vases. Both have the heavier rim and lower wall profile; in addition, in these and many contemporary phialai, the wall and floor do not merge as in 6th-century examples. **424**, from a 5th-century context, shows the same characteristics in a very small size. **425** is a lovely work, with crisp scalloped walls, probably 5th century in date.[83]

There are no examples, either from the Sanctuary or from other contexts in Ancient Corinth, that may be securely dated to the first half of the 4th century. **426** probably belongs within that period, but the context has a long span, from the 6th through the 4th century. There are abundant phialai from later 4th-century contexts. **427–430** find parallels in closely datable strata of the third quarter of the century.[84] They are also very important, for they were found in the foundation trench of wall 245, indicative, perhaps, of a ritual associated with the construction of a dining room. The 4th-century profile is still low, the floor and wall are once more continuous, the rim is defined and in many examples is offset by grooves. Some examples have an inturned rim, similar to the profile of the small echinus bowl (see **117**, **175**). The omphaloi are low, set off from the floor, and almost always flat topped. From the later 4th century on, phialai are undecorated.[85]

431 and **432**, from the debris in Room Ka (Building K–L:24–25), may be slightly later than the above, for the central depression is losing its definition.[86] Group 7 contains several phialai that have a range in dates.

[81] For 6th-century phialai, see C-53-209 (Brann, *Hesperia* 25, 1956, p. 363, no. 45, pl. 56; well 1953-1). A larger unpublished example, C-34-2516, has the same profile and is decorated with a late incised palmette chain. It comes from a grave, 1934-11, which contained aryballoi and other LC pottery.

[82] KP 548 and KP 549 (*Corinth* XV, iii, no. 1036), from Stelai Shrine A of the Potters' Quarter, have similar omphaloi, but the rim is not so well defined as that of **421**. The context of **421**, lot 1991, has pottery going to the end of the 6th century; the developed form of the type 3 kalathiskos is not found in that lot, nor are other shapes characteristic of the early 5th century. See the discussion under kalathiskoi (Shape Studies, VII), p. 24 above.

[83] There are several dated 5th-century phialai: C-39-226 and C-39-227, from well 1939-1, unpublished; C-34-1159 and C-34-1162 (Pease, *Hesperia* 6, 1937, p. 287, nos. 120, 121, fig. 20; well 1934-10). The profile of rim and wall of many 5th-century phialai resembles a contemporary form of bowl. See T 2871 (*Corinth* XIII, p. 148, grave 388-13).

[84] See C-75-161 and C-75-162, from the Forum, well 1975-4; other pottery of this group is published in Williams and Fisher, *Hesperia* 45, 1976, pp. 117–124 (C-75-162 is no. 49, pl. 21).

[85] C-75-162 (footnote 84 above) is one of the last examples to be decorated, with interior bands and dots on the rim.

[86] See KP 703 (*Corinth* XV, iii, no. 2247), from the Potters' Quarter, Terracotta Factory, quite similar to **432**.

117 is probably from the end of the 4th century, but 118 and 119 resemble the Room Ka examples and may date to the early 3rd century.

Group 9, ranging throughout much of the 3rd century, contains three examples, 173–175. The omphaloi are small, the central depressions weak, the resting surfaces very narrow, the rims less well defined.[87] The contraction of the resting surface resembles the change in contemporary saucers.

The phiale appears to lose its importance and popularity as a cult or votive vessel in the later 3rd century. Group 10 contained no phialai; the huge amount of pottery in Group 11 revealed fragments of only three. This may be accidental, since both fills are from dining rooms. But generally in strata associated with the later Hellenistic phase of the Sanctuary, phialai are absent.

There is a group of phialai discussed by K. Slane in the last section of Catalogue II (675–681). The contexts of the fragments do not give an indisputable date of manufacture of the pieces. The profiles and fabrics, however, of these relatively large examples differ considerably from those that are clearly pre-146 B.C. Since Slane recognized and studied these phialai, it is more appropriate that she publish them, although we are not sure whether they are Greek (Hellenistic) or Roman.

XII. KANTHAROI

Corinthian

433	goblet?		Fig. 10, Pl. 46	first quarter 4th century
434	one-piece		Pl. 46	second quarter 3rd century?
435	cyma		Fig. 10, Pl. 46	second quarter to mid-3rd century
436	articulated		Fig. 10, Pl. 46	mid-3rd century or slightly later
437	West Slope?		Fig. 10, Pl. 47	later Hellenistic?

Imported

83	Attic	Group 6	Pl. 12	4th century
84	Attic	Group 6	Fig. 10, Pl. 12	4th century
120	Attic	Group 7	Pl. 15	early 3rd century

There is only one early kantharos from the Demeter Sanctuary, a very small fragment of Etruscan bucchero, published in 1974 and not included here.[88] Fragments of Hellenistic kantharoi in Corinthian fabric, identifiable by handle and foot fragments, are conspicuous in later levels.

There is a very real question about the beginning date for the Hellenistic varieties of Corinthian kantharoi. No Corinthian examples have been found in any of the recently excavated fills dated to the third quarter of the 4th century.[89] Similarly, no Corinthian fragments were found in the fill of the Trapezoidal Stoa, Group 6, which did have several Attic fragments, 83 and 84.[90] Group 7, the votive pit B, also contained no Corinthian kantharoi but one Attic handle, 120. Both these groups have other forms of drinking vessels. Edwards noted the presence of kantharoi in the South Stoa shop wells but not in the deposits associated with the construction of the building.[91] Since the Stoa wells contained unstratified dumped fills, they give no

---

[87] There is a similar example from the Katsoulis well (well 1965-3, unpublished), C-65-387, with a slightly more projecting rim. The example is unfortunately not closely datable within the Hellenistic period, owing to the long span of the contents of that well.

[88] MacIntosh in Williams, MacIntosh, and Fisher, *Hesperia* 43, 1974, p. 39, no. 30: C-73-301.

[89] See the material from the Forum drain, 1971-1: Williams and Fisher, *Hesperia* 41, 1972, pp. 155–163; well 1975-4: Williams and Fisher, *Hesperia* 45, 1976, pp. 117–124 (a votive pit). A Corinthian version of the Attic cup-kantharos with molded rim (*Agora* XII, nos. 696–704) was found in cistern 1979-1, C-1979-115, but with simpler foot, closer to the kotyle foot (cistern noted in Williams, *Hesperia* 49, 1980, pp. 120–121). This cistern was put out of use by the building of the South Stoa; the pottery is consistent with other deposits of the third quarter of the 4th century. There are a few fragments of cup-kantharos rims in the Demeter Sanctuary, as lot 3230:15 (Group 11), but it was never a popular shape in Corinth. The 5th-century votive kantharoi from Vrysoula, based on a Boeotian form, stand apart as a special class with neither past nor future (Pemberton, *Hesperia* 39, 1970, pp. 276–277, 290–291, nos. 16, 17, 72–76).

[90] Small lip fragments of cyma kantharoi might be mistaken for late skyphoi, but no kantharos feet, no ring handles in Corinthian fabric exist in the context pottery of Groups 6 and 7.

[91] *Corinth* VII, iii, p. 83, discussing the articulated kantharos form, but the observation is applicable to all the profiles.

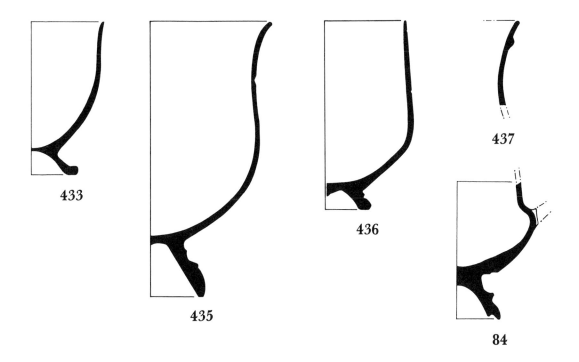

FIG. 10. Kantharoi. Scale 1:2

intrinsic evidence for the introduction of the kantharos locally made. Given the lack of kantharoi in con-struction fills and the current lowering of the date of the building of the South Stoa, it now seems that the Hellenistic forms of Corinthian kantharoi may not have appeared in Corinth until *ca.* 300 B.C. or later,[92] that is, after similar forms had been established in Athens.[93]

Two forms of kantharoi resemble older drinking vessels that disappear in the 3rd century. The one-piece type has a wall profile similar to the black ovoid kotyle; the cyma kantharos resembles the skyphos with

[92] There are three kantharoi, not from South Stoa wells, that seem to come from pre-300 B.C. contexts. From the Potters' Quarter is a one-piece example with knotted handles, KP 213 (*Corinth* VII, iii, no. 384, p. 76), published now in *Corinth* XV, iii as no. 1166, p. 217, dated there to the first half of the 4th century. It is called eclectic there, the body similar to a footed mug, the reserved foot as on a kotyle. The wall does not curve in as typical for the one-piece, nor is the foot well articulated. It may show the same sort of experimentation as does **433**. Although the Potters' Quarter seems to have been destroyed by the later 4th-century earthquake, there are later vessels from that site. KP 213 did not have a secure context.

Also from the Potters' Quarter is KP 2702 (*Corinth* VII, iii, p. 76, note 77), published in *Corinth* XV, iii as no. 1237, p. 227. The clay does not appear to be Corinthian. It is much harder than the usual Corinthian, with a hard thin glaze; the core is 7.5YR 7/4 (pink). The ribbing rises very close to the top of the wall, unlike similar work on the cyma or Acrocorinth varieties, where it stops lower on the wall. The ribbing is bounded by a groove and a ridge; the separate grooves of the rim zone are lacking. The wall also passes more continuously into the flaring lip. The lack of incision or painted decoration, conspicuous on most kantharoi, is also curious. The quality of the ribbing and the stamped eggs are more suggestive of an early 4th- than of the later 4th-century date proposed in both publications. It is a large vessel, with an estimated lip diameter of 0.125 m. and is, I am sure, an import, found without good context.

The kantharos found in grave 1960-7, C-60-227 (*Corinth* VII, iii, no. 451, p. 82), giving the name to the Acrocorinth shape, also is not Corinthian. The clay is highly micaceous, 5YR 5/6 (reddish yellow) in the core, very hard, close to Attic. The unguentarium and the silver obol found with the kantharos date the grave to the third quarter of the century, but the kantharos is foreign. The shape is made elsewhere.

None of the other kantharoi given later 4th-century dates comes from closed, stratified, secure contexts.

[93] The related Attic types are discussed in *Corinth* VII, iii, under the various shapes: one-piece, pp. 74–76; cyma, pp. 76–82; articulated, pp. 83–86.

compound curve. If kantharoi were first produced shortly after 300 B.C., they may have been intended as replacements for the older vessels which had become very impractical in shape.

The earliest examples from the Sanctuary are Attic: **83**, **84**, **120**. Parallels for each are cited under the individual entries. Of the Corinthian kantharoi, the cyma and articulated are the most popular forms, but as with so much of the Hellenistic pottery, found primarily on the Lower Terrace, few mended sufficiently for publication. The two examples, **435** and **436**, can be placed within the series arranged by Edwards, although the absolute dates may have to be lowered. **434** may be a one-piece type, but it has a ribbed body, exceptional for the shape. One fragment of a wall with thorn decoration was found in lot 6181 (6181:1), M–N:19.[94]

There are two curious pieces included here as possible kantharoid vessels. **437** is a handsome puzzle; the fabric may be Corinthian, as it resembles the fabric used in some hemispherical bowls and lamps of the later Hellenistic period, demonstrable as local.[95] The decoration of that incomplete vase is much more elaborate than is customary for the shape. **433** is a hybrid or experimental *hapax*, placed in this section by its foot profile. The foot is conical and spreading, the wall nearly vertical with a slight concavity under the simple lip, reminiscent of the late 5th-century change in the skyphos profile. The handle is not preserved. The decoration seems to derive from semiglazing of Classical kotylai and skyphoi. The general profile most resembles the Vrysoula goblet.[96] The context of **433**, lot 2110, is very consistent, with a great amount of pottery dating from the mid-5th through the first quarter of the 4th century, with but a few earlier pieces.[97] Thus **433** must belong to that period and is placed in the later part of it, on the basis of the resemblance to the goblet.

XIII. ONE-HANDLED CUPS

Corinthian

438	type 1		Pl. 47	mid- to third quarter 5th century
439	type 1		Fig. 11, Pl. 47	4th century
121	type 1	Group 7	Pl. 15	later 4th century
440	type 2		Fig. 11	first half 4th century
86	type 2	Group 6	Fig. 11, Pl. 12	third to fourth quarter 4th century
87	type 2	Group 6	Fig. 11, Pl. 12	third to fourth quarter 4th century
441	type 2		Fig. 11	third or early fourth quarter 4th century
442	type 2		Fig. 11, Pl. 47	third or early fourth quarter 4th century
122	type 2	Group 7	Fig. 11, Pl. 15	*ca.* 300 B.C.
123	type 2	Group 7	Pl. 15	*ca.* 300 B.C. or slightly later
Imported				
85	Attic	Group 6	Pl. 12	mid-4th century

The one-handled cup is a problematic shape, with a chronologically vague development. There are two forms. The first is a thin-walled cup, glazed inside, semiglazed by dipping on the exterior, with a thin or even false ring foot, convex wall turning in slightly to a rounded lip, and a small horizontal loop handle set at the top of the wall. It appears in the second quarter of the 5th century[98] and continues into the 4th, becoming

[94] Lot 6181, a burnt stratum within Building M–N:19, contains pottery of the 4th and earlier 3rd centuries; how far into the 3rd century it went cannot be precisely stated. No moldmade relief bowl fragments were found, but that may be accidental. Typical 3rd-century material, including a later unguentarium (6181:3), a later stewpot (6181:2), small late pyxis fragments, and plates, suggests a terminal date at the middle of the century.

[95] See the discussion of this fabric by C. Edwards, *Hesperia* 50, 1981, pp. 200–201 (Fabric A).

[96] Pemberton, *Hesperia* 39, 1970, p. 277, no. 18, pp. 291–292, nos. 78–87.

[97] O:24, lot 2110. One of the latest datable fragments is a badly preserved Attic plate rim, close to *Agora* XII, no. 1048, p. 309, of 400–375 B.C. (2110:1). The kalathiskoi in the lot are mostly of type 3, without interior floor circles (116 of these), as well as 22 of type 4, earlier than the examples in Groups 6 and 7. There are at least 8 ovoid black-glazed kotylai, all without contraction, 2 black-glazed skyphoi, 23 semiglazed, only 3 ray based. There are also 2 plain kotylai (2110:2, 2110:3), with well-articulated ring feet, early in the series. The pottery thus seems to go into the first quarter of the 4th century but not beyond that.

[98] See T 3025, from the North Cemetery (*Corinth* XIII, grave 294-1). Group 3, however, has no fragments of this shape, although ray-based and semiglazed kotylai and skyphoi do appear in that deposit. The pottery from the first level of the Punic Amphora

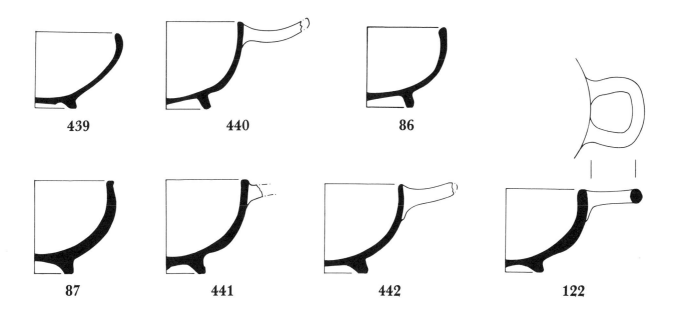

439   440   86

87   441   442   122

Fig. 11. One-handled cups. Scale 1:2

less common after the first quarter.[99] Type 1 seems to be most popular in the second half of the 5th century.[100] There is no clear development or change in shape, except for a gradual contraction of the foot and a swifter rise of the wall to the lip, in place of the gentler convex curve, thus creating a more diagonal profile.[101] Compare the Sanctuary examples **438** of the mid-5th century with **121** of the 4th.

439 is only partially preserved. It comes from the debris over the floor of Building M–N:19 (Room P); the material is mostly 4th century (see the saucer **464** and the cooking pot **651**), with only a few fragments of earlier material. The profile of the one-handler **439** appears to be a hybrid or transition between the type 1 one-handler and the echinus bowl. The heavier inturning lip suggests the cup form, but the light ring foot derives from the echinus bowl. The latter normally has a wall higher than that of **439**, and so far as I can determine, it always has a strong ring foot. I tend to believe that **439** is a type 1 cup, but without evidence for the handle, it may be an early echinus bowl.[102]

Type 2 has a thicker wall, more vertical in its upper half; the lip is flat, the foot begins as a well-defined ring, nearly vertical on its outer face. There may often be a slight projecting of the lip. The cup is entirely glazed, except for a few examples with reserved undersurfaces decorated with black circles and pink wash,

---

Building, excavated in the Forum in 1978 (Williams, *Hesperia* 48, 1979, p. 114), compounds the problem of the date. Although some of the material appears to go well into the second quarter of the 5th century (Attic imports: red figure, glaux cup, krater fragments), there are ray-based kotylai and skyphoi, one semiglazed vessel, but no one-handlers.

[99] The evidence is inconclusive. One of the best sources of the shape is the graves of the North Cemetery, but they drop in number after 400 B.C. A few examples of type 1 have been found in 4th-century contexts: C-37-188, from drain 1937-1, unpublished; C-71-92, from drain 1971-1 (Williams and Fisher, *Hesperia* 41, 1972, p. 159, no. 31, pl. 26). The first is dated to the second quarter of the 4th century, the second to the third quarter. Both types 1 and 2 of the one-handlers were found in cistern 1979-1, also of the third quarter of the 4th century (C-1979-117, type 1; C-1979-116, type 2).

[100] For example, C-39-56–C-39-79, from well 1939-1, mostly third quarter of the 5th century.

[101] Compare examples from the North Cemetery: T 568 and T 569, from grave 321, nos. 1 and 2 (*Corinth* XIII, pl. 46), second quarter of the 5th century, with T 2637, T 2638, of grave 429, nos. 2 and 3 (*Corinth* XIII, pl. 72), from the early 4th century. The North Cemetery examples appear to decrease in size, but C-37-188 (footnote 99 above) is over 0.05 m. in height, 0.123 m. in lip diameter.

[102] See also the Attic example, C-71-89, from drain 1971-1 (footnote 99 above), unpublished, with a clearly inturned lip. For the large echinus bowl see p. 41 below, for the small version, pp. 41–42 below.

similar to some kotylai and skyphoi. The type appears in the early 4th century, but the exact date is as yet unclear.[103] It continues into the 3rd century.

As with type 1, the shape allows no precise dating. Two examples from Group 6 show differences in profile. **86** has a foot wider in relation to the height, a more open wall profile, and well-offset foot. **87** has a high wall, narrower foot, and slightly projecting lip. Neither has the handle preserved. It is impossible to determine if one is earlier than the other.[104] **441** resembles **87**.

Group 7 contains several one-handlers, with examples of both profiles of type 2, **122** and **123**. There are also examples of type 1 in the group, illustrated by **121**. Since 6th- and 5th-century pottery was found in this stratum, albeit in less quantity than the later material, I cannot give a firm date for this type 1 cup. It shows peculiarities, however, in its better defined ring foot, nippled undersurface, and high wall. There appears to be influence on **121** from the type 2 cup. I can only suggest a later 4th-century date for it.[105]

442, from late 4th-century destruction debris in Room 2–3 of Building K–L:24–25, has the lower type 2 profile and seems slightly earlier than the example of that type from Group 7 (Pit B), **122**. The foot is better defined, the handle less triangular in **442**. **441**, from Building N:21–22, has the higher wall profile of type 2. **123**, Group 7, showing the same higher profile, has a poorer wall-surface finish and a peculiar contraction of the upper wall to the lip. But **123** may not be much later than **441**. **441** has a pronounced nipple, strongly contracted handle roots, and a narrower foot, although the heights of **441** and **123** are almost the same.

The two profiles of type 2 appear to be contemporaneous; one does not succeed the other. They may have had a span of about one hundred years, without consistent changes in profile. Differences may be attributable more to workshops than to dates, and the utilitarian nature of the vase (used as a scoop or ladle as well as a drinking cup?) may account for the lack of interest in altering it.

The final date of the shape is also unclear. It is uncertain whether any of the one-handled cups from Group 7 may be assigned to the terminal date of that group. No fragments of the shape were found in Groups 8 or 9, but that may be fortuitous. Both the later groups contained fragments of other drinking vessels, but the one-handled cup was never so popular as the skyphos. The one-handled cup is not, however, a shape associated with 146 B.C. destruction debris.

Although there are several fragments of Attic one-handlers in the context pottery, it was apparently a shape not often imported into Corinth. Only one is sufficiently preserved to deserve publication, **85**, from the mid-4th century. The Corinthian forms have no Attic equivalent. There is some similarity in the lip and foot of some type 2 cups with Attic profiles, but the Attic versions are wider in relation to the height, and thus are shallower. In addition, the Corinthian one-handler may have lasted longer than the Attic.[106]

XIV. BOWLS, LEKANIDES, AND OTHER DISHES

Corinthian, pre-Hellenistic forms

443	flat rimmed		Pl. 47	first half 6th century
236	figured, lekanoid		*Fig. 30, Pl. 24	MC or LC
237	figured		Fig. 12, Pl. 24	LC or later
54	semiglazed, small	Group 4	Pl. 8	second quarter 5th century
62	semiglazed, small	Group 5	Pl. 9	third or fourth quarter 5th century

[103] One was found in Forum well 1937-1, C-37-422, unpublished.

[104] These same differences appear in two examples from drain 1971-1 (footnote 99 above, p. 37). C-71-108 has the lower, wider profile; C-71-95 is taller, with a less offset foot. Another contemporary fill, pit 1937-1, also has the two variants: C-37-2548, C-37-2553, C-37-2554 show the lower profile; C-37-2549, C-37-2550, C-37-2551 the higher. Both variants of type 2 also came out of the 1979-1 cistern: C-1979-145 with the lower wall, C-1979-116 the higher profile.

[105] See reference to late type 1 in footnote 99 above, p. 37.

[106] For the Attic one-handled cup, see *Agora* XII, pp. 124–127: "it does not seem to go down into the Hellenistic period" (p. 124). There are also versions of the cup in Corinthian fabric with two handles, found in the Forum; these have not been identified in the Sanctuary. But the rim and foot sherds are identical; without evidence for one or two handles, they cannot be distinguished.

293	Sam Wide		Pl. 32	third quarter 5th century
294	Sam Wide		Pl. 32	third quarter 5th century
136	lekanis	Group 7	Pl. 16	early 3rd century
137	lekanis lid	Group 7	Pl. 16	early 3rd century

Corinthian, Hellenistic forms[107]

447	large echinus		Fig. 12, Pl. 47	early 3rd century
185	large echinus	Group 10	Fig. 12	later 3rd century
88	small echinus	Group 6	Fig. 12, Pl. 13	early 4th century
89	small echinus	Group 6	Pl. 13	late 4th century
124	small echinus	Group 7	Fig. 12, Pl. 16	fourth quarter 4th century
125	small echinus	Group 7	Fig. 12, Pl. 16	first quarter 3rd century
448	small echinus		Pl. 47	second quarter to mid-3rd century
126	unglazed echinus?	Group 7	Fig. 12, Pl. 16	4th century
160	semiglazed	Group 8	Pl. 18	early 3rd century
186	semiglazed	Group 10	Fig. 12, Pl. 20	mid- or third quarter 3rd century
449	outturned rim		Fig. 12, Pl. 47	early 4th century
90	outturned rim	Group 6	Pl. 13	third quarter 4th century
450	outturned rim		Pl. 47	late 4th century
451	outturned rim, small		Fig. 12, Pl. 47	early 3rd century
452	outturned rim, small		Fig. 12	late 3rd or early 2nd century
453	conical		Pl. 47	second half 3rd century
187	conical	Group 10	Fig. 12, Pl. 20	*ca.* 200 B.C.
454	hemispherical		Fig. 12, Pl. 47	late 3rd or early 2nd century

Imported

444	Lakonian		Fig. 12	6th century?
445	Attic saltcellar		Fig. 12, Pl. 47	late 6th century
446	Attic echinus		Fig. 12, Pl. 47	mid-4th century
91	Attic outturned rim	Group 6	Fig. 12, Pl. 13	third quarter 4th century

*Decoration only; see catalogue entry.

Most of the pre-Hellenistic bowls from the Sanctuary are single examples of the type. Although 6th-century levels have many fragments of black-glazed bowls, only one example, **443**, was sufficiently preserved to warrant publication. Two decorated examples, a lekanoid form, **236**, and an interesting coarse-ware example, **237**,[108] are among the few figured bowls found. It is not a shape much favored by Corinthian painters. One import from Lakonia, **444**, without shape parallel, can be dated only by context. Originally it was very large, possibly even a krater, not a bowl.

Two examples of the very popular semiglazed bowls of the 5th century are published, **54** and **62**.[109] It is possible that these are not miniatures but small saltcellars, superseded by the small echinus bowls or beveled-rim bowls. The unglazed lekanis also appeared in the 5th century; fragments of this type may be found in almost every stratum of the dining rooms, but only two examples, late in the series, mended sufficiently for publication, **136** and **137**. It is stated in *Corinth* VII, iii that the lekanis continued to 146 B.C.;[110] this is not sure. In 146 B.C. destruction levels excavated in the Forum, no fragments of unglazed lekanides were found.[111] Fragments of these bowls appear in debris of that date in the Sanctuary, but there is earlier material also in all

[107] Some of the shapes begin in the earlier 4th century, but because the types continue into the Hellenistic period, they are included in this group.

[108] The coarse-ware example, **237**, is technically placed in the wrong section; it is catalogued with the Corinthian black-figured (fine-ware) vases, rather than with the coarse ware. The criterion used was the decorative technique, rather than the fabric, hence the anomaly.

[109] *Corinth* XIII, pp. 148–149. Many of these little bowls have been found in domestic contexts, as in the 5th-century well 1939-1. There are examples from drain 1937-1 and pit 1937-1, but none were found in Forum drain 1971-1. The form of bowl may thus have gone out of use by the end of the third quarter of the 4th century.

[110] Pp. 94–96.

[111] For example, Forum Southwest well 1975-1. But it must be noted that the lekanis is not often found in the Forum.

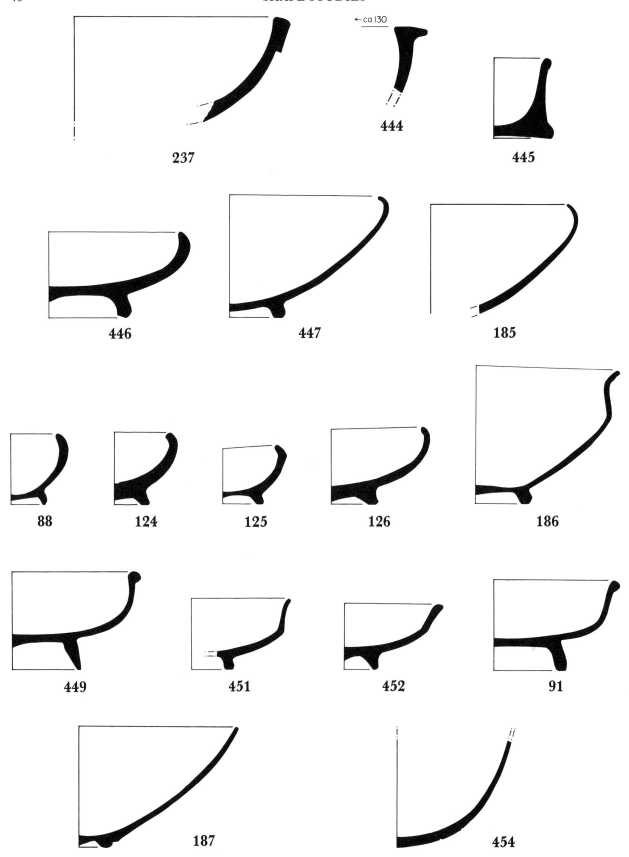

FIG. 12. Bowls. Scale 1:2

those strata.[112] Although many Corinthian vessels have counterparts elsewhere, especially in Athens, assisting the chronology of the form, the unglazed lekanis does not have parallels. The Attic version does not survive the 4th century.[113] The example in *Corinth* VII, iii (C-47-822), dated to 146 B.C., comes from a destruction dump in a building of Forum Southeast,[114] a fill with earlier and Roman vessels. The late characteristics that it displays can be seen in other 3rd-century pots: the pinched-on handle has its counterpart in the undecorated kotylai of the 3rd century (see **114, 157, 404**). The change of profile from continuous curve to slight carination echoes contemporary profiles of semiglazed bowls and bowls with outturned rims. The last lekanides are so small that the late form of pyxis with slipover lid may have been a replacement (see **179–181, 202**). As Edwards states, the full development and chronology of the lekanis bowl are as yet not clear.[115]

Relatively greater numbers of Hellenistic forms of bowls appear in the catalogue; they seem to be in greater proportion in the later strata than are the bowls in 6th- and 5th-century levels. Also, publication of a number of examples may help establish the shape development of some of the problematic forms. The various types of bowls are discussed separately below; small bowls with beveled rims, moldmade relief bowls, and saucers appear below in Shape Studies, XV–XVII.

Large echinus bowl

The large echinus bowl appears about the middle of the 4th century.[116] C-71-52 and C-71-53 of Corinthian fabric and C-71-50 of Attic were found in the pottery deposit of Forum drain 1971-1.[117] They are solid bowls with substantial walls, high thick ring feet, and wide convex walls with a continuous curve to the tapered lips. They are fully glazed. The earliest bowls have a maximum diameter only slightly more than twice the foot diameter. This ratio changes in time: the foot contracts in both diameter and height; the wall becomes higher and in some examples has a less pronounced curve to the lip; the lip slants up instead of directly into the center of the bowl. The outer wall is glazed by dipping, not fully painted. If the change to steepness and foot constriction is accurate, the shape development compares with that of the saucer. The Attic version of the vessel has a lower profile and is thus more open; the foot has a diameter greater than that of contemporary Corinthian bowls.[118]

The large echinus bowl is not so popular a shape in the Sanctuary as plain saucers and semiglazed bowls. Three examples appear in the catalogue. The first, appropriately, is Attic, since the shape was produced there first; **446** is mid-4th century, although much of the context material is later in date. **185** from Group 10 is incomplete, but the angle of the wall requires a later 3rd-century date; **447** may be earlier.

Small echinus bowl

This saltcellar or condiment bowl (?) appears in the 4th century, as early as the first quarter.[119] It may replace the small 5th-century bowl (**54, 62**), which disappears in the later 4th century. The small echinus bowl comes from Athens,[120] undergoes some changes in shape, and disappears in the later 3rd century. It is not clearly associated with 146 B.C. destruction material.

88, from Group 6, is an excellent example of the type, with a solid ring foot, high convex wall, and good glazing. It is close to an example found in 1947[121] but with a better defined foot. The high wall may imitate the original Attic shape. **88** is probably fairly early in the series, before the middle of the 4th century. **89** from the same group has a more typical profile: lower and wider wall, slight nippling, lower foot, all characteristics of a late 4th-century date. The two bowls from Group 7, Pit B, **124** and **125**, also exhibit variations

---

[112] This wide range of dates parallels the dating of the South Stoa wells, on which so much of the Hellenistic chronology in Corinth has depended. See the Introduction, pp. 3–4.

[113] *Agora* XII, pp. 165–167.

[114] *Corinth* VII, iii, no. 558, p. 95, pls. 18, 57 (well 1947-3).

[115] *Corinth* VII, iii, p. 95.

[116] *Corinth* VII, iii, pp. 29–33; large echinus bowls are nos. 15–34.

[117] Not illustrated in Williams and Fisher, *Hesperia* 41, 1972 with material from the drain.

[118] *Agora* XII, nos. 825–842, pp. 131–132 (incurving rim).

[119] *Corinth* VII, iii, no. 64, p. 32 (from well 1937-1); small echinus bowls are nos. 46–71.

[120] *Agora* XII, nos. 939–950, pp. 137–138.

[121] C-47-264 (*Corinth* VII, iii, no. 53, p. 32).

of shape. **124** is taller, with a narrower foot; **125** is poorly made, probably later than **124**, made in the early 3rd century.

The last example, **448**, is also 3rd century, but how late is as yet unclear. The foot is narrow, but the wall is not so low as the examples that are given the latest date in *Corinth* VII, iii.[122] There are other changes in the profile of the small echinus bowl that may be used as dating criteria; in some the turn to the lip is angled, approximating the beveled saucer. Bowls from a deposit with fairly limited dates may show different profiles.[123] Such differences in contemporary bowls as well as changes in profile characteristics may or may not be chronologically significant. It is still very difficult to give any example a very specific date.

126, from Group 7, is comparable in size to a saucer; it has no glaze. The wall is lower than is typical for the echinus bowl in this intermediate size; it may be a 4th-century (or later?) variant. The saucer size is not so popular in the Sanctuary as the large and small versions.

Semiglazed bowls[124]

With only two examples in the catalogue, one of which is incomplete, it might appear that this popular Hellenistic shape was not used in the Sanctuary. In fact, fragments of these bowls, recognizable by the distinctive rim and banding, are conspicuous from the later 4th century on. One may note the fragments in Groups 8 and 10; without the profile sufficiently preserved, dating is difficult and consequently publication unwarranted.

A number of different profiles appear in examples of the third quarter of the 4th century: C-71-51 and C-71-266 from Forum drain 1971-1,[125] and C-75-171 and C-75-172 from Forum well 1975-4.[126] Not only do the profiles vary among these contemporary examples, but they are also quite different from examples published in *Corinth* VII, iii. C-75-171 has a concave neck before the rim; C-75-172 has a strongly projecting, almost flat rim. Only C-71-51 seems close to Edwards' earlier forms.[127] Moreover, the examples from the Forum excavations all have feet narrower than expected and often lack exterior banding. There may be a discernible evolution from a continuous curve to a greater articulation of shoulder, rim, and lip. But it is also possible that there are different but contemporary variations of the profile with little chronological significance. Compare the two forms of type 2 one-handled cups.

Fragments of semiglazed bowls are found in 146 B.C. destruction levels in the Sanctuary. **186** is from such a fill, Group 10. It does not have the exaggerated articulation of bowls dated to the mid-2nd century in *Corinth* VII, iii.[128] The foot is wider in relation to height and lip diameter than in examples cited as *ca.* 146 B.C. Whether or not this is significant is unclear.[129] **160** is from Group 8 and lacks the full profile but appears to retain a more continuous curve from wall to lip. No additional examples with enough of the profile surviving could be inventoried.

Bowl with outturned rim

This form has a long history in Corinth, undergoing extensive changes.[130] It comes from Athens;[131] many Corinthian versions imitate the source by adding pink to the undersurface. **449** is the earliest example in the catalogue. It shows a continuous curve, flaring out and up to the heavily rolled rim derived from the

---

[122] C-60-65 (*Corinth* VII, iii, no. 52, p. 32, *ca.* 250 B.C., from well 1960-4); C-47-443 (*ibid.*, no. 67, *ca.* 200 B.C., from well 1947-5). The date could conceivably be lowered into the early 2nd century for the latter.

[123] C-37-2536 and C-37-2537 (*Corinth* VII, iii, nos. 49, 57, p. 32, pls. 2, 44; both from pit 1937-1). The first has a continuous curve, the second a far more angular shoulder.

[124] *Corinth* VII, iii, pp. 28–29.

[125] C-71-266 is published in Williams and Fisher, *Hesperia* 41, 1972, p. 159, no. 35, pl. 26.

[126] Both are in Williams and Fisher, *Hesperia* 45, 1976, pp. 120–121, nos. 40, 41, pl. 21. A third example, C-75-173, has the profile of the first example but with bands on the exterior.

[127] C-31-201 (*Corinth* VII, iii, no. 11, p. 29, pls. 1, 43; well 1931-8).

[128] C-34-21 from fill 1934-1 and C-47-235 from well 1934-5 (*Corinth* VII, iii, nos. 5, 6, p. 29, pls. 1, 43).

[129] See C-75-303, unpublished, from a late Hellenistic well in the Forum (well 1975-1). It has a profile similar to **186**.

[130] *Corinth* VII, iii, pp. 33–34; these bowls are nos. 72–94.

[131] *Agora* XII, nos. 777–808, pp. 128–130.

Attic prototype. The stamping of the floor suggests a date in the first quarter of the 4th century, as does the context.[132]

In **90**, from Group 6, the wall is beginning to lose the continuous curve in favor of a strong vertical turn to the rim. In time, this turn will become a true carination. **90** is very similar to C-71-46, from Forum drain 1971-1.[133] In addition, the rim is not a single roll but is tooled below its outer face, giving a sharp edge. The Attic example, **91**, is contemporary.

450 from room 2 (V) of Building M:21–22 is a variant of the bowl. The foot is less pronounced, although not so slight as in the carinated form; the lower wall is losing convexity; the upper wall is less vertical and has a slight concavity before terminating in a rounded lip. This example may be a transition between the two forms of bowls with outturned rims.[134]

The smaller version with strong carination begins in the 3rd century[135] and lasts through the Hellenistic period. There is an Attic equivalent.[136] **451** is the earlier of the two examples in the catalogue. It retains full glazing, with miltos on the inner foot (characteristics inherited from the larger bowl); the wall and rim are sharply offset; the foot diameter is wider in relation to the maximum diameter. **452** is later, perhaps early 2nd century, with a less well defined foot and loss of articulation.

Conical bowl

Only two incomplete examples appear in the catalogue; it was never very popular in the Sanctuary, indeed is fairly rare generally in Hellenistic levels in Corinth.[137] **453** is fairly well preserved. **187** has been reconstructed in plaster; in no area is a continuous original profile preserved. Both are probably not past the early 2nd century.

Hemispherical bowl

This is an even rarer form.[138] It has the profile of the moldmade relief bowl but has, in place of the relief design, West Slope decoration. The one fragmentary example from the Sanctuary, **454**, may be *ca.* 200 B.C. in date.

XV. SMALL BOWLS WITH BEVELED RIMS

Corinthian

455		Fig. 13, Pl. 47	third quarter 4th century
456		Fig. 13, Pl. 47	third quarter 4th century
457		Fig. 13, Pl. 47	third quarter 4th century
92	Group 6	Fig. 13, Pl. 13	late fourth quarter 4th century
93	Group 6	Fig. 13	late fourth quarter 4th century
127	Group 7	Fig. 13, Pl. 16	first or early second quarter 3rd century
128	Group 7	Fig. 13, Pl. 16	first or early second quarter 3rd century
161	Group 8	Fig. 13, Pl. 18	mid-3rd century

[132] Lot 6838: room 4 of Building M–N:20–26 (Room Ga). Fragmentary skyphoi in the context pottery show the beginning of the compound curve (6838:1).

[133] Not published with the other material from that drain in Williams and Fisher, *Hesperia* 41, 1972.

[134] The context, lot 6208, contains mostly 4th-century material: C-69-267, a one-handled cup (cited below under **441**); **387**, a blister-ware oinochoe; and **455**, a small bowl with beveled rim. **450** is not necessarily from the terminal date of the context, at the end of the third quarter of the century.

[135] *Corinth* VII, iii, p. 34; the earliest examples are dated to *ca.* 250 B.C.

[136] Thompson, *Hesperia* 3, 1934, p. 317, A9–A13; p. 327, A71, A72; p. 347, C3; p. 370, D2–D6; p. 395, E33–E44.

[137] Rare in comparison with the numbers of other forms of Hellenistic bowls. Conical bowls in *Corinth* VII, iii, are nos. 532–549 and 943, pp. 90–92, 187.

[138] *Corinth* VII, iii, nos. 527–531, 944, pp. 90, 187. Few additional examples have been found in recent excavations.

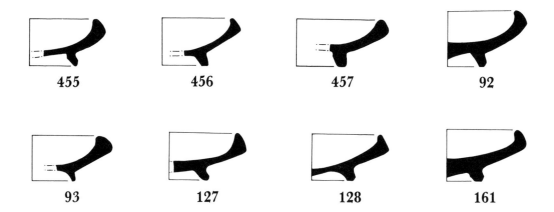

455   456   457   92

93   127   128   161

Fig. 13. Small bowls with beveled rims. Scale 1:2

This low profiled saltcellar[139] appears in Corinth in the third quarter of the 4th century, with a profile more open than that of the small echinus bowl. Two deposits found in recent Forum excavations, both dated to the same period, contain examples of the beveled bowl.[140] The echinoid saucer[141] of the first half of the 4th century may be the forerunner of the beveled bowl. The echinoid saucer comes from an Attic form imported into Corinth[142] and does not last beyond the middle of the century, according to present evidence.

C-75-175 from Forum well (votive pit) 1975-4 shows the combination of echinoid bowl with heavier bevel; the foot is not so solid as the vertical bracelet foot of most beveled bowls. C-71-97, from Forum drain 1971-1, has this heavier foot; it also has a double profile of the rim. C-71-273 from the same drain has the most typical profile of the three, with a straight flaring wall and well-articulated shoulder bevel. Thus the three bowls found in contemporary deposits show quite different profiles.

Formulation of a consistent shape development in the beveled bowl proved to be impossible. There appears to be no one canonical form in any period. The wall profile may be virtually horizontal before the carination of the rim[143] or quite diagonal,[144] even though the examples are contemporary. There are also saucers which one might call beveled bowls, others, echinoid saucer-bowls.[145] Many of the beveled bowls

[139] *Corinth* VII, iii, pp. 34–35, nos. 95–100. Since it is so difficult to date examples of this shape, the date assigned to each example in the catalogue is the latest date of the context.

[140] C-71-97 and C-71-273, from Forum drain 1971-1 (Williams and Fisher, *Hesperia* 41, 1972, p. 159, no. 36, pl. 26 is the former). C-75-175, from well (votive pit) 1975-4, unpublished.

[141] *Corinth* VII, iii, nos. 35–45, p. 32.

[142] Attic example from Forum well 1971-1, C-71-3 (unpublished), with parallels in *Agora* XII, nos. 887, 888, p. 135, pl. 33. The Corinthian version has the ring foot typical of many 4th-century Corinthian shapes, as against the wide cut-out disk foot of the Attic version.

[143] C-37-2546 (*Corinth* VII, iii, no. 99, p. 35), from pit 1937-1, of the third quarter of the 4th century.

[144] C-71-273, from Forum drain 1971-1 (see footnote 140 above).

[145] C-46-15 and C-35-645, classified in *Corinth* VII, iii, in the saucer group of the echinoid bowls (nos. 38 and 40, p. 32). The first is from South Stoa well XV (well 1946-1) and so may be later than 350 B.C. The second is from a well in the terrace of the South Stoa (well 1935-4), found with a skyphos, C-35-114 (*Corinth* VII, iii, no. 350, p. 70) which appears to be later than the date assigned to it of 375–350 B.C. The same well contained a gray-ware fish plate, C-35-962 (unpublished), probably post-146 B.C., and a wall fragment from an imitation Cypriot amphora, C-35-984 (unpublished). Other material from the well, consequently, is after mid-century. Thus neither of the bowls is limited by context to the earlier 4th century.

Well 1935-4, containing C-35-645, has not been relocated. It must lie somewhere in front of shops XIII–XVI, in the terrace between the South Stoa and the central shops. It may have been open for a considerable length of time in the roadway in front of the Stoa. See the well excavated in 1971, also apparently open in front of the South Stoa, towards the west end (Williams and Fisher, *Hesperia* 41, 1972, p. 171, the well in the courtyard of Building II, well 1971-2). See also remarks in the Introduction, footnote 20 above, p. 4.

have a rounded rather than sharp bevel, thus resembling the small echinus bowls.[146] Generally the beveled bowl has a wider profile, more open than the former type, but both shapes are totally black glazed, both have ring feet, both have inturning rims.[147]

The beveled bowls from the Demeter Sanctuary do not give any assistance in defining shape development. The Hellenistic strata, however, do help confirm a terminus in the 3rd century. Group 8 has one example, **161**; later groups have only a few or no fragments, suggesting that the beveled bowls are no longer used by the end of the 3rd century.

From Group 6, two examples show different profiles. **92** has a higher wall and solid ring foot; the wall is slightly convex, not straight. **93** has a lighter foot (from the echinoid-bowl predecessor?) and a straight, almost horizontal wall. The two from Group 7, **127** and **128**, are similar, closer to **93** with the more horizontal wall. **161** from Group 8 actually resembles **92**, with a more diagonal wall but slighter foot. It is possible that **161** is earlier than the bulk of the material in that group, thereby explaining the resemblance to **92**. But as noted above, bowls from limited contexts vary considerably in profile. The changes and resemblances described may not, indeed probably do not, indicate chronological differences.

The remaining examples, **455–457**, come from debris of Classical dining rooms on the Lower Terrace, the result of the later 4th-century earthquake. Each has a different profile. **455** has a rounded bevel and is more echinoid. **456** has a straight flaring high wall and fairly sharp bevel. The wall of **457** is more horizontal than that of **456**.

The Corinthian potters may never have adopted a canonical version of the beveled bowl, unlike the kotylai, skyphoi, saucers, and other shapes. The similarity in size and profile between this vessel and the small echinus bowl caused crossover of characteristics. The two forms probably had identical functions in the dining rooms. Both these small shapes disappeared in the 3rd century; production of the beveled form probably stopped slightly before that of the small echinus bowl. The two dishes were replaced by what?

XVI. MOLDMADE RELIEF BOWLS

Corinthian

458	figured		Pl. 48	late 3rd century?
459	figured		Pl. 48	early 2nd century
193	imbricate	Group 11	Fig. 14, Pl. 21	first or early second quarter 2nd century
460	imbricate		Pl. 48	second quarter 2nd century
194	linear leaf	Group 11	Pl. 21	second quarter 2nd century
461	shield		Pl. 48	2nd century

Imported

462	gray ware, imbricate	Pl. 48	2nd century
463	gray ware, long petal	Pl. 48	2nd century

The moldmade relief bowl appears in Corinth in the last third of the 3rd century. A fill excavated in Forum Southeast in 1980, with a coin of Ptolemy III, had no fragments of the ware. It contained much fine-ware pottery, mostly kantharoi, but also fragments of saucers, a very late black-glazed skyphos, and a West Slope plate with offset rim.[148]

There are many more moldmade bowls in the Demeter Sanctuary than the eight listed above would indicate.[149] Most are very fragmentary; most are also very common types, as the list given in Group 11

[146] See p. 42 above in the discussion of echinus bowls (Shape Studies, XIV).

[147] See *Agora* XII, pp. 137–138, discussing the Attic equivalent, the footed saltcellar: "The need to establish typological arrangements may sometimes divide classes of shapes too rigidly." The similarities of the saltcellar with the small bowl, especially of echinoid profile, are noted there.

[148] Lot 1980-129. The skyphos is numbered 1980-129:1, the plate 1980-129:3. See Williams and Russell, *Hesperia* 50, 1981, p. 19, note 25.

[149] For discussion of these bowls, their types and tentative dating, see *Corinth* VII, iii, pp. 151–187.

Fig. 14. Moldmade relief bowl
193. Scale 1:2

indicates. Only the best preserved or most unusual are included in the catalogue. Two in Corinthian clay appear to show outside influence: the charioteers of **458** may derive from an Argive model; the pinwheel of **461** finds its best parallel in gray ware.

The foliage and imbricate forms seem to be more popular in the Sanctuary than the figured bowls. Whether this preference is important cannot be ascertained. Demeter and Kore do not seem to be represented on moldmade bowls. Neither do the Archaic figured Corinthian drinking vessels show the goddesses. The preference may therefore be entirely accidental.

The absence of long-petal bowls[150] is also interesting, for there are a number of examples of other linear types: **460, 461**, and **194. 463** is an imported bowl bearing the petals. Current dating of the long-petal form in Corinth has been pushed back from the *ca.* 150 B.C. date often cited, in order to account for the many examples of the type now known in Corinth. The other linear forms presumably began at about the same time. Since the Sanctuary does not appear to have had any significant activity during the interim period,[151] the late bowls all ought to be well-established types of the later first and second quarters of the 2nd century. The absence of the long-petal form is fortuitous.

The two gray-ware examples appear to be the only imports in this shape. Although the Forum excavations of 1980 produced a number of bowls in different fabrics,[152] all but the gray ware are absent in the 2nd-century Sanctuary types. Even Attic examples are virtually absent; there is one in lot 6206 (6206:5). This absence may be interpreted in different ways. It may indicate the use of inexpensive drinking vessels in the later Hellenistic period, assuming that imports cost more. Or, the presence of imports in the Forum may be evidence for activity during the interim period in that area of Corinth but not in the Sanctuary. The interpretation may be argued either way on the basis of the extant material.

The dating of the eight examples is very tentative. Figured bowls continue from the later 3rd century to 146 B.C. Only the linear bowls seem to belong to the 2nd century alone. The gray-ware bowls are problematic. **462** may be assigned to the workshop of Menemachos, the first of the "Delian" ateliers.[153] **463** comes from the Monogram group, ". . . [qui] se situerait au centre de cette production."[154] If one accepts the conventional beginning date of 166 B.C. for the Delian production, **462** could have been used in the Sanctuary before its destruction in 146; the mold, however, must have been worn. The second is more difficult. By Laumonier's dating, it would have to belong to the interim period or be brought in during the Roman revival.[155] Since there seems to be little evidence for activity in the Sanctuary between 146 and 44 B.C., **463** either must be from the period of reorganization (too late?), or the date for the beginning of the production of gray ware, 166 B.C., is too low.[156] **461** also seems to depend on the Monogram workshop but is of Corinthian clay and surely was made before 146.

No elucidation for the dating of moldmade bowls may be gained from the Sanctuary examples; the contexts are neither closed nor sufficiently limited. Probably the establishment of a chronology for the Corinthian examples will arise from the interrelationships between Corinthian bowls found in sites with more clearly stratified material or from the imports to Corinth of moldmade bowls from dated workshops.

---

[150] There is one fragmentary Corinthian long-petal bowl from M:17–18, lot 3222, a Roman dump in Building M:16–17 (3222:1).
[151] See the discussion in the Introduction, p. 2 above.
[152] Edwards, *Hesperia* 50, 1981.
[153] Laumonier, *Délos* XXXI, pp. 21–68.
[154] *Ibid.*, p. 12; pp. 129–213 for the workshop.
[155] Laumonier (*Délos* XXXI, p. 12) suggests a span of 40–50 years for the duration of a workshop.
[156] "166 à 69 seraient donc les limites logiques approximatives de cette production . . ." (*ibid.*, p. 7).

XVII. SAUCERS

Corinthian

94	Group 6	Fig. 15, Pl. 13	third quarter 4th century
95	Group 6	Fig. 15, Pl. 13	third quarter 4th century
129	Group 7	Fig. 15, Pl. 16	third quarter 4th century
464		Fig. 15	third quarter 4th century
465		Fig. 15, Pl. 48	fourth quarter 4th century
466		Pl. 48	*ca.* 300 b.c.
130	Group 7	Fig. 15, Pl. 16	first quarter 3rd century
467		Fig. 15, Pl. 48	first quarter 3rd century
131	Group 7	Fig. 15, Pl. 16	first or early second quarter 3rd century
132	Group 7	Fig. 15, Pl. 16	second quarter 3rd century
133	Group 7	Fig. 15, Pl. 16	second quarter 3rd century
162	Group 8	Fig. 15, Pl. 18	second quarter or mid-3rd century
468		Fig. 15	second quarter or mid-3rd century
176	Group 9	Fig. 15, Pl. 19	third to fourth quarter 3rd century
195	Group 11	Fig. 15	early 2nd century

A saucer was found in Forum drain 1971-1 that is a paradigm of the shape.[157] The fabric is thin, the foot a vertical bracelet, the undersurface slightly nippled, the wall a gentle convex curve to the rounded lip; the entire saucer is glazed. In size and profile it is very similar to a saucer published in *Corinth* VII, iii.[158] Both must date to the third quarter of the 4th century, when the saucer was first made in Corinth, with a sensible, serviceable profile. Edwards identifies the following changes in the saucer shape as criteria for dating: constriction of the foot; elevation of the wall; change of profile from a convex to a straight or angled wall; conversion of the ring foot to a rounded low one (and even to a proto-conical form); speed of decoration by dipping. These changes are visible in the saucers from the Demeter Sanctuary, but one must be careful not to apply them too rigidly. Most of the examples are poorly made, often uneven in height or diameter, making the profiles on opposite sides of the vessel very different.

Of the saucers from Group 6, **94** may be slightly earlier than **95**, indeed is the earliest of all the examples. The foot is almost a perfect vertical ring, the wall is very low, the nipple barely perceptible. **95** has a slightly flaring foot, is more nippled, and has a higher profile. Both are completely glazed.

The five saucers from Group 7 show a range of dates. **129** is the earliest, very similar in profile and other characteristics to **95**, although it is much larger. Slightly later than **129** are **464** and **465**. **464** has a more convex wall; the foot is losing its straight descent and becoming more rounded on the interior. **465** has a foot diameter wide for its height and maximum diameter, but it is poorly made, with uneven dimensions. Its wall appears to have a flare straighter than that of **464**. Both are still completely glazed. The later 4th-century date for both is suggested by the contexts. Both were found in fill over floors of early Hellenistic dining rooms, built after the late 4th-century earthquake.[159]

466 comes from a corridor in N:19, between Buildings M–N:19 (Room P) and M:16–17 (Northwest Stucco Building). The lot, 5635, contains a wall fragment of a cyma kantharos of Corinthian fabric (5635:1), thus giving a lower date after 300 b.c. to the context. There is earlier material in that lot, however, including Classical skyphos and kotyle fragments; the saucer need not be at the lowest date. It is glazed overall, nippled, poorly made; the foot is rounded, quite diagonal on the interior face. The maximum diameter exceeds 0.12 m., making it a fairly large example, but the foot is still wide, the wall not elevated. A low open profile is retained thereby. I am inclined to date it slightly later than **464** and **465**, at about 300 b.c.

---

[157] C-71-73, not published.

[158] C-37-2584, from pit 1937-1 (*Corinth* VII, iii, no. 148, p. 43). No saucers have yet appeared in contexts datable before mid-century.

[159] **464** is from Building M–N:19, **465** from Building K–L:23–24, room 3. See p. 3 above for the earthquake.

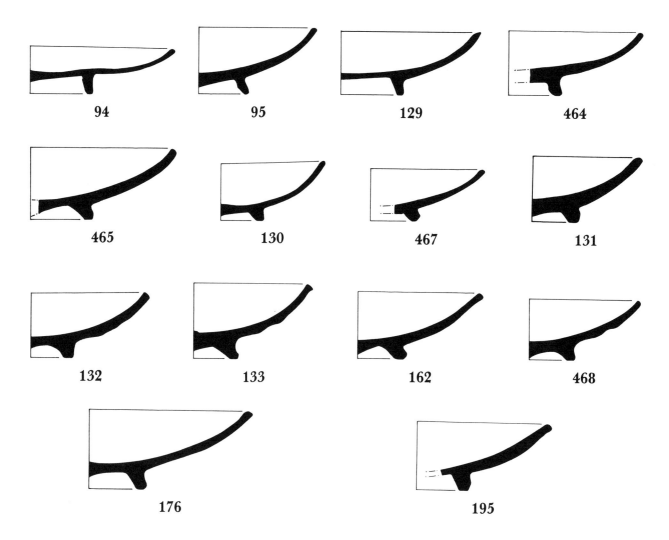

FIG. 15. Saucers. Scale 1:2

130, Group 7, and **467**, from the lower fill of a cistern in Building L–M:28, are similar in profile, although **467** is larger. These are the first examples that show glazing by dipping: only the upper walls have paint. The feet are small and rounded; the walls, although somewhat convex in profile, are taller in relation to foot and lip diameters. **467** also shows a slight break in the wall profile. Since it is so poorly made, that angularity of the wall may be accidental. Both ought to be dated in the early 3rd century, later than **464–466**.

The remaining three saucers from Pit B also belong to the 3rd century. **131**, slightly lower in height than **467**, has a heavier and wider foot and a narrower lip diameter, giving it a steeper profile. It may therefore be slightly later. **132** and **133** should be assigned to the second quarter of the century, at the lower date of Pit B. Both are poorly made, with exterior wheel ridges, badly formed feet, and uneven heights. In both the foot shows the change to the proto-conical form; that is, the interior of the foot is not well offset from the resting surface but merges with it.

162 from Group 8 has a mixture of characteristics, making it difficult to date. The undersurface is highly nippled, the foot heavy and rounded on the exterior, concave inside. The wall changes direction slightly, as on **467**; the foot diameter is still wide and serviceable. Since Group 8 has a fairly long time span, **162** could come from any part of the 3rd century. It is assigned to the second quarter or slightly later because of characteristics that appear to be contemporary with the details of the latest saucers in Group 7; the angled wall is probably not accidental and would compare with the growing steepness of **131**. The retention of the heavy nippling on **162**, however, shows that the foot is not so late as the proto-conical foot found on **131** and **132**.

468, from an unstratified context, is also difficult to date, for it is the most miserably made of all the Sanctuary saucers. The nipple is still fairly pronounced, as on **162**, and the interior of the foot, still offset from the resting surface, is early. The general characteristics of **468** seem closest to **162**.

The last two examples are from Groups 9 and 11. **176** is very large, with an estimated lip diameter of 0.178 m. The relatively narrow diameter (0.06 m.) of the foot indicates profile constriction. Although there is a definite break between the resting surface and the interior, the latter is quite scooped out and shows the proto-conical form. **195**, although poorly preserved, is more advanced in late characteristics. The undersurface seems to be slightly higher than the top of the exterior face of the foot, a detail indicative of the conical-foot profile. The wall is not continuous but angled, the foot is slight, the fabric thick. The saucer may thus be later than **176**.

No saucers with full profiles found in the Sanctuary are so constricted in proportions as some examples assigned to 146 b.c.[160] This is accidental, for most of the latest material came from dining rooms of the Lower Terrace, where fill was not extensive and where the pottery was very badly damaged. Group 10 contained fragments of saucers but all very incomplete and therefore not helpful.

The numbers of saucers in the Sanctuary are high; it was a popular shape. One assumes that it was used in the dining rooms and had no cult or votive associations.

XVIII. PLATES

Corinthian

26	figured	Group 2	Pl. 5	MC
238	figured		Fig. 16, Pl. 25	MC
239	figured		Pl. 25	MC
240	figured		Pl. 25	MC
241	figured		Pl. 25	MC
242	figured		Pl. 25	MC
243	figured		Pl. 25	MC
27	figured	Group 2	Fig. 16, Pl. 5	late MC or LC
244	figured		Pl. 25	LC
245	figured		Pl. 26	LC
246	figured		Pl. 26	LC
247	figured		Pl. 26	LC
196	figured	Group 11	Pl. 21	LC
28	patterned	Group 2	Pl. 5	6th century?
469	patterned		Pl. 48	early 5th century
282	figured		Pl. 30	first half 5th century
283	figured		Fig. 16, Pl. 30	third or early fourth quarter 5th century
284	figured		Pl. 30	late 5th or early 4th century
295	Sam Wide		*Fig. 35, Pl. 32	third quarter 5th century
296	Sam Wide		Pl. 32	third quarter 5th century
297	Sam Wide		Pl. 32	third quarter 5th century
470	undecorated		Fig. 16	4th century?
177	offset rim	Group 9	Pl. 19	fourth quarter 3rd century
188	fish plate	Group 10	Fig. 16, Pl. 20	early 2nd century?

[160] For examples C-48-101 from well 1948-3 and C-47-813 from well 1947-3 (*Corinth* VII, iii, nos. 168 and 169, p. 43).

189	flat rim	Group 10	Fig. 16	2nd century?
197	flat rim	Group 11	Fig. 16, Pl. 21	2nd century
472	offset rim		Pl. 48	late 2nd century?
473	offset rim?		Fig. 16	mid-2nd century or later?

Imported (all Attic except 198)

324	black figured		Pl. 35	early 5th century
325	black figured		Fig. 16, Pl. 35	early 5th century
471	rolled rim		Fig. 16	mid- to third quarter 4th century
198	fish plate	Group 11	Pl. 21	2nd century?

*Decoration only; see catalogue entry.

The numbers of inventoried plates are deceptive; there are not that many plates in proportion to other shapes in the Sanctuary, but they assume importance either for their decoration (6th- and 5th-century examples) or for the dating of fills (Hellenistic plates). Thus a disproportionate number of them have been inventoried, above their true popularity. There are 23 inventoried fragments of 6th-century plates, of which 13 are published. Most of the better preserved Hellenistic plates are published, including those with chronological significance. There are more fragments in the stored pottery but with poor decoration or poor preservation, or both. Some of the plates may have been votive offerings, but many may have been used in the dining rooms. Although there is not a high percentage of the shape in the Sanctuary, there are relatively more fragments than one finds in contemporary fills in the Forum.

The first 13 examples were made in the 6th century and include five works by the Chimaera Painter or his workshop, **26, 238–241**. There is also an interesting red-ground example, **244**. Interest in decorating the shape continued into the 5th century, with a large example related to the Vrysoula workshop, **283**, and small products of the Sam Wide group, **295–297**. Since the pre-Hellenistic plate has been well analyzed, the arguments and chronology are not repeated here.[161]

One Attic plate, **471**, represents the 4th century. There is one undecorated Corinthian example, **470**, that is difficult to date but may be contemporary with **471**. It was originally black glazed, but was burnt, reddening the glaze and disintegrating it. The foot has a wide diameter; the wall is short and convex, the rim similar to the everted 6th-century profile. But the foot is a solid ring, not the low round form of the Archaic plate foot, nor the false or disk foot found in the 5th century. The example seems therefore to have some early, some late characteristics. **470** is tentatively given a 4th-century date, on the basis of the later characteristics and the context in which it was found.

The first Hellenistic plates in the catalogue appear in Group 9. No fragments of the characteristic forms of the Hellenistic profiles were found in the strata of the later 4th-century destruction debris of the dining rooms.[162] Hellenistic plate rims take many forms, but in general the later plates have ring feet of diameters narrow in relation to height and maximum diameter. The walls and rims are distinctive; the walls reach a greater height than earlier types. There is more correspondence of the plate profiles with contemporary bowls and saucers than with the plates of the 6th and 5th centuries.

The first type of Hellenistic plate is the form with offset rim.[163] Two, **177** and **472**, have canonical West Slope decoration. The first is only a rim fragment but shows the design of boxed rectangle with added X and thus helps to date the context, Group 9, to the late 3rd century.[164] The second, **472**, is more problematic. It is Corinthian but shows a late motif of crosshatching. The plate should date to the end of the 2nd century.[165] From the same context as **472** comes another puzzle, **473**. The wall profile most resembles the offset-rim

[161] See Callipolitis-Feytmans.

[162] See *Corinth* VII, iii, p. 36. Only the offset-rim form has examples from 3rd-century contexts. In the dining rooms, other early Hellenistic shapes such as saucers, echinus bowls, bowls with beveled rims, and so forth, were found.

[163] *Corinth* VII, iii, nos. 127–130, pp. 39–40.

[164] See C-48-53 (*Corinth* VII, iii, no. 129, p. 40, pl. 45, of the fourth quarter of the 3rd century?), from South Stoa Well IX, well 1948-2. Should the design of **177** and the South Stoa plate prove to be earlier or later than the date assumed here, the date of Group 9 could be affected.

[165] For crosshatching: Thompson, *Hesperia* 3, 1934, p. 441, found only in the last deposit, group E, nos. 59 and 60. See also J. Hayes, *Late Roman Pottery*, London 1972, pp. 8–9 on group E.

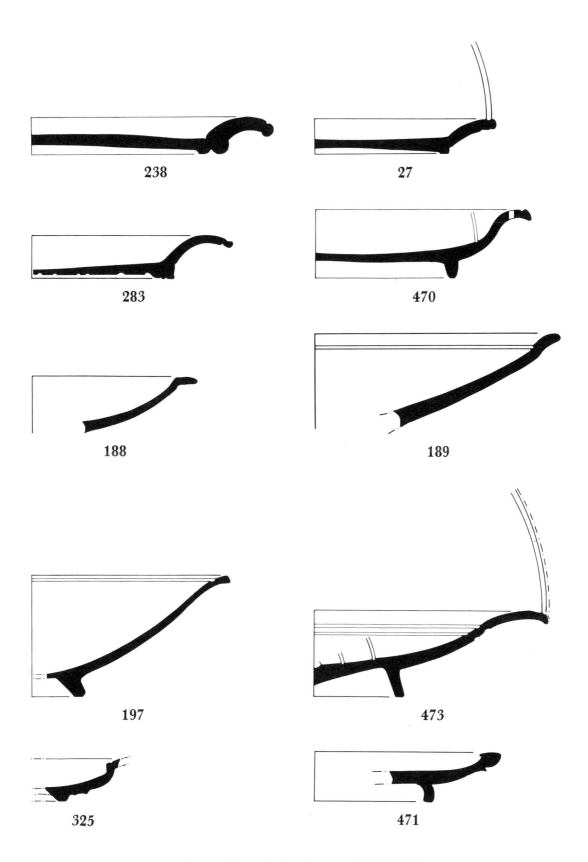

Fig. 16. Plates. Scale 1:2, except **188**, **189**: 1:4

plate, but it is larger, heavier in fabric, and has a much taller ring foot. Moreover, it lacks the normal West Slope decoration; instead, it has grooves on both faces of the wall and rim. It was originally entirely glazed. The Attic form of plate with offset rim is entirely different and offers no parallel for **473**.[166] Moreover, **473** is hastily made, with a thin coat of paint replacing the elaborately incised and painted decoration of the shape. **473** is probably late Hellenistic, at 146 B.C. or later.

189 and **197** are flat-rimmed plates, both from 2nd-century contexts (Groups 10 and 11). **197** from the later group has a slight convexity in the wall; **189** is straight. Edwards was unable to isolate any 3rd- or early 2nd-century examples of this profile;[167] the Sanctuary also provided no examples. The profile resembles the saucer; like that dish, it gains steepness in the wall and narrowing in the foot. But without contexts more defined than South Stoa wells and 146 B.C. destruction debris, the development of this plate cannot be well documented.

From the same two groups come two fragmentary plates, possibly fish plates with beveled rims.[168] Only one fish plate with the heavy Attic form of rim has been noted in the Sanctuary (lot 6643:1). Neither example has the foot and central floor depression preserved. **188** from Group 10 seems closest to a plate from New Museum Well A, C-40-433.[169] **188**, however, has a tooled line to offset the rim on its exterior surface, unlike any other example. **198** is even more peculiar. The fabric is not Corinthian, although the profile resembles the Corinthian fish plate. The plate is glazed overall, in contrast to the usual dipping of Corinthian examples. The rim is far more pronounced than the Corinthian forms. It may be 2nd century, but its place of manufacture is unknown.[170]

XIX. LEKYTHOI

Corinthian

44	black glazed	Group 3	Pl. 7	early second quarter 5th century
51	black glazed	Group 4		second quarter 5th century

Imported, Attic

45	cylinder, black figured	Group 3	Pl. 7	second quarter 5th century
46	cylinder, palmette	Group 3	Pl. 7	second quarter 5th century
326	cylinder, black figured		Pl. 36	second quarter 5th century
327	cylinder, white ground		Pl. 36	second quarter 5th century
366	cylinder, white ground		Pl. 43	mid-5th century
367	squat, red figured		Pl. 43	late 5th century
96	squat, palmette	Group 6	Pl. 13	second quarter 4th century

It is not surprising that few lekythoi appear in the catalogue; aryballoi are also conspicuous by their absence (see Shape Studies, XX). Only two Corinthian lekythoi are included, of the early 5th-century black-glazed form. Very few additional fragments remain in the context pottery.

Most of the lekythoi are Attic imports; the overwhelming majority are the late black-figure palmette type, represented by **46**.[171] Additional fragments of the type can be found in many 5th-century strata. Fragments of the lekythoi with ivy-chain patterns were also found; no examples were required for dating, and so none were inventoried. The latter decorative pattern was not so popular as the palmette design.

The black-figured examples belong to the same period. It appears as if there was a sudden vogue of dedication or use of these Attic lekythoi in the Sanctuary, *ca.* 475–450 B.C. The dilemma concerns their function.

[166] Thompson, *Hesperia* 3, 1934, group D, p. 370, no. 1, fig. 55; group E, p. 395, nos. 22–26, fig. 83.
[167] *Corinth* VII, iii, nos. 107–126, pp. 37–38; the examples are dated only to the mid-2nd century.
[168] *Corinth* VII, iii, nos. 134–137, pp. 41–42.
[169] Well 1940-1; *Corinth* VII, iii, no. 137, p. 42.
[170] There are some very fragmentary "normal" fish plate examples in Corinthian fabric: lot 6206:1 and lot 6205:6, too small to be published.
[171] See *Corinth* XIII, p. 142, group 2.

Were the lekythoi in fact given as votives, or did they contain some oil or perfume, necessary for a brief period in the Sanctuary rites? There is no Archaic vessel that could be the predecessor of these lekythoi in function; there is, however, a successor, the blister-ware aryballos. The sudden appearance of the lekythoi, imported from Athens, could be in response to a new cult requirement. The sudden disappearance can be explained by the introduction of the blister-ware vessels replacing the more expensive imports. This is only a speculative interpretation.

The black-figured lekythoi are not of the first order; **326** comes from the Class of Athens 581. In the third quarter of the century someone brought to the Sanctuary a white-ground lekythos, **366**, with quite lovely painting on it. The two red-figured examples complete the Attic imports: one has an ugly sphinx, **367**; the other has a palmette, **96**.

The lekythos was never an important Corinthian shape; the aryballos apparently served in its place. But the lack in the Sanctuary finds of the small container in either form, until the 5th century, is puzzling. Even the cheapest, simplest type of small closed ointment vessel, the little banded lekythos,[172] is almost totally absent from the Demeter Sanctuary.

XX. ARYBALLOI, ALABASTRA

Corinthian aryballoi

249	figured		Pl. 26	EC
250	figured		Pl. 26	MC
251	figured		Fig. 17, Pl. 26	MC
252	figured		Pl. 26	MC
253	figured		Pl. 26	LC
475	blister ware		Pl. 48	third quarter 5th century
97	blister ware	Group 6	Fig. 17, Pl. 13	third quarter 4th century
476	blister ware		Pl. 48	late third quarter 4th century
477	blister ware		Pl. 48	first or second quarter 3rd century
478	blister ware		Pl. 48	2nd century?

Imported

474	Attic alabastron?		Pl. 48	before end of 4th century

The five inventoried Archaic Corinthian aryballoi are almost the sum total of all aryballoi of that period found in the Demeter Sanctuary. Only a few more remain in the context pottery. Thus one of the most popular, most exported, most typical of all the Corinthian shapes is virtually absent from the Sanctuary. The aryballos apparently had no function in the cult and was not considered to be an appropriate votive. One usually assumes that almost anything can be dedicated to any deity. One would expect that aryballoi, especially the later quatrefoil or warrior types which were probably inexpensive (mass produced, small, simply decorated), would be numerous in the Sanctuary. But they are not. Is the aryballos then to be associated with other deities in Corinth and excluded from the proper offerings to Demeter and her daughter?[173]

The five examples of blister-ware aryballoi present almost the full range of the shape:[174] **475** with moderate ribbing, **97** with narrow linear ribs,[175] **476** with incisions replacing ribs, and **477** and **478** without any decoration and made of extremely thin fabric.[176] The latter two are similar to the latest example in *Corinth*

---

[172] See Pemberton, *Hesperia* 39, 1970, pp. 293–294.

[173] Aryballoi are found in other areas of Corinth; great numbers were excavated in the Potters' Quarter. Many were recovered on Temple Hill; Hera at Perachora also received her share (*Perachora* II, nos. 1555–1672).

[174] For the shape see *Corinth* VII, iii, nos. 750–775, pp. 146–148.

[175] **97** is very similar to the blister-ware aryballos from Forum drain 1971-1, C-71-357 (unpublished).

[176] **477** measures 0.0015 in thickness at the shoulder, 0.001 m. at the base. The 5th-century example, **475**, is 0.0035 m. thick at the shoulder (between ribs) and 0.003 m. at the base.

251

97

Fig. 17. Aryballoi. Scale 1:2

VII, iii, C-47-228.[177] There is a change in profile. **97** and **476** have a low ovoid wall, resulting in a domed profile. In **477** the body has become almost biconical; in **478** it is biconical, resembling the profile of a lagynos. The neck also gains height in the later examples. The blister-ware aryballos is wheelmade; the neck is usually made separately from the body.

The date for both **477** and **478** is later than the 300 B.C. terminus given for the shape in *Corinth* VII, iii. The examples from drain 1971-1[178] give a date for similarly ribbed aryballoi, thereby lowering the chronology as outlined in *Corinth* VII, iii. Second, there are sufficient numbers of fragmentary blister-ware aryballoi in Hellenistic strata to suggest that the vessel was still produced in that period. **477** was probably made before the year 250 B.C., on the basis of context; **478**, having a later profile, may even be as late as mid-2nd century, also on the basis of context.

Edwards has suggested that the blister-ware aryballos went out of production when superseded by the imported unguentarium;[179] the thin fabric of **478** may show imitation of unguentarium fabric. There are not, however, many unguentarium fragments in the Sanctuary.[180] If these two shapes competed for the same function, as oil containers at the dining table,[181] the lack of unguentaria in the Sanctuary would argue for continuation of the aryballoi in the Hellenistic period. Otherwise, it would seem that what was necessary in the dining rooms from *ca.* 450 to 300 B.C. was not necessary later. Or, perhaps the two shapes did not have the same function. Yet, one may well ask what was used in 6th-century dining rooms, since few lekythoi and Archaic aryballoi have been found.

The last vessel on the above list is of Attic fabric: a small, pointed, closed vessel, which most resembles an alabastron. It is, so far, without parallel and cannot be dated of itself. The context of **474** ends in the late 4th century, but has earlier material in it.

---

[177] No. 775, p. 148, pls. 35, 64. It might have been biconical, but the bottom is not preserved. There is another Hellenistic example, C-69-301, from a cave in the Fountain of the Lamps in the Gymnasium, without full profile (neck and handle missing). The context, lot 6071, is late Hellenistic and early Roman, thus possibly giving more evidence for survival until 146 B.C. It is biconical in shape, with blisters on the shoulder; the fabric fired orange, and there are traces of a thin exterior wash. The fabric is very thin: Th. 0.002 m. at the shoulder, 0.001 below.

[178] See footnote 175, p. 53 above.

[179] *Corinth* VII, iii, p. 145.

[180] See Shape Studies, XXI.

[181] See the aryballoi found in the Theater Cave at Isthmia (the cave had dining facilities and couches): O. Broneer, *Isthmia*, II, *Topography and Architecture*, Princeton 1973, pp. 37–40, pl. 19:d.

XXI. ASKOI, UNGUENTARIA

Corinthian				
98	blister-ware duck askos	Group 6	Pl. 13	late 4th century
200	blister-ware duck askos	Group 11		last quarter 4th century
199	spouted askos	Group 11	Pl. 21	2nd century?
134	unguentarium	Group 7	Pl. 16	early 3rd century?
Imported				
135	Attic guttus askos	Group 7	Fig. 18, Pl. 16	third quarter 4th century
201	unguentarium	Group 11	Pl. 21	later Hellenistic?

The askoi are all documented shapes. The Attic example, **135**, from Pit B, has many parallels that date it to the later 4th century, probably the late third quarter. The vessel is thus earlier than much of the material from its context. The two very fragmentary duck askoi are identical with a more complete example excavated in 1960.[182] Edwards suggests that there was a limited time of production, in the last quarter of the 4th century. As more of these theriomorphic askoi in blister-ware fabric are recognized, however, the length of production may have to be expanded. **98** ought not to be much later than 300 B.C., given the bulk of the material in that group; the second duck askos came from a later group, with debris in it dated to after 146 B.C. It must then be considerably earlier than most of the material in that context if production of blister-ware askoi was so limited. The last askos, a double-spouted vessel, also from Group 11, has an unpublished parallel from South Stoa Well VII.[183] There is no way to determine a specific date for either example. The askos generally was never an important shape, either in Corinth or specifically in the Sanctuary.

Fig. 18. Attic guttus askos **135**.
Scale 1:2

The unguentarium is also not a popular shape in the Sanctuary. The shape appears in Corinth in the later 4th century. A grave located on the road to Acrocorinth contained a small example, C-60-228.[184] It is made of a fine buff clay, decorated with dull brown bands on the shoulder and neck, and is surely Corinthian. The grave is dated to the third quarter of the 4th century by a coin. There is also a similar form of unguentarium of later date, with the same wide sloping shoulder but in a slightly rosier clay, found in the North Cemetery.[185] In the early 3rd century, a more brittle, blue-gray fabric appears, the fabric of **134** of Group 7, without shoulder bands. A North Cemetery grave also produced one in this fabric.[186] **134** has in the fabric many white and orange nuclei that swirl on the surface, creating an attractive natural pattern. The core is part gray, part orange; there are orange streaks on the interior surface. The North Cemetery example is similar. The fabric is especially thin, as in later blister ware, which it resembles in texture and color. There is also affinity with the imitation Cypriot found in Corinth in the later 4th century.[187] Blister ware was surely a Corinthian production; the other two classes are probably Corinthian also.

There are a few unguentarium fragments in Hellenistic strata of the Sanctuary in the more typical smooth gray fabric, often with red or red and white bands on the shoulder. Examples have been noted in several lots: 3228:1, 3231:2, 6181:3, 6206:2. No whole profiles were preserved.

---

[182] C-60-68 (*Corinth* VII, iii, no. 776, p. 149, pl. 64; well 1960-4).

[183] C-47-899. The well, 1933-3, is deposit 99 in *Corinth* VII, iii.

[184] Deposit 58 in *Corinth* VII, iii, grave 1960-7, published in H. S. Robinson, "Excavations at Corinth," *Hesperia* 31, 1962 (pp. 95–133), pp. 118–120, pl. 46:b. The kantharos from this grave is discussed in footnote 92 above, p. 35.

[185] T 2716 (*Corinth* XIII, grave 496-16, pl. 77).

[186] T 2701 (*Corinth* XIII, grave 495-7, pl. 78).

[187] For imitation Cypriot, see Williams, *Hesperia* 38, 1969, pp. 57–59, pl. 18:a–d.

201 is more problematic. Part of it comes from Group 11 which contained Roman material, but one joining fragment was found in lot 3228, ending by 200 B.C. The concave stem and slightly conical foot, thickened outside, the black glaze of the interior, the dark orange-brown micaceous clay with a fine surface polish, all differ from the usual unguentaria found in Corinth. The brown shoulder bands are characteristic of the early buff examples made in Corinth. **201** is probably an import.

There is a rim in lot 6716; the terminal date of the lot is in the early Roman period. It was too small a fragment to be inventoried, but it should be noted. It has a thin, red glaze inside and on the rim. It resembles in fabric and glaze C-48-12, from South Stoa Well XXII, identified by J. Hayes as Cypriot. C-66-222, from Katsoulis well 3 (well 1965-3), is also very similar.

XXII. PYXIDES, LIDS

Corinthian, figured pyxides

254	concave		Pl. 27	EC
255	concave		Pl. 27	MC
256	tripod		Fig. 19, Pl. 27	LC
257	convex		*Fig. 31, Pl. 27	MC?
258	convex		Pl. 27	MC
259	convex		Pl. 27	MC
260	convex		*Fig. 31, Pl. 27	LC
261	convex		Pl. 27	LC
262	convex		Pl. 28	LC
263	convex		*Fig. 31, Pl. 28	LC
264	convex		Pl. 28	fourth quarter 6th century

Corinthian, banded or patterned pyxides

482	tripod		Pl. 49	later 6th century
483	tripod		Pl. 49	later 6th century
484	flanged		Pl. 49	early 5th century
485	flanged		Fig. 19	mid-5th century
486	pyxis		Pl. 49	6th century

Corinthian, figured lids

265	pyxis		Figs. 19, *31, Pl. 28	EC
266	pyxis		Pl. 28	MC
267	pyxis		Pl. 28	MC
268	pyxis		*Fig. 31, Pl. 28	MC
29	pyxis	Group 2	Fig. 25, Pl. 5	LC
269	kotyle-pyxis		Pl. 28	MC
270	pyxis		Pl. 28	EC?
271	lekanis		Pl. 28	LC (after mid-century?)

Corinthian, banded or patterned lids

487	pyxis		Pl. 49	second half 6th century
488	pyxis		Pl. 49	second half 6th century
489	pyxis		Pl. 49	late 6th or early 5th century
490	?		Pl. 49	6th century
285	pyxis		Pl. 30	second quarter or mid-5th century

Corinthian, Hellenistic

179	pyxis	Group 9	Pl. 19	later 3rd century
180	pyxis	Group 9	Fig. 19, Pl. 19	late 3rd century
181	pyxis, lid	Group 9	Fig. 19, Pl. 19	late 3rd century
202	pyxis	Group 11	Pl. 21	early 2nd century
178	West Slope lid	Group 9	Pl. 19	late 3rd century?

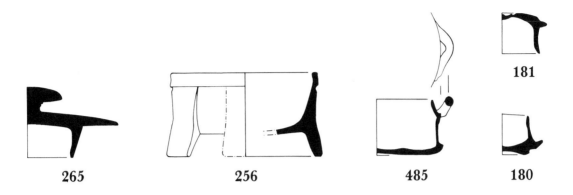

FIG. 19. Pyxides and lids. Scale 1:2

Imported, Attic

328	Nikosthenic pyxis, black figured	Pl. 36	third quarter 6th century
369	lekanis-like pyxis, red figured	Pl. 43	*ca.* 380–360 B.C.

*Decoration only; see catalogue entry.

The number of pyxis fragments from the Demeter Sanctuary is high; what function the shape served cannot be definitely stated. Pyxides of the convex form in particular are found in almost every Archaic and Classical level. Moreover, some of the 6th-century examples show very fine decoration.[188]

The pyxides are arranged chronologically, divided according to shape and figured or non-figured forms. The convex form is the most popular, since it begins as a Corinthian shape in the MC period, the time of great growth in the Sanctuary. The concave pyxis disappears by the end of the MC period. The tripod pyxis survived the 6th century; there is one late example from an early 5th-century grave in the North Cemetery.[189] The most popular form of powder pyxis in the Archaic period is absent from the Sanctuary, as it seems to have been used almost exclusively as a grave gift.[190] **487**, however, although taller than the grave powder pyxis, has very similar decoration. The powder pyxis continued into the Classical period, although with a different, taller shape (see the lid **285**), and apparently disappeared in the 4th century, only to be reborn in the later 4th century in a Hellenistic version.

The convex pyxis began in the MC period, with a number of variant forms,[191] and changed shape and decoration throughout the 6th, 5th, and 4th centuries, when it too finally ended. All the inventoried examples from the Sanctuary have figure decoration. There are also many small examples of the white style; none were catalogued since they lack decorative interest and do not assist dating. In the late 5th and 4th centuries a form of convex pyxis with upright handles was popular; it shows a fairly routine decoration with buds on the

---

[188] Fragments of convex pyxides may be mistaken for oinochoai and vice versa.

[189] T 1673 (*Corinth* XIII, grave 271-1, pl. 39).

[190] T 1586 (*ibid.*, grave 157-t), T 3241 (grave 159-12), T 1557, T 1559 (grave 168-8 and 9), T 3055 (grave 224-5), T 1864 (grave 225-1). See also C-60-125–C-60-127 (P. Lawrence, "Five Grave Groups from the Corinthia," *Hesperia* 33, 1964 [pp. 89–107], grave E, p. 96, nos. 24–26, pl. 19); found in a grave with one tripod pyxis and eight convex white-style pyxides. Yet, a few of this "grave" form of pyxis were found in the Tocra excavations (Boardman and Hayes, *Tocra* I, nos. 229–232, pl. 15).

[191] *NC*, pp. 305–308.

wall and palmettes on the shoulder. Several fragments of these remain in the context pottery from Classical levels.[192]

In the Archaic period, the pyxis is by far the most popular of the small non-drinking vessels in the Sanctuary. There are very few fragments, for example, of kothons; open or lidded bowls are not so frequently found; plates, although popular, are not so numerous. Only the most interestingly decorated pyxides are published. There are many additional figured fragments in the context pottery, with poor or totally indecipherable designs. Since none of the figured examples are well preserved, little can be said about shape development.

The popularity of the Corinthian pyxis obviated imports. Thus it was a little surprising to find a fairly rare form of Attic black-figured pyxis, the Nikosthenic type, **328**.[193]

The lids show variety also. The form with inset flange is appropriate for a pyxis, although it may have been used for other vessels also. The domed type without flange fits a kotyle-pyxis, and later a lekanis or other flanged container. Representative examples of lid shapes are included, all of which are figured. There are many more whose designs have disintegrated. The great numbers of lids with 5th-century conventionalizing patterns have not been catalogued; **285** from a powder pyxis represents the best of the type. **490** is a peculiar example; it is unclear to what sort of container it belonged.

The Hellenistic period produced new pyxis shapes. One decorated lid from that period was found in the Sanctuary, **178**. It has zones demarcated by grooves and is decorated with West Slope patterns in incision, raised clay, and added white. There is a parallel from a pottery deposit in Shop I of the South Stoa.[194]

The late form of pyxis seems to begin in the third quarter of the 4th century.[195] In the Sanctuary, however, the type does not seem to become popular until the 3rd century (Groups 9 and 11). Few examples of the earliest form can be found. In Group 9, the "high-keeled" form is already noticeable (**179**); the lower wall has a wide-flaring diagonal profile rising to the ledge, well advanced in comparison to late 4th-century examples with the lower diagonal wall. The set, **180** and **181**, is later, probably made at the end of the 3rd century.[196] The high keel has disappeared, replaced by a false foot and a very low wall. There is a final stage for the shape of the bowl, not illustrated by a catalogue example. In lot 3233 (M:16–17), two small fragmentary examples show a disk foot (3233:2) and a low ring foot (3233:1); the ledge for the lid projects horizontally immediately above the foot, and the wall is set back from the ledge. **180** shows the evolution to this late stage. The lid gains a domed profile in the later stages.[197] **181** is poorly made, but the grooves still have appreciable depth, although they are not symmetrically placed. **202**, from Group 11, is later and may belong to the 2nd century. The grooves have become incisions; the top is domed.

In *Corinth* VII, iii, the terminal date for this shape is the later 3rd century,[198] but the vessel is found in all the late Hellenistic debris of the dining rooms, in greater numbers than the small unglazed lekanis (see p. 39 above). It is possible that this form of pyxis continued to 146 B.C.[199] The function of this pyxis is also

---

[192] See the published example from Forum drain 1971-1, C-71-191 (Williams and Fisher, *Hesperia* 41, 1972, p. 161, no. 46, pl. 27).

[193] Almost all the fragments of the Nikosthenic pyxis were found in N–O:26, north and east of Room J, in different years of the excavation. Presumably the vessel was used or displayed in that area.

[194] C-34-36, unpublished (fill 1934-1).

[195] *Corinth* VII, iii, pp. 96–97, with the first examples dated to 350 B.C. A very early form of this pyxis, with a flat base, was found in the votive pit of the third quarter of the 4th century (well 1975-4), in the roadway west of the Forum bath building, C-75-177 (Williams and Fisher, *Hesperia* 45, 1976, p. 121, no. 44, pl. 21). The earliest examples in the North Cemetery, T 2371 and T 2369 (*Corinth* XIII, deposit 36e and f, pl. 73), have a developed keel. The example from grave 491-8, T 1159 (*ibid.*, pl. 76), is also later; the skyphos in that grave seems later in profile than the skyphoi in Forum well 1975-4 (C-75-167, Williams and Fisher, *Hesperia* 45, 1976, p. 120, no. 38, pl. 21). Grave 491 may not be quite so late as suggested, in the late fourth quarter of the 4th century, not the early third century (*Corinth* XIII, p. 291).

[196] A fill excavated in Forum Southeast, lot 1980-129, with pottery of the middle and the third quarter of the 3rd century (and a coin of Ptolemy III), contained an example with a fairly high keel (1980-129:2).

[197] *Corinth* VII, iii, p. 97.

[198] *Ibid.* Edwards notes that the shape continued in Athens into the 1st century B.C.

[199] Very few were found in South Stoa wells, but that may be a result of the function of the vases as votive or sacral, making them less common in domestic contexts.

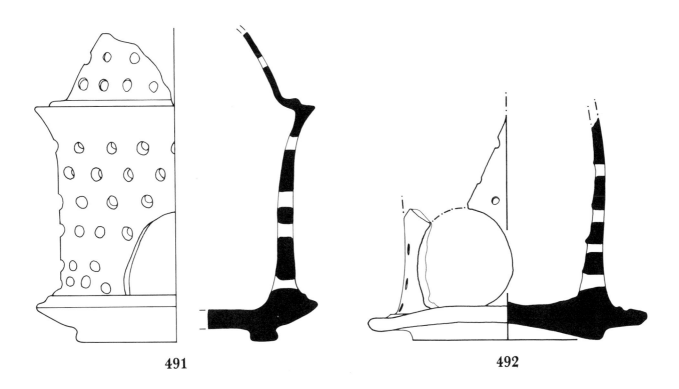

491   **492**

FIG. 20. Perforated cylindrical vessels. Scale 1:2

unclear; they are found in votive deposits (Group 9) but also in contexts with little clearly defined votive material.[200]

XXIII. PERFORATED CYLINDRICAL VESSELS

Corinthian

491	Fig. 20, Pl. 49	Hellenistic
492	Fig. 20, Pl. 49	Hellenistic

Imported

493	Pl. 49	Hellenistic
494	Pl. 49	Hellenistic
495	Pl. 49	Hellenistic

In many of the Hellenistic and mixed Greek and Roman strata of the Sanctuary, there are fragments of cylindrical vessels pierced with numerous holes. Although no complete profile is preserved, the many fragments allow restoration of the general shape. There is often a foot, recessed behind a projecting ring or flange

---

[200] See footnote 199 above, p. 58. The findspots of the small pyxides in the Sanctuary do not clarify their purpose. They have not been found extensively elsewhere in Corinth, except in graves or dumps of votive nature. Yet their presence in the Sanctuary dining room debris suggests some sort of use other than a purely religious one.

from which a tall cylindrical wall rises, either to a second flange at the top of the wall or to a ridge or other offset, above which is a domed top. At the base of the wall there is an oval or square opening, five to six centimeters in both height and width. The wall and often the top are pierced all around with many holes. **491** is the best preserved example; it has a ring foot set well back from the strong flange, which is also the maximum diameter. Both the lower and upper flanges have rings on the upper surfaces, further decorating the articulation of the vessel. There are, however, many variations of the parts of the vase, described below.

Feet. On **491** there is a solid ring foot with wide resting surface. **492** has a disk foot of the same diameter as that of the wall and is concave underneath. **493** has no foot. Many of these fragments, found in lot 1945,[201] show a variety of feet: 1945:1 with flat resting surface below the wall and no separate foot; 1945:2, a squared torus foot at the lower edge of the flange; 1945:3, a torus foot turning directly into the wall without a separate flange; 1945:4, a flaring ring foot, also rising directly into the cylindrical wall.

Walls. The cylindrical wall may be slightly concave as **491**, turning directly into the upper projecting flange, the profile thus resembling an epichysis. It may also be somewhat convex, as **492**, the walls of which appear to merge continuously with the domed top, without a separate upper flange dividing the wall from the top. **493** has a cylindrical wall, flaring out to the shoulder flange.

Tops. **491** and **493** have the pierced dome set back from the upper flange. 1945:5 has a vertical wall, flaring out slightly to form a ridge, not a well-defined flange, above which is a second smaller ridge; both are cut with vertical outer faces, rather like the steps of the lids of unglazed lekanides. The domed top is not pierced. 1945:6 shows the top of a pierced, slightly convex wall, with a narrow rounded flange, above which is a slightly rising, narrow strip of clay, essentially an inner flange, with finished inner edge. Clearly the vessel was open at the top. It may have had a lid, but a handle scar covering both the outer and inner flanges shows that there was a strap handle probably passing over the open top to the other side. **495** is conical, with five holes pierced in it; a strap handle rises vertically, within the loop of which is a round knob, like the top of a spouted askos.

Holes and doors. The small holes are made before firing, punched through from the outside, normally in random placement. **491** is neater than many, showing horizontal but no vertical arrangement. Many examples show no scraping of the inside of the holes; the wads of clay formed around the interiors remain. **491** shows that the holes from the top of the door up are scraped; those below the top of the door are not. The holes on **493** begin above the level of the door and cease well below the flange. The vessel normally has one door, usually oval; a few are more square. The doors were also made before firing.

Fabric. There are at least three different fabrics. The most common is a pale buff clay, represented by the first two examples in the catalogue. The clay is fairly soft and is typically Corinthian: 10YR 7/3 (very pale brown) for the core of **491**; 2.5YR 8/2–4 (white to pale yellow) for the core of **492**. 1945:6 has an orange core, fired buff on the surface, that one also finds in Corinthian: 7.5YR 8/6 (reddish yellow). The clay shows no mica, and all these examples are unslipped.

There is also a redder clay, both hard and softer. 1945:3 is lightly micaceous, 7.5YR 7–6/6 (reddish yellow), very hard, without inclusions or slip. **493** is slightly grittier, with a few inclusions and a little mica, 5YR 7–6/6 (reddish yellow). The last two examples are similar but softer in texture; the clay is also micaceous. **495** is 7.5YR 7/6, **494** is 5YR 6/8 (both reddish yellow). In addition, **494** has a pale, thin exterior slip of 10YR 7/4, as if to make it appear to be Corinthian. These four examples appear to be imports.

One fragment, 1945:5, is very different. The fabric has small black inclusions, is of slightly gritty quality, and has a light surface wash. The core is 5YR 7/4 (pink). The texture is close to Argive, but Argive clay normally fires a darker color.

All the vessels appear to be wheelmade. The fabric is very thick below, decreasing steadily to the dome. **491** is 0.014 m. thick above the lower flange, 0.006 m. below the upper flange, and 0.003 m. at the top break. A few (probably imports) appear to be slipped. No example shows any paint or decoration.

---

[201] The fragments in lot 1945, although of great importance for shape and fabric, were too small to inventory and would not reproduce clearly in photographs. The sherds have been numbered and remain in the context pottery, if re-examination should be necessary.

Function. These vessels have been found only in the Demeter Sanctuary, nowhere else, so far, in Ancient Corinth. Consequently they must have had some particular function in the Sanctuary, whether for ritual or for dining. Most of the contexts are not helpful for discerning purpose or date. Lot 1945, containing many fragments, is from a well on the Middle Terrace, with all periods represented in the material. Some fragments have been found in dining-room fills; Building M:16–17 contained a number of them, including three of the four catalogued examples. The cistern in Building L–M:28 also contained sherds (6720:1). It is not clear that the findspots are relevant. The absence of material from Groups 8 and 9, consisting primarily of votive material, cannot be used as evidence of a non-votive function. For in a votive deposit of figurines, containing very little pottery and that little primarily votive in type, one large wall fragment was found (lot 2063:1, from the wall and upper flange). The few vases in that deposit were type 4 kalathiskoi, a few pieces of Attic, and the miniature lebes gamikos, *333*. Very few fine-ware fragments were found in lot 2063. Thus the figurine deposit offsets the "evidence" of Groups 8 and 9.

The function of these vessels seems to be that of lamp holder. Similar vases found in Cyprus, found with lamps in them, have been so identified.[202] The openings in our examples appear to be smaller than their counterparts in Cyprus, yet they are of sufficient size to allow lamps of types IX and X to be placed inside. The other possible function is as a thymiaterion receptacle, with type 4 kalathiskoi as the holder of the incense.[203] The many holes would allow the light or scented smoke, depending on the function, to escape. It is, however, only right to note that none of the fragments of this vessel bears any trace of carbonized material. Whatever the function, the vessel enjoyed a certain popularity in the later years of the Sanctuary.[204]

Date. Most of the fragments have been found in late fills, from the Hellenistic period, or mixed fills of very late dump containing both Greek and Roman material. Lot 2063, noted above, has one fragment of an upper wall and flange, resembling *491*. The pottery does not appear to go far into the 3rd century but should be given a lower limit in the first half of the century, on the basis of the type 4 kalathiskoi. There is, however, very little pottery in that context; a more precise date must be determined by the many figurines.

The presence of many of these vessels in mixed strata, such as the fills in Building M:16–17, suggests that they were popular in the later Hellenistic period. There is enough variation in profile to presume manufacture for several generations. Thus, they may have been introduced, possibly from Cyprus, for an as yet unverifiable function, in the earlier 3rd century; they would have had, if that is correct, about one hundred years of use in the Sanctuary. The evidence is, at this point, too slim to propose any more specific chronology. Nor can any sequence of shape changes be outlined, since full profiles are lacking. It is also difficult to account for what seems to be the manufacture of these vessels in at least two non-Corinthian fabrics, for to my knowledge there are no published examples from other mainland sites. They remain, despite the many hundreds of fragments, somewhat enigmatic.

---

[202] D. Bailey, *British Museum Catalogue of Lamps* I, Oxford 1975, Z495 and Z496, pp. 225–227, pls. 98–99, without flanges or holes in the dome. The example he cites from Priene also has no holes in dome or wall. But note the bronze lamp holder, with many fine small holes, found in Tomb 2 at Vergina (*Alexander The Great: History and Legend in Art*, Thessaloniki 1980, p. 40) and a second, less elaborate example, from Grave A, Derveni (*Treasures of Ancient Macedonia*, Thessaloniki 1979, no. 160, pl. 33). The example in the British Museum from Cyprus is dated "probably fourth or third c. B.C." Bailey cites others from Cyprus; there are others, unpublished, in various museums, all said to be from Cyprus.

[203] There are very few examples of thymiateria in the Sanctuary pottery: one or two possible examples of the Vrysoula type (Pemberton, *Hesperia* 39, 1970, pp. 289–290), too small for inventory; a few stems of Attic thymiateria are also present. Yet the Romans certainly used incense in the Sanctuary: see K. Slane, *Corinth* XVIII, ii, forthcoming.

[204] Another suggestion has been that they are beehives. But the objects identified as ancient beehives do not have the holes that these vessels have, nor are the Sanctuary vessels combed on the interior. See A. J. Graham, Excursus II, "Evidence for Beekeeping," in J. E. Jones, A. J. Graham, and L. H. Sackett, "An Attic Country House," *BSA* 68, 1973 (pp. 355–452), pp. 397–412. The vessels identified by Graham as gliraria are more similar, but no Demeter Sanctuary vessels have their characteristic spiral track on the interior (A. J. Graham, "The Vari House—an Addendum," *BSA* 73, 1978, pp. 99–101).

XXIV. MISCELLANEA, UNKNOWN SHAPES (FINE WARES)

Miscellanea

215	bottle	Fig. 21, Pl. 23	MC
248	red-ground plaque	Pl. 26	LC
329	Attic epinetron	Pl. 36	*ca.* 480 B.C.
333	Attic miniature lebes gamikos	Fig. 21, Pl. 37	second quarter 4th century
480	"feeder"	Pl. 48	late 4th century?
481	"feeder"	Fig. 21, Pl. 48	late 4th or early 3rd century?
479	blister-ware filter vase		3rd century?
496	ladle	Pl. 49	?

Unknown shapes

272	closed vase	Pl. 28	EC?
273	closed vase	Pl. 28	6th century
274	closed vase	Pl. 28	LC
311	Attic closed vase	Pl. 34	later 6th century
312	Attic closed vase	Pl. 34	later 6th century
368	Attic lid, plate?	Pl. 43	530–520 B.C.
370	Attic head-kantharos?	Pl. 43	second quarter 5th century
497	West Slope vessel	Fig. 21, Pl. 49	mid-2nd century?
498	imported West Slope vessel	Pl. 49	Hellenistic
499	Gnathian closed vase	Pl. 49	late 4th century

The unknown fragments are all puzzles; the profile and possible interpretation of each is discussed in each catalogue entry.

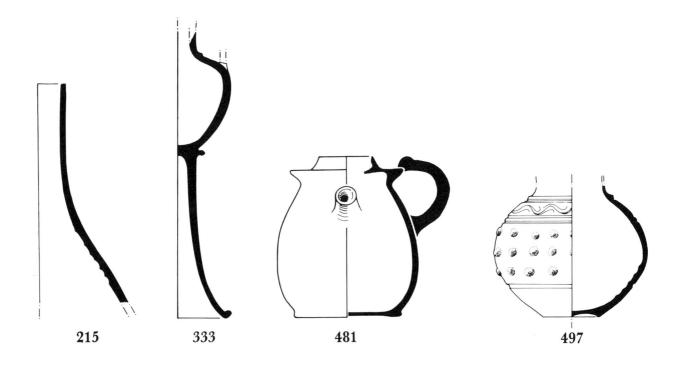

215   **333**   **481**   **497**

FIG. 21. Miscellanea. Scale 1:2

A few remarks on the miscellanea: The one bottle has a *Frauenfest* scene;[205] that subject occurs on a number of different shapes and may be significant for the cult. Very few plaque fragments were found in the Sanctuary, many fewer than at Perachora. The one example in the catalogue is the best preserved plaque; the others are corner scraps, without extant decoration. As with aryballoi and other shapes, the plaque is a votive type popular in other Corinthian cults but apparently not appropriate for Demeter. No Corinthian epinetra have been found, although one might think it a dedication appropriate for the two goddesses. The blister-ware filter vase is no longer such a rarity; more examples have been found in excavations in the Forum.[206] And the one ladle finds companions in the material from the Potters' Quarter.[207]

The "feeder" presents problems of date and function. First, this type of vessel seems to start suddenly in the later 4th century.[208] Second, most of the examples come from the Demeter Sanctuary. There are three from the Potters' Quarter, one from the North Cemetery, one from Forum drain 1971-1, one from Forum well 1975-4, one from the Baths of Aphrodite, and one from Katsoulis well 3 (well 1965-3).[209] The contexts of all the above, where closely datable, seem to be in the third quarter of the 4th century.

The two inventoried examples from the Sanctuary come from contexts of the late 4th to earlier 3rd century (lots 6181, 6723). There are quite a few fragments in the later groups of Catalogue I: 11 in Group 6, none in 7, five in 8, none in 9, two in 10, and one in 11. A few more examples remaining in the context pottery have been numbered in order to give support for the popularity of the shape: 3227:1, 3231:1, 5625:3, 5648:3, 6205:1, 6723:6, 72-128:1. Many of these contexts have terminal dates of the late 4th or early 3rd centuries, although a few go into the later Hellenistic period (3227, 3231). There are many more fragments than the above, recognizable by the distinctive stopper mouth and wall spout, the heavier parts that usually survive.

The presence of so many "feeders" in later strata can be explained by the earlier material that exists in each context. Yet, one wonders why, if there was a vogue for so many of them in the later 4th century, it would last for only 30 to 50 years? They are usually found in the fills of dining rooms; were they used in the meals in those rooms? They are probably misnamed and should be identified as containers for some type of liquid necessitating slow pouring, after filtering into the vessels. It is difficult to prove that the vases continued to be manufactured throughout the Hellenistic period, for there appears to be almost no change in shape. The Forum drain example, C-71-522, is not so dumpy in profile as the Demeter examples; it reaches its maximum diameter higher on the wall. All examples, except one very small one from the Potters' Quarter, have rotellai or pellets at the top of the handle, where preserved. It is tempting to connect the shape with a metal prototype, which, however, does not exist, so far as I know. There are somewhat similar vases in non-Corinthian relief wares.

The small Gnathian fragment, from a closed, thin-walled convex vase, has the characteristic decoration. Similar white, purple, and incised patterns appear on the shoulder of an epichysis excavated in 1975.[210] Gradually, more South Italian vessels, imported into Corinth in the 4th century and later, are being recognized.

---

[205] See I. Jucker, "Frauenfest in Korinth," *Antike Kunst* 2, 1963, pp. 47–61, no. 6.

[206] The only early example, C-47-853, is published in *Corinth* VII, iii, no. 778, p. 149, pls. 36, 64 (well 1947-3). There was also one found at Kenchreai: B. Adamschek, *Kenchreai*, IV, *The Pottery*, Leiden 1979, GR 47, p. 21, pl. 5.

[207] See *Corinth* XV, iii, nos. 1992–1995, p. 333, pl. 72.

[208] There is a curious fragment of a wall, with a high ovoid profile, partly glazed inside (on the lower area), decorated with black and red bands on the exterior, and bearing a spout on the wall in the form of a lion's head. It is C-74-115, unpublished, without good context, but probably to be dated on the 5th century on the basis of the black and red bands. It may resemble the kotyle-feeders from the North Cemetery (T 1662; *Corinth* XIII, grave 336-e) and the Potters' Quarter (KV 914; *Corinth* XV, iii, no. 1722). None of these forerunners foreshadows the 4th-century form.

[209] Potters' Quarter: KP 700, KP 671, both small, and KP 237 (*Corinth* XV, iii, nos. 2207, 2213, 2203).

North Cemetery: T 2484 (*Corinth* XIII, grave 457-5, pl. 75), small.

Forum drain 1971-1: C-71-522, large.

Forum well 1975-4: C-75-91, small (*Hesperia* 45, 1976, p. 121, no. 46, pl. 21).

Baths of Aphrodite: C-60-264, mouth of a large example, from well II (well 1960-6), abandonment fill. Some of the material goes into the 3rd century, but there is earlier pottery also. See Robinson (footnote 184 above, p. 55), p. 125.

Katsoulis well 3: C-66-175, mouth only. Found in fill E, which included a West Slope hemispherical bowl, C-65-377 (see under **454** and Fig. 36), hence later Hellenistic; but the "feeder" need not be that late.

[210] See C-75-222, mentioned in Williams and Fisher, *Hesperia* 45, 1976, p. 118.

XXV. MINIATURES

Krateriskoi		
48	Group 3	Pl. 7
52, 53	Group 4	Pl. 8
508–512		Pl. 50
Oinochoai, jugs		
30, 31	Group 2	Pl. 5
139	Group 7	Pl. 17
166, 167	Group 8	Pl. 18
513–519		Pl. 50
Kotylai		
561–568		Pl. 52
Kylikes		
569–572		Pl. 52
Bowls		
573–580		Pl. 52
Plates		
581–583		Pl. 52
Kana		
584–587		Pl. 52
Dishes		
588, 589		Pl. 52
Pyxides		
590–592		Pl. 52
Kothon		
593		Pl. 52
Aryballos		
150	Group 7	Pl. 17
Proto-unguentarium?		
594		Pl. 52

A small selection from the thousands of miniatures is published in order to give an overview of the types found in the Demeter Sanctuary. The greatest number were found in the deep strata of the Archaic and Classical periods in the Middle Terrace, during the excavations of 1961 through 1965. But no area of the Sanctuary is without some few fragments of miniatures. Although vessels which seem purely cultic in nature, offering trays and likna, and three shapes which must have been the standard or obligatory types, phialai, hydriai, and above all kalathiskoi, are the dominant votive shapes, other vessels were also dedicated in roughly the same proportion as the large shapes of the form. Thus, kotylai and jugs are the most popular of the miniatures.

The miniatures become less varied in shape in the later period of the Sanctuary. In the Archaic strata, especially in Room D (Room R:23–24), the types are quite varied, the decoration often painstaking and attractive. In the later 4th century, not only do a lot of the types disappear (kotylai, pyxides, plates) but also many hitherto with paint or patterns are entirely plain.[211] At this same time the three major votive forms of miniatures also lose painted decoration.

The types of votives find parallels in other Sanctuaries of Demeter. The shrine at Knossos,[212] for example, produced many kotylai (called skyphoi), krateriskoi, jugs, and cups.[213] One also notes in that sanctuary the

---

[211] See the examples from the Forum votive pit (well 1975-4): Williams and Fisher, *Hesperia* 45, 1976, pp. 117, 122–123, nos. 50–60, pl. 22. Half are glazed; the rest are not.

[212] Coldstream, *Knossos*.

[213] Some of the cups, so designated at Knossos, are similar to our one-handled jugs. *Ibid.*, pl. 15, from Deposit E.

popularity of small hydriai in the Hellenistic period. Curiously, however, phialai and kalathiskoi are conspicuously absent from Knossos. The excavations at Perachora also turned up many parallels for our votives, especially in oinochoai and kotylai.[214]

Three shapes, small hydriai, kalathiskoi, and phialai, discussed in Shape Studies, III, VII, and XI, are not included here.

Krateriskoi. There is one fairly large example, **48**, from Group 3 of the early 5th century. It could have functioned as a cup but is included as a votive miniature because of the nature of the deposit. Of the small examples, all are column-krateriskoi except **508**, with horizontal handles at mid-body; it is banded, not fully glazed. The krateriskoi have different profiles: the first, with high wall, represented by **52, 53, 510, 511**; the second, with a lower, more open profile, by **509** and **512**. There is probably no chronological difference between the two, because **509** and **510**, from the same 6th-century context (Room D, lot 1991) have the differing profiles. There are hundreds more of these krateriskoi in Archaic and Classical contexts; the shape apparently ceased in the late 4th or early 3rd century.[215]

Oinochoai, jugs. Most are small versions of well-known types. Although miniatures of these shapes were found consistently throughout the Sanctuary, they never gained the popularity of the small hydriai.

Kotylai. The examples show differences in decoration which may reflect changes in the standard size of the shape and thus have chronological significance. Differences in profile, however, are less trustworthy, for on such a small scale, changes in proportion may be quite accidental. Nonetheless, the list has a tentative chronological arrangement. These little kotylai abound in 6th- and 5th-century levels, in patterned, glazed, and plain varieties; they appear to die out in the late 4th century, apparently because no tiny version of the ovoid or plain form was made. No miniatures classifiable as skyphoi were found.

Kylikes. The first two examples, **569** and **570**, are fairly large, but given the usual size of a standard cup, they ought to be called miniature. No one of the four examples has a true parallel. Although the first two have the offset rim of the Archaic Corinthian kylix, the handles are unusual. Few cups of miniature size were found in the Sanctuary, echoing the general lack of interest in or use for this shape.

Bowls. This is also not a popular votive, possibly because of similarity with the kalathiskos. The first two, **573** and **574**, are miniature editions of the flat-rimmed bowl of the 6th century (see **434**). The third, **575**, resembles the 5th-century semiglazed form (see **54, 62**) and may even be its predecessor. It is possibly erroneous to classify it as a miniature; it could have functioned as an early saltcellar (as may also **54** and **62**). **576** is a handmade version of the lekanis, so popular in Classical and Hellenistic times; as many of these unglazed lekanides were fairly small, few miniatures were made. **577** and **578** are well-made standed bowls, possibly meant as miniature perirrhanteria. **579** and **580** are miniatures of the bowl with beveled rim and thus belong to the 4th or early 3rd century. They are smaller than the standard form and without any glaze; neither is well made.

Plates. Miniature plates are more abundant in the Sanctuary than some other shapes (pyxides, kylikes, bowls), reflecting the popularity of the large-size plates. The popularity is limited, however, to the 6th and 5th centuries. The three catalogued examples are typical of the Sanctuary plate miniatures; the decoration is limited to bands of color or linear patterns. They are datable only by context; they show little difference in profile.

Kana, dishes. The six examples are probably all from the 6th century. Two are from Room D, **584** and **589**; three are from a surface context, **585, 587,** and **588**; and one is from a context with a long span of time, **586**. The first four have reflex handles on the rim; the type could be called a miniature kanoun. The last, **589**, may not be a dish at all but a molded stand for some other small vessel.

Pyxides. There are fewer of the type than might be expected, given the popularity of the standard convex pyxis. The first two, **590** and **591**, are tiny versions of that shape, made with a precision of profile and decoration. Several similar intact examples come from later 6th- and 5th-century contexts. The third example is

---

[214] *Perachora* II, esp. pls. 117–119.
[215] Note the lack of miniatures other than phialai, hydriai, and kalathiskoi in Groups 7 through 11.

a carefully banded pyxis lid, not quite large enough for a small pyxis. Its classification as a miniature is perhaps arbitrary.

Kothons. There are very few additional examples in the context pottery; the shape was not functional in the Demeter Sanctuary in any size. Both miniatures are crisp editions of the form; neither can be dated.

Aryballos. No Archaic miniatures were found, although they were dedicated at Perachora and elsewhere in Corinth.[216] This lack is not surprising, given the absence of the regular size of aryballos in the Sanctuary. The one example is a small fine-ware version of the blister-ware form, probably late 4th century in date.

Proto-unguentarium. There are some small unguentaria of Corinthian fabric published in *Corinth* VII, iii.[217] **594** has vestigial handles on the upper wall, resembling an amphoriskos. But the glaze bands on the shoulder are more typical of the unguentarium. It is the only example found in the Sanctuary and is published for that reason. It was made in the early Hellenistic period.

XXVI. COARSE-WARE KITCHEN VESSELS

Hydriai			
629		Pl. 57	6th century
630		Pl. 57	before early 4th century
Pithos			
107	Group 6	Pl. 14	Classical
Krater			
631		Pl. 57	Classical
Lekanai			
632	deep	Pl. 57	late Archaic
633	shallow	Pl. 57	early Classical
634	shallow	Pl. 57	early 5th century?
Oinochoai			
635	trefoil lid	Pl. 57	probably 6th century
636	trefoil	Pl. 57	Archaic
637	trefoil	Pl. 57	Archaic
638	trefoil	Pl. 57	probably Classical
Mortars			
639		Fig. 22, Pl. 58	early 5th century
640		Pl. 58	mid-4th century?
108	Group 6	Fig. 22, Pl. 14	4th century
641		Pl. 58	later Hellenistic
Tray			
642		Fig. 22, Pl. 58	4th century
Bowl			
643		Pl. 58	6th century
Strainer			
644		Pl. 58	Hellenistic?

Little can be said about the development of any of the coarse-ware vessels from the Demeter Sanctuary.[218] Since most are large vessels, they had to be smashed for burial; thus only small parts of each were recovered. Representative examples of the popular types appear in the catalogue in order to give some evidence of the furnishings for the dining-room meals. The evidence is, unfortunately, very incomplete, very fragmentary. The history of the Corinthian kitchen may not be written from the material of the Demeter Sanctuary.

[216] *Perachora* II, nos. 2810–2820; in the Asklepieion, C. Roebuck, *Corinth*, XIV, *The Asklepieion and Lerna*, Princeton 1951, pl. 3: fig. 1.

[217] C-48-119 (well 1948-3), C-63-662, C-63-654 (*Corinth* VII, iii, nos. 584–586, p. 99, pls. 20, 58; Pemberton, *Hesperia* 54, 1985, nos. 26 and 2 for latter two [graves 1963-8, 1963-9]).

[218] For a discussion of coarse-ware fabric and the technique of manufacture, see Lawrence in *Corinth* VII, ii, pp. 94–95.

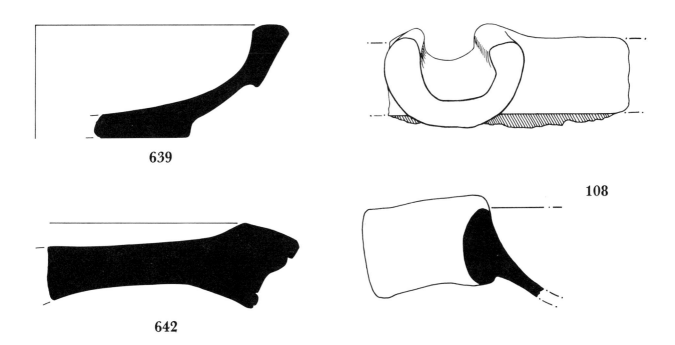

639

108

642

Fig. 22. Coarse-ware kitchen vessels. Scale 1:2

Hydriai. One Archaic hydria handle, decorated in typical Archaic fashion with pellets and stamps, represents hundreds of similar large coarse-ware hydriai, known only from rim and handle sherds. The second example, although small, preserves the fairly typical profile found in many contexts: high ovoid body, tall concave neck, flaring rim concave inside. The listings of the pottery shapes in the 11 groups of Catalogue I indicate the importance of this shape in coarse ware. Groups 1 and 4 had no kitchen material at all; thus only Groups 5 and 7 lacked coarse-ware hydriai. The absence of the shape in fine ware (see p. 9 above) is compensated for by its popularity in the more utilitarian fabric.

Lekanai. Lekanai in both coarse and fine fabric are ubiquitous. The deep fine-ware lekanai, represented by **381–383** and **75**, are the most popular. Note the 23 rims preserved in Group 6. Many coarse-fabric examples were also made. **633** in particular is a handsome vessel, with a fine polished slip hiding the inclusions. In both coarse and fine clay, these vessels of both deep and shallow profiles must have taken the place of kraters so conspicuously absent. Sufficient numbers are found in later contexts to suggest that the household lekanis continued to be made in the Hellenistic period (see Groups 8, 11).

Oinochoai. Large oinochoai of coarse ware were also important in the Sanctuary. The few examples in the catalogue date to the Archaic and Classical periods. The type may have been superseded in the later 4th century and Hellenistic period by the cooking-fabric pitchers (see **151**, **152**, **646**, **647**). Coarse-ware oinochoai are not numerous in the later strata. Together, these two types of vessels must have been the chief pourers for the myriad drinking vessels throughout the history of the Sanctuary.

Mortars. The development of the mortar has been outlined by Edwards, who has classified two profiles which show changes.[219] The rims of his first type show great variation and may indicate that several different forms ran concurrently. Since most of the Sanctuary examples are limited to fragments of rims or spool handles, it is impossible to work out a chronological sequence of profiles. Only comparisons are given for dating specific examples.

[219] *Corinth* VII, iii, pp. 109–111.

639 has a disk foot, unarticulated below, a low, slightly convex wall, and a distinctive rim, flat on the outer face, projecting slightly away from the wall below, and terminating in a wide, convex top face. It is very similar to an example from a 5th-century well, C-34-929.[220] By its context, **639** probably should be dated to the first half of the century.

A more common and lasting form of rim is represented by **640** and **108**, in which the rim has a convex outer face, rising to a peak at the top with no appreciable top face. The inner bowl merges with that peak. The outer wall may be straight or slightly concave and flare out to form the lower edge of the rim, as on **640**. Or there may be a distinct lower face of the rim, projecting clearly from the wall, as on **108**. The former profile appears in the Archaic period.[221] Without the full profile one cannot date **640** precisely. By context it ought to belong to the 4th century, probably the first half. There is a slight overhang on the underside, not so pronounced as that on C-53-269.[222] The beads of the handle are more defined than on the latter.

108, from Group 6, has a close parallel in C-68-120, from the Sacred Spring, dated to the late 5th century. Thus the mortar was found in a fill of the late 4th century or slightly later (see p. 91 below), but it seems to be earlier than much of the pottery in that context. The spout flares slightly, indicative of a date in the first half of the 4th century.[223]

The last example, **641**, comes from the late cistern in Building M–N:25–26, which produced so much later kitchen material. **641** is only a fragment, with a rising flat rim and a projecting horizontal collar, with "pie-crusted" finger holds. The fabric is thin, softer than pre-Hellenistic mortars. It is probably 2nd century in date.[224]

Although only four examples appear in the catalogue, the mortar must have been a necessary element of the Archaic, Classical, and Hellenistic dining rooms. Analysis of the material in the groups of Catalogue I indicates that fragments of at least one mortar were found in Groups 2, 3, 6, 7, 8, and 11. There are many more throughout the contexts of all periods.

Tray. The curious flat object, **642**, has been called a tray for lack of a better term. There are more of this shape; Group 6 has two or three, although without the elaborate outer rim profile. They are not known from other sites in Ancient Corinth.

Other shapes. Low coarse-ware bowls are represented by **643**. The strainer **644** is unique. The tripod krater **631** may have been an elaborate base for a dedication, as its closest comparison surely was.[225] It is included in this section on the basis of its fabric.

XXVII. COOKING-FABRIC VESSELS

Krater or lekane

645			Fig. 23, Pl. 58	later Hellenistic

Pitchers

151	round mouthed	Group 7	Fig. 23	4th century
152	round mouthed	Group 7	Pl. 17	early 3rd century
646	round mouthed		Fig. 23, Pl. 58	Hellenistic
647	trefoil		Pl. 58	Hellenistic?

[220] Pease, *Hesperia* 6, 1937, p. 299, no. 194, fig. 32 (well 1934-10).

[221] Examples in the Anaploga Well (*Corinth* VII, ii), from the LPC period on: C-62-651 (An 307), C-62-653 (An 273), C-62-654 (An 272), C-62-655 (An 266), C-62-652 (An 286; pl. 110 for comparative profiles).

[222] *Corinth* VII, iii, no. 624, p. 110 (well 1953-2).

[223] *Ibid.*, p. 109.

[224] *Ibid.*, p. 111, mortar II.

[225] See MF 9500, R. E. Carter, "A Terracotta Tetrapod Dedication at Corinth," *Hesperia* 22, 1953, pp. 209–214. Tripod bases for basins, kraters, and other vessels are known in metal. See for example the fragmentary ones found at Perachora (*Perachora* I, pl. 70) and the more complete examples from Trebenischte (B. D. Filow, *Die archaische Nekropole von Trebenischte*, Berlin/Leipzig 1927), esp. nos. 83–87, figs. 76, 83. The bronze vessels have a collar flange above the feet, often with incisions (perfunctory ribbing or tongue pattern) on the collar, as in **631**.

Unflanged cooking pots, large

648	flaring rim		Pl. 58	6th century
649	flaring rim		Fig. 23, Pl. 58	4th century
172	flaring rim	Group 8	Pl. 19	third or fourth quarter 4th century?
650	flat rim		Fig. 23, Pl. 59	end of 4th century?
651	flat rim		Pl. 59	end of 4th century
652	flat rim		Fig. 24, Pl. 59	Hellenistic
190	flat rim	Group 10	Pl. 20	Hellenistic

Unflanged cooking pots, small

49	flaring rim	Group 3	Pl. 7	early 5th century
653	flaring rim		Fig. 24, Pl. 59	4th century
654	flaring rim		Fig. 24, Pl. 59	later 4th century
655	flat rim		Fig. 24, Pl. 59	3rd century?
656	vertical rim		Fig. 24, Pl. 59	Hellenistic

Flanged cooking pots

109	chytra I?	Group 6	Fig. 24, Pl. 14	later 4th century?
657	chytra II?		Pl. 59	later Hellenistic?

Casseroles (lopades)

110	type I	Group 6	Pl. 14	4th century
111	type I	Group 6	Fig. 24, Pl. 14	4th century
658	type I?		Figs. 24, 37, Pl. 59	late 4th century?
112	type II	Group 6	Fig. 24, Pl. 14	mid-4th century
659	type II		Pl. 59	later 4th century
660	type II		Fig. 24, Pl. 59	early 3rd century?

Open saucepan

153		Group 7	Fig. 24, Pl. 17	later 4th century?

The amount of cooking ware in the Demeter Sanctuary is great. The examples in the catalogue typify the shapes found, with the exception of lids. No lids were included, as they did not contribute to the understanding of the shape.[226] The unflanged cooking pot and the flanged casserole are the two most popular forms; fragments from large walls suggest that there were also many kraters, although only one was sufficiently preserved for publication. The round-mouthed pitcher is also well represented. Most examples of the fabric come from the 4th century and later, since the most complete examples were found in the dining rooms and cisterns of the Lower Terrace. But 6th- and 5th-century levels also have the material, as **648** and **49**.

We still are not absolutely sure that the vessels were made with Corinthian clay in Corinth.[227] There is, however, a type of fabric that is characteristic of most of the vessels: somewhat gritty in texture, although often given a smoothing of the surface; micaceous, more in the Archaic, less in later periods; often with burnishing strokes on the exterior until the end of the 4th or beginning of the 3rd century. The colors vary considerably. There is a red fabric that is popular in the 4th century, a gray and an orange-brown in the Hellenistic, but one cannot determine the date from color or surface finish. Moreover, the cooking pots and casseroles are all blackened on the exterior from use, so that on many the color has changed, become mottled, and the surface is cracking. Those examples which do not seem to have the fabrics typical of most cooking ware found in Ancient Corinth are noted in the catalogue. But it is possible that all the vessels are not Corinthian.

Many of the wares are partly or wholly wheelmade. The cooking pots and casseroles appear to have the upper articulated areas (rims, flanges, shoulders) made on the wheel; the walls are without wheel marks. Pitchers are usually totally wheelmade. The method of manufacture is more clearly seen on the interior surface, as the exterior is often wiped with a thin film that gives a finer texture, but which thereby conceals the marks. Some of the later vases appear to have more white inclusions; but this too is variable.

[226] *Corinth* VII, iii, lids, pp. 129–131.
[227] *Ibid.*, pp. 117–118; *Agora* XII, pp. 35–36.

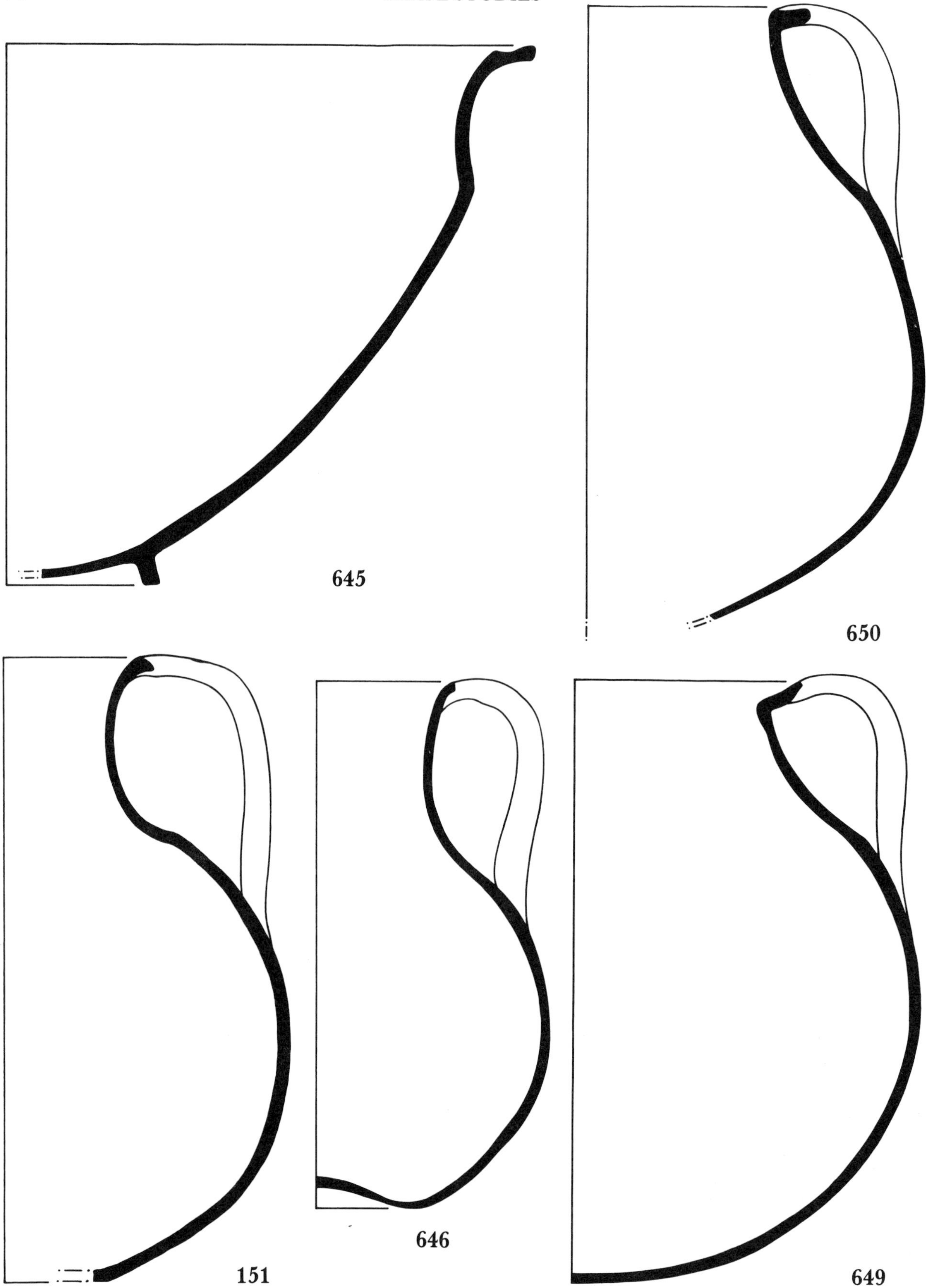

SHAPE STUDIES

645

650

151

646

649

FIG. 23. Cooking-fabric vessels. Scale 1:2

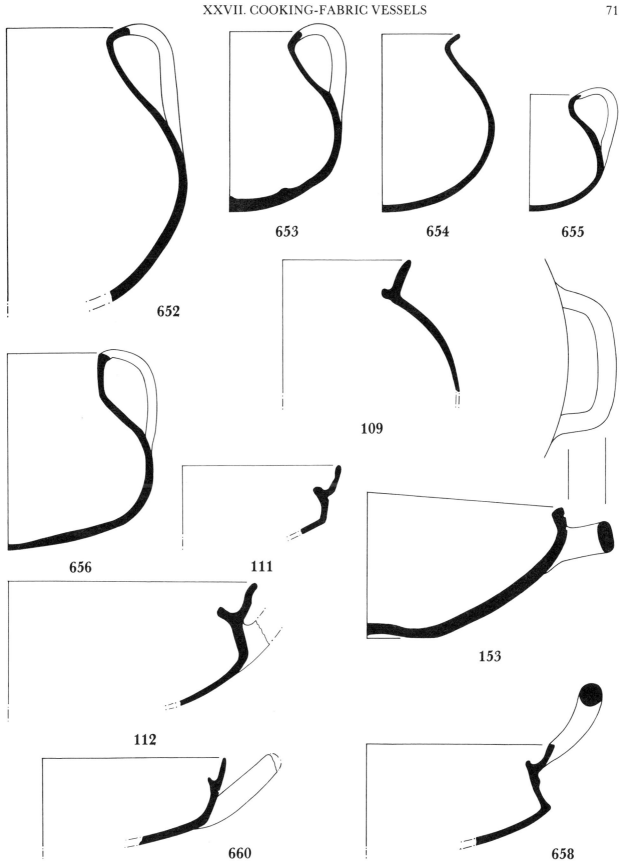

FIG. 24. Cooking-fabric vessels. Scale 1:2

Each shape is presented separately; the shape not discussed in *Corinth* VII, iii, the unflanged cooking pot, has been studied more thoroughly than the others. The catalogue entries do not note whether wheel- or handmade, since many combine the two processes. The date of each example is only probable, based on context and any dated parallels.

Lekane.[228] The one example is Hellenistic. The earlier version of the shape may be found in two 4th-century examples, C-71-541, from Forum drain 1971-1, without the offset concave area and having a flaring rim with convex face and two canted loop handles on the upper wall. The second 4th-century example was found in the Sacred Spring, C-69-102.[229] The shape continues into the Roman period.[230]

Pitchers.[231] There are no examples in the catalogue predating the 4th century, but a fragment from the upper body and rim in lot 5695, M:16 (5695:1), dates by context to the earlier 5th century. The profile of the preserved upper wall suggests a globular body, merging continuously with a sloping shoulder; the neck is tall and concave, ending in a much thickened, flaring rim. There is no discernible shoulder offset, unlike the mid-5th-century example, C-35-640.[232] C-37-569, from the early 4th-century drain 1937-1, is also without the shoulder stop;[233] there are variants of the type.

The three examples in the catalogue exhibit the changes in form as set forth by Edwards. **151** is the oldest, belonging to the 4th century, with a shallow depression originally on the bottom, a strongly concave neck, and a wide-flaring triangular rim. Very similar in both fabric and profile is a smaller pitcher, C-72-120, dated by context to the later 4th century.[234] **152**, from the same group as **151**, shows retention of the neck form and sharply flaring rim, but the latter has become lighter and merges more with the neck on the under face. It may be 25 or 50 years later. C-60-288 has a similar rim but a proportionately higher neck.[235]

646, from the Hellenistic cistern in Building M–N:25–26, has a deeper central depression, a less concave and lower neck, and a plain flaring lip, not offset from the neck. The fabric also seems to be slightly grittier. There are no exact parallels; C-75-302 from well 1975-4 is perhaps the closest in profile, although smaller. Both are later than **152**.[236] None of the three examples from the Sanctuary shows burnishing marks or glaze strokes on the exterior. There are additional fragments in a number of lots of the 4th century and Hellenistic era. Together with coarse-ware oinochoai, the round-mouthed cooking-fabric pitcher must have been an important pouring vessel in the dining rooms.

Many fewer examples of trefoil pitchers were found. The one published here (**647**) is very warped, probably from overexposure to heat, and provides no firm data to contribute to the understanding of the shape.[237]

Unflanged cooking pots, large. In order to discuss the types of deep cooking pots, it is clearest to divide them into two groups, flanged and unflanged. The presence of one or two handles, especially in the un-flanged form, seems to have no significance for dating. Both types have rounded bottoms and no feet, prob-ably to facilitate setting them on the grills. Changes in the wall profile and in the form of rim can be noted in the unflanged form and are given below.

The 6th-century profile of the large unflanged vessels is globular; the shoulder is not well offset from the wall and also merges with a flaring rim, sometimes thickened on the exterior. On the interior face, the rim and wall merge by a continuous rounding of the surface as the direction changes; there is no sharp break

[228] *Corinth* VII, iii, p. 134.

[229] See Williams (footnote 46 above, p. 22), p. 5, no. 3, pl. 1.

[230] C-67-161, from the Gymnasium (J. Wiseman, "Excavations in the Gymnasium," *Hesperia* 38, 1969 [pp. 64–106], pp. 74–75 and note 18, pl. 22:D).

[231] *Corinth* VII, iii, round-mouthed pitchers type I, pp. 139–142.

[232] As dated by Edwards (*Corinth* VII, iii, no. 733, p. 141, pls. 34, 63; well 1935-7).

[233] This example belongs to Edward's type III, owing to the addition of a disk foot. All the pitchers from that early 4th-century drain are so classified by Edwards (*Corinth* VII, iii, p. 137, note 22).

[234] Williams and Fisher, *Hesperia* 42, 1973, p. 24, no. 23, pl. 11 (pit 1972-1).

[235] *Corinth* VII, iii, no. 724, p. 141 (well 1960-6).

[236] Both types of rim continue to appear in 3rd-century contexts. A fill containing many kantharos fragments, excavated in the Forum in 1980, lot 1980-129, contained one with the lighter rim (1980-129:4) and one with the older, heavier form (1980-129:5). This fill is also noted in the discussion of the moldmade relief bowls, p. 45 above.

[237] For trefoil pitchers see *Corinth* VII, iii, pp. 142–143.

between the two parts. **648**, found in a 6th-century context, and two found in a 6th-century well, C-37-2058 and C-37-2059,[238] show the profile.

There are no large examples as yet clearly datable to the late 6th or early 5th century. At some time in the 5th century, the profile becomes more squat, more ovoid, with the maximum diameter just below the shoulder. There is now a clear demarcation between shoulder and wall. The rim remains flaring but has a number of different forms: it may be much thickened on the exterior, very thin and elongated, or even slightly undercut on the exterior. But no vessels of this period have strong articulation inside between the rim and the inner wall. The type is visible in C-39-275, from well 1939-1; C-37-547 and C-37-550, from well 1937-1; and C-37-558 and C-37-567 from drain 1937-1, all unpublished. The rims remaining in the context pottery of the latter two deposits are quite varied, but in all the flaring profile remains. No clear differences exist in the vessels represented by these examples which span about a hundred years.

In the late 4th century, the pots show changes. The profile becomes more globular, the maximum diameter is retained longer, while the offset between shoulder and wall seen in the previous examples is kept. Many of the rims echo the forms described above, but some also are flat, projecting horizontally, and a sharp break between the inner edge of the rim and the wall beneath becomes noticeable. C-37-2508, from pit 1937-1, shows the older form, but C-71-15, a contemporary example from well 1971-1, has a flat rim and rounded profile. Both are unpublished. Of the rims left in the context pottery from Forum drain 1971-1 (lot 7079), several also show the new form, but more, the older flaring rim. **172**, part of a 3rd-century group, also has the older rim. Either **172** is older than much of the pottery in that group, or the flaring rim survived into the 3rd century. Late 4th-century contexts show that the two forms seem to have continued together for a while. The new flat-rim cooking pots are without burnishing strokes. No example of the new type in drain 1971-1 has that decoration, although several of the flaring-rim vessels in that context do have the markings. The flat rim may vary from a thin and quite sharp profile to one that is heavier and slightly concave on the under face.[239]

650–652, all from late 4th-century or Hellenistic contexts, show the later profile. It is difficult to posit a definite date for any of them. It is possible that ratios of diameter to height may be significant, but there are not, as yet, sufficient numbers of well-preserved pots from limited contexts for such calculation.

190, from Group 10, has a different profile. The body wall originally was taller than the three pots **650–652**, the offset less pronounced, the sloping shoulder more concave and vertical; the flat rim is grooved, with the lip slightly peaked. It has no apparent parallel.

649, with a flaring rim, is also difficult. The profile appears to be 4th century in its offset shoulder and thickened flaring rim. But the fabric differs from the usual Corinthian vessels, with greater amounts of white inclusions, pitting the surface badly; there is also a total lack of mica. The handle is smaller and more angular than is customary.

Unflanged cooking pots, small. If the small examples echo the profiles of the larger vessels, **49** of Group 3 would indicate that the change from the 6th-century globular wall to the later ovoid form may have taken place in the early 5th century. **653** continues the ovoid profile; the shoulder is offset, the rim simple and flaring. Its context is the debris within Building M–N:20–26, room 3 (Room Da), created either by the earthquake or by destruction of the building after the earthquake in order to build the Hellenistic successor. The beveled bowl **456** (Shape Studies, XV), from the same context, helps suggest a date for **653** in the later 4th century. Thus, as in the larger vessels, the lower profile and flaring rim continue through much of the 4th century. **654** comes from a contemporary context. It has an almost identical twin in C-1979-140 (unpublished), from cistern 1979-1 in the Forum, of the same third quarter 4th-century date; the latter is of blister-ware fabric. In both, the rim is nearly flat, but the squatter profile is retained.

[238] Campbell, *Hesperia* 7, 1938, p. 599, nos. 159–160, fig. 21; well 1937-3.
[239] In lot 877, P:24, whose material is concentrated in the later 4th century and goes into the 3rd (with earlier material also), there are nine unflanged rims in the context pottery. Of these, two have the flaring rim (877:2, 877:3) and seven the flat (877:4–877:10). Both small- and large-size cooking pots are represented. Group 7 has two large pots (rims only) still in the context pottery; both have the flat form (880:1, 880:2). One might assume that the flat rim becomes prevalent in the 3rd century; **172** cautions against too strong an assumption. One cannot know how long the pots were used and to which limit of a given group they should be assigned. All the flat rims in lot 877 are without burnishing marks.

655, almost a miniature, yet blackened by use, comes from a Hellenistic context with earlier material in it. The vessel shows the newer flat rim and slightly more globular shape, although none of the small versions regains the full globular profile. **656** is an oddity, without parallels in fabric or shape.

Flanged cooking pots. The flanged vessels are varied in profile, form of rim, and handles. The one-han-dled form has two shapes, chytra I and II.[240] The first, found in the 6th century if not earlier,[241] has a low and globular body, slightly diagonal thin rim with rounded lip, and a flange that is usually horizontal. It continues into the Hellenistic period with little change, except for a slightly higher profile. Two unpublished examples from Forum drain 1971-1 give the shape: C-71-116 has a slight offset on the shoulder; C-71-115 has a thicker rim but is otherwise similar. C-60-60, possibly from a slightly later context,[242] is not fully preserved but probably also was higher than the 6th-century example.

No representative of chytra I appears in the catalogue, for it was not so popular as the unflanged form, and only rim fragments remain in the context pottery. The type continues well into the Hellenistic period. The cistern in Building L–M:28, lot 6723, contains one such rim (6723:4); the context pottery of Group 8 also contains one (3217:1), as does the pottery remaining in lot 4482, from the Hellenistic cistern of Building M–N:25-26 (4482:1). The latter deposit also yielded the second form of flanged vessel (chytra II), discussed below. The lack of popularity of this form of deep-flanged cooking pot is clearly indicated by the rim forms in lot 877. There are nine unflanged rims remaining in the context pottery, but only one flanged (877:1; see discussion of unflanged above, especially footnote 239, p. 73).

The later form, chytra II, has a low ovoid profile, a thicker rim flattened on top; the inner face of the rim is concave and turns in to form a small flange. All the examples known are datable in the later Hellenistic period. **657**, from the Hellenistic cistern noted above, represents type II. Since there seems to be a range in the dates of the pottery from that context, this example does not serve to date the introduction of the late rim form. What the relationship between the two types is remains unclear.[243] Chytra II is found in the Roman period at Corinth but with a heavier and beveled rim.

The low ovoid profile of chytra II is found in the vessels designated as stewpots;[244] the same form of rim and flange is also present. The upper wall and shoulder in some examples seem to have slightly greater convexity than that found on chytra II. If only rims are left, without the evidence for the wall profile or for the type of handles (two vertical, or one vertical and one horizontal contrasting with the plain strap handle of chytra II), one cannot be sure whether the fragment comes from a stewpot, which has at least 3rd-century examples,[245] or from a chytra II.

109 is problematic. The rim and flange resemble a chytra I, although thicker than most examples, but the convexity of the shoulder is closer to the profile of a stewpot. Moreover, the horizontal grooves of the upper wall are best compared with the grooves on stewpots C-47-826 and C-34-1613, both of which have been dated to the mid-2nd century.[246] **109** cannot be that late; it belongs to Group 6 with a lower limit not after 300 B.C. **109** is probably an earlier stewpot form.[247]

Casseroles (lopades). There is no attempt here to refine the shape changes as given in *Corinth* VII, iii,[248] for without the evidence for the handles, one cannot be sure whether shape I or shape II is preserved. No

---

[240] *Corinth* VII, iii, chytra I, pp. 120–122; chytra II, p. 122.

[241] See C-53-134 (*Corinth* VII, iii, no. 648, p. 121; Brann, *Hesperia* 25, 1956, p. 368, no. 69, pl. 58; well 1953-1).

[242] *Corinth* VII, iii, no. 649, p. 121, from a well of the 4th to 3rd centuries (well 1960-4).

[243] See *Corinth* VII, iii, p. 122. There is a rim-and-handle fragment in lot 6206, L–M:21, a context of the earlier 2nd century at the latest, with a chytra II rim and wide strap handle (6206:3). Whether it is a chytra II or a stewpot with two different handles cannot be determined from this small fragment.

[244] *Corinth* VII, iii, pp. 122–124, for stewpots.

[245] In lot 6723, from a cistern in Building L–M:28, with material of the 4th and earlier 3rd centuries, there is one fragment, 6723:5, showing a rather vertical wall, rising rim and flange, and the handle root for a loop handle, vertically oriented. It can only be a stewpot, but the rim is thinner than the examples discussed by Edwards.

[246] *Corinth* VII, iii, nos. 656 and 658, pp. 123, 124 (wells 1947-3 and 1934-5).

[247] Lot 6181, a burnt stratum in Building M–N:19, goes to the mid-3rd century. Fragment 6181:2 is a cooking-fabric wall, with a vertical loop handle and groove on the wall. It must be a stewpot, datable to before *ca.* 250 B.C. **109** may support the beginning of this shape by the late 4th century at least.

[248] *Corinth* VII, iii, type I, pp. 124–125; type II, pp. 125–126.

fragments of the type III form, without handles, have been discerned in the Hellenistic strata of the Sanctuary.[249] Types I and II appear together, from the early 5th century on. Few have been inventoried, although they and the unflanged cooking pots are the most popular cooking-fabric vessels. Type I casseroles appear to be more prevalent than type II in the Sanctuary.

For type I, **658** is not canonical. The articulation of the wall and the curious handles are without parallel in typical Corinthian casserole forms. The contexts provide no clues for the date of **658**; lot 5620 ranges throughout the 4th century and 5625 goes far into the 3rd century. The two examples from Group 6 are normal, with parallels elsewhere, but comparisons between examples from similar contexts (**110** from Group 6: slight groove and lightly diagonal turn of the rim; C-71-525 from Forum drain 1971-1: slight groove and vertical rim; C-75-301 from Forum well 1975-4: strong groove and diagonal rim) show that there is no single canonical profile. The presence of a deeper groove in the other type I casserole of Group 6, **111**, is not necessarily of chronological significance.

All type II casseroles from the Sanctuary have good parallels in other contexts. **659**, however, seems not to have the usual fabric and is slipped on the interior. All the casseroles show heavy use.

Open saucepan. There is only one example in the catalogue, for it was not a common shape in the Sanctuary or anywhere else in Corinth. **153**, from Group 7, has no close parallel, but an example noted in *Corinth* VII, iii (C-47-870)[250] is close, although with flatter rim and square handles. Both probably derive from the fine-ware lekanis, omitting the foot and reflex handles. There is also in lot 5625, M–N:19, another fragment of a saucepan, with rim and oval handle (5625:4), very similar to C-34-25.[251] The material of lot 5625 goes well into the 3rd century, with fragments of kantharoi (5625:5, 5625:6). Thus the suggestion by Edwards that C-34-25 is 3rd century, later than C-47-870 and **153**, seems upheld by that small fragment.

XXVIII. PERIRRHANTERIA

Corinthian

661	Base, shaft, rim	Pl. 60	mid-6th century
662	Base	Pl. 60	earlier 6th century
663	Base, shaft	Pl. 60	before 500 B.C.
664	Base	Pl. 60	Archaic
665	Base	Pl. 60	early 5th century
666	Base	Pl. 60	Classical
667	Base	Pl. 61	Classical
668	Base, shaft	Pl. 61	Classical
669	Shaft	Pl. 61	6th century
670	Shaft, bowl	Pl. 61	late 6th century
671	Shaft	Pl. 61	Classical
672	Rim	Pl. 61	Classical?
673	Rim	Pl. 61	Classical
674	Rim	Pl. 61	Classical

The 14 examples of perirrhanteria[252] in the catalogue are but a few of the many fragments found in the Sanctuary. Only the best preserved of the representative types are published. Many of the remaining examples are fragmentary rims, similar to **672** and **673**, or base fragments without whole profiles. Uncatalogued

---

[249] *Ibid.*, pp. 127–128. Most recently, see K. W. Slane, "Two Deposits from the Early Roman Cellar Building" *Hesperia* 55, 1986 (pp. 271–318), esp. p. 305.

[250] *Corinth* VII, iii, p. 129 (well 1947-2).

[251] *Ibid.*, no. 687, p. 129, pls. 30, 62 (well 1934-3).

[252] For Archaic perirrhanteria in particular, see Weinberg, *Hesperia* 23, 1954. The study by M. Iozzo, "Corinthian Basins on High Stands," *Hesperia* 56, 1987, pp. 355–416, appeared too late for consideration. Many of the Sanctuary fragments appear in that article, and the references are cited accordingly.

stamped sherds duplicate the designs on catalogue entries. Over 70 lots of context pottery contain additional perirrhanteria, found in almost all parts of the site.

All the fragments are made of thick fabric with many inclusions, usually self-slipped on the exterior surfaces and painted or stamped. **670** is an exception, a very small example made of fine clay, included here for its shape. The large size of the functioning basin necessitated the heavier clay. The different elements, base, shaft, bowl, were often made separately. The clean break on the outside of the top of the foot on **661** and the finished edge before the area of attachment of the shaft on the inside on that same example indicate the process of fabrication. **666** is wheelmade. Whether the others, without visible wheel marks, were hand-made or moldmade with the relief bands in the mold, the cording and stamping added after application of the slip, is not as yet clear and cannot be determined from this material. Archaic slips are often thicker than Classical ones, thus more resistant to soil action, but **663** of the later 6th century shows a deteriorating surface.

A tentative chronology can be proposed for the high pedestal feet of **661–666**. It is based on those examples from the Demeter Sanctuary and other Corinthian contexts with findspots fairly limited in date or with decoration allowing dating.

The earliest form of base is very simple: a narrow vertical face and long, low, sloping upper face without decoration. One was found in a LPC context, C-31-186;[253] a smaller example, C-35-335, is not datable by its context but has the same profile.

In the 6th century the two faces become more distinct. The outer face grows in height and is slightly diagonal in orientation; it remains undecorated. The outer face is carefully offset from the upper sloping face which retains a width greater than the outer face, so that relief bands and stamps may be applied. **661** shows this form. It is characteristic to have relief bands on the outer edge of the upper face, often with rouletting, plain, or painted, or both.[254] These bands do not create the articulation between the faces, however; the offset is distinct without them. Stamped patterns on these profiles indicate dates throughout much of the 6th century. **661** is probably mid-6th, by the plumpness of the palmette leaves; **662** has the same base profile but seems earlier in the form of the palmette leaves of the stamp. C-37-2076, found in a well of the second half of the century, shows the profile with only plain relief bands on the upper face and at the base of the columnar shaft.[255] Many of these perirrhanteria have the best slips, thick and smooth, giving a firm lustrous surface over the coarse clay to hold the stamps.

This offset profile appears to weaken in the later 6th century. A relief band or projecting ledge creates the distinction between the two faces. In profile, however, the two faces begin to merge. **663** and **664** show this new form, which continues into the 5th century. The older articulated type continues also, apparently disappearing by the end of the century. **664** also shows stamping on the outer face, not found in the articulated profile. C-50-17, from a late 6th- or early 5th-century context,[256] confirms the time for the popularity of this profile.

665 shows the continuation of the merging of the two faces and combines both the older stamped designs and the popular black and red paint of Classical examples. It is possible that the black-and-red convention was introduced at the end of the century or in the early 5th, contemporary with other vases using the combination, such as the type 3 kalathiskoi. Stamped designs probably ended in the earlier 5th century. C-75-306, from a context of the second quarter of the century,[257] has none; the three rings of the upper face are red and black, as **665**. The slips become thinner, often worn away, possibly because they need no longer support the stamping.

---

[253] *Corinth* VII, i, no. 182, p. 50, pl. 25 (well 1931-7).
[254] See C-31-446 from well 1931-14 (Weinberg, *Hesperia* 23, 1954, p. 126, note 111, pl. 28:a), with plain bands; C-72-282, without good context, with dotted ovolos and relief bands painted brown.
[255] Campbell, *Hesperia* 7, 1938, p. 603, no. 184, fig. 26 (well 1937-3).
[256] Weinberg, *Hesperia* 23, 1954, p. 127, note 120, pl. 28:g.
[257] From pit 1975-1, lot 75-132.

In the later 5th century, a new type of offset base is made. C-34-931 shows the form, having a sharp distinction between outer and upper faces.[258] The outer face has become much higher than in any previous examples; the upper face is decorated only with wide, shallow relief bands. **666** continues this profile but with an even higher, almost vertical outer face; the upper face has shrunk in width. The rings are sharply cut, more resembling steps, comparable to the steps that encircle the knobs of lekanis lids. **666** may be later than C-34-931, possibly 4th century by its context. A similar profile, with red and black on the bands of the upper face, is found on a fragment from well 1940-1, still in the context pottery.[259] It is likely that that example is 4th century.

The square-base form, illustrated by **667**, does not appear to be so popular as the pedestal feet just discussed. One example from the Potters' Quarter may be dated to the later Archaic period by its stamps;[260] **667** must be later by its context. The fluted examples, **668** and **671**, are at least Classical, if not later, dated by the findspots, comparative material, and the stone examples from which they surely derive.

The rims as yet do not lend themselves to similar analysis. The Archaic rim **661** and the Classical one **672** show little variation in profile.

Stamped patterns on the perirrhanteria from the Demeter Sanctuary are common motifs: corded bands, chevrons, rosettes, palmettes, ovolos. There are no figural stamps. Figured scenes appear to have been most popular in the 7th and early 6th centuries, before the growth of the Sanctuary and concomitant need for the vessels.

Perirrhanteria were made throughout the Classical period, for fragments were found in a well whose material was concentrated in the 4th century and lasted until the early 3rd.[261] It is not yet possible to isolate any examples as specifically Hellenistic. One of the strata in the cistern of Building M–N:25–26 (lot 4480), containing mostly kitchen material of the Hellenistic period, also yielded one black-and-red painted rim. But there is also earlier material in the cistern, including a later 4th-century Panathenaic amphora (**306**), ray-based skyphoi, and other conventionalizing material.[262] That perirrhanterion rim could be Classical. Generally, clay perirrhanteria found in Corinth come from Archaic and Classical strata and are not characteristic of Mummian destruction debris. What, if anything, was used in the Hellenistic period cannot as yet be identified. The chronology of the shape needs a detailed study, possible only when more complete examples from defined contexts appear.

The reconstructed dimensions of **661** (D. base 0.44 m., D. shaft 0.28–0.30 m., D. basin 0.60 m.) show the typical proportions, with the bowl projecting farther than the foot. The height of the shaft would probably be slightly greater than the foot diameter but not so great as the bowl diameter. A conservative estimate for the total height of the vessel would be over 0.80 m., making it a functioning vessel. We cannot be sure, however, what its function was.

The use of the term perirrhanterion implies that these large basins were used in the Sanctuary for ritual cleansing, not actual bathing.[263] The name refers to function, not shape, for the same form of basin was apparently used for washing,[264] and even for mixing and kneading clay.[265] It is the context, therefore, that gives the proper name and function.

Sufficient numbers of these vessels were found in and around the dining rooms of the Lower Terrace (as well as the open areas of the Middle Terrace) to suggest possible use in those buildings. The following is a sample of such findspots.

[258] Pease, *Hesperia* 6, 1937, p. 297, nos. 174, 175, figs. 25, 28 (well 1934-10).
[259] New Museum well A.
[260] KN 162 (Weinberg, *Hesperia* 23, 1954, p. 128, note 121, pl. 30:f); not in *Corinth* XV, iii.
[261] See footnote 259 above.
[262] Not all the material cited here is from lot 4480, but the layers in the cistern had joins throughout (lots 4478–4482).
[263] See R. Ginouvès, *Balaneutikè* (*Bibliothèque des Écoles Françaises d'Athènes et de Rome* 200), Paris 1962: louterion, pp. 77–79; perirrhanterion, pp. 299–310.
[264] *Ibid.*; representations on Attic vases, pls. 18, 19 for washing, pl. 41 for ritual cleansing.
[265] See Pease, *Hesperia* 6, 1937, p. 297.

Dining rooms, late 4th-century debris on floors:
  Building K:23 (Ra), lot 73-121
             K–L:24–25, rooms 2 and 3 (Ka), lot 72-139
             K–L:25–26, room 2 (Ja), lot 72-134
             L:26–27, room 1 (Ha), lot 72-129
             M–N:20–26, room 4 (Ga), lot 6840
             N:21–22, room 2, lot 4398
6th and 5th-century contexts in dining rooms:
  Building M:21–22, room 2 (Room V), lot 6832
             M–N:20–26, room 3 (Da), lot 6830
             M–N:20–26, room 4 (Ga), lot 6839
             N–O:22–23, lot 2186
             N–O:24–25 (Room L), lots 2091, 2110, 2141, 2216
             N–O:25–26 (Room J), lots 2074, 2083, 2225, 75-248
Contexts in open (cult?) areas:
  Room   P–Q:24 (Room B), lots 897, 899
             P–Q:26, floor 1 (Room E), lot 2230
             R:23–24 (Room D), lots 1985, 1988

One fragment of **661** (e) was found in the packing for the north couch of the Classical Building N–O:25–26. Some of the other fragments of **661** were found in and around that area, although a few wandered westward (O–P:20–21). That perirrhanterion may have been used in the Archaic predecessor of the Classical dining room. It is, however, dangerous to argue too strongly for the functions of these vessels on the basis of findspots. Broken vases were not necessarily discarded in the area of use. The number of fragments does suggest, nevertheless, some use in the Sanctuary ritual.

CATALOGUE I (1–202): CONTEXT GROUPS

GROUP 1 (1–21)

Grid location R:21   Lot 6231   Upper Terrace, pocket of votive pottery, in stereo, in south half of grid square (pocket 1970-1)   Pl. 1:a

2.55 kg., 49 vessels
    oinochoai: 0.3 kg. (2)
    kotylai: 0.45 kg. (8)
    kalathiskoi, fine ware: 1.2 kg. (34)
    kalathiskoi, coarse ware: 0.6 kg. (5)

The pottery was found in a small natural fissure in the rock of the stepped theater on the Upper Terrace.[1] A few kalathiskoi were lodged above the main deposit, but most of the vessels were found closely packed together, resting on bedrock under surface fill. No architecture could be associated with the vases.

The group consists of 49 vases, as listed above. By size, all can be classified as miniatures or small votives. There was no other material. This deposit gives the first sure evidence of the functioning of the Sanctuary. Although there is earlier material, belonging to the Mycenaean and Geometric periods,[2] that material does not have votive functions. This deposit is the first extant example of the many deliberate discardings of votives. Moreover, the predominant shape in the deposit is the kalathiskos, the chief vase found in all periods and areas of the Sanctuary, apparently the most common offering to Demeter.[3]

The date of most of the pottery is LPC. The kalathiskoi have LPC parallels, but votive miniatures tend to change less rapidly than other vases, and some of them could be later. One kotyle (**4**) may be early EC. There is also a problematic one-handled kotyle (**8**); the vase is as yet without parallel and may not fit into the chronology of kotyle profiles.

Group 1 represents a cleaning of some area of the Sanctuary, with deliberate burning of a few and breaking of many of the vases. It was probably deposited in the early part of the Early Corinthian period. Thus the Sanctuary was already functioning, if on a limited scale, by the mid-7th century.

1. Conical oinochoe   Pl. 4

C-70-479. H. 0.095, D. 0.075 m. Mouth slightly chipped.

Flat resting surface; conical body with slight convexity; tall cylindrical neck; trefoil mouth; flat strap handle attached on upper wall and back of mouth. Resting surface reserved; wide glaze band on lower body with three added-purple lines; zone of dicing; upper body with glaze band, added purple; rays from base of neck to beginning of band. Glaze fired red; peeling from neck, handle, mouth.
Cf. C-39-2 (*Corinth* VII, i, no. 147, p. 45, pl. 22).
Late Protocorinthian

2. Conical oinochoe   Pl. 4

C-70-480. P.H. 0.04, D. 0.073 m. Neck, mouth, handle missing.

Shape as **1**. Small triangles on lower wall; rest of wall black; incised tongues on upper wall with traces of added purple but no preserved added white.
Late Protocorinthian

3. Small ray-based kotyle   Fig. 6, Pl. 4

C-70-522. H. 0.051–0.053, D. 0.069, D. foot 0.031 m. Complete.

Small ring foot; convex flaring wall turning in slightly to rounded lip; two loop handles. Undersurface with central

---

[1] Bookidis and Fisher, *Hesperia* 41, 1972, p. 284, note 4. A second deposit, lot 6232, was found one meter south of this group but with less pottery. It contained mostly kalathiskoi, was not closely datable, and is probably later than Group 1. All the pottery found in Group 1 has been inventoried; all is published or noted in the catalogue.

[2] The Mycenaean pottery from the Demeter Sanctuary has been published: Rutter, *Hesperia* 48, 1979, pp. 348–392.

[3] Similar kalathiskoi were found in the southeast deposit of the Temple of Hera at Perachora: *Perachora* I, pp. 98–101.

black dot, two black circles; edge of foot black; lower wall with well-spaced rays off black band; central wall with file of silhouette dogs between three black bands above and below; handle zone with six groups of seven "worms"; two black lines at lip; interior black.

Cf. C-37-590 (*Corinth* VII, i, no. 160, p. 47, pl. 23).
Late Protocorinthian

4. Small ray-based kotyle   Pl. 4

C-70-521. H. 0.068, D. 0.089, D. foot 0.044 m. Many joining fragments; small part of lip missing.

Shape as **3**. Black circles on undersurface; edge of foot black; zone of rays on lower wall; band at top of rays running into glaze of upper wall; two added-red, one added-white line over glaze below handles; no lines at lower edge of glaze zone; area between handle roots reserved; handles black; interior black with added-white line below lip. Glaze fired streaky brown to black.

Cf. C-40-128, from well 1940-2 (well partially published: S. Weinberg, "A Cross-Section of Corinthian Antiquities," *Hesperia* 17, 1948 [pp. 197–241], pp. 214–229, as well group D; C-40-128 not included). Published examples from well 1940-2, D46–D52, have the canonical red and white below the handles and at edge of glaze zone; C-40-128 and **4** do not have the lower lines.
Beginning of Early Corinthian?

5. Small ray-based kotyle   Pl. 4

C-70-524. H. 0.05, D. 0.066, D. foot 0.032 m. Many joining fragments; one handle, part of lip missing.

Shape as **3**. Two circles on undersurface; rays on lower wall; band of glaze above rays; wall glazed; reserved band at handle zone; interior glazed; reserved line at top of wall; no added colors. Glaze fired red to black. Similar in group: C-70-477.

Cf. C-31-136 (*Corinth* VII, i, no. 179, p. 49, pl. 24).
Late Protocorinthian

6. Small ray-based kotyle   Fig. 6, Pl. 4

C-70-523. H. 0.048, D. 0.062, D. foot 0.026 m. Handles missing.

Shape as **3** but with flatter resting surface of foot; slightly stronger inturn to lip. Decoration as **5** but with added-white line at lower edge of glaze and below handles. Glaze fired red to black.
Late Protocorinthian

7. Small kotyle   Pl. 4

C-70-525. H. 0.048, D. 0.071, D. foot 0.028 m. Part of wall missing.

Shape as **6**. Glaze overall except reserved handle zone, edge of foot, undersurface; no added colors. Traces of interior burning. Similar in group: C-70-526.
Late Protocorinthian

8. Small kotyle(?)   Fig. 6, Pl. 4

C-70-478. H. 0.048, D. 0.057, D. foot 0.027 m. Intact.

Ring foot, not well set off from wall; tall, almost straight flaring wall with inturn to lip; one loop handle. Edge of foot, undersurface reserved; glazed over exterior except reserved band of handle zone; two added-purple lines on lower wall; interior glazed.

Tall profile suggests EC, but single handle is exceptional; the handle is small and not a full loop.

9. Flaring kalathiskos   Pl. 4

C-70-485. H. 0.055, D. 0.069, D. resting surface 0.033 m. Many joining fragments; part of wall missing.

Flat resting surface; concave flaring wall; rounded lip. Thin bands of diluted glaze in groups of two, three, two, two, on exterior wall; interior with two bands below lip. Glaze fired orange. Similar in group: C-70-505.

10. Flaring kalathiskos   Pl. 4

C-70-486. H. 0.053, D. 0.075, D. resting surface 0.029 m. Many joining fragments; part of wall missing.

Shape as **9**, with wider, slightly outward thickened rim. On exterior wall, three groups of bands: diluted glaze, added red, diluted glaze; rim glazed; interior with glaze lines on lower, middle, upper wall. Similar in group: C-70-484, C-70-487, C-70-503.

11. Flaring kalathiskos   Pl. 4

C-70-490. H. 0.052, D. 0.07, D. resting surface 0.037 m. Intact.

Shape as **9**, with more concave wall, rounded rim. Three groups of two narrow bands of black glaze on lower, middle, upper exterior wall; rim with five groups of five black dots; interior with wide black band at bottom of wall, below rim. Thin peeling glaze. Similar in group: C-70-492.

12. Flaring kalathiskos   Pl. 4

C-70-501. H. 0.051, D. 0.078, D. resting surface 0.049 m. Part of wall missing.

Shape as **9**, with lower wall, rounded lip. Exterior wall with five bands of glaze; glaze at beginning of lip, possibly with added purple; interior floor with circle, three bands; lip reserved. Thin peeling glaze. Similar in group: C-70-488, C-70-497, C-70-498, C-70-512.

13. Flaring kalathiskos   Pl. 4

C-70-502. H. 0.044, D. 0.065, D. resting surface 0.029 m. Intact.

Shape as **9**, with straight flaring wall, rounded lip. Exterior wall with three pairs of glaze lines; interior with three broad bands; dots on lip. Glaze fired red. Similar in group: C-70-494, C-70-509, C-70-510.

14. Flaring kalathiskos   Pl. 4

C-70-489. H. 0.037–0.04, D. 0.068–0.069, D. resting surface 0.028–0.031 m. Intact.

Shape as **9**, more concave wall, slightly thickened rim. Exterior wall with three bands of glaze; interior with three, top one close to rim and running into dots on rim. Thin peeling glaze, uneven banding. Similar in group: C-70-504, C-70-506, C-70-511, C-70-514.

15. Flaring kalathiskos   Pl. 4

C-70-483. H. 0.035, D. 0.064, D. resting surface 0.03 m. Many joining fragments; part of wall missing.

Flat resting surface with groove on lower wall creating false foot; low, very slightly convex flaring wall; rounded lip. Exterior wall with six bands of glaze; interior with spiral on floor (intentional?), seven bands on wall; traces of glaze circles on resting surface. Possibly added red on some bands. Glaze fired red. Traces of burning. Similar in group: C-70-491, C-70-495, C-70-507, C-70-508, C-70-513.

16. Flaring kalathiskos   Pl. 4

C-70-500. H. 0.029, D. 0.05, D. resting surface 0.016 m. Intact.

Shape as **15**. Traces of glaze on exterior; interior with glaze on floor, four lines on wall. Thin, peeling glaze. Similar in group: C-70-493, C-70-499.

17. Flaring kalathiskos   Pl. 4

C-70-496. H. 0.028, D. 0.048, D. resting surface 0.026 m. Intact.

Very small version of **11**. Lower wall with two thin lines; upper wall with line, band; line just below rim; interior with two bands, line on upper wall, one below rim. Dots on rim. Thin glaze, partly red.

18. Kalathiskos, type 1   Pl. 4

C-70-481. H. 0.05, D. 0.084, D. resting surface 0.05 m. Many joining fragments; part of wall and of one handle missing.

Inset disk foot with three grooves on it; concave flaring wall, rounded lip; two handles, not well articulated, set horizontally at midwall. No decoration.

Cf. footed example from southeast deposit, *Perachora* I, pl. 30: 5, later than **18**; note heavier rim, handle zone design. **18** is probably a very early example of type 1.

19. Kalathiskos, type 1   Pl. 4

C-70-482. H. 0.027, D. 0.05, D. resting surface 0.04 m. Intact.

Flat resting surface; low concave wall slightly rounded at bottom; outward thickened rim; no handles. Exterior wall with low glaze band and added red; upper wall and rim glazed, possibly with added red; interior with glaze on floor, lower and upper wall; two bands on resting surface. Thin glaze, fired brown, peeling.

20. Handmade kalathiskos   Pl. 4

C-70-3. H. 0.043–0.045, D. 0.078–0.08, D. resting surface 0.048 m. One handle missing. Handmade; coarse clay with inclusions.

Flat resting surface; concave wall, thickened at bottom; outward thickened rim; flat top; horizontal handle at midwall (originally two). Attached pellets between handles; third pellet in center of floor.

21. Handmade kalathiskos   Pl. 4

C-70-517. H. 0.043–0.045, D. 0.077–0.081, D. resting surface *ca*. 0.05 m. Intact.

Fabric and shape as **20**; projecting lug handles; no pellets. Extensive burning on resting surface.

Three additional kalathiskoi of coarse clay without handles: C-70-2, with pellets on floor; C-70-515, with pellets on rim; C-70-516, plain.

GROUP 2 (**22–32**)

Grid location R:23–24   Lot 1990   Room D, lowest fill to stereo

7.8 kg. (0.75 kg. inventoried)

    kraters: 0.1 kg. (1 black glazed)

    oinochoai: 0.5 kg. (7: 2 conical, 2 ray based, 3 banded)

    kotylai: 1.25 kg. (33: 4 figured, 6 ray based, 14 banded, 3 black glazed, 3 plain, 1 LPC, 2 uncertain)

    phialai: 0.4 kg. (29)

    cups and bowls: 0.25 kg. (2 cups with offset rim, 1 with wishbone handles, 1 Attic cup, 1 kothon, 3 bowls or cups with flattened rims, 2 feet of large bowls)

    miscellaneous fine wares: 0.3 kg. (footed dish, 3 powder-pyxis lids, fragments of closed vessels)

    plates: 0.3 kg. (3)

kalathiskoi: 3.5 kg. (92: 50 flaring, 11 type 1, 23 type 2, 8 uncertain)
miscellaneous votives: 0.3 kg. (15: 2 krateriskoi, 4 oinochoai, 1 jug, 1 lekanis, 1 dish, 1 plate, 3 offering trays, 2
        handmade bowls)
coarse wares: 0.9 kg. (4: 1 amphora or hydria, 1 lekane, 1 mortar, 1 bowl)

These vases are not from a deposit. Rather, they form a fairly cohesive group from the lowest stratum in Room R:23–24 (Room D), in fill 0.15–0.20 m. deep over bedrock. The stratum may be the packing for a floor. The vases represent the growth of the Sanctuary in the first half of the 6th century. The earliest vessels in the context pottery are fragments of LPC kotylai; the latest, **23** and **25**, were probably made before mid-century. The major shape in the group is the kalathiskos. The flaring perforated form predominates; type 1 and early type 2 examples are also present.

The broken, incomplete state of most of the Group 2 vases is typical, not just for the pottery of Room D but also for the Sanctuary generally. Whether offered as votives or used in the dining rooms, the pottery was deliberately shattered and buried. Sherds from the same vase come from different areas, for the earth containing the buried fragments was moved about, to be used as fill during the different and continuous building periods in the Sanctuary. One fragment of **23** was found in P:26, one of **26** in M:17–18.

Room D, which was very rich in material, contained some of the finest Archaic figured pieces, such as **26**. Other examples from the same area were found in its other 6th-century strata, lots 1985, 1989, 1991. The pottery is mostly votive, but some of the larger fine wares, kotylai and plates, might have been used in the dining rooms. Room D, not clearly defined by walls as a room or building, may have been an open sacred area of the Archaic Sanctuary, possibly with an altar.[4]

22. Kotyle   Fig. 6, Pl. 5

C-62-764. H. 0.067, est. D. 0.108, D. foot 0.069 m.
Five joining fragments; complete profile; no handles.

Flaring ring foot; inner disk; flat undersurface; wide convex flaring wall turning vertical to rounded lip. Undersurface: central circles; lines radiating to arcuated band; outer face of disk brown (diluted glaze); dicing on resting surfaces of disk and foot. Brown band on outer foot. Lower wall with narrow zone of straight lines between glaze bands. Zone of dicing below animals. Animal frieze between brown lines: feline facing left, added purple on rib cage, belly, haunches; steer to right, added purple on rib cage. F.o.: incised circles, dots. Handle zone: broad brown band below; dot rosettes alternating with four vertical lines; brown band at lip. Interior black; reserved line near top of wall; brown band below lip. Interior glaze peeled; no trace of added colors.

Careful shaping of foot, clarity of banded and linear decoration in contrast with less careful incision and painting of animals. Use of brown and added purple unusual. For foot profile cf. C-39-23 (*Corinth* VII, i, no. 367, p. 80, fig. 30).

Late Corinthian

23. Kotyle   Pl. 5

C-62-763. Joining fragment from P:26 (lot 2046). P.H. 0.043, est. D. 0.097 m. Four joining fragments of upper wall, lip, one handle.

Interior glazed brown. At bottom break, brown ground line for zone of silhouette goats(?) walking right; f.o. of hailstones. Added red over brown glaze above. Handle zone: vertical "worms" with added red below, brown above.

Similar kotylai from Well I of Potters' Quarter. Cf. also C-53-137 (Brann, *Hesperia* 25, 1956, p. 358, no. 21, pl. 54).

Late Corinthian

24. Cup with offset rim   Pl. 5

C-62-948. H. 0.055, est. D. lip 0.14, D. foot 0.048 m. Many joining fragments; much of wall, one handle missing; plaster restoration.

Sloping ring foot; wide, almost straight flaring wall, thickened at shoulder; slightly concave vertical offset rim; tapered lip; loop handle set horizontally on shoulder. Interior glazed to top of rim where there is a reserved band; added-purple circle in center of floor (in place of medallion); three more on floor and wall, one on interior of rim. Exterior glazed from foot to shoulder; black bands at bottom and top of rim; handle black.

Cf. C-53-160 and C-53-156 (Brann, *Hesperia* 25, 1956, p. 361, nos. 31, 33, pl. 54).

Middle Corinthian or early Late Corinthian

25. Phiale   Fig. 9, Pl. 5

C-62-769. H. 0.018, D. 0.07 m. Center with omphalos missing.

---

[4] Stroud, *Hesperia* 34, 1965, pp. 11–12.

Good central depression; flat resting surface; flaring convex wall turning vertical to rounded lip. Glaze fired brown. Three bands around omphalos: brown, brown, added red; brown design of four zigzags alternating with dot rosettes; bands on upper wall: brown, brown, added red. Added red on top of outer wall; rest of exterior reserved. Full convex profile.

Before 550 B.C.

26. Plate Pl. 5

a) C-62-770. H. 0.018, est. D. 0.265 m. Many joining fragments, preserving parts of outer floor, feet, rim. b) C-65-509 (M:17–18, lot 3222). Max. dim. 0.055 m. Fragment from outer floor.

Double ring foot; low flaring rim, convex above, with groove on upper face before thick rounded lip.

a. Wide black circle on undersurface; feet with added purple (over black); lip black with traces of added purple; added purple at juncture of floor and rim; black lines at beginning of rim and before outer groove. Floor: black ground line; one well-preserved forepaw and leg, part of other forepaw, one back paw of a crouching sphinx, lion, or Chimaera. Traces of added purple on legs.

b (not illustrated). Black band on undersurface. Floor: double-circle incised rosette. Polished surfaces on both fragments.

Profile: Callipolitis-Feytmans, fig. 17, esp. no. 57. Decoration: P. Lawrence, "Corinthian Chimaera Painter," *AJA* 63, 1959 (pp. 349–363), pl. 87, esp. fig. 2. Late Chimaera Painter (Lawrence).

Middle Corinthian

27. Plate Fig. 16, Pl. 5

C-62-272. H. 0.02, est. D. 0.20 m. Three joining fragments; about half of floor, part of rim preserved. Published: Stroud, *Hesperia* 34, 1965, pl. 3:e.

Flat undersurface; flat ring foot, barely articulated inside; flaring straight rim with grooves on both faces before slightly convex lip. Glaze fired red, thin and peeling. Undersurface: two wide glaze circles. Foot and outer face of rim black; inner face of rim with linear tongues; added purple over grooves; purple band at juncture of foot and rim. Floor: outer circle of dicing. Two heraldic crouching sphinxes, each with lowered foreleg holding central palmette; other foreleg probably raised (now missing). Long hair; poloi; thin proportions. Added purple on wings, chest, neck, face. Between legs of right-hand sphinx, a human figure facing right, sitting on a rosette (a padded dancer, resting?); added purple on body. F.o.: incised rosettes, some with double circles; incised blobs; dots.

No similar profile in Callipolitis-Feytmans. Typical Corinthian rim, but unarticulated foot is unusual.

Late Middle Corinthian or Late Corinthian

28. Plate(?) Pl. 5

C-62-766. Est. D. to preserved edge 0.13 m. One fragment from floor.

Horizontal floor of plate or disk, thickened in center; small area of preserved outer face. Side A has groove 0.023 from edge; side B has groove just before edge. Edge is badly eroded; it might be the outer edge of a small foot.

Side A, from center: black circle; added-purple band (over black); black dicing; black band with added-white dot rosettes; two black lines; reserved zone with black dot rosettes; two black lines; added purple in groove; zone of dicing; added-purple band; black line at outer edge; traces of black on edge.

Side B, from center: black dot; two black lines; added-purple band; two black lines; black zone with added-white dot rosettes; black dicing; reserved zone with black dot rosettes; black band; wide added-purple band to groove.

6th century?

29. Pyxis lid Fig. 25, Pl. 5

C-62-768. H. 0.021, D. 0.077 m. Part of rim missing.

Low flat knob narrowing to lid; sloping lid; low, well-inset vertical flange. Interior reserved. Top of knob: central glaze dot; three circles. Lid: glaze around knob; glaze lines limiting animal frieze. Animal frieze to right after break: goat to right, panther to right, goat to left, head and tail of panther to right over break. F.o.: incised rosettes, dots. Glaze almost completely peeled.

Late Corinthian

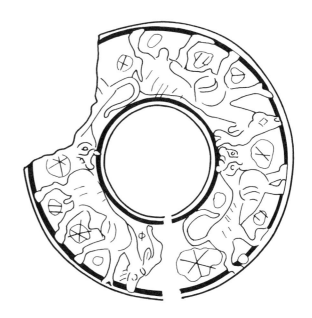

FIG. 25. Pyxis lid **29**. Scale 1:2

30.   Miniature conical oinochoe   Pl. 5

C-62-771. H. 0.036, D. 0.028 m. Handle missing.

Flat resting surface; conical body; tall neck; trefoil mouth. Black line at base of wall; zone of dicing; black line; black tongues at top of wall; black line at bottom of neck; black tongues on neck; added purple (over glaze) on mouth.

31.   Miniature conical oinochoe

C-62-765. H. 0.021, D. 0.023 m. Intact.

Shorter version of **30**, with squatter body, lower neck. Upper half of vase glazed. Glaze thin and cracking; string marks on resting surface.

32.   Kalathiskos, type 1   Fig. 5, Pl. 5

C-62-767. H. 0.024, D. base 0.032, D. rim 0.036 m. Intact.

Flat resting surface with groove midway; concave wall; flaring triangular rim with four grooves on upper face; two well-formed loop handles. Black at base of wall; added-purple (over black) band; handle zone of black "worms"; added purple on upper wall and rim. Interior with glaze bands on floor, lower wall, upper wall.

Good example of type 1, showing origin in flat-bottomed pyxis-kalathos. See **532** for very similar but larger example.

Probably earlier 6th century

GROUP 3 (**33–49**)

Grid location Q:26   Lot 2260   Pottery pocket in the northeast corner of Room E   (P–Q:26; Pit 1965-2) Pl. 1:c, d

14.07 kg. (2.9 kg. inventoried)
  krater: 0.09 kg. (1 black glazed)
  oinochoai: 0.5 kg. (9: 1 black globular, 1 black ovoid, 2 round mouthed, 1 wide mouthed, 4 banded)
  kotylai and skyphoi: 1.7 kg. (24: 1 figured kotyle, 1 Conventionalizing, 7 ray based, 7 semiglazed, 2 banded, 4 plain;
      1 ray-based skyphos; 1 uncertain)
  lekanides: 0.2 kg. (4 bowls, 1 lid)
  bowls: 0.08 kg. (3: 1 with flattened rim [or cup?], 2 small unglazed)
  miscellaneous fine wares: 0.35 kg. (4: 1 amphora lid, 1 tripod-pyxis, 1 concave pyxis, 1 plate)
  Attic fabric: 0.5 kg. (8)
  kalathiskoi: 6.4 kg. (99: 1 flaring, 1 transitional, 14 large type 3, 76 type 3, 3 undecorated, 4 very small type 3).
  miscellaneous votives: 0.78 kg. (11: 2 hydriai, 1 krateriskos, 2 oinochoai, 2 phialai, 1 lekythos, 2 offering trays, 1
      handmade bowl)
  coarse wares: 3.2 kg. (8: 2 amphorai, 3 hydriai, 2 oinochoai, 1 mortar)
  cooking fabric: 0.17 kg. (2 stewpots or pitchers)
  lamps: 0.1 kg. (2)

The pottery of Group 3 was found densely packed, with little earth between the vases, against the east wall of Room P–Q:26 (Room E). A few upright Corinthian pan tiles originally fenced in the deposit, laid down in the second quarter of the 5th century. A joining fragment of **45** was found near by,[5] suggesting either that the tiles did not completely seal the deposit or, more likely, that the pot was broken before discarding and the fragments scattered. By the end of the century, the pocket was covered by the upper floor of the room (lot 2230).

Most of the pottery is votive in function, primarily kalathiskoi, including large examples of type 3. Other votive shapes are small oinochoai, a krateriskos, and a small hydria. The lekythoi may also be dedicatory; the drinking cups might have been used in a Classical dining room, as also the fragmentary kitchen ware.[6] There are also lamps and terracotta figurines in the deposit.

This group is especially important for dating the introduction of the black-and-red form of kalathiskos, type 3, used for over one hundred years in the Sanctuary. The group contains only one example not of the

---

[5] The fragment is from lot 2046 (P:26), located south of wall 13, the north retaining wall of the Middle Terrace.

[6] Only one cooking pot, **49**, mended sufficiently for cataloguing. The numbers of drinking vessels and kitchen wares throughout the Sanctuary lead one to hypothesize that the former may have been used in the dining rooms only once or twice (ritually?) and that the latter replaced various forms of fine-ware shapes absent from the Sanctuary (see pp. 15, 67, 72 above). These were then discarded with the more commonplace votives.

canonical type 3 form, **38**, thereby helping to confirm the date of the new type at the beginning of the century. Along with it came an undecorated version, **39**. In the uninventoried context pottery are two tiny red-and-black banded examples. The large size of **35–37** was an experiment in the first years of the shape and never became popular; the smaller version, 0.04–0.06 m. in height, must have been considered adequate for cult purposes and surely less expensive. Another example of the larger size is a fragmentary base remaining in the context pottery of Group 4 (see p. 87 below and note 9).

The appearance of the ray-based drinking vessels, **40** and **43**, with the semiglazed version, **41** and **42**, in the same rather chronologically limited context shows a longevity in the former type greater than hitherto suspected. In addition, the absence of the one-handled cup from the group shows that a mid-5th-century date may be necessary for the introduction of that form of drinking cup.[7]

Only a few fragments in the context pottery may be dated to the later 6th century. Most of it belongs to the first and early second quarter of the 5th century and was discarded before the middle of the century.

33. Round-mouthed oinochoe   Pl. 6

C-65-126. H. 0.079, D. 0.075, D. foot 0.054 m. Complete except handle restored in plaster.

Thin, sloping ring foot; flat undersurface; globular wall turning continuously into sloping shoulder; low concave neck; flaring rim concave on outer face; thickening in place of drip ring. Black glazed overall except reserved undersurface; no trace of added color.

Absence of a true drip ring and lack of added color would suggest a late 5th-century date (*Corinth* XIII, p. 134), but the thin foot and strongly globular profile are earlier characteristics. This and **34** are smaller than the usual oinochoai of the type and thus may lack added colors and articulation.

First quarter 5th century

34. Round-mouthed oinochoe   Pl. 6

C-65-127. P.H. 0.07, D. 0.094, D. foot 0.061 m. Many joining fragments; mouth, neck, handle missing; plaster restoration.

Shape as **33** but with high ovoid wall; drip ring at upper break. Black glazed overall; no trace of added colors.

First to second quarter 5th century

35. Kalathos, type 3   Fig. 5, Pl. 6

C-65-124. H. 0.094–0.096, D. 0.11, D. resting surface 0.061 m. Many joining fragments; complete profile; plaster restoration.

Slightly concave resting surface; bevel at bottom of wall; concave wall with reflex handles at midpoint; flaring triangular rim. Undersurface and bevel reserved; lower wall decoration of black and added-red bands with two black lines between; handle zone with black and added-

red pomegranate chain between black lines; upper wall banded as lower; added red on rim; black lip. Interior with black bands on outer floor, midwall, top of wall. Size and decoration unusual.

First quarter 5th century

36. Kalathos, type 3   Pl. 6

C-65-123. H. 0.09–0.093, D. 0.102–0.103, D. resting surface 0.066 m. Many joining fragments; complete profile; plaster restoration.

Shape as **35**. Lower wall, black and added-red bands, with brown (diluted glaze) lines between; handle zone with S-maeander between brown lines; upper wall banded as lower; rim and lip black. Black bands on interior floor and upper wall.

First to second quarter 5th century

37. Kalathos, type 3   Pl. 6

C-65-122. H. 0.071, D. 0.095, D. resting surface 0.044 m. Many joining fragments; complete profile; plaster restoration.

Shape as **35**; deep wheel groove on bevel; lip slightly thickened inward. Lower wall with black and added-red bands, with diluted glaze lines between; black blob buds in handle zone between black and added-red lines; upper wall black; black bands on rim, lip. Black bands on interior on outer floor, upper wall.

First to second quarter 5th century

38. Kalathiskos   Fig. 5, Pl. 6

C-65-580. H. 0.046, D. 0.059, D. resting surface 0.036 m. Intact.

Shape as **35** but smaller; less articulated rim. Lower wall with bands: black, added red, black; upper wall above

---

[7] This differs from the North Cemetery dates. Only a few ray-based kotylai were found in the 5th-century graves: *Corinth* XIII, p. 124. A date of 475 B.C. is suggested for the beginning of the one-handlers: *Corinth* XIII, p. 129. The latter also continue well into the 4th century, not ending at the beginning of that century as stated therein (see pp. 36–37 above). The differences may indicate that tastes in grave furnishings diverged from fashions in household or votive pottery. The first level of the Punic Amphora Building in the Forum, the pottery of which is similar in date to Group 3, also contained no one-handled cups and only one semiglazed kotyle; but over twenty ray-based kotylai were found in that context, demonstrably of the second quarter of the 5th century. See Williams, *Hesperia* 48, 1979, p. 114.

handles: two black bands; added-red rim. Interior with black bands on outer floor, upper wall.

Type 3 shape but no handle-zone design. Probably transitional between types 2 and 3, supporting the date of introduction of type 3 at the beginning of the 5th century.

39. Kalathiskos, type 3   Pl. 6

C-65-581. H. 0.045, D. 0.059, D. resting surface 0.037 m. Rim slightly chipped.

Shape as **35**; undecorated. The small plain form of type 3 is introduced at the same time as the larger banded form.

40. Ray-based kotyle   Fig. 6, Pl. 6

C-65-119. H. 0.108, rest. D. 0.129, D. foot 0.072 m. Half of wall, one handle restored.

Sloping ring foot; flat undersurface; tall, gently convex flaring wall turning in slightly to tapered lip; loop handle. Two black circles on undersurface; added red on inner foot, reserved on resting surface; black and added red on outer face of foot; two thirds of wall with well-spaced black rays, ending in long thin lines; upper third of wall black, with pairs of added-red lines at bottom, middle, top of black. Interior black with added red on midwall, outer floor.

See T 1665 (*Corinth* XIII, grave 265-1, pl. 37). The type is longer lived than previously thought. Over twenty were found in the first level of the Punic Amphora Building, of the second quarter of the 5th century.

41. Semiglazed kotyle   Fig. 6, Pl. 7

C-65-121. H. 0.079, D. 0.104, D. foot 0.065 m. Many joining fragments; part of wall, floor restored in plaster.

Shape as **40**, with slighter foot, lower wall. Black on outer undersurface and edge of foot; added red on inner and outer faces of foot; black line at bottom of wall; lower wall reserved; upper black with two pairs of added-red lines at lower edge and midzone; one added-red line at lip. Interior black with red at midwall, outer floor.

Semiglazed kotyle introduced before ray-based form disappeared. See *Corinth* XIII, pp. 124–126.

Second quarter 5th century

42. Semiglazed kotyle   Pl. 7

C-65-120. H. 0.065, D. 0.087, D. foot 0.058 m. One chip in wall, completed in plaster.

Shape as **41** but smaller; wall lower in relation to diameters. Reserved area of lower wall narrower than **41**; no black on undersurface; no added-red lines over black area; red line at lower edge of black. Changes may be due to smaller size; profile is still the full earlier form.

Second quarter 5th century

43. Ray-based skyphos   Fig. 7, Pl. 7

C-65-117. H. 0.102–0.105, D. 0.126, D. foot 0.08 m. Many joining fragments; small part of floor and wall restored in plaster.

Heavy torus foot; flat undersurface; tall convex flaring wall becoming vertical at top; tapered lip; two loop handles. Undersurface with two black bands; inner foot added red; outer foot black; added-red line at top of foot; closely set lines in place of rays on lower wall; upper wall black with added-red line at bottom of black; two pairs of added-red lines below handle at top of wall. Interior black; added-red line at top of wall.

The Attic foot was grafted onto the Corinthian kotyle. See T 1713 (*Corinth* XIII, p. 124, grave 296-1, pl. 41). One additional skyphos in group: C-65-118.

Early 5th century

44. Black-glazed lekythos   Pl. 7

C-65-125. H. 0.10, D. 0.043, D. foot 0.034 m. Handle, most of rim restored in plaster.

Flat resting surface with string marks; false ring foot; low ovoid wall with little gain of diameter; concave flaring rim beginning with projection from top of wall; no neck ring; funnel-shaped upper face of rim narrowing to small opening; rounded lip. Black glazed overall, except reserved resting surface, peeling. Poor surface finish.

See *Corinth* XIII, p. 140, especially T 2804 (grave 297-3, pl. 42).

Early second quarter 5th century

45. Attic black-figured lekythos   Pl. 7

C-65-42. P.H. 0.08, est. D. 0.044 m. Joining fragment from lot 2046, P:26. Three joining fragments; foot, most of shoulder, neck, rim, handle missing.

Tapering lower body; cylindrical wall without flare at shoulder. Black on lower wall; wide black band as ground line; charioteer in long white robe, in four-horse chariot, to right; behind horses a white marker. Top of wall with black running maeander between black lines; shoulder with black linear tongues. Streaky glaze, uncontrolled incision, poor drawing.

Second quarter 5th century

46. Attic palmette lekythos   Pl. 7

C-65-41. P.H. 0.082, D. 0.039, D. foot 0.032 m. Half of foot, all of neck, rim, handle missing.

Disk foot with small hollow center; body as **45**. Thin peeling glaze. Outer foot, undersurface reserved; lower wall black; upper wall with poorly executed palmette-and-lotus chain: added white in volutes, lines enclosing palmettes, white dots in calyces. Black linear tongues on shoulder.

See *Corinth* XIII, p. 163, group ii.
Second quarter 5th century

47.   Small hydria   Fig. 1, Pl. 7

C-65-500. P.H. 0.066, D. 0.071, D. foot 0.046 m. Vertical handle, one side handle; neck and rim missing.

High ring foot; high ovoid body; sloping shoulder offset from wall; canted-loop side handle with attached disk in center. Polished surface, now peeling; no decoration.
First quarter 5th century

48.   Krateriskos   Pl. 7

C-65-128. H. 0.064, D. (top of wall and rim) 0.085, D. foot 0.052 m. Many joining fragments; one handle, part of rim restored in plaster.

Sloping ring foot; flat undersurface; slightly convex wall; vertical concave rim offset from wall; flaring flattened lip;

vertical handles from wall to lip. Black glazed overall except undersurface. Added-red line on outer foot, top of wall, lip; on interior of outer floor, midwall, below lip.

Much larger than the typical krateriskos. Possibly used as a drinking cup.
End of 6th or early 5th century

49.   Unflanged small cooking pot   Pl. 7

C-65-650. P.H. 0.095, est. D. 0.13, est. D. rim 0.075 m. Many joining fragments; part of wall, shoulder, rim preserved. Orange cooking fabric, lightly micaceous. Burning inside and out; encrusted.

High ovoid wall; squat profile; sloping shoulder offset from wall, turning up to flaring rim with rounded lip. Scar of lower handle attachment on shoulder. No burnishing strokes.
Probably early 5th century

GROUP 4 (50–60)

Grid location O–P:22   Lot 4351   Pit E (Pit 1965-3)   Pl. 2

0.7 kg. (0.65 kg. inventoried)
   11 inventoried vessels; 26 uninventoried sherds.
   Too few to weigh the individual shapes separately.

The pit from which Group 4 came measures 1.95 m. east–west and 0.90 m. north–south.[8] The south wall was constructed of field stones 0.30–0.35 m. wide; the east wall was a thin stone slab set on edge; the north wall was made of gravelly fill; the west wall was not preserved. Four pan tiles, found in fragmentary condition, set inside the walls, sealed off the pit from the overlying earth. There were bits of carbon in the fill of the pit, but no traces of burning were apparent. Thus the pit was not a holocaust sacrificial area. Although the pan tiles originally sealed the pit, there was later disturbance of them but without any contamination of the contents.

The major shape is the kalathiskos, thus signaling the votive nature of the group. The Attic black-figured vase **50** and the Corinthian lekythos **51** may also have been votive dedications; the krateriskoi are miniature votives. All the well-preserved pottery from the pit appears in the catalogue; the context pottery contains only a few sherds of additional kalathiskoi, including the base of a large example,[9] a few ray-based kotyle fragments, a handle from an Attic kylix, and a lekanis-lid knob. There is also a scarab, MF 12156.

The group is contemporary with Group 3 and shows the same approximate lower limit in the second quarter of the 5th century, but it has a slightly earlier upper limit; there are more kalathiskoi of type 2. The group helps to support the date for the introduction of the type 3 kalathiskos at the end of the 6th or beginning of the 5th century.

50.   Attic black-figured oinochoe   Fig. 3, Pl. 8

C-65-174. P.H. 0.083, D. 0.076, D. foot 0.061 m. Mouth and handle missing.
   Published: Stroud, *Hesperia* 37, 1968, pl. 98:m, n.

Low, recessed disk foot, concave on undersurface, flaring to cylindrical wall; sloping shoulder, sharply offset from wall; narrow neck with drip ring; stub of vertical strap handle on outer shoulder. Undersurface and foot reserved;

---

[8] Stroud, *Hesperia* 37, 1968, pp. 311–312.
[9] Lot 4351:1; see **35–37** of Group 3.

reserved ribbon pattern on lower wall; two black lines; black pomegranate chain on upper wall; black line at shoulder; drip ring added purple, with short black linear tongues radiating from it; stub of handle, beginning of mouth black. On shoulder, to right from handle: man in cloak facing right; three women in added white, wearing short peploi, holding hands, dancing right toward bearded man in cloak seated on stool to left, playing a lyre. Added-purple and added-white dots on clothing. Careless incision and painting; lyre has no strings, hand on lyre has six fingers.

See Vanderpool, *Hesperia* 7, 1938, p. 380, no. 12, fig. 15; oinochoe of Vraona type (*ABV*, p. 443, no. 1), second quarter 6th century. **50** is later, by shape and by style. See especially the example by the Gela Painter (*ABV*, p. 475, no. 29 and p. 443, no. 3).

End of 6th or beginning of 5th century

51. Black-glazed lekythos

    C-65-582. P.H. 0.094, D. 0.042, D. foot 0.027 m. Neck, rim, handle missing; large gouge in wall.

False foot; flat resting surface with string marks; low ovoid body; wall continuous with neck; no drip ring. Very poorly glazed overall, with drips on resting surface.
    See **44**, Group 3; **51** is later, at the end of the series.
    Second quarter 5th century

52. Krateriskos   Pl. 8

    C-65-172. H. 0.027, D. 0.032, D. resting surface 0.021 m. Intact.

Flat resting surface; concave lower wall turning convex; vertical rim slightly concave; flat lip; two krater handles pressed against rim. Thin, peeling glaze overall.

53. Krateriskos

    C-65-589. H. 0.025, est. D. 0.032, D. resting surface 0.021 m. Part of wall, rim, one handle missing.

Shape as **52**. Glaze overall, fired mostly red.

54. Small bowl   Pl. 8

    C-65-173. H. 0.029, D. 0.062, D. foot 0.036 m. Completed from three fragments.

Disk foot with string marks; convex flaring wall, turning in slightly to simple lip. Interior glazed; exterior partly glazed by dipping. This type may not be a miniature; see footnote 109 above, p. 39.
    Second quarter 5th century

55. Kalathiskos   Pl. 8

    C-65-583. H. 0.057, D. 0.063, D. foot 0.038 m. Part of wall, rim missing.

Narrow disk foot, flaring to bevel of lower wall; concave wall with two poor lug handles; flaring triangular rim. Wall: black, added red, black bands; black dots in handle zone; black band; black rim; black band on upper interior wall. Bevel, foot, undersurface reserved. Type 2 shape; type 3 decoration.

56. Kalathiskos   Pl. 8

    C-65-584. H. 0.04, D. 0.054, D. resting surface 0.031 m. Intact.

Slightly concave resting surface; low sharp bevel; concave wall without handles; flaring triangular rim. Wall: black, black, added-red bands; black rim; black line on interior midwall, two on upper wall. Bevel and resting surface reserved. Glaze fired red to black. Type 3 shape; type 2 decoration.

57. Kalathiskos, type 3   Fig. 5, Pl. 8

    C-65-586. H. 0.052, D. 0.067, D. resting surface 0.042 m. Completed from many fragments.

Shape as **56**, with two pinched-on handles. Wall: black, black, added-red, black bands; black Z-maeander in handle zone; black, black bands; added-red rim; black bands on interior on mid- and upper wall. Bevel and resting surface reserved. Peeling glaze. Early type 3.

58. Kalathiskos, type 3   Pl. 8

    C-65-585. H. 0.051, est. D. 0.065, D. resting surface 0.036 m. Part of wall, rim missing.

Shape as **56**, with two lug handles. Wall: black, added-red, black bands; black zigzag in handle zone; black, added-red bands; black rim; added-red lines on interior on outer floor, upper wall. Bevel and resting surface reserved. Glaze fired red to black. Singular use of added red on interior. Early type 3.

59. Kalathiskos, type 3   Pl. 8

    C-65-587. H. 0.046, D. 0.06, D. resting surface 0.034 m. Two joining fragments, slightly chipped.

Shape as **56**, with two badly finished reflex handles. Wall: added-red, black, added-red bands; black dots in handle zone; added-red, black bands; added-red rim; black lines on interior on floor, upper wall. Bevel and resting surface reserved. Peeling glaze. Not so early as **56–58**.

60. Kalathiskos   Pl. 8

    C-65-588. H. 0.035, D. 0.046, D. resting surface 0.03 m. Five joining fragments; part of wall and rim missing.

Very small undecorated version of the above. No handles.

GROUP 5 (61–72)

Grid location Q:25   Lot 887   Pit A (Pit 1961-2)   Pl. 3:a

3.30 kg. (0.55 kg. inventoried)
  kraters: 0.1 kg. (1 black glazed; 1 lekane)
  oinochoai: 0.1 kg. (5: 1 conical, 1 Conventionalizing, 3 uncertain)
  kotylai and skyphoi: 0.35 kg. (9: 2 figured kotylai, 2 ray based, 2 semiglazed, 1 plain, 1 banded; 1 red-figured
    skyphos)
  lids: 0.1 kg. (4: 2 pyxis, 2 lekanis)
  miscellaneous fine wares: 0.25 kg. (14: 2 small bowls, 1 black-glazed bowl, 1 flattened-rim bowl, 1 one-handler,
    2 blister-ware aryballoi, 4 plates, 1 powder pyxis, 1 lamp, 2 Attic sherds)
  kalathiskoi: 1.5 kg. (45: 9 flaring, 4 type 2, 1 large type 3, 28 type 3, 3 undecorated)
  miscellaneous votives: 0.2 kg. (10: 1 hydriskos, 1 krateriskos, 1 cup, 3 phialai, 4 offering trays)
  kitchen vessels: 0.7 kg. (2 basins, 2 fragments of cooking fabric)

The pit containing Group 5 was rectangular, 2.40 m. north–south, 1.20 m. east–west.[10] Poros blocks set on edge made up the north and west sides of the construction; the east was of field stones, the south wall consisted of three large stones. Over these walls were Corinthian pan tiles laid in two layers. The earth fill was hard packed, with a quantity of sherds and a few figurines.[11] The fill was 0.65 m. deep at the north end, less at the south, and went to bedrock. At the north end of the construction, set in the fill close to bedrock, were seven kalathiskoi, 64–70. There were traces neither of burning nor of animal bones; thus, as with Pit E (Group 4), Pit A was not a holocaust pit.

The contents of this pit do not have so limited a date as the pottery of Groups 3 and 4. The inventoried objects give a range from the late 6th to the last quarter of the 5th century. This dating is supported by fragments remaining in the context pottery: a later 5th-century blister-ware aryballos with flat ribs (887:4), a semiglazed skyphos with an angular torus foot (887:2), a sherd with a fairly linear palmette (887:1) of the later 5th century, and a fragment of a large plain kotyle (887:5). There are also earlier fragments: perforated flaring kalathiskoi, a ray-based conical oinochoe, 6th-century kotyle fragments. The greater number of the uninventoried fragments are from type 3 kalathiskoi. The bulk of the pottery, therefore, is from the 5th century, going into the last quarter, with a few fragments from the 6th century.

61. Red-figured skyphos   Pl. 9

C-61-227. P.H. 0.093 m. Five joining fragments, preserving part of upper wall, lip. Hard micaceous clay; 5YR 6/6 (reddish yellow).

Published: Stroud, *Hesperia* 34, 1965, pl. 2:b.

Convex upper wall, rounded lip just beginning to show outward flare. On wall, boy facing left, wrapped in himation, right arm inside cloak, left arm probably stretching back, extending the cloak; fillet originally in hair. Very straight lines for folds; cursory detail. Upper border of eggs. Thin, peeling glaze; peeling miltos on figure, border.

The clay is closer to Attic than to Corinthian. The figure is typical of cloaked youths on the reverses of skyphoi and bell-kraters. The hand, distinctive in the downturned mouth and straight drapery folds, can be detected in other Attic fragments found in Corinth: see **339** and C-37-525 (I. McPhee, "Attic Red Figure of the Late 5th and 4th Centuries from Corinth," *Hesperia* 45, 1976 [pp. 380–396], p. 388, no. 21, pl. 88). There are also fragments in a non-Attic clay by the same or a similar hand. Ian McPhee will discuss these fragments in a forthcoming article.

Fourth quarter 5th century

62. Bowl   Pl. 9

C-61-388. H. 0.024, D. 0.054, D. foot 0.035 m. Two joining fragments; part of wall missing.

Disk foot with string marks; slightly convex flaring wall; outward thickened rim. Glazed inside; partly glazed by dipping on exterior wall. See T 1640 (*Corinth* XIII, grave 344-7, pl. 52).

Third or fourth quarter 5th century

63. Flaring kalathiskos   Pl. 9

C-61-226. H. 0.023, D. 0.037, D. resting surface 0.023 m. Intact.

---

[10] Stroud, *Hesperia* 34, 1965, pp. 6–7.
[11] Figurines: MF 10537–MF 10544, MF 10942, MF 10943. There is also a lamp, L 4186, a 5th-century miniature.

Flat resting surface; slightly concave flaring wall; rounded lip. Two glaze bands on exterior wall, outer floor, and upper interior wall. Lip glazed. Glaze fired partly red; banding uneven. A miniature of the older flaring form of kalathiskos.

64. Kalathiskos, type 3   Fig. 5, Pl. 9

C-61-390. H. 0.048, D. 0.064, D. resting surface 0.038 m. One chip from rim.

Published: Stroud, *Hesperia* 34, 1965, pl. 2:c.

Concave resting surface; beveled lower wall; concave wall with two good lug handles; flaring triangular rim; lip inward thickened. Wall: added-red, black bands with black line between; black zigzag in handle zone; black on upper wall continuing over rim; interior: black lines on outer floor, upper wall, lip. Bevel and undersurface reserved. Good type 3 kalathiskos.

65. Kalathiskos, type 3

C-61-391. H. 0.043, D. 0.055, D. resting surface 0.034 m. Intact.

Published: Stroud, *Hesperia* 34, 1965, pl. 2:c.

Shape as **64**. Wall: black, added-red bands, black zigzag in handle zone, black band, added-red rim; interior: black lines on outer floor, upper wall. Good type 3 kalathiskos.

66. Kalathiskos, type 3   Pl. 9

C-61-392. H. 0.035, D. 0.057, D. resting surface 0.036 m. Intact.

Published: Stroud, *Hesperia* 34, 1965, pl. 2:c.

Shape as **64**, with lower wall, pinched-on handles. Wall: black, added-red bands, black band of upper wall goes over lip; interior: black lines on outer floor, upper wall; no handle-zone design. The decoration is sloppy, the shape less precise.

Later 5th century

67. Kalathiskos, type 3   Pl. 9

C-61-393. H. 0.044, D. 0.068, D. resting surface 0.04 m. Slightly chipped.

Published: Stroud, *Hesperia* 34, 1965, pl. 2:c.

Shape as **64**, with lower wall. Wall: black, added-red bands with black line between, 5-stroke maeander in handle zone; black band continuing over rim; interior:

black lines on outer floor, mid- and upper wall. Banding goes over bevel. More open profile than typical of type 3.

68. Kalathiskos, type 3   Pl. 9

C-61-394. H. 0.048-0.05, D. 0.065, D. resting surface 0.042 m. Intact.

Published: Stroud, *Hesperia* 34, 1965, pl. 2:c.

Shape as **67**, with similar wall; handles are merely bumps. Wall: black, added-red bands with diluted-glaze line between, Z-maeander between black lines, placed above handles, black band continuing over rim; interior: black lines on outer floor, upper wall. Peeling glaze; wheel grooves. Degenerating shape and decoration.

Late 5th century

69. Kalathiskos, type 3

C-61-395. H. 0.046, D. 0.058, D. resting surface 0.035 m. Intact.

Published: Stroud, *Hesperia* 34, 1965, pl. 2:c.

Shape as **68**. Decoration as **68**, with Z-maeander above handles; interior has lines on wall, not on floor. Glaze fired red; wheel grooves.

Late 5th century

70. Kalathiskos, type 3   Fig. 5, Pl. 9

C-61-396. H. 0.044, D. 0.053, D. resting surface 0.033 m. Intact.

Published: Stroud, *Hesperia* 34, 1965, pl. 2:c.

Similar to **68** and **69**, but with very low bevel. Wall: added-red, black bands with diluted-glaze line between, black zigzag between black lines; black band continuing over rim; interior: black lines on outer floor, top of wall. Peeling glaze.

Late 5th century

71. Kalathiskos, type 3   Fig. 5, Pl. 9

C-61-387. H. 0.034, D. 0.049, D. resting surface 0.028 m. Intact.

Flat resting surface; rounded bevel; concave wall without handles; flaring triangular rim. No decoration. Well-formed, plain version of early type 3.

72. Kalathiskos

C-61-389. H. 0.018-0.019, D. 0.024, D. resting surface 0.016-0.018 m. Intact.

Shape as **71** with taller wall. No decoration.

GROUP 6 (**73–112**)

Grid location N–P:20–25   Lots 1950, 1982, 2111, 2233, 2249, 2250, 4355, 4356, 4369.   Construction fill of Trapezoidal Stoa

49.74 kg. (10.74 kg. inventoried)
    kraters: 0.7 kg. (6: Archaic and Classical)
    lekanai: 6.2 kg. (23)
    oinochoai: 1.6 kg. (44: 4 Archaic, 11 Conventionalizing, 11 plain, 2 imitation blister ware, 4 spouted necks, 3 ribbed, 4 olpai, 1 epichysis, 4 lids)
    kotylai and skyphoi: 5.8 kg. (69 kotylai: 14 ray based, 22 semiglazed, 15 plain, 16 ovoid, 2 white ground; 28 skyphoi: 1 Archaic, 27 black glazed)
    cups and miscellaneous bowls: 1.35 kg. (11 one-handlers; 5 small semiglazed bowls, 2 with outturned rim, 4 plain, 2 banded, 2 offset rims, 4 uncertain)
    echinus bowls and bowls with beveled rims: 0.7 kg. (10 echinus bowls; 9 bowls with beveled rims)
    plain saucers: 0.7 kg. (10)
    plates: 0.4 kg. (1 Archaic, 16 Conventionalizing)
    blister ware: 1.2 kg. (9 oinochoai, 10 aryballoi, 1 askos)
    lekanides: 0.5 kg. (9 bowls, 15 lids)
    stands: 0.39 kg. (11)
    "feeders": 0.3 kg. (11)
    hydriskoi: 0.2 kg. (38)
    kalathiskoi: 2.4 kg. (96: 1 basket handle, 5 flaring, 1 type 1, 1 type 2, 30 type 3, 57 type 4, 1 handmade)
    phialai: 0.2 kg. (19)
    miscellaneous votives: 1.0 kg. (48: 1 amphoriskos, 12 krateriskoi, 3 oinochoai, 10 one-handled jugs, 1 three-handled jug, 5 kotylai, 9 bowls and dishes, 1 pyxis, 1 lid, 4 plates, 1 stand)
    offering trays: 1.8 kg. (51 kernos type, 12 liknon type)
    Attic fabric: 1.5 kg. (26)
    coarse wares: 13.8 kg. (18: 4 amphorai, 4 hydriai, 2 pithoi, 1 mortar, 2 bowls, 3 trays, 1 jar, 1 lid)
    cooking fabric: 3.4 kg. (47: 1 pitcher, 8 flanged pots, 18 unflanged, 17 lopades, 3 lids)
    perirrhanteria: 1.3 kg. (6)
    unidentifiable shapes: 1.4 kg.
    lamps: 2.9 kg. (61)

The fill brought in for construction of the stoa on the Middle Terrace was dug in different campaigns from 1962 through 1965. The context pottery was subsequently amalgamated. The vases in the group are extremely varied, including votives, decorated fragments, fine wares of all shapes, and kitchen vessels. Most of the latest material appears in the catalogue; fragments of earlier date are published in Catalogue II (**227**, **254**, **260**, **276**, **292**, **298**, **323**, **354**, **357**, **413**, **602**) as they are valuable for the decoration but are without significance for establishing the date of the construction of the building.

Much of the material belongs to the later 4th century, with parallels in Forum drain 1971-1, Forum well 1975-4, and other deposits.[12] There is also similarity with late 4th-century destruction debris in the Sanctuary dining rooms: lots 6826, 6827, 72-128, 72-129, 72-134, 72-139, 72-140, etc. Presumably, much of the pottery destroyed by the earthquake(s) in the third or early fourth quarter of the 4th century[13] was discarded in earth which was used as construction fill to level the ground for the stoa.

Although most of the pottery is later 4th century in date, a few pieces, especially **82** (Attic calyx-cup), **99** (small hydria), and a few of the kalathiskoi, belong to the beginning of the 3rd century and represent the lowest limit of the group. There is one Pegasos/Trident coin, 64-80, that has been tentatively dated to 279–252 B.C. (lot 2111). The stoa may thus have been constructed in the early 3rd century.

---

[12] Forum drain 1971-1: Williams and Fisher, *Hesperia* 41, 1972, pp. 154–163. Forum well 1975-4 (votive pit): Williams and Fisher, *Hesperia* 45, 1976, pp. 117–124. Other deposits: *Corinth* VII, iii, deposits nos. 80, 90.

[13] For the earthquakes, see Williams and Fisher, *Hesperia* 45, 1976, pp. 115–116.

73. Attic red-figured bell-krater   Fig. 2, Pl. 10

C-68-244. Additional fragments from L:17, lots 5613, 5693. **a)** P.H. 0.088, p.W. 0.084 m. Eight joining fragments: part of upper wall, beginning of flaring rim preserved. **b)** P.H. 0.062, est. D. 0.27 m. Many joining fragments; part of upper wall, rim, lip preserved.

    Published: Bookidis, *Hesperia* 38, 1969, pl. 79:a.

Vertical upper wall, continuous with flaring rim; rounded lip; groove under lip on outer face.

    a. Interior glazed; reserved band below flaring rim. Exterior: horse and youthful rider to right; added-white tympanum at right, originally with yellow (diluted-glaze) dots and line; two ivy leaves in field.

    b. Interior as fragment **a.** Exterior rim with chain of myrtle leaves; reserved band below. Wall: heads and upper torsos of two draped youths facing each other; discus with dotted X as device between them. Miltos on figures. Peeling, thin brown glaze.

    Near Group G (*ARV*², pp. 1462–1471) and the Filottrano Painter (*ARV*², pp. 1453–1455; McPhee).

    Second quarter 4th century

74. Attic red-figured bell-krater   Pl. 11

C-61-478. Additional fragments from Q:24–25, Q:25, R:25, R:26, S:25, N–O:26, O–P:22–23; lots 882, 886, 1953, 1961, 2013, 2067, 4356. **a)** P.L. 0.087, est. D. 0.30 m. Three joining fragments from rim. **b)** Max. dim. 0.25 m. Many joining fragments from upper wall; plaster restoration. **c)** P.H. 0.133, p.W. 0.221 m. Many joining fragments from midwall. **d)** P.H. 0.16, p.L. 0.236 m. Many joining fragments from lower wall, part of one handle.

Convex lower wall; concave upper wall; flaring rim; rounded lip offset from inner wall. Interior black glazed.

    a (not illustrated). Rim: hooked spirals on upper rim; ivy-berry chain on outer rim face.

    b. Part of ivy chain of rim; at left, a head to left; beginning of unidentifiable object to right of head; large area of black glaze above handle; ivy border at right break, with beginning of wall scene.

    c. Amazon with spotted trouser on horse, attacked left and right by griffins; part of neck, body, leg of left griffin (added white only remaining on neck); wing visible at left break. Added white better preserved on right griffin: neck, with white strokes for mane, foreleg, and part of back; raised wing at right break. Object below with added white: fallen shield?

    d. Right part of handle, originally in 90° angle. Lower border with egg and dart; palmette at left, originally filling area below handle. Right of handle, draped youth, to right, before stele. According to usual scheme, second youth facing him preserved in head of fragment **b.**

For the Amazon-griffin design, see the Olynthos krater 38.329 (*Olynthus* XIII, no. 37, p. 90, pls. 45–47).

    Mid-4th century

75. Deep lekane   Pl. 10

C-65-652. P.H. 0.083, est. D. rim 0.34 m. Two joining fragments from upper wall, rim, one handle.

Wall becoming convex at lower break, vertical in handle zone, turning slightly concave and merging with heavy flaring rim, slightly overhanging. Horizontal handle, round in section, on upper wall, canted slightly upward. No decoration.

    The rim is slighter than two larger examples with comparable profiles, C-1979-243, from a late 5th- or early 4th-century context, and C-72-121, of the later 4th century (Williams and Fisher, *Hesperia* 42, 1973, p. 24, no. 24, pl. 10). The handles of **75** are closer to the former example in placement and direction.

    Earlier 4th century?

76. Blister-ware oinochoe   Pl. 10

C-65-557. P.H. 0.075, D. rim 0.062 m. Four joining fragments; parts of shoulder, neck, rim, and handle preserved.

Originally a globular body; sloping shoulder not offset from wall; short neck; flaring rim; double strap handle from outer shoulder to rim. Shallow slanting ribs on shoulder.

    Early 4th century

77. Blister-ware oinochoe   Pl. 10

C-65-558. P.H. 0.082, est. D. rim 0.07 m. Six joining fragments; parts of upper wall, shoulder, neck, mouth, handle preserved.

Shape as **76.** Finger depressions in place of ribs on lower shoulder. See C-40-390 (Weinberg [under **4**], p. 233, E10, pl. 85). See also **387.**

    Third quarter 4th century

78. Beveled oinochoe (epichysis)   Fig. 3, Pl. 10

C-65-517. P.H. 0.052, D. bevel and shoulder 0.051, D. foot 0.042 m. Neck, handle, mouth missing.

Concave undersurface; ring foot with vertical outer face; bevel of lower wall; concave wall; bevel of shoulder; sloping rounded shoulder with shallow ribs; neck ring below narrow, originally tall neck. Black glazed overall except resting surface.

    Related to the high-shouldered oinochoe C-31-129, from well 1931-7, and C-37-2502, from pit 1937-1; neither is published. See also **385.**

    Probably late 4th century

79. Attic(?) oinochoe   Pl. 10

C-65-549. P.H. 0.025 m. Neck fragment; no preserved edge.

Concave narrow neck; black glazed on exterior, upper part of interior. On neck, a myrtle wreath in thick added white. From an oinochoe or lekythos. For the design see *Agora* XII, no. 131, p. 245, pl. 7, 325–310 B.C.

Late 4th century

80. Large krateroid skyphos   Fig. 7, Pl. 12

C-65-481. Additional fragments from P–Q:20–22, M:17–18, M–O:17–20, O:20–21, O–P:22–23, O:22; lots 2156, 3206, 3222, 4348, 4352, 4369. H. 0.277, est. D. lip 0.27, D. foot 0.14 m. Many joining fragments; about half preserved; plaster restoration; no complete handle.

Heavy torus foot; flat undersurface (center missing); wall with compound curve; flaring lip. Black glazed overall; glaze worn off resting surface of foot. Lower wall undecorated; above, narrow vertical ribs to maximum diameter of wall, which has an unribbed band 0.02 m. wide. Ribs on upper wall; narrow horizontal band of eggs; top of wall and lip plain. On non-joining fragment of band a graffito:

XOIP[

Glaze fired red in some areas.

Two other large skyphoi: J. L. Caskey, "Objects from a Well at Isthmia," *Hesperia* 29, 1960 (pp. 168–176), pp. 168–172, from Isthmia; C-37-582 from drain 1937-1.

Third quarter 4th century

81. Skyphos   Fig. 7, Pl. 12

C-62-337. H. 0.087, D. (maximum and lip) 0.086, D. foot 0.043 m. Many joining fragments; complete vertical profile; plaster restoration.

Shape as **80**; slightly nippled undersurface; preserved handle with contracted roots, set slightly canted. Black glazed overall except undersurface with two glaze circles, miltos between them.

Third quarter 4th century

82. Attic calyx-cup   Pl. 12

C-64-423. P.H. 0.019 m. One fragment of resting surface, lower wall.

Recessed undersurface with nipple; grooved resting surface, no foot; flaring wall with very shallow ribs. In center of floor a satyr mask. Black glazed overall; burnt on bottom.

See Miller, *Hesperia* 43, 1974, p. 231, nos. 16, 17, pl. 31. *Agora* XII, no. 695, p. 285, pl. 28, is similar but earlier; **82** has shallower ribbing.

First quarter 3rd century

83. Attic kantharos   Pl. 12

C-64-421. P.H. 0.044, est. D. 0.079 m. Many joining fragments; part of upper wall, shoulder, rim, lip, lower part of one handle preserved; plaster restoration.

Convex wall with maximum diameter at shoulder; vertical concave rim inset from shoulder, ending in slightly flaring rounded lip; wide strap handle attached at shoulder. Black glazed overall. Bowl insufficiently preserved to show stamping.

4th century (lack of profile precludes closer dating)

84. Attic kantharos   Fig. 10, Pl. 12

C-65-535. P.H. 0.073, D. 0.085, D. foot 0.046 m. Broken at rim.

Pedestal foot with central ledge; concave above stem; convex foot below; conical interior with wide groove before resting surface of foot; groove at base of wall; wide convex flaring body with maximum diameter at shoulder; beginning of inset concave rim; attachment scar for strap handle at shoulder. Wall ribbed. Black glazed overall except reserved resting surface, inner groove of foot, narrow band below ledge on foot.

Without rim, uncertain if of plain or molded form. No stamping in bowl. For proportions: *Agora* XII, no. 704, p. 286, fig. 7, pl. 29, 320–310 B.C.

4th century

85. Attic one-handled cup   Pl. 12

C-65-550. P.H. 0.032, est. D. rim 0.11 m. Four joining fragments; one third of rim and upper wall, handle preserved.

Convex wall rising to flattened lip; loop handle of horseshoe shape. Black glazed overall; rouletting in bowl at break. See *Agora* XII, no. 759, pl. 56, for similar rouletting.

Mid-4th century

86. One-handled cup, type 2   Fig. 11, Pl. 12

C-65-551. H. 0.042, D. 0.089, D. foot 0.053 m. Four joining fragments; handle, part of wall missing.

Vertical ring foot; nippled undersurface; convex flaring wall turning vertical to flattened lip. Black glazed overall, peeling.

Third to fourth quarter 4th century

87. One-handled cup, type 2   Fig. 11, Pl. 12

C-65-539. H. 0.051, D. 0.086–0.088, D. foot 0.042 m. Handle, part of rim missing.

Shape as **86** but without nipple; flattened lip with slight outward projection. Originally glazed overall, now peeled.

Third to fourth quarter 4th century

88. Small echinus bowl   Fig. 12, Pl. 13

C-62-342. H. 0.039, rest. D. 0.064, D. foot 0.039 m.
Full profile, half restored in plaster.

Ring foot; flat undersurface; convex flaring wall, turning
in continuously to rounded lip. Black glazed overall.

Early 4th century

89. Small echinus bowl   Pl. 13

C-65-552. H. 0.033, D. 0.065, D. foot 0.04 m. Intact
except for slightly chipped lip.

Shape as **88** but with nippled undersurface; more angular turn to lip; slightly higher wall. Black glazed overall;
peeling; poor surface finish.

Late 4th century

90. Bowl with outturned rim   Pl. 13

C-65-555. a) P.H. 0.051 m. b) P.H. 0.037, est. D. rim
0.21 m.

Both a and b (not illustrated) mended of two fragments,
preserving upper wall and rim.

Wide convex flaring wall with beginning of carination
from convex lower wall to concave upper wall; outward
thickened rim; rim tooled on outer edge, not fully rolled.
Originally black glazed overall; glaze fired red in places
and peeling.

Rim profile close to C-71-46, from Forum drain
1971-1, unpublished.

Third quarter 4th century

91. Attic bowl with outturned rim   Fig. 12, Pl. 13

C-65-556. H. 0.049, est. D. 0.14, D. foot 0.08 m. Five
joining fragments; most of wall missing; plaster
restoration.

High ring foot; flat undersurface, no nipple; nearly
straight, flaring wall turning out widely from foot, rising
vertically to flaring, outward thickened rim. Black glazed
overall except resting surface; miltos on latter and on juncture of foot and wall. Four impressed unlinked palmettes
in center of floor; abortive rouletting around them; outer
floor rouletted. Palmettes extremely thin and linear.

For the shape: *Agora* XII, no. 806, p. 293, fig. 8,
pl. 32.

Third quarter 4th century

92. Small bowl, beveled rim   Fig. 13, Pl. 13

C-65-538. H. 0.03, D. 0.085, D. foot 0.042 m. Complete profile; three fifths preserved.

Diagonal ring foot; nippled undersurface; slightly convex
flaring wall; rounded bevel, turning in to tapered lip.
Black glazed overall, peeling.

Late fourth quarter 4th century

93. Small bowl, beveled rim   Fig. 13

C-65-554. H. 0.024, est. D. 0.09, est. D. foot 0.05 m.
One fragment of vertical profile; floor missing.

Small ring foot; straight flaring wall; sharp bevel turning
in to tapered lip. Originally black glazed overall, peeling.
Lower profile than **92**.

Late fourth quarter 4th century

94. Saucer   Fig. 15, Pl. 13

C-65-540. H. 0.024, est. D. 0.16, D. foot 0.068 m.
Three joining fragments; much of wall missing; foot
complete.

High vertical ring foot; slightly nippled undersurface;
low, wide, convex wall; rounded lip. Black glazed overall,
glaze thin and peeling.

Third quarter 4th century

95. Saucer   Fig. 15, Pl. 13

C-64-420. H. 0.036, est. D. 0.13, D. foot 0.054 m.
Two joining fragments; one third of wall, all of foot
preserved.

Profile as **94**, with smaller foot, diagonal inner face of
foot, higher wall. Black glazed overall.

Third quarter 4th century

96. Attic squat lekythos   Pl. 13

C-65-516. P.H. 0.068, D. 0.048, D. foot 0.037 m. Top
of neck, rim missing; hole in wall below handle.

Low ring foot; globular body merging with shoulder;
drip ring below neck; concave neck; strap handle from
upper wall to neck. Red-figure palmette, not on axis with
handle. Black glazed elsewhere except undersurface;
glaze peeling. See *Olynthus* XIII, no. 113, p. 153,
pl. 105.

Second quarter 4th century

97. Blister-ware aryballos   Fig. 17, Pl. 13

C-65-537. P.H. 0.062, D. 0.092 m. Many joining
fragments; complete profile; part of floor, most of rim
and handle missing.

Flat resting surface; low ovoid body continuous to narrow short neck; broken at flare to rim; scar of strap handle on upper wall. Narrow incised ribs from upper wall
to base. Orange surface.

Third quarter 4th century

98. Blister-ware duck askos   Pl. 13

C-64-437. P.L. 0.038 m. Two joining fragments; only
upper back, stump of tail preserved.

Groove dividing one side of duck horizontally; short
incised lines on upper half for feathers. For a more

complete example see C-60-68 (*Corinth* VII, iii, no. 776, p. 149, pl. 64). See also **200**, Group 11.

Late 4th century

99. Small hydria   Fig. 1, Pl. 13

C-65-546. H. 0.103, D. 0.066, D. foot 0.032 m. One side handle, part of rim missing; hole in lower wall.

Narrow ring foot; nippled undersurface; ovoid body with maximum diameter just above midwall; sloping offset shoulder turning into narrow concave neck; neck flaring to horizontal rim; slightly peaked lip; side handle of 90° form; vertical round handle attached at upper wall and under rim.

Ca. 300 B.C.

100. Kalathiskos, type 3   Fig. 5, Pl. 13

C-65-590. H. 0.039–0.041, D. 0.053–0.057, D. resting surface 0.030–0.032 m. Intact.

Flat resting surface; rounded bevel; concave wall with two pinched-on handles, merging with slightly flaring, almost vertical rim. Wall: black, added-red bands; zigzag in handle zone; added-red, black bands, black going over rim and lip; one black band on upper interior wall. Uneven banding; poorly thrown.

Very late type 3.

101. Kalathiskos, type 3   Pl. 13

C-62-344. H. 0.048, D. 0.059, D. resting surface 0.031 m. Many joining fragments; part of wall, rim missing; completed in plaster.

Slightly concave resting surface; concave flare to rounded bevel; vertical wall rising to flaring rounded rim; peaked lip; two poor handles on midwall. Lower wall black; gray-purple line at midwall, going over handles; upper wall black; rim black. Interior burnt.

One of the latest of type 3 kalathiskoi.

102. Kalathiskos, type 3   Pl. 13

C-62-340. H. 0.025, D. 0.036, D. resting surface 0.021 m. Intact.

Slightly concave resting surface; low bevel; concave wall; flaring rim. Well-articulated miniature type 3, without handles or decoration.

Late 5th or early 4th century

103. Kalathiskos, type 4   Pl. 13

C-62-339. H. 0.04, D. 0.054, D. resting surface 0.036 m. Intact.

Flat resting surface; rounded bevel; gently concave wall; slightly flaring rounded rim; no handles; no decoration.

104. Kalathiskos, type 4   Pl. 13

C-65-559. H. 0.038, D. 0.052, D. resting surface 0.035 m. Slightly chipped.

Shape as **103**, with more rounded bevel, simpler rim.

105. Kalathiskos, type 4

C-62-338. H. 0.037, D. 0.049, D. resting surface 0.023 m. Intact.

Shape as **103**; low bevel; vertical wall; horizontal flaring rim; peaked lip.

Later than **103** and **104**.

106. Kalathiskos, type 4   Fig. 5, Pl. 13

C-65-560. H. 0.035, D. 0.049, D. resting surface 0.032 m. Slightly chipped.

Shape as **103**; minimum diameter just below rim.

107. Coarse-ware pithos   Pl. 14

C-62-347. P.H. 0.187, est. D. *ca.* 0.85 m. Two fragments (joining but too heavy and large for mending) from wall and rim. Heavy inclusions, thin slip, through which inclusions show.

Vertical wall; projecting rim with straight diagonal outer face; short bevel to broad flat upper face. Exterior wall with grooves, deeply cut wavy line between them. Incised on rim: delta with alpha inside.

Classical

108. Coarse-ware mortar   Fig. 22, Pl. 14

C-64-436. L. of spout 0.07, p.L. of rim 0.138 m. One fragment of rim and spout. Small inclusions; no slip.

Shallow, open, convex wall; heavy projecting rim undercut from wall, rounded outer face rising to rounded lip, concave inner face continuous with interior wall; spout projecting from rim, open above, oval in plan, widening out. At inner break of bowl, increase in grits for grinding surface.

4th century

109. Chytra I or stewpot   Fig. 24, Pl. 14

C-64-433. P.H. 0.068, est. D. rim 0.14 m. Two joining fragments; part of shoulder, rim, flange preserved. Red cooking fabric.

Highly convex shoulder; diagonal, straight collar rim rising sharply from shoulder; rounded lip; slightly convex inner face of rim; rounded flange flaring in to bowl at inner base of rim. Three shallow horizontal grooves on shoulder. Traces of burning on both interior and exterior.

Rim and flange resemble chytra I; shoulder has stewpot profile. See discussion, p. 74 above.

Later 4th century?

110.   Casserole, type I   Pl. 14

C-64-434. P.H. 0.043, p.L. 0.104 m. One fragment of wall, shoulder, rim, flange, and handle. Gray-brown cooking fabric.

Shallow diagonal wall with little convexity; sharp turn to vertical shoulder; rim lightly set off (no strong groove), with slight outward flare ending in tapered lip; inner rounded flange 0.008 m. wide, rounded edge; round handle attached to rim, rising diagonally above it. Traces of burning on both interior and exterior.

4th century

111.   Casserole type I   Fig. 24, Pl. 14

C-65-547. P.H. 0.036, est. D. 0.16 m. One fragment of lower wall, shoulder, rim, flange; no handle. Gray cooking fabric.

Shallow diagonal wall with sharp carination to vertical shoulder; deep groove setting off diagonal flaring rim from wall; wide, well-defined flange.

4th century

112.   Casserole type II   Fig. 24, Pl. 14

C-64-435. P.H. 0.068, est. D. 0.27 m. One fragment of wall, shoulder, rim, flange, stub of handle. Orange cooking fabric.

Shallow wall, with slight convexity; rounded protruding shoulder; flaring rim with compound curve (convex to concave) terminating in slightly thickened rounded lip; interior flange, slightly rising rounded edge; stub of round handle, attached to shoulder, rising diagonally. Closest parallel: C-47-889 (*Corinth* VII, iii, no. 675, p. 126, not illustrated).

Mid-4th century

GROUP 7 (113–153)

Grid location P:24:25   Lot 880   Pit B (Pit 1961-1)   Pl. 1:b

11.83 kg. (4.48 kg. inventoried)
  oinochoai: 0.25 kg. (6: 1 squat, 3 olpai, 2 ribbed)
  kotylai and skyphoi: 1.5 kg. (13 kotylai: 1 semiglazed, 5 Conventionalizing, 7 plain; 8 black-glazed skyphoi)
  cups and bowls: 1.3 kg. (7 one-handlers; 2 small echinus bowls, 4 beveled-rim bowls, 2 with thickened rim, 2 small
        semiglazed bowls, 2 unglazed)
  phialai: 0.5 kg. (17)
  saucers: 0.8 kg. (10)
  pyxides and lekanides: 0.41 kg. (4 lekanis bowls, 3 lids, 3 powder pyxides, 5 stands)
  miscellaneous fine wares: 0.2 kg. (1 unguentarium, 1 hydria, 2 plates)
  small hydriai: 0.29 kg. (5)
  kalathiskoi: 1.55 kg. (61: 5 flaring, 8 type 3, 1 small type 3, 47 type 4)
  miscellaneous votives: 0.4 kg. (13: 1 krateriskos, 6 jugs, 1 kotyle, 2 bowls, 1 kanoun, 1 dish, 1 aryballos)
  offering trays: 0.38 kg. (17)
  Attic fabric: 0.35 kg. (7)
  coarse ware: 0.8 kg. (2 mortars)
  cooking fabric: 3.05 kg. (4 pitchers, 4 unflanged pots, 4 lopades, 1 dish, 5 lids, 1 uncertain)
  lamps: 0.05 kg. (1)

In the eastern room of the Trapezoidal Stoa on the Middle Terrace was a sacrificial pit[14] containing a great deal of pottery: votives, fine wares, kitchen material, and figurines.[15] All the later datable pottery appears in the catalogue.

Unlike Pits A and E (Groups 5 and 4), Pit B was used for animal sacrifice. The pit measured 1.00 × 0.85 m. and was filled with ash to bedrock. The stone walls were burnt; the bones in the fill were from young pigs and goats. The pottery, including many intact votive kalathiskoi, was without stratigraphy. It was apparently dumped into the pit at one time. Since the pit contained both votive and dining-room material, one might hypothesize that in the mid-3rd century the use of the pit for holocaust sacrifice ceased

[14] Stroud, *Hesperia* 34, 1965, pp. 10–11. A few of the vases, **129–133, 151,** are published in *Corinth* VII, iii, deposit no. 45, p. 211.
[15] Figurines: MF 10486–MF 10494, MF 10496–MF 10505, MF 10934, MF 11239, MF 11261, MF 11338–MF 11342, and MF 13805; also cover tile FC 95 and pan tile FP 245.

and it became a convenient bothros for discarding the vases. Very few of the pots show any burning, and so a ritual involving casting pottery into the pit during sacrifices of pigs seems precluded.

Most of the pottery seems to date from the late 4th century, with a few pieces going into the 3rd. If the building containing the pit was built in the early 3rd century (see Group 6), the votives and food vessels thrown into the pit would date from the early period of building use and could also come from neighboring buildings. The latest material in the pit consists of a few of the saucers, especially **132** and **133**, and the Attic skyphos **116**.

It has been argued that some of the saucers belong to the first quarter of the 2nd century.[16] The profiles do not appear to be that late. Moreover, there is evidence for proposing a terminal date before the middle of the 3rd century for the pit. There are no moldmade relief-bowl fragments, no West Slope sherds, no Corinthian kantharoi; none of the characteristic later Hellenistic vessels were found in the pit, types which can be found in other strata of the Sanctuary (see Groups 8–11). The votive vessels that became popular in the later Hellenistic period, the small powder pyxides and the later forms of small hydriai, are also conspicuously absent.

Consequently, most of the material is contemporary with Group 6. A few later pieces give the terminal date of this group in the first half of the 3rd century.

113. Plain kotyle   Fig. 6, Pl. 15

C-61-427. H. 0.076, D. 0.088, D. foot 0.038 m. Many joining fragments; vertical profile complete; plaster restoration.

Low false ring foot; nippled undersurface; tall convex wall with slight inturn to rounded lip; two loop handles, set horizontally. Undecorated. Wheel grooves on surface.
End of 4th century

114. Plain kotyle   Fig. 6, Pl. 15

C-61-209. H. 0.056, D. 0.069, D. resting surface 0.031 m. Intact; warped.

Nearly flat resting surface; tall convex flaring wall, becoming vertical to rounded lip; two pinched-on handles at lip. Undecorated. Stacking line on upper wall.
First quarter 3rd century

115. Skyphos   Fig. 7, Pl. 15

C-61-426. H. 0.086, D. 0.078, D. foot 0.04 m. One handle, part of upper wall restored in plaster.
Cited: Williams, *Hesperia* 48, 1979, p. 124, under no. 35, where it is erroneously listed as C-1961-246.

Low torus foot; nippled undersurface; stemmed lower wall; compound curve to convex upper wall; flaring lip; round handle set on upper wall, slightly canted; contracted handle roots. Peeling black glaze overall.
End of 4th century

116. Attic skyphos   Fig. 7, Pl. 15

C-61-206. H. 0.102, D. 0.104, D. foot 0.044 m. Many joining fragments; vertical profile complete; plaster restoration.
Published: Stroud, *Hesperia* 34, 1965, pl. 3:a, left.

Shape as **115** but with greater stem, more abrupt curve to upper wall. Black glazed overall, except ledge of foot; undersurface reserved with two glaze circles.
For parallel: Miller, *Hesperia* 43, 1974, p. 231, no. 19, pl. 31.
Late first or second quarter 3rd century

117. Phiale   Pl. 15

C-61-418. H. 0.023, D. 0.101 m. Complete profile; plaster restoration.

Narrow resting surface; shallow central depression; low, flaring convex wall; slightly inturned rim; low, rounded button omphalos well offset from floor. Undecorated. Similar to **173** and **432**.
End of 4th century

118. Phiale   Fig. 9, Pl. 15

C-61-417. H. 0.018, D. 0.108 m. Complete profile; plaster restoration.

Resting surface and wall as **117**; slight articulation of outward thickened rim, set off by groove below; rounded omphalos, not well offset from floor. Undecorated.
Early 3rd century

119. Phiale   Pl. 15

C-61-374. H. 0.011, D. 0.054 m. Intact.

Flat resting surface with string marks; no central depression; low, straight flaring wall; rounded lip; low nipple omphalos. Undecorated. Similar to **175** (Group 9).
Early 3rd century

120. Attic kantharos   Pl. 15

C-61-470. P.L. 0.046 m. One fragment from upper wall, part of handle.

---

[16] *Corinth* VII, iii, p. 44: **130**, no. 186 therein, is dated to the early first quarter of the 2nd century.

On upper part of strap handle, attached satyr mask. The kantharos was the articulated form. Black glaze overall, peeling. Mask very worn.

For parallel: R. S. Young, "*Sepulturae intra urbem*," *Hesperia* 22, 1951 (pp. 67–134), p. 129, pyre 13, nos. 3 and 4, pl. 54.

Early 3rd century

121. One-handled cup, type 1   Pl. 15

C-61-467. H. 0.049, est. D. 0.09, D. foot 0.04 m. Three joining fragments; half preserved, no handle.

Ring foot; nippled undersurface; convex flaring wall turning vertical to rounded lip. Interior glazed; top third of exterior glazed by dipping. Similar type 1 cup in group: C-61-468.

Late example, probably towards end of 4th century

122. One-handled cup, type 2   Fig. 11, Pl. 15

C-61-208. H. 0.045–0.048, D. 0.089, D. foot 0.046 m. Complete.

Low ring foot; nippled undersurface; low, convex wall turning up to flattened lip; loop handle set at top of wall with roots contracted. Originally glazed overall, peeled.

Ca. 300 B.C.

123. One-handled cup, type 2   Pl. 15

C-61-421. H. 0.052, rest. D. 0.09, D. foot 0.046 m. Most of wall, much of handle restored in plaster.

Shape as **122** but higher profile. Wall contracts noticeably to flattened lip; contracted handle roots. Glazed overall.

Ca. 300 B.C. or slightly later

124. Small echinus bowl   Fig. 12, Pl. 16

C-61-213. H. 0.039, D. 0.069, D. foot 0.038 m. Intact.

Flaring ring foot; nippled undersurface; convex flaring wall turning continuously to rounded lip. Originally glazed overall, peeled.

Last quarter 4th century

125. Small echinus bowl   Fig. 12, Pl. 16

C-61-423. H. 0.028–0.031, rest. D. 0.067, D. foot 0.04 m. Half restored in plaster.

Very low ring foot; slightly nippled undersurface; convex flaring wall turning in strongly to rounded lip. No trace of glaze. Wider profile than **124**.

First quarter 3rd century

126. Bowl   Fig. 12, Pl. 16

C-61-384. H. 0.039, D. 0.105, D. foot 0.048 m. Part of wall restored in plaster.

Small ring foot; nippled undersurface; convex flaring wall turning in to tapered lip. Unglazed; wheel marks on surface; stacking line on exterior. Unglazed version of echinus bowl?

Probably 4th century

127. Small bowl, beveled rim   Fig. 13, Pl. 16

C-61-450. H. 0.027, D. 0.087, D. foot 0.047 m. One third missing including center of floor; restored in plaster.

Ring foot with wheel groove on interior face; straight flaring wall; sharp bevel, turning in to tapered lip. Peeling black glaze overall.

First or early second quarter 3rd century

128. Small bowl, beveled rim   Fig. 13, Pl. 16

C-61-215. H. 0.025, D. 0.084, D. foot 0.048 m. Slightly chipped.

Shape as **127** but slightly wider bevel, nippled undersurface. Peeling glaze overall. Higher profile than **127**.

First or early second quarter 3rd century

129. Saucer   Fig. 15, Pl. 16

C-61-381. H. 0.033, D. 0.152, D. foot 0.068 m. Three joining fragments, half preserved; plaster restoration.

Published: *Corinth* VII, iii, no. 146, p. 43.

Low, vertical ring foot; slightly nippled undersurface; wide convex wall, ending in slightly tapered lip. Glazed overall.

Third quarter 4th century

130. Saucer   Fig. 15, Pl. 16

C-61-383. H. 0.030–0.033, D. 0.114, D. foot 0.044 m. Three joining fragments; one third of wall restored in plaster.

Published: *Corinth* VII, iii, no. 186, p. 44.

Shape as **129**; lower rounded foot; strong nipple, less convex wall; rounded lip. Interior glazed; one half of exterior glazed by dipping.

First quarter 3rd century

131. Saucer   Fig. 15, Pl. 16

C-61-425. H. 0.034, rest. D. 0.118, D. foot 0.052 m. One fragment, preserving one third of vase; plaster restoration.

Published: *Corinth* VII, iii, no. 184, p. 44.

Shape as **129**; thicker foot, less convexity to wall. Peeling black glaze overall.

First or early second quarter 3rd century

132. Saucer   Fig. 15, Pl. 16

C-61-424. H. 0.033–0.035, D. 0.128, D. foot 0.048 m. One fragment, preserving two thirds of vase; plaster restoration.

Published: *Corinth* VII, iii, no. 181, p. 44.

Ring foot; uneven exterior, flat resting surface, concave diagonal inner face of foot (proto-conical); nippled undersurface; wide, wheel-ridged wall, slightly convex; rounded lip. Interior glazed; most of exterior glazed by dipping, but peeling.

Second quarter 3rd century

133. Saucer   Fig. 15, Pl. 16

C-61-382. H. 0.038–0.04, D. 0.135, D. foot 0.049 m. Two joining fragments; half restored in plaster.
Published: *Corinth* VII, iii, no. 179, p. 44.

Shape and glaze as **132**; glaze peeling, wheel-ridged exterior.

Second quarter 3rd century

134. Unguentarium   Pl. 16

C-61-469. P.H. 0.053, D. rim 0.043 m. Three joining fragments preserving part of shoulder, neck, rim. Thin fabric (0.002 m. at shoulder), resembling blister ware: gray-to-orange core, with orange and white particles throughout the fabric, creating swirls of orange and white on the surface.

Sloping shoulder; tall narrow neck; sharp flaring rim, lip projecting inward.
Profile of an early bulbous unguentarium. Thin fabric close to Hellenistic blister ware; see **477, 478**. For shape, see discussion, pp. 55–56.

Early 3rd century?

135. Attic guttus askos   Fig. 18, Pl. 16

C-61-214. H. 0.086, D. 0.087, D. foot 0.066, D. rim 0.043 m. Part of lower wall restored.
Published: Stroud, *Hesperia* 34, 1965, pl. 3:a, center.

Low ring foot with wide resting surface; flat undersurface; low ovoid wall, narrowing to shoulder; well-defined shoulder ridge; sloping shoulder merging with tall concave neck; wide-flaring, overhanging rim, convex on upper face; one ring handle, with two vertical grooves, attached on upper wall below shoulder ridge. Black glazed overall.
See *Agora* XII, no. 1194, pl. 39. **135** does not have so tall a neck as the askos from Menon's cistern: Miller, *Hesperia* 43, 1974, p. 231, no. 21, pl. 31, first quarter 3rd century. There is no Corinthian version of the shape known.

Third quarter 4th century

136. Lekanis   Pl. 16

C-61-451. H. 0.031, D. 0.086, D. foot 0.041 m. Six joining fragments; part of flange missing.

Ring foot, unevenly made; nippled undersurface; straight flaring wall, slightly carinated about midpoint; change of direction to flat rim, slightly outward thickened; low inset flange rising diagonally to interior; parts of two handles: pinched-on lumps of clay. Poor surface finish. Undecorated.
For the shape: *Corinth* XIII, pp. 147–148; *Corinth* VII, iii, pp. 94–96. Closest parallel: C-53-248, from well 1953-2, unpublished.

Early 3rd century

137. Lekanis lid   Pl. 16

C-61-211. H. 0.04, D. 0.08 m. Four joining fragments; chipped.

Flat knob, slightly concave on top; short thick stem; domed lid; rounded lip. Two steps cut around knob; two light grooves near outer edge. **137** fits **136** very well, although no adjusting marks visible. The quality of **137** is higher than that of **136**.

Early 3rd century

138. Small hydria   Fig. 1, Pl. 17

C-61-447. H. 0.081, D. 0.056, D. foot 0.033 m. One side handle, part of foot missing.

High false ring foot; ledge on upper foot; high ovoid body; slightly offset sloping shoulder; short straight neck, flaring to heavy horizontal rim with peaked lip; vertical round handle from shoulder to top of neck; two side handles set well below shoulder, of 90° form. Clay fired partly orange. Earlier profile than **99** (Group 6).

Mid-4th century

139. Miniature jug   Pl. 17

C-61-210. H. 0.063, D. 0.058, D. foot 0.037 m. Intact.

Disk foot; high ovoid wall merging with sloping shoulder; short concave neck not set off from shoulder; flaring rim; vertical strap handle from shoulder to rim. Upper half of jug glazed by dipping. Similar in Group 7: C-61-204.
See T 2483 (*Corinth* XIII, grave 457-3, pl. 75).

Third quarter 4th century

140. Miniature jug   Pl. 17

C-61-422. H. 0.042, D. 0.041, D. resting surface 0.032 m. Intact.

Flat resting surface; low, ovoid wall narrowing to slightly concave neck; flaring rim with rounded lip; round handle from wall to rim. Undecorated.
Possibly related to the oinochoe with shoulder stop (see p. 18) but without the trefoil mouth. The wall of **140** sags more than the examples in Group 8, **166** and **167**.

Early 3rd century?

141. Kalathiskos, type 4   Fig. 5, Pl. 17

C-61-379. H. 0.043, D. 0.049, D. foot 0.031 m. Intact.

Vestigial disk foot; rounded bevel; straight wall narrowing to flaring rim convex on outer face; peaked lip; two pinched-on handles at midwall.

142.   Kalathiskos, type 4

C-61-441. H. 0.037, D. 0.05, D. resting surface 0.03 m. Slightly chipped.

Flat resting surface; concave flare to rounded bevel; wall narrowing to strong flaring rim, convex on upper face; peaked lip; no handles. Similar in Group 7: C-61-376.

143.   Kalathiskos, type 4   Pl. 17

C-61-377. H. 0.032, D. 0.049, D. resting surface 0.031 m. Slightly chipped.

Shape as **142**, more horizontally flaring rim; rounded lip; no handles. Similar in Group 7: C-61-434, C-61-437.

144.   Kalathiskos, type 4   Pl. 17

C-61-445. H. 0.038, D. 0.053, D. resting surface 0.031 m. Part of rim missing.

Flat resting surface; low, rounded bevel; straight vertical wall; flaring diagonal rim, concave on upper face; rounded lip; two pinched-on handles at midwall. Similar in Group 7: C-61-444.

145.   Kalathiskos, type 4

C-61-442. H. 0.043, D. 0.054, D. foot 0.038 m. Intact.

Shape as above, with disk foot. Similar in Group 7: C-61-378, C-61-435.

146.   Kalathiskos, type 4   Pl. 17

C-61-433. H. 0.035, D. 0.049, D. foot 0.03 m. Intact.

Shape as above; wall merging with rim; no handles.

147.   Kalathiskos, type 4

C-61-436. H. 0.037, D. 0.049, D. foot 0.028 m. Intact.

Shape as above; narrower foot, more rounded bevel.

148.   Kalathiskos, type 4   Fig. 5, Pl. 17

C-61-440. H. 0.038, D. 0.051, D. foot 0.037 m. Intact.

Shape as above, with slightly concave wall.

149.   Kalathiskos, type 4   Fig. 5, Pl. 17

C-61-446. H. 0.038–0.041, D. 0.051, D. foot 0.032 m. Intact.

Shape as above, with higher foot. Traces of burning on rim; thickness of interior irregular. Similar in Group 7: C-61-438, C-61-439, C-61-443.

150.   Miniature aryballos   Pl. 17

C-61-207. H. 0.037, D. 0.046 m. Half of mouth missing.

Flat resting surface; low, ovoid wall; low neck; flaring rim; rounded lip; handle from shoulder to mouth. Upper area glazed; wall scored with irregular diagonal incisions. Miniature imitation of blister-ware aryballos.

Late 4th century

151.   Cooking-fabric pitcher   Fig. 23

C-61-385. Rest. H. 0.217, D. 0.205, D. rim 0.112 m. Many joining fragments; holes restored in plaster including resting surface. Red cooking fabric; traces of burning.

Published: Stroud, *Hesperia* 34, 1965, pl. 3:b; *Corinth* VII, iii, no. 736, p. 142.

Central depression on bottom not preserved but originally narrow and shallow; tall globular wall; slight offset for concave neck; flaring triangular rim without articulation from neck; flat strap handle springing from upper wall, rising level to rim attachment.

For parallel: C-72-120 (Williams and Fisher, *Hesperia* 42, 1973, p. 24, no. 23, pl. 11) dated third or fourth quarter of 4th century by context. **151** has a more flaring rim.

152.   Cooking-fabric pitcher   Pl. 17

C-61-492. P.H. 0.198, est. D. 0.19, D. rim 0.106 m. Many joining fragments, preserving parts of wall and shoulder, all of neck, rim, and handle. Red-brown cooking fabric; traces of burning.

Wall shape as **151**, depression not preserved; less offset to shoulder; lower concave neck, thinner rim, with slight flattening of upper face. Later than **151** by rim change.

Probably early 3rd century

153.   Cooking-fabric bowl or   Fig. 24, Pl. 17
          saucepan

C-61-386. H. 0.068–0.081 (depression not in center); D. 0.216 m. Many joining fragments; full profile; holes in wall restored in plaster. Red cooking fabric; burnt on exterior and interior.

Published: Stroud, *Hesperia* 34, 1965, pl. 3:c.

Shallow central depression; low, slightly convex flaring wall, turning to rounded rim, descending diagonally into bowl; two grooves on exterior wall; two horizontal handles, rectilinear in section, attached below grooves, set slightly canted, square in plan.

Similar profile: C-47-870 (*Corinth* VII, iii, p. 129) but with stronger grooving and flatter rim; looped, not square, handles, placed at rim. Shape related to fine-ware lekanis.

Later 4th century?

GROUP 8 (154–172)

Grid location N–O:17–18   Lot 3217   Votive deposit overlying Building N–O:17–18 (Pit 1965-1)   Pl. 3:b

12.05 kg. (1.45 kg. inventoried)
amphoras: 0.15 kg. (1)
oinochoai: 0.3 kg. (7: 3 small globular, 1 handle only, 3 squat)
kotylai, skyphoi, and other drinking vessels: 0.9 kg. (16: 5 plain kotylai, 2 ray based, 2 ovoid; 3 black-glazed skyphoi;
        3 kantharos handles; 1 Archaic cup)
phialai: 0.2 kg. (8)
bowls: 0.45 kg. (13: 3 plain, 2 semiglazed, 1 with beveled rim, 1 small echinus, 4 small semiglazed, 2 stands)
saucers: 0.15 kg. (3)
lekanides: 0.2 kg. (4)
"feeders": 0.25 kg. (5)
miscellaneous fine wares: 0.4 kg. (9: 1 Geometric fragment, 1 blister-ware oinochoe, 1 blister-ware aryballos, 2
        plates, 1 pitcher, 3 uncertain)
small hydriai: 2.3 kg. (41)
kalathiskoi: 1.25 kg. (48: 3 flaring, 5 type 3, 40 type 4)
miscellaneous votives: 0.3 kg. (10: 3 krateriskoi, 1 oinochoe, 3 jugs, 1 lid, 1 dish, 1 aryballos)
offering trays: 0.2 kg. (7)
Attic fabric: 0.4 kg. (6)
coarse wares: 2.7 kg. (10: 3 amphoras, 1 hydria, 3 lekanai, 1 basin, 1 mortar, 1 uncertain)
cooking fabric: 1.5 kg. (14: 1 lekane, 1 pitcher, 3 flanged pots, 5 unflanged pots, 2 lopades, 2 lids)
lamps: 0.4 kg. (9)

Group 8 was found at the southern edge of the Lower Terrace to the west of the stone stairway. The deposit lay over the remains of Building N–O:17–18, whose east wall formed the eastern boundary for the pottery and other objects. On the south the limit was a line of tiles and a slab of poros, set on edge, running 1.15 m. west to east. The north limit was a line of fallen stones, 0.90 m. north of the tile barrier; fallen stones and tiles formed a similar western limit. But the boundaries did not define a constructed pit like those of Groups 4, 5, and 7.

The pottery appeared to have been thrown in, already broken. There was carbon in the fill; in the southwest corner of the area was a considerable amount of burnt earth as well as a few burnt sherds (some with burning over the broken edges). At some point the western limit collapsed, and some of the vessels were dislodged, to be recovered from where they scattered west of the boundary. More pots were found high up in the fill, next to the broken tiles of the western boundary. Clearly the area was disturbed, not sealed in any fashion. The greatest mass of material was found along the western limits, some in the center, less along the south and east sides.

The deposit is composed mostly of fine wares, some kitchen material, figurines, and a few lamps.[17] Most of the pottery is votive, with a high percentage of type 4 kalathiskoi and small hydriai. All the datable material appears in the catalogue; there are additional fragments of kantharoi, skyphoi, and bowls. There are also earlier fragments: scraps of 6th- and 5th-century vessels, and a late Attic black-figured kylix with a graffito, 159.

The saucer, 162, kalathiskoi, 168–171, and hydriai, 163–165, require a date later than comparable material from Group 7; but the hydriai do not show the extreme profile of those in Group 9. The date, therefore, should lie between the two groups; the pottery was discarded perhaps in the third quarter of the 3rd century.

---

[17] Lamp: L 4813, type 25. Figurines: MF 12534—MF 12536, MF 13408, MF 13420, MF 13431, MF 13479.

154.   Globular oinochoe   Fig. 3, Pl. 18

C-65-602. H. 0.093, D. 0.065, D. foot 0.035 m. Part of mouth missing.

Disk foot; globular wall merging with shoulder; short concave neck; cutaway mouth; handle from shoulder to mouth with pellets at mouth attachment. Unglazed.
Later 3rd century

155.   Globular oinochoe   Pl. 18

C-65-603. H. 0.079, D. 0.054, D. foot 0.032 m. Back of mouth, handle missing.

Shape as **154** but with higher, more flaring foot; vertical rim.
Both **154** and **155** show profiles similar to the hydriai in Group 8.
3rd century

156.   Wide-necked pitcher   Fig. 4, Pl. 18

C-65-608. P.H. 0.128, D. rim 0.085 m. Many joining fragments; part of shoulder, handle, neck, rim preserved; plaster restoration.

Narrow, sloping shoulder; tall cylindrical neck with ring at area of handle attachment; slightly flaring rim; rounded thickened lip; vertical strap handle from shoulder to upper neck. Exterior surface originally polished; no decoration.
See *Corinth* VII, iii, pp. 112–113. For close parallel: C-1976-114, from fill in basin room, lot 1976-101 (Williams, *Hesperia* 46, 1977, p. 52 for this fill), unpublished.
3rd century

157.   Plain kotyle   Pl. 18

C-65-592. H. 0.056, est. D. lip 0.084, D. foot 0.034 m. One fragment preserving vertical profile, part of one handle.

Flat resting surface; tall, convex flaring wall, turning concave before rounded lip; part of one pinched-on handle. Very contracted base.
See C-75-285 (from well 1975-5: Williams, *Hesperia* 46, 1977, p. 68, no. 5, pl. 24).
First quarter 3rd century

158.   Skyphos   Fig. 7, Pl. 18

C-65-606. P.H. 0.07, D. foot 0.041 m. Four joining fragments; foot, lower wall, beginning of upper wall preserved.

Small torus foot; nippled undersurface; compound-curve wall with stemmed lower body; strong change to convex upper body. Black glazed overall except for miltos at base of wall, on resting surface, between glazed circles of undersurface. Very stemmed body, thick bottom. See late example in Group 7, **116**, Attic.
Late first or second quarter 3rd century

159.   Attic black-figured kylix   Pl. 18

C-65-294. P.H. 0.038, D. foot 0.085 m. Foot, floor preserved.

Wide stem foot with flat upper face, slightly flaring vertical face; hollow conical stem, continuous with foot and bowl; no rings or grooves on stem. Resting surface reserved; lower stem interior glazed, upper reserved; outer edge of foot reserved; outer stem glazed. On floor: satyr running right (tail tip at left break), left arm holding torch(?). On outer edge of resting surface, graffito:
CΜΙΚΥΘΙΟΝ[. . .]Ν ΜΕ
interrupted by break at foot.
For shape: Vanderpool, *Hesperia* 15, 1946, p. 309, nos. 187, 188, pls. 56, 58.
Early 5th century

160.   Semiglazed bowl   Pl. 18

C-65-607. P.H. 0.051, est. D. lip 0.13 m. Two joining fragments from upper wall and rim.

Deep convex wall; concave rim; rounded lip. Glazed inside; added-red bands on lip, below rim on exterior.
Probably early 3rd century

161.   Small bowl, beveled rim   Fig. 13, Pl. 18

C-65-604. H. 0.029, est. D. 0.084, D. foot 0.039 m. Two joining fragments; vertical profile complete, one third preserved.

Ring foot with angled outer face; nippled undersurface; straight flaring wall; sharp bevel turning in to tapered lip. Black glaze overall, thin and peeling.
Mid-3rd century

162.   Saucer   Fig. 15, Pl. 18

C-65-591. H. 0.036, est. D. 0.135, D. foot 0.052 m. Two joining fragments; vertical profile complete, one third preserved.

Ring foot, round on outer face; nippled undersurface; convex wall with change of direction at midwall; rounded lip. Glazed interior; most of exterior glazed by dipping. Poor surface finish; glaze fired red.
Second quarter or mid-3rd century

163.   Small hydria   Pl. 18

C-65-599. P.H. 0.094, D. 0.075, D. foot 0.036 m. Many joining fragments; part of neck, whole rim, vertical handle, part of one side handle missing.

Narrow ring foot; high ovoid wall; sloping shoulder offset from wall; narrow concave neck; two side handles on upper wall of 90° form. Profile similar to **99** of Group 6. The later form is shown in the next two examples.
Early 3rd century

164. Small hydria   Fig. 1, Pl. 18

C-65-600. H. 0.09, D. 0.063, D. foot 0.032 m. Part of rim missing.

False ring foot; high, ovoid body, merging with shoulder; concave neck; flaring horizontal rim; two pinched-on side handles just below shoulder; round vertical handle from shoulder to below rim.

Mid-3rd century

165. Small hydria   Pl. 18

C-65-601. H. 0.072, D. 0.054, D. foot 0.028 m. Part of rim missing.

Shape as **164** but higher foot, grooved outer edge of rim; side handles at shoulder of 90° form; flattened vertical handle.

Mid-3rd century

166. Miniature jug   Pl. 18

C-65-593. H. 0.034, D. 0.041, D. resting surface 0.03 m. Slightly chipped.

Flat resting surface; low, ovoid wall; wall tapering to flaring rounded rim, grooved on under face; strap handle from upper wall to mouth.

167. Miniature jug   Pl. 18

C-65-594. H. 0.036, D. 0.034, D. foot 0.026 m. Intact.

Shape as **166**, with maximum diameter slightly higher on wall; rim with more diagonal flare. Both **166** and **167** are similar to, though slightly later than, **140** of Group 7.

168. Kalathiskos, type 4   Pl. 18

C-65-595. H. 0.038, D. 0.051, D. resting surface 0.032 m. Part of wall, rim missing.

Flat resting surface; low, rounded bevel; nearly vertical wall with two pinched-on handles; flaring rim; rounded lip.

169. Kalathiskos, type 4   Pl. 18

C-65-596. H. 0.043, D. 0.051, D. resting surface 0.029 m. Intact.

Shape as **168** but taller, slightly concave wall; no handles.

170. Kalathiskos, type 4   Pl. 18

C-65-598. H. 0.032, D. 0.047, D. resting surface 0.03 m. Intact.

Shape as above, more vertical wall. Burnt inside and out. **170** has the profile most typical of the kalathiskoi in the group.

171. Kalathiskos, type 4   Fig. 5, Pl. 18

C-65-597. H. 0.037, D. 0.051, D. resting surface 0.03 m. Part of upper wall, rim missing.

Shape as above; less flaring rim, very slight bevel. The latest of the kalathiskoi in Group 8.

172. Unflanged cooking pot   Pl. 19

C-65-651. P.H. 0.124, D. 0.16, D. rim 0.102–0.105 m. Many joining fragments; parts of wall, shoulder, rim, all of handle preserved. Orange cooking fabric, fired gray on exterior; white particles in the fabric; no burnishing strokes. Burnt on exterior.

High, ovoid wall; sloping, slightly concave shoulder only lightly offset from wall; flaring rim convex below, offset from shoulder, nearly flat on vertical face; one strap handle, convex on outer face, attached at lower shoulder and at rim, rising slightly above rim. Transitional to later type, without the typical flat rim.

Probably third or fourth quarter 4th century

GROUP 9 (173–184)

Grid location S–T:21   Lot 6503   Hydria dump of stepped theatral area   Pl. 3:c

5.63 kg. (0.98 kg. inventoried)
  kotylai and skyphoi: 0.4 kg. (15: 3 ray-based kotylai, 1 semiglazed, 2 plain, 1 banded; 3 late black-glazed skyphoi,
        5 uncertain)
  phialai: 0.2 kg. (4)
  saucers and plates: 0.4 kg. (6: 4 saucers; 1 Conventionalizing plate, 1 Hellenistic plate)
  pyxides and lekanides: 0.53 kg. (20: 15 powder pyxides and lids, 2 lekanis lids, 1 Hellenistic lid, 2 stands)
  miscellaneous fine wares: 0.45 kg. (9: 4 Conventionalizing oinochoai, 2 plain bowls, 1 banded bowl, 1 kanoun,
        1 pierced cylindrical vessel)
  small hydriai: 1.4 kg. (16)
  kalathiskoi: 0.3 kg. (12: 6 type 3, 5 type 4, 1 uncertain)
  miscellaneous votives: 0.5 kg. (20: 3 krateriskoi, 4 jugs, 4 dishes, 9 offering trays)
  cooking wares: 0.45 kg. (1 hydria handle, 1 pitcher, 1 unflanged pot, 1 stewpot[?], 1 lid)
  lamps: 1.0 kg. (24)

Group 9 is made up primarily of small votive vessels and terracotta figurines.[18] It was found on the Upper Terrace, in the small stepped theatral area, in a pocket of earth at the east end of step 5, caught in the angle of the step and bedrock. The material was apparently thrown down, without any care. There were no traces of burning. The findspot is about 10 meters south of Group 1.

The material contains quite a few earlier sherds from the 6th and 5th centuries and two intrusive Roman fragments; but much of the pottery, particularly the votives, dates from the late 4th to the late 3rd century, probably deposited by 200 B.C. Other material includes a late 4th-century coin (Pegasos/Trident, coin 70-129) and a number of lamp fragments, one of which seems to be a variant of type 28 B.[19]

Kalathiskoi and small hydriai are the predominant shapes, but the hydriai are conspicuously later than most of the kalathiskoi. They become a primary votive type in the Hellenistic period. Small pyxides and other votive shapes are also well represented. There is kitchen material but not much proportionately of customary dining-room vessels. Kantharoi and moldmade relief bowls are absent,[20] and there are relatively few kotylai and skyphoi. Moreover, much of the non-votive fine ware is earlier than the latest material, represented by the small hydriai and powder pyxides. These peculiarities suggest that the group is a secondary dump, the votive material taken from some cult area (?) and discarded in fill with earlier sherds, which was then moved to this second area.

173. Phiale   Pl. 19

C-70-563. H. 0.021, est. D. 0.11 m. One half preserved.

Narrow resting surface; good central depression; convex flaring wall; groove at top articulating outward thickened rim; low, wide, flat button omphalos; ridge on floor around omphalos. String marks on bottom. Undecorated.
    Similar to **117** (Group 7) and **432**.
    Late 4th or early 3rd century

174. Phiale   Fig. 9, Pl. 19

C-70-564. H. 0.017, D. 0.09 m. Intact.

Very narrow resting surface, limited to area around shallow central depression; straight flaring wall, turning up and becoming slightly concave below flat rim; slightly rounded omphalos. Undecorated.
    Later 3rd century

175. Phiale   Pl. 19

C-70-565. H. 0.011, D. 0.054 m. Rim chipped.

Flat resting surface with string marks; no central depression; straight flaring wall, turning in slightly to rounded lip; nipple omphalos. Undecorated.
    Similar to but shallower than small example from Group 7: **119**.
    Mid-3rd century

176. Saucer   Fig. 15, Pl. 19

C-70-520. H. 0.041, est. D. 0.178, D. foot 0.06 m. Three joining fragments; complete profile.

Ring foot, almost vertical on outer face, wide resting surface, diagonal inner face; nippled undersurface; wide, convex flaring wall; rounded lip. Glazed inside; upper third of exterior wall glazed. Glaze fired red, peeling.
    Third to fourth quarter 3rd century

177. Plate with offset rim   Pl. 19

C-70-518. P.L. 0.044, est. D. 0.18 m. One rim fragment.

Slightly convex on upper surface; groove before rounded lip. Rim decoration of incised boxed rectangles, with X over rectangles. Originally glazed.
    A late West Slope design. See C-48-53 (*Corinth* VII, iii, no. 129, p. 40, pl. 45; well 1948-2).
    Fourth quarter 3rd century

178. Lid   Pl. 19

C-70-519. P.H. 0.028, est. D. 0.10 m. Three joining fragments; outer edge preserved; broken before knob.

Descending slope of lid, with little convexity, to vertical flange, not inset. Interior reserved; exterior glazed, fired mostly red. Two deep grooves on lid, 0.015 m. apart. Between grooves, running pattern of eggs in raised clay with added-white interior dots; between eggs, clusters of raised clay dots.
    Lid of similar shape but glazed inside, with similar grooves, decorated with West Slope pattern of ivy chain: C-34-36, from South Stoa Shop I, unpublished. C-34-36 is probably Attic; **178** is Corinthian.
    Late 3rd(?) century

---

[18] MF 70-27, MF 70-59, MF 70-64, MF 70-65.

[19] Lamp L 70-66. See R. H. Howland, *The Athenian Agora*, IV, *Greek Lamps and their Survivals*, Princeton 1958, nos. 401–405, pp. 93–94, pls. 14, 41, esp. no. 403. The Demeter lamp is neither Attic nor Corinthian, and certainly not of blister-ware fabric.

[20] The absence of moldmade bowls can not be used to help date the introduction of that form of Hellenistic vessel, since other Hellenistic material is also not present in the group, although certainly in existence.

179. Pyxis bowl   Pl. 19

C-70-566. H. 0.032, D. 0.054, D. resting surface 0.027 m. Slightly chipped.

Gently concave resting surface; straight flaring wall; vertical rim inset from horizontal flange above wall; tapered lip. Wheel grooves on surface.

Later 3rd century

180. Pyxis bowl   Fig. 19, Pl. 19

C-70-567. H. 0.023, D. 0.046, D. resting surface 0.029 m. Intact.

Disk foot, lower wall than that of **179**; slightly diagonal flange; vertical rim; tapered lip. Very uneven dimensions; poor finish. **181** is the lid.

Late 3rd century

181. Pyxis lid   Fig. 19, Pl. 19

C-70-568. H. 0.02, D. 0.048 m. One third of vertical flange missing.

Lightly domed top with two central grooves, sloping to projecting rim; vertical flange set in from rim. Poorly thrown; poor finish. **181** is the lid of **180**.

Late 3rd century

182. Small hydria   Fig. 1, Pl. 19

C-70-212. H. 0.122, D. 0.073, D. foot 0.034 m. Intact.

False ring foot; tall body; high, ovoid wall, merging with shoulder; tall, narrow concave neck, flaring to triangular rim; two smeared-on side handles; round vertical handle from shoulder to top of neck. Poor surface finish.

Second half 3rd century

183. Small hydria   Fig. 1, Pl. 19

C-70-213. H. 0.081, D. 0.058, D. foot 0.031 m. One slight chip from rim.

Shape as **182**; groove on neck is accidental.

Second half 3rd century

184. Small hydria   Fig. 1, Pl. 19

C-70-214. P.H. 0.098, D. 0.072, D. foot 0.037 m. Rim and vertical handle missing.

Shape as above but with greater maximum diameter in relation to foot diameter and height of wall. Very poor surface finish.

Late 3rd century

GROUP 10 (**185–190**)

Grid location L–M:28   Lot 6712   Pottery over the floor of room 2, Building L–M:28 (Ca)

4.25 kg. (0.7 kg. inventoried)

    kotylai and other drinking vessels: 0.4 kg. (18: 3 ray-based kotylai, 7 semiglazed, 2 plain; 5 late black-glazed sky-
        phoi; 1 kantharos)

    bowls: 0.3 kg. (6: 1 echinus, 2 semiglazed, 1 conical, 2 uncertain)

    saucers and plates: 0.45 kg. (7: 3 saucers; 2 fish plates, 1 offset-rim plate, 1 flat-rim plate)

    pyxides and lekanides: 0.15 kg. (4: 2 powder pyxides; 1 lekanis lid, 1 stand)

    miscellaneous fine wares: 0.4 kg. (1 krater, 2 Archaic oinochoai, 2 aryballoi, 2 "feeders", 2 offering trays)

    kalathiskoi: 0.3 kg. (15: 3 flaring, 2 type 2, 10 type 3)

    Attic fabric: 0.2 kg. (8 +)

    coarse and cooking ware: 2.05 kg. (1 amphora rim, 2 amphora toes, 3 pitchers, 1 jar, 1 cooking pot, 2 lopades)

Building L–M:28 is a dining-room complex on the Lower Terrace, built at the end of the 4th century after the earthquake(s) destroyed earlier dining rooms near by.[21] The building has three rooms; room 2 is the main dining area with couches placed against the walls, accommodating eight diners. The whole complex measures 8.05 × 7.80 m. Room 2 is 4.65–4.88 × 4.67 m.

The pottery of Group 10 represents the material on the floor of room 2, when the building went out of use in the mid-2nd century. The material was not sealed; fragments of three of the vessels were found in other levels of the complex.[22]

[21] The complex is discussed in Bookidis and Fisher, *Hesperia* 43, 1974, pp. 275–278, with fig. 4.

[22] **185**: joining fragment from lot 6713, layer 2 over floor in room 2; another joining fragment from lot 6715, layer 3 of same room. Both lots contain Roman material, of the early 1st century after Christ. **186**: joining fragments from lots 6716, from room 3, floor level; 6719, room 1 over the cistern; and 6722, the upper fill of the same cistern (cistern 1971-1). See Bookidis and Fisher, *Hesperia* 43, 1974, p. 277, note 16. **188**: joining fragment from lot 6715.

The amount of pottery found on the floor is not great. The lot contains fragments of earlier material, including Classical black-glazed sherds, blister ware, and figurines. There is also one 5th-century outline fragment, C-71-583 (not published). Only the latest material is included here, showing the kind of pottery used in the dining room during the Hellenistic period, up to the Mummian destruction. A coin of Philip V of Macedon (220–178 B.C.) from the stratum confirms the use date of the building.[23]

185. Large echinus bowl   Fig. 12

C-71-176. Joining fragments from lots 6713, 6715. **a)** P.H. 0.058 m. Six joining fragments, preserving parts of upper wall and lip. **b)** P.H. 0.05, est. D. lip 0.19 m. One fragment of upper wall and lip.

Wide, convex flaring wall, turning in to tapered lip. Streaky glaze on interior; upper exterior wall glazed by dipping. Steep angle of ascent of wall.

Later 3rd century

186. Semiglazed bowl   Fig. 12, Pl. 20

C-71-181. Joining fragments from lots 6716, 6719, 6722. H. 0.072, D. rim 0.157, D. foot 0.058 m. Many joining fragments; completed in plaster.

Published: Bookidis and Fisher, *Hesperia* 43, 1974, pl. 59.

Low, heavy ring foot; nippled undersurface; low, convex flaring wall with carination to concave rim; flaring tapered lip. Glazed inside; bands on upper rim and shoulder; glaze fired red, peeling. Foot not very contracted.

Mid- or third quarter 3rd century

187. Conical bowl   Fig. 12, Pl. 20

C-71-585. Restored height of whole 0.065 m. **a)** D. base 0.034 m. One fragment of base of bowl. **b)** P.W. 0.04 m. One fragment of lower wall. **c)** P.H. 0.07, est. D. lip 0.18 m. Seven joining fragments of wall and lip. **d)** P.W. 0.04 m. Two joining fragments of lip.

Low ring foot articulated from exterior wall by scraped groove; nippled undersurface; flaring wall only slightly convex; rounded lip. Interior glazed, fired red (deliberate?); exterior glaze a thin black, peeling; only stain of added white remaining.

Order of fragments and restored decoration established by comparison with similar bowls: C-34-37 and C-47-107 (*Corinth* VII, iii, nos. 532 and 536, pp. 91–92, pls. 40, 55). In base of bowl, incised tendrils between (missing) white petals. Lowest wall zone, white pendent dotted buds with incised scallops below. Middle zone, incised wavy tendrils. Zone at top of wall, incised boxed rectangles, interrupted by checkerboard of red and white squares. Each decorative zone divided by grooves.

Ca. 200 B.C.

188. Fish plate with beveled rim   Fig. 16, Pl. 20

C-71-177. Joining fragment from lot 6715. P.H. 0.063, est. D. 0.19 m. Five joining fragments of upper wall, rim.

Convex flaring wall; projecting horizontal rim with slightly convex upper face; rim set off from exterior wall by groove. Central depression not preserved. Thin glaze on interior; exterior wall glazed by dipping of upper half.

Identification as fish plate not secure; rim more strongly articulated than rim of flat-rim plate. See C-40-433 (*Corinth* VII, iii, no. 137, p. 42).

Early 2nd century?

189. Flat-rim plate   Fig. 16

C-71-178. P.H. 0.102, est. D. 0.25–0.26 m. Four joining fragments of upper wall, rim. Plaster restoration.

Straight flaring wall; horizontal rim slightly convex on upper face, set off from inner wall by groove. Lower break at beginning of turn to foot. Interior glazed; exterior wall glazed by dipping on upper part. Wheel grooves on interior.

No chronology is yet discernible for the flat-rim plate. Examples appear to be limited to the 2nd century. See *Corinth* VII, iii, pp. 37–38.

190. Unflanged cooking pot   Pl. 20

C-71-180. P.H. 0.12, D. rim 0.11 m. Many joining fragments; plaster restoration. Part of wall, neck, all of rim preserved. Red cooking fabric; encrusted.

Convex wall, probably globular profile, merging with slightly concave neck, without strong articulation of shoulder; projecting rim with vertical straight face, flat on upper face; slight peaking of outer lip; attachment of one handle to rim preserved. Wheelmade.

Although not completely preserved, **190** differs from the more usual profile of unflanged cooking pot by its more articulated rim and lack of shoulder. As yet, **190** has no identifiable parallels.

[23] Coin 71-222. See Bookidis and Fisher, *Hesperia* 43, 1974, pp. 298, 302, no. 49.

GROUP 11 (191–202)

Grid location M:16–17   Lot 3230   Fill in room 1 of Building M–N:16–17 (Northwest Stucco Building)

12.30 kg. (4.35 kg. inventoried)

    kraters and lekanai: 0.75 kg. (10: 3 Archaic, 3 plain, 1 West Slope; 3 lekanai)

    hydriai: 0.1 kg. (1)

    oinochoai: 0.25 kg. (10: 2 conical, 4 black figure, 2 Conventionalizing, 2 ribbed)

    kotylai and skyphoi: 0.4 kg. (11: 6 Archaic kotylai, 1 Conventionalizing; 4 late black-glazed skyphoi)

    kantharoi: 0.4 kg. (8: 1 molded rim, 1 hexamilia, 4 cyma, 2 articulated)

    moldmade relief bowls: 0.45 kg. (16 +)

    other bowls: 0.25 kg. (8: 2 echinus, 4 outturned rims, 2 beveled rims)

    saucers: 0.25 kg. (5)

    plates: 0.6 kg. (17: 1 Archaic, 2 Conventionalizing, 10 fish plates, 3 flat rim, 1 uncertain)

    pyxides: 0.5 kg. (10: 1 Archaic, 4 Conventionalizing, 5 powder pyxides)

    miscellaneous fine wares: 0.25 kg. (6: 1 askos, 2 Archaic aryballoi, 1 thymiaterion, 1 feeder, 1 handle)

    blister ware: 0.1 kg. (1 askos, 12 sherds of aryballoi, lamp, oinochoai)

    pierced cylindrical vessels: 0.15 kg. (2)

    unguentaria: 0.45 kg. (6)

    kalathiskoi: 0.4 kg. (13: 9 flaring, 1 type 3, 1 type 4, 2 handmade)

    miscellaneous votives: 0.8 kg. (27: 1 hydria, 2 oinochoai, 4 jugs, 3 phialai, 1 cup, 9 bowls, 1 lid, 6 offering trays)

    Attic fabric: 0.7 kg. (27)

    coarse wares: 0.25 kg. (6: 1 wall, 1 footed wall, 1 mortar, 1 thymiaterion, 2 handles)

    cooking fabric: 3.9 kg. (23: 2 pitchers, 5 flanged, 2 unflanged cooking pots, 2 lekanai, 8 bowls, 1 lopas, 1 lid,
        2 uncertain)

    lamps: 0.4 kg. (6)

    stamped amphora handles: 0.95 kg. (3)

The pottery of Group 11, as Group 10, comes from a dining-room complex. The amount is greater; over nine baskets were collected from the central area of the building.[24] The complex measures 8.23 × 6.18 m., the first well-preserved dining room found in the excavations.[25]

Group 11 represents the end of the Greek period in the Demeter Sanctuary and the beginning of Roman control. Ten of the 12 inventoried vessels of this section are late Hellenistic debris from the dining room, destroyed in 146 B.C. Roman pottery, C-65-322 and C-65-323,[26] indicates the filling in of the room over one hundred years later when there was a collapse of the south wall. There was a final collapse of the walls at an even later date. The context pottery also contained a good deal of earlier material, mixed in with the original debris (as did Group 10), and more was added later with the Roman packing. Two LC vases, a krater, **192**, and a plate, **196**, represent this earlier material.

About half the material found in the context consists of terracotta figurines.[27] Four tins of kalathiskoi were collected; numerous phialai, offering trays, and other votives were also found, and since repetitive, discarded. There is also a large amount of table ware, from all periods, suggestive of the meals served in this and other complexes: oinochoai, skyphoi, plates, bowls, etc.

The complex was originally built in the later Classical period, with subsequent remodeling, and used until 146 B.C. It is thus not surprising to have such a long range of pottery, not only from use accumulation

---

[24] Most of the pre-Hellenistic pottery was discarded. Only the more contemporary (Hellenistic and Roman), imported, or decorated early material was retained.

[25] The building is described by Bookidis in Stroud, *Hesperia* 37, 1968, pp. 315–317, pl. 96:N, Banquet Hall.

[26] See *Corinth* XVIII, ii.

[27] Figurines: MF 13422, MF 13432, MF 13436, MF 13456, MF 13464, MF 13465, MF 13505, MF 13507–MF 13509. There are also stamped amphora handles: C-65-314, C-65-316, C-65-318, C-65-321, C-68-160; a sima, FS 988; and a poros molding, A 590.

but also from filling. Probably, pottery was dumped periodically around the building and so was contained within the earth shoveled into the complex during the Roman clean-up. Three of the inventoried examples have joining fragments from other lots in the building: fragments of **192** were found in lots 3220 and 3226,[28] part of the unguentarium **201** comes from lot 3228,[29] and fragments of the moldmade bowl **194** were discovered in lot 3233.[30]

This context was fairly rich in fragments of Hellenistic moldmade relief bowls, although, unfortunately, most of the material was very fragmentary. To give an indication of the type of material, the descriptive sherds remaining in the context pottery have been numbered; the list, with the type of decoration, follows:

lot 3230:1 Poseidon and Amphitrite   lot 3230:8 fronds
   2 Erotes and krater   9 palmettes
   3 trophies   10 two standing figures
   4 pine cones   11 linear leaf
   5 imbricate   12 net
   6 imbricate   13 net
   7 grapes and vines   14 net

191. Attic West Slope amphora   Pl. 21

C-65-486. P.H. 0.104 m. Five joining fragments; part of shoulder, neck, handle preserved.

Sloping shoulder; short, concave neck offset from shoulder by two grooves; broad, flat vertical handle attached below flare of neck to rim. Black glaze overall, thin and peeling. On shoulder: boxed rectangles with X across, stopped by checkerboard at left in black and added white. On neck: bow end of a garland in added white, now peeled. On handle: satyr-head mask in place of usual twisted form of handle. See Thompson, *Hesperia* 3, 1934, p. 375, no. D26, fig. 60.

Mid-2nd century or later

192. Red-ground krater   Pl. 21

C-65-563. Joining fragments from M:16 and L:18; lots 3226, 3220. P.H. 0.044, P.W. 0.136 m. Three joining fragments from wall.

Convex wall of large krater. Interior glazed. Exterior: black lower wall; reserved band with thin added-red line above (for ground of figure zone). Figure zone covered with buff-orange wash. Legs and lower skirts of nine women preserved, moving right, in chain dance. Lower skirt in outline technique, central brown fold, edge of overfall at top break, some figures with added red in dress or with border of overfall decorated with incised running zigzags or maeanders.

Late Corinthian (very late)

193. Moldmade relief bowl: imbricate Fig. 14, Pl. 21

C-68-280. H. 0.075-0.08, est. D. 0.14 m. Many joining fragments; full profile; plaster restoration.

Published: Bookidis, *Hesperia* 38, 1969, pl. 79:c.

Recessed central medallion; deep convex bowl; wall turning vertical before slightly flaring rim. Glazed overall; worn mold. Central medallion with one leaf preserved from a four-leaf design. On wall: imbricate pattern of small, pointed, veined leaves in ring around medallion; six long acanthus leaves (three preserved), with striated spines, laid radially to medallion; small, pointed, veined leaves covering rest of wall to border, not overlapping. Top of wall: two ridges with tendril between; slight groove 0.02 m. below flaring rim.

See *Corinth* VII, iii, pp. 158-159 for discussion of the decoration and C-1980-137 (Edwards, *Hesperia* 50, 1981, p. 197, pl. 45).

First or early second quarter 2nd century

194. Moldmade relief bowl: linear leaf Pl. 21

C-65-565. Fragment **b** from lot 3233. a) P.H. 0.039, est. H. of whole 0.085 m. Four joining fragments of base and lower wall. **b**) P.H. 0.058, est. D. 0.13 m. One fragment of wall and rim. Double-dipping streak on **b**.

Noted: Edwards, *Hesperia* 50, 1981, p. 198.

Shape as **193**. Central medallion; six-arm pinwheel. Wall: radially from base, four overlapping zones of six leaves; central line of leaves in first and third zones, second and fourth zones, is continuous; leaves of third zone with multiple divisions. Above leaves: band of eggs between ridges, ending 0.02 m. from rim. Thin brown-to-black glaze overall.

No comparable pattern in *Corinth* VII, iii; **194** has a more complicated pattern than the linear bowls published therein.

Second quarter 2nd century

---

[28] Lot 3220: fill north of Building M:17-18; lot 3226: test through the center of the building. 3226 contains Roman material.
[29] Lot 3228: post-destruction fill, without any Roman material discernible.
[30] Lot 3233: fill under the pottery of this group.

195. Saucer   Fig. 15

C-65-568. H. 0.035, est. D. 0.142–0.145, est. D. foot 0.054 m. Five joining fragments; one fourth preserved, complete profile of wall; center of floor missing.

Heavy ring foot; wide resting surface; diagonal inner face of foot; low convex wall with change of direction at mid-wall, turning up to rounded lip. Interior glazed; exterior glazed by dipping on top of wall only; drip on undersurface. Glaze peeling; poor finish.

Early 2nd century

196. Figured plate   Pl. 21

C-65-514. Max. dim. 0.086, est. D. floor 0.18 m. One fragment of floor and foot.

Single ring foot, broken at beginning of rim. Undersurface: two outer glaze bands, second running into glaze on foot, traces of added purple on it. Floor: outer band with added purple; horse and rider moving left; traces of purple on horse's face and body, rider's body; staff or goad in rider's hand. F.o.: incised star. Limited incision; thin proportions. Polished surface of floor; glaze fired mostly red.

Late Corinthian

197. Flat-rim plate   Fig. 16, Pl. 21

C-65-490. H. 0.065, est. D. 0.22, D. foot 0.062 m. Five joining fragments; vertical wall profile complete; center of floor missing.

Published: Bookidis, *Hesperia* 38, 1969, pl. 79:d, left.

Wide ring foot of narrow diameter; tall diagonal wall beginning slightly convex and turning slightly concave before flaring rim; rim flat on top, offset by groove from upper wall. Interior glazed; upper exterior wall glazed by dipping. Glaze mostly peeled.

2nd century

198. Fish plate   Pl. 21

C-65-566. P.L. 0.089, est. D. 0.20 m. Three joining fragments from wall and rim. Soft, lightly micaceous clay: 7.5YR 7/6 (reddish yellow) core.

Flaring wall slightly convex, set off by ridge from overhanging rim; rim convex on upper face; rounded lip. Thin gray wash on both surfaces, peeling.

Profile of **198** resembles C-63-737 (*Corinth* VII, iii, no. 131, p. 41, pls. 5, 46), a local version of the Attic heavy-rimmed fish plate; but the latter has a groove between the wall and rim, and the rim is more pronounced in its overhang. **198** is neither Attic nor Corinthian; see discussion of fabric and profile, p. 52.

2nd century?

199. Spouted askos   Pl. 21

C-65-320. P.L. body 0.09 m. Three joining fragments from upper part of vessel; plaster restoration.

Upper part of biconical body; central vertical handle or knob with peaked top; most of one of the two diagonal spouts whose outer edges are continuous with the lower half of biconical body. Groove around upper body; flange around center of body, visible at lower break; groove before flange. Glaze inside upper part of spout and over exterior.

For a complete example: C-47-899, from South Stoa Well VII, unpublished (well 1933-3).

2nd century?

200. Blister-ware duck askos

C-65-564. P.L. 0.042 m. One fragment from end of body, beginning of tail.

Tail oriented sideways, curling from rounded wall of askos. On upper surface: incised chevrons and horizontal chain of S-spirals. For more complete example: C-60-68 (*Corinth* VII, iii, no. 776, p. 149, pl. 64); see also **98**, Group 6.

Last quarter 4th century

201. Unguentarium   Pl. 21

C-65-567. Joining fragment from M:18, lot 3228. P.H. 0.17 m. Two joining fragments; base, part of wall preserved to shoulder. Fine micaceous clay: 5YR 6/4 (light reddish brown) core.

False ring foot, deeply concave beneath; high ovoid wall, beginning as stem inset from foot; maximum diameter creating shoulder, contracting to missing neck. Exterior surface originally polished; interior black glazed; three horizontal streaky bands on shoulder. Imported.

See discussion of shape and fabric, p. 56.

Later Hellenistic?

202. Pyxis lid   Pl. 21

C-65-489. H. 0.038, D. 0.084 m. Six joining fragments; full profile; part of flange missing.

Domed lid; two grooves near center, two at outer edge, more resembling wheel grooves than added decoration; projecting rim; slightly inset vertical flange. No glaze.

Early 2nd century

CATALOGUE II (203–681): FABRIC AND DECORATION

DECORATED FINE WARES

CORINTHIAN BLACK FIGURE (203–274)

The 79 inventoried examples (72 in this section; 5 in Group 2 and 2 in Group 11 above) represent the varied quality of the Corinthian figured vases in the later 7th and 6th centuries. They do not statistically represent the wealth of decorated vases. There are hundreds more fragments, mostly from kotylai and pyxides (or oinochoai) which could not be inventoried. The sherds are small and disintegrating, with only the stain of the original designs remaining. They are also, for the most part, examples of the hasty work produced in the later MC and LC periods.

Very few artists of the first rank are represented by vases from the Sanctuary. Curiously, five plates from the Workshop of the Chimaera Painter were found (**26** in Group 2 and **238–241**). Other artists are the Royal Library Painter (**223**), the Samos Group (**221, 224**), the Lion Group (**249**), the Heraldic Lions Painter (**265**), the Patras Painter (**225, 226**), and the Geladakis Painter (**214**). But many of the fragments were not easily attributed to the well-known and distinctive hands of the MC and LC periods. One might hypothesize that those hands produced more expensive vases; the average visitor to the Sanctuary could only afford a less expensive work.

Statistics for the figured shapes generally correspond to those for the non-figured: mostly kotylai, plates, pyxides, some kraters and oinochoai. Conspicuously absent are alabastra, and almost as scarce are aryballoi. Five of the latter are published here (**249–253**); the context pottery contains only a few additional mouths, one fragment of a Warrior type, a few in black-and-white style. Figured bowls are also rarities, although there are great numbers of fragmentary coarse-ware bowls and later, fine-ware lekanides. Figured phialai, rare in any case, do not match their plain counterparts. Figured kraters, especially of the LC period, may have been too expensive; there are many fragments of black-glazed and plain kraters and lekanai that were sufficient for the needs of the 6th-century drinkers. **205**, with its simple dolphin, is the best of the Sanctuary examples; the others, with very careless animal scenes, are represented by **206**. **207** and **208**, probably from the same vase, represent a very small but well-decorated krater. Narrative scenes are quite scarce in all shapes. Six vases show chains of dancing women (**192** of Group 11; **215, 217, 226, 227,** and **235**).

There is very little PC and almost as little EC. The Sanctuary certainly was in existence in the 7th century (see Group 1), but it experienced its major growth in the 6th century, when the first architectural remains are discernible. The numbers of MC and LC fragments from Room R:23–24 (Room D, Group 2 and lots 1985, 1988, 1989, 1991) testify to the expansion. There are slightly more MC than LC entries in this section. This has no statistical significance: many of the LC sherds were too poorly preserved or decorated to warrant publication.

It must be stressed that the published pieces give a somewhat distorted view of the Corinthian black figure from the Sanctuary. All the figured fragments (of this and all other decorated styles) were extracted from the context pottery over the years and repeatedly examined for joins. A few (**226, 255,** etc.) show some success in this effort, but most of the work was fruitless. Too much is still missing; the great volume of material made it possible to isolate only the best preserved and most distinctive fragments.

P. Lawrence helped greatly with the material of the Chimaera Painter and related hands. Most of the attributions are by D. A. Amyx; where the author ventured an ascription, Amyx checked it. All scholars who work with Corinthian vases are in his debt.

203. Red-ground hydria   Pl. 22

C-61-175. P:24–25; lot 875 (second half 4th century after Christ). P.H. 0.044, p.W. 0.048 m. One fragment of upper wall, beginning of shoulder.
    Published: Stroud, *Hesperia* 34, 1965, pl. 5:b, left.

Convex wall, offset from sloping shoulder. From a closed vessel, probably a hydria. Interior reserved. Exterior with buff slip. Wall: woman to right, left hand out with palm up, right holding reins of horse. Face and arms in added white over black; incised contour of figure except

face and left hand; pupil of eye in added red; eye, ear, and brow outlined in fine black line; added-red strands hanging from added-red band in hair; dress in added red. Horse behind woman; mane in added red. Above figures, black line at shoulder; feet and tail of bird to right on shoulder; added red on bird's body.
Late Corinthian

204.   Krater handle-plate   Pl. 22

C-65-445. P:26; lot 4408 (5th century). L. (edges preserved) 0.115, p.W. 0.067 m. Three joining fragments; broken at handle attachment.

Bearded head to left; wavy incision for hair, turning directly into beard; four straight incisions for nose and mouth. Added purple on face just below hair line. Line of glaze at outer edge of undersurface and along sides. Glaze thin, mostly peeled.
Middle Corinthian

205.   Krater   Pl. 22

C-61-414. P:24; lot 877 (early 3rd century). P.L. 0.11, p.W. 0.093 m. Four joining fragments of upper wall.

High ovoid wall, broken above at turn to neck. Interior glazed; added-purple band at upper break. Exterior: Wide black zone on lower wall; possible added-purple line at top. Dolphin to left, incised along lower body; three incised curving lines separating head from body; added purple between lines. F.o. of incised rosette with double circle.
Middle Corinthian

206.   Krater   Pl. 22

C-62-946. R:23–24; lot 1985 (*ca.* 500 B.C.). a) P.H. 0.103, p.W. 0.101 m. Five joining fragments; part of wall, scar of one handle root preserved. b) P.H. 0.09, p.W. 0.15 m. Six joining fragments from lower wall.

a. Reserved zone of lower wall at bottom break; wide zone of black; two pairs of added-purple lines at bottom and center of black zone; two of added white and one of added purple at top of zone. Bird or siren to left; added purple on alternate wing sections, tail. Black around handle root. Bird to right; no added purple preserved. Black band at top break. Interior glazed; added-purple band at top break.

b. Reserved zone and black zone as fragment a. At bottom of black, added white bands not preserved on a: other bands as a. Bottom of bird's tail; interior as a.
Late Corinthian

207.   Krater   Pl. 22

C-64-430. O–P:18–20; lot 2150 (second half 4th century after Christ). P.H. 0.057, est. D. 0.138 m. One

fragment from top of wall, neck, rim; scar of handle attachment to rim at left break.

High ovoid wall; low, slightly concave neck; projecting square rim with vertical outer face, flat upper face, undercut below. Interior glazed (red) and peeling; traces of added-purple bands. Exterior with animal frieze at break: panther head; incised rosette. Above animal frieze, three bands of black, added purple, black; vertical lines rising from top band enclosing tongues alternately of black and added purple. Band at top of wall; neck with added purple. Outer face of rim with black stepped zigzag; top of rim with black S-maeander between black lines. **207** and **208** are probably from the same krater.
Late Corinthian

208.   Krater   Pl. 22

C-65-451. O:18; lot 4349 (4th century after Christ). P.H. 0.047, p.W. 0.034 m. One fragment of wall.

See **207**. Interior with red glaze as **207**. Exterior: Pairs of narrow bands of black and added purple above and below wide band. Animal frieze: body and rear legs of lioness to left; added purple on belly, ribs. F.o.: dotted circle rosette, incised blob, dots. Quality of fabric, color of glaze, type of incision similar to **207**.
Late Corinthian

209.   Red-ground krater   Pl. 22

C-64-411. O–P:18–20; lot 2150 (second half 4th century after Christ). P.H. 0.029, p.W. 0.072 m. Two joining fragments of wall.

Convex wall. Interior glazed, peeling. Buff wash on exterior. Chest and neck of black horse; incised reins; muzzle of horse's head at left of rider. Lower break: back of a white horse, black mane at right break, with rider. Boy poorly incised, holds a thin spear. Traces of added purple on neck of black horse.
Late Corinthian

210.   Conical oinochoe   Pl. 22

C-62-761. R:23–24; lot 1989 (later 6th century). P.H. 0.049 m. One fragment of shoulder and neck.

Shoulder: crosshatching around diamond; three lines; umbrella pattern. Neck: three lines; dotted crosshatching set off by vertical lines; three lines; file of water birds to left; two lines at upper break.
Probably Late Protocorinthian

211.   Conical oinochoe   Fig. 26, Pl. 22

C-64-216. N:26; lot 2074 (mid- to third quarter 5th century). P.H. 0.09, D. 0.025 m. One fragment of tall neck. Burnt; most of color gone.

Beginning of outward flare of shoulder preserved at lower break; beginning of mouth at upper break. Area

211

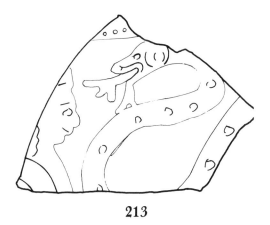

213

FIG. 26. Corinthian black-figured oinochoai. Scale 1:1

behind handle reserved. On neck: zones of wavy lines above and below figured zone, set off below and above by three horizontal lines. Figured zone: *potnia theron* to right, with outstretched sickle wings, holding long-necked birds by necks. F.o.: incised rosettes and dots.

See C-35-27 (*Corinth* VII, i, no. 199, p. 58, pl. 28).
Early Corinthian

212.   Broad-bottomed oinochoe   Pl. 22

C-71-569. M:23; lot 6829 (late 6th century). P.H. 0.064, p.W. 0.063 m. Two joining fragments of shoulder and wall.

Wall vertical at lower break, turning into convex sloping shoulder. Interior unglazed. Lower animal frieze: goat's ear and horn, lowered neck, to left. Black bands, separated by zone of dicing. Upper animal frieze: crouching sphinx to left; wing of bird or siren. Traces of added purple on upper area of wing, goat's neck. F.o.: incised rosettes, incised blobs, many dots. **212** could also be from a large convex pyxis.
Middle Corinthian

213.   Oinochoe   Fig. 26, Pl. 22

C-62-938. R:23–24; lot 1985 (*ca.* 500 B.C.). P.H. 0.051, p.W. 0.07 m. One fragment from convex shoulder of large oinochoe, either high ovoid or broad-bottomed type.

At top break, beginning of upward turn to neck; at top of inner wall trace of glaze. Glaze mostly peeled on exterior. Animal frieze: head and shoulder of sphinx or siren facing

snake. Body of snake with incised circles; spiral on face; forked tongue coming from mouth; bearded. Probably part of symmetrical group of sphinx–snake–sphinx.
Middle Corinthian?

214.   Olpe   Pl. 22

C-72-196. M:17–18, M:16–17; lots 3222 (first half 3rd century after Christ) and 3226 (1st century after Christ). a) P.H. 0.07, p.W. 0.076 m. Lower wall fragment. b) P.H. 0.091, p.W. 0.068 m. Three joining fragments of wall. c) P.H. 0.068, p.W. 0.066 m. Two joining fragments of wall.

Interior wheel ridged. Glaze thin and brown.

a. Tips of rays; wide band between rays and animal frieze, possibly with added-white and added-purple lines. Animal frieze: grazing goat to right; forepaws and chest of feline to left. Added purple on feline chest.

b. Two animal friezes separated by glaze band with added white–purple–white on it. At lower break, top of band of fragment **a**. Lower animal frieze: rear legs and body of feline to right, added purple on flanks, belly. Upper animal frieze: tail, body, feet of bird to right; added purple on wing.

c. Two animal friezes separated by glaze band as **b**. Lower animal frieze: tails and backs of animals. Upper animal frieze: forelegs and one back paw, body of feline to left; added purple on shoulder. F.o.: incised rosettes, incised blobs, many small dots. Strong bold drawing.

Geladakis Painter, fairly late (Amyx). See Amyx, *CorVP*, A-39 *bis*, p. 322.
Middle Corinthian

FIG. 27. Corinthian black-figured bottle **215**. Scale 1:1

215.   Bottle   Figs. 21, 27, Pl. 23

C-64-223. P–Q:20–22; lot 2156 (4th century after Christ, Byzantine). P.H. 0.118, D. neck 0.031 m. Five joining fragments from shoulder, neck.

Long sloping shoulder turning without articulation to tall cylindrical neck; flat lip; suspension holes at top of neck. Interior unglazed; wheel ridged. Exterior with three figure zones extant. Below: top of palmette; head and wing of sphinx to left; right figure unclear, probably woman to right in long cloak. Band of S-maeander. Middle zone: two antithetical sphinxes with palmette between; added purple on chests, faces, wings, center of palmette. Band of dicing. Top zone: chain dance with four women preserved, moving right; no discernible added white on bodies; added purple on upper dresses, lower

skirts; two of four hands hold branches. F.o.: incised rosettes and blobs, plain dots, closely set. Band of dicing. Lip black. Glaze almost gone, incision thin.

For the shape see Jucker (footnote 205 above, p. 63), pl. 19:1.

Middle Corinthian

216.   Pyxis-kalathos   Pl. 23

C-62-731. R:23–24; lot 1988 (late 6th century). P.H. 0.038, p.W. 0.046 m. One fragment of upper wall, rim.

Concave wall; outward projecting triangular rim; peaked lip. Interior: Wide bands of peeling glaze on wall; traces of added purple at top. Exterior: Black band at lower break; wide band of black with added purple; silhouette bird between vertical wavy lines. Upper wall and rim with black bands. For the shape: *Perachora* II, pp. 166–167.

Early or Middle Corinthian

217.   Pyxis-kalathos   Fig. 28, Pl. 23

C-61-279. P–Q:24, P:21–22; lots 896 (second half 4th century after Christ), 73–130 (late 6th century). H. 0.128, est. D. 0.19, est. D. resting surface 0.15 m. Five joining fragments; full vertical profile; floor missing; about one third preserved.

Concave undersurface, no foot; bevel at base of wall; concave wall; heavy flaring triangular rim; peaked lip. Traces of glaze on interior wall; reserved band below rim. Exterior: Bevel and rim glazed; band of dicing; lowest register: chain of dancing women to right, nine preserved; dicing; middle register: two antithetical lions; top register: back and hindquarters of bull or goat to left, lion to right, bull to right. F.o.: incised blobs, plain dots. Proportions of animals compact. In all zones, heads go over glaze bands. Glaze thin, brown, mostly peeling.

Early Corinthian

218.   Pyxis-kalathos   Pl. 23

C-65-446. O–P:21; lot 4363 (late Roman). P.H. 0.048, p.W. 0.06, est. D. 0.155 m. One fragment of upper wall, rim.

Shape as **217**; rim with three grooves on upper face. Interior: Wide black band on wall, traces of added purple and black on rim. Exterior: Sphinx to right facing palmette. Added purple on wings, face, polos, calyx, and palmette leaves. F.o.: incised and plain dots. Added-purple band, zone of dicing above figure zone; black band under rim.

Middle Corinthian

219.   Pyxis-kalathos   Pl. 23

C-65-447. Grid O–P:21; lot 4363 (late Roman). P.H. 0.034, est. D. 0.095 m. One fragment of wall, rim.

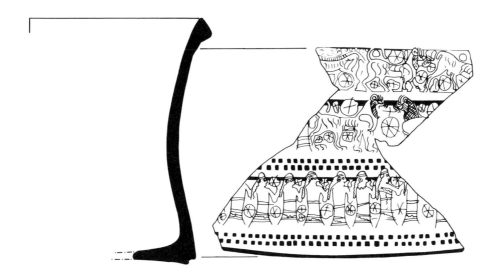

FIG. 28. Corinthian black-figured pyxis-kalathos **217**. Scale 1:2

Straight, not concave, wall; flaring triangular rim, rounded on upper face. Interior: Bands of glaze, added purple on one. Exterior: Horse race to right; nose of horse at left break; horse and rider, rider with staff or goad; flanks of third horse at right break. Added purple on chest and face of rider. Bands of glaze above figure zone and on underside of rim; S-maeander on upper face of rim. Glaze fired mostly red.

Late Corinthian?

220. Kotyle with narrative scene Fig. 29, Pl. 23

C-62-940. R:23–24; lot 1985 (*ca.* 500 B.C.). P.H. 0.034, p.W. 0.035 m. One fragment of upper wall, lip.

Interior glazed, peeled. Exterior: At left break, diagonal spear or trainer's staff (?); boxer to right, broken below genitals, bearded, fillet in hair, raised right arm behind with strapped hand, left arm extended. At right break, the rim, upper bowl, and ring handle of tripod; object above tripod at break possibly another strapped hand (although spacing in relation to tripod and preserved boxer problematic). Fine controlled drawing, precise incision.

Middle Corinthian

221. Kotyle with narrative scene Pl. 23

C-62-367(a), C-62-368(b), C-62-841(c). P–Q:24–25, R:23–24, P:23–24; lots 893 (first quarter 4th century), 1985 (*ca.* 500 B.C.), 1993 (mid-4th century). a) P.H.

0.032, p.W. 0.056 m. Two joining wall fragments.
b) P.H. 0.025, p.W. 0.021 m. One wall fragment.
c) P.H. 0.035, p.W. 0.034 m. One wall fragment.

Interior glazed (brown), cracking, trace of one added-purple band.

a. Two horses galloping right, near one in outline, far one in brown, legs of rider visible at left break. This team overlaps a single brown horse, with lower torso and legs of its rider preserved. Horses' bodies tubular; very elongated legs. Thin diagonal brown lines at right break, under horses' forelegs.

b. Heads of a pair of horses, near one brown, far one in outline. Curving brown line for back of outline horse, in front of other horses' heads, its rider with raised arm and hand holding spear at right.

c. Unclear. Cart or platform at lower right, with added purple at lower edge, poles and yoke(?) extending to left, reins(?) above. Object at top break not elbow of raised arm, too thin in comparison with arm of **b**. Object at right on platform, half silhouette, half coursed masonry(?) in outline. Neat drawing and incision.

Samos Group, unattributed (Amyx). See Amyx, *CorVP*, no. 6, p. 192.

Middle Corinthian

222. Kotyle with narrative scene Fig. 29, Pl. 23

C-62-733. R:23–24; lot 1988 (late 6th century). P.H. 0.046, p.W. 0.053 m. One fragment of upper wall, lip.

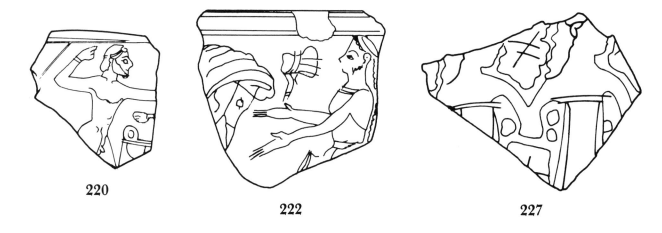

220

222

227

Fɪɢ. 29. Corinthian black-figured kotylai. Scale 1:1

Interior with streaky glaze; added-purple band below lip. Exterior: Brown bands below lip. At left break, horse's head, bowed to right. Woman facing horse: face, neck, shoulder, arms, hair fillet preserved. Her face and arms are in outline; black hair, added purple on dress; both arms extended to horse; both hands are right hands, with long fingers. Incised ornament in field between horse and woman.

Middle Corinthian?

223. Kotyle Pl. 23

C-62-304. O–R:23–24; lot 1955 (second half 4th century after Christ). P.H. 0.043, p.W. 0.028 m. One lower wall fragment.

Interior glazed thin brown. Exterior: Tips of rays; neat band of dicing; thin ground line. Rear legs and belly of feline to right; added purple on belly, thighs. F.o.: incised rosettes, two with double circles; dots.

Royal Library Painter. See Amyx, *CorVP*, no. A-17, p. 127.

Early Corinthian

224. Kotyle Pl. 23

C-65-459. P:21; lot 4370 (mid-6th century). P.H. 0.062, est. D. lip 0.134 m. Seven joining fragments of wall, lip.

Interior glazed thin black; reserved band at top of wall. Exterior: Lower wall black; two black bands above. Upper wall: two heraldic roosters facing enscrolled palmette and lotus. Extensive use of added purple on roosters and palmette. No f.o. Black band below lip.

Samos Group (Amyx). Same hand as *NC*, no. 953

(Berlin 3925) and Isthmia, IP 1289 (fragment). See Amyx, *CorVP*, no. B-2, p. 191.

Middle Corinthian

225. Kotyle Pl. 23

C-62-371. R:23–24; lot 1985 (*ca.* 500 B.C.). P.H. 0.078, p.W. 0.081 m. One wall fragment.

Interior glazed streaky brown. Exterior: Tips of rays; three brown bands; animal frieze: feline to left with elongated body; two front legs, one back paw preserved; added purple in ribs. Large f.o.: incised rosettes; "bow ties"; dots.

Patras Painter. See Amyx, *CorVP*, no. A-50, p. 188. For the painter, see *Corinth* VII, ii, pp. 38–40, list of vases.

Middle Corinthian

226. Kotyle Pl. 23

C-61-463. P:24, P–Q:20–22, O–P:22–23; lots 877 (early 3rd century), 2156 (4th century after Christ, Byzantine), 4352 (4th century after Christ). P.H. 0.065, est. D. lip 0.18 m. Three joining fragments of upper wall, lip.

Interior glazed streaky brown orange; reserved band at top of wall. Exterior: Head of woman wearing polos, under handle; arms extended, holding wreath (at bottom right break); part of chain dance. Large crowded f.o.: incised rosettes with circle; incised blobs, "bow ties", etc. No traces of added color.

Late Patras Painter. See Amyx, *CorVP*, no. A-31, p. 187.

Late Middle Corinthian to Late Corinthian

227. Kotyle Fig. 29, Pl. 23

C-65-520. O–P:22–23; lot 4356 (late 4th century). P.H. 0.049, p.W. 0.06 m. One wall fragment.

Interior black with two added-purple bands. Exterior: Head and upper body of a woman, part of a chain dance; curly hair, high ear, fat chin; traces of added purple on dress. Crowded f.o.: dots, incised blobs.

Not the Patras Painter. For similar but cruder work see *CVA*, Bibl. Nat. 1 [France 7], inv. no. 4839, pls. 15 [299]:19 and 22, 16 [300]:1.

Middle Corinthian

228. Kotyle Pl. 23

C-62-947. R:23–24, P–Q:25; lots 1988 (late 6th century), 73-141 (third quarter 5th century). P.H. 0.073, p.W. 0.117 m. Four joining fragments of wall.

Interior black; two added-red bands. Exterior: Tips of rays; three bands of black, added red, black. Animal frieze: bird or siren with outstretched wing, long tail, long feet. Added red and white on alternate tail feathers, added red on section before feathers, on horizontal section of wing. Dense f.o.: incised rosettes (one with circles), X-blobs, dots. Very thick, heavy style, long proportions, much angular incision.

Middle Corinthian

229. Kotyle Pl. 24

C-62-872. P–Q:24; lots 896 (second half 4th century after Christ), 897 (mid-4th century), 898 (*ca.* 500 B.C.), 2003 (mid-5th century). **a)** P.H. 0.13, p.W. 0.155. Five joining fragments of wall, lip. **b)** P.H. 0.064, p.W. 0.095 m. Four joining fragments of wall. **c)** P.H. 0.043, p.W. 0.054 m. One fragment of lower wall; joins **b** at lower right in very narrow area.

Interior black; two added-purple bands at midwall.

a. Tips of elongated rays; two black bands. Animal frieze: rear legs of animal to left; tail, lower body, legs of bird to right; legs, tail, body of feline to right. Added purple on feline. F.o.: incised rosettes, "bow ties", plain dots. Handle zone: vertical wavy lines between black bands.

b. Animal frieze: forelegs, neck, head of goat to right. Added purple on neck, dots on second leg. Right break: tip of tail. Tips of rays, two bands as fragment **a**.

c. Tail and rump of animal to right (end of tail at right break on **b**). Second division of hindquarters with added-purple dots; other areas with solid purple. Interesting, distinctive artist who likes large areas of purple; loose curvilinear incision, rubbery feet, scattered f.o.

Middle Corinthian

230. Kotyle Pl. 24

C-62-364. R:23–24, Q:26; lots 1985 (*ca.* 500 B.C.), 1991 (late 6th century), 2230 (late 5th century). P.H. 0.052, p.W. 0.065 m. Three joining fragments of wall.

Interior brown. Exterior: Double row of rays; three brown bands. Animal frieze: bird between long-chinned (or bearded?) sirens. Added purple on neck and cheek of right one. F.o.: incised rosettes with circle, incised and plain dots. Two brown bands above. Small style, not delicate. Minimal, rather careless incision. Popular MC lower-wall design; see *CVA*, Louvre 6 [France 9], inv. no. N 3103, pl. 6 [390]:22–24.

Middle Corinthian

231. Kotyle Pl. 24

C-65-526. P:26, N:21; lots 2046 (late 5th century), 4408 (5th century), 4450 (4th century). **a)** P.H. 0.08, est. D. lip 0.14 m. Two joining fragments of wall, lip, handle. **b)** P.H. 0.041, p.W. 0.05 m. One wall fragment.

a. Tall wall, slight incurve to lip; loop handle. Interior black; two added-purple bands at midwall, two below lip. Exterior: Tips of rays; two black bands. Animal frieze: panther head at left break; bird to right; added-purple and added-white tail feathers; added purple on body, purple dots on chest and neck. At right, volutes of a scroll palmette. F.o.: dots of varying sizes, X-blobs; added purple on some. Added-purple and black bands below handle; vertical wavy lines in handle zone; outer handle black; added purple at lip.

b. Black band at lower break. Panther to left. F.o.: dots and X-blobs. Rather gaudy flavor, incision often imprecise, compact proportions.

Middle Corinthian?

232. Kotyle Pl. 24

C-65-457. O–P:22–23; lot 4352 (4th century after Christ). P.H. 0.079, est. D. lip 0.14 m. One fragment of wall, lip.

Tall wall, strong inturn to lip. Interior black; lip reserved. Exterior: Black with added red at lower break; two black bands. Animal frieze: volute lotus and palmette; sphinx to left (with second one originally left of palmette). Added purple on palmette and lotus, on neck and body of sphinx. F.o.: one incised blob; dots. Black bands below lip. Poor drawing and incision, rough style.

Late Kotylai, descended from Samos Group (Amyx): Amyx, *CorVP*, no. 5, p. 250.

Late Corinthian

233. Kotyle Pl. 24

C-62-692. R:23–24, Q:20–22, Q:26; lots 1985 (*ca.* 500 B.C.), 1988 (late 6th century), 2088 (second half 4th century after Christ), 73-137 (first quarter 5th century). **a)** P.H. 0.075, est. D. lip 0.11 m. Seven joining fragments of wall, lip, handle roots. **b)** P.H. 0.02 m. One fragment of upper wall. **c)** P.H. 0.031 m. Two joining fragments of upper wall, lip. **d)** P.H. 0.031 m. One fragment of upper wall.

Tall wall with inturn to lip; small loop handle. Interior brown and peeling.

a. Rays, running through brown band to animal frieze. Wide band with added purple at edges; two brown lines. Animal frieze: three sphinxes wearing poloi; body of one under handle to left, two others to right. Patches of added purple scattered on bodies. Wormy f.o., sometimes incised. Added-purple band at lip; handle black.

b. Face of sphinx to right.

c. Face of sphinx at left break; body and wing of second at right; both facing right.

d. Body of sphinx to right. Incision and added purple often miss intended area.

Long proportions; tails are whalelike.

Vermicular Painter (Amyx). See Amyx, *CorVP*, no. 2, p. 249. For the painter see Williams and Fisher, *Hesperia* 42, 1973, p. 14, under no. 15.

Late Corinthian, very late

234. Cup with offset rim   Pl. 24

C-62-365. R:23–24; lot 1985 (*ca.* 500 B.C.). P.H. 0.078 m. One fragment of wall, rim.

Wide convex flaring wall; thin flaring offset rim; tapered lip. Interior black; one wide added-purple band at mid-wall; top of inner rim reserved. Exterior: Two wide black bands; two diluted lines above each band. Upper wall: bird with turned-back head; added purple on neck, center of body. Line below rim; exterior rim reserved. Fragments of only five additional bird cups in the context pottery.

See Boardman and Hayes, *Tocra* I, group III, no. 292, p. 36.

Late Middle Corinthian or Late Corinthian

235. Phiale   Pl. 24

C-62-730. R:23–24; lots 1988 (late 6th century), 2217 (early 4th century). a) Max. dim. 0.044, est. D. lip 0.09 m. One fragment of bowl, lip. b) Max. dim. 0.022 m. One fragment of bowl.

Flaring convex wall turning vertical to rounded lip.

a. Exterior: Two brown bands at top of wall. Interior: Vertical rows of dots, alternating with dot rosettes; added-purple band; group of six vertical lines; brown band; zone of dancing women (three preserved), moving left, in silhouette. F.o.: hailstones. Two added-purple and brown bands above figure zone; dots on lip. Added purple over glaze.

b. One dancer preserved; arm of second; top of vertical lines below figure zone.

See *Perachora* II, no. 2569, pl. 109, for similar example.

Late Corinthian

236. Lekanoid bowl   Fig. 30, Pl. 24

C-62-939. R:23–24; lot 1985 (*ca.* 500 B.C.). P.H. 0.077, est. D. rim 0.25 m. Four joining fragments of upper wall, rim.

Deep convex flaring wall; offset rim flaring diagonally; rounded inner flange. Rim, flange, top 0.025 m. of inner wall reserved; glaze below on inner wall. Exterior with parts of two figured zones. Lower animal frieze: panther head; ear and back of second animal to left. Upper animal frieze: panther to right; griffin with outstretched wings to right. F.o.: incised blob rosettes; dots. Two glaze bands above; black Z-maeander below rim. Glaze peeled.

Middle Corinthian or Late Corinthian

237. Coarse-ware figured bowl   Fig. 12, Pl. 24

C-65-442. P:26, N:22, Q:26; lots 2012 (early 5th century), 4408 (5th century), 4461 (late 4th century), 73-137 (first quarter 5th century). a) P.H. 0.068, est. D. rim 0.235 m. One fragment of upper wall rim. b) P.H. 0.081 m. Three joining fragments of wall, rim. c) P.H. 0.038 m. One fragment of lower wall. Corinthian clay with inclusions; glaze fired red and black; no slip.

Wide convex flaring wall; heavy folded rim with vertical outer face, flat top. Vertical rim face: opposing triangles alternately painted and stamped. Flat rim face with S-maeander.

a (not illustrated). Interior: Three glaze bands below (limiting floor tondo); enclosed tongues above; two bands at top of bowl. Exterior: Animal frieze with bird's wing at break; bull to right. Silhouette f.o. of star, dots, loops.

b. Interior: Bands and tongues as a. Tondo: figure to right, right arm in front of body, hand and wing overlapping inner band. Exterior: Glaze below. Animal frieze: hindquarters of feline to left; boar to right.

c (not illustrated). Interior: Two inner bands; beginning of tondo design, unclear. Exterior: Long snout and open mouth of animal to right; raised forelegs of animal galloping to left; beginning of body at right break.

Such decorated coarse-ware fabric is rare, but the figure style and stamped design are Corinthian.

Late Corinthian or later

238. Plate   Fig. 16, Pl. 25

C-69-185. Lot 6215, stairway cuts (6th century after Christ). H. 0.019, est. D. rim 0.27, est. D. foot 0.21 m. Many joining fragments; parts of floor and rim restored in plaster.

Double ring foot; flaring convex rim with groove before rounded lip; one suspension hole preserved. Undersurface: Three wide concentric black bands; added purple on feet; lip originally black and added-purple bands. Floor: Two heraldic lions, bodies turned out, heads turned to

Fig. 30. Corinthian black-figured lekanoid bowl **236**. Scale 1:1

center, tails intertwined. Left-hand lion with one foreleg against tondo border, one on rim; right-hand lion originally in same pose. Squared-off ruff; big heart-shaped ear. Added purple on neck. F.o.: neatly incised rosettes, one with double circles.

By the Chimaera Painter. See Amyx, *CorVP*, no. A-17, p. 169; Lawrence (under **26**), pl. 87, fig. 4.

Middle Corinthian

239. Plate   Pl. 25

C-62-762. R:23–24, O:25, P–Q:22–23; lots 1989 (later 6th century), 2092 (mid-4th century), 2106 (mid to second half 4th century after Christ). a) H. 0.022, est. D. rim 0.33, est. D. foot 0.23 m. Three joining fragments of floor, foot, rim; one suspension hole preserved. b) P.L. 0.091 m. One rim fragment. c) Max. dim. 0.031 m. One fragment of outer tondo. d) Max. dim. 0.055 m. One fragment from near center of floor. e) Max. dim. 0.071 m. One fragment of floor and lower rim.

Shape as **238**.

a. Undersurface: Two concentric narrow bands near center, outer one with added purple. One added-purple band midway; two black at outer edge; added purple on feet. Floor: Hair, neck, chest of sphinx to left, one paw against outer tondo over two concentric black bands. Black bands on lower and upper rim.

b (not illustrated). Banding as fragment a. No preserved floor decoration.

c (not illustrated). Banding as a. Floor with either peak of wing or part of incised rosette.

d (not illustrated). Bands as a. Floor with part of wing; added purple on main section and alternate feathers.

e (not illustrated). Banding as a.

Workshop of the Chimaera Painter (Lawrence). See Amyx, *CorVP*, no. 7, p. 173: Chimaera Group, unattributed.

Middle Corinthian

240. Plate   Pl. 25

C-72-244. N–O:26; lot 72-209 (later 6th century). Max. dim. 0.106, est. D. tondo 0.17 m. One fragment of tondo, beginning of rim.

Undersurface: Narrow concentric circles as **239**. Floor: Frontal face of panther, deep pouches under eyes; neatly incised ruff. At left, wing of sickle shape; the original figure must have been a panther-bird protome. The glaze and any added colors have peeled.

Compare the pouches under the eyes of the sphinxes on the Copenhagen plate: Lawrence (under **26**), pl. 89, fig. 14.

By the Painter of Louvre E574 (Lawrence).

Middle Corinthian

241. Plate   Pl. 25

C-65-449. O:15–17; lot 4403 (late Roman). Max. dim. 0.07 m. One fragment of center of floor.

Undersurface: Central dot; concentric lines of glaze. Floor: Part of torso, left wing, upraised left thigh of Boread or Gorgon in *Knielauf* position to right. Running spiral on hem of short skirt; lines for folds fanning from waist; running loops on neckline.

For comparable profiles of **238–241** and **26** (Group 2) see Callipolitis-Feytmans, p. 153, fig. 17.

Chimaera Group, unattributed (Amyx). See Amyx, *CorVP*, no. 10, p. 173.

Middle Corinthian

242.   Plate   Pl. 25

C-64-404. P:26, K–L:23; lots 2042 (late 5th century), 73-102 (mid-5th century with Roman intrusion). H. 0.016, est. D. rim 0.20 m. Two joining fragments of floor, rim.

Double ring foot, inner one considerably smaller than outer; rim almost horizontal; rounded lip with offsetting groove on upper surface. Undersurface: Added-purple band at outer edge, going over inner foot; foot black, added purple on outer face of foot. Undersurface tondo: Frontal panther; face, neck, shoulder, one raised forepaw preserved. Traces of added purple on forehead, chest; incision of face without details of Chimaera Painter style. Floor tondo: Added-purple bands at outer edge. F.o.: incised rosettes; beginning of larger object at inner break, indiscernible. Black rays on upper face of rim; added purple on lip; two suspension holes preserved. Glaze peeled.

Middle Corinthian

243.   Plate   Pl. 25

C-61-235. O:24–25; lot 890 (2nd century after Christ). H. 0.019, est. D. rim 0.25 m. Two joining fragments of floor, rim.

Profile as **242**, with slightly wider inner foot. Undersurface: Wide concentric bands; added purple at edge and over inner foot; outer foot glazed. Floor: Three glaze bands on outer floor; inner tondo design missing; two concentric circles at inner break. Outer floor design of chain of incised palmettes; traces of added purple on calyces, alternate leaves; incised dots in circles created by looped volutes. Outer edge of palmettes incised. Rays on rim, glaze band below; glaze on outer lip. Glaze fired red. Coarse work.

Middle Corinthian by profile

244.   Red-ground plate   Pl. 25

C-65-472. N:22, lot 4460 (late 4th century). P.H. 0.019, est. D. foot 0.162 m. Many joining fragments; half of foot and floor, beginning of rim preserved. Surface on both sides covered with peeling thin wash, more buff than red (7.5YR 6/6, reddish yellow). Same color on LC krater C-72-149 (Williams and Fisher, *Hesperia* 42, 1973, p. 10, no. 12, pl. 3).

Double ring foot; beginning of convex flaring rim. Undersurface: Wide concentric bands of black; feet black. Floor: Black rooster to left, elaborately incised wings and tail; added purple on alternate tail sections.

Late Corinthian

245.   Plate   Pl. 26

C-68-218. L–N:15–20; lot 5613 (11th century after Christ). H. 0.014, est. D. rim 0.21 m. One fragment of floor, foot, rim.

Single wide ring foot; flaring straight rim; rounded lip without offsetting groove; floor and rim not clearly offset. Foot and under face of rim black. Undersurface: Two concentric black lines at inner break. Animal frieze: lion to right facing ram to left. Thin body of lion; strange incisions on paws; squared-off ruff. Either the ram is stooping before the lion or spacing was misjudged. F.o.: incised rosettes and dots. Floor: Black bands; coils of snake or sea monster. Stain of added purple on outer section of body. F.o.: incised rosettes, blobs. "Worm" pattern on upper face of rim.

Late Corinthian by profile

246.   Plate   Pl. 26

C-64-414. O–P:19–20; lot 2240 (second half 4th century after Christ). Max. dim. 0.083 m. One fragment of outer floor.

Ring foot; beginning of rim. Undersurface undecorated. Floor: Brown outer bands. Animal frieze: sphinx to right, facing horizontal palmette; traces of added red on neck and shoulder of sphinx and on palmette leaves. Hailstone f.o. Poor drawing and incision; debased version of MC plate. See Callipolitis-Feytmans, fig. 4.

Late Corinthian

247.   Plate   Pl. 26

C-62-372. R:23–24; lot 1985 (*ca.* 500 B.C.). P.H. 0.014, est. D. floor 0.108 m. Four joining fragments, preserving most of floor, small area of lower rim.

Double foot with flat and narrow resting surfaces. Undersurface: Central black dot; four concentric black circles, added purple between second and third; black bands on outer area; black on feet. Floor: Three concentric circles; red rays to three black circles at midfloor, outer one with added purple. Narrow animal frieze: 11 elongated silhouette dogs(?), all to right except one. F.o.: dots and blobs. Black band on lower rim; beginning of rim design at break, zigzag?

Late Corinthian

248.   Red-ground plaque   Pl. 26

C-65-477. J–L:14; lot 4411 (4th century after Christ). P.H. 0.104, p.W. 0.096 m. Three joining fragments of lower left plaque, about one fourth preserved. Thick, rather coarse clay; thin wash on top surface and over edges.

Black border of irregular width. Legs of nude male to right; trace of added white on foot, for sandal? Thin diagonal glaze line at left for staff or spear. Hole on undersurface, beneath foot, not pierced to surface. Undersurface reserved.

Late Corinthian

249. Aryballos Pl. 26

C-62-756. R:23–24; lot 1989 (later 6th century). P.H. 0.025, p.W. 0.02 m. One wall fragment.

From convex lower wall; beginning of curve to resting surface at bottom break. Lion to left in stretched position; glaze at right for something on his back; Chimaera? Crosshatched mane; curved lines of ruff. One incised dot as f.o. Glaze fired brown; any added colors gone.

Lion Group (Amyx). See Amyx, *CorVP*, no. 4, p. 122: Lion Group, unattributed.

Early Corinthian

250. Aryballos Pl. 26

C-64-61. P:26; lot 2012 (early 5th century). P.H. 0.025, p.W. 0.047 m. Two joining fragments, from convex lower wall.

Top of bands at lower break. Nude man running left, legs far apart; one hand visible at right; rear leg overlaps part of incised rosette. Surface stained.

Middle Corinthian

251. Aryballos Fig. 17, Pl. 26

C-64-424. O:26–27; lot 2051 (later 3rd century). H. 0.064, D. 0.061, D. rim 0.042 m. Six joining fragments; full profile; part of wall, rim missing.

Flat resting surface; low globular body without shoulder offset; low neck; projecting rim sloping in above; vertical overhanging outer rim face; short strap handle from shoulder to lower rim. Seven concentric black circles on resting surface. Oriented opposite handle: siren with outstretched wings, to left; added purple on wings. F.o.: incised rosettes with circles; incised blobs; dots. Handle black; vertical rim black with reserved central band; upper rim with two wide bands of black; added purple on inner one. *NC*, shape B2.

Middle Corinthian

252. Aryballos Pl. 26

C-65-512. O–P:13–15; lot 4385 (second half 2nd century after Christ). P.H. 0.026, D. rim 0.04 m. One fragment of neck, rim, handle.

Short narrow neck; vertical rim not so undercut as **251**; sloping upper face of rim; wide handle rising to peak before attachment at top of rim. Upper rim: inner glaze lines; reserved rosette pattern; outer band. Crosshatching

on vertical face of rim, sides, top of handle. On back of handle, female head, poorly drawn in outline, to left.

See CP-2355 for the type (*Corinth* VII, ii, no. 85, p. 32, pl. 14).

Middle Corinthian

253. Aryballos Pl. 26

C-68-198. M:17; lot 5658 (early 5th century). H. 0.054, D. 0.053 m. Part of rim and handle missing.

Flat resting surface with slight central depression; globular body, offset from nearly horizontal shoulder; narrow low neck; strap handle from shoulder to lower edge of rim; vertical overhanging rim; sloping upper face of rim. Central black blob in resting surface depression; irregular circles around it. Wall: sketchy, badly executed quatrefoil design, without incision or added color. Rim, upper handle black. A poor descendant of a lovely type.

Late Corinthian

254. Concave pyxis Pl. 27

C-61-240. P–Q:24–25, O:24; lots 892 (4th century after Christ), 1950 (4th century). P.H. 0.097, p.W. 0.086 m. Two joining fragments of wall.

Concave wall; broken below at beginning of floor, above at beginning of flare to lip. Interior: Wide brown bands. Exterior: Rays; band of dicing; animal frieze; dicing; added-red line over brown band. Animal frieze: goat grazing to right, added purple on neck, following curve of incised shoulder, face with incised contour line; outstretched wing and narrow tail of bird; added purple on upper wing, alternate wing feathers. F.o.: rosettes neatly incised, dots.

Early Corinthian

255. Concave pyxis Pl. 27

C-73-357. O:21–22, N:22, P:21–22; lots 4372 (later 4th century), 4461 (late 4th century), 73-130 (late 6th century). P.H. 0.084, p.W. 0.064 m. Four joining fragments, preserving part of wall, small area of lip.

Concave wall, flaring to rounded lip. Interior: Black on most of lower wall; added-purple bands over black; reserved bands below lip, above floor. Lip black. Exterior: Lower wall before frieze with black pattern, obscured. Figured frieze: padded dancer to left, bearded, wearing incised loin cloth, right arm raised, left arm in front of torso; added purple on face, padding, thighs. Feline to right, incised rump, short leg, high arching tail; added purple between alternate ribs. F.o.: incised rosettes (two with double circles); added purple in centers and on alternate petals; dots; incised blobs. Two black bands above frieze; added-purple and black wavy lines in top zone.

255 and **27** (Group 2) are the only Sanctuary vases with padded dancers. The painter of **255** is often careless but exuberant, fond of added purple.

Middle Corinthian

256. Tripod pyxis   Fig. 19, Pl. 27

C-62-307. P–Q:24, O–R:23–24; lots 898 (*ca.* 500 B.C.), 1955 (second half 4th century after Christ). H. 0.045, est. D. base 0.09, est. D. lip 0.08 m. Two non-joining fragments. **a)** Two joining fragments preserve complete vertical profile, beginning of bowl. **b)** One fragment, broken off in figure zone at beginning of bowl.

Flaring foot flat on resting surface, rising without articulation into slightly concave wall; thickened rim with vertical outer face, flattened lip.

a. Bowl interior: Red glazed with reserved band at top. Lip red. Undersurface, inner face of foot, resting surface reserved. Lower wall: black, added red, black, added red bands (red directly on clay). Animal frieze: bird to left between antithetical sirens. F.o.: dots, incised blobs. Vertical lines at edge of zone; one black, one added-red band above; vertical rim glazed.

b. Bowl and rim as fragment **a**. Animal frieze: panther to right. F.o. as **a**. Interior glaze fired mostly red; exterior black.

Severeanu Painter (Amyx). See Amyx, *CorVP*, no. A-3, p. 256; *CVA*, Bucharest 2 [Romania 2], p. 11; *Münzen und Medaillen Auktion 60, September 1982*, no. 10.

Late Corinthian

257. Convex pyxis   Fig. 31, Pl. 27

C-61-176. P:24–25; lot 875 (second half 4th century after Christ). P.H. 0.057, p.W. 0.06 m. Two joining fragments from wall; possibly an oinochoe.

Convex wall. Bands above and below figure zone. Figure in short tunic to left, left arm across body, holding staff(?). Warrior advancing right, right arm raised, left forward with shield, left leg advancing, right stretched back, wearing Corinthian helmet with long crest, breastplate, greaves. Lower leg and foot of fallen warrior under his advancing leg. F.o.: incised rosettes, dots. Glaze almost completely peeled.

Middle Corinthian?

258. Convex pyxis   Pl. 27

C-64-59. P:26; lot 2012 (early 5th century). Max. dim. 0.073 m. One fragment of shoulder.

Slightly convex sloping shoulder, beginning of downward curve at lower break. Bands of black; added purple on central one. Animal frieze: griffin to right, facing palmette. Traces of added purple on palmette; added purple and added white on alternate leaves; added purple on griffin's neck and wing; stain of added white on neck band, shoulder section. F.o.: incised rosettes, some with central circles; small dots.

Near the Stobart Painter (Amyx).

Middle Corinthian

259. Convex pyxis   Pl. 27

C-64-408. P–Q:20–22; lot 2156 (4th century after Christ, Byzantine). P.H. 0.058 m. Fragment of shoulder with attached head, rim.

Rounded sloping shoulder; low vertical neck; flat bridge from rim to attached head. Interior: neck black; added purple bands; Z-maeander on rim. Wall animal frieze: tail and f.o. only. Added-purple band, dicing above. Shoulder animal frieze: sphinxes on either side of head; traces of added purple on each. F.o.: incised rosettes, dots. Head very worn.

Middle Corinthian

260. Convex pyxis   Fig. 31, Pl. 27

C-65-519. O–P:22–23; lot 4356 (late 4th century). P.H. 0.053, p.W. 0.068 m. One fragment of convex wall.

Published: E. G. Pemberton, "A Late Corinthian Perseus from Ancient Corinth," *Hesperia* 52, 1983, pp. 64–69.

Interior apparently unglazed. Exterior: below, goat to left, tail and bent leg joint of panther to right; broad glaze band, wheel groove below band; above, foot of figure at left break; legs and genitals of man running right, wing on ankles; thigh of rear leg, genitals incised. In field between legs:

ΠΕΡΣΕΥΣ

(in Corinthian epichoric alphabet; see Fig. 31).
Scar of handle attachment at upper right. Under handle, either foot and skirt of figure or outer edge of palmette design.

Perseus, presumably being chased by the Gorgon sisters. For the subject in Corinthian art, see the publication cited above.

Late Corinthian

261. Convex pyxis   Pl. 27

C-65-38. R:24, N–O:25–26; lots 2217 (early 4th century), 75-248 (mid-5th century). P.H. 0.105 m. Two joining fragments from part of foot, wall, shoulder.

Published: Stroud, *Hesperia* 37, 1968, pl. 91:d; Pemberton, *Archaeology* 31, Nov.–Dec. 1978, p. 28; F. Lorber, *Inschriften auf korinthischen Vasen (Archäologische Forschungen* 6), Berlin 1979, no. 132, p. 84, pl. 41.

Floor missing; concave inner foot; resting surface and outer edge of foot missing; upper face of foot well offset from wall; high ovoid wall turning continuously into rounded shoulder. Head originally attached at right. Polished surface. Undersurface reserved; upper face of foot black. Wall: added-red band at base; row of black dots; checkerboard pattern on most of wall, five rows of black and reserved squares between added-red lines;

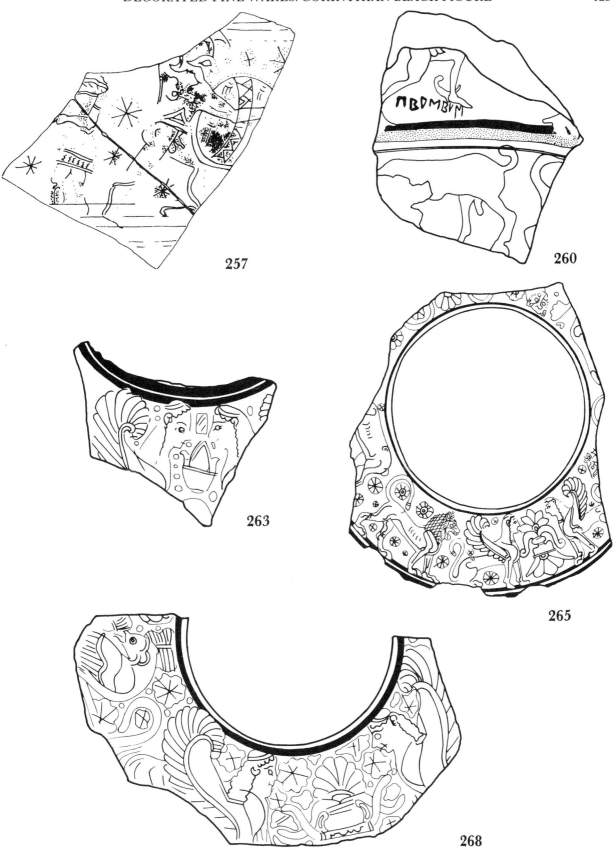

FIG. 31. Corinthian black-figured pyxides and lids. Scale 1:1

wide added-red line above. Red directly on surface. Shoulder: three female faces, in outline and incision. At left break, hair with fillet, forehead, eye, and nose of woman to right, overlapping a frontal face. Third woman in profile to left, scale design on dress; black hair, reserved fillet; incision between hair and neck and from nose to lower break. Left of this figure, added red over black, significance unclear. In field between third woman and attached head:

HEPA

(in Corinthian epichoric alphabet), vertical and retrograde (see Pl. 27). Raised clay and scoring for head attachment at right; black shoulder of dress; scale pattern on torso, extended hand in outline to left.

See the head **624**; the latter does not fit the scar of this shoulder, but it could be from elsewhere on the same pyxis; fabric, color, scale are similar.

Late Corinthian

262. Convex pyxis   Pl. 28

C-62-370. R:23–24; lot 1985 (*ca.* 500 B.C.). P.H. 0.06, p.W. 0.112 m. Two joining fragments from convex wall.

Lower wall: lines in place of rays; two bands. Upper-wall animal frieze: bird to right, added purple on breast, central wing section; sphinx to left, added purple on breast, outer wing, alternate wing feathers, between ribs; bird or siren to right, added purple on alternate tail feathers, center of tail, central section of wing, added-purple dots on chest, upper wing. F.o.: incised blobs. Above animal frieze, three lines, lowest with added purple; tips of shoulder tongues or lines. Careless technique; streaky glaze; sloppy incision; added purple in irregular patches.

Late Corinthian

263. Convex pyxis   Fig. 31, Pl. 28

C-65-492. Q:26; lot 2230 (late 5th century). P.H. 0.037, p.W. 0.056 m. One shoulder fragment.

Two antithetical sphinxes, lotus between. Black bands above. F.o.: incised blobs.

Late Corinthian

264. Convex pyxis   Pl. 28

C-61-273. P–Q:24–25; lot 893 (first quarter 4th century). H. 0.041, D. 0.078, D. foot 0.051 m. Complete.

Low ring foot, wide resting surface, slightly convex undersurface; low globular body merging with shoulder; raised flat rim. Two central black circles on undersurface; band from undersurface over inner face of foot; exterior foot black. Wall: black band; two glaze lines; file of nine silhouette birds to right, no incision or added colors. F.o.: dots and blobs. Dicing on shoulder. Vertical rim, face black; flat top with continuous black zigzag between black lines; lip black. Peeling glaze.

Probably last quarter 6th century

265. Pyxis lid   Figs. 19, 31, Pl. 28

C-62-793. R:23–24; lot 1991 (late 6th century). H. 0.037, est. D. 0.105 m. Half missing; full profile.

Well inset, high flange tapering to resting surface; lid horizontal below, slightly domed upper surface; short stem of knob with wide flare rising into domed top of knob. Flange, undersurface reserved. At edge of lid two lines. Animal frieze (beginning with well-preserved area): ram to left (partly missing); lion to right; antithetical sphinxes with palmette and lotus between; lion to left; ram to right facing feline to left; palmette and lotus; feline to right facing ram to left (first animal). Symmetrical design of eight animals arranged in relation to axial palmette motifs. Added purple used extensively on all figures; added white disappeared. F.o.: incised rosettes with and without double circles. Above animal frieze, dicing between two lines; rays on upper lid. Knob: added-purple and black pinwheel on top; dicing on outer edge of knob. Precise miniature style; exquisite detail.

Heraldic Lions Painter (Amyx). See Amyx, *CorVP*, no. 7, p. 119.

Early Corinthian

266. Pyxis lid   Pl. 28

C-65-458. M:17–18, O:18; lots 3222 (first half 3rd century after Christ), 4350 (late Roman). P.H. 0.02, est. D. 0.136 m. Two joining fragments of rim, flange; knob missing.

Shape as **265**, with shorter flange, closer to lid edge. Undersurface, flange reserved. Dots on lip; two bands at outer edge, inner one with added purple. Animal frieze: feline to left, ram to left. Added purple on lion's ribs, belly, neck, and ram's neck. F.o.: incised rosettes. Above animal frieze, S-maeander between glaze bands, each with added-purple line; rays at top.

Related to the Carrousel Painter (Amyx). See Amyx, *CorVP*, B-7, p. 167.

Middle Corinthian

267. Pyxis lid   Pl. 28

C-65-460. O–P:22–23; lot 4352 (4th century after Christ). P.H. 0.017, est. D. 0.08 m. One third of lid and flange preserved; knob missing.

Shape as **265**; flange more inset from edge of lid. Flange, undersurface reserved. Dots on lip. Animal frieze: panther to left; goat to left; panther to right; siren to right. Added purple on all figures: bellies, ribs, necks. F.o.: incised and plain dots. Above animal frieze, two bands; tongues attached to added-purple band.

Poor imitation of the Carrousel Painter (Amyx). See Amyx, *CorVP*, no. C-7, p. 167. A second, smaller lid by the same hand: C-64-470, Q:20–22, lot 2088.

Middle Corinthian

268. Pyxis lid Fig. 31, Pl. 28

C-62-804. R:23–24; lot 1991 (late 6th century). Max. dim. 0.108 m. Part of lid, flange preserved; outer edge lost; no knob.

Shape as **267**. Undersurface, flange reserved. Animal frieze: bird to right with turned-back head; antithetical sphinxes with palmette between. Crowded f.o.: incised rosettes, swags, dots. Added purple used extensively on figures and palmette. Above animal frieze: two bands, first with added purple; black tongues; band about missing knob. Rather careful incision on figures; careless on palmette and f.o.
Middle Corinthian

269. Kotyle-pyxis lid Pl. 28

C-64-196. P–Q:20–22; lot 2156 (4th century after Christ, Byzantine). P.H. 0.012, est. D. 0.094 m. Part of lid, beginning of flange preserved.

Flange broken away, set very close to edge; convex domed lid, originally with narrow-stemmed high knob. Undersurface, flange reserved. Bands at outer edge. Animal frieze: lion to right; antithetical sphinxes with siren between; feline (tail only) to right. Added purple on faces of siren and sphinxes, lion's neck, alternate wing feathers. F.o.: incised rosettes; dot rosettes; plain dots. Above animal frieze, tongues between bands. Precise incision. Note straight line across shoulder of wing; overly large heads, very narrow bodies. Glaze mostly red, peeling.
Middle Corinthian

270. Powder-pyxis lid Pl. 28

C-62-760. R:23–24; lot 1989 (later 6th century). H. 0.025, est. D. 0.07 m. Full vertical profile.

Flat resting surface; rounded, outward thickened base; vertical wall inset from base; outward thickened rim; horizontal flat top of lid, inset from rim. Interior reserved. Base and rim black with added-purple lines. Two black lines on lower and upper wall. Wall animal frieze: bird with turned-back head; goat to left in silhouette. No f.o. Top of lid: legs and belly of unidentifiable animal in silhouette.
Early Corinthian?

271. Lekanis lid Pl. 28

C-61-167. P–Q:25, P:26; lots 871 (12th century after Christ, coin), 2042 (late 5th century). H. 0.025, D. 0.064 m. Three joining fragments; half of lid, all of knob preserved.
Published: Stroud, *Hesperia* 34, 1965, pl. 4:h.

No separate flange; domed convex lid, turning down to vertical termination in rounded lip; flaring knob without stem; conical above with central cone. Interior reserved. Outer edge: S-maeander between lines. Animal frieze:

birds to right, one with turned-back head; added purple in central section of wing; purple dots on neck; incised circles as eyes. Sparse f.o. Two bands around knob; outer knob glazed; recessed top banded with added purple around glazed cone. Glaze fired red.
Late Corinthian (after mid-century?)

272. Closed vase Pl. 28

C-62-722. R:23–24, M:22–23; lots 1988 (late 6th century), 6828 (mid-5th century). **a)** P.H. 0.057, p.W. 0.051 m. One wall fragment. **b)** P.H. 0.042, p.W. 0.049 m. One wall fragment.

Large closed vessel, highly convex, with at least two figured zones. Polished surface; glaze fired red.
a. Antithetical deer; heads and ears with incised contours; added purple on neck. No f.o. Band above; bottom of rosette in upper figure zone.
b. From same area as fragment **a**. Neck, back, flanks of lion to left; tip of tail incised; added purple on ribs. Band above. Incised foot and belly of feline to right.
Early Corinthian?

273. Closed vase Pl. 28

C-61-262. P–Q:24–25; lot 893 (first quarter 4th century). P.H. 0.049, p.W. 0.057 m. One fragment from upper wall, shoulder. Clay slightly micaceous, very hard. Core: 7.5YR 7/4 (pink); slip: 5YR 7/6 (reddish yellow). Possibly not Corinthian.
Published: Stroud, *Hesperia* 34, 1965, pl. 5:b, right.

Gently convex wall; rounded shoulder. Slipped exterior. Wall: woman to right, right hand raised; face, hand in added white directly on slip; brown contour lines and details. Two incised lines in hair as fillet. Black dress with incised scale pattern. In field to right:

$$[\cdot\cdot]\mathsf{K}A[\cdot\,]$$

Two brown lines above figure; running-leaf design on shoulder.

274. Red-ground closed vase Pl. 28

C-65-501. O:19, N–O:19–20; lots 2239 (late Roman), 2247 (4th century after Christ). P.H. 0.031, p.W. 0.04 m. Two joining fragments from sloping shoulder.

Shoulder with little convexity, very thin fabric. At left: horse's neck and head to left, pulling chariot; driver's hands with whip, reins; guidepost at right break. Behind at right of horse, helmeted warrior rushing right, carrying shield in outline. Lower right: line of incised glaze for tail of second horse. In field between warrior and charioteer's hands:

$$C\,)\,A$$

Added purple on horse's neck, warrior's helmet, outline of shield. Black band limiting scene at top break.
Late Corinthian

CORINTHIAN CONVENTIONALIZING (275–285)

The 11 examples published in this section represent a type of pottery known from the Vrysoula Classical deposit.[1] The five oinochoai, two phialai, three plates, and one lid are typical of the unpublished vases decorated in this style, still in the context pottery. One shape from the Vrysoula deposit is not represented in the Sanctuary: the lekythos, decorated with the characteristic animals or floral patterns, or both. The lekythos in general is absent from the Sanctuary pottery.[2] Apparently some shapes were not appropriate for the goddesses.

The two phialai, **280** and **281**, introduce a new shape into the repertoire of vases decorated in the Conventionalizing style. **280** is especially interesting for its peculiar sirens. They resemble the felines on the plate **283**; both types of animals are similar to the beast on the Vrysoula oinochoe C-64-176 and lekythos C-64-162.[3] All seem to be related to the same workshop, that of the Merlin Painter.[4] The oinochoe **276**, without animals, decorated with palmettes, maeanders, and other Conventionalizing motifs, probably also came from the same studio.

It was known that the floral decoration on these vases continued into the 4th century, especially on oinochoai, pyxides, and lids.[5] **279** shows that the figure style also survived well into that century. I know of no later examples, fortunately. The early Hellenistic potters in Corinth adopted instead the more conventional Hellenistic decorative forms of stamping, West Slope, and other widespread methods.[6]

275. Ray-based oinochoe   Pl. 29

C-64-476. N–O:24, O:24, N:24, N–O:24–25; lots 2094 (early 4th century), 2110 (first quarter 4th century), 2140 (second half 5th century), 2142 (first quarter 4th century), 2144 (mid-4th century), 2244 (first quarter 4th century), 72-207 (second quarter 5th century). **a)** P.H. 0.14, est. D. foot 0.13, est. D. wall 0.21 m. Thirteen joining fragments of foot and wall. **b)** P.H. 0.085, p.W. 0.151 m. Five joining fragments of wall. **c)** P.L. 0.075 m. One fragment of shoulder.

Wide flaring ring foot, with resting surface only at outer edge; flaring convex wall turning vertical above to flat shoulder; neck ring at top break of fragment **c**. Polished surface. Glaze thin, peeling, fired red in places. Resting surface, undersurface reserved. Outer foot banded in black, added red, black. Wall: wide black rays with extended tips; bands of black, added red; running spiral with dots above and below, between black bands; black alternately upright and pendent volute palmettes, with eight or nine petals; stopped three-stroke maeander at top of wall between black lines. Shoulder: four black lines; dotted spiral as on wall; running maeander below black neck ring. Interior reserved.

See KP 2424 and KP 2429 for the dotted-spiral motif (*Corinth* XV, iii, nos. 968, 969, oinochoai but much smaller).

First or early second quarter 5th century

276. Broad-bottomed oinochoe   Pl. 29

C-65-499. N–O:23, N:22–23, O:22–23, M:21, N:23; lots 2152 (4th-century pottery, 2nd-century coin), 2173 (mid-4th century), 2183 (late 5th—early 4th century), 2185 (late 5th—early 4th century), 2250 (end of 4th century), 4458 (late 4th century), 4474 (mid-4th century), 4477 (late 5th century), 4488 (second half 5th century). **a)** P.H. 0.095, est. D. base 0.23 m. Two joining fragments of base, lower wall. **b)** P.H. 0.154 m. Eight joining fragments of wall. **c)** P.H. 0.11 m. Four joining fragments of upper wall, shoulder. Restored height of preserved fragments 0.183 m.

Flat resting surface; wall inset from base with rounded projection; cylindrical wall merging with rounded shoulder. Resting surface reserved. Base wall projection black; lower wall with added-red and black lines. Zones of decoration, each limited by black line, as follows: 1) Seven-stroke stopped maeander. 2) Tendril of alternating upright and pendent palmettes each with seven petals; chevrons between tendrils. 3) Running spirals with chevrons between spirals. 4) Five-stroke stopped maeander. 5) Enscrolled horizontal palmette of seven petals. 6) Seven-stroke stopped maeander, punctuated by checkerboards. 7) Running maeander. 8) Two rows of buds. 9) Two rows of five-stroke stopped maeanders; beginning

---

[1] Pemberton, *Hesperia* 39, 1970, pp. 265–307.

[2] See Shape Studies, pp. 52–53. The Vrysoula forms of goblet and kantharoi are also unrepresented in the Sanctuary. Only one fragment of a goblet was found: C-65-494, not published, from lot 2230, the floor of Room E. The terminal date of that lot, at the end of the 5th century, helps confirm the date established for the Vrysoula pottery. See Catalogue I: Group 3.

[3] Pemberton, *Hesperia* 39, 1970, pp. 271–273, no. 1, pl. 66 and p. 274, no. 5, pl. 66.

[4] *NC*, no. 1553, fig. 195, p. 337, for the British Museum vase giving the name to the workshop.

[5] For example, C-71-191 (Williams and Fisher, *Hesperia* 41, 1972, p. 161, no. 46, pl. 27; drain 1971-1).

[6] There is a curious example of outline style on an Attic jug: Braun, *AM* 85, 1970, p. 145, no. 120, pl. 59:2, 4.

of running spiral at upper break of fragment **c**. All decoration in black.

Clubbed ends of petals. Use of chevrons as in Merlin Painter's workshop: see Pemberton, *Hesperia* 39, 1970, pp. 273, 282–283.

Late third or early fourth quarter 5th century

277. Broad-bottomed oinochoe Pl. 29

C-70-203. M:23–24; lot 6508 (miscellaneous finds). P.H. 0.067, D. 0.098 m. Many joining fragments, preserving parts of base, wall, stub of handle, lower shoulder.

Slightly concave resting surface; flare to bevel; concave wall; offset sloping shoulder without outer shoulder ring; stub of vertical strap handle on outer shoulder. Black band under bevel to resting surface; resting surface reserved; lower wall banded; black, two added-red lines above. Traces of black cavorting animals on wall, in silhouette. Linear enscrolled palmettes on shoulder.

See C-64-177 (Pemberton, *Hesperia* 39, 1970, p. 273, no. 2, pl. 66). **277** is slightly later.

Fourth quarter 5th century

278. Broad-bottomed oinochoe Pl. 29

C-61-202. P:24–25; lot 878 (third quarter 4th century). H. 0.084, D. resting surface 0.07 m. Many joining fragments; center of floor, parts of wall missing.

Flat resting surface; rounded bevel at base of wall; wall barely concave, narrowing to shoulder; offset sloping shoulder without ring; tall cylindrical neck with base drip ring; trefoil mouth; high strap handle from shoulder to mouth. Resting surface reserved. Lower wall: lower bands black, two brown, black, two brown (brown is diluted glaze). Upper wall: very linear, black palmette leaves on either side of curvilinear stem. Two brown lines on shoulder; on upper shoulder black wave pattern; brown on drip ring; lower neck brown; upper neck, mouth, handle black. Sharp profile lost; wall elongated.

Second quarter or mid-4th century

279. Broad-bottomed oinochoe Pl. 30

C-61-460. P–Q:24; lot 899 (mid-4th century). P.H. 0.067, est. D. resting surface 0.11 m. Five joining fragments of parts of base, wall, shoulder.

Flat resting surface; rounded bevel set off from wall by groove; low, ovoid wall merging with sloping shoulder. Black from bevel to midwall; brown line. On upper wall: very linear palmette leaves as **278**. On shoulder: winged bust, with parts of two others; added-purple torso; brown lines for tall neck, head, eyes; dark and light brown for wings. Unarticulated profile. The end of the Corinthian Conventionalizing figure style.

Mid-4th century

280. Phiale Fig. 32, Pl. 30

C-64-407. N–O: 24–25, O:24; lots 2094 (early 4th century), 2110 (first quarter 4th century). **a)** Max. dim. 0.091, est. D. 0.18 m. Three joining fragments of floor, rim. **b)** Max. dim. 0.078 m. One floor fragment.

Low profile; slightly convex resting surface; flaring convex wall, turning vertical to outward thickened rim, with groove setting off rim from outer wall; center with omphalos missing.

a. Outer rim black; rest of exterior reserved. Dots on upper face of rim; black band on inner wall. Floor: black line delineating inner tondo; added-red dots inside line; more traces of added red to inner break, pattern unclear. Outer floor: palmettes of 11 petals, with small side palmettes, between sirens(?). Palmettes oriented to center of floor, sirens to rim. Siren at left: head to left, wing outstretched from thin body which curls down to rim; originally black with incised scales and feathers for wing and hair; incised circles on body (see **283**). Traces of second siren at right break.

b (not illustrated). Palmettes, siren with incised circles. Traces of added brown and added red on sirens.

See the decoration on the shoulder of a pyxis in Bonn: G. Weicker, *Seelenvogel*, Leipzig 1902, p. 143, figs. 66, 67; and **283** below.

Probably third quarter of 5th century (by profile)

281. Phiale Pl. 30

C-65-507. M–N:12; lot 4409 (4th century after Christ, Byzantine). Max. dim. 0.06 m. One fragment of outer floor, rim.

Shape as **280**; groove between inner wall and rim. Black and added-red buds on rim; inner wall black; exterior reserved. On floor: trailing glaze strokes, for smoke? Possibly related to the Sam Wide group, see pp. 134–136 below.

Later 5th century

282. Plate Pl. 30

C-65-441. M–N:12; lot 4409 (4th century after Christ, Byzantine). Max. dim. 0.085 m. One fragment of outer floor, beginning of rim.

No foot; flat resting surface with two grooves near outer edge; beginning of convex rising rim. Polished surface; exterior and undersurface reserved. Floor: head, wing, one foreleg of sphinx to left, confronting second sphinx of whom part of face, breast, raised leg are preserved. Legs raised over top of lotus (see **27**, Group 2); bud rosette between faces. Figures in black, outline technique; diluted glaze for details of face, wing feathers; added-white band in hair. Outer floor black. Good, controlled drawing.

First half 5th century

FIG. 32. Corinthian black-figured phiale **280**. Scale 1:1

283. Plate   Fig. 16, Pl. 30

C-61-241. P–Q:24–25, L:28, M–N:24; lots 893 (first quarter 4th century), 6847 (miscellaneous finds). a) H. 0.027, D. 0.22, D. foot 0.152 m. Many joining fragments, preserving half of floor, most of rim; plaster restoration. b) Max. dim. 0.045 m. One floor fragment.

Disk foot; inset undersurface; undersurface and foot with grooves; flaring rim becoming horizontal at rounded lip; groove before lip on upper face; one suspension hole. Outer face of rim, foot, undersurface reserved. Glaze fired mostly red.

a. Dots on lip; added red on groove; ivy-berry chain on lower rim; glaze bands at juncture of rim and floor. Floor: central black band; black line; added-red band; two black lines. Outer floor: very thin felines walking right, oriented to rim, turned-back heads, frontal faces. Incised detail over glaze of bodies: circles on bodies, lines on neck, roughly incised features.

b (not illustrated). Part of rump of feline.

See **280** above; pyxis KP 1170 (*Corinth* XV, iii, no. 1023, pls. 45, 107); oinochoe C-64-176 (Pemberton, *Hesperia* 39, 1970, p. 271, no. 1, pl. 66).

Third or early fourth quarter 5th century

284. Plate   Pl. 30

C-65-427. N–O:23; lot 4474 (mid-4th century). Max. dim. 0.10 m. One floor fragment.

No foot; flat resting surface with wheel grooves; wide, shallow groove before outer edge. Undersurface reserved. Floor: design of outer area limited by black band outside, added red inside, diluted black line above added red. In field: cavorting animals in silhouette drawing. At left, bird: neck, head, long beak, back-swept wing, body at left break. Right: four legs, body, tail, to right. Under right animal, X with chevrons in angles.

Late 5th or early 4th century

285. Powder-pyxis lid   Pl. 30

C-64-396. N–O:23; lot 2152 (4th-century pottery, 2nd-century coin). P.H. 0.05, D. 0.091 m. Many joining fragments, lower edge not preserved.

Vertical flange slightly concave, descending from raised rounded rim, outward thickened; flat lid top. Interior reserved. Flange: glaze at lower break; central added-red band with two diluted glaze lines above and below; black band continuing over rim. Top: central black bud rosette; two lines of diluted glaze; band of added red; chain of ivy-berry pattern in black.

Second quarter or mid-5th century B.C.

CORINTHIAN OUTLINE STYLE (286–292)

Three of the catalogued vases have been published in *Archaeology*,[7] wherein some discussion of the style was presented. The outline style on 5th-century Corinthian vases was known from a few earlier examples.[8] The excavations of the Demeter Sanctuary have found sufficient numbers of the vases to prove a local popularity of the technique. As yet, no vases so decorated are known to have been exported.

The method of decorating varies. **287** has a surface slip; **288**, **289**, and **292** show polishing of the surface before painting. **287**, **292**, and probably **288** and **289** have polychrome effects. The drawing, where clearly discernible, is of the highest quality, except on **286**. On some vases, the figures suggest possible activities in the Demeter cult (**292**) or mythological subjects relevant for the goddesses of the Sanctuary (**287**).[9]

Outline style is a more appropriate term for the vases than Corinthian white ground. Since Corinthian clay normally fires quite pale, the creamy white and chalky slips used in Attic pottery were not necessary. Contour lines are usually in a shade of brown. The artist of **287** used dark brown for horses (**h**), a red brown for humans (**c, j**), and a black brown for non-human objects (**d, i**, and probably **k**). The painter of the kotyle **292** may have used brown for male (**b**) and purple for female (**c, d**).[10] The artist of the krater with architectural decoration, **290**, used black throughout the preserved fragment, but the rest of the scene, whatever it was, may have been rendered with additional colors.

Given the fragmentary state of the extant pieces, it is impossible to establish workshop relationships. Nor can the vases be well dated. The kotyle, **292**, is similar in subject to the oinochoe found in the Forum in 1934.[11] But the kotyle is earlier; the lack of foreshortening on most of the boy's body, the stiff rendering of folds, the more archaic eye of Persephone, all require an earlier date. The Forum oinochoe comes from a well of 460–420 B.C., although whether at the upper or lower date is unclear. Only one of the fragments of the Sanctuary kotyle has a dated context; the context of **d** includes nothing later than the third quarter of the 5th century, with earlier material in the lot. I suggest tentatively a date of 480–450 B.C. for the vase.

287 has one fragment, **b**, from a context no later than the third quarter of the 5th century. The krater was made before 425 B.C. and probably before mid-century. **288** has one fragment, **c**, from a similar context. The context of the architectural krater, **290**, spans most of the 5th century.

All the vases in this style were probably made in the 5th century, more specifically in the second and third quarters, thus contemporary in their lower limit with the vases of the Sam Wide group, with which there are some technical similarities. The style of drawing and technique might have been influenced by the white-ground work of Attic vase painters, but the shapes differ. **287** is a large skyphoid krater, which may also be the shape of the other large vessels. **292** appears to be unique; I know of no Attic white-ground kotylai.[12] The style of decoration never attained the popularity it enjoyed in Athens but was reserved for a few vases, probably of cult importance.

---

[7] Pemberton, *Archaeology* 31, Nov.–Dec. 1978, pp. 27–33.

[8] C-36-836, found in the Forum (Pease, *Hesperia* 6, 1937, p. 312, fig. 41; probably from well 1936-1): thin fragments, probably not from a krater; brownish slipped surface, showing a hand and part of a border. C-34-362, from Forum well 1934-10 (*ibid.*, p. 311, no. 235, fig. 40): oinochoe with a torch race. Altar MF 71-19, from Forum excavations, lot 6768: small altar with a horse's head. There are at least three more vases with outline-style decoration from the Demeter Sanctuary, not published here because of the poor condition of the fragments. These are C-64-417 and C-71-570, possibly from the same vase as **289**; C-64-400, C-65-167, and C-72-212 all from the same krater; C-68-331, possibly the same as **291**. There are several additional sherds without any decoration but which by size and fabric may be undecorated pieces belonging to the type.

[9] For the interpretation of the letter forms on **287**, see Stroud, *Hesperia* 37, 1968, p. 322, reading fragment **l** as Ere]bnos, the lord of the underworld, and thus identifying the scene as the rape of Persephone. A. L. Boegehold ("Korinthiaka: A Neglected Gorgon" (*GRBS* 15, 1974, pp. 32–35) read the letters as Sth]enoi, one of the Gorgon sisters, identifying the scene as showing Perseus, the ugly sisters, and possibly He[rmes (**j**).

[10] A similar distinction in color for outlines of the different sexes is visible on the Pitsa plaque of a family sacrificing: red brown for females, black brown for males (J. Charbonneaux, *Archaic Greek Art*, New York 1971, fig. 357). The plaque is signed by a Corinthian.

[11] For the Forum oinochoe C-34-362, see footnote 8 above.

[12] For the shapes in Attic white ground, see J. Mertens, *Attic White-Ground*, New York 1977. She notes black-figured white-ground skyphoi (pp. 89–95) but no outline white-ground kotylai or skyphoi.

286. Hydria   Pl. 31

C-73-28. T–U:19; lots 73–96 (1st century after
Christ), 73–99 (second half 4th century after Christ).
Two non-joining fragments from shoulder, top of wall.
a) P.H. 0.04, p.W. 0.086 m. b) P.H. 0.049, p.W.
0.077 m. Two joining fragments. Gray clay: 10YR 7/2
(light gray).

Surface of fragment **b** fired a lighter color than **a**. Clay
color not typical of Corinthian, but texture characteristic
of Corinthian. Fragments appear to be handmade; no
slip.

a. Bearded man, to left; top of garment at lower break;
incised line for fillet in hair; object behind him probably a
flying cloak (although appears fishlike).

b. Woman in brown outline, to right; chin visible at
top right edge; left arm stretched to right; lines of breasts
visible. Dark object at waist, below which are traces of
legs. At left, single added-red line.

Drawing is very poor, not resembling the rest of the
fragments in outline style.

5th century

287. Krater   Pl. 31

C-64-226 (**b–m**), C-65-491 (**a**). Thirteen fragments
from a very large skyphoid krater; each fragment discussed separately with specific grid and lot.

Published: Stroud, *Hesperia* 37, 1968, pl. 93:a;
Daux, *BCH* 89, 1965, p. 760, fig. 17; Pemberton, *Archaeology* 31, Nov.–Dec. 1978, p. 33; Boegehold (footnote 9 above, p. 129).

a (C-65-491). M–O:27–29; lot 2210 (4th century after
Christ). P.H. 0.062, est. D. 0.30 m. Fragment of foot.
Traces of burning at top break, continuing over break
to interior. Core: 5YR 7/7 (reddish yellow); surface
slip: 10YR 8/4 (very pale brown), applicable to all
fragments. Interior reserved on all fragments. Polished
creamy slip on exterior; core buff in center, orange
close to surface (sandwich effect).

Heavy torus foot; beginning of straight flaring wall. Two
brown lines on inner face of foot; resting surface reserved;
band on outer face of foot and at juncture of wall and
ledge of floor. Exterior gouged.

b (C-64-226 b + l). N–O:23, N:22; lots 2152 (4th-cen-
tury pottery, 2nd-century coin), 4391 (later 5th century). P.H. 0.11, p.W. 0.076 m. Three joining fragments of lower wall.

Ground line: egg-and-dart between brown glaze lines;
eggs alternately of brown and added red, darts brown;
eggs vary in size. Both border lines in two parallel narrow bands overlapping each other. Wall design above
border: dark brown wheel with five, not four, spokes;
floor of chariot in added red between brown outlines;

above red, an area of streaky orange (diluted glaze), not
drapery, possibly the low side of chariot. Overlapping
orange, small patch of brown with four lines at end (tassel? tip of cloak?). At upper left, thin lines of brown for
horses' tails.

c (C-64-226 n). M:22–23; lot 6827 (late 4th century).
P.H. 0.057, p.W. 0.04 m. One fragment of lower wall.
Border as fragment **b**. Foot outlined in reddish brown
above (color used for humans; compare dark brown
outline for horses on **h**); darker brown contour below, for
sole of sandal; broad brown strap across instep, beginning of second narrower strap for ankle band.

d (C-64-226 j). M:17–18; lot 3222 (first half 3rd century after Christ). P.H. 0.063, p.W. 0.043 m. One
fragment of lower wall; surface scratched.
Border as fragment **b**. Object drawn in black outline resting on border: possibly foot and beginning of leg of metal
cauldron or tripod. At left, a long thin diagonal brown
line (not a staff); orange tassel ending in tiny brown dots:
decoration of metal object?

e (C-64-226 e). N:21–23; lot 2170 (second half 4th
century after Christ). P.H. 0.045, p.W. 0.08 m. One
fragment of lower wall; surface gouged.
Border as fragment **b**. Thin orange line above border.

f (C-64-226 f). N:28; lot 2259 (5th century). P.H.
0.071, p.W. 0.045 m. One fragment of lower wall; surface chipped.
Border as fragment **b**.

g (C-64-226 k; not illustrated). N–O:22; lot 4475
(third quarter 4th century). P.H. 0.030, p.W. 0.024 m.
One fragment of lower wall.
Border as fragment **b**.

h (C-64-226 a). N–O:23; lot 2152 (4th-century pottery, 2nd-century coin). P.H. 0.065, p.W. 0.071 m.
One fragment of middle wall.
Upper rear legs of two horses galloping left, pulling
chariot of fragment **b**(?). Front pair of legs in light-
orange wash (diluted glaze); rear pair darker; interior
details in thin brown lines; dark brown outline of legs.

i (C-64-226 d). N:23; lot 2178 (early 4th century).
P.H. 0.066, p.W. 0.055 m. One fragment of middle
wall.
At bottom break, horizontal band in dark outline; upper
course of stepped altar, letters]ON[between bands. Fire
on altar: stacked logs drawn as dark circles of brown,
alternating with lighter areas rendered in raised clay;
round dots of added red for hot flames or charcoal; light
brown and orange (diluted glaze) for flames and smoke.

j (C-64-226 h). N:23; lot 4477 (late 5th century). P.H.
0.092, p.W. 0.094 m. One fragment of upper wall.

At top break, two handle scars for horizontal handle; handles outlined in brown. Two neatly drilled holes for ancient repair with plugs; holes carefully placed in empty field, although right one close to one letter. Letters HB[in field.

At left, head facing right; fillet over brown curly hair; wing, with apex partially hidden by head. Red-brown contour line for face; brown contour line and added-red details for wing. Added white in face: to correct mistake of original contour line, apparently too narrow, white used as eraser. Added white used nowhere else on fragments. At right lower break, thin contour line of red brown, either figure's outstretched bent left arm or elbow of second person facing winged figure. Figure is probably male; hair style more appropriate for male than female.

k (C-64-226 m). M:20; no lot. P.H. 0.039, p.W. 0.04 m. One fragment of upper wall; traces of burning at top and right, going over break.

At left break, hole for ancient repair (see **j**). Fragment shows part of pole or quiver, with fluttering brown tassels; broad black band under burnt area at top, connecting with vertical outline at right. More black bands below; two cross each other. Thin, light-brown lines under black bands; at top right, another outline horizontal to break.

l (C-64-226 g). O–P:13–15; lot 4385 (second half 2nd century after Christ). P.H. 0.079, p.W. 0.074 m. One fragment of upper wall.

Outer part of wing of figure facing left; ends of feathers in added red and gray brown; interior detail in thin, gray-brown strokes. In field (retrograde; see Pl. 31):

BNOϟ

At lower right break, thin, vertical, light-brown stroke.

m (C-64-226 c). N–O:23; lot 2152 (4th-century pottery, 2nd-century coin). P.H. 0.056, p.W. 0.078, est. D. lip 0.34 m. One fragment of lip.

Rounded lip, no rim or separate articulation. Glaze on lip, top of inner wall. Scars of handle roots preserved.

Estimated height of whole vase 0.40 m. There is not enough preserved to reconstruct the figure scenes with any certainty; there may have been two separate scenes, separated by the handles. The letters on fragment **l** may be read as [Ere]bnos, an underworld figure, or as [Sth]e-noi, one of the Gorgons (see footnote 9, p. 129 above). The abduction of Persephone by Hades, coming in a chariot, or the killing of Medusa by Perseus are possible interpretations. The quality of the vase, in both technique and drawing, makes this an exceptional work.

Second quarter 5th century

288. Krater   Pl. 31

C-69-299. Four fragments from a large krater; each fragment discussed separately with specific grid and lot.

a (b). M–N:23; lot 6838 (early 4th century). P.H. 0.064, p.W. 0.079 m. Two joining fragments of lower wall.

Soft orange clay, not fired as hard as **287**. Exterior not slipped but polished, surface flaking. Interior glazed (fired red) with added-red bands. At bottom: border with egg-and-dart; border outline in brown glaze; eggs in diluted glaze, peeling; area around eggs in added red; darts in added white. Above, at right, part of outer rim of chariot wheel in brown; left, three or four rear legs of two horses, galloping left; legs in dark brown outline, filled in with lighter brown (see **287h**). Patch of thin brown glaze below hooves, just above border.

b (a). Stairway cuts; lot 6215 (6th century after Christ). P.H. 0.054, p.W. 0.052 m. One fragment of upper wall.

Garland of elongated buds in light brown, apparently suspended from two objects at sides of break. Left object of angular shape, drawn with brown contour line and reserved; object re-emerges at lower left, filled in with added red. Right object rounded; brown contour line, continuing to lower right break. Outside of brown line, traces of diluted glaze. The fragment may be an excerpt from some type of architecture.

c (d). L–M:23–24; lot 6841 (later 5th century). P.H. 0.035, p.W. 0.058 m. One fragment of upper wall.

Large patch of peeling added red, with brown outline. Polelike object in brown passes diagonally across field.

d (c). No grid or lot. P.H. 0.034, p.W. 0.04 m. One fragment of upper wall.

Large area of mostly peeled added red; thin brown contour line on right side; added red continues horizontally at top right. The fragment possibly represents a figure in a red garment, with outstretched arm.

Less can be said about this krater than the first, but fragment **a** is sufficiently similar to fragment **h** of **287** that we may suggest two vases with the same scene, made in two different workshops, at the same time.

Second quarter 5th century

289. Krater   Pl. 32

C-65-429 (**b**), C-65-432 (**a**), C-72-254 (**c**). Three fragments from a large krater; each fragment discussed separately with specific grid and lot.

a. M–N:25; lot 4435 (early Roman). P.H. 0.06, p.W. 0.056 m. One fragment of lower wall.

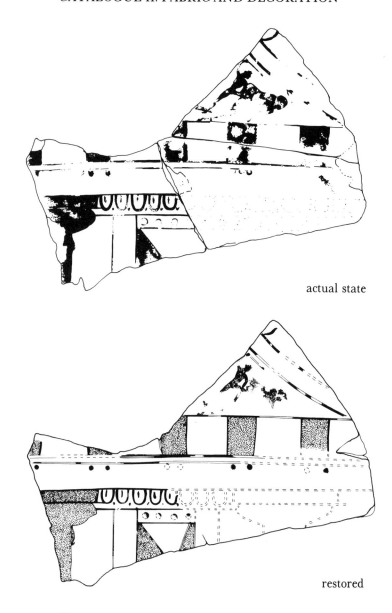

actual state

restored

FIG. 33. Corinthian outline-style krater **290**. Scale 1:2

Glaze fired partly red, partly black; a diluted gray glaze used for details; interior of all fragments glazed brown. Pale clay, fired buff on surface; surface polished, not slipped.

Fragment with lower part of skirt with added-purple contour; gray and red decoration of hem; interior folds rendered in thin gray. No indication of feet, but ascent of hem to right suggests figure flying or running to right. Added-purple and added-red bands at bottom break for border(?).

b. M–N:25; lot 4434 (early Roman). P.H. 0.078, p.W. 0.051 m. Two joining fragments of middle wall.

On either side, large patches of red with areas of added white and added purple: folds? Band of added white on lower right red area might indicate textile pattern. Upper left patch has straight lower edge. In center, thin curving lines of red which converge near lower break. Diagonal line of red at lower right could be a staff.

c (not illustrated). L:26-27; lot 72-129 (third quarter 4th century). P.H. 0.04, p.W. 0.024 m. One fragment of upper wall.

Area of red glaze, mostly peeled, with added purple over it.

Nothing can be made of fragments **b** and **c** of this krater; there are additional pieces, not in this catalogue, with large patches of red but no discernible designs (see footnote 8 above, p. 129).

5th century

290. Krater   Fig. 33, Pl. 32

C-64-188. N–O:24–25; lot 2141 (second half 5th century). P.H. 0.114, p.W. 0.185 m. Three joining fragments, from convex wall.

Published: Stroud, *Hesperia* 37, 1968, pl. 91:c; Daux, *BCH* 88, 1964, p. 696, fig. 11; Pemberton, *Archaeology* 31, Nov.–Dec. 1978, p. 31.

Orange core; paler at surface; surface neither slipped nor polished. Very worn; decoration in black glaze, peeling. Interior reserved. On exterior, depiction of temple. At left break, Doric column; egg-and-dart molding below architrave; below molding, entrance to temple, rosettes above the open doors. Area at right worn, with faint traces of glaze, probably indicating a second column. Above, metope-triglyph frieze: the triglyphs in silhouette, with round guttae below. At upper right, pediment of temple, with fighting figures in it. Glaze line at top right break over pediment could be part of floral peak akroterion.

If the apical akroterion is shown, the pediment would not fill the width of the fragment; thus both the front and part of one flank would be shown on the extant piece. Such a reconstruction, however, would require placing the door off center. Alternatively, the line over the pediment could be accidental, and thus only the façade would be shown, with the doors open, two columns before it.

The architecture is not very accurate: the metopes are placed over the columns; the capitals are too wide for the shafts. But the drawing of the doors indicates a very early example of perspective drawing.

Probably mid-5th century

291. Krater   Pl. 32

C-65-434. N–O:22; lot 4475 (third quarter 4th century). P.H. 0.061, p.W. 0.065 m. One fragment of wall.

Orange core; soft clay; no exterior slip; interior reserved. Four parallel lines in added red, running from upper right to lower left, over a brown-black curling band and outlined object with scalloped edge: neither a lyre nor a chariot. Another outline at lower left; beginning of large patch of brown at lower break. Despite the poor condition, the drawing is visibly formal and very painstaking.

For an additional fragment possibly from **291** see footnote 8 above, p. 129.

Classical

292d

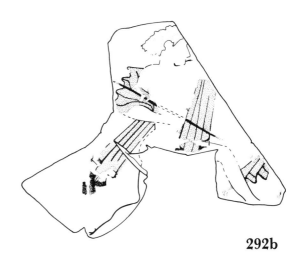

292b

FIG. 34. Corinthian outline-style kotyle **292**. Scale 1:2

292. Kotyle   Fig. 34, Pl. 32

C-65-291, C-69-180, C-69-182. Four fragments from a large kotyle, each fragment discussed separately with specific lot and grid.

Published: Pemberton, *Archaeology* 31, Nov.–Dec. 1978, p. 33.

a (C-69-182). N–O:17–18; lot 6199 (late 5th or early 4th century). P.H. 0.038, D. foot 0.12 m. Six joining fragments; part of lower wall, foot preserved.

Pale clay, core: 7.5YR 8/4 (pink), fired orange in spots; pale surface, polished, not slipped: 10YR 8/3 (very pale brown).

Ring foot with wide resting surface; straight flaring wall. Undersurface: brown pinwheel design. Inner and outer faces of foot brown; resting surface reserved. Concentric bands of brown glaze on inner wall and floor; no decoration on preserved exterior wall. For pinwheel design: C-37-1037 (Campbell, *Hesperia* 7, 1938, p. 589, no. 99); design apparently most popular before 450 B.C.

b (C-65-291 a). M–O:17–20, N–O:17–18; lots 3206 (Byzantine), 6199 (late 5th or early 4th century). P.H.

0.107, p.W. 0.138 m. Eleven joining fragments; part of wall, lip preserved.

Three concentric bands of brown on inner wall. Exterior: boy running right, staff in right hand, another object in left; right leg to rear, left in front. Body outlined in brown; brilliant added-red cloak around back and over both upper arms; folds rendered in black. Raised left leg overlaps cloak of boy running in front of him; traces of added red at extreme right break. Details of face, hair, arms have gone.

c (C-65-291 c). O:22–23; lot 2249 (end of 4th century). P.H. 0.025, p.W. 0.036 m. One fragment of wall.

Broad brown band on interior, same width as lowest one on fragment **b**. On exterior: foot of figure running or flying right; outline in added purple; purple ankle bone.

d (C-69-180). N:18; lot 6198 (third quarter 5th century). P.H. 0.18, p.W. 0.07, est. D. 0.24 m. Two joining fragments of upper wall, lip.

Head facing left; nose outlined in added purple; eye, hair, crown in brown. Eye not in triangular form. Crown with spiky projections; band decorated with a maeander. In field (see Fig. 34):

ΦΒΡΣ[.

Three additional wall fragments, without figured decoration, preserved, not published. For the subject, compare the oinochoe with the torch race: C-34-362 (Pease, *Hesperia* 6, 1937, p. 311, no. 235, fig. 40). **292** is earlier by style and context.

Second quarter 5th century or slightly earlier

SAM WIDE GROUP (293–297)

The workshop producing these miniature vases was isolated in 1901 by Sam Wide[13] and originally published as Boeotian. Although Pease compared the drawing on the Forum oinochoe with the style of the Sam Wide figures,[14] the vessels were still identified as Boeotian as late as 1949.[15] In 1952, Ure re-identified the fabric rightly as Corinthian.[16] Sufficient numbers of them have been found in the Potters' Quarter and in the Demeter Sanctuary to verify Corinthian origin. In 1970, Boardman proposed giving the group the name of the scholar who first discussed these vases.[17]

Stillwell and Benson list 19 examples of the group, excluding those from the Demeter Sanctuary and the related vases with lotus designs.[18] The range of shapes is not great: two-handled stemless cups, plates, bowls or shallow footless dishes, pyxides and lids, and lekanides and lids if the lotus-design vases are included. Curiously, the examples from the Demeter Sanctuary do not include cups, the most popular shape in the Potters' Quarter examples.[19] The phiale **281** is possibly a member of the group; the trailing glaze strokes decorating that vase might indicate smoke and so compare with **293** and **295**. If it is a Widean work, it introduces a new shape into the repertory. All the vases are small, not truly functional in size.

None of the vases in the group appears to be slipped. A few show polychromy, although no Sanctuary examples are so decorated.[20] The drawing never approaches the quality of the large outline vases. The drawing style is unmistakeable, especially in the distinctive features: big heads, tiny torsos and limbs, fringed eyelashes, thick contour lines. Stillwell rightly stresses the humor often found in this group.[21]

[13] S. Wide, "Eine lokale Gattung boiotische Gefässe," *AM* 26, 1901, pp. 143–156.

[14] Pease, *Hesperia* 6, 1937, p. 312. For the Forum oinochoe, C-36-836, see footnote 8 above, p. 129.

[15] A. D. Ure, "Boeotian Haloa," *JHS* 69, 1949, pp. 18–24.

[16] A. D. Ure, "The God with the Winnowing-fan," *JHS* 72, 1952, p. 121.

[17] J. Boardman, "A Sam Wide Group Cup in Oxford," *JHS* 90, 1970 (pp. 194–195), p. 194.

[18] *Corinth* XV, iii, pp. 368–371. The appendix on the style of the group is by Stillwell; she listed 13 examples, Benson added 5 (note 1); the pyxis in Athens (*NC*, no. 1515) is surely Widean, not just related (*Corinth* XV, iii, p. 370, note 7). There are at least six examples of the related lotus vases (called rosebuds by Stillwell). That brings the total number to 30, with the 5 examples published here.

[19] The cup is not a popular shape in the Sanctuary in any technique, fabric, or period. See p. 31 above.

[20] Only **294** shows a thin wash of color for the dress of the figure. CP-989, a cup found in 1930 in the Peribolos of Apollo (see *Corinth* XV, iii, p. 368, no. 9), shows a figure of an archer (Herakles?) drawn in thick black outline, the body having a diluted (yellow) glaze.

[21] *Corinth* XV, iii, p. 369.

FIG. 35. Sam Wide plate **295**. Scale 1:1

The Wide group has been placed in the later 5th century, probably belonging to the third quarter of that century.[22] **295** helps to confirm that date, for one fragment of it was found in a context dating at the latest approximately 400 B.C. The similarities in technique with the Vrysoula pottery and the outline vases in the previous section are also chronologically valuable.

293. Dish   Pl. 32

C-65-450. O:18; lot 4349 (4th century after Christ). Max. dim. 0.056, est. D. floor 0.084 m. One fragment of floor, wall, rim.

Flat resting surface, no foot; vertical wall; diagonally flaring rim. Resting surface, outer wall reserved. Inner wall glazed; glaze fired red. On floor: hand holding short flaming torch, with poppy hooked around raised index finger; smoke rising from torch. Glaze at lower break possibly from dress on shoulder of missing figure.

For profile: KV 694 (*Corinth* XV, iii, no. 1215; Callipolitis-Feytmans, p. 164, no. 63, fig. 24).

294. Dish   Pl. 32

C-65-440 (**a**), C-65-506 (**b**). M–N:12; lot 4409 (4th century after Christ, Byzantine). Two non-joining fragments. **a**) Max. dim. 0.033 m. One fragment of

foot, floor. **b**) Max. dim. 0.055, est. D. foot 0.04 m. One fragment of foot, floor.

Low ring foot; flat floor; shallow open profile; upper edge not preserved. Foot black; undersurface reserved.

a. Head of woman to left; hair in knot; top of right arm at lower break, extended to side. Fringed eye; heavy chin, no mouth. Winglike object at left perhaps part of omphaloid basket held by outstretched arm.

b. Outstretched left arm; long dress with overfall (horizontal line in center); over arms a filmy cloak in diluted glaze; dress decorated with dots and triangles. Traces of glaze lines at lower left break; large black drip at right.

295. Plate   .   Fig. 35, Pl. 32

C-64-219. N–O:23, M–N:25; lots 2152 (4th-century pottery, 2nd-century coin), 4440 (late 5th century).

---

[22] *Ibid.* Boardman summarizes the argument for the dating ([footnote 17 above, p. 134] p. 195). The London cup with the very peculiar male sphinx has been interpreted as a Corinthian mockery of Kleon. See E. L. Brown, "Kleon Caricatured on a Corinthian Cup," *JHS* 94, 1974, pp. 166–170; such an interpretation has significant bearing on the date.

Max. dim. 0.121, est. D. floor 0.15 m. Two joining fragments of floor.

Published: Stroud, *Hesperia* 37, 1968, pl. 87:b.

Flat plate, no foot. Woman to left, with left arm raised behind, holding torch and stalk of wheat (?); traces of added red on hair. Added-red band at juncture of floor and wall; undersurface grooved. Glaze fired red orange, peeling.

296. Plate   Pl. 32

C-64-208. N–O:24; lot 2143 (early 4th century). Max. dim. 0.069 m. Two joining fragments of floor. Traces of burning.

Published: Stroud, *Hesperia* 37, 1968, pl. 87:c.

Floor: lower face and upper torso of woman to left, broken off above nose; V-neck peplos, folds indicated by glaze lines; heavy chin, pronounced lips, curly hair; right arm bent back to face, holding a poppy. Glaze fired orange; undersurface with concentric grooves in center.

Combination of large head, tiny arms holding objects typical of Widean format.

297. Plate   Pl. 32

C-64-225. N–O:23; lot 2152 (4th-century pottery, 2nd-century coin). Max. dim. 0.111, H. 0.02 m. Two joining fragments; vertical profile preserved.

Published: Stroud, *Hesperia* 37, 1968, pl. 87:d; Pemberton, *Archaeology* 31, Nov.–Dec. 1978, p. 30.

Footless vessel; low rounded wall; flaring horizontal rim, not sharply offset from wall; lip not preserved. Resting surface reserved; grooves on undersurface. Black and added-red bands at juncture of floor and wall; interior wall with added red; rim black. Floor: head, upper torso, right arm of woman to left. Dress with scale pattern (aegis?); necklace, snake bracelet; snake rising from right shoulder. Dotted stephane, over which is forward projection of helmet or spiky crown. In right hand, pine cone or phallus. Fringed eyelash especially Widean. Athena? Note the scale dress of Hera on **261**. Stroud noted that **296** and **297** are by the same hand.

CORINTHIAN RED FIGURE (298–304)

Corinthian red-figured pottery has been most recently studied and published by Herbert and McPhee.[23] The analyses of clay, technique, style, and relation with Attic red figure are not repeated here. Four of the seven fragments discussed in this section were previously published by Herbert. Four additional fragments presented in that publication are not republished, but I list below the grid and lot references for them:

Corinth VII, iv, no. 33: C-65-541. O–P:13–15; lot 4385 (second half 2nd century after Christ)

no. 155: C-65-521. O:23; lot 4347 (end of 4th century)

no. 162: C-64-398. N–O:23; lot 2152 (4th-century pottery, 2nd-century coin)

no. 164: C-72-246. K–L:24–25; no lot

There are considerably more fragments of Corinthian red figure in the Sanctuary pottery. Most are too small and too poorly preserved for publication. The technique is not well suited to Corinthian clay, and the action of the soil in the Sanctuary has destroyed most of the slip, black glaze, and miltos on each sherd, making the scenes virtually illegible.

Herbert rightly notes the popularity of the skyphos shape among the Corinthian red-figured fragments in the Sanctuary.[24] That there may have been dedicatory functions for these skyphoi is, however, unclear. If the votive kalathiskoi are excluded, the majority of vessels from the Sanctuary are in the drinking category. One may also compare the popularity of imported red-figured skyphoi (**61, 343–360**).

The findspots of the fragments are not particularly revealing. All the pieces of the hydria **298** are from the Middle Terrace; the vase was possibly used in a Classical building under the Trapezoidal Stoa (Building N–P:20–25; see Group 6). Also from the Middle Terrace are **303, 304,** and parts of **300**. Unpublished fragments come from the dining-room fills of the Lower Terrace, as did C-72-246, noted above. Very few sherds were found in the Upper Terrace; one, **301**, belongs to the late Roman destruction fill of the Mosaic Building (T–U:19); a few others were found in surface levels. No particular pattern is discernible from the excavated contexts. Therefore, we cannot be sure if the Corinthian red-figured pottery from the Demeter Sanctuary is votive or utilitarian.

[23] *Corinth* VII, iv; I. McPhee, "Local Red Figure from Corinth, 1973–1980," *Hesperia* 52, 1983, pp. 137–153.

[24] *Corinth* VII, iv, p. 66.

298. Hydria Pl. 33

C-61-475. Q:25, R:25, O:22–23; lots 881 (third quarter 4th century), 1953 (Byzantine), 2250 (end of 4th century), 73-139 (second quarter 4th century). **a)** P.H. 0.064, p.W. 0.13 m. Four joining fragments of lower wall. **b)** P.H. 0.07, p.W. 0.06 m. Five joining fragments of lower wall. **c)** P.H. 0.037, p.W. 0.062 m. Three joining fragments of upper wall, shoulder. **d)** P.H. 0.015, p.W. 0.037 m. One fragment of upper wall. **e)** P.H. 0.044, p.W. 0.036 m. Two joining fragments of upper wall, shoulder.

Published: *Corinth* VII, iv, no. 123, pp. 57–58, pl. 20.

Hydria with high ovoid wall merging with flat shoulder. Interior reserved.

a (d). Lower wall black. Border of figure zone: spiral tendril with dots and leaves, between horizontal bands. At upper right, back hoof of horse; large round object (vase?). Spiral ends at right break: end of figured panel on front of hydria.

b (c). Horses galloping left; forelegs of two horses overlapping body of third. At top left, mane of one horse, upper neck of another. Ground line at lower break.

c (a). At left, back of head and mane of horse. At right, rider in chariot(?), extended right arm, probably holding goad; lowered left hand with reins; upper chest with lines for folds of chlamys; beginning of chin at upper right break.

d (e). At left, neck and mane of horse moving left; part of rider at right.

e (b). At right break, muzzle of horse going left; peeling glaze. Spasmodic use of relief contour; raised relief line for interior details; diluted (yellow) glaze for horses' reins.

Style close to some fragments of Herbert's Sketch Painter. Compare hand of fragment **c** with C-37-257 (*Corinth* VII, iv, no. 80, p. 49, pl. 14).

Early 4th century

299. Bell-krater Pl. 33

C-65-523. N–O:23; lots 2152 (4th-century pottery, 2nd-century coin), 4474 (mid-4th century). P.H. 0.098, p.W. 0.132 m. Six joining fragments of wall, beginning of rim.

Published: *Corinth* VII, iv, no. 20, p. 34, pl. 3.

Convex wall, flaring rim. Interior with thin peeling glaze. At left, woman facing right, preserved to just above waist; hair pulled up in a knot, ribbon in hair; wearing a chiton and carrying a flat-topped chest; scarf falling from right hand. Circular objects on top of chest. At right, youth facing right; nude torso, petasos behind neck, strap across torso; cloak encircling lower torso and coming over

right arm; right hand on hip, visible at lower break. Laurel wreath on rim.

Flat interior relief lines (peeling); no contour lines. Diluted yellow glaze for strap on youth's torso; white on hair fillet. Attributed by Herbert to the Pelikai Painter.

Late 5th century

300. Bell-krater Pl. 33

C-65-522. M:17–18, Q–T:16–20, and surface areas; lot 3222 (first half 3rd century after Christ), 4377 (theatral area, surface), 6214 (surface). **a)** P.H. 0.073, p.W. 0.135 m. Two joining fragments of lower wall. **b)** P.H. 0.026, p.W. 0.06 m. One fragment of lower wall. **c)** P.H. 0.049, p.W. 0.047 m. One fragment of midwall.

Published: *Corinth* VII, iv, no. 39, p. 41, pl. 9.

Convex wall, becoming vertical in upper part. Interior black glazed.

a (a). Black band and pink line below as border. At left, palmette under handle. At right, woman moving right; dress billowing to left under palmette; curved modeling lines of chiton over bent right leg, straight lines of dress over advancing left leg; dress decorated with small circles, spiral pattern on border; lower quills of wings preserved. Herbert suggested identification of this figure as Nike. Drapery of second figure visible at right break.

b (c). Foot, chiton hem of figure moving right on ground line; curvilinear pattern over chiton folds; horizontal lines at top break for edge of cloak.

c (b). At top left, breast of frontal woman in thin pleated chiton; dotted cloak covering upper left arm (at right break), passing behind torso, across waist, thrown over extended lower left arm.

No contour lines; for the use of relief line see *Corinth* VII, iv, p. 41. Microscopic examination shows that the vase was covered with a thin yellow slip. Diluted glaze for some dress folds on fragments **a** and **c**. Traces of added white on palmette leaves, wing on **a**. Attributed by Herbert to the Hermes Painter, although glaze and slip of **300** are inferior.

First quarter 4th century

301. Skyphos Pl. 33

C-73-99. T–U:19; lot 73-100 (second half 4th century after Christ). P.H. 0.072, p.W. 0.053 m. Fragment of wall and rim.

Concave wall, rim slightly everted. Interior black glazed. At right, tip of palmette decoration. Profile head and frontal torso of woman looking left; sleeveless chiton; hair in knot with pink snood over it; diluted brown for curls around face; traces of added white on hair; dress shows multitude of linear folds, some in full glaze, some in diluted (yellow) glaze; both breasts point left. Rim border of dotted eggs between black lines.

Slight contour line; little relief visible in interior lines; sketch lines on the body very visible. Closer to the Hermes Painter than to the Pelikai Painter; rendering of chiton different from that of both artists. Relief line of facial contour typical of Hermes Painter.

Very early Corinthian red figure. For another early skyphos see C-37-439 (*Corinth* VII, iv, no. 151, p. 66, pl. 25). The incipient concavity below the rim requires the early date.

Ca. 420–410 B.C.

302. Skyphos   Pl. 33

C-62-943. R:25; lot 1953 (Byzantine). P.H. 0.049, p.W. 0.056 m. One fragment of upper wall.
    Published: *Corinth* VII, iv, no. 124, p. 58, pl. 20.

Interior glazed streaky black. At right, large volute palmette (under handle). At left, crested helmet and part of aegis of Athena, facing left. Contour line around aegis; strong relief line for interior details, especially on aegis. Attributed by Herbert to the Hermes Painter.

End of 5th century

303. Skyphos   Pl. 33

C-73-327 (**a**), C-73-328 (**b**). M–N:23–24; no lot. **a**) P.H. 0.074, p.W. 0.082 m. Two joining fragments of lower wall. **b**) P.H. 0.077, p.W. 0.14 m. Four joining fragments of lower wall.

Interior glazed, peeling, fired gray brown.

a. Reserved band with added pink as ground line

above black originally on lower wall, now peeled, leaving brown stain. At left, right foot with raised heel. At right, flying loose drapery on figure, moving right.

b. Glaze of lower wall at lower break; ground line as fragment **a**. At left, foot and lower cloak of figure facing right; second figure facing left; foot of figure visible at lower right break, wearing cloak, holding staff or spear (thin vertical line between peeled glaze areas). Drawing of figures on **b** inferior to those of **a**; figures of **b** probably cloaked youths on lesser side of skyphos.

No contour lines; flat interior details; hooks at end of drapery lines on figures of **b**. See **304**.

End of 5th or beginning of 4th century

304. Skyphos   Pl. 33

C-70-204. M:23–24; lot 6508 (miscellaneous finds). **a**) P.H. 0.081, p.W. 0.074 m. Five joining fragments of wall. **b**) P.H. 0.06, p.W. 0.046 m. One fragment of wall, rim.

Slight flare of rim. Interior glazed, peeled, fired gray brown.

a (**b**). Handle palmette of tall curving leaves, angular calyx.

b (**a**). Wall design faded; both glaze and miltos gone, figures cannot be discerned. Top of wall with running dotted zigzag between bands.

This may belong to **303**; the interior glaze and thinness of fabric are similar.

End of 5th or beginning of 4th century

NON-CORINTHIAN BLACK FIGURE (305–329)

The pieces published in this section are representative of the imported black-figured material from this site. All are Attic except **323**, of an undetermined fabric. Most are later than the Corinthian black-figured vases. Only two, **318** and **319**, date to before 550 B.C.; the rest come from the late 6th century and the first decades of the 5th.

Drinking shapes, kylikes and skyphoi, are the predominant types. There are many fragments of late palmette cup-skyphoi in the context pottery; none have been inventoried, as all are very poorly preserved. There are also several late black-figured lekythoi from the early 5th century. **326**, **45** (Group 3), and **327**, white ground, illustrate this import. Many fragments have parallels in the material from the Rectangular Rock-cut Shaft in the Athenian Agora.[25] The Nikosthenic pyxis **328**, the epinetron **329**, and the later Panathenaic amphora fragments **305–307** stand out as rarities among the Attic black-figured imports.

It appears that cost was the determining factor for the choice of these vases. Late black figure was surely less expensive than contemporary red figure. If a visitor to the Demeter Sanctuary wanted to bring with him an imported vase, possibly with a certain popularity (especially a drinking vessel), a black-figured skyphos would be more affordable than a red-figured cup. Dedications of red-figured vases increased in number only after the technique was mass-produced and thus less costly. It was surprising, however, to find such a relatively high amount of Attic fabric in the Sanctuary, given the typical inexpensive vessel found in the excavations. It is also noteworthy, although probably coincidental, that many of the vessels in this section

[25] Vanderpool, *Hesperia* 7, 1938, and especially Vanderpool, *Hesperia* 15, 1946.

seem to have Dionysiac scenes. That fact is probably due to the appropriateness of the subject for drinking vessels and not specifically related to the worship of Dionysos in the Sanctuary.[26]

I am very grateful to Mary Moore, who gave her time and expertise to examine the fragments and identified several shapes, classes, and hands.

305. Panathenaic amphora   Pl. 34

C-61-397. P–Q:24; lot 896 (second half 4th century after Christ). **a)** P.H. 0.045, p.W. 0.085 m. Three joining wall fragments. **b)** P.H. 0.067, p.W. 0.09 m. Three joining wall fragments.

a. Wall decoration showing the overfall of Athena's peplos. Thick added-white decoration. Trace of black glaze at upper right break.

b. At right break, probably the tapering and swelling of the peplos at the waist; the diagonal line represents the narrow cloak behind Athena's back, looped over the right arm; the left-hand area is the falling end of the cloak. Athena faces right.

See British Museum B 610 (*ABV*, p. 417; *CVA*, British Museum 1 [Great Britain 1], pl. 4 [34]:3), for similar cloak arrangment. Probably from the same vase as **306**.

After 359 B.C.

306. Panathenaic amphora   Pl. 34

C-65-448. N:26; lot 4478 (later Hellenistic). P.H. 0.064, p.W. 0.091 m. One fragment from neck.

Concave neck of large Panathenaic amphora. Long rays between lines, over which is crested helmet to right, with spiraling support to cap.

After 359 B.C.; see J. D. Beazley, *The Development of Attic Black-Figure*, London 1951, p. 98.

307. Panathenaic amphora   Pl. 34

C-64-442. O:26–27; lot 2051 (later 3rd century). P.H. 0.12, Th. bottom 0.011, Th. top 0.005 m. Ten joining fragments of upper shoulder, part of neck.

Sloping shoulder turning continuously into neck; relatively narrow neck with raised molding; scars of upper attachment of handle on neck at left, lower attachment at right. Upper part of preserved interior glazed to just below molding area. Long tongues between lines; one small part of lower border preserved; reserved bands on either side of molding; molding black; black panels behind handles; above molding very linear palmettes, alternating between full palmettes and three-petaled type. Uneven application of glaze.

Although the drawing of the rays is similar to the rays of **306**, the thickness and curvature of the fragment and the surface of the interior differ; it is unlikely that **306** and **307** are from the same amphora.

See British Museum B 610 (under **305** above) for the neck floral. **307** is sloppier.

308. Attic hydria   Pl. 34

C-64-197. N:22–23; lot 2177 (later 5th century). P.H. 0.048, p.W. 0.06 m. One fragment of shoulder.

Flat, almost horizontal shoulder of hydria. Thin black lines at lower edge; satyr running right, right arm bent, left extended in front of body; added purple on tail, beard (mostly peeled). Sketchy, effective drawing.

Later 6th century

309. Attic hydria   Pl. 34

C-64-75. Q–R:26–29; lot 2038 (first half 4th century after Christ). P.H. 0.068, p.W. 0.075 m. One fragment of upper wall, beginning of shoulder.

Vertical wall, contracting at lower break; convex turn to flat shoulder. On wall: woman's raised arm and hand in added white over black, bracelets on wrist, palm turned back to missing face. Male to right, shaggy incised hair in a knot, short-sleeved chiton, cloak over left arm, falling behind back; arms extended in front of body, holding kithara; top of kithara frame in added white visible above head, cross bar at forehead extending to break. Branches in field. Glaze line at shoulder; feet(?) of figure on shoulder.

See Louvre C 10629 (*CVA*, Louvre 11 [France 18], pl. 151 [824]:3) for similar subject, style; but **309** is looser in drawing. Apollo, followed by Leto?

Late 6th century

310. Attic oinochoe   Pl. 34

C-73-260. K–L:23; lot 73-102 (mid-5th century with Roman intrusion). P.H. 0.053, p.W. 0.036 m. One wall fragment.

From wall of small closed vessel, with high ovoid wall, turning continuously into shoulder at top break; probably an oinochoe. Surface badly chipped. At left, left half of woman in peplos, facing left, left arm down, hand across body. Second woman, better preserved, in same pose at right; right arm raised, face to left; added white on arms, face, added purple on blouse. In front of women, nude youth stooping to left, arms in front of body, lifting some object to left of break. Glaze and incision of his upper right arm do not match.

Third quarter 6th century

311. Attic closed vessel   Pl. 34

C-69-302. N–O:17–18; lot 6199 (late 5th—early 4th century). P.H. 0.058, p.W. 0.071 m. Five joining fragments of wall.

---

[26] For Dionysos in the Demeter Sanctuary see Stroud, *Hesperia* 37, 1968, pp. 329–330.

From wall of large globular closed vessel, an oinochoe or small neck amphora. At left, bearded cloaked man facing right, staff in right hand, left arm extended; added purple on beard. At right, second cloaked figure facing left; lower chest, upper legs preserved; end of cloak hanging from left shoulder at right break. Sketchy, quick incision.

Later 6th century

312. Attic closed vessel   Pl. 34

C-61-464. P:24, P–Q:20–22; lots 877 (early 3rd century), 2156 (4th century after Christ, Byzantine). **a)** P.H. 0.034, p.W. 0.05 m. One wall fragment. **b)** P.H. 0.017, p.W. 0.022 m. One wall fragment.

High ovoid wall of closed vessel, turning continuously into shoulder.

a. Maenad, head to left, right arm across chest, left arm out with palm facing outwards; skin originally with added white; added-purple fillet in hair; added-white and added-purple dots on cloak and skirt. Grapes and dotted branch in field.

b. Head of satyr to right; added-purple beard; stain of added white below. In field, branch; arm or other object at upper right break.

Later 6th century

313. Attic skyphos   Pl. 34

C-64-401. P:26; lot 2046 (late 5th century). **a)** P.H. 0.134, est. D. lip 0.21 m. Many joining fragments; plaster restoration. **b)** P.H. 0.054, p.W. 0.056 m. Five joining fragments of wall. **c)** P.H. 0.065, p.W. 0.05 m. Four joining fragments of wall.

Tall convex wall, continuous with concave rim, rounded lip. Interior glazed, reserved band on lip. Exterior lip black; horizontal band on rim with dots on either side; two bands at top of wall. Figures on wall as follows:

a. Woman moving left in cloak; stain of added white on neck, extended right arm, left hand (in front of torso); legs without added white. Winged phallus flying right towards figure moving left, preserved from waist down, in cloak over chiton, which is decorated with crosses. Ground line visible at lower break. Branches in field.

b. Woman (maenad?) facing left, preserved from shoulder to waist, in voluminous cloak; stain of added white on left hand in front of body and on extended right arm and hand, holding drinking horn (?). Branches behind right arm; glaze of undetermined object at left break.

c. Figure in chiton and cloak moving right, rear leg and lower body preserved; ground lines at lower break; beginning of second figure at left break.

There are uninventoried fragments of skyphoi with similar late black-figure designs; the type had a certain popularity in the Sanctuary.

Early 5th century

314. Attic skyphos   Pl. 35

C-65-419. N:22; lot 4391 (later 5th century). P.H. 0.046, D. foot 0.086 m. Foot, part of lower wall preserved.

Ring foot; convex wall becoming vertical at top break. Undersurface with traces of added miltos; black central dot and concentric circle; two thin glaze lines. Inner face of foot black; resting surface reserved; outer foot and lower wall black; black band as ground line. Skinny, voluted palmette at left break. Figure facing right, in long dress and cloak, tassels at tip of cloak. Second figure facing right, leaning on staff, feet crossed. Third figure facing right, with dress as first figure. Sketchy incision, no added colors; interior glazed.

See Vanderpool, *Hesperia* 15, 1946, p. 294, nos. 81–95: Ure type K 2. **314** is poorer in quality than any examples from the Athenian Agora deposit.

Early 5th century

315. Attic cup-skyphos   Pl. 35

C-62-852. P:23–24; lot 1993 (mid-4th century). P.H. 0.057, est. D. lip 0.112 m. Six joining fragments of upper wall, lip.

Convex wall, contracting for foot at lower break; short concave rim; rounded lip. Scar of handle attachment at left break. Interior glazed; reserved band below lip. Exterior: two lower bands; two heraldic sphinxes; added white originally on faces; no incision. On either side, voluted palmettes attached to handles; added white on calyx; no incision. Brown line at offset of rim; rim and lip black.

For the type see P. N. Ure, *Sixth and Fifth Century Pottery from Rhitsona*, London 1927, grave 112.68, p. 64, pl. 19, type E 3.

Early 5th century

316. Attic deep cup   Pl. 35

C-64-35. P–Q:26–27, P:26; lots 2009 (3rd to first half 4th century after Christ), 4408 (5th century). P.H. 0.063, est. D. lip 0.25 m. Two joining fragments of wall, rim.

Vertical wall; short concave offset rim; rounded lip. Interior glazed; reserved band at lip; exterior with line at offset of rim; rim black. On wall: bearded satyr, preserved to waist, right arm raised, facing right; elbow of second figure at right break. See **317**.

317. Attic deep cup   Pl. 35

C-62-301. O–R:23–24; lot 1955 (second half 4th century after Christ). P.H. 0.022, p.W. 0.035 m. One wall fragment.

Interior glazed. Exterior: woman standing to left, left arm bent back, wearing short jacket. No trace of white on flesh. Probably from the same vessel as **316**.

See Vanderpool, *Hesperia* 15, 1946, p. 135, no. 30, pl. 23:8.

318. Attic Siana cup　　　　　　　　Pl. 35

C-65-453. O:18; lot 4349 (4th century after Christ). P.H. 0.02, p.W. floor 0.059 m. One fragment from upper stem, inner floor.

Flaring conical stem; central cone in stem; flat floor with only beginning of upward flare preserved. Undersurface reserved; cone glazed; interior and exterior of stem glazed; exterior wall glazed. Glaze fired red. Floor: all figures face right; woman holding two wreaths; dress of second figure behind her; elbow and arm of third at right break; hand of fourth at left break. All arms show stain of added white. Dress elaborately decorated with stars, crosshatching, triangles, and incised circles, in horizontal bands alternating with undecorated bands in added purple.

Attributed to the C Painter by H. A. G. Brijder.

Second quarter 6th century

319. Attic Siana cup　　　　　　　　Pl. 35

C-65-444. P:26, L:19; lots 2012 (early 5th century), 4408 (5th century), 73-107 (mid-5th century). Max. dim. 0.128, est. D. inner tondo 0.106 m. Four joining fragments of floor of cup; about one fourth of floor preserved; inner break at beginning of stem.

Exterior: Black around missing foot; outer bands of added white, purple, white; black rays; S-maeander with three black lines above and below as border for figure zone of wall. Lower legs and feet of two males walking left. Interior: Legs of Herakles and Nemean lion. Tondo border of three black lines; tongues alternately of added purple and black between black lines; outer lines; black on inner wall. Glaze fired partly red.

By the Heidelberg Painter. See very similar example in Taranto (*ABV*, p. 66, no. 55; *CVA*, Taranto 3 [Italy 35], pl. 26 [1569]:4342).

Second quarter 6th century B.C.

320. Attic band cup　　　　　　　　Pl. 35

C-62-843. P:23-24; lot 1993 (mid-4th century). P.H. 0.027, p.W. 0.025 m. One fragment of upper wall, rim.

Convex upper wall; concave offset rim. Interior glazed. On wall: siren to left, added white on chest; added-purple line on wing; added white by feathers. Rim glazed.

Mid- or third quarter 6th century

321. Attic lip cup　　　　　　　　Pl. 35

C-65-452. O:18; lot 4349 (4th century after Christ). P.H. 0.028, p.W. 0.029 m. One fragment of rim.

Offset concave rim. Interior glazed; reserved band below lip; lip black. On rim: satyr to right, right arm extended; added purple in hair and beard; black object at right

break, with added white, unclear: bent arm of maenad and part of dress?

Third quarter 6th century

322. Attic lip cup　　　　　　　　Pl. 35

C-62-363. R:23-24; lot 1985 (*ca.* 500 B.C.). P.H. 0.031, p.W. 0.036 m. One fragment of wall, rim, lip.

Convex wall, slightly concave rim, rounded lip. Interior glazed; reserved band below lip; lip black. On exterior wall: added-purple line at top of wall. On rim: silhouette warrior advancing left, shield raised, no weapon in right hand; beginning of second figure at left break.

Third quarter 6th century

323. Cup　　　　　　　　Pl. 35

C-73-360. O:22-23, Q:26; lots 2249 (end of 4th century), 73-137 (first quarter 5th century). **a)** P.H. 0.024, p.W. 0.037 m. One wall fragment. **b)** Max. dim. 0.037 m. One wall fragment. Hard, non-micaceous clay; core: 5YR 6-5/6 (reddish yellow), streaky surface slip. C-50-67 has a very similar surface slip but a core redder in color; latter is possibly Euboean, according to L. Siegel, *Corinthian Trade in the 9th through 6th Centuries B.C.*, diss. Yale University 1978, no. 225, p. 280.

From the wall of an open deep cup, neither Corinthian nor Attic.

a. Chariot, with part of charioteer in silhouette; reins visible at top; tails of two pairs of horses at right; left-hand tails in added white, brown; right-hand pair in brown, added purple; hoof at left break.

b. Part of wheel, horses' tails. Good drawing, careful incision, colorful surface.

Later 6th century

324. Attic plate　　　　　　　　Pl. 35

C-65-414. N:22; lot 4391 (later 5th century). Max. dim. 0.08 m. One fragment of outer floor.

Undersurface with streaky glaze; beginning of thickening for foot discernible. On floor: figure in blousing chiton turned to left, left arm and torso preserved. In field: branches and dots, two of larger dots with added white (now peeled). At right, beginning of cloak(?) of second figure. See **325.**

325. Attic plate　　　　　　　　Fig. 16, Pl. 35

C-64-438. N:22, lot 2171 (mid-5th century). P.L. 0.073, est. inner D. of floor 0.165 m. One fragment of outer floor, foot, lower rim.

Ring foot; outer narrow ledge from which rises convex lower rim, flaring out horizontally at break. Surface slightly polished. Foot and ledge glazed, fired partly red. Interior wall with peeling miltos. Upper rim surface glazed. On floor: outer band of dots; tondo with dotted branches and an arm(?). From the same plate as **324.**

Cleiboulos Workshop; see D. Callipolitis-Feytmans, *Les plats attiques*, Paris 1974, no. 9, p. 471, fig. 71, pls. 87–92, esp. pl. 90, no. 20 (Athens, N.M. Akr. 2459).
Early 5th century B.C.

326.   Attic lekythos   Pl. 36

C-73-259. L:23; no lot. P.H. 0.083, D. 0.047 m. Foot, upper neck, rim, handle missing.

Tapering lower body; cylindrical wall with maximum diameter at shoulder; offset sloping shoulder continuous with concave neck; scar of handle preserved. Lower body black; wide band; thin line as ground for figure zone. Above figure zone, black line at shoulder; debased lotus buds on shoulder; strokes on neck; two motifs separated by dots. Figure zone: satyr to right; maenad to right holding krotala; Dionysos seated to right, head to left; maenad running right, head turned to left. Vine branches in field. Maenads' skin in added white; added white on Dionysos' beard and cloak.

Class of Athens 581 (Moore).
Early 5th century B.C.

327.   Attic white-ground lekythos   Pl. 36

C-65-312. M:16–17; lot 3229 (late Hellenistic). P.H. 0.049, p.W. 0.037 m. One fragment of wall.

Hard, creamy white slip on surface; glaze is thin, often orange. On wall: white-ground figure zone 0.042 m. high; two glaze lines below, one above; maeander on wall below figure zone. Figure zone: outstretched arm at left break holding knotted club; figure facing left in long dress, holding skirt in left hand, staff with animal skin in right hand. Added red on tassels at bottom of skin; added-red dots on outer areas of upheld skirt; peeled added-white dots on vertical section of upper dress. Glaze of face thin; possible stain of added white on glaze of right arm. In field, dots of imitation inscription.

Second quarter 5th century

328.   Nikosthenic pyxis   Pl. 36

C-65-545, C-72-241. O:26, N:26, N:28, N–O:25–26, K–L:23; lots 2057 (second or early third quarter 5th century), 2075 (early 5th century), 2196 (end of 5th century), 2198 (late 5th century), 2253 (early 4th century), 72-208 (second quarter 5th century), 73-102 (mid-5th century with Roman intrusion), 75-248 (mid-5th century). **a)** P.H. 0.055 m. One lower-wall fragment. **b)** P.H. 0.036 m. One lower-wall fragment. **c)** P.H. 0.048, est. inner D. 0.15 m. Five joining fragments of wall, rim, flange; plaster restoration. **d)** P.H. 0.06 m. Four joining fragments of wall, rim, flange. **e)** P.H. 0.031 m. One fragment of wall, rim, flange.

Tall cylindrical wall, contracting to stem and (missing) foot; wide, projecting ledge for flange, with horizontal surface to hold lid; short vertical rim with flattened lip, continuous with inner wall. Interior glazed; flange and rim glazed; lip reserved. Figured scene on exterior wall:

a (C-65-545). Linked lotus-bud chain below, narrow bands above. Figure zone shows legs, all to left; one front leg, two hind legs, belly of horse, behind which are legs and spear of a youth; second youth at right break.

b (C-72-241 d). Lotus chain as fragment **a**; leg of youth to right; glaze at upper break uncertain pattern; foot to left at right break.

c (C-72-241 a + c). From left: two youths to left, second with spear, added-purple hair; woman in chiton(?) to left, added-white fillet, right hand close to face; youth to right (face missing), added-purple hair, spear; bird flying left; youth with horse, spear, facing right; two additional youths holding spears, facing right, first with added-purple hair, second with added-white fillet.

d (C-72-241 b). Athena to left, right hand raised, left holding spear (tip preserved); flesh originally in added white; added-purple aegis; high crested helmet. Traces of glaze at left and right breaks.

e (C-72-241 e; not illustrated). Added-purple hair of youth, to left at left break; glaze at right break for spear tip.

For comparison, see the pyxis Eleusis 576 (*Paralipomena*, p. 106), a larger, more elaborate example of the Nikosthenic shape, by Painter N. The subject of **328** may be a gathering of athletes in honor of Athena; they are not soldiers, for they carry only one spear and are without armor. A Panathenaic reference?

Third quarter 6th century

329.   Attic epinetron   Pl. 36

C-64-312. O:26, P:26, O:27; lots 2026 (mid-5th century), 2046 (late 5th century), 2212 (mid- or third quarter 5th century). P.L. 0.187, p.W. 0.135 m. About one half preserved; lateral edge below figure scene preserved. Many joining fragments; plaster restoration.
Published: Stroud, *Hesperia* 37, 1968, pl. 92:d.

Transverse band of rays, bounded by black, decorating open end. Upper area decorated with incised scale pattern. Glaze band limited by lines, separating scales from figured zone. Scene: Woman to left, wrapped in cloak, left arm raised within cloak; added white on face. Man to right, seen from back, wearing himation, right arm up with two fingers extended. Woman facing him, in chiton and cloak, left arm wrapped in cloak, right raised to first man; added white on flesh, added-purple fillet in hair. At right break, man to right, leaning on staff (now missing), wearing cloak, right hand on hip. Ribbon(?) hanging between first two figures. Probably one additional figure in the scene, now lost.

Attributed to a follower of the Sappho and Diosphos Painters (Elaine Banks, M.A. thesis University of Maryland, 1972), probably representing a homecoming scene.
Ca. 480 B.C.

NON-CORINTHIAN RED FIGURE (330–370)

Of the 41 examples discussed in this section,[27] one in Group 5 (**61**), and the two in Group 6 (**73, 74**), all but three are Attic imports. **341** is a South Italian epichysis; **331** and **365** do not appear to be Attic, but their origins are unknown. **61** is unclear. The quality varies more than the imported black-figure work. The Sanctuary yielded several interesting examples of early red figure (**334, 335, 368**), some very fine 5th-century fragments, especially among the skyphoi, and some distinctive, if not high-caliber, later material (**73, 360, 369**).

The Apulian epichysis **341**, the white-ground lekythos **366** (included in this section), and the miniature lebes gamikos **333** stand out as special vases, as surprising as the Panathenaics in the black-figure section. Kraters, skyphoi, and kylikes constitute the bulk of the red-figure shapes, both in the catalogue and in the many uninventoried fragments, repeating the popular shapes in the imported black figure. The numbers of skyphoi of about 470–430 B.C. is high; the large size of some is also noteworthy (**350–355, 358**). The painters represented range from among the very best (Makron, **361**; a Dourian hand, **363**; Penthesilean style, **344, 345**); Pistoxenos Painter, **364**; Lewis Painter, **346–349**), to the mediocre (**333**, Painter of Athens 1256).

All the fragments, in the catalogue and those not inventoried, were examined by Ian D. McPhee. He identified several of the shapes (**369, 370**) and attributed some fragments. I am grateful to him.

330. Attic hydria   Pl. 37

C-61-480. O:24–25, N–O:24–25, N–O:23, M–O:27–29; lots 890 (2nd century after Christ), 2141 (second half 5th century), 2142 (first quarter 4th century), 2143 (early 4th century), 2152 (4th-century pottery, 2nd-century coin), 2157 (4th century after Christ), 2210 (4th century after Christ). **a)** P.H. 0.10, p.W. 0.097, Th. bottom 0.005, Th. top 0.007 m. Five joining fragments of shoulder, wall. **b)** P.H. 0.047, p.W. 0.066, Th. bottom 0.005, Th. top 0.006 m. One wall fragment. **c)** P.W. 0.079, Th. bottom 0.006, Th. top 0.009 m. Three joining fragments of upper shoulder. **d)** P.H. 0.076, est. D. rim 0.18–0.19, Th. bottom 0.01 m. Two joining fragments of neck, rim. **e)** P.L. 0.087 m. One fragment of upper neck.

Convex wall; long sloping shoulder continuous with wall and neck; concave wide neck; flaring rim with convex overhanging outer face, rounded peaked lip, flat horizontal inner face.

a (d). Upper zone: front leg of stool with plump cushion on it; diluted glaze for details. Above chair, bottom of kalathos, probably held by draped figure facing left, wrapped tightly in cloak, left hand on hip. Reserved band between zones. Lower zone: top of sakkos of woman facing left; dotted wreath or fillet at right.

b (e). Upper zone: curving object, probably leg of a chair. Lower zone: boy wrapped in cloak, looking right, head inclined; figure holding tray with fruits or cakes (arm holding tray visible below). Curving line of glaze at right break probably for sleeve.

c (c). Enscrolled palmette-and-lotus border of figure zone; reserved line below. Head of woman facing right, wearing sakkos. Dotted wreath or fillet hanging from top of zone. Head of figure facing left at right break.

d (a) and **e** (b; not illustrated). Inner neck glazed to shoulder; wall and shoulder reserved inside. Inner face of mouth and lip glazed. On rim: enclosed eggs with miltos in reserved area; miltos on band at tip of rim before lip. Underside of rim reserved; streaky glaze on outer neck. Enscrolled palmette border for top of figure zone.

Miltos on some figures. Very low relief line for interior details, no contour line. Heavy accumulation of glaze around reserved areas.

The two-row hydria is not common but was reasonably popular in the Polygnotan Group, as was the type of palmette and lotus on the neck.

Third quarter 5th century

331. Hydria   Pl. 37

C-61-474 (**b**), C-62-944 (**a**). Q:25, R:25; lots 881 (third quarter 4th century), 885 (first half 4th century), 1953 (Byzantine), 6215 (stairway cuts). **a)** P.H. 0.048, D. foot 0.055 m. Two joining fragments of most of foot, lower wall. **b)** P.H. 0.05, D. rim 0.061 m. Three joining fragments of shoulder, neck, mouth, top of vertical handle. Fine clay with slight mica, a few fine, dark inclusions; core: 5YR 7–6/6 (reddish yellow).

Ring foot: outer face with compound curve, strongly concave inner face, wide resting surface (0.005 m.); inset undersurface. Convex flaring wall; sloping shoulder continuous with short concave neck; flaring undercut rim with compound curve of vertical face of rim, peaked lip set off from inner face; sloping convex upper surface merging into neck; oval handle, attached to neck below rim. Undersurface and face of inner foot black; resting surface black with reserved bands either side; outer foot black; lower and upper borders of figure zone with dots

---

[27] There are fewer than 41 vases actually represented in the catalogue. Several fragments published separately seem to be from the same vessel, but because there was no absolute certainty, it seemed safer to describe the fragments individually, noting the likelihood of derivation from the same vessel.

and eggs; upper wall, neck, mouth, handle, interior of neck glazed.

Figure zone: **a**. Two feet and lower skirts of two figures facing each other; traces of miltos on dress of left-hand figure.

b. Face of woman to left, badly preserved, possibly with miltos on face; hair surrounded by undulating reserved line. No relief contour. Sloppy drawing; dots used to separate toes. Clay and drawing seem neither Attic nor Corinthian; fabric similar to **365**.

End of 5th or beginning of 4th century

332.   Attic hydria   Pl. 37

C-73-59. Q:25; lot 73-139 (second quarter 4th century). P.H. 0.079, p.W. 0.112, Th. 0.003 m. Many joining fragments preserve part of wall, part of one side handle. Highly micaceous clay: core 5YR 7-6/4 (pink to light reddish brown). Thin fabric, laminating on interior; exterior glaze chipped, interior unglazed.

Convex wall contracting for shoulder; part of one side handle, turning up at sharp angle. Parts of elaborate enscrolled palmette on exterior wall. Glaze is thin; no contour lines, no miltos.

Color, amount of mica, and fracturing in layers unusual for Attic but can be found in some 4th-century workshops.

Second quarter 4th century (**332** is one of the latest pieces in the lot)

333.   Attic miniature lebes gamikos   Fig. 21, Pl. 37

C-64-224. R:20; lot 2063 (early 3rd century). P.H. 0.151, D. base 0.060, D. bowl 0.058 m. Two joining fragments of stand and bowl; handles, neck, mouth missing.

Narrow hollow stand, flaring out for base with rounded edge; sharp projecting ledge at juncture of stand and bowl; convex wall with maximum diameter near shoulder, turning into sloping shoulder; base ring around narrow neck; scars of two vertical loop handles on shoulder, not on axis, creating wider front scene. Interior reserved; base black, lower stem with black tongues and dots. On stand, side A (Pl. 37: views A–C): woman, looking right, holding up in either hand chests (small *kibotoi*), under which are scarves; B (Pl. 37: view D): figure wrapped in cloak, facing right. Top of stand: glaze line, row of dots; molding black, with reserved area on inside of top face and lower bowl. On bowl, side A (Pl. 37: view B): woman (bride) seated on chair to left, looking right, draped from waist down, cloak behind her, extending edge of cloak with left hand, right arm out. Thick added white for flesh; applied clay dots on right wrist for bracelet, also for necklace and for diadem. On either side of her, Erotes, with added-white bodies, incised wings.

Right-hand Eros with wreath in left hand, box in right. Left-hand Eros with mirror in right hand, holds bride's hand with left. Under left handle, woman facing right with chest and scarf in right hand, bowl with scarf in left. Under right handle, woman to left with box and scarf in left hand, fan in right. On side B (Pl. 37: view D): winged woman flying left with mirror. Applied clay dots at top of bowl, above obverse. On shoulder: tongues with dots between tips; neck ring and neck black. No contour, no relief lines. Details are sparse; dots for ears and mouths, few indications of drapery folds.

By the Painter of Athens 1256; *ARV*² , p. 1506 (McPhee).

334.   Attic calyx-krater   Pl. 38

C-61-228. O-P:25, O:24-25, P:27, M:26, P:26, O:26-27, O-Q:22-23, P-Q:20-22, N:27, N-O:19-20, L:26-27; lots 889 (first quarter 4th century), 890 (2nd century after Christ), 2050 + 2010 (lots combined; late Roman), 2021 (early Roman), 2049 (early 4th-century pottery, coin of Ptolemy I), 2155 (4th century after Christ), 2156 (4th century after Christ, Byzantine), 2204 (first half 4th century), 2247 (4th century after Christ), 72-128 (third quarter 4th century). **a**) P.H. 0.139, p.W. 0.11, Th. 0.006 m. Four joining fragments of vertical wall, beginning of thickened rim. **b**) P.H. 0.04, p.W. 0.046 m. Three joining fragments of wall. **c**) P.H. 0.07, p.W. 0.08, est. outer D. 0.47 m. One fragment of upper wall, rim, lip. **d**) P.H. 0.061, p.W. 0.09 m. Three joining fragments of top of wall, rim, lip. **e**) P.H. 0.048, p.W. 0.093 m. One fragment of rim, lip. **f**) P.H. 0.08, p.W. 0.061 m. Two fragments of upper wall, rim, lip.

Published: E. G. Pemberton, "An Early Red-figured Calyx-krater from Ancient Corinth," *Hesperia* 57, 1988, pp. 227–235.

Vertical wall; thickened, slightly concave vertical rim; heavy, round, outward thickened lip. Interior glazed. Exterior glaze fired red in places.

a. Bearded male (Hephaistos or Dionysos), riding on ithyphallic donkey to right, wearing short decorated cloak over short tunic; right arm extended behind; right hand holding ends of reins, rendered in added purple (now peeled); incised line of hair. In field over head, reserved line for ivy branch, originally with added-purple leaves on either side. Reserved band on lower rim; beginning of glaze just above it. Good relief line, heavy contour line; diluted glaze for some markings on donkey. Preliminary sketch lines on donkey.

b. Satyr head to left; hair incised; added-purple dots for wreath in hair. Ivy branch in field as fragment **a**.

c. On wall, ivy branch without leaves; beginning of object at lower break. Reserved band at top of wall. On rim, five-petal encircled palmette with buds between. Thin line at top of rim. Lip black; reserved band at top of inner wall.

d, e, f. Rim and lip as **c**. On wall of **f**, part of scroll design, probably for handle zone.

Pioneer Group; stylistic links to the Leiden amphora PC 85 (*ARV*², p. 32, no. 1) and the Bonn fragment (*ARV*², p. 33, no. 2).

Very early Attic red figure, *ca.* 510 B.C.

335. Attic krater   Pl. 38

C-71-201. I:19; no lot. P.H. 0.047, p.W. 0.045, Th. 0.006 m. One fragment of vertical wall, probably from a column krater.

Interior glazed. On wall: stacked folds of lower chiton or long cloak, ending in double border; part of back of garment at bottom break, to right of leg. Thick black horizontal lines very carefully placed. At lower left, front curving wing of boot with fine added-purple lines placed below the bottom. Good relief line, fine, narrow contour line.

Figure faces left with garment overlapping boot. There is probably no back wing; the simpler and older form of Attic winged shoe is represented (N. Gialouris, «Πτερόεντα πέδιλα», *BCH* 77, 1953, pp. 293–321), as used by the Brygos Painter (J. Boardman, *Athenian Red-Figured Vases: The Archaic Period*, London 1975, fig. 252:1). The length of the garment, with a glimpse of the skirt on the opposite side, suggests identification of the figure as female. The style recalls the Nikoxenos Painter.

First decade 5th century

336. Attic volute-krater   Pl. 38

C-73-356. N:24; lot 73-134 (second half 4th century). P.H. 0.068, p.W. 0.058 m. Four joining fragments from wall.

Convex wall, interior glazed. Exterior: necks, upper bodies, forelegs of four running horses, to right; at left bottom break, flying skirt of figure moving rapidly to left behind horses. Fine contour line, good interior relief line; diluted glaze on manes. Glaze is thin.

Mid-5th century

337. Attic krater   Pl. 38

C-70-369. O–P:27–28; lot 6656 (early Roman). Max. dim. 0.036 m. One wall fragment.

Interior glazed. Exterior: male head to left, looking up, with fillet tied behind, its ends sticking up at right break; dot of added purple in hair; two lines for eyebrow; heavy glaze lines for moustache; diluted glaze for beard and curls on temple. Lines at lower left break probably for

clothing. Fine contour line; heavy interior relief line. The man is probably a banqueter.

Mid-5th century

338. Attic bell-krater   Pl. 38

C-70-368. O–P:27–28; lot 6656 (early Roman). P.H. 0.058, p.W. 0.065, Th. 0.006 m. Two joining fragments of bell-krater wall or very large skyphos.

Interior glazed. Draped figure in chiton and cloak, glaze lines decorating cloak border, facing nude male holding lyre across body (parts of two strings preserved at top break). Very fine contour line on all parts of figures. Surface damaged, peeling.

Third quarter 5th century

339. Attic bell-krater   Pl. 38

C-64-478. Q:22–23, O:23, N–O:23; lots 2165 (4th century after Christ), 4347 (end of 4th century), 4474 (mid-4th century). **a)** P.H. 0.062, p.W. 0.076 m. Two joining fragments of upper wall. **b)** P.H. 0.044, p.W. 0.039 m. One upper wall fragment. **c)** P.H. 0.044, est. D. 0.30 m. Two joining fragments of upper wall, rim.

Upper vertical wall of convex bell-krater, turning to flaring rim, heavy rounded lip. Slight offset of rim from exterior wall; groove 0.011 m. from lip on underface. Interior glaze thin and streaky. Miltos on all reserved areas except interior bands, peeling. No contour lines; very slight relief line.

Exterior: **a.** Youth turned to right, wearing himation over left shoulder, possibly seated.

b. Woman facing left, wearing peplos.

c. Top of wall with reserved band. On underface of rim, single-leaf laurel garland; reserved band above. Reserved bands on interior upper wall, just below lip.

Style of drawing (large, dotted eye, downturned mouth) similar to **61** of Group 5 and to non-Attic red-figured examples in Corinth: C-71-259 and C-71-581, both bell-kraters with the single-leaf laurel garland.

End of 5th century

340. Small Attic bell-krater   Pl. 38

C-64-399. O:24, N–O:24–25, N–O:23; lots 2110 (first quarter 4th century), 2141 (second half 5th century), 2152 (4th-century pottery, 2nd-century coin). P.H. 0.123, p.W. 0.081 m. Four joining wall fragments.

Low ovoid profile. Interior glazed; glaze is peeling inside and out. Exterior: border of enclosed eggs; figure running right wearing chiton with loops hanging from belt; swirling fussy folds. No relief contour.

End of 5th century

341. Apulian epichysis   Fig. 3, Pl. 38

C-61-459. P–Q:24; lot 896 (second half 4th century after Christ). **a)** P.H. 0.044, est. D. 0.11 m. Five joining fragments; parts of base, wall, shoulder preserved. **b)** P.L. 0.089 m. Five joining fragments of upper wall, shoulder. Hard, non-micaceous clay; core: 2.5YR 6/4 (light reddish brown), surface: 5YR 6/6 (reddish yellow).

Published: H. Lohmann, "Zu technischen Besonderheiten apulischer Vasen," *JdI* 97, 1982 (pp. 191–249), p. 237, fig. 36. Noted: J. R. Green, "Ears of Corn," *Studies in Honour of Arthur Dale Trendall,* Sydney 1979 (pp. 81–90), p. 87, note 5.

Disk base; groove 0.022 m. from outer edge; slightly rounded surface of base near outer edge; low, concave wall inset from protruding base and shoulder by grooves; protruding shoulder ring; rounded shoulder offset from shoulder ring by groove.

a. Undersurface reserved; upper face of base ring black; reserved band around groove; wall black with incised chain and tendrils, with added-white buds; black continues to underface of shoulder ring; upper face with black enclosed eggs; miltos in groove between shoulder and ring. On shoulder: horizontal enclosed palmette; legs of seated figure, right leg preserved from thigh to foot, crossing over left foot; peeled added white for sandals.

b. Shoulder palmette as fragment **a.** Right arm of figure on **a**, winged; added white for bracelet, decoration on wings. Circular object in field. Some relief contour. Probably Eros.

See *RVAp* Suppl. I (Institute of Classical Studies Bull. Suppl. 42), London 1983, p. 108, no. 372 b. Minor vases from the Darius Workshop: Liverpool Group (Trendall).

Late third quarter 4th century

342.   Attic ray-based kotyle   Pl. 39

C-68-201. N–O:24–25, M–O:17–20, N–O:19–20, O:20, N–O:23, N:16, N–O:17–18; lots 2094 (early 4th century), 3206 and 3207 (Byzantine), 4362 (late Roman), 4474 (mid-4th century), 5643 (mid-5th century), 6199 (late 5th or early 4th century). **a)** P.H. 0.065, Th. 0.003 m. Seven joining fragments of lower wall. **b)** P.H. 0.054, Th. 0.003, est. D. lip 0.18–0.19 m. Two joining fragments of upper wall, lip.

Wide, gently convex wall, vertical at top, ending in simple lip. Interior glazed; reserved band below lip with miltos. Exterior: lower wall with tips of rays, miltos between.

a. Border of stopped maeander, punctuated by cross squares. Figure running right, in chiton; lower border of cloak over chiton visible at upper break; edge of hem flaring over right heel. Chiton folds in series of spreading lines, interspersed black dots. Miltos originally on all reserved areas, now peeling.

b. Sleeved left arm; hand grasping tall staff or spear. Glaze to right of figure fired red and peeling.

Fine contour and relief lines on both fragments; preliminary sketch.

The painter is in the Lewis Painter Group, probably the Group of Ferrara T.981 (*ARV²*, p. 978), especially Athens 13936 (*ARV²*, p. 979, no. 11), also a ray-based kotyle. The linearity of the folds recalls the Euaion Painter.

Second quarter 5th century

343.   Attic glaux skyphos   Pl. 39

C-65-614. O:20–21, N–O:17–18; lots 4348 (Late Roman, Byzantine), 6199 (late 5th, early 4th century). P.H. 0.074, est. D. lip 0.11 m. Two joining fragments of wall, lip.

Convex, flaring wall, contracting to (missing) foot below; above, turning in to simple rounded lip. Interior glazed. Exterior: Lower wall glazed; reserved line; olive plant, wing of owl. Carelessly painted.

The glaux skyphos is a frequent import in Corinth, but this is the only example found in the Sanctuary.

See F. P. Johnson, "A Note on Owl Skyphoi," *AJA* 59, 1955, pp. 119–124, esp. pl. 35, fig. 17.

Second quarter 5th century

344.   Attic skyphos   Pl. 39

C-62-322. O–Q:23–24; lot 1965 (second half 4th century after Christ). P.H. 0.0325, p.W. 0.04 m. One fragment of upper wall.

Interior glazed. Exterior: Reserved band at top of figure zone; at top break part of running garland of lip decoration. Below, female head to left, wearing dotted sakkos. Light contour line, good interior relief line; preliminary sketch visible.

Penthesilean in style.

Second quarter 5th century

345.   Attic skyphos   Pl. 39

C-65-654. N:23; lot 4477 (late 5th century). P.H. 0.018, p.W. 0.021 m. One fragment from upper wall.

Interior glazed. Exterior: head to right, probably male; diluted glaze for locks on temple. Strong contour line. Penthesilean in style, but probably not from the same skyphos as **344**; size, interior glaze differ.

Second quarter 5th century

346.   Attic skyphos   Pl. 39

C-65-423 (**a**), C-65-518 (**b**). N:20, M–N:25; lots 4421 (second half 5th century after Christ or later), 4440 (late 5th century). **a)** P.H. 0.038, est. D. lip 0.18–0.19 m. One fragment of upper wall, rounded lip. **b)** P.H. 0.023, p.W. 0.028 m. One wall fragment.

Interior glazed.

Exterior: **a**. Man to left, right arm extended, probably holding staff or spear (edge of it at left break); fillet in hair; double line for upper eyelid; thick glaze for curls in front of ear; slightly curving line of nose; rounded tip of nose; slightly protruding lower lip.

b. Woman to right; stephane or polos on hair; features drawn as on fragment **a**. Both faces with strong raised contour line; fine relief line. Miltos on figures. The male on **a** is probably a komast.

By the Lewis Painter (Polygnotos II; *ARV*², pp. 972–975). **347**–**349** are probably from the same skyphos.

Second quarter 5th century

347. Attic skyphos   Pl. 39

C-64-439. Q–S:17–20; lot 2107 (end of 4th century after Christ, Byzantine; Turkish coins). P.H. 0.074, p.W. 0.033 m. Two joining wall fragments.

Interior glazed. Exterior: Left hand and lower arm of a woman holding up chiton skirt; folds rendered in fine but strong relief line, with randomly placed small dashes. Thick relief line for fingers; contour line; miltos.

For the gesture see the Lewis Painter skyphos in Mississippi (*ARV*², p. 974, no. 26; H. R. W. Smith, *Der Lewismaler*, Leipzig 1939, pl. 15:a). See **346**, **348**, and **349**.

348. Attic skyphos   Pl. 39

C-65-611. N–O:16–17; lots 4404 (mid-3rd century), 5613 (11th century after Christ). P.H. 0.048, p.W. 0.049 m. Two joining wall fragments.

Interior glazed. Exterior: Woman running right; preserved is the skirt of a chiton with blousing overfall and nebris represented by dotted area; protruding knee shown at right break. Folds of chiton in fine relief line, close together but not parallel; diluted dots randomly placed between folds. Contour and relief line as **346**, **347**; slight traces of sketch under glaze around contours; miltos.

This fragment and **349** are probably from the same figure, on the side opposite the figures of **346** and **347**.

349. Attic skyphos   Pl. 39

C-65-612. N–O:16–17; lot 4404 (mid-3rd century). P.H. 0.034, p.W. 0.03 m. One lower-wall fragment.

Interior glazed. Exterior: Heel of foot; flaring hem of skirt of figure running right. At left break, spiral and tip of side tendril of palmette under handle. Good relief line, thick contour line, including palmette; preliminary sketch on heel. Miltos on figure.

See **346–348**.

350. Attic skyphos   Pl. 39

C-70-367. O–P:27–28; lot 6656 (early Roman). P.H. 0.074, p.W. 0.059 m. Two joining wall fragments.

Vertical wall. Very streaky, thin glaze on interior. Exterior: Frontal figure in peplos or chlamys: right arm extended to left, holding lyre; one curved sidepiece, part of sound box preserved. Area at top break not from design but peeled glaze. Fine contour line. Glaze stripe along contour particularly pronounced.

351–**353** are probably from the same skyphos: thickness, interior details, quality of line, glaze stripe around contours all similar. The skyphos would be extremely large.

The style seems to be derived from that of the Lewis Painter.

Just after mid-5th century

351. Attic skyphos   Pl. 39

C-65-412. N:23; lot 4394 (later 4th century). P.H. 0.044, p.W. 0.042 m. One fragment of wall, lip.

Vertical wall; simple rounded lip. Streaky interior glaze; reserved band on interior below lip. Exterior: Below black lip, band of egg pattern. Woman's head to left, hair tied up in knot, wispy strands in diluted glaze on nape, fillet around head. Two lines for upper eyelid; fat round ear. Contour, relief lines, and glaze stripe as **350**.

352. Attic skyphos   Pl. 39

C-65-615. M–O:27–29; lot 2210 (4th century after Christ). P.H. 0.036, p.W. 0.052 m. One upper-wall fragment.

Streaky interior glaze. Exterior: Chin, neck, upper chest of male looking left, right arm extended. Reserved area deteriorating, with loss of interior detail. Line of pectoral muscle continues into extended arm; curving lines of collarbone meet for median line. Good contour lines.

See **350**, **351**, and **353**.

353. Attic skyphos   Pl. 39

C-68-339. L:17–18; lot 5692 (late Roman). P.H. 0.024, p.W. 0.026 m. One wall fragment.

Glaze on interior as **350–352**. Exterior: nose, edge of eye of figure facing right; at right, raised wrist and palm turned toward face.

354. Attic skyphos   Pl. 40

C-61-462 (**a, b**), C-73-355 (**c**). O:24–25, O–Q:23–24, O:24, O–P:23, O:22–23; lots 890 (2nd century after Christ), 1965 (second half 4th century after Christ), 2110 (first quarter 4th century), 2145 (later 2nd century after Christ), 2250 (end of 4th century). **a**) P.H. 0.124, est. D. at lower border 0.20 m. Many joining wall fragments. **b**) P.H. 0.093, p.W. 0.086 m. Two joining wall fragments. **c**) Max. dim. 0.117 m. Two joining wall fragments.

Interior glazed.

Exterior: **a.** Border of stopped maeander punctuated every fourth one by cross or saltire squares. At left (side A), legs and cloven hooves of cow or bull, behind which are the skirt and feet of a figure moving left. Thin line at left break for staff. Palmette with side scrolls, under handle, separating two scenes of skyphos. At right (side B), figure in cloak standing right, with seven-string lyre in right hand. Beginning of object at right break, unclear. Reserved areas once with miltos, now flaking.

b. Top of border visible below. Figure in cloak to left, leaning on staff, feet close together, right heel raised. Beginning of handle-zone palmette at right break; beginning of another object at left break, rock(?).

c. Border below. At left, part of vertical palmette as fragment **b**. Figure in chiton (Nike?), moving to right (side A). Little relief line for interior details; no contour lines except around legs and hooves of animal on **a**.

The vase may be reconstructed as having on the main side a scene of sacrifice, moving left, toward the figure on **c**. The reverse had originally three figures, two preserved (both male): the lyre player of **a** at the left, the staff holder of **b** at the right. **355** is probably from the same vase. **354** is very large; compare **350**.

Just after mid-5th century

355. Attic skyphos   Pl. 40

C-72-269. L:24; no lot. P.H. 0.028, p.W. 0.02 m. One vertical wall fragment.

Interior glazed. Exterior: Head of woman facing left, broken at mouth. Relief contour on nose and mouth. Drawing, quality of glaze and fabric, size, and thickness, all suggest that it is from the same vase as **354**. The style is very close to **351**.

356. Attic skyphos   Pl. 40

C-64-207. Q:22, Q:20–22; lots 2052 (later 5th century), 2087 (second half 4th century after Christ). P.H. 0.127, D. foot 0.128 m. Four joining fragments of foot, wall.

Torus foot; tall, lightly convex wall, becoming vertical at top break. Interior glazed, fired brown. Undersurface with miltos; no concentric circles; inner foot black; resting surface reserved; outer foot, lower wall glazed, with scraped groove at juncture of wall and foot; plain reserved line as ground. On wall: figure in profile to left, weight on right leg, left crossed behind right, heel raised; right arm bent behind back; originally leaning on a staff. Figure wears cloak, probably falling from left shoulder, with thick glaze at lower border; soft shoes. Good contour line; thick relief line for modeling lines around waist and buttocks; thinner lines for falling folds. Preliminary sketch very visible.

Mid-5th century

357. Attic skyphos   Pl. 41

C-64-440. N–O:23, Q:26, O:22–23, N–O:23, K–L:21–22; lots 2152 (4th-century pottery, 2nd-century coin), 2230 (late 5th century), 2249 (end of 4th century), 4474 (mid-4th century), 6214 (surface), 6219 (1st century after Christ). **a)** P.H. 0.13, est. D. foot 0.15 m. Six joining fragments; part of foot, lower wall preserved; plaster restoration. **b)** P.H. 0.057, p.W. 0.076 m. Two joining fragments of lower wall. **c)** P.H. 0.06, p.W. 0.074 m. Two joining fragments of lower wall.

Heavy torus foot; flat undersurface; scraped groove between foot and wall; slightly convex wall. Undersurface with miltos; no concentric circles preserved; inner foot black, resting surface with miltos; outer foot, lower wall black; groove reserved. Interior glazed.

Exterior: **a.** Border zone of stopped maeander, punctuated by cross squares. Palmette, enclosed by tendril, with elaborate buds (at top break, towards left). At left break, figure standing to right wearing chiton and himation (black upper border). No contour lines; preliminary sketch visible.

b. Border as fragment **a**. Frontal leg at left break; two legs of figure having weight on frontal right leg, left crossed behind right, foot off ground; lower edge of short cloak.

c. Border as **a** and **b**. At left, toes of one foot to right, tip of staff. At right, two feet to left.

The form of the bud is very similar to that found in the workshop of the Penthesilea Painter: cf. Mississippi skyphos (*ARV*² , p. 899, no. 143), which also has the same sort of handle palmette.

Mid-5th century

358. Attic skyphos   Pl. 41

C-64-192. O:22–23; lot 2163 (late Roman). P.H. 0.087, p.W. 0.052 m. One fragment of vertical wall.

Interior glazed, with large X graffito on wall (modern?). Exterior: at left, arms extended to right holding white floral wreath (now peeled), end of sleeve visible on upper arm. At right, figure bending to right, wearing belted dress, holding hydria(?), base preserved. Miltos on figure. Relief contour on right arm of figure (missing) at left and for hydria. At upper break, bottom of top border, probably with eggs. Possibly Nike with wreath and Amymone (McPhee).

Third quarter 5th century

359. Attic skyphos   Pl. 41

C-64-477. O:26; lot 2066 (second half 4th century after Christ). P.H. 0.051, p.W. 0.039 m. Three joining fragments of upper wall, lip.

Vertical upper wall, slight concavity below rounded lip: beginning of flaring rim. Interior glazed. Exterior: Lozenge panel at right, limiting figure zone, preceding handle. Head to left, eye preserved; hair may have been white originally, now peeled. Below lip, enclosed dotted-egg pattern. Miltos on all reserved areas. Exterior glaze thin.

The lozenge panel is often found on skyphoi and cups of the Marlay Painter and his group (*ARV²*, pp. 1276–1282).

About 430–420 B.C.

360. Attic skyphos   Pl. 41

C-65-417 (**b**), C-65-496 (**a**). P:24–25, P–Q:24–25, O:23–24, N–O:23, N–O:22; lots 875 (second half 4th century after Christ), 892 (4th century after Christ), 1964 (4th-century pottery, Roman coin), 4347 (end of 4th century), 4473 (mid-4th century), 4475 (third quarter 4th century). **a**) H. 0.105, D. foot 0.086, est. D. lip 0.13 m. Many joining fragments preserving profile except handles. **b**) P.H. 0.041 m. Two joining fragments of wall, lip.

Torus foot; center of undersurface not preserved; wall with compound curve, without noticeable stemming; flaring rim with simple rounded lip; scar of one handle. Undersurface with miltos; no concentric circles; inner foot black; resting surface reserved; outer foot and lower wall continuously black. All reserved areas in figure zone originally with miltos, now mostly peeled. Stacking line slightly above midwall, above which no miltos is preserved; glaze is very reddish, thin, peeling.

Wall: **a**. Below handle, 12-petal palmette (asymmetrical), clubbed, with spiraling volutes on either side. Left of palmette (side A), feet of two confronted figures, lower edge of staff. Right of palmette (side B), youth in cloak with staff, facing second figure, whose feet are preserved.

b (side A). Hand with staff, facing boy in cloak, probably the upper parts of the figures on fragment **a**, left of palmette. Spiraling volutes of handle-zone palmette at right.

Akin to the skyphoi of the F. B. Group; cf. *ARV²*, pp. 1494–1495 (McPhee).

First or early second quarter 4th century

361. Attic kylix   Pl. 41

C-69-184. M:21–22; no lot. P.H. 0.028, p.W. 0.05 m. One wall fragment.

Upper convex wall of wide cup. Interior glazed. Exterior: At left break, a hand originally holding horizontally a wreath or branch, in added purple, of which only the stain now remains. At right, youth in sleeveless dress and cloak, looking right; wash for hair, darker dots for wreath in hair. Fine contour and relief lines; preliminary sketch visible.

By Makron. Compare Akropolis 325 and 320 (*ARV²*, p. 460, no. 20 and p. 474, no. 239).

First quarter 5th century

362. Attic kylix   Pl. 41

C-65-424. N:22; lot 4391 (later 5th century). P.H. 0.035, p.W. 0.063 m. Three joining wall fragments.

From a wide cup; interor glazed. Exterior: Male advancing left, cloak around shoulders, right arm holding staff across body; probably leading a bull whose chest is preserved at right break. In field to left of figure, stain of horizontal sigma, from *pais* or *kalos*. Much interior detail (breast line, ribs, thigh) in diluted glaze. Clumsy drawing of fingers, ribs. Uneven relief line, thick in places. Some relief contour. Preliminary sketch visible.

First quarter 5th century

363. Attic kylix   Pl. 42

C-65-439 (**a**), C-65-613 (**b**). O:23, M–N:12; lots 4347 (end of 4th century, 4409 (4th century after Christ, Byzantine). **a**) Max. dim. 0.073, Th. outer edge 0.005, est. D. inner tondo 0.10–0.12 m. One floor fragment; inner break at stem of foot. **b**) Max. dim. 0.033, Th. 0.006 m. One fragment of outer floor.

Glaze rather thin and brown.

a. Floor: Neat stopped maeander framing tondo. Nude male facing right, right arm bent, lower arm and hand brought across chest. Interior details finely drawn in diluted glaze; fine contour and relief lines. Preliminary sketch visible. Exterior: Reserved band for border. Cloven rear hooves and legs of animal, beginning of another figure at left break.

b. Floor: four fingers and tip of thumb of left hand, holding discus. Contour and relief lines as fragment **a**. Fingers rendered as ovals in heavy relief lines. Exterior glazed.

Dourian quality. R. Guy cited as comparable the white-ground lekythos in Cleveland (*Paralipomena*, p. 376, no. 266 *bis*), with similar thigh and rib markings.

First quarter 5th century

364. Attic kylix   Pl. 42

C-64-69. P–Q:24–25, O–Q:23–24, R:26, P:26, Q:25–26, M–N:23–24; lots 869 (surface), 896 (second half 4th century after Christ), 897 (mid-4th century), 1965 (second half 4th century after Christ), 2035 (4th century after Christ), 2046 (late 5th century), 2048 (2nd or 3rd century after Christ), 6842 (late 4th century), 73-138 (end of 5th century). **a**) P.H. 0.081, est. D. lip 0.25 m. Many joining fragments of wall, lip. **b**) Max. dim. 0.07 m. Two joining wall fragments. **c**) Max. dim. 0.084 m. Two joining wall fragments. **d**) Max. dim. 0.032 m. One wall fragment. **e**) P.H. 0.02, p.W.

0.031 m. One fragment of wall, lip. **f**) Max. dim. 0.043 m. One fragment of wall, lip. **g**) P.H. 0.015, p.W. 0.018 m. One fragment of wall, lip.

From a wide cup with convex wall, turning up to simple lip.

a. Interior glazed, reserved line below lip, lip black. Reserved bands on either side of stopped maeander bordering tondo. Tondo: foot to right, edge of skirt. Exterior: Bearded male, in long dress and cloak, seated to right, holding staff in right hand; diluted glaze and added white for hair and beard. Warrior, in short chiton, breastplate, crested helmet, large round shield on left arm, seen from rear, head turned to left facing seated man. Top of shield slightly burned; details of warrior worn. In field between figures, stain only preserved:

OΓAIϞ

b. Interior: small part of tondo border maeander. Exterior: warrior seen from rear, in short chiton; parts of breastplate, greaves, shield preserved, running right.

c. Interior: small area of tondo border maeander. Exterior: greaved legs of warrior with spear, advancing right; left foot and ankle of second figure advancing right.

d. Interior glazed. Exterior: lower left part of shield with object extending either from it or behind it to left, explained by Dyfri Williams (personal communication) as part of protective leather apron attached to shield rim.

e. Interior glazed. Exterior: head of helmeted warrior looking right.

f. Interior glazed. Exterior: reserved area without contour line at left break.

g. Interior glazed. Exterior: reserved area with contour line at left break, probably the back of a helmet; shields have no contour lines.

Very fine drawing; good, thin contour and relief lines; relief especially heavy for details of greaves, toes, facial features; diluted glaze, thinner relief lines used for armor, shields, body markings. Scene probably shows a hoplitodromos, with bearded man as judge.

By the Pistoxenos Painter. R. Guy noted that the line of the greaves stops before the calf line, as rendered on figures by that painter (*ARV*², p. 860, nos. 5 and 8; p. 862, no. 26).

Second quarter 5th century

365. Kylix   Pl. 43

C-61-236, C-62-321. Q:25, O–P:25, P–Q:24–25, O:23–24, M–N:25; lots 886 (at least 3rd century after Christ), 889 (first quarter 4th century), 892 (4th century after Christ), 1964 (4th-century pottery, Roman coin), 4434 (early Roman), 6215 (stairway cuts). **a**) Max. dim. 0.144, est. D. lip 0.25 m. Five joining fragments of floor, wall, lip. **b**) P.H. 0.035, p.W. 0.102 m. Two joining fragments of upper wall, lip. **c**) P.H.

0.044, p.W. 0.051 m. One fragment of upper wall, lip. **d**) P.H. 0.048, p.W. 0.041 m. One fragment of upper wall, lip. **e**) Max. dim. 0.05 m. One wall fragment. **f**) P.H. 0.02, p.W. 0.03 m. One fragment of upper wall, lip. Fairly soft, highly micaceous clay; core 5YR 7–6/6 (reddish yellow).

Wide shallow cup; floor turning continuously into incurving, simple lip. Brown glaze, thin and peeling; miltos added to figures.

a (C-62-321). Interior: Tondo border of maeander and saltire. Youth seated on himation to left, head to right, left hand raised, right arm out. Scalloped reserved band setting off hair; dilute glaze for locks. Double line for upper eyelid, dot for nose, three lines to indicate fingers. Plump proportions. Very slight relief line for inner details. No contour line. Preliminary sketch on this figure only. Upper wall glazed; reserved band below lip. Exterior: Reserved band and line as ground. Woman facing right, both arms extended. Surface damaged, but there does not appear to be anything in her hands. Nude youth facing her, left leg advanced, one arm raised. Low object behind his right leg. Heavy glaze bands, swirls, hasty lines indicate folds and parts of dress.

b (C-61-236 b). No tondo design. Exterior: Enscrolled palmette with flat petal tips. Nude youth, seen from rear, upper back and head preserved, right arm out. Two curving lines for spine; loop for right shoulder blade. At right break, wing of figure turned to right; large dots across upper wing, irregularly spaced lines for feathers. Fragment **b** may go to left of **a**, in which case central figure would be Nike.

c (C-61-236 a). No tondo design. Exterior: Nude youth, seen from rear, turned to left. Single line for upper eyelid, dot for mouth; less detail in hair than tondo figure of **a**. Anatomical details as **b**. At right break, staff(?) of next figure.

d (C-61-236 c). No tondo design. Exterior: part of volute palmette.

e (C-61-236 d). Interior: top of tondo border of stopped maeander. Exterior: part of volute palmette.

f (C-61-236 e). Exterior: tips of palmettes.

The clay is not characteristic of 4th-century Attic pottery; the glaze is very thin, fired black to brown, and has a metallic quality. If Attic, the cup would belong in the area of the Jena Painter, but it exhibits oddities of style (McPhee). See **331** for similar fabric.

Early 4th century

366. Attic white-ground lekythos   Pl. 43

C-64-418 (**b**), C-64-409(**a, c**). N:21–23; lots 2170 (4th century after Christ), 2178 (early 4th century), 4491 (third quarter 4th century). **a**. P.H. 0.070, p.W. 0.061 m. Three joining wall fragments. **b**. P.H. 0.037, p.W. 0.036 m. One wall fragment. **c**) P.H. 0.056, p.W. 0.031 m. One wall fragment.

From a cylindrical lekythos. Chalky white slip, poor brown-black glaze on exterior; interior reserved.

a. Black-glazed lower body, maeander border, two lines above. In field, woman standing to right, wearing chiton and himation, painted in diluted (orange) glaze with brown glaze for folds. Feet outlined in brown glaze. She holds a scepter or staff. At right, large rock in outline, on which sits a figure wearing a purple garment. Flowers on rock.

b (not illustrated). At left break, hand in black outline, grasping staff or spear; near top break, bit of black glaze, possibly for a letter.

c (not illustrated). Maeander border, reserved field.

Mid-5th century

367.   Attic squat lekythos   Pl. 43

C-73-306. N:24; lot 73–134 (second half 4th century). P.H. 0.084, est. D. 0.07 m. Many joining fragments; foot, handle, rim missing.

Globular body; ledge separating narrow cylindrical neck from shoulder; scar of one handle on upper wall. Glaze fired brown to black, uneven. Glazed over exterior. On wall: crouching sphinx to right with minimal detail; below, reserved band. Head of sphinx on axis with handle.

Late 5th century

368.   Attic lid(?)   Pl. 43

C-71-238. N:22; lot 2172 (later 5th century). Max. dim. 0.08, Th. outer break 0.004, Th. inner break 0.01 m. Two joining fragments.

Probably from a convex lid. Outer break probably at descending flange of lid. Flat undersurface with wide black-glazed band from outer break to just before inner break. Slightly curved upper surface, on which is frontal eye, incised line around black iris, slightly open at inner corner; profile face turned to left, line of nose preserved. Incision above for contour of hair. Relief contour along nose.

Very early red figure, *ca.* 530–520 B.C.

369.   Attic lid from lekanis-like pyxis   Pl. 43

C-61-476. O–P:24–25; lot 874 (4th century after Christ). P.H. 0.021, D. knob 0.067 m. Knob, part of lid preserved.

Low, wide knob with convex outer face, groove on top face; beginning of sloping lid; area under knob depressed. Knob black glazed except grooved ring and lower outer face with miltos; interior glazed. On preserved lid exterior: tails and backs of felines, with black dots for spots; between them a volute; tip of griffin wing.

See *Olynthus* XIII, pl. 86 (*ARV*² , p. 1501, no. 1) for the type.

Ca. 380–360 B.C.

370.   Attic head-kantharos(?)   Pl. 43

C-64-213. N–O:23; lot 2152 (4th-century pottery, 2nd-century coin). P.H. 0.027, est. D. lip 0.11–0.12 m. One fragment of wall, lip.

Slightly concave wall, flaring out to simple lip. Reserved line on lip; interior glazed. Exterior: Boy in cloak facing right; stain of white fillet in hair. Thin contour line for cloak.

The flaring lip suggests this fragment as the upper wall of a head-kantharos; see fragmentary head vases **600–602**.

Second quarter 5th century

NON-FIGURED FINE WARES (371–499)

This section might be termed a "catch-all", for in it appear all the regular fine wares not included in the first 11 groups or appropriate for one of the divisions of the figured pottery. A few of the examples in this section have patterns: "worms", bands, or the like; the Hellenistic vessels with West Slope decoration or relief figures also appear here. There were not enough of these later decorated wares to warrant a separate section for them. But generally, the vases are plain, glazed, or have only simple decorative patterns. They are published either because the shape is intrinsically important or unique and contributes to the discussion of that shape, or because the specific vessel helps to establish a date for a building, useful for the discussions in the forthcoming volume on the architecture of the Sanctuary.

All fine-ware fabrics appear in this section, arranged by shape,[28] subdivided by date; if no fabric is indicated, the vessel is Corinthian. There are several Attic imports, one Laconian bowl (**444**), a Gnathian

---

[28] The order of the shapes usually follows that of Talcott and Sparkes (*Agora* XII), but there is one exception. Plain saucers appear before plates, so as to be closer to the contemporary bowls of echinus shape or with beveled rims, all of which show similar changes in the profiles.

fragment (**499**), and several of unknown origin (**437**, possibly Corinthian; **493–495, 498**). The shapes are discussed fully in Shape Studies, pp. 9–78 above. Comparative material is given for the entry only if not covered in the earlier discussions.

Miniatures appear in a separate section, but all the phialai except the late Hellenistic group (**675–681**) appear here.

371. Amphora

C-65-313. M:16–17; lot 3227 (late 3rd—early 2nd century). P.H. 0.044, est. inner D. neck 0.09 m. One fragment of neck, rim.

Vertical neck; flaring rim in two degrees; flat top; groove at outer edge of rim. Rim stamped with half circles on either side of groove; outer face originally stamped with dotted circles. On upper face of rim, a red dipinto:

].B..BPĄ[

See **372**.

372. Amphora   Pl. 44

C-70-352. O–P:27–28; lot 6656 (early Roman). P.H. 0.066, est. inner D. neck 0.09, est. outer D. 0.14 m. One fragment of neck, rim.

Shape as **371**; scar for handle attachment (round handle) on neck below rim. Stamped circles preserved. Dipinto on upper rim face, in Corinthian epichoric alphabet:

[. . .]ΙΑΣΙΣ:ΑΝΕΘΕΚΕ:
ΤΑΔ[. . .]

The two fragments are very similar in size and decoration and are presumably from the same vessel. The width of the upper face of the rim inside the groove differs, however: in **371** it is 0.015 m., in **372** 0.017–0.019 m. Neither context provides a date for the fragments.

373. Imitation Cypriot amphora   Pl. 44

C-61-471. P:24–25; lot 878 (third quarter 4th century). P.H. 0.07, est. D. rim 0.09 m. Three joining fragments of neck and rim. Split fabric, irregular surface, resembling blister ware. Core: 2.5YR 6–5/0 (gray); outer core: 2.5YR 6/6 (light red).

High cylindrical neck; flaring rim with diagonal upper face; horizontal bands of light and dark gray and red on neck. For the shape: Williams, *Hesperia* 38, 1969, pp. 57–59, fig. 8, pl. 18. There are very few fragments of this ware in the Sanctuary, in contrast to its popularity in the Forum.

Third quarter 4th century

374. Hydria

C-64-65. R:26, Q:25–26; lots 2013 (second half 4th century after Christ), 2048 (2nd or 3rd century after Christ). P.H. 0.046, est. D. rim 0.155 m. Two fragments of neck, rim. A few inclusions in the fabric, not enough to designate it as coarse ware; polished surface.

Vertical neck; flaring funnel rim with convex exterior, concave interior; flat lip. Around outer lip, stamped circles; on inner lip, dipinto in brown glaze, in Corinthian epichoric alphabet:

]ΡΕΤΑ : ΚΑΜΟΦΙΑ : ΤΑΔΑΜΑΤΡ[

For the profile: *NC*, p. 327, fig. 172.

Probably Archaic

375. Hydria

C-64-467. N–O:24; lots 2142 (first quarter 4th century), 2144 (mid-4th century). Max. dim. 0.111, est. D. rim 0.14 m. Two joining fragments of rim, upper handle attachment. No slip; soft worn clay.

Published: Pemberton, *Hesperia* 50, 1981, p. 102, no. 1, pl. 29:a.

Horizontally projecting rim; outer convex face, flat horizontal top face (lip), with raised round molding at outer edge. Molding mostly covered by extra strip of clay for handle attachment to rim. Ends of strip with "rivets", rosettes on top face; spool-shaped thumb-rest at top of handle, with rosettes on outer faces. Three mock rivets on inner rim, aligned with handle. Vertical incisions (tooling) on upper part of outer rim face and on raised molding; impressed eggs on lower area of outer rim. Handle-attachment scar below thumb-rest.

The type of metal-imitating elements suggests a 6th-century date.

376. Hydria   Pl. 44

C-73-25. R–S:27; no lot. P.H. 0.049, est. inner D. 0.105 m. One fragment of neck, rim. No slip; polished surface.

Horizontally projecting rim; raised outer molding as on **375** but bigger; beginning of vertical handle attached to neck. On outer rim face, eggs; on raised molding, vertical incisions as **375**. Red dipinto on upper face:

Archaic?

377. Hydria

C-64-446. P–Q:26–27; lot 2009 (3rd—first half 4th century after Christ). P.H. 0.088 m. One fragment of handle, area of wall attachment.

Published: Pemberton, *Hesperia* 50, 1981, pp. 102–103, no. 2, pl. 29:b.

Three quarters of a handle, vertically fluted; inner face plain. At base of handle, originally attached to sloping shoulder, two crouching heraldic sphinxes; forelegs raised on undetermined object; heads frontal; angular wings extending well past handle. Moldmade; figures worn.

Imitating metal but without any known similar figures preserved in metal. Compare the sirens on many metal hydriai and other shapes.

Late 5th century

378. Hydria

C-62-278. R:25; lot 1953 (Byzantine). P.H. 0.107, est. D. rim 0.09 m. Two joining fragments; parts of shoulder, neck, rim, handle preserved. White slip.

Published: Pemberton, *Hesperia* 50, 1981, p. 103, no. 3, pl. 29:c.

High ovoid body; sloping shoulder continuous with tall, narrow concave neck; horizontally projecting rim, undercut; outer face of rim convex; rounded offset lip; inner face with gentle slope into neck; round handle from shoulder to rim just below rim. On outer rim face, stamped eggs; white slip on exterior and upper interior of body. Neck made separately.

Proportions and profile of rim and neck similar to small hydriai in Group 9 (**182–184**). Parallel: C-53-273, from well 1953-2, unpublished; similar profile but without slip or molding.

Hellenistic

379. Krater Pl. 44

C-64-410. P:19–20, M:17; lots 2151 (second half 4th century after Christ), 5652 (mid-5th century). P.H. 0.051, est. D. 0.29 m. Three joining fragments of small area of upper wall, rim.

Wall inset from lower edge of folded rim; straight inner wall. Wall black glazed inside and out; reserved band at top of inner wall; top of rim black; lip reserved. Outer face of rim with oblique maeander in added white and pink, surrounded by black.

C-1976-279 a and b, LC handle-plates from Temple Hill, have the same maeander design; see also Louvre hydria E 695 (*NC*, no. 1444, LC) with the same design on the shoulder above the front panel. The wall of **379** was probably without figures.

Late Corinthian or later

380. Lekane Pl. 44

C-61-461. P–Q:24; lot 896 (second half 4th century after Christ). P.H. 0.189, D. 0.32 m. Many joining fragments; part of lower wall, whole foot missing. Plaster restoration.

Convex flaring wall, turning vertical above maximum diameter; flaring rim, flat on upper surface; rounded lip. Added-red band on lower wall; black and added-red

triangles on top of rim, edged by added red. Interior reserved. One suspension hole preserved on rim; no handles extant.

Classical

381. Lekane Fig. 2

C-61-415. P:24; lot 877 (early 3rd century). H. 0.165, rest. D. 0.244, D. foot 0.092 m. Complete profile; much of upper wall, rim restored in plaster. Burnt on part of exterior.

Heavy ring foot with wide, flat resting surface, convex outer profile, concave inside; undersurface slightly convex; gently convex flaring wall; projecting rim with flat upper face. Two suspension holes on rim; no handles preserved. Gray (diluted glaze) and added-red bands on wall; gray bands on outer face and inner edge of upper face of rim; black and added-red triangles on upper face of rim. Interior, foot, undersurface reserved.

Classical

382. Lekane Pl. 44

C-69-314. M–N:19; lot 5625 (later 3rd century), 6182 (fourth quarter 4th century), 6189 (later 4th century). P.H. 0.093, est. D. 0.44–0.45 m. Seven joining fragments (one photographed); most of wall profile to rim, one handle preserved. Thin surface slip or polish.

Shallow lekane; convex flaring wall, horizontal outturned rim with long reflex handle at top of wall, hole in center of handle. On flat, upper handle face, three leafy branches incised with circles between; one interrupted by central hole. Single circle on rim.

Similar examples: C-30-47 (*Corinth* VII, i, no. 378, p. 82, pl. 45); C-34-928 (Pease, *Hesperia* 6, 1937, p. 299, no. 189, fig. 32). There are other fragmentary examples of this type of lekane with similar decoration in the Demeter Sanctuary: Classical contexts, lots 4347, 4382.

Classical

383. Lekane Pl. 44

C-73-305. K–L:23–24; lot 73–116 (late 4th century). H. 0.141, rest. D. 0.37, D. foot 0.17 m. Mended from many fragments; half preserved; complete profile.

Flaring ring foot with wide resting surface; flaring convex wall; projecting rim with straight vertical face, flat, broad upper face. No handles preserved. No decoration.

Classical (probably 4th century)

384. Broad-bottomed oinochoe Pl. 44

C-70-393. J:20–21; lot 6516 (third quarter 5th century). P.H. 0.036, est. D. resting surface 0.06 m. Three joining fragments of resting surface, wall, shoulder; plaster restoration.

Recessed, slightly concave bottom; rounded bevel; lightly concave wall; sloping shoulder without shoulder ridge; upper break at neck. Bevel and lower wall black; black band; added-red band; black band at shoulder; linear black tongues on shoulder. Small version of the Vrysoula oinochoe.

Third quarter 5th century

385. Beveled oinochoe (epichysis)   Pl. 44

C-61-429. P:24; lot 877 (early 3rd century). P.H. 0.073, D. (both bevels) 0.071, D. foot 0.055 m. Many joining fragments; handle, mouth, center of floor missing; plaster restoration.

Low ring foot with vertical outer face; flat undersurface; concave wall with bevels above and below; sloping shoulder with groove before bevel; tall cylindrical neck with groove as drip ring. Black glaze overall, now peeling. Light crosshatched grooving on shoulder. See **78**, Group 6.

End of 4th or beginning of 3rd century

386. Chous   Fig. 3, Pl. 44

C-65-476. N:26; lot 4482 (early Hellenistic). H. 0.163, D. 0.11, D. foot 0.062 m. Many joining fragments; completed in plaster, including entire handle.

Ring foot; nippled undersurface; tall globular wall; wall merging with shoulder and neck; wide concave neck flaring into trefoil mouth; strongly projecting thumb-rest. Thin peeling black glaze overall except resting surface of foot. Narrow, shallow, but well-spaced ribs on wall; groove on shoulder at top of ribs. There are very few Corinthian versions of the Attic chous. The shallow ribbing and small foot are the dating criteria.

Fourth quarter 4th century

387. Blister-ware oinochoe   Pl. 44

C-69-186. M:22; lot 6208 (late 4th century). H. 0.111, D. 0.118, D. mouth 0.06 m. Many joining fragments; part of wall, floor missing.

Flat bottom; globular body merging with shoulder; short, narrow neck with straight flaring rim, rising to rounded lip; strap handle with central vertical groove. Shoulder and wall have bumps, not ribs, set more or less diagonally. Neck made separately; line of attachment on interior with rough clay globules. Similar to **77**, Group 6.

Late third to fourth quarter 4th century

388. Blister-ware oinochoe   Pl. 44

C-61-154. P–Q:25; lot 871 (coin of 12th century after Christ). P.W. 0.057, p.L. 0.063 m. Two joining fragments of wide sloping shoulder.

Larger than **387**. Chain of incised ivy with exaggerated heart-shaped leaves, bordered by incised half moons. See

the askos decoration, C-34-1645 (*Corinth* VII, iii, no. 777, p. 149, pl. 64). There is a more complete example, C-31-235, from well 1931-8, unpublished.

Fourth quarter 4th century

389. Globular oinochoe   Fig. 3, Pl. 45

C-61-428. P:24, lot 877 (early 3rd century). P.H. 0.113, D. 0.08, D. foot 0.048 m. Many joining fragments; mouth, handle missing; plaster restoration.

Ring foot, undercut to form central disk on undersurface; tall globular wall; well-offset sloping shoulder; short, narrow cylindrical neck; mouth apparently spouted with pellets at handle attachment; scar of lower handle attachment on lower shoulder.

The shape is as yet without parallel, but finish, foot, and wall profile suggest a 5th-century date. The closest wall profile is that of the more convex olpai of the 6th century. The context is too wide to assist dating.

First half 5th century(?)

390. Small oinochoe with shoulder stop   Fig. 3

C-65-169. O:18; lot 4349 (4th century after Christ). H. 0.087, D. 0.074, D. mouth 0.043–0.047, D. foot 0.046 m. Intact.

Published: *Corinth* VII, iii, no. 275, p. 55, pl. 48.

Recessed resting surface, no true foot; low ovoid profile merging with shoulder; shoulder stop of slight ridge; mouth barely pinched to form trefoil shape; strap handle from upper wall to mouth, rising above mouth. Surface uneven.

Early 3rd century(?)

391. Attic mug   Pl. 45

C-62-874. O:24; lot 1952 (5th century, 1 late Roman fragment). H. 0.078, est. D. 0.084, D. foot 0.061 m. Many joining fragments. Traces of burning.

Disk foot, with groove offsetting it from wall; concave undersurface; globular body; concave neck flaring to simple lip. Thin black glaze, peeling; reserved undersurface. Vertical grooves on wall for ribbing. Graffito on undersurface:

MNAM[

Higher, early profile without true ring foot. See *Agora* XII, no. 202, p. 250, fig. 3.

Second quarter 5th century

392. Pitcher with inset rim   Pl. 45

C-72-215. K–L:25–26; lot 72-134 (third quarter 4th century). P.H. 0.114, D. 0.148 m. Many joining fragments; small part of shoulder, one third of neck, one half of rim, upper handle preserved; plaster restoration.

Sloping shoulder; high, straight cylindrical neck; heavy flaring rim with concave underside, convex outer face;

rounded lip; concave interior face (for holding lid) to neck opening; wide strap handle with convex outer face, attached to rim.

The context is 4th century. Similar examples from later 4th-century deposits, all unpublished, discussed p. 18 above.

393. Narrow-necked pitcher Pl. 45

C-65-529. N:26; lots 4481 and 4482 (early Hellenistic). P.H. 0.126, D. 0.072 m. Many joining fragments; part of shoulder, neck, rim, handle preserved; plaster restoration.

Rounded shoulder continuous with tall, narrow concave neck; flaring overhanging triangular rim, peaked lip; flat strap handle from shoulder to upper neck, with only vestigial ridge on neck. For the name (different from name in *Corinth* VII, iii, nos. 633–642), see footnote 41 above, p. 19.

Hellenistic

394. Glazed kotyle Pl. 45

C-61-473. Q:25; lots 881, 885 (third quarter 4th century). P.H. 0.094, est. D. lip 0.094 m. Many joining fragments; most of wall and lip preserved; lower break just above foot.

Convex flaring wall turning in slightly to rounded lip. Black glaze overall, except added pink above foot.

Without full profile, dating is inconclusive, but beginning of rounder profile of wall and slightly inturned lip suggest a late 5th- or early 4th-century date. See *Agora* XII, pp. 81–84; *Corinth* XIII, pp. 127–128. Added pink or red is found later in Corinthian kotylai than in Attic examples.

395. Attic glazed kotyle Fig. 6, Pl. 45

C-64-397. P:23; lot 4483 (later 4th century). H. 0.085, D. 0.08, est. D. lip 0.07, D. foot 0.036 m. Many joining fragments; vertical profile preserved.

Narrow ring foot; tall, high ovoid wall turning in to rounded lip. Reserved: undersurface, with central dot and circle; lower wall with poor crosshatching; area between handle roots; top of inner wall. Black glazed elsewhere. See *Agora* XII, no. 323, p. 258, pl. 15.

Second quarter 4th century

396. Glazed kotyle Pl. 45

C-70-206. J:21; no lot. H. 0.093, D. 0.098, est. D. lip 0.086, est. D. foot 0.048 m. Many joining fragments; about one third preserved; vertical profile complete.

Shape as **395** but more contracted. Black glazed overall except added pink on lower wall, outer areas of foot; inner foot pink above, black below; undersurface with central dot and circle, pink between.

Mid- or third quarter 4th century

397. Glazed kotyle Fig. 6

C-65-315. M:18; lot 3228 (later 3rd century). P.H. 0.095, D. foot 0.056 m. Many joining fragments, preserving foot, lower wall.

Splayed ring foot, rounded on outer face; nippled undersurface; tall diagonal wall just beginning to change to convex at upper break. Originally black glazed overall, now peeling.

Late 4th century; not so extreme as the following examples.

398. Glazed kotyle Pl. 45

C-65-622. M:18; lot 3228 (later 3rd century). P.H. 0.074, D. foot 0.04 m. Three joining fragments, preserving foot, part of lower wall to area of maximum diameter.

Spreading ring foot; broad, flat resting surface; slight stem; high ovoid wall. Glazed overall.

Later than **397**; late 4th, beginning of 3rd century

399. Glazed kotyle, West Slope decoration Fig. 6, Pl. 45

C-65-621. M:18; lot 3228 (later 3rd century). H. 0.137, D. 0.123, D. foot 0.074, est. D. lip 0.101 m. Many joining fragments, preserving foot, two fifths of wall, small area of lip, most of one handle.

Spreading ring foot, carelessly turned with uneven surface; low conical interior, nippled undersurface; high ovoid wall, very narrow at foot; upper wall turning in to rounded lip; horizontal loop handle in horseshoe shape, slightly canted, set at top of wall. Two horizontal grooves on exterior below lip. Black glaze overall, quite thin, scraped from grooves; stacking line visible on lower wall. On upper wall, incised decoration of wheat(?) pattern.

Ovoid kotyle shape but decoration of articulated kantharos shape. Compare the Gnathian kotylai with even more elaborate decoration (*CVA*, British Museum 1[Great Britain 1], pls. 5 [41]:4, 12, 18 and 7 [43]:17). See also the Attic example: Schlörb-Vierneisel (footnote 70 above, p. 26), p. 91, grave 158 (hS87), no. 1, pl. 57:1, dated to the fourth quarter of the 4th century.

Probably mid-3rd century

400. Glazed kotyle, West Slope decoration

C-65-623. M:18; lot 3228 (later 3rd century). P.H. 0.036, est. D. lip 0.15 m. Three joining fragments, from upper wall and contracting rounded lip.

From the same shape as **399**. Thin peeling glaze overall. Two horizontal grooves below lip. On exterior wall, incised decoration of wheat or sprays, poorly preserved.

Probably mid-3rd century

401. Plain kotyle   Pl. 45

C-62-773. R:23–24; lot 1991 (late 6th century). H. 0.12, D. 0.155, D. foot 0.09 m. Many joining fragments, completed in plaster.

Low ring foot; tall, slightly convex flaring wall, vertical at rounded lip; loop handle. No decoration; stacking line below handles.

For profile see *Corinth* XIII, pp. 106–108.
Later 6th century

402. Plain kotyle   Fig. 6

C-69-270. N:21; lot 6217 (later 4th century, 2 Roman sherds). H. 0.073, est. D. lip 0.085, D. foot 0.037 m. Many joining fragments, plaster restoration; full profile including handle.

Narrow ring foot; nippled undersurface; tall, convex flaring wall without inturned lip; loop handle. No decoration; stacking line below handle.
Late 4th century

403. Plain kotyle   Pl. 45

C-71-171. L–M:28; lot 6723 (late 4th or early 3rd century). H. 0.067, est. D. lip 0.08–0.09, D. foot 0.037 m. Four joining fragments; vertical profile preserved.

Small false ring foot; tall, convex flaring wall with slight inturn to lip. No decoration. See **113**, Group 7, for similar profile.
End of 4th, beginning of 3rd century

404. Plain kotyle   Pl. 45

C-65-628. M:18; lot 3228 (later 3rd century). H. 0.073, D. 0.104, D. foot 0.042–0.044 m. Many joining fragments; holes in wall, lip.

Disk foot; string marks on bottom; convex flaring wall turning in slightly to rounded lip; two strips of thick clay pinched on to top of wall as handles, slightly canted. No decoration; poor surface finish. Very similar in profile to C-75-285 (well 1975-5), unpublished.
Later 3rd century

405. Plain kotyle   Fig. 6, Pl. 45

C-70-366. T:16–17; lot 6640 (early Roman). P.H. 0.076, est. D. lip 0.12 m. Seven joining fragments; upper wall, handle preserved.

Tall, convex flaring wall, becoming vertical at rounded lip; canted handle with horizontal groove around upper face. No decoration; encrusted.

The wall profile suggests the kotyle; the handle is anomalous. The context extends from early Hellenistic into early Roman.

406. Plain kotyle   Pl. 45

C-70-597. T:16–17; lot 6640 (early Roman). P.H. 0.163 m. Six joining fragments of wall, lip. Fabric with a few small inclusions.

Tall convex wall, turning in above the maximum diameter; rounded lip. Scar of handle attachment at top right break. No decoration; interior wheel ribbed.

407. Plain kotyle   Pl. 45

C-70-598. T:16–17; lot 6640 (early Roman). P.H. 0.039, est. D. lip 0.158 m. Three joining fragments of upper wall, lip.

Vertical wall with slight inturn to rounded lip. Horizontal groove 0.006 m. below lip. Scar of handle attachment at left break; daub of red paint (intentional?) around it.

408. Plain kotyle   Pl. 46

C-70-600. T:16–17; lot 6640 (early Roman). P.H. 0.028, L. of handle 0.081 m. Three joining fragments preserving handle, part of lip. Slight traces of burning.

Upper wall and lip as **407** but without horizontal groove. Horizontal handle, round in section, triangular in form, pinched at corners. A few dots of black paint.

409. Plain kotyle   Pl. 46

C-70-599. T:16–17; lot 6640 (early Roman). P.H. 0.035, est. D. foot 0.11 m. One fragment of foot, beginning of wall.

Heavy ring foot with wide resting surface; beginning of convex flaring wall. No decoration. **409** may be from the same vase as **408**; clay and surface similar.

410. Skyphos   Fig. 7, Pl. 46

C-61-406. P:24–25; lots 877 (early 3rd century), 878 (third quarter 4th century). H. 0.087, rest. D. rim 0.085, D. foot 0.046 m. Many joining fragments, completed in plaster.

Small torus foot, splayed on inside; flat undersurface; slightly stemmed lower wall; full compound curve of upper wall; flaring rim; rounded lip; slightly canted handle with root contraction. Black glaze overall, peeling.

There are a number of skyphoi at a similar stage of development, from the late 4th-century debris of the dining rooms: C-72-217, L:26–27, lot 72-129 (Williams, *Hesperia* 46, 1977, p. 68, no. 1); C-72-218, K–L:24–25, lot 72-139; C-71-87, M:22–23, lots 6826, 6827 (Bookidis and Fisher, *Hesperia* 41, 1972, p. 297, no. 9, pl. 58); C-61-472, P:24–25, lot 878. It is superfluous to illustrate them all. See also C-71-105 (Williams and Fisher, *Hesperia* 41, 1972, p. 157, no. 27, pl. 25), from drain 1971-1, and **81**, Group 6.
Third or early fourth quarter 4th century

411. Attic skyphos   Pl. 46

C-71-175. L–M:28; lot 6723 (late 4th—early 3rd century). P.H. 0.133, est. D. rim 0.15 m. Many joining fragments; plaster restoration; much of wall, both handles, foot missing.

Shape as **410** but more noticeably stemmed; lip more flaring. Black glaze overall; wheel grooves.

The lot contained a coin, 71-372, Pegasos/Trident, dated 303–287 B.C.

Early 3rd century

412. Skyphos   Fig. 7, Pl. 46

C-69-262. O:20–21; lot 6205 (early 3rd century). H. 0.10, est. D. rim 0.10, D. foot 0.038 m. Many joining fragments; full profile preserved.

Cited: Williams, *Hesperia* 48, 1979, p. 124, under no. 35.

Shape as **411**; more contraction of foot in relation to rim diameter; very thick bottom. Added pink on undersurface with central dot; black glazed elsewhere. See **116**, Group 7 and **158**, Group 8.

Late first or second quarter 3rd century

413. Cup with offset rim   Fig. 8, Pl. 46

C-65-171. O–P:22–23; lot 4355 (late 4th century). P.H. 0.051, est. D. at break 0.11, D. foot 0.035 m. Many joining fragments; foot, most of wall to shoulder preserved.

Published: Stroud, *Hesperia* 37, 1968, p. 328, pl. 98:g; M. L. Lazzarini, "I nomi dei vasi greci nelle iscrizioni di vasi stessi," *Archeologia classica* 25–26, 1973–1974 (pp. 341–375), p. 357, no. 24; *SEG* XXV, 343; XXIX, 332.

Low ring foot with slightly convex undersurface; wide, almost straight flaring wall, beginning to round and thicken for shoulder. Black glaze overall except at lower edge of foot, undersurface. Graffito around wall at upper break; see above publications.

See C-36-743 (*Corinth* VII, i, no. 213, p. 57, pl. 29) and C-62-505 (*Corinth* VII, ii, An 157, pl. 69) for the profile.

Early Corinthian

414. Cup with wishbone handles   Fig. 8, Pl. 46

C-62-374. R:23–24; lot 1985 (*ca.* 500 B.C.). H. 0.049, D. 0.104, D. foot 0.064 m. Many joining fragments; center of bowl missing, completed in plaster.

Ring foot; flaring wall beginning convex, with carinated turn to vertical lip; two slightly canted wishbone handles (one complete). Black glaze overall, thin and peeling; fired partly red; no traces of added colors.

For 6th-century cups with wishbone handles, see C-53-157 (Brann, *Hesperia* 25, 1956, p. 361, no. 35), closest in wall profile, but with more sloping foot and flattened rim. C-53-225, from the same deposit (p. 361, no. 34), has a more convex profile turning in to rounded lip. C-39-193, from well 1939-1, unpublished, could be either 6th or 5th century by context; it has a sloping ring foot, higher wall profile, and slightly flattened rim. None of the above is truly similar to **414**. The context of **414** extends through the 6th century.

6th century; lack of any parallel precludes closer dating.

415. Phiale   Fig. 9, Pl. 46

C-62-716. R:23–24; lot 1985 (*ca.* 500 B.C.). H. 0.026, D. 0.071 m. Three joining fragments; complete.

Wide resting surface; good central depression; convex flaring wall turning vertical to rounded lip; low rounded omphalos. Black glaze on omphalos; six interior bands alternately added purple (over glaze) and black; black band at top of outer wall. Traces of burning. Similar examples from lot: C-62-357, C-62-358.

Small version of the deep phiale of the early and mid-6th century.

416. Phiale

C-62-353. R:23–24; lot 1985 (*ca.* 500 B.C.). H. 0.019, D. 0.07 m. Two joining fragments; completed in plaster.

Shape as **415** but with broader omphalos, more offset from floor; slightly lower wall. Added purple on omphalos; six added-purple (over glaze) bands in bowl, two at top of exterior wall.

Mid-6th century

417. Phiale   Pl. 46

C-62-356. R:23–24; lot 1985 (*ca.* 500 B.C.). H. 0.021, D. 0.06 m. Two joining fragments; completed in plaster.

Flat bottom, no central depression; tall, convex flaring wall with profile of **415**; small rounded omphalos. Undecorated.

Mid-6th century

418. Phiale

C-61-309. P–Q:24; lot 898 (*ca.* 500 B.C.). H. 0.02, D. 0.068 m. Slightly chipped.

Shallow central depression; wall profile as above; rounded omphalos. Added-red bands, now peeled, around omphalos, on midwall, top of wall, top of exterior wall. Wheel grooves on exterior.

Slightly later than **417**.

419. Phiale   Pl. 46

C-61-311. P–Q:24; lot 898 (*ca.* 500 B.C.). H. 0.015, D. 0.053 m. Intact.

Very shallow central depression; wall and lip as **418**; very small nipple omphalos. Two added-red and brown bands around omphalos and on upper wall; brown dots on lip, running into added-red band on exterior wall. Similar examples from lot: C-61-308, C-61-310, C-61-312, C-61-313.

Mid- or later 6th century

420. Phiale   Fig. 9

C-62-738. R:23–24; lot 1988 (late 6th century). H. 0.015, D. 0.049 m. Slightly chipped.

Flat bottom, with string marks; no central depression; low, convex flaring wall; slightly thickened rim; wide rounded omphalos. Fabric and glaze fired red. Red omphalos; inner floor with added red; upper wall red. Heavy rim indicates change to new profile.

End of 6th century or slightly later?

421. Phiale   Fig. 9, Pl. 46

C-62-781. R:23–24; lot 1991 (late 6th century). H. 0.034, rest. D. 0.114 m. Many joining fragments; completed in plaster.

Wide resting surface; deep central depression; tall, convex flaring wall; outward thickened rim, flat on top; high wide omphalos, flat on top, well offset from floor. Added red on omphalos continuing onto floor; black dicing; black band and line; black blob buds; zone of dotted loops attached to upper black line; black band to rim; added red on rim; exterior reserved. One of the latest pieces in this lot.

The wall profile is still that of 6th-century phialai, but the rim and omphalos anticipate the 5th-century form.

422. Attic phiale

C-73-359. K–L:23; lot 73-102 (mid-5th century, Roman intrusion). Max. dim. 0.094 m. Three joining fragments; broken at omphalos and at beginning of upward turn of wall.

Floor decoration over black glaze: inner and outer bands of added white enclosing added-white tongues around omphalos; outer floor with large buds or leaves outlined in added white and filled in with added purple; areas between buds originally orange. Added colors mostly peeled. See **423**.

Early 5th century

423. Attic phiale   Pl. 46

C-64-402. P:26; lot 2012 (early 5th century). Max. dim. 0.05 m. One floor fragment.

Floor decoration over black glaze: two zones of added-red

buds encircled by added white, divided by added-white line. Smaller than **422**. For both these Attic examples see Vanderpool, *Hesperia* 15, 1946, p. 326, nos. 297–299, pl. 67.

Early 5th century

424. Phiale   Pl. 46

C-64-44. P:26; lot 2011 (late 5th century). H. 0.01, D. 0.038 m. Slightly chipped.

Wide resting surface; well-defined central depression; low, convex flaring wall, turning vertical to outward thickened rim; tall rounded omphalos, set off from floor; interior floor and wall strongly set off from each other. Two brown bands around omphalos; brown band on lower wall; one on rim; exterior reserved. Well-executed tiny example.

Later 5th century

425. Phiale   Pl. 46

C-65-422. M:21; lot 4458 (late 4th century). H. 0.012, D. 0.048 m. Intact.

Wide resting surface; shallow central depression; low vertical wall turning into seven scallops, ending in rounded lip; rounded, offset nipple omphalos. Black bands on floor around omphalos; added red on outer floor; black bands at top of interior and exterior wall.

5th century (?)

426. Phiale   Fig. 9

C-61-416. P:24; lot 877 (early 3rd century). H. 0.021, D. 0.104 m. Two joining fragments; plaster restoration.

Narrow resting surface; shallow central depression; convex flaring wall turning vertical to rounded lip; uneven groove of outer wall perhaps an attempt to offset lip; low button omphalos, well offset from floor. Undecorated. Resting surface narrower than typical of 5th-century phialai.

First half 4th century

427. Phiale   Fig. 9, Pl. 46

C-72-88. Foundation trench of wall 245; J:14. H. 0.032–0.035, D. 0.196 m. Many joining fragments, almost complete.

Narrow resting surface; deep central depression with straight sides; low, convex flaring wall turning vertical to outward thickened rim, set off from wall by pared line (groove); flat-topped button omphalos, rising vertically from floor. Unevenly fired, buff to orange. Undecorated. See **428–430**.

428. Phiale   Fig. 9

C-72-86. Context as **427**. H. 0.035–0.041, D. 0.176 m. Intact.

Taller, more flaring wall than **427**; similar rim; rounder and lower button omphalos. Unevenly fired, buff to orange. Undecorated.

429. Phiale

C-72-87. Context as **427**. H. 0.036–0.041, D. 0.174 m. Many joining fragments; almost complete.

Profile similar to **428**; uneven grooves below rim as **427**. Unevenly fired, buff to orange. Undecorated. Stacking line on exterior.

430. Phiale Fig. 9, Pl. 46

C-72-89. Context as **427**. H. 0.023–0.026, D. 0.17 m. Many joining fragments; part of wall, rim missing.

Wide central depression with deep groove around it; low flaring wall, rising to flat, outward thickened rim, articulated by two uneven grooves below; very low, wide button omphalos. Lower profile than **427–429**. Undecorated.

427–430 are the largest phialai found in the Sanctuary; there was no other pottery in the foundation trench, in which they were apparently carefully placed.

Third quarter 4th century (by profile)

431. Phiale

C-72-210. Building K–L:24–25, Room 3, on hearth. H. 0.023, D. 0.104 m. Many joining fragments; almost complete.

Narrow resting surface; shallow central depression; low, convex flaring wall; flat-topped rim barely articulated by incised line on outer wall; offset rounded omphalos. Undecorated. Stacking line on exterior.

Late 4th century

432. Phiale Pl. 46

C-72-211. Context as **431**. H. 0.019, D. 0.094 m. Many joining fragments; almost complete.

Shape as **431** but lower wall profile; inturned rim; flat button omphalos. Wheel grooves on exterior. Slightly later than **431**; see **117**, Group 7 and **173**, Group 9.

Early 3rd century

433. Goblet or kantharos Fig. 10, Pl. 46

C-72-245. O:24; lot 2110 (first quarter 4th century). **a)** H. 0.081, est. D. lip 0.084, D. foot 0.052 m. Many joining fragments; one third preserved; vertical profile without handle. **b)** P.H. 0.027, p.W. 0.039 m. Two joining fragments of upper wall, lip (not illustrated).

Wide, splayed ring foot with vertical edge (almost a stem foot); conical underneath; tall wall beginning convex, turning vertical at maximum diameter, with slight flare to rounded lip. Interior glazed. Exterior wall black to reserved zone at base of wall; black line above foot; outer foot with added red, edge reserved; undersurface with central black dot, black bands.

The closest parallel for the foot is in the Vrysoula goblet (Pemberton, *Hesperia* 39, 1970, p. 277, no. 18, pp. 291–292, nos. 78–88). The wall profile is of neither the late kotyle nor the late skyphos form. For full discussion of this curious vase, see p. 36 above.

First quarter 4th century (by context)

434. One-piece kantharos Pl. 46

C-65-627. M:18; lot 3228 (later 3rd century). P.H. 0.065, D. foot 0.047 m. Five joining fragments; part of foot, wall preserved.

Ring foot, in two degrees, wide resting surface; nippled undersurface; tooled groove between foot and wall (in later examples to become a true stem); low ovoid wall, curving in to (missing) rounded lip. Flat, narrow vertical ribs on wall. Originally black glazed overall, now peeling.

Foot of one-piece form, but no other ribbed examples known. See C-31-206 (*Corinth* VII, iii, no. 380, p. 76, pl. 15) for profile.

Second quarter 3rd century?

435. Cyma kantharos Fig. 10, Pl. 46

C-65-498. N–O:16–17; lot 4404 (mid-3rd century). H. 0.146–0.15, D. lip 0.136, D. foot 0.06 m. Many joining fragments, about half preserved; handles missing; plaster restoration.

Pedestal foot; stem ring; low ovoid wall; groove and ridge 0.033 m. below lip marking change to concave rim; flaring tapered lip. Interior completely glazed; exterior glazed to stem. Reserved: conical undersurface with central black dot; resting surface of foot; stem; black band on ledge. Scratched vertical incisions for ribs on lower wall; X panel incised below handles; upper wall below groove with incised wavy tendril; no trace of added white for ivy leaves.

High convex profile of foot is unusual. For profile: C-47-62 (*Corinth* VII, iii, no. 411, p. 80); for decoration: C-47-282 (no. 413, p. 80).

Probably second quarter to mid-3rd century.

436. Articulated kantharos Fig. 10, Pl. 46

C-65-625. M:18; lot 3228 (later 3rd century). H. 0.098 est. D. lip 0.09, D. foot 0.052 m. Many joining fragments, preserving most of foot, one third of wall, small area of lip, no handles; some plaster restoration.

Ring foot with fillet (not a true foot in two degrees); semiconical inside; nippled undersurface; straight flaring wall, carinated at point of maximum diameter (one third of height), turning in slightly without convexity to rounded lip; scar of lower attachment for vertical strap handle. Two horizontal grooves on upper wall, at areas of lower and upper handle attachments. Glazed overall; glaze fired mostly red; no trace of decoration.

For similar profile: C-47-88 (*Corinth* VII, iii, no. 473, p. 85); but **436** is slightly sharper in articulation and has neater grooving.

Mid-3rd century or slightly later?

437. Imported kantharos(?) with   Fig. 10, Pl. 47
West Slope decoration

C-65-292. N–O:19–20; lots 2239 (late Roman), 3207 (late Hellenistic, two Byzantine sherds), 3209 (1st century after Christ). **a)** P.H. 0.046, est. D. lip 0.11 m. Four joining fragments of upper wall, rim. **b)** Max. dim. 0.031 m. Wall fragment (not illustrated). Hard, slightly gritty fine clay with a few bits of mica; fabric: 7.5YR 7/4 (pink), glaze: 5YR 3/4 (dark reddish brown). Possibly Corinthian; the clay is harder than typical of Corinthian but not so fine as Attic.

Concave wall, beginning to flare at lower break, terminating above in projecting molding; straight flaring rim ending in rounded lip. On wall: boxed rectangles alternating with checkerboard in brown and black glaze; reserved band above design to molding; molding and rim brown; interior glazed.

No parallels for the shape. The estimated diameter and thinness of the fabric (0.003 m.) make it more suitable for a kantharos than for an amphora or krater. Two other fragments of the same fabric: C-47-357, kantharos (*Corinth* VII, iii, no. 397, p. 79) and C-63-742, conical bowl (no. 535, p. 92). The fabric also seems close to fabric A found in hemispherical moldmade relief bowls and lamps of Corinth type X, group 1 (see C. M. Edwards, *Hesperia* 50, 1981, pp. 200–201). See **498**.

Later Hellenistic?

438. One-handled cup, type 1   Pl. 47

C-70-392. J:20–21; lot 6516 (third quarter 5th century). H. 0.036, D. 0.082, rest. D. foot 0.043 m. Most of wall, foot, all of handle missing; plaster restoration.

Shallow ring foot; convex flaring wall with slight inturn to rounded lip. Glazed inside; upper half of exterior wall glazed by dipping.

Mid to third quarter 5th century

439. One-handled cup, type 1   Fig. 11, Pl. 47

C-69-264. M–N:19; lot 6182 (fourth quarter 4th century). H. 0.042, D. 0.092, D. foot 0.048 m. Many joining fragments; half of wall preserved, no handle; plaster restoration.

Published: Bookidis and Fisher, *Hesperia* 41, 1972, p. 291, no. 2, pl. 57.

Low ring foot with thin disk on undersurface; low, convex flaring wall with strong inturn to rounded lip. Interior glazed; upper one third of exterior wall glazed (red and peeling) by dipping. The profile of the upper wall and lip resembles an echinus bowl. See discussion, p. 37 above.

4th century

440. One-handled cup, type 2   Fig. 11

C-65-421. N–O:22; lot 4476 (third quarter 4th century). H. 0.043–0.048, D. 0.085, D. foot 0.048 m. Many joining fragments; half of handle, part of wall, foot missing.

Diagonal ring foot; nippled undersurface; convex wall vertical at lip; flattened lip; handle slightly contracted. Black glaze overall, peeling.

First half 4th century

441. One-handled cup, type 2   Fig. 11

C-69-271. N:21; lot 6217 (later 4th century, 2 Roman sherds). H. 0.049–0.052, est. D. lip 0.09, D. foot 0.04 m. Many joining fragments; half of foot, wall, most of handle missing.

Published: Bookidis and Fisher, *Hesperia* 41, 1972, p. 294, no. 7, pl. 57.

Shape as **440** but with higher wall profile, lower foot. Black glaze overall except undersurface. Similar one-handlers: C-69-267, M:22, lot 6208; C-72-216, L:26–27, lot 72-129.

Third or early fourth quarter 4th century

442. One-handled cup, type 2   Fig. 11, Pl. 47

C-72-219. K–L:24–25; lot 72-139 (third to fourth quarter 4th century). H. 0.046, D. lip 0.086, D. foot 0.047 m. Many joining fragments; much of foot, bottom of bowl, half of wall, part of handle missing; plaster restoration.

Shape as **441** but with more rounded lip, more contracted handle. Black glaze overall, now peeled.

Third or early fourth quarter 4th century

443. Flat-rimmed bowl   Pl. 47

C-62-772. R:23–24; lot 1991 (late 6th century). H. 0.053, D. rim 0.13, D. foot 0.082 m. Many joining fragments; full profile; completed in plaster.

Flaring ring foot with wide resting surface; convex flaring wall turning vertical to flattened rim, thickened in and out. Black glaze overall, thin and peeling. Added-purple bands (no white) on outer foot, upper wall, under rim, on lip, outer floor, inner midwall.

First half 6th century

444. Laconian bowl (or krater)   Fig. 12

C-75-281. P:26; lot 2040 (*ca.* 500 B.C.). P.H. 0.038, est. D. rim 0.26 m. One upper wall and rim fragment. Hard, slightly rough clay without inclusions; core: 5YR 6/3 (light reddish brown).

Slightly convex flaring wall; outward thickened, wide rim, flat on top. Hard black glaze inside and out. No published parallels for shape. Identified as Laconian by Laura Siegel.

6th century (by context)

445. Attic saltcellar   Fig. 12, Pl. 47

C-62-783. R:23–24; lot 1991 (late 6th century). H. 0.043, D. 0.063, rest. D. lip 0.062 m. Many joining fragments; full profile; completed in plaster.

Slightly concave resting surface, no foot; tall concave wall outward thickened at lower edge, terminating in outward thickened lip. Black glazed except reserved resting surface and lip. For profile: *Agora* XII, no. 922, p. 136, pl. 34.

Late 6th century

446. Large Attic echinus bowl   Fig. 12, Pl. 47

C-69-263. O:20–21; lot 6205 (early 3rd century). H. 0.045, est. D. 0.16, est. D. foot 0.088 m. Four joining fragments; preserving one fifth of whole.

Ring foot; groove on inner face of resting surface; nippled undersurface; wide, convex flaring wall turning in to tapered lip. Black glaze overall, except reserved band at base of wall and on resting surface; miltos on groove of resting surface. On floor: five circles of rouletting around six alternately linked, stamped palmettes; central circle. See *Agora* XII, no. 830, p. 295, pl. 33, fig. 8.

Mid-4th century

447. Large echinus bowl   Fig. 12, Pl. 47

C-65-488. M:18; lot 3231 (later 3rd century?). H. 0.065, est. D. 0.17, D. foot 0.058 m. Many joining fragments; one third preserved; plaster restoration.

Small ring foot; convex flaring wall, taller than **446**; strong inturn to tapered lip. Interior glazed; exterior glazed on upper third of wall.

Early 3rd century (by profile)

448. Small echinus bowl   Pl. 47

C-65-629. M:18; lot 3228 (later 3rd century). H. 0.04, est. D. lip 0.07, D. foot 0.029 m. Two joining fragments; half missing.

Small ring foot; nippled undersurface; convex flaring wall with pronounced turn and thickening of wall to rounded inturned lip. Originally glaze overall; glaze fired red, peeling.

Second quarter to mid-3rd century

449. Bowl with outturned rim   Fig. 12, Pl. 47

C-71-136. M–N:23; lot 6838 (early 4th century). H. 0.053, D. 0.138, D. foot 0.074 m. Many joining fragments; part of foot, wall, rim missing.

Tall ring foot; no nippling; wide, convex flaring wall with continuous curve to round rolled rim. Black glaze

overall, peeling; miltos on undersurface with wide concentric band of glaze. In center of floor: circle, four stamped palmettes linked in diamond configuration, three light grooves over which are 14 unlinked palmettes, very thin and linear. Stamp very worn.

Not yet with double curve to wall, a trait noticeable by the mid-4th century: C-37-2589 (*Corinth* VII, iii, no. 73, p. 34, pls. 3, 44). Older high foot still present in **449**.

Early 4th century

450. Bowl with outturned rim   Pl. 47

C-69-268. M:22; lot 6208 (late 4th century). H. 0.036, est. D. lip 0.15, est. D. foot 0.063 m. Four joining fragments; most of foot, three fourths of wall and rim missing.

Ring foot; flaring lower wall only slightly convex, turning up and becoming slightly concave before barely outturned rounded lip. Graffito (single stroke) on undersurface. Glazed overall.

Ring foot and glazing from older form of bowl; slight concavity of upper wall and loss of thickened lip indicate Hellenistic profile. See discussion, p. 43 above. **450** may represent the transition between the two profiles.

Late 4th century (by context)

451. Small bowl with outturned rim   Fig. 12, Pl. 47

C-69-269. N:19; no lot. H. 0.039, est. D. rim 0.114, est. D. foot 0.046 m. Two joining fragments; one fourth preserved.

Ring foot; wide, straight flaring wall rising from strong carination to concave rim and slightly outturned lip. Originally black glaze overall, peeling, with miltos on inner foot and undersurface.

Complete glazing and use of miltos (imitating Attic) suggest a date early in the series.

Early 3rd century

452. Small bowl with outturned rim   Fig. 12

C-65-487. M:16–17; lot 3232 (probably to 146 B.C.). H. 0.037, est. D. rim 0.108, D. foot 0.038 m. Five joining fragments; one third preserved.

Published: Bookidis, *Hesperia* 38, 1969, p. 303, note 11, pl. 79:d, right.

Narrow ring foot; nippled undersurface; straight flaring wall becoming concave above carination; rounded flaring rim. Glazed inside; rim dipped on exterior; thin glaze mostly red and peeling.

Less articulated rim, lack of strong carination, relatively narrow foot all suggest date later than **451**.

Late 3rd or early 2nd century

453. Conical bowl   Pl. 47

C-65-624. M:18; lot 3228 (later 3rd century). P.H. 0.046, p.W. 0.044 m. Four joining fragments from wall and lip.

Straight flaring wall, simple rounded lip. Thin, reddish, peeling glaze overall. Decoration limited to interior of bowl, in incision and added white. Below: horizontal incised chain of berries, black dots once with added white. Narrow band of added white above. Zone below lip: incised boxed rectangles stopped by checkerboard; traces of added white in alternate squares of checkerboard. Narrow added-white band below lip.

Second half 3rd century

454. Hemispherical bowl with West   Fig. 12, Pl. 47
      Slope decoration

C-65-525. M:16–17; lot 3227 (late 3rd or early 2nd century). P.H. 0.057. Four joining fragments; plaster restoration.

Bottom and lower wall of round open bowl, without articulation of resting surface. Glazed inside and out, thin and peeling, scraped away from grooves limiting zones of decoration. Decoration limited to exterior wall; interior not sufficiently preserved to determine presence of decoration on floor. Designs in incision and added white; stain of white preserved. From bottom: traces of white petals; bead and reel in added white; incised horizontal wheat pattern, with added-white dots inside center area; broken below lip.

For the shape, see C-65-377, the profile of which is shown in Figure 36 (*Corinth* VII, iii, no. 944, p. 187, pl. 84), with the same lower motifs. For the wheat, see the kotylai above, **399** and **400**.

Later 3rd or early 2nd century

455. Small bowl, beveled rim   Fig. 13, Pl. 47

C-69-266. M:22; lot 6208 (late 4th century). H. 0.026, est. D. 0.088, est. D. foot 0.052 m. Three joining fragments; one third preserved; center of floor missing.

Ring foot; convex flaring wall without sharp articulation of bevel, turning in to tapered lip. Black glaze overall. Echinoid profile.

Third quarter 4th century

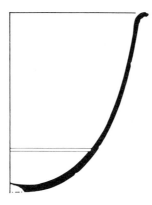

Fig. 36. Hemispherical bowl, C-65-377. Scale 1:2

456. Small bowl, beveled rim   Fig. 13, Pl. 47

C-71-137. M:22–23; lots 6826 and 6827 (late 4th century). H. 0.026, D. 0.087, D. foot 0.051 m. Four joining fragments; most of floor missing; plaster restoration.

Published: Bookidis and Fisher, *Hesperia* 41, 1972, no. 10, p. 298, pl. 58; cited: Williams, *Hesperia* 48, 1979, p. 124.

Shape as **455**, with more articulation of bevel, higher foot. Black glaze overall, peeling.

Third quarter 4th century

457. Small bowl, beveled rim   Fig. 13, Pl. 47

C-72-220. K–L:24–25; lot 72-139 (third to fourth quarter 4th century). H. 0.027, est. D. 0.10, est. D. foot 0.052 m. Two non-joining fragments, each mended of several fragments; plaster restoration. Only larger fragment illustrated.

Shape as **456**, with more horizontal wall. Black glaze overall, peeling. Similar profile: C-72-222, L:26–27, lot 72-128.

Third quarter 4th century

458. Moldmade relief bowl, figured   Pl. 48

C-64-37. P–Q:26–27; lot 2009 (3rd to first half 4th century after Christ). P.H. 0.038, p.W. 0.062 m. Two fragments of upper wall. Peeling black glaze; worn mold.

Traces of two chariots moving right; between them at left lower break a rosette; above, enclosed eggs between ridges; upper border design at break not discernible. Charioteers apparently not winged. Peeling black glaze overall; worn mold.

The chariot motif, rosette, and enclosed egg pattern suggest an Argive model. C-73-191, from a late Hellenistic and Roman fill in Shop 5, Lechaion Road east, shows the chariots and rosette. See also Siebert (footnote 21 above, p. 4), M48, pl. 27 and the related Nikai motif, on Ep2, pl. 43.

Late 3rd century?

459. Moldmade relief bowl, figured   Pl. 48

C-65-644. M:16–17; lot 3233 (early Roman). Two non-joining fragments. a) Max. dim. 0.079 m. Five joining fragments of medallion and lower wall. b) Max. dim. 0.088 m. Four joining fragments of upper wall, rim.

a. Medallion enclosed by two concentric ridges; medallion design indiscernible. Ten palmettes with curled leaves laid radially to medallion; rosettes between upper parts of palmettes.

b. Part of one rosette preserved; undetermined objects on the upper wall; rim zone with running tendril between ridges, three dots in each loop. In one small area the tendril appears to be stopped by a rosette. Peeling glaze overall, partly red; worn mold.

For similar palmettes, see C-35-978 (*Corinth* VII, iii, no. 862, p. 170).

Early 2nd century

460. Moldmade relief bowl, imbricate　　Pl. 48

C-65-645. M:18–19; lot 3223 (late Roman). P.H. 0.041, p.W. 0.055 m. Two joining fragments of convex wall.

Variant imbricate pattern on wall, of overlapping scales in double ridges, central vertical row of four to seven dots in each section. Thin glaze, fired red to black, overall.

For linear imbricate designs, see *Corinth* VII, iii, p. 158.

Second quarter 2nd century

461. Moldmade relief bowl, shield　　Pl. 48

C-65-646. M–O:17–20; lot 3206 (Byzantine). Two non-joining fragments from convex lower wall. **a)** Max. dim. 0.041 m. **b)** Max. dim. 0.032 m.

a. Lower wall, turning into area of medallion, with six-arm pinwheel, dots, set off from bowl by circle. Above circle, dots, two concentric ridges.

b. Wall fragment with concentric ridges, dots. Peeling glaze overall.

The offset of the lowest part of the bowl by circle or ridge, with decoration between it and the medallion, is fairly common on shield bowls in both Corinthian and other fabrics. The pinwheel is not a common Corinthian motif, although the triskeles is used as a medallion motif or within the circles of shield bowls: see CP-1930, C-37-1569, C-33-102, C-31-479 (*Corinth* VII, iii, nos. 923, 928, 930, 931, p. 184, pl. 81). Delian bowls have six- and nine-arm pinwheels, as on C-38-699, and examples in *Délos* XXXI, nos. 4303 and 4328, pl. 45.

2nd century

462. Imported moldmade relief bowl,　　Pl. 48
　　　 imbricate

C-65-303. M:18–19; lot 3223 (late Roman). P.H. 0.076, p.W. 0.079 m. Four joining fragments of wall, lip. Micaceous fabric: 5YR 5/1 (gray).

Noted: Williams (*Hesperia* 47, 1978), p. 22, note 32.

Convex wall with ridge before inturned lip. On wall: imbricate pattern of overlapping pointed leaves; above ridge, row of eight-petal rosettes. Gray glaze overall.

For similar leaves, see *Délos* XXXI, nos. 371, pl. 1, and 5158, pl. 9. See also the discussion of gray ware in Corinth and the chronological problems raised by it in Williams, *Hesperia* 47, 1978, pp. 21–23.

Workshop of Menemachos, 2nd century

463. Imported moldmade relief bowl, long　　Pl. 48
　　　 petal

C-65-647. M:18–19; lot 3223 (late Roman). P.H. 0.041, p.W. 0.054, est. D. lip 0.11 m. One fragment of upper wall, rim. Micaceous fabric: 10YR 7-6/1 (gray).

Shape as **462**. Lower wall: rounded tips of long petals, vertical dots between; above, enclosed pendent eggs, separated by incised darts, bounded by horizontal ridges. Thin peeling blue to dark gray glaze overall.

For the petal/dot motif: *Délos* XXXI, nos. 4666, 8541, pl. 43; for the egg and dart, *Délos* XXXI, no. 226, pl. 42, no. 1592, pl. 45, and others.

Monogram workshop, 2nd century

464. Saucer　　Fig. 15

C-69-297. M–N:19; lots 6182 and 6189 (late 4th century). H. 0.035, est. D. 0.144, D. foot 0.06 m. Seven joining fragments; half preserved; center missing.

Published: Bookidis and Fisher, *Hesperia* 41, 1972, p. 291, no. 1, pl. 57.

Ring foot, slightly rounded; convex flaring wall, ending in rounded lip. Black glaze overall, peeling. Similar profile: C-72-221, K–L:25–26, lot 72-134.

Third quarter 4th century

465. Saucer　　Fig. 15, Pl. 48

C-73-316. K–L:23–24; lots 73-115 and 73-116 (late 4th century). H. 0.035–0.039, D. 0.154, D. foot 0.069 m. Many joining fragments; completed in plaster.

Ring foot: vertical outer face, wide resting surface, diagonal inner face; nippled undersurface; flaring wall with little convexity; rounded lip. Black glaze overall.

Fourth quarter 4th century

466. Saucer　　Pl. 48

C-69-265. N:18; lot 5635 (early 3rd century). H. 0.036, est. D. 0.17, D. foot 0.064 m. Five joining fragments; one fourth preserved; plaster restoration.

Shape as **465**, slightly lower foot. Glaze overall, peeling; poor surface finish.

Ca. 300 B.C.

467. Saucer　　Fig. 15, Pl. 48

C-71-174. L–M:28; lot 6723 (late 4th—early 3rd century). H. 0.028–0.032, est. D. 0.124, est. D. foot 0.055 m. Many joining fragments; one third preserved; center of floor missing; plaster restoration.

Shape as **466** with change of direction in wall. Glazed on interior; top third of exterior wall glazed by dipping.

First quarter 3rd century

468. Saucer   Fig. 15

C-72-53. N:12–13; no lot. H. 0.031–0.033, D. 0.124, D. foot 0.05 m. Many joining fragments; half preserved.

Shape as **467**; small foot; nippled undersurface; wheel ridges on wall. Interior glazed; most of exterior wall glazed; badly finished surface.

Second quarter to mid-3rd century

469. Plate   Pl. 48

C-65-473. N:22; lot 4460 (late 4th century). H. 0.015, est. D. 0.135, D. resting surface 0.11 m. Four joining fragments; full profile.

Flat resting surface with groove near outer edge; low rim beginning diagonally, flaring with little convexity to rounded lip; shallow groove below lip on upper face. Three brown lines on resting surface; two brown lines on outer rim. Floor: four central brown circles; reserved ribbon made by radiating opposing triangles; brown line; outer floor with brown dot rosettes; brown line and added-red band at edge of floor. Lower rim: groups of "worms"; four brown lines above. Brown is diluted glaze.

Probably early 5th century

470. Plate   Fig. 16

C-61-404. P:24–25; lot 878 (third quarter 4th century). H. 0.038, rest. D. rim 0.24, rest. D. foot 0.154 m. Many joining fragments; completed in plaster.

Wide vertical ring foot; flat undersurface; low convex wall; flaring convex rim, concave underneath; rounded lip with groove on upper surface setting it off from rim. Two suspension holes. Originally glazed overall, now peeled. Surface burnt.

Lip and rim profile suggestive of 6th-century date; foot and glaze suggestive of 4th. The plate cannot be closely dated by context.

471. Attic plate with rolled rim   Fig. 16

C-70-205. J:21; no lot. H. 0.028, est. D. rim 0.21, est. D. foot 0.13 m. Six joining fragments of foot, wall, rim; center missing.

Vertical ring foot; slightly convex flaring wall; shallow groove at turn to upper concave wall; ledge; flaring rolled rim; no grooves on upper surface, which is flat. Black glaze overall; no traces of stamping. See *Agora* XII, no. 1056, p. 310, fig. 10.

Mid- to third quarter 4th century

472. Plate with offset rim   Pl. 48

C-65-319. M:16–17; lot 3410 (probably early Roman). Est. D. rim 0.175 m. Four joining fragments, preserving part of wall, rim; broken at groove for central medallion of floor.

Slightly convex flaring wall; flaring horizontal rim offset from upper wall face by two grooves; groove on outer edge of rim before lip. Originally glazed overall; glaze scraped from grooves. On upper rim, crosshatching interrupted by checkerboard. Not sufficiently preserved to discern bowl decoration.

For crosshatching as a late West Slope design: Thompson, *Hesperia* 3, 1934, p. 441, found only in examples of the last group, E59, E60.

Late 2nd century?

473. Plate with offset rim   Fig. 16

C-65-609. M:16–17; lot 3410 (probably early Roman). H. 0.044, est. D. rim 0.25, D. foot 0.105 m. Many joining fragments; full profile; plaster restoration.

Vertical ring foot; nippled undersurface; convex flaring wall; grooves on both exterior and interior faces offsetting concave rim; rounded lip offset by groove from rim. Grooves on floor with narrow central depression, too narrow for use as fish plate. Glaze overall, peeling.

Interior grooves suggest West Slope decorative system, but there are no traces of paint for such designs. Exterior grooves without known parallel. Size and width of rim also unusual. Variant of West Slope plate?

Mid-2nd century or later?

474. Attic alabastron(?)   Pl. 48

C-65-410. M:21; lot 4458 (late 4th century). P.H. 0.038, Th. upper break 0.006 m. One fragment from base of pointed closed vessel, without foot or resting surface.

Exterior wall black glazed; careful horizontal ribbing ringing the wall; interior reserved. No known parallels.

475. Blister-ware aryballos   Pl. 48

C-61-168. O–P:25; lot 872 (late 5th-century pottery; Roman lamp). P.H. 0.033, D. 0.074 m. Many joining fragments; part of wall, all of neck, rim, handle missing.

Flat resting surface; low ovoid body curving continuously to neck. Well-modeled, convex ribs evenly spaced on wall.

Third quarter 5th century

476. Blister-ware aryballos   Pl. 48

C-61-400. P:24–25; lot 878 (third quarter 4th century). H. 0.068, rest. D. 0.10, D. rim 0.04 m. Most of resting surface, part of wall restored in plaster.

Shape as **475** with lower, ovoid wall; domed profile; low, concave, narrow neck merging with flaring rim; rim slopes down on upper face; strap handle from upper wall to rim. Vertical incisions on wall, irregularly but closely spaced.

At lower limit of lot; third quarter 4th century

477. Blister-ware aryballos   Pl. 48

C-65-631. M:18; lot 3228 (later 3rd century). H. 0.065, D. 0.087, D. rim 0.032 m. Many joining fragments; part of wall and resting surface missing; plaster restoration.

Slightly concave resting surface; short, almost biconical wall turning continuously into shoulder; tall, narrow, tapering neck; projecting rim horizontal below, diagonal above to neck opening; strap handle with central vertical groove (pseudo-double handle), attached from shoulder to rim. Blisters on exterior. Very thin fabric.

First or second quarter 3rd century

478. Blister-ware aryballos   Pl. 48

C-65-309. M:18; lot 3222 (first half 3rd century after Christ). P.H. 0.074, D. 0.089, D. resting surface 0.05 m. Rim and most of handle missing.

Slightly concave resting surface; wall as **477** but more pronouncedly biconical; two grooves on upper wall in handle area. Thin wash on surface, mostly peeling; blisters on surface. Very thin fabric as **477**. Biconical shape and context require a date later than **477**. Surface burnt.

2nd century?

479. Blister-ware filter vase

C-65-630. M:18; lot 3228 (later 3rd century). P.H. 0.06, D. rim 0.063 m. Three joining fragments; shoulder and neck preserved. Wheelmade.

Convex shoulder; funnel neck with diagonal flare to flat horizontal rim, inward thickened. Neck made separately from rest of vessel, with floor, through which were punched six holes, 0.005 m. in width. Strap handle at base of neck. No surface wash; blisters on surface. Very thin fabric (0.002 m. at shoulder).

For a more complete example, see C-47-853 (*Corinth* VII, iii, no. 778, p. 149, pls. 36, 64) dated to 146 B.C. **479** may be earlier.

480. "Feeder"   Pl. 48

C-71-170. L–M:28; lot 6723 (late 4th, early 3rd century). H. 0.098–0.102, est. D. 0.087, D. foot 0.057 m. Many joining fragments; much of wall with spout missing; vertical profile complete; plaster restoration.

Very low ring foot; low ovoid wall, narrowing to flaring rounded flange; diagonally rising rim. Mouth made separately with stopper; ten holes pierced through stopper on one side. Strap handle, concave on outer face, from upper wall to rim; pellet at top of handle.

Most of the examples of feeders (see discussion, p. 63 above) have the stopper holes only on one side. Of those that have the spout preserved, always on the side, never on axis with the handle, some have the spout on the side with the holes, others do not.

480 has a more gentle curve than the example from Forum drain 1971-1, C-71-522. Differences may not indicate chronological variance.

Late 4th century?

481. "Feeder"   Fig. 21, Pl. 48

C-69-313. M–N:19; lot 6181 (mid-3rd century). H. 0.085, D. 0.076, D. foot 0.058 m. Stopper missing; edge of spout, flange chipped.

Profile as **480**, except disk foot; diagonal spout on side; bolster at top of handle. Spout on side away from holes of stopper. Surface originally polished but now burnt, flaking.

Late 4th or early 3rd century?

482. Tripod pyxis   Pl. 49

C-62-782. R:23–24; lot 1991 (late 6th century). H. 0.028, D. 0.062, D. foot 0.058 m. Two joining fragments; one foot restored in plaster.

Flaring foot, not offset from wall; high recessed undersurface; low concave wall; flaring flat rim; bowl undercut from rim inside. Exterior and undersurface reserved. Wide "worms" on rim; traces of X and petal pattern (see **483**) on floor. Badly burnt, obscuring patterns; glaze has peeled.

Probably later 6th century

483. Tripod pyxis   Pl. 49

C-64-217. N–O:23; lot 2152 (4th-century pottery, 2nd-century coin). H. 0.035, est. D. 0.09 m. Three joining fragments, one third preserved; full profile.

Shape as **482**. Exterior and undersurface reserved. On rim: "worms"; on floor: long X, intersected by a cross with petals at its tips in added red over glaze.

Later 6th century

484. Flanged pyxis   Pl. 49

C-61-408. P:24; lot 877 (early 3rd century). H. 0.074, est. D. inner flange 0.20 m. Four joining fragments; vertical profile, part of one handle preserved; floor missing.

No foot; rounded outward thickening of lower wall; vertical wall; thickened rounded rim with groove below; diagonal flange flaring into bowl; part of vertical reflex handle on rim. Base of wall: added red (over glaze), black band above; most of wall with zone of six or seven "worm" lines alternating with wide stripes of brown; some traces of added red on stripes; pattern bordered by glaze lines above and below. Dots on rim and handle; flange glazed including lip; trace of glaze inside at beginning of floor. Glaze fired mostly red, peeling.

See T 2980 (*Corinth* XIII, grave 333-4, pl. 50). **484** is probably earlier.

Early 5th century

485.   Flanged pyxis   Fig. 19

C-70-237. I–J:21–22; lot 6511 (mid-5th century). H. 0.031, D. 0.075, D. inner flange 0.061 m. Many joining fragments; full vertical profile, one handle preserved.

Shape as **484** but smaller; flat resting surface. Resting surface, handle reserved. Base of wall black; wall banded with added red, black, black, the latter continuing over rim; upper half of rim reserved; flange black including lip. On floor: central circle; wide bands of black and added red separated by glaze lines; interior wall with added-red band, glaze line below. Added red directly on clay. Typical black-and-red Conventionalizing decoration.

  Mid-5th century (by context)

486.   Powder-pyxis bowl   Pl. 49

C-62-696. R:23–24; lot 1985 (*ca.* 500 B.C.). P.H. 0.013, D. 0.086 m. Resting surface, lower wall preserved; upper wall broken away, break worn smooth resembling finished surface.

Flat resting surface, with one central groove, one near outer edge; vertical wall inset from base, creating projecting rounded ledge. Interior: central glaze circle; one at juncture of floor and wall. Exterior: two lines on wall; resting surface with added red (over glaze), glaze in groove, glaze line just inside groove, glaze band in center, central groove with added red. Colors worn and peeling.

  6th century

487.   Powder-pyxis lid   Pl. 49

C-62-780. R:23–24; lot 1991 (late 6th century). H. 0.086, D. 0.113 m. Many joining fragments; vertical profile complete; half restored in plaster.

Domed top (center restored in plaster); two molded rings near center, third near rim; projecting rounded rim with four narrow grooves on upper face; slightly concave flange set in from rim, outward thickened at bottom. Interior reserved. Flange: red above rounded edge; wide zone of vertical stripes between bands; dicing above; band below rim; traces of added red on rim grooves and rings; "worm" pattern possibly between rings. Added red appears to be over glaze, but glaze fired red. Colors peeling; surface encrusted; patterns obscured.

  Designs similar to those on powder pyxides found in graves but **487** is much larger than the latter. Similar pyxis identified as a bowl, not a lid: T 1138 (*Corinth* XIII, grave 258-4, pl. 34). The size of the rings makes it difficult to turn **487** upside down and call it a bowl; it does not rest steadily.

  Second half 6th century

488.   Powder-pyxis lid   Pl. 49

C-62-779. R:23–24; lot 1991 (late 6th century). H. 0.043, D. 0.073 m. Many joining fragments; about

two thirds preserved; center of lid missing; plaster restoration.

Shape as **487**; nearly flat top of lid; vertical flange set back only slightly from rim. Interior reserved. Flange: bands of added red, black, added red, black, with glaze lines between. Upper rim with groove, added red on it; four lines of glaze, before missing center of lid. Added red over glaze.

  Second half 6th century

489.   Pyxis lid   Pl. 49

C-64-429. N:26; lot 2075 (early 5th century). H. 0.042, D. 0.107 m. Three joining fragments; about three fourths preserved; complete profile.

Tapering flange set in from edge; sloping top with two ridges set off by grooves at outer edge; knob in form of eight pomegranates laid radially to central conical ring. Undersurface reserved; black checkerboard on outer edge of lid; added red in grooves; black band on upper lid around knob; pomegranates alternately added red and black; central ring scored, painted black. Exterior surface polished; colors peeling.

  Late 6th or early 5th century (by context)

490.   Lid   Pl. 49

C-62-720. R:23–24; lot 1985 (*ca.* 500 B.C.). H. 0.035, est. D. 0.12 m. Five joining fragments; full profile.

High domed center with rounded knob narrowing in stem; flat horizontal lid with wide groove near outer edge, ending in rounded lip; no flange. Interior and exterior surfaces covered with careful, thin wheel grooves. Interior reserved. Exterior: two added-purple (over black) bands near edge on either side of wide groove; black circle around juncture of domed knob and lid; X-pattern of pairs of added-purple lines from knob to lip; top of knob originally glazed. No parallels for shape or decoration.

  6th century (by context)

491.   Perforated cylindrical vessel   Fig. 20, Pl. 49

C-64-447. Q:20–22; lot 2087 (second half 4th century after Christ). P.H. 0.162, D. 0.156, D. foot 0.112, D. wall 0.129 m. Many joining fragments preserve foot, lower flange, part of wall with opening, top flange, and beginning of domed top. Center of floor missing.

Low ring foot with wide, flat resting surface, set well back from projecting flange; flange with slightly convex lower surface, raised ring around set-back cylindrical wall; wall gently concave, flaring out continuously to form projecting flange at top of wall; raised ring around base of domed top. At bottom of wall, oval door opening 0.05 m. high, 0.064 m. wide. Holes through wall and top, made before firing, in horizontal but not vertical alignment. Holes not scraped clean inside on wall from level of top of door down; those above and those on dome are free of wadded clay. No decoration.

Hellenistic

492. Perforated cylindrical vessel   Fig. 20, Pl. 49

C-65-610. M:18; lot 3228 (later 3rd century). P.H. 0.121, D. 0.153, D. foot 0.105 m. Two joining fragments preserve all of foot, lower flange, floor, part of wall with opening.

Disk foot, gently concave on undersurface; flange as **491**; cylindrical wall lightly convex, turning in at top for dome; probably no upper wall flange. Holes, door opening as **491**. Door: est. H. 0.053, 0.055 m. wide. No holes are scraped clean.

Hellenistic

493. Perforated cylindrical vessel   Pl. 49

C-69-320. K–L:21–22; lot 6219 (1st century after Christ). **a)** P.H. 0.123, D. 0.155 m. Many joining fragments preserve base, much of wall. **b)** P.W. 0.106 m. Two joining fragments of upper wall, beginning of top. Hard, gritty fabric, with traces of mica and a few inclusions; 5YR 7–6/6 (reddish yellow).

a. Flat resting surface, no foot; wall contracting above edge of base, forming sharp bevel; cylindrical wall. Finished surface at left break for top of door; parts of two rows of holes preserved, more at top break, scraped clean on interior. Holes begin above level of door.

b (not illustrated). Wall flaring to projecting flange; beginning of domed top, set in from flange, preserving one hole, parts of others. Preserved top of wall without holes. Slight misfiring, surface darker in a few areas. Interior of both fragments have wheel ridges; exterior also with wheel grooves.

Hellenistic.

494. Perforated cylindrical vessel   Pl. 49

C-65-626. M:18; lot 3228 (later 3rd century). P.H. 0.057, est. D. flange 0.14 m. One fragment of cylindrical wall, upper flange, beginning of dome. Lightly micaceous soft clay: 5YR 6/8 (reddish yellow); buff exterior slip: 10YR 7/4 (very pale brown).

Cylindrical wall preserving six holes, part of seventh, in random placement; projecting flange set off from wall with slightly convex lower face, flat diagonal top face, with groove setting flange off from slanting top; top thickened at inner break, probably becoming level. Top without holes.

Clay slightly softer than the other red fabric noted in these vessels (see p. 60 above) but with sufficient mica to suggest that it is not Corinthian. The buff clay slip is also not found in vessels of this type in typical Corinthian clay, even those of the more orange color. The clay of

this piece resembles that of the next; both are probably imported.

Hellenistic

495. Perforated cylindrical vessel   Pl. 49

C-65-656. N–O:13–17; lot 4417 (late Roman). P.H. with handle 0.063 m. One fragment of top. Lightly micaceous clay, 7.5YR 7/6 (reddish yellow). See **494**.

Conical top, rising to rounded knob as on spouted askos; wide strap handle rising vertically (but not symmetrically) attached at either side below knob. Five preserved holes, more at lower break. There is a very similar fragment, C-65-653, M:16–17, lot 3227.

Hellenistic

496. Ladle   Pl. 49

C-65-465. N–O:13–15; lot 4387 (4th century after Christ). P.L. 0.106 m. Five joining fragments, from bowl and handle attachment. Handmade.

Rounded bowl with beginning of vertical flare for rising sides of ladle; attachment for long handle visible on lower surface. Black on sides of handle. Dipinto in added red on bowl, turning 90° on one side:

ᛃᒋᘑᒋᐱᛉᒋᐱᒋᘓ

Height of the bowl is unknown, but one curving side suggests a fairly deep bowl, although probably not so deep as a kyathos. The context provides no date for the ladle.

497. Open vessel with West Slope   Fig. 21, Pl. 49
       decoration

C-68-200 (**a**), C-65-293 (**b**). O:20, M:18–19, M–N:19; lots 3215 (early Roman?), 5615 (late Roman), 5624 (5th and 4th century and **497**). **a)** P.H. 0.076, est. D. 0.08, D. resting surface 0.028 m. Many joining fragments; base, part of wall, shoulder, beginning of neck preserved. **b)** Max. dim. 0.035 m. One fragment of midwall.

Recessed undersurface; false base ring, not articulated on exterior; short globular body merging with sloping shoulder; neck set off from shoulder by vertical ledge. Neck opening probably as narrow as resting surface. Without evidence for length of neck, shape, and direction of handle, shape is unclear. Perhaps a juglet or small askos?

a. Black glaze overall, interior and exterior. Midwall decorated with thorns (clay nodules), set off above and below by grooves; zone below neck ledge with incised wavy stem for ivy chain; leaves in added white, now peeled. Glaze scratched from grooves.

b (not illustrated). Wall fragment with thorns.

Similar profile: C-28-70 (*Corinth* VII, iii, p. 2, note 3: "small closed shape"), with Hellenistic scale pattern. The use of thorns seems to be late Hellenistic. The lot contains Classical pottery with the exception of this fragment.

Mid-2nd century

498.   Open vessel with West Slope decoration   Pl. 49

C-65-648. O:18; lot 4349 (4th century after Christ). P.H. 0.038, rest. D. lip 0.10 m. One fragment of upper wall, concave neck, molded rim. Hard, non-micaceous clay: 5YR 7/6 (reddish yellow).

Convex wall turning in at top; ridge at top of wall as offset for low concave neck; flaring molded rim with lower flat ridge; slightly convex molding, light groove, rounded thickened lip. Hard, metallic glaze overall, a mottled red brown. Shallow ribbing on wall, stopping at right break, where there is a scar of a handle attachment; the lip above is not broken. On neck, incised tendril with leaves and dots in thick creamy applied clay.

The fabric resembles that of **437** but is darker and seems more compact. **498** is neither Corinthian nor Attic. The shape also is problematic, for the rim and neck pro-

file do not appear to be kantharoid (rim diameter greater than wall diameter), although the fragment is of suitable thinness (0.003 m.).

Hellenistic, possibly 3rd century?

499.   Gnathian closed shape   Pl. 49

C-65-511. O:23; lot 4347 (end of 4th century). P.H. 0.032, p.W. 0.030 m. One wall fragment, no preserved edge. Fine, non-micaceous clay: 5YR 7/6 (reddish yellow). From closed shape; oinochoe?

Exterior black glazed; interior reserved. On exterior: below, incised eggs with added white inside, between two pairs of horizontal incised lines; row of added-white dots above; at upper break, chain of added-purple and added-white leaves, with one large added-white circle; added-white clusters of berries. Added white peeled, only stain preserved.

See Gnathian oinochoe with similar designs: *CVA*, British Museum 1 [Great Britain 1], pl. 6 [42]:19.

Probably late 4th century

MINIATURES (500–594)

The miniatures are arranged by shape and chronologically within each shape; the chronology is, however, very tentative. Only the phialai are not included here; because it was impossible to ascertain at what size a phiale becomes a miniature, the very small examples are not separated from the others.

500.   Small hydria   Pl. 50

C-61-256. P–Q:24–25; lot 893 (first quarter 4th century). H. 0.063, D. 0.063, D. foot 0.042 m. Part of vertical handle, rim missing; hole in shoulder.

Wide false ring foot; short wall with high ovoid profile; offset shoulder, almost horizontal; short concave neck flaring to triangular rim; loop side handles; vertical round handle from shoulder to neck. Added purple over black on foot; black on lower wall; black dicing at top of wall; black linear tongues on shoulder; added-purple band on neck; rim and handles black. Added purple and black peeling.

See T 3202 (*Corinth* XIII, grave 160-9, pl. 24), first quarter 6th century, with more globular body. **500** is later, probably second half of 6th century.

501.   Small hydria   Pl. 50

C-61-203. P:24–25; lot 878 (third quarter 4th century). H. 0.071, D. 0.06, D. foot 0.029 m. Foot chipped; one side handle and part of rim missing.

Disk foot; high ovoid wall, taller than **500**; horizontal offset shoulder; vertical neck, flaring to horizontal rim, grooved on upper face; side handles diagonally set; vertical round handle from shoulder to rim. Added red on foot; black band on midwall; black blob buds on upper

wall continuing onto side handles; added-red band at shoulder; black linear tongues on shoulder; neck and rim black.

Compare similar profile of **47**, Group 3 (Fig. 1).

First half 5th century

502.   Small hydria   Pl. 50

C-73-320. P–Q:24–25; no lot. P.H. 0.065, D. 0.063, D. foot 0.036 m. Five joining fragments; neck, rim, all handles missing; holes in wall and foot.

Ring foot with outer ledge (accidental); high ovoid body merging with convex sloping shoulder; drip ring at base of neck. Added red on foot; brown band below handles; handle zone bounded by added-red lines, with unattached black ivy leaves off right-angled stems; brown and added-red lines on lower shoulder; linked brown spirals; added red at top of shoulder and on drip ring.

Similar example, C-61-220, Q:25, lot 881.

More contracted foot suggests late 5th- or early 4th-century date.

503.   Small hydria   Pl. 50

C-64-405. O:25–26; lot 2079 (earlier 4th century). H. 0.09, D. 0.064, D. foot 0.036 m. Many joining fragments; part of wall, neck, rim missing.

Flaring disk foot; wall and shoulder as **502**; tall narrow neck, flaring to rounded lip; canted side handles; round vertical handle from outer shoulder to neck. Poor surface finish; unevenly fired.

Early 4th century

504. Small hydria

C-61-399. P:24–25; lot 878 (third quarter 4th century). H. 0.084, D. 0.054, D. foot 0.034 m. One side handle, vertical handle, part of rim missing.

Nipple on undersurface (accidental?); high false ring foot; wall and shoulder as **502**; narrow concave neck, flaring to horizontal rim with peaked lip; 90° side handle. Poor surface finish; warped.

See **138**, Group 7, for similar profile (Fig. 1); **138** not at lower terminus of that group. Form of rim and side handle later than **138**.

Later 4th century

505. Small hydria Pl. 50

C-62-317. R:23–24; lot 1962 (early 3rd century). H. 0.067, D. 0.051, D. foot 0.028 m. Intact, except hole in upper wall.

Disk foot; high ovoid wall merging with sloping shoulder; shorter profile than **504**; tall narrow neck, flaring to horizontal rim with grooves on inner and outer faces; 90° side handles; ribbon for vertical handle, from shoulder to rim.

Late 4th, beginning of 3rd century

506. Small hydria Pl. 50

C-65-577. M:18; lot 3228 (later 3rd century). H. 0.117, D. 0.072, D. foot 0.041 m. Many joining fragments; part of wall missing.

Disk foot; biconical ring above foot; high ovoid wall merging with shoulder and neck; tall narrow neck, flaring to triangular rim; unarticulated side handles on shoulder; vertical handle poorly attached from shoulder to under rim; wheel grooves on surface.

Profile more exaggerated than **182–184** of Group 9. Probably at end of 3rd century (or later?). Lot 3228 does not appear to go down to 146 B.C., although some of its contents are difficult to date; see **399, 400, 479, 492, 494**.

507. Small hydria Pl. 50

C-65-579. M:17–18; lot 3222 (first half 3rd century after Christ). P.H. 0.083, D. 0.053, D. foot 0.028 m. Broken at beginning of flare to rim; vertical handle missing.

Disk foot; tall profile, high ovoid wall without convexity, merging with sloping shoulder; narrow concave neck;

pinched-on side handles; lump of clay for lower attachment of vertical handle.

The last of the series, with almost no articulation of the profile.

2nd century

508. Krateriskos Pl. 50

C-61-193. P:24–25; lot 878 (third quarter 4th century). H. 0.031, D. rim 0.042, D. foot 0.024 m. Intact; slightly burnt.

Low disk foot; concave to top of wall; concave flaring rim, not offset from wall; rounded lip; two reflex handles at top of wall. Shape based on calyx-krater. Bands on bottom of base, top of wall, upper rim, below lip; dots on lip; two bands on upper interior wall.

509. Krateriskos Pl. 50

C-62-788. R:23–24; lot 1991 (late 6th century). H. 0.025, D. rim 0.048, D. foot 0.026 m. Three joining fragments; rim chipped; one handle missing.

Flat resting surface; flaring wall, concave to convex; diagonal flaring rim offset from wall; rounded lip; two vertical handles pressed to rim. Black glaze overall. Shape based on column-krater.

510. Krateriskos

C-62-789. R:23–24; lot 1991 (late 6th century). H. 0.032, D. rim 0.044, D. foot 0.027 m. Intact.

Shape as **509** but high profile; ring foot with disk on undersurface. Black glaze overall, now peeled.

511. Krateriskos Pl. 50

C-62-851. P:23–24; lot 1993 (mid-4th century). H. 0.033, D. rim 0.047, D. foot 0.028 m. Intact.

Shape as **509, 510**, with flat resting surface, taller, more vertical rim. Black glaze overall, now peeled.

512. Krateriskos

C-64-47. P:26; lot 2012 (early 5th century). H. 0.022, D. rim 0.043, D. foot 0.018 m. Slightly chipped.

Shape as **511**; flat projecting rim; vestigial handle-plates. Black glaze overall, peeling.

513. Squat oinochoe Pl. 50

C-62-790. R:23–24; lot 1991 (late 6th century). H. 0.043, D. 0.034, D. foot 0.028 m. Handle missing.

Low disk foot; short globular body; tall cylindrical neck; trefoil mouth. Handle scar preserved at beginning of shoulder. Glaze band on base; two on upper body, one at base of neck; added purple on neck and mouth (directly on clay).

6th century

514.   Rounded conical oinochoe   Pl. 50

C-64-76. Q:27; lot 2060 (early 5th century). H. 0.039,
D. 0.037 m. Resting surface chipped.

Flat resting surface; convex conical body; short cylindrical neck; trefoil mouth; strap handle. Bands on lower
wall; design of upper wall indiscernible; black neck and
mouth. Glaze has peeled.

Later 6th century

515.   Broad-bottomed oinochoe   Pl. 50

C-62-778. R:23–24; lot 1991 (late 6th century). P.H.
0.051, D. 0.066 m. Handle, trefoil mouth missing.

Flat resting surface; false ring foot grooved from wall,
very slight articulation of inner face; wide globular body,
merging with shoulder; short neck with drip ring. Added
purple (over black) on foot; black band at bottom of wall;
zone of dicing with black band above and below on shoulder; added purple at base of neck; handle stub black;
traces of black at neck break, on exterior and interior.

6th century

516.   Broad-bottomed oinochoe

C-61-286. P–Q:24; lot 898 (ca. 500 B.C.). H. 0.058, D.
0.062, D. foot 0.058 m. Part of mouth missing.

Shape as **515** without drip ring; trefoil mouth; strap handle. Black glazed except resting surface; added-purple
band on shoulder, foot, lip. Purple directly on clay.

Later 6th century

517.   Two-handled pitcher   Pl. 50

C-61-277. P–Q:24; lot 896 (second half 4th century
after Christ). H. 0.034, D. 0.039, D. resting surface
ca. 0.017 m. Intact.

Resting surface uneven, merging directly into globular
wall; straight flaring rim; rounded lip; two vertical strap
handles, not rising above rim. No decoration.

Classical

518.   One-handled pitcher or mug   Pl. 50

C-61-238. P–Q:24–25; lot 892 (4th century after
Christ). H. 0.022, D. 0.031, D. resting surface
0.022 m. Intact.

Flat resting surface; low globular wall; diagonally flaring
rim; rounded lip; one handle, rising slightly over wide
mouth. No decoration.

Very small version of wide-mouthed oinochoe: *Corinth*
XIII, p. 130.

5th century

519.   Squat jar   Pl. 50

C-62-758. R:23–24; lot 1989 (later 6th century). H.
0.027, D. 0.044, D. rim 0.026 m. Intact.

Flat resting surface; low ovoid body, narrowing to

vertical rim with flat horizontal lip; no handles. No
decoration.

6th century

520.   Perforated kalathiskos

C-62-348. R:23–24; lot 1985 (*ca.* 500 B.C.). P.H.
0.099, D. rim 0.145 m. Many joining fragments; parts
of mid- and upper wall, rim preserved.

Published: Stroud, *Hesperia* 34, 1965, pl. 4:e, left.

Narrow vertical wall, expanding to heavy, flaring, triangular rim with peaked lip. Three rows of triangular
holes; lower break at beginning of fourth row. Grooves
between each row on upper wall; three narrow grooves
on wall. Three wide bands of added red between diluted
glaze lines on exterior; red rim; added red between glaze
lines on interior, below first two rows of holes and above
third; glaze lines below first row, between second and
third row, and at top of wall. Added red directly on clay.
Glaze fired mostly red; extensive burning on interior.

521.   Perforated kalathiskos   Pl. 51

C-65-307. M:17–18; lot 3222 (first half 3rd century
after Christ). P.H. 0.05 m. Several joining fragments;
part of wall and rim with protome preserved.

Part of tall, vertical upper wall, flaring to small diagonal
rim with protome preserved. Triangular holes. Bands of
diluted glaze inside and out, wide band of added red over
glaze above row of holes on exterior; glaze on rim. Protome of woman's head with stepped wig, top of wig with
incised diamond pattern; round face, large nose and eyes;
features very worn. Traces of glaze on hair and face.
Back of head very smooth, without detail.

See **603–620** below for other protomes from kalathoi.
Most of the heads found in the Sanctuary are from kalathoi, not pyxides; they lack the upper attachment characteristic of the latter shape. Heads decorated only flaring kalathoi, not types 1–3, nor the basket variety.

522.   Perforated kalathiskos

C-61-247. P–Q:24–25; lot 893 (first quarter 4th century). H. 0.046, D. rim 0.067, D. resting surface
0.025 m. Intact.

Published: Stroud, *Hesperia* 34, 1965, pl. 4:c, left.

Flat resting surface; tall, slightly concave wall expanding
to rounded flaring rim. One row of vertical slits. Four
bands of glaze outside; added-red rim; four bands inside
wall. Glaze fired mostly orange, peeling; extensive burning on interior.

523.   Perforated kalathiskos

C-62-805. R:23–24; lot 1991 (late 6th century). H.
0.022–0.025, D. 0.041–0.042, D. resting surface
0.025 m. Intact.

Uneven dimensions. Similar to **522** but with lower, more open profile; small diagonal rim. One row of vertical slits. Bands of glaze at bottom and top of wall; three glaze lines in zone of holes; interior floor glazed; five lines of glaze on interior wall; rim with five groups of five dots. Glaze fired red, peeling; wheel grooves on surface.

None of the four perforated examples can be dated except generally by context: late 7th through 6th centuries.

524. Flaring kalathiskos   Pl. 51

C-61-242. P–Q:24–25; lot 893 (first quarter 4th century). H. 0.042, D. 0.07, D. resting surface 0.035 m. Slightly chipped rim.

Flat resting surface; gently concave flaring wall; flaring triangular rim. Pairs of bands on interior floor, top of interior and exterior wall, bottom of exterior wall; single band at midwall on exterior and interior; alternately black and added purple. Nine groups of four to five black triangles on rim. Colors peeling, but vase and decoration beautifully executed and finished.

525. Flaring kalathiskos

C-62-256. R:23–24, lot 1985 (*ca.* 500 B.C.). H. 0.043, D. 0.053 m. Rim slightly chipped.

Published: Stroud, *Hesperia* 34, 1965, pl. 4:c, right.

Shape as **520**, with heavier rim, taller wall. Twelve neat bands of added red (directly on clay) on wall and rim; outer rim with added red; four bands on interior; possibly more, but lower wall and floor badly encrusted.

526. Flaring kalathiskos   Pl. 51

C-62-813. R:23–24; lot 1991 (late 6th century). H. 0.046, D. 0.06, D. resting surface 0.03 m. Rim, lip slightly chipped.

Shape as **525**, except wider body, flaring to rounded lip. Two pairs of grooves on exterior, probably not intentional. Exterior with six glaze bands; interior with at least three, but lower wall encrusted. Glaze fired orange, now peeling; extensive burning overall.

527. Flaring kalathiskos

C-61-304. P–Q:24; lot 898 (*ca.* 500 B.C.). H. 0.03, D. 0.042, D. resting surface 0.02 m. Intact.

Small version of **526**. Added red brown on interior at midwall, on lip, on exterior wall. Banding uneven; daubs of color on wall.

528. Flaring kalathiskos

C-62-723. R:23–24; lot 1988 (late 6th century). H. 0.025, D. 0.039, D. resting surface 0.019 m. Intact.

Small version of **524**. Three glaze lines on exterior, one on rim; floor glazed; two lines on mid- and upper interior wall. Glaze fired brown, now peeling. Neatly executed.

529. Kalathiskos, type 1   Pl. 51

C-62-706. R:23–24; lot 1985 (*ca.* 500 B.C.). H. 0.037, D. 0.072, D. resting surface 0.068 m. One chip from rim.

Flat resting surface; low, very concave wall, merging with flaring, sharp, flat rim; two lug handles formed by pushing clay up from below. Exterior: two brown lines at bottom; one line below handles, one going over handles, one below rim with traces of added red below it; rim with added red. Interior: floor with central brown circles, two brown bands, added red on outer floor; two brown lines on midwall, added red above, brown line at top. Added red directly on clay. Glaze fired brown, peeling.

530. Kalathiskos, type 1   Pl. 51

C-62-713. R:23–24; lot 1985 (*ca.* 500 B.C.). H. 0.037, D. 0.059, D. resting surface 0.04 m. Intact.

Flat resting surface; tall concave wall; flaring rim, convex on upper surface; two narrow loop handles. Higher profile than **529**. Exterior: three bands below, three above handle zone, alternately black and added purple; handles with black line; six black darts between handles. Interior: floor with two glaze circles; glaze line at midwall; three lines on upper wall and rim, first and third of added purple. Added purple partially peeled.

531. Kalathiskos, type 1   Pl. 51

C-62-831. R:23–24; lot 1991 (late 6th century). H. 0.035, D. 0.067, D. resting surface 0.054 m. Intact.

Flat resting surface; lower wall slightly convex, upper concave, expanding to flaring rounded rim; two good lug handles. Exterior: two black bands below handles, one above; black S-maeander in handle zone; rim black, continuing onto upper interior wall. Interior: floor with two black circles; two black bands on wall.

532. Kalathiskos, type 1

C-62-830. R:23–24; lot 1991 (late 6th century). H. 0.036, D. 0.055, D. resting surface 0.053 m. Two joining fragments; part of wall, rim restored in plaster.

Flat resting surface; gently concave wall; strong triangular rim; two good lug handles. Exterior: added-purple band between black lines; black "worms" in handle zone; black line, added-purple band on upper wall; outer rim black, top of rim and handles with added purple. Interior: central floor with glaze circle, peeled; two black bands on wall. Added purple over glaze.

For a tiny, almost identical example, see **32**, Group 2.

533. Kalathiskos, type 2   Pl. 51

C-62-774. R:23–24; lot 1991 (late 6th century). H. 0.058, D. 0.082, D. resting surface 0.041 m. Many joining fragments; part of wall, rim restored in plaster.

Slightly concave resting surface; wide, slightly rounded bevel; straight wall; flaring triangular rim with peaked lip; two lug handles (one missing). Exterior: paired glaze band and line on lower wall, reversed and repeated above handles; added red on rim. Interior: four glaze circles on floor, first and third of diluted glaze; upper wall with black band, diluted-glaze lines above and below. Some glaze fired black to orange; added red over glaze.

534. Kalathiskos, type 2

> C-61-300. P–Q:24; lot 898 (*ca.* 500 B.C.). H. 0.05, D. 0.072, D. resting surface 0.046 m. Rim slightly chipped.
> Published: Stroud, *Hesperia* 34, 1965, pl. 4:d, left.

Shape as **533** but more rounded bevel; concave wall; strongly triangular rim; two lug handles. Glaze bands on lower and upper wall, rim, on interior floor, upper interior wall. Glaze fired brown, peeling.

535. Kalathiskos, type 2

> C-61-246. P–Q:24–25; lot 893 (first quarter 4th century). H. 0.049, D. 0.07, D. foot 0.047 m. Rim slightly chipped.
> Published: Stroud, *Hesperia* 34, 1965, pl. 4:d, right.

Disk foot with convex outer face; sharp bevel; lightly concave wall merging with nearly vertical rim; two loop handles. Exterior: foot black; black and added-purple bands below and above handles; added purple on rim. Interior: two black circles on floor; black band at mid-wall; added purple at top of wall. Purple over black, but unevenly applied; banding is irregular. Addition of a foot, rare in type 2, is suggestive of the krateriskos.

536. Kalathiskos, type 2   Pl. 51

> C-61-245. P–Q:24–25; lot 893 (first quarter 4th century). H. 0.047–0.049, D. 0.067–0.068, D. resting surface 0.043 m. Part of wall, rim missing.

Flat resting surface; sharp bevel; wall and rim as **535**, with rim less articulated; two big, well-formed reflex handles. Exterior: two black bands on lower wall, two above handles; handles outlined in black; rim with added purple over black. Interior: two black circles on floor; two black bands at midwall and at top of wall. Glaze often thin, unevenly applied.

537. Kalathiskos, type 2   Pl. 51

> C-62-827. R:23–24; lot 1991 (late 6th century). H. 0.043–0.044, D. 0.06, D. foot 0.042 m. Rim and foot slightly chipped.

Low ring foot; sharp bevel; concave wall merging with almost vertical rim; rounded lip; two good lug handles. Exterior: glaze on foot and bevel; two lines over bevel, two below handles, two at top of wall; outer rim glazed.

Interior: inner rim with added red (over glaze); black circle in center of floor, two pairs of circles at mid- and outer floor; two bands at midwall, two at upper wall. Glaze fired red brown.

538. Kalathiskos, type 2

> C-61-162. P–Q:25; lot 871 (12th century after Christ). H. 0.042, D. 0.067, D. resting surface 0.038 m. Part of wall and rim missing.

Flat resting surface; low sharp bevel; lightly concave wall; flaring diagonal rim; no handles. Exterior: two glaze lines on lower and upper wall; four groups of three "worms" at midwall; added red (over glaze) on rim. Interior: glaze circle on floor, band on upper wall. Glaze thin, fired mostly orange.

Similar example from Southeast Deposit, *Perachora* I, pl. 30:1.

539. Miniature kalathiskos, type 2   Pl. 51

> C-62-255. R:23–24; lot 1977 (4th-century coin). H. 0.024, D. 0.041, D. resting surface 0.025 m. Intact.

Flat resting surface; rounded bevel; low concave wall; rounded triangular rim; no handles. Exterior: brown line and added-red band on bevel; midwall with black opposing cones between lines; upper wall with added-red band and two black lines; thin line on rim. Interior: added red on outer floor and upper wall; black at top of wall. Added red directly on clay.

540. Miniature kalathiskos, type 2

> C-62-743. R:23–24; lot 1988 (late 6th century). H. 0.024, D. 0.037, D. resting surface 0.024 m. Intact.

Shape as **539** but sharper articulation of rim; two lug handles. Three glaze lines on wall, one on rim, one on interior floor, three on interior wall. Glaze mostly peeled.

541. Kalathiskos, transitional to type 3   Pl. 51

> C-62-832. R:23–24; lot 1991 (late 6th century). H. 0.047, D. 0.064, D. foot 0.04 m. Rim and foot chipped.

Small disk foot; high, slightly rounded bevel; concave wall; flaring triangular rim, slightly rounded on upper face; two reflex handles, not well formed. Exterior: added-purple band with two glaze lines above and below; glaze buds attached to glaze band in handle zone, second glaze band above; added purple on rim. Interior: glaze bands on outer floor, midwall top of wall. Added purple over glaze; glaze fired mostly red.

Neat banding and handle zone pattern of type 3, but profile is type 2.

542. Kalathiskos, type 3   Fig. 5, Pl. 51

> C-61-465. P–Q:24; lot 898 (*ca.* 500 B.C.). H. 0.044, D. 0.059, D. resting surface 0.03 m. Intact.

Slightly concave resting surface; high sharp bevel; gently concave wall; flaring rounded rim with peaked lip; two small lug handles. Exterior: added-red and black bands with glaze line between; picket-fence pattern in handle zone between glaze lines; upper wall and rim black. Interior: black circle on floor, glaze band on upper wall. Neat banding. Glaze mostly peeling. Very early type 3.

543. Kalathiskos, type 3 Fig. 5, Pl. 51

C-61-156. P–Q:25; lot 871 (12th century after Christ). H. 0.049, D. 0.057, D. resting surface 0.038 m. Slightly chipped.

Shape as **542** but more concave wall; straighter rim; two pinched-on handles. Exterior: black and added-red bands with glaze line between; three-stroke stopped black maeander between lines in handle zone; two black bands on upper wall, upper one merging partially with black on rim; dicing on rim. Interior: black circle on outer floor; two black lines at midwall, one on upper wall.

Lot 871 contained 12 type 3 kalathiskoi, all found together, represented by this and **550**, an undecorated example. All 12 are very similar in profile, belonging to the second and third quarters of the 5th century. **543** seems to be the earliest.

544. Kalathiskos, type 3 Pl. 51

C-61-298. Q:25; no lot. H. 0.045, D. 0.057, D. resting surface 0.035 m. Part of wall, rim missing.

Shape as above, with rim and wall less set off from each other. Exterior: bands of added red, glaze, red; two-stroke black maeander in handle zone, with black line below, added red above; top of wall with black, continuing over rim. Interior: black line at top of wall. Encrusted. Loss of sharp profile, contrasting with **542, 543**. **544** and **549** were found in the east face of wall 1.

545. Kalathiskos, type 3 Fig. 5, Pl. 51

C-61-281. P–Q:24; lot 897 (mid-4th century). H. 0.046, D. 0.052, D. resting surface 0.04 m. Rim slightly chipped.

Flat resting surface; high bevel with diameter equal to rim; concave wall with minimum diameter just under rim: contracted profile; heavy, horizontally flaring rim with vertical outer face, peaked lip. Exterior: black, added-red bands; black line between them; Z-maeander between lines; upper wall black, continuing over rim. Glaze line near top of interior wall. Glaze thin and peeling.

Lot 897 continues into 4th century. Exaggerated profile of **545** probably later than **544**; see **100**, Group 6 (Fig. 5).

Probably earlier 4th century

546. Kalathiskos, type 3

C-61-401. P:24–25; lot 878 (third quarter 4th century). H. 0.047, rest. D. 0.065, D. resting surface 0.04 m. Most of rim restored.

Shape as **545**, except for wall merging with very flaring rounded rim; two pinched-on handles. Exterior: bands of black, added red, black; outer rim black. Top of interior wall black. The bands merge and drip over each other; poor surface finish. See **547**.

547. Kalathiskos, type 3 Pl. 51

C-61-403. P:24–25; lot 878 (third quarter 4th century). H. 0.046, D. 0.059, D. resting surface 0.032 m. Half of wall, rim restored in plaster.

Flat resting surface; rounded bevel; nearly vertical wall, merging with flaring rounded rim; two pinched-on handles. Clay fired gray; the added red is nearly gray purple. Exterior: black from resting surface past bevel; added-purple below handles; black in handle zone and over handles; upper wall and rim black. Black band on upper interior wall. Profile close to type 4.

546 and **547** are the last of the type 3 kalathiskoi, later 4th century. Lot 878 extends to *ca.* 325 B.C.

548. Small kalathiskos, type 3 Pl. 51

C-61-219. Q:25; lot 881 (third quarter 4th century). H. 0.021, D. 0.03, D. resting surface 0.018 m. Intact.

Tiny version of **544**, including two handles. On wall: bands of black, added red; black zigzag in handle zone; upper wall with two black lines, continuing over rim; black band on upper interior wall.

549. Small kalathiskos, type 3

C-61-299. Q:25; no lot. H. 0.035, est. D. 0.048, D. resting surface 0.027 m. Half preserved.

Shape as **548**, with less articulation of parts; no handles; no decoration. Found with **544** in the east face of wall 1.

550. Small kalathiskos, type 3 Pl. 51

C-61-165. P–Q:25; lot 871 (12th century after Christ). H. 0.031, D. 0.04, D. resting surface 0.027 m. Intact; partly burnt.

Sharply articulated; small, undecorated type 3; no handles. Found with **543** and other kalathiskoi of second and third quarters of the 5th century.

For type 4 kalathiskoi, see Groups 6, 7, and 8. It was unnecessary to include additional examples in this catalogue.

551. Basket kalathiskos

C-61-180. P:24; lot 877 (early 3rd century). H. 0.026, D. 0.047, D. resting surface 0.036 m. Intact.

Published: Stroud, *Hesperia* 34, 1965, pl. 4:a, center.

Flat bottom; concave wall; horizontal flaring rim; basket handle, convex on upper surface, attached to juncture of upper wall and rim. Exterior: two pairs of brown lines on lower and midwall; brown lines with vertical strokes connecting them on rim; lines on handles. Interior reserved.

552. Basket kalathiskos

C-62-306. O–R:23–24; lot 1955 (second half 4th century after Christ). H. 0.021, D. 0.046, D. resting surface 0.033 m. Intact.

Similar to **551** except with less concave wall. Four glaze lines on exterior wall (peeled), two on rim; circle on top of handle, lines below.

553. Basket kalathiskos   Pl. 51

C-61-305. P–Q:24; lot 898 (*ca.* 500 B.C.). H. 0.02, D. 0.043, D. resting surface 0.038 m. Intact.

Flat resting surface; wall contracting to minimum diameter just below flaring diagonal rim; flat basket handle. Added-red bands on lower and upper wall, on rim; lines at end of handle. Added red mostly peeled. Traces of burning.

554. Basket kalathiskos   Pl. 51

C-61-229. O–P:25; lot 889 (first quarter 4th century). H. 0.022, D. 0.039, D. resting surface 0.027 m. Part of rim, handle missing.

Flat resting surface; slightly rounded lower wall (incipient bevel); barely concave wall; horizontal flaring rim. Higher profile than **551–553**. Four bands on wall, black except second in added red; dicing between added-red and black lines on rim.

555. Basket kalathiskos

C-62-699. R:23–24; lot 1985 (*ca.* 500 B.C.). H. 0.028, D. 0.042, D. resting surface 0.024 m. Intact.

Similar to **554**, with minimum diameter below rim; flat basket handle. Exterior: three added-red bands with three added-red lines between; added red on rim; traces of lines on handles. Color peeling; banding stops at bevel.

556. Basket kalathiskos   Pl. 51

C-62-350. R:23–24; lot 1985 (*ca.* 500 B.C.). H. 0.02, D. 0.044, D. resting surface 0.025 m. Part of rim, most of handle restored in plaster.

Flat resting surface; convex wall; flaring diagonal rim; flat basket handle. Originally black glaze overall, now peeling.

557. Basket kalathiskos

C-61-166. P–Q:25; lot 871 (12th century after Christ). H. 0.04, D. 0.061, D. resting surface 0.048 m. Half of rim, handle missing.
  Published: Stroud, *Hesperia* 34, 1965, pl. 4:f, right.

Flat resting surface; rounded lower wall, becoming straight and contracting to minimum diameter below flaring diagonal rim. Exterior: black and added-red

bands with black line between; zone of Z-maeander between lines; zone of black and added-red cones between zigzag line; dicing above; upper wall with added red; black Z-maeander at top of wall; flaring underside of rim with black dots; black band; black dots on lip; inner rim added red with added-white dots.

558. Handmade kalathiskos   Pl. 51

C-62-700. R:23–24; lot 1985 (*ca.* 500 B.C.). H. 0.047–0.05, D. 0.085–0.087, D. resting surface 0.047 m. Intact. Handmade, of rough clay with inclusions.

Flat resting surface; low flaring wall; flat rim with five pellets on it; no handles. Burnt inside and out.

559. Handmade kalathiskos

C-62-262. R:24; lot 2000 (late 6th century). H. 0.048–0.05, D. 0.079, D. resting surface *ca.* 0.035 m. Intact.

Fabric and shape as **558**, with two lug handles on upper wall, pellets on rim. Resting surface burnt.

560. Handmade kalathiskos

C-62-685. R:23–24; lot 1985 (*ca.* 500 B.C.). H. 0.034–0.037, D. 0.063, D. resting surface *ca.* 0.03 m. Intact.

Fabric as **558, 559**. Wall lower than the above; thickened rounded rim with seven pellets; two pinched-on handles on upper wall. Slightly burnt inside.

561. Kotyle   Pl. 52

C-62-864. R:24; lot 2000 (late 6th century). H. 0.029, D. 0.05, D. foot 0.021 m. Intact.

Narrow false foot with flat resting surface; low convex wall, turning in slightly to lip; two horizontal handles. Four uneven black bands on foot and wall; resting surface black; vertical lines in handle zone; interior glazed. Glaze is peeling. Similar example: T 3201 (*Corinth* XIII, grave 160-5, pl. 24).
  First or second quarter 6th century

562. Kotyle

C-61-183. P:24; lot 877 (early 3rd century). H. 0.026, D. 0.049, D. foot 0.018 m. One handle restored in plaster.
  Published: Stroud, *Hesperia* 34, 1965, pl. 4:a, extreme left.

Shape and date as **561**; similar decoration but with one less band on wall.

563. Kotyle   Pl. 52

C-61-407. P:24; lot 877 (early 3rd century). H. 0.026, D. 0.047, D. foot 0.032 m. Both handles, part of wall restored in plaster.

Convex undersurface; ring foot; low convex wall; tapered lip. Foot glazed; undersurface with central circle, band on outer area; silhouette animals between glaze bands on wall; "worms" on handle zone; interior glazed with two reserved bands at top of wall. Low, wide profile.

Mid-6th century?

564. Kotyle   Pl. 52

C-62-817. R:23–24; lot 1991 (late 6th century). H. 0.033, D. 0.041, D. foot 0.022 m. One handle, part of wall restored in plaster.

Central disk on undersurface; narrow ring foot; tall convex wall turning in slightly to tapered lip; two horizontal loop handles. Undersurface with central circle; inner and outer faces of foot black; wall with glaze line, black band, dicing, black band, "worms" in handle zone; interior glazed. High profile. See C-73-186 (Williams, MacIntosh, and Fisher [*Hesperia* 43, 1974], p. 17, no. 16, pl. 4).

Mid-6th century

565. Kotyle

C-61-260. P–Q:24–25; lot 893 (first quarter 4th century). H. 0.03, D. 0.044, D. foot 0.027 m. Intact.

Ring foot; gently convex wall; two horizontal loop handles. Circle on undersurface; foot glazed on inner and outer faces; wall with glaze band, two glaze lines, added-red band, opposing triangles of glaze in handle zone; interior glazed. Glaze fired red. See T 2951, a larger example (*Corinth* XIII, grave 200-1, pl. 31).

Mid- or later 6th century

566. Kotyle   Pl. 52

C-61-259. P–Q:24–25; lot 893 (first quarter 4th century). H. 0.046, D. 0.061, D. foot 0.037 m. Many joining fragments; part of wall missing.

Shape as **565**, with taller wall, slight inturn of wall to lip. Added red on foot; edge of foot black; undersurface with three glaze circles; brown line at bottom of wall; added red between glaze lines above; added-red and black bud chain, with red line above; "worms" in handle zone; outer handles black; added red on lip; interior glazed; reserved band at top of inner wall. Glaze fired brown.

Late 6th or early 5th century

567. Kotyle   Pl. 52

C-62-795. R:23–24; lot 1991 (late 6th century). H. 0.037, D. 0.056, D. foot 0.036 m. Handles broken off.

Barely articulated ring foot; slight disk on undersurface; low convex wall; tapered lip. Central black circle on undersurface; inner and outer foot black; added-red and black bands on wall, separated by diluted glaze lines; black zigzag in handle zone; added red on lip; interior glazed, reserved band at top of inner wall. Uneven banding. See T 2902 (*Corinth* XIII, grave 253-1, pl. 35).

Late 6th century or later

568. Kotyle   Pl. 52

C-62-265. P:23–24; lot 1993 (mid-4th century). H. 0.033, D. 0.053, D. foot 0.032 m. Slightly chipped.

Shape as **567** with two horizontal handles set slightly below lip. Black circle on disk; inner and outer foot glazed; six bands on wall; interior glazed with reserved band at top of wall. Glaze thin.

5th century

569. Three-handled cup

C-62-259. R:23–24; lot 1991 (late 6th century). H. 0.042, D. 0.07, D. foot 0.033 m. Foot chipped.

Published: Stroud, *Hesperia* 34, 1965, pl. 5:c, d.

Flaring foot, semiconical below; low convex flaring wall; concave rim; flaring rounded lip; three strap handles rising above lip. Added red on foot; two black bands at shoulder; horizontal black stripes on handles. Interior: central added-red circle, black band with added-red lines on either side, two diluted glaze lines on outer floor; upper rim with red and black lines; black dots on lip. Added red directly on clay.

6th century

570. Two-handled cup   Pl. 52

C-64-191. N:24; lot 2188 (first half 5th century). H. 0.046, D. 0.065, D. foot 0.035 m. Intact.

Flaring disk foot; convex flaring wall; lightly concave rim; rounded lip; two strap handles from rim offset to lip. Diameter of rim and shoulder equal. Taller profile than **569**. Foot glazed; glaze line at shoulder; glaze zigzag in handle zone; lip glazed; glaze band on floor, line on upper wall, and on top of handles. Glaze fired red.

6th century?

571. Stemmed kylix   Pl. 52

C-64-77. Q:25–26; lot 2044 (second half 5th century and Roman). H. 0.023, D. 0.038, D. foot 0.022 m. Handles broken off; foot chipped.

Flat resting surface; flaring stemmed foot; low diagonal flaring wall; slightly concave rim; flaring rounded lip. Glaze on foot and shoulder; dots on lip; added red (directly on clay) on inner rim with glaze line below; outer bowl with four black petals, red stems, glaze line below; added red at bottom of bowl. Compare the lotus cups of the Sam Wide group (footnote 18 above, p. 134).

5th century

572. Stemless kylix   Pl. 52

C-65-493. Q:26; lot 2230 (late 5th century). H. 0.031, est. D. 0.062, D. foot 0.038 m. Four joining fragments; half preserved with one handle.

Ring foot; low convex wall, turning in slightly to rounded lip; handle set below lip and canted upward. Glazed inside; three circles on undersurface; exterior wall black to handle zone; reserved band in handle zone, with black five-stroke stopped maeander; handle and lip black.

5th century

573. Flat-rimmed bowl   Pl. 52

C-62-821. R:23–24; lot 1991 (late 6th century). H. 0.023, D. 0.055, D. foot 0.035 m. Slightly chipped.

Flaring ring foot; straight flaring wall, turning vertical to flattened outward-projecting rim. Black glaze overall, except undersurface; added red on foot. Glaze is peeling. Low open profile. See larger example, **443**.

574. Flat-rimmed bowl

C-62-849. P:23–24; lot 1993 (mid-4th century). H. 0.022, D. 0.049, D. foot 0.032 m. Slightly chipped.

Profile as **573** but heavier foot; rim not projecting, groove on top of flat rim. Glazed overall, except undersurface. Glaze fired red to black, peeling.

6th century

575. Bowl with incurving rim   Pl. 52

C-62-799. R:23–24; lot 1991 (late 6th century). H. 0.03, D. 0.063, D. foot 0.032 m. Intact.

Convex undersurface; ring foot; straight diagonal wall with slightly incurving rim. Band on rim, two lines on interior of wall; exterior reserved. Predecessor of small semiglazed bowls (and therefore not a miniature)? A saltcellar? See **54**, Group 4 and **62**, Group 5.

Later 6th century

576. Lekanis or bowl   Pl. 52

C-64-45. P:26; lot 2011 (late 5th century). H. 0.016–0.02, D. 0.045 m. Slightly chipped. Handmade.

Wide, flat resting surface; low, slightly convex wall; two reflex handles in wishbone form; uneven profile. Stain on lip; handles glazed.

577. Standed bowl or basin   Pl. 52

C-61-405. P:24–25; lot 878 (third quarter 4th century). H. 0.035–0.038, D. 0.071, rest. D. foot 0.048 m. Many joining fragments; foot, part of wall restored in plaster.

Stem foot, with narrow resting surface; short concave stem; low, convex flaring wall; projecting rim, rounded lip; three grooves on under face of rim and flat upper edge of rim. Glaze on edge of foot, outer face; added purple (over glaze) on rim; center of bowl with bands of added purple, black, purple; glaze line on outer floor. For a black-figured example, see *Perachora* II, no. 1941, pl. 71, in a more practical size.

578. High-footed bowl

C-61-189. P:24; lot 877 (early 3rd century). H. 0.03, D. 0.053, D. foot 0.034 m. Slightly chipped.

Published: Stroud, *Hesperia* 34, 1965, pl. 4:a, extreme right.

Low stem foot with flat resting surface, outer edge rounded; convex flaring wall; slightly projecting rim, flat on top. Added red on foot and over whole rim directly on clay.

Probably Classical

579. Bowl with beveled rim   Pl. 52

C-61-191. P:24–25; lot 878 (third quarter 4th century). H. 0.02, D. 0.056, D. foot 0.033 m. Intact.

Ring foot; low diagonal wall, turning into rounded bevel. Four deep wheel grooves on exterior wall, probably deliberate. No glaze.

580. Bowl with beveled rim

C-61-412. P:24; lot 877 (early 3rd century). H. 0.018, D. 0.058–0.062, D. foot 0.043 m. Chipped; warped.

Shape as **579** but very uneven; profile slightly wider and lower. One deep groove on wall. No glaze.

581. Plate   Pl. 52

C-62-296. O–P:23; lot 1954 (late 4th century). H. 0.009, D. 0.072, D. resting surface 0.048 m. Part of rim missing.

Flat resting surface; horizontal projecting rim, convex on upper surface; two suspension holes in rim. Exterior reserved. Floor: two central black circles, added-red lines bordering black zigzag pattern, black band at rise to rim. On rim, zigzag pattern between added-red lines; lip black. Added red directly on clay.

582. Plate   Pl. 52

C-64-48. P:26; lot 2012 (early 5th century). H. 0.01, D. 0.058, D. foot 0.043 m. Slightly chipped.

Wide, flaring disk foot; flaring rim with compound curve; rising rounded lip, with upper face thickened at inner edge. Stain of black on outer foot; rest of exterior reserved. Floor: black bands, two outer black lines; added red over rounded rise of rim; three black lines, black blobs on rim.

Later 6th century

583. Plate

C-62-294. R:25; lot 1953 (Byzantine). H. 0.009, D. 0.055, D. foot 0.047 m. Intact.

Flat base; rim with slight projection, convex upper surface. Exterior reserved. Floor: central added-red circle, black on outer floor; traces of color on rim, peeled.

584. Kanoun

C-62-351. R:23–24; lot 1985 (*ca.* 500 B.C.). H. 0.017, rest. D. 0.075, D. resting surface 0.06 m. Half restored in plaster; originally three handles, not two (thickening at right break for handle).

Flat resting surface; low, slightly diagonal wall; slightly flaring rounded rim; reflex handle attached to rim. Spiral grooves on resting surface and floor. Added purple (over black) on resting surface and floor; added-purple bands on exterior and interior wall.

6th century

585. Kanoun   Pl. 52

C-62-295. R:25; lot 1953 (Byzantine). H. 0.011, D. 0.061, D. resting surface 0.058 m. Slightly chipped.

Shape as **584**, with straighter wall, plain lip; two suspension holes. Spiral groove on floor only. Handles of lumps of clay, with slash in center. Resting surface reserved; glaze bands on exterior wall; added purple (over black) on floor; glaze dots on inner wall.

586. Kanoun

C-61-430. P:24; lot 877 (early 3rd century). H. 0.012, D. 0.064, D. resting surface 0.053 m. One handle, part of wall restored in plaster.

Shape as **584** but smaller, no grooves. Resting surface reserved; added purple (directly on clay) on exterior wall, floor; inner wall with glaze bands, five groups of stripes.

587. Kanoun   Pl. 52

C-62-293. R:25; lot 1953 (Byzantine). H. 0.016, D. 0.052, D. resting surface 0.041 m. Intact.

Shape as **584** but higher wall. Poorly finished; string marks in center of resting surface. Black at top of exterior wall; wide added-red (directly on clay) band on floor, black on interior wall, on handles.

588. Dish   Pl. 52

C-62-254. R:25; lot 1953 (Byzantine). H. 0.01, D. 0.058, D. resting surface 0.052 m. Slightly chipped.

Flat resting surface; vertical low wall; slightly outward thickened rim; no handles. Resting surface reserved; outer wall glazed; central glaze circle on floor, with added-red band, glaze band on outer floor, on top of interior wall. Glaze fired red brown; added red directly on clay.

589. Dish or stand   Pl. 52

C-62-352. R:23-24; lot 1985 (*ca.* 500 B.C.). H. 0.017, D. 0.044 m. Small area of wall restored in plaster. Extensively burnt; clay very hard and gray from burning.

Flat resting surface; low straight wall contracting slightly to flat narrow rim. Stamped egg and dart on exterior; no glaze.

6th century

590. Globular pyxis, flat rim   Pl. 52

C-61-287. P-Q:24; lot 898 (*ca.* 500 B.C.). H. 0.022, D. 0.035, D. foot 0.029 m. Intact.

Ring foot; low globular wall; raised rim, flat on top. Interior reserved. Undersurface: two glaze circles; black on inner face of foot; added red on outer foot (red directly on clay). Wall: two black lines; black and added-red bands; dicing at center of wall; added-red band; top of rim with black line; lip black.

Probably late 6th century

591. Globular pyxis, flat rim

C-62-264. P:23-24; lot 1993 (mid-4th century). H. 0.019, D. 0.032, D. foot 0.026 m. Intact.

Published: Stroud, *Hesperia* 34, 1965, pl. 4:b, extreme right.

Shape as **590**. Undersurface: three black circles; black on inner, added purple on outer foot (purple over black). Wall: black, added-purple bands with three diluted-glaze lines between each dicing on shoulder; added-purple, black bands; two diluted-glaze lines on top of rim; lip black. Interior reserved. Very careful, delicate work.

592. Pyxis lid   Pl. 52

C-62-820. R:23-24; lot 1991 (late 6th century). H. 0.027, D. 0.057 m. Slightly chipped.

Flat knob, tapered below; slightly sloping lid; recessed low flange narrowing to lip. Interior reserved. On lid from outer edge: two added-red lines (directly on clay); black band; two black lines; added-red band; black line; black to knob; two added-red, one black line on top of knob.

6th century

593. Kothon   Pl. 52

C-62-325. O-Q:23-24; lot 1965 (second half 4th century after Christ). H. 0.016, D. 0.043, D. foot 0.02 m. Intact.

Flat resting surface; wide, low convex wall rounding to rim descending into interior; one horizontal reflex handle. Exterior reserved. One black circle on interior floor; black lines on inner rim; added red on top of rim (directly on clay); handle black.

594. Proto-unguentarium(?)   Pl. 52

C-69-103. M-N:19; no lot. H. 0.061, D. 0.047, D. foot 0.024, D. mouth 0.02 m. Several joining fragments; part of wall missing.

False ring foot; flat resting surface; high ovoid wall, merging with sloping shoulder; concave neck without offset from shoulder; flaring rim with flat upper face; two unarticulated handles smeared onto shoulder. Glaze bands on foot, below handles, on shoulder, lower neck; inner mouth glazed.

PLASTIC WARES (595–602)

All fragments of plastic vases found in the Sanctuary are included; there are eight in the catalogue, with citation of two more very similar to one of the published examples. The Corinthian animal vases are the usual types, as is the komast vase. There are three fragments of Attic head vases and one other import. A red-figured fragment, **370**, may belong to one of the head vases.

595.   Siren   Pl. 53

C-62-261. R:23–24; lot 1985 (*ca.* 500 B.C.). H. 0.087, L. 0.072 m. Tail, one foot slightly damaged; surface worn, encrusted.

Published: Stroud, *Hesperia* 34, 1965, pl. 7:a.

Typical siren vase; suspension holes at end of hair; worn glaze. See *CVA*, Cambridge 1 [Great Britain 6], pl. 6 [243]:3, late 7th century. For dating, see *Perachora* I, pp. 238–239.

596.   Hare   Pl. 53

C-62-260. R:23–24; lot 1991 (late 6th century). H. 0.043, L. 0.068 m. Tail missing; hole in top of head.

Published: Stroud, *Hesperia* 34, 1965, pl. 7:b.

Typical example of a well-known type; decorated with zigzag line on belly, vertical rows of dots. See *CVA*, Cambridge 1 [Great Britain 6], pl. 6 [243]:1, almost identical; first half 6th century. See also R. Higgins, *British Museum Terracottas* II, London 1959, no. 1675, p. 42, pl. 29. For dating see *Perachora* I, pp. 236–237.

Similar fragment: C-62-854, P:23–24, lot 1993. Also, the bottom of either a hare or ram, C-64-66, R:26, lot 2013.

597.   Ram   Pl. 53

C-68-305. L:18–19; lot 5639 (late 4th—early 3rd century). P.H. 0.054, p.L. 0.064 m. Three joining fragments, preserving most of right side, bottom, head. Chest, most of left side missing. Moldmade except head.

Traces of suspension holes through horns. On body, groups of three rows of vertical dots; zigzag line on belly; glaze on tail, legs, around head and neck; glaze fired orange. See *CVA*, Cambridge 1 [Great Britain 6], pl. 6 [243]:2, different body markings.

First half 6th century

598.   Seated figure   Pl. 53

C-65-543. P:20–21; lot 4367 (late 4th—early 3rd century). P.H. 0.132 m. Two joining fragments; right side damaged; surface eroded. Micaceous clay; core 2.5Y 6/0 (gray); surface 7.5YR 7/6 (reddish yellow). Moldmade.

Figure seated in high-backed chair; flat back and sides.

Left arm resting on knee, right arm at side or breast (damaged); projection of chest at break for breasts? High headdress with veil over it; eroded traces of folds on right side of neck. Facial features blurred except for very sharp nose. Flat rim at top of head; small area of resting surface preserved. Roughly finished interior.

For the type, see Higgins (under **596**) nos. 63–70, pls. 13, 14.

599.   Komast vase   Pl. 53

C-65-30. O–P:19–20; lot 2240 (second half 4th century after Christ). P.H. 0.065, p.W. 0.064 m. One fragment, broken at neck, below belly in front, upper back in rear. Rough finish, probably not moldmade.

Hollow; hole through neck. Breaks on front suggest proper left arm came across body to center of chest; proper right arm originally hanging down. At lower break, round navel with small hole, not piercing whole wall. Big belly, rounded back. No traces of glaze on back; front glazed, fired red to black.

See *Perachora* I, no. 199, pl. 104, similar but with a straight back.

600.   Attic head vase   Pl. 53

C-64-91. O:26; lot 2026 (mid-5th century). P.H. 0.057 m. Part of hair, jaw on left side, neck, bottom preserved.

Hollow; unglazed inside. Flat base reserved. Black hair, black band at base of neck.

601.   Attic head vase   Pl. 53

C-62-945. P:23–24; lot 1993 (mid-4th century). P.H. 0.051 m. Part of face preserved, including proper right eye, cheeks, mouth, chin, part of neck.

Traces of glaze on eye; incised pupil. Suggestion of smile indicates late Archaic date.

602.   Attic head vase   Pl. 53

C-65-548. O:22–23; lot 2249 (end of 4th century). P.H. 0.028 m. Lower part of spout, beginning of hair preserved.

At top, inner break with beginning of black glaze covering interior of upper spout. At lower break, wreath in added white, three rows of applied clay dots; top of hair.

HEADS ATTACHED TO VASES (603–628)

The majority of the examples of attached heads or protomes in the catalogue (**259, 521, 603–628**) come from large kalathoi of the flaring form, often with perforations. That moldmade heads were so used is clear from **521**, a kalathiskos; these attachments on kalathoi have hitherto not been noticed. There may have been several heads on a rim; **608** and **611** both have extant "sisters", demonstrably from the same vase. Several of the heads are very large, especially **603** and **618**. In the context-pottery lots there are very heavy rims, strong enough to support such decoration.

There are a number of ways to recognize these kalathos heads; the simplest is by the preservation of the flaring rim of the vase, below the head, and the separate wall visible at the back of the figure. Plate 53 shows the backs of the kalathos head **612** and the pyxis head **621**; the finished interior shoulder of the latter vase contrasts with the protruding wall of the former. Often the head snaps off, leaving just the top of the rim, but the bands decorating the rim may be discerned. On others, the lower break is at the juncture of flaring rim and wall, leaving a slight gap or split at the lower break; this split is not so wide as the opening in the bottom of a head once filled with wads of clay and attached to a separately made body. Unlike the pyxis head, the kalathos head necessarily shows no scar for an upper attachment. The back is often covered with paint; pyxis heads are without paint.

Only the heads clearly identifiable as once on kalathoi or pyxides are published, for if the head from a kalathos breaks off well above the rim, it is impossible to distinguish whether it is from a figurine or a kalathos. This difficulty is compounded by the use of the same type for heads on figurines, pyxides, or kalathoi, as seen in **615** and **620**.

The range of types is interesting. Since the kalathos heads are freestanding, they are sometimes decorated as figurines are, with attached pellets (**604**) or necklaces (**609, 616**). Some even have arms, rendered either as cursory projections (**607, 609**) or as more fully extended limbs (**616**, broken). The pyxis head **624** shows arms rendered by incision and outline; it may belong to the curious pyxis **261**. The set of three pyxis heads, **625**, from a very large vase, shows cursorily modeled breasts, as does the enigma, **626**, which also has vestigial arms.

No examples can be dated before 600 B.C.; the earliest, **603**, probably belongs to the early MC period, with similarities to a MC pyxis in Oxford. The lack of EC heads is not surprising, since there is generally a lack of EC pottery in the Sanctuary. Most of the Demeter Sanctuary heads are later MC and LC, going down into the later 6th century. Some of the examples are easily dated, for they compare with types still preserved on MC or LC pyxides or with figurines found in datable contexts. The others have been placed within the series, using the criteria provided by D. A. Amyx.[29] A few are difficult to date, because of their poor condition (especially **609** and **616**), but are included for their interesting details. No example was found in a limited context.[30]

The catalogue entries are arranged first by type, from kalathos or pyxis, then within each group by chronological order, with two exceptions. **521** is presented under miniature perforated kalathiskoi; it illustrates clearly the use of attached heads on kalathoi. For the one remaining pyxis with attached head, see **259**. The description of the preserved remains of the vessel is omitted to save space; decorative details of the vase are noted, for often the decoration of the lower area of the head continues onto the vase. The preserved height of the whole fragment is given, followed by the height of the face, taken from under the chin to the beginning of the hair. The last two items are included here for lack of any other more appropriate or correct section.

---

[29] D. A. Amyx, "Corinthian Vases in the Hearst Collection," *University of California Publications in Classical Archaeology* I, no. 9, 1943, pp. 207–240, esp. pp. 213–215. See also *NC*, chap. 16, pp. 232–247; R. H. Jenkins in *Perachora* I, pp. 197–224; *Corinth* XV, ii, classes VIII and IX, pp. 55–83; K. Wallenstein, *Korinthische Plastik*.

[30] The shapes do not assist dating, for no pyxis head may be attached to its original vase with the possible exception of **624**. The flaring kalathos was apparently in use throughout much of the 7th and 6th centuries, disappearing by the time of Group 4. See p. 22 above.

603. Kalathos head   Pl. 53

C-65-168. O–P:22–23; lot 4352 (4th century after Christ). P.H. 0.07, H. face 0.033 m. Proper right cheek and nose damaged.

Long heavy face; arched eyes; thick, spreading nose; small mouth with protruding upper lip; heavy chin; ears worn away. Incised waves on brow; three long locks separating behind ears, with horizontal incisions; no polos. Neck not visible in profile. Small vent holes on either side of head, piercing whole head; two transverse vent holes between locks on both shoulders; one hole in crown of head. Added-red band at juncture of rim and wall, on inner wall at break. Added red between locks, at bottom for dress; traces of black brown on hair; no paint preserved on face.

See *NC*, no. 884, pl. 47 for head of similar shape (Wallenstein, *Korinthische Plastik*, IV/A 8, pl. 8:2 and 5).

Middle Corinthian

604. Kalathos head   Pl. 53

C-62-826. R:23–24; lot 1991 (late 6th century). P.H. 0.061, H. face 0.018 m. Encrusted; worn.

Heavy face; arched eyes, defined only by paint; nose and mouth worn; deep jaw; no defined chin. Low forehead curls rendered in paint; three strands of hair either side of face. On both shoulders, two clay disks, with separate pellets on disks. At proper right, broken projection, probably for arm (see **616**). Black hair, eyes, forehead curls; added red on polos, dress. Added-red and black bands on underside of rim, beginning of exterior wall; dicing at lower break.

Facial type resembles **603**. See also *Perachora* I, p. 244, for discussion of ornaments.

Middle Corinthian

605. Kalathos head   Pl. 53

C-62-257. R:24; lot 1969 (early 5th century). P.H. 0.062, H. face 0.023 m. Nose, proper left cheek damaged; encrusted.

Heavy deep face; arched eyes; straight mouth with protruding upper lip; bridge of nose begins below hair; ears set vertically. Horizontal waves on brow; stepped wig. No paint on face or hair; stain on back. Marks on proper left side suggest damage when head was taken from mold. Facial type resembles **603**.

Middle Corinthian

606. Kalathos head   Pl. 54

C-65-569. O–P:19–20; lot 2240 (second half 4th century after Christ). P.H. 0.046, H. face 0.019 m. Polos broken away; worn.

Face slightly more tapering than **605**; arched eyes; thin triangular nose; slightly smiling mouth with projecting upper lip; prominent chin; ears set diagonally. Two rows of waves receding from brow; stepped wig. Traces of added red on neck, back of head.

Middle Corinthian or early Late Corinthian

607. Kalathos head   Pl. 54

C-65-170. O:18; lot 4350 (late Roman). P.H. 0.036, H. face 0.014 m.

Shallow oval head; arched eyes; narrow prominent nose; slightly smiling mouth; wide chin; no ears. "Wing" at proper right for arm. Horizontal forehead waves, high above eyes; shallow wig; polos almost gone. Black dress, hair, polos, black over whole back; traces of added red on eyes, two added-red lines for necklace.

The heavy shape resembles **605**.

Middle Corinthian

608. Kalathos head   Pl. 54

C-65-32 a. N–O:19–20; lot 2247 (4th century after Christ). P.H. 0.052, H. face 0.019 m.

Shallow, slightly tapering face; arched eyes; small nose; slightly smiling mouth with protruding upper lip; horizontally set ears. Closely set waves on forehead; two braids on either side of face; low polos. Mold damaged; chin projects too sharply; face recut on proper left. Traces of red on back, red for dress and polos; peeled bands on outer wall.

C-65-32 b (not illustrated), M:17–18, lot 3222, from the same mold.

Middle Corinthian

609. Kalathos head   Pl. 54

C-65-469. N:13–15; lot 4405 (4th century after Christ). P.H. 0.078, H. face 0.018 m. Nose and mouth damaged; badly stained.

Deep tapering face; eyes narrower than **608**; prominent large nose; small mouth. Receding forehead waves; stepped wig. Body with two arms; applied necklace on chest, mostly gone; trace of polos on back of head. Traces of black paint on hair; added purple on arms, chest, mostly peeled. Pyxis head, N–O:25–26, lot 75-249:1, from same mold.

Middle Corinthian

610. Kalathos head   Pl. 54

C-65-36. P:27; lot 2245 (late 6th century). P.H. 0.075, H. face 0.02 m. Nose damaged.

Tapering face; narrow eyes with distinct lids; long nose; horizontal mouth with slightly protruding upper lip; no defined jaw; no ears. Diagonal waves on forehead; stepped wig; high polos, with veil over it. Projecting arms broken away. Added red for peplos, polos, latter with dicing front and back. Added-red line on lower back.

See KT 3–4 (*Corinth* XV, ii, class VIII, 21, pl. 8) for the same type, more worn. The polos of **610** is higher.

Middle Corinthian

611. Kalathos head — Pl. 54

C-62-784. R:23–24; lot 1991 (late 6th century). P.H. 0.056, H. face 0.019 m. Encrusted, worn.

Facial type as **610**, slightly wider eyes. Receding waves on forehead; stepped wig; low polos. Orange-brown bands on wall; added red on rim. Traces of orange on face; added red on polos; traces of paint on back.

C-61-280, P–Q:24, lot 896, is from the same kalathos.

Middle Corinthian

612. Kalathos head — Pls. 53, 54

C-64-200. P:19–20; lot 2151 (second half 4th century after Christ). P.H. 0.075, H. face 0.025 m.

Deep but narrow face; flat narrow eyes; pronounced nose; small horizontal mouth; big, vertically set ears. Waves high on brow; stepped wig; low polos. Moldmade necklace of two strands, attached to disks. Added-red rim, becoming red of dress; added red on polos; brown hair; brown black on back; no traces of paint on face.

From the same mold: MF 12152, O–P:22–23, lot 4355; KT 9–11 (*Corinth* XV, ii, class IX, 7, pl. 13). MF 3893 is also very similar (*Corinth* XII, no. 77, pl. 5).

Late Corinthian I

613. Kalathos head — Pl. 54

C-64-201. P:19–20; lot 2151 (second half 4th century after Christ). P.H. 0.063, H. face 0.025 m. Chin damaged.

Published: Daux, *BCH* 89, 1965, p. 693, fig. 9, left (Wallenstein, *Korinthische Plastik*, VI/A 4b).

Face similar to **612**, slightly broader, wider mouth. Hair as **612**, with wig behind very high vertically set ears; low polos, mostly broken away. Hole on proper left side of body does not go through the fabric. Black hair, black overall on back; added red on dress, traces of red on lower back. Colors mostly peeled.

Late Corinthian I

614. Kalathos head — Pl. 54

C-64-199. O–P:18–20; lot 2150 (second half 4th century after Christ). P.H. 0.053, H. face 0.027 m. Proper right brow and forehead damaged.

Published: Daux, *BCH* 89, 1965, p. 693, fig. 9, right (Wallenstein, *Korinthische Plastik*, VI/A 5).

Similar to **613**, slightly more tapering face; projecting chin. Traces of black on hair, on crown surrounded by polos (now broken away); black on back and on interior where rim and wall split.

Late Corinthian I

615. Kalathos head — Pl. 55

C-65-33. N–O:19–20; lot 2247 (4th century after Christ). P.H. 0.048, H. face 0.018 m.

Narrow tapering face; diagonally set eyes; triangular nose; narrow, straight mouth; hair as **614**, low polos. On inside wall below head a black checkerboard; outer rim with added purple (over black) for dress, purple on polos; black for eyes, brows, hair.

A popular type: C-61-186, P:24, lot 877 and C-65-31, from the same context as **615**, come from the same mold and are kalathos heads but with different paint schemes. See also MF 2524 (*Corinth* XII, no. 80, pl. 5), MF 8343, from well 1937-3 (unpublished), and MF-72-20 (Williams and Fisher, *Hesperia* 42, 1973, p. 8, pl. 3). See also Wallenstein, *Korinthische Plastik*, V/B12 a–c, which includes MF 2524 and two heads found at Perachora.

Late Corinthian I

616. Kalathos head — Pl. 55

C-62-880. R:23–24; lot 1985 (*ca.* 500 B.C.). P.H. 0.043, H. face 0.015 m. Three joining fragments; very worn.

Head as **615**, features almost gone. Stepped wig, preserved only on proper left; low polos; applied strip of clay with disk for necklace; on projection on proper left side for arm. No preserved paint except for slight trace on inside of rim.

MF-69-65 from Temple Hill, without datable context, has the same head.

Late Corinthian I

617. Kalathos head — Pl. 55

C-64-186. P:26; lot 2042 (late 5th century). P.H. 0.056, H. face 0.016 m.

Published: Daux, *BCH* 89, 1965, p. 693, fig. 9, center (Wallenstein, *Korinthische Plastik*, VI/A3).

Shallow face, long and tapering; slightly arched eyes; short nose; narrow mouth; projecting chin; low, vertically set ears. Separated locks on forehead; stepped wig; polos. Orange-brown glaze on hair, eyes, brows, necklace; glaze on back of head; added purple (over glaze) on dress, polos, inner rim.

Late Corinthian I

618. Kalathos head — Pl. 55

C-62-828. R:23–24; lot 1991 (late 6th century). P.H. 0.081, H. face 0.028 m. Encrusted; proper right side of head damaged.

Oval face; heavy eyes with rounded lids; narrow nose; small mouth with full lips; heavy chin. Tilt of head to right, unevenly attached to rim. Heavy roll of hair without detail on forehead; trace of fillet; twisted strands of hair on either side of face; edge of cloak over head. Traces of added red and black on back of head; added red for dress, fillet; black for cloak, eyes, brows, hair. Very large example.

For heads of similar type, but smaller: KT 9-25 and KT 9-32 (*Corinth* XV, ii, class IX, 11 and IX, 12, pl. 13); *Perachora* I, no. 236, pl. 107. See also Wallenstein, *Korinthische Plastik*, VII/A2 a–d.

Late Corinthian II

619. Kalathos head   Pl. 55

C-68-159. M:16; no lot. P.H. 0.061, H. face 0.027 m.

Similar to **618**, slightly broader through the eyes, not so deep a head. Three layers of hair across brow, originally with small indentations; two braided strands on either side of face; fillet; ridge at proper left is part of low polos. Inner and outer wall with added-red lines; added red on eyes, lids, brows, necklace, dress.

C-68-349, lot 5613 (surface finds) is from the same mold but is probably a figurine head, not from a vase.

Late Corinthian II

620. Kalathos head   Pl. 55

C-65-34. N–O:19–20; lot 2247 (4th century after Christ). P.H. 0.054, H. face 0.013 m. Very worn.

Narrow, tapering face; diagonally set eyes; long nose; smiling mouth; low set ears. Waves on forehead placed very high; cursory hair on sides of face. Cloak over head, with incisions on border; rosettes or flowers (very worn) over cloak, by temples. Added purple (over glaze) on polos, dress; brown hair, cloak; orange brown on back.

Pyxis head C-62-284, R:25, lot 1953, from the same mold. Very close and probably from the same mold is KT 9-64 (*Corinth* XV, ii, class VIII, 47, pl. 11). See Wallenstein, *Korinthische Plastik*, VII/A7 a–c, including latter example, one in Tübingen, and one in New York, all from pyxides.

Late Corinthian II

621. Pyxis head   Pls. 53, 55

C-72-56. I:15; no lot. P.H. 0.078, H. face 0.026 m.

Left of head, bud from bud chain decorating shoulder; at lower break, two bands limiting top of figure zone. Wide face with little taper; narrow eyes with defined lids; wide nose; thin, horizontal mouth; projecting chin. Receding waves on brow; stepped wig. Black for dress, necklace, hair, eyes. Traces of red wash on shoulder: red-ground pyxis.

Late Corinthian I

622. Pyxis head   Pl. 55

C-73-302. K–L:23–24; lot 73-118 (third quarter 5th century). P.H. 0.075, H. face 0.023 m. Nose and chin damaged.

Tapering face; pronounced eyelids; slight smile, slightly protruding upper lip; chin originally pointed. Well-defined receding waves on forehead; stepped wig behind vertical ears. Polos with central medallion of eight petals, in added red; traces of added-red maeander on polos. Added purple (over black) for cloak, covering polos; black hair; brown at bottom break for dress.

Similar, probably from same mold: KT 9-7 (*Corinth* XV, ii, class VIII, 35, pl. 11; Wallenstein, *Korinthische Plastik*, V/B3).

Late Corinthian I

623. Pyxis head   Pl. 55

C-62-258. O–R:23–24; lot 1955 (second half 4th century after Christ). P.H. 0.054, H. face 0.015 m.

Wide face with little taper; bulging eyes without lids; short nose; smile; projecting chin. Hair as **622**; polos. V-neck dress or cloak; moldmade necklace. Added purple (over black) for cloak; black hair, top of polos. Colors mostly peeled.

From same mold, but different pyxis, a head from N–O:26, lot 72-208:1.

Late Corinthian I.

624. Pyxis head   Pl. 56

C-64-422. O–P:21; lot 2161 (early 4th century). P.H. 0.072, H. face 0.027 m. Mouth and chin damaged; badly worn.

Long, heavy face; large eyes; smile; low-set, vertical ears. Simple waves on brow; bulging hair without divisions (vertical groove at proper left accidental); no polos; added-white fillet. Added purple (over black) for dress; cloak on shoulders indicated by incision. On chest, arms and hands rendered by incision and outline, with added white. Black on top of head, hair, eyes. Beginning of wall with added-red line; black-and-white checkerboard below.

See **261**, pyxis with female outline heads, attached protome (missing) with similarly rendered arms. **624** does not fit that scar but could be from another side of the pyxis; the fabric is similar.

Other pyxis heads have the arms indicated, although usually without the details of **624**. See T 1513 (*Corinth* XIII, grave 157-m, p. 183, pl. 87); the California vase published by Amyx (footnote 29 above, p. 179), p. 208, pl. 32:a, b.

Late Corinthian I?

625. Pyxis heads   Pl. 56

C-65-175. Surface; lot 4377 (4th century after Christ).
a) P.H. 0.08 m. Two joining fragments. **b)** P.H.

0.081 m. Two joining fragments. **c)** P.H. 0.053 m. Head missing. H. of faces 0.019 m.

Three heads from the same pyxis. Flat body; two knobs as breasts; slight articulation of neck and shoulders; no arms. Narrow tapering face; small eyes; prominent nose; small straight mouth, heavy lips. Heavy frame of hair on forehead, incisions indicating curls; side tresses with vestigial steps; high polos supporting bridge to rim. Added-purple and black dots on polos; black hair, eyes, brows; added-purple mouth, earrings, necklace; added purple (over black) for dress; incised vertical zigzags for folds, running incised maeander on sides and top of dress.

The facial type resembles **620**.

Late Corinthian II

626. Head   Pl. 56

C-62-271. R:23–24; lot 1985 (*ca.* 500 B.C.). P.H. 0.06, H. face 0.015 m. Nose damaged.

Small, slightly tapering face; small eyes with pronounced lids; triangular nose; horizontal mouth. Receding waves on brow; stepped wig; grooves between steps continue onto sides of hair; fillet and polos. Two pointed projections for arms; modeled breasts. Two holes pierce the head on either side of face; seven holes in polos, pierced diagonally down to below brim of polos in back. Black hair, eyelids, brows, necklace.

C-62-283, R:25, lot 1953, is very similar in facial type, body with arms, holes. These are not plastic vases; there is no outlet hole, and they are solid to below the neck. For lid handles?

Late Corinthian I?

627. Sphinx handle   Pl. 56

C-61-190. P:24–25; lot 878 (third quarter 4th century). P.W. 0.072, p.H. 0.082 m. Handmade.

Published: Stroud, *Hesperia* 34, 1965, pl. 7:c (Wallenstein, *Korinthische Plastik*, VI/B16).

Broken at attachment to lid. Sphinx with long neck, turned head, polos, curving wings, gripping onto handle attachment. Incision on hair, no detail on wings. Front rotella of five-petal rosette; back one broken off. Traces of added red on wing, polos.

Probably mid-6th century B.C.

628. Gorgon head   Pl. 56

C-62-354. R:23–24; lot 1985 (*ca.* 500 B.C.). P.H. 0.038 m. Lower break at left may be a finished surface.

Typical gorgon head; black on hair, entire back of head; added red on eyelids, mouth. I am not sure that this is from a vase.

Archaic

KITCHEN VESSELS: COARSE WARE AND COOKING FABRIC (629–660)

The catalogue entries are divided into two parts: kitchen coarse ware and cooking fabric. The analysis of shape development for the vessels in each part is presented in Shape Studies, XXVI and XXVII. The fabric of the kitchen vessels is not described; all have inclusions,[31] although, as is typical of Corinthian, the clay fires to different colors. The slips, where present, are mentioned. The color of the cooking-fabric vessels is noted in order to make clear the range of fired colors, even though most are presumed to be Corinthian in origin. The problem of the origin of cooking fabric is discussed in the Shape Studies. Mica, characteristic of most cooking-ware pots found in Corinth, is not mentioned unless it is absent.

There are other vessels which might be called kitchen equipment, such as banded lekanai, certain types of jugs, and so forth. They probably were household items, used in the dining rooms of the Sanctuary. But since they are made of fine clay, they are included in the section on non-figured fine ware.

Perirrhanteria are discussed separately; although they are similar in fabric to the coarse-ware vessels, they presumably had cult, not dining-room, functions.

COARSE WARE (629–644)

629. Hydria handle   Pl. 57

C-62-786. R:23–24; lot 1991 (late 6th century). P.L. 0.191 m. Three joining fragments; full handle, small part of rim preserved. No slip.

Flat, diagonal flaring rim; handle attached on convex shoulder (part of inner face preserved), at top of rim; vertical handle round in section. Five pellets attached on rim at handle; outer handle with six irregularly spaced stamps of 12-ray burst or linear rosette. Between second and third stamps, faint impression of standing figure to right.

6th century (by context)

---

[31] There is one coarse-ware bowl, **237**, decorated with Late Corinthian figure style. It is included not here but rather in the Corinthian black-figure section because the figure style was considered to be more important than the fabric.

630. Hydria   Pl. 57

C-61-488. P:24–25; lot 893 (first quarter 4th century).
P.H. 0.102, D. 0.133, D. rim 0.083 m. Two joining
fragments preserve upper wall, shoulder, neck, rim,
vertical handle, and one side handle. Thin self-slip.
Neck and rim made separately from body.

High ovoid wall, beginning to contract at lower break,
turning continuously into rounded shoulder; low, wide,
slightly concave neck; flaring rim, convex on outer face,
inward sloping on top face. Vertical handle oval in section; small horizontal handle: a wad of clay, pierced vertically, set slightly canted (accidental?).

Classical, before the early 4th century (by context)

631. Tripod krater   Pl. 57

C-64-222. N–O:23; lot 2152 (4th-century pottery,
2nd-century coin). P.H. 0.11, D. bowl at break
0.235 m. Two joining fragments; two feet, base of bowl
preserved. Self-slip; handmade.

Two (of three) animal paws for feet. Feet conical inside,
0.08 m. wide at maximum dimension; attached to bottom
of concave band or collar 0.035–0.04 m. high, as support
for bowl, with vertical incisions. Flat-bottomed bowl,
broken off at beginning of flaring sides.

Similar but more elaborate bowl with four animal
paws: MF 9500 (Carter [footnote 225 above, p. 68], from
South Stoa in front of shop XXVI). Probably later than
631.

Probably Classical (by context)

632. Deep lekane   Pl. 57

C-61-284. P–Q:24; lot 898 (*ca.* 500 B.C.). P.H. 0.071,
p.W. 0.076, est. D. 0.15–0.16 m. One fragment of upper wall, rim. No slip.

Tall cylindrical wall; projecting lug handle of triangular
shape; flat, unarticulated rim. Stamping above handle:
multiple X alternating with volute palmette of four petals. Design of palmette is very loose, late in the series.

Late Archaic (by stamp, context)

633. Shallow lekane   Pl. 57

C-73-58. R:25, Q–R:26–29, O:28, N–O:24, Q:25; lots
1966 (later 4th century), 2038 (first half 4th century
after Christ), 2220 (late 5th or early 4th century),
2143 (early 4th century), 72-122 (miscellaneous
finds), 73-139 (second quarter 4th century B.C.).
a) P.H. 0.056, est. inner D. 0.36 m. Three joining
fragments of upper wall, rim. **b**) P.H. 0.028, p.W.
0.045 m. One rim fragment. **c**) P.H. 0.072, p.W.

0.160 m. One fragment of outer handle-plate and part
of handle. Fine, smooth buff slip.

a. Vertical wall; heavy projecting rim with diagonal outer face; bevel to flat upper face, widening at right break
for horizontal handle attached to rim. Incised vertical
strokes on vertical face; horizontal groove below; diagonal strokes on bevel to top face with curving groove
(following flare to handle). Near inner edge of top face,
incised leaves on either side of stem. Added-red dipinto
on horizontal face:]Þ[•]ΧΑ: ΑΛΒ[

b (not illustrated). Incised design as **a**; no dipinto.

c. End of large loop handle, set vertically, flaring outward from body of bowl, reinforced at top by large handle-plate, inner rim of which is not preserved. Outer face
of plate with incised vertical strokes along top and bottom
(see fragment **a**); stamped palmette and lotus, enclosed,
above beginning of each handle root. Top face of plate:
line outlining outer edge; similar stamp at either end.

Probably early Classical (by context)

634. Shallow lekane   Pl. 57

C-61-490. P:24; lot 877 (early 3rd century). P.H.
0.083, Th. wall 0.011, est. D. rim 0.20 m. Two joining
fragments of upper wall, rim, handle. Self-slip.

Shallow profile; convex wall, turning in at bottom break;
wide triangular handle attached to top of wall above
which rises narrow rounded rim. Three faces of handle
flat, hole in center. On wall, three low-relief bands,
bounded by grooves above and below, central band corded. Outer face of rim with three bands, top and bottom
ones corded. Pellet attached to apex of handle on top face.
Non-joining fragment of upper bowl and rim, from
N:26, lot 2242 (2242:1), which ends in the later 5th
century.

Closest parallel: unpublished example from well
1937-1 (lot 1937-1:113), of the late 5th or early 4th
century. The handle of the latter is less rigidly triangular,
curving to the apex; the fragment lacks any decoration.
The cording on **634** may require an earlier date.

Early 5th century?

635. Trefoil-oinochoe lid   Pl. 57

C-62-305. O–R:23–24; lot 1955 (second half 4th
century after Christ). Max. dim. 0.088 m. Two joining
fragments, some outer edges missing. No slip.

Usual trefoil shape but with vertical handle, oval in
section, stubs preserved. Attached pellets around handle
area; stamping of boxed triangles around outer edge. Underside plain.

Probably 6th century

636. Trefoil oinochoe Pl. 57

C-65-642. N:23; lot 4393 (early 5th century). P.H. 0.132, D. neck 0.119 m. Six joining fragments of neck, beginning of shoulder, handle. Thin surface wash.

Offset flat shoulder; wide vertical neck turning into trefoil mouth; vertical handle from top of shoulder to mouth, oval in section.

Archaic (by context)

637. Trefoil oinochoe Pl. 57

C-61-489. P–Q:24; lot 898 (*ca.* 500 b.c.). P.H. 0.136, D. neck 0.102 m. Four joining fragments; part of shoulder, neck, most of trefoil mouth, vertical handle preserved. Thin surface wash.

Convex sloping shoulder, offset from wide neck; trefoil mouth; vertical handle from lower shoulder to mouth, oval in section. Five pellets (originally six) attached on spine of handle.

A more convex shoulder than **636**, but without full profile, it cannot be used as dating criterion.

Archaic (by context)

638. Trefoil oinochoe Pl. 57

C-73-358. P–Q:25; lots 73-138 (end of 5th century), 73-139 (second quarter 4th century). P.H. 0.082, D. neck 0.099 m. Many joining fragments; parts of shoulder, neck, mouth preserved. Thin creamy slip on exterior, interior of neck. Traces of burning.

High diagonal shoulder, set off from short neck; trefoil mouth separately made of thickened clay. Attached pellets in center of each foil on inner surface of mouth.

Probably Classical (by context)

639. Mortar Fig. 22, Pl. 58

C-64-431. N–O:25–26; lots 2075 (early 5th century), 75-248 (mid-5th century). H. 0.058, est. D. 0.31, est. D. resting surface 0.18 m. Two joining fragments; complete profile. Light buff slip.

Disk foot, set off by light groove above vertical face from shallow convex bowl; heavy folded rim with flat diagonal outer face, wide convex lip, concave inner bowl. About 0.04 m. below rim on interior bowl is additional grit over slip for roughened grinding surface.

For parallel: C-34-929 (Pease, *Hesperia* 6, 1937, p. 299, no. 194, fig. 32).

Early 5th century

640. Mortar Pl. 58

C-72-195. I–J:15; lot 72-111 (4th century). P.H. 0.052, est. inner D. 0.28 m. Three joining fragments; part of upper wall, rim preserved. No slip.

Slightly concave profile of wall; heavy projecting rim undercut from wall on exterior; convex outer face rising to narrow peaked lip; one spool handle preserved, with three inner beads, attached to rim. At left break, beginning of projection for spout. Additional grit on bowl at lower break.

For a comparable profile: C-53-269 (*Corinth* VII, iii, no. 624, p. 110). **640** is probably earlier.

Mid-4th century?

641. Mortar Pl. 58

C-65-576. N:26; lot 4478 (later Hellenistic). P.H. 0.035, p.L. 0.078 m. One fragment of upper wall, rim. No slip. Photograph taken to show rim of fragment from above.

Shallow bowl, rising to lightly thickened vertical rim with flat lip; projecting horizontal collar, attached 0.01 m. below lip, encircling bowl. On upper surface of collar, finger holds attached by wads of clay, resembling pie-crusting.

See C-47-242 and C-47-399 (*Corinth* VII, iii, nos. 626, 627, p. 111, pls. 22, 59; wells 1934-5 and 1936-13); C-1976-198 in cooking fabric (Williams, *Hesperia* 46, 1977, p. 70, no. 19); and a Delian example (*Exploration archéologique de Délos*, XXVII, *L'Îlot de la Maison des Comédiens*, P. Bruneau, ed., Paris 1970, D225, pl. 49).

Later Hellenistic

642. Tray Fig. 22, Pl. 58

C-64-475. O:24–25; Q–R:26–29, N–O:26; lots 890 (2nd century after Christ), 2038 (first half 4th century after Christ), 2067 (third quarter 4th century). **a**) H. 0.045, L. floor to rim 0.415 m. Four joining fragments of outer floor, rim. **b**) One fragment of outer-floor rim. L. floor to rim 0.167 m. Th. wall 0.023, est. D. rim 0.50 m. Buff slip; floor burnt. Only part of **a**, with dipinto, illustrated (Pl. 58).

At inner break, thickening of floor descending to support or foot; concave profile of undersurface, turning continuously to rim; heavy molded rim, with flat top surface, slightly offset from shallow, barely diagonal floor. Outer face of molded rim: half-round relief band below, offset by grooves; cyma reversa; fascia above; beveled turn to flat top face. On rim of fragment **a**, dipinto of phi, two lambdas(?). No sign of grits on floor.

The term "tray" is used for lack of any better interpretation. The bowl is much shallower than that of a mortar or perirrhanterion. For parallel of the rim molding: C-1978-255, some sort of large flowerpot(?) from Forum Southwest, destruction debris of the third quarter 4th century.

4th century (by context)

643. Bowl   Pl. 58

C-62-836. R:23–24; lot 1991 (late 6th century). H. 0.038, rest. D. 0.133 m. One fragment preserves one third of bowl, with full profile; fully restored in plaster. No slip.

Flat resting surface, no foot; diagonal wall with slight convexity; heavy rim outward thickened, wide convex upper surface. Pellets attached at wide intervals on upper rim face.

6th century (by context)

644. Strainer   Pl. 58

C-65-297. M:17–18; lot 3222 (first half 3rd century after Christ). L. 0.11, W. 0.062, H. 0.012–0.025 m. Slight chipping of edges. Handmade; no slip.

Jaw-shaped strainer with rising edges; holes punched throughout, about 0.004 m. in diameter, in semicircular pattern, following configuration of strainer shape.

COOKING FABRIC (645–660)

645. Lekane or krater   Fig. 23, Pl. 58

C-65-532. N:26; lots 4479, 4480 (Hellenistic). H. 0.192, est. D. 0.39, est. D. foot 0.11 m. Many joining fragments; complete profile, plaster restoration. Orange fabric; slight traces of slip. Wheelmade.

Ring foot; tall, convex flaring wall turning concave above, offset by ridge; projecting rim with flat top face, vertical outer face, sharp break between inner rim and interior wall. Scar of one handle root for horizontal reflex handle below wall ridge. Burning on exterior.

Similar: C-65-400, from Katsoulis well 3 (well 1965-3), unpublished, with slightly lower wall; C-47-256 (*Corinth* VII, iii, no. 705, p. 134, pls. 33, 63; well 1934-5), with heavier lip, grooved outer face of rim.

Probably later Hellenistic (by context)

646. Round-mouthed pitcher   Fig. 23, Pl. 58

C-65-533. N:26; lot 4482 (early Hellenistic). H. 0.18–0.19, D. 0.17–0.174, rest. D. rim 0.105 m. Many joining fragments; complete profile; plaster restoration. Gray-brown fabric.

Deeply recessed undersurface; tall globular wall; slight offset at shoulder; concave neck, merging continuously with slightly thickened round lip; single strap handle, convex on outer face, from upper wall to lip, rising slightly above lip.

Similar: C-75-302, from well 1975-4, unpublished, with similar profile but smaller in size.

Hellenistic

647. Trefoil pitcher   Pl. 58

C-65-475. N:26; lot 4482 (early Hellenistic). H. 0.205, D. 0.20 m. Many joining fragments; fully restored in plaster except missing rim. Gray fabric; badly warped.

Slightly recessed undersurface; wide convex wall merging continuously with shoulder and low concave neck, terminating in trefoil mouth; single strap handle from upper wall to neck.

See C-35-557 and C-48-35 (*Corinth* VII, iii, nos. 747,

748, p. 143, pls. 34, 63; well 1948-4). The warped shape of **647** is probably the result of intense burning.

Hellenistic?

648. Unflanged cooking pot, flaring rim   Pl. 58

C-61-491. P-Q:24; lot 898 (*ca.* 500 B.C.). P.H. 0.091, est. D. rim 0.13 m. One fragment of upper wall, shoulder, rim. Burning on interior, over break. Orange fabric.

Convex wall turning continuously into sloping shoulder, thickened flaring rim. Thin, peeling paint on exterior; burnishing strokes on shoulder.

6th century (by context)

649. Unflanged cooking pot, flaring   Fig. 23, Pl. 58
rim

C-61-432. P:24; lot 877 (early 3rd century). H. 0.215, D. 0.26, D. rim 0.165. Many joining fragments; full profile; plaster restoration. Gray fabric, without mica.

Noted: *Corinth* VII, iii, p. 121, note 7.

Rounded bottom; globular wall with slight offset below sloping shoulder; flaring rim with convex outer face, diagonal inner face. One strap handle, convex on outer surface, attached from upper wall, offset to rim, rising slightly above the rim. The restoration of the second handle is doubtful.

No specific parallel in shape or fabric; the lack of mica is not typical of cooking pots found in Corinth.

Probably 4th century (by context)

650. Unflanged cooking pot, flat rim   Fig. 23, Pl. 59

C-69-253. L:18; lot 5640 (later 4th century). Rest. H. 0.214, D. 0.25, D. rim 0.155 m. Many joining fragments, half preserved; bottom, gaps filled in with plaster. Brown-red fabric; burnt; poor surface.

No resting surface; globular wall, offset from sloping shoulder; flat, horizontally projecting rim set off from wall inside and out; one wide strap handle with flat outer face.

Latest piece in lot?

End of 4th century?

651. Unflanged cooking pot, flat rim   Pl. 59

C-69-298. M–N:19; lot 6182 (fourth quarter 4th century). P.H. 0.197, est. D. rim 0.17 m. Many joining fragments; profile preserved from lower wall to rim, including one handle; plaster restoration. Red fabric; burnt.

Published: Bookidis and Fisher, *Hesperia* 41, 1972, p. 291, no. 3, pl. 57.

Shape as **650** with slightly more convex outer face of handle.

End of 4th century

652. Unflanged cooking pot, flat rim   Fig. 24, Pl. 59

C-65-474. N:26; lot 4482 (early Hellenistic). Rest. H. 0.162, D. 0.19, D. rim 0.135 m. Many joining fragments; resting surface, holes restored in plaster. Red fabric; burnt.

Shape as above two, with less offset to shoulder; two handles preserved.

Hellenistic

653. Unflanged small cooking pot,   Fig. 24, Pl. 59
flaring rim

C-71-88. M:22–23; lot 6826 (late 4th century). H. 0.094, rest. D. 0.122, D. rim 0.08 m. Many joining fragments; one third preserved with complete profile; plaster restoration. Red fabric; burnt, encrusted.

Rounded resting surface; high ovoid wall with slight offset before sloping shoulder; flaring rounded rim; strap handle attached below offset and at rim, rising slightly above rim.

4th century

654. Unflanged small cooking pot,   Fig. 24, Pl. 59
flaring rim

C-69-79. O:18; lot 6193 (later 4th century). H. 0.094, D. 0.123, D. rim 0.082 m. Several joining fragments; part of neck, rim, and all of handle missing. Red fabric.

Shape as **649**, offset even less pronounced; scars for handle attachment at midwall and rim. For shape parallel: C-1979-140, cistern 1979-1, third quarter 4th century (unpublished).

Later 4th century

655. Unflanged small cooking pot,   Fig. 24, Pl. 59
flat rim

C-65-438. N–O:16–17; lot 4404 (mid-3rd century). H. 0.064, D. 0.082, D. rim 0.053 m. Intact, except for small rim chips. Very gritty red fabric; burnt, encrusted.

Small version of **652**; two strap handles rising above rim. Probably 3rd century; context date clarified by **435**, cyma kantharos.

656. Unflanged small cooking pot,   Fig. 24, Pl. 59
vertical rim

C-65-531. N:26; lot 4482 (early Hellenistic). H. 0.106, D. 0.155, D. rim 0.108 m. Many joining fragments; complete profile; plaster restoration. Gray-brown micaceous fabric: 10YR 5/3 (brown); burnt, encrusted.

Rounded resting surface; low globular wall; offset sloping shoulder; vertical rim set off from shoulder; flat narrow lip; flat strap handle from below shoulder to lip, rising slightly above it. No parallels in fabric or shape.

Hellenistic

657. Flanged cooking pot (chytra II)   Pl. 59

C-65-530. N:26; lot 4480 (Hellenistic). P.H. 0.09, D. 0.121, D. rim 0.096 m. Many joining fragments; most of rim, wall preserved. Plaster restoration. Orange fabric; burnt, encrusted.

Low ovoid wall, contracting to rim; straight flaring rim rising sharply from shoulder, with flattened lip; inner rim concave to rounded flange projecting into bowl; flange not sharply articulated. No trace of strap handle.

Parallel: C-46-38 (*Corinth* VII, iii, no. 653, p. 122; well 1946-1).

Later Hellenistic?

658. Casserole I   Figs. 24, 37, Pl. 59

C-68-304. M–N:19; lots 5620 (later 4th century), 5624 (later 3rd century). Rest. H. 0.06–0.073, D. rim 0.205–0.212 m. Many joining fragments; center missing, restored in plaster as are parts of wall, rim. Red fabric; burnt.

Rounded wall; carination to concave contracted shoulder; shoulder and rim divided by narrow ridge, not groove; flaring rim, convex outside, flattened diagonal lip, concave inner face to strong flange rising diagonally. Diameter and height of shoulder and rim equal, creating

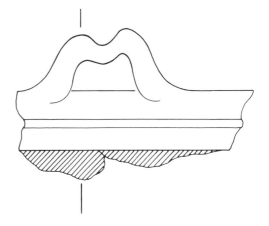

FIG. 37. Casserole I **658**. Scale 1:2

biconical profile. Rounded handles attached to rim, rising diagonally above rim; central depression in handles creating M shape.

No parallel for profile. For handles: C-53-268 (*Corinth* VII, iii, p. 124, note 11, an import; well 1953-2). **658** has fabric typical of most cooking-fabric vessels in Corinth.

659. Casserole II   Pl. 59

C-73-307. K–L:23–24; lot 73-116 (late 4th century). P.H. 0.06, est. D. rim 0.20 m. Many joining fragments; most of bowl, shoulder, rim, one handle preserved; plaster restoration. Orange-red fabric, heavily micaceous: 2.5YR 6/6-8 (light red); thinner (0.003 m.) and finer than typical cooking ware. Traces of fine red slip on interior. Burnt.

Deep rounded wall; bulging round shoulder, contracting to light groove separating shoulder from rim; straight rim, diagonally flaring, convex to concave inner face;

strong rounded horizontal flange; loop handle, round in section, attached to shoulder, rising diagonally above rim.

Similar fabric: C-71-48, drain 1971-1 (Williams and Fisher, *Hesperia* 41, 1972, p. 161, no. 48, pl. 27), with different profile. Similar profile: C-36-986 (*Corinth* VII, iii, no. 681, p. 126; well 1936-3).

Probably later 4th century

660. Casserole II   Fig. 24, Pl. 59

C-71-173. L–M:28; lot 6723 (late 4th—early 3rd century). P.H. 0.05, est. D. rim 0.20 m. Many joining fragments; parts of wall, rim, half of one handle preserved; plaster restoration. Red fabric; burnt.

Straight flaring wall; sharp turn without bulge to vertical upper wall (no articulation for shoulder), merging with rim; thin groove separating upper wall from rim; rim rising vertically to rounded lip; narrow flange; part of one loop handle, round in section, attached to upper wall.

Early 3rd century?

PERIRRHANTERIA (661–674)

The perirrhanteria are arranged by the part of the vessel from which each fragment derives: base, shaft, and rim, subdivided chronologically in each section. The one example with fragments from the different parts of the vessel appears first. The clay of each is coarse, with many inclusions, except for the very small (votive?) example, **670**, of fine clay. The fabric is not described, but the slip is noted. Dating of each example is usually by context; any parallels in profile or decoration are given. For the development of the profile and the changes in decoration, see Shape Studies, XXVIII.

661. Perirrhanterion   Pl. 60

a, b. Base

C-62-755. R:23–24, N–O:24–25, O:20–21; lots 1988 (late 6th century), 2094 (early 4th century), 4348 (late Roman, Byzantine). **a)** P.H. 0.088, est. D. 0.44 m. One fragment of vertical and horizontal faces of foot, broken at beginning of shaft. **b)** P.H. 0.083 m. (not illustrated). Two fragments of vertical face of foot, broken near shaft. Self-slip on exterior.

Published: Iozzo, *Hesperia* 56, 1987, no. 71.

Flat resting surface; nearly vertical, plain outer face, carefully offset from sloping upper face, decorated with three relief bands at outer edge, upper and lower corded; above, stamped enclosed volute palmettes with seven petals; incised line as lower limit; corded band at base of shaft. Palmette stamp very worn.

See C-31-446 (Weinberg, *Hesperia* 23, 1954, p. 126, note 111, pl. 28:a; Iozzo, *Hesperia* 56, 1987, no. 66). The palmettes of **661** are plumper, probably later.

c–g. Shaft

C-64-471 (**c**), C-65-649 (**d**), C-75-320 (**e–g**). O:26, M–N:25–26, P:20–21, M–N:25, N–O:25–26; lots 2083 (later 6th century), 4344 (Roman, Byzantine), 4367 (late 4th or early 3rd century), 4434 (early

Roman), 75-248 (mid-5th century). Five fragments, three with same design, non-joining. Est. D. of shaft 0.28–0.30 m. **c)** P.H. 0.133, p.W. 0.117 m. **d)** P.H. 0.072, p.W. 0.084 m. **e)** P.H. 0.063, p.W. 0.053 m.; **f)** p.H. 0.094, p.W. 0.085 m.; **g)** p.H. 0.074, p.W. 0.046 m. Slip as **a, b**.

Published: C-64-471 (**c**) Iozzo, *Hesperia* 56, 1987, no. 80; C-65-649 (**d**) Iozzo, *Hesperia* 56, 1987, no. 67.

c. At lower break, thin fillet; three relief bands, upper and lower corded as **a, b**. At upper break, stamped chevrons of eight parallel V's, lower limit of zone an incised line. Groove of upper limit at top right break. Worn stamp.

d. At lower break, palmettes as **a, b**, corded band above. At top right break, incised line.

e–g. Three bands, lower and upper corded; stamped ten-petal rosettes; incised line as upper limit.

h. Rim

C-64-472. N:26; lot 2074 (mid- to third quarter 5th century). P.W. 0.102, p.L. 0.14, est. D. 0.60 m. One fragment of outer bowl, rim. Self-slip on interior of bowl, rim.

Published: Iozzo, *Hesperia* 56, 1987, no. 21, fig. 1 (profile).

Shallow concave bowl rising to heavy projecting rim, with flat horizontal upper face, molded vertical face, slightly rounded narrow underface, undercut to meet bowl exterior. Outer rim face with two sets of relief bands, separated by concave zone, upper and lower in each set corded.

Mid-6th century (by context, lots 1988, 2083, style of palmettes)

662. Base   Pl. 60

C-62-373. R:23–24; lot 1985 (*ca.* 500 B.C.). Max. dim. 0.078 m. One fragment of foot. Pale slip on exterior, cracking. Traces of burning.
Published: Iozzo, *Hesperia* 56, 1987, no. 64.

From upper surface of foot, probably very wide; see **661 a, b**. Two plain relief bands, zone of stamped palmettes similar to those of **664**, but more closely set, so that the volutes enclose a heart-shaped area with a dart or central spine; five small leaves projecting from calyx.

An example from Perachora may have palmettes from the same stamp (*Perachora* II, no. 3365a, pl. 126; Weinberg, *Hesperia* 23, 1954, pl. 29:g).

Earlier 6th century

663. Base and lower shaft   Pl. 60

C-62-362. R:23–24; lot 1985 (*ca.* 500 B.C.). P.H. 0.142, est. D. 0.35 m. Ten joining fragments of base, lower shaft. Thin self-slip on exterior; inclusions show.
Published: Iozzo, *Hesperia* 56, 1987, no. 83.

Foot with less offset between the two faces than **661**. Rounded resting surface. Corded relief band 0.024 m. above edge of foot; stamped zone of rosettes, ovolos, pendent from upper corded band; additional band at top of foot, separated from lower one by plain band. Columnar shaft; five bands below, top and bottom corded; stamped rosettes above, at wide intervals. Worn stamps.

See C-47-786 (Weinberg, *Hesperia* 23, 1954, p. 129, note 128, pl. 30:e; well 1947-4).

Before 500 B.C. (by context)

664. Base   Pl. 60

C-64-60. P:26; lot 2012 (early 5th century). Max. dim. 0.117, est. D. 0.28 m. One fragment preserving base profile. Part of outer face broken away. Self-slip on exterior.
Published: Iozzo, *Hesperia* 56, 1987, no. 78.

Continuous foot profile as **663**, broken above at beginning of vertical shaft. Flat resting surface; outer face with faint traces of stamped volute palmettes; upper face set off by ledge, cut back from outer face, decorated with chevrons of four parallel V's; three relief bands, upper and lower carelessly corded; one corded band at top break surrounding shaft.

C-62-275, O:24, lot 1950, with similar profile (Iozzo, *Hesperia* 56, 1987, no. 81); eight-petal rosettes on both faces, poorly corded bands. For palmette of **664**, see C-40-36 (Weinberg, *Hesperia* 23, 1954, p. 124, note 106, pl. 28:b; Iozzo, *op. cit.*, no. 65); for profile, see C-50-17 (Weinberg, *Hesperia* 23, 1954, p. 127, note 120, pl. 28:g; Iozzo, *op. cit.*, no. 82).

Archaic.

665. Base   Pl. 60

C-68-350. L:15–16; lot 5719 (mid-5th century). P.H. 0.083, est. D. 0.26 m. Six joining fragments of foot. Self-slip on exterior; surface flaking.
Published: Iozzo, *Hesperia* 56, 1987, no. 89.

Rounded resting surface; low diagonal outer face, sloping upper face; broken above at beginning of shaft. At bottom of sloping face, three low, wide relief bands, outer two black, upper added red, with grooves between. Zone of stamped enclosed seven-petal rosettes, with slightly squared tips. Black band around missing shaft.

Early 5th century (by context and by designs)

666. Base   Pl. 60

C-69-315. M–N:19; lots 5625 (later 3rd century), 6189 (later 4th century). P.H. 0.144, est. D. 0.28 m. Three joining fragments of foot, broken above at beginning of shaft. Pale buff slip on exterior. Wheelmade. Photographed before final joins.
Published: Iozzo, *Hesperia* 56, 1987, no. 100, fig. 4 (profile).

Flat resting surface; very high foot, outer face diagonal, short upper face sloping to shaft; upper face with three plain relief bands, grooves between each; one plain band with grooves on either side encircling missing shaft.

Classical, probably 4th century (by context)

667. Base   Pl. 61

C-65-324. N–O:17–18; lot 3411 (early Hellenistic). P.H. 0.128, est. L. each side *ca.* 0.40 m. One fragment, preserving almost one fourth of square base (half of two sides), beginning of shaft. Flaking buff slip on all surfaces except resting surface.
Published: Iozzo, *Hesperia* 56, 1987, no. 121.

Square base with flat resting surface, vertical outer face; flat horizontal face with added red, from which rises footing for circular shaft, broken at ascending turn. Non-joining fragment from another corner, K–L:22, lot 73-101:1.

Similar profile: KN 162 (Weinberg, *Hesperia* 23, 1954, p. 128, note 121, pl. 30:f; Iozzo, *Hesperia* 56, 1987, no. 120; not in *Corinth* XV, iii), decorated with stamps, not paint, dated to the earlier 6th century. **667** is later.

Classical (by context)

668. Upper base, beginning of shaft   Pl. 61

C-64-474. P:26; lot 2049 (early 4th-century pottery; coin of Ptolemy I). P.H. 0.063, est. D. inner shaft 0.10 m. One fragment of upper base, lower shaft. Self-slip on exterior.

Base and shaft continuous. Undersurface preserves beginning of resting surface. Parts of five flutes preserved from bottom of shaft, continuing onto base, spreading in width. At outer break, flattening of arris, probably for outer raised band; added red and gray on arris and surrounding area.

668 duplicates in clay a type well documented in stone. See Ginouvès (footnote 263 above, p. 77), pl. 20; it is also known in representations on Classical vases: *ibid.*, pl. 14, fig. 41; pl. 27, fig. 84, and so forth.

Probably Classical

669. Shaft   Pl. 61

C-62-279. R:25; lot 1953 (Byzantine). Max. dim. 0.095 m. One fragment of wall of shaft. Self-slip on exterior; burning at lower left break.

Published: Iozzo, *Hesperia* 56, 1987, no. 86.

Chain of stamped pendent dotted ovolos, unevenly spaced, of different sizes; above, two relief bands, upper one corded.

See Weinberg, *Hesperia* 23, 1954, pl. 29:f (*Perachora* II, no. 3367, pl. 126).

6th century

670. Shaft, beginning of bowl   Pl. 61

C-64-473. O:25; lots 2089 (early 5th century), 2090 (later 6th century). P.H. 0.116, D. shaft 0.067 m. Two joining fragments of shaft, beginning of bowl. Fine clay; thin slip or polish on exterior, flaking.

At bottom break, slight splaying of shaft for turn to base; circular hollow shaft; projecting fascia at top, above which is the shallow, concave projecting bowl. At lower break, stamps of five-petal volute palmettes; traces of added red around stamps; chevron of three parallel V's. Both stamps very worn. At midshaft, three rows of irregularly spaced triangular marks, carelessly applied, bounded above by faint groove. Suspended from added-red fascia, added-red and gray loops, with central vertical lines in same colors, similar lines between loops. Colors alternate irregularly. Bowl reserved.

Probably late 6th century

671. Shaft   Pl. 61

C-64-221. N-O:23; lot 2152 (4th-century pottery, 2nd-century coin). P.H. 0.15, est. D. 0.12 m. Three joining fragments of lower area of shaft, almost half the circumference preserved. Self-slip on exterior.

Broken below at beginning of base. Band of added-brown paint at base of flutes; 10 preserved flutes, probably 22 or 24 when complete; traces of added brown on arrises.

For similar larger shaft: C-1976-152, Forum Southwest (Iozzo, *Hesperia* 56, 1987, no. 116), Classical stratum.

Classical

672. Rim   Pl. 61

C-62-277. R:25; lot 1953 (Byzantine). P.L. 0.153, est. D. 0.60 m. One fragment of rim, beginning of bowl. Thin buff slip on all surfaces; inclusions showing.

Published: Iozzo, *Hesperia* 56, 1987, no. 26, fig. 1 (profile).

Concave shallow bowl, rising to flat horizontal face of rim; vertical face with six relief bands, painted alternately black and added red; central flat area of vertical rim with black and red dentils.

Similar rims are found in contexts of the Archaic through Hellenistic periods.

673. Rim   Pl. 61

C-70-596. M-O:27-29, P-Q:25; lots 2210 (4th century after Christ), 73-141 (third quarter 5th century). P.L. 0.152, est. D. 0.57 m. Two joining fragments of rim. Thin buff slip on all surfaces.

Published: Iozzo, *Hesperia* 56, 1987, no. 44, fig. 2 (profile).

Profile as **673**. On vertical face, six relief bands with wide stripes of added red, black, red; black over horizontal face of rim. At inner broken edge of horizontal face, graffito:

Classical   ﬔ ﬔ

674. Rim   Pl. 61

C-64-432. P:26; lot 2042 (late 5th century). P.W. 0.092, est. D. 0.43 m. One fragment of rim and bowl. Self-slip on all surfaces.

Profile as **672, 673**. On vertical rim face, projecting spool handle, with stamped horizontal palmettes at either end; three narrow relief bands, upper and lower ones corded. Misjudged spacing; central band cut away for the palmettes, the leaves of which are obscured.

See C-48-177 (Weinberg, *Hesperia* 23, 1954, p. 126, note 116, pl. 28:c; Iozzo, *Hesperia* 56, 1987, no. 16, fig. 1 [profile]) and C-67-136, from the Gymnasium (Classical context; Iozzo, *op. cit.*, no. 10). Both are of higher quality than **674**; both may be earlier.

Classical (by context).

POST-CLASSICAL PHIALAI (675–681)
Kathleen Warner Slane

In the study of the Roman context pottery from the Sanctuary of Demeter a group of large mesomphalic phialai was identified. They were thought to be late Roman (4th century) on the basis of the context of the examples originally identified, but the discovery of parallels at Morgantina in Sicily and of a possible antecedent in the Corinth excavations in 1981 has suggested that these phialai are late Hellenistic in date. They may fill the gap between the end of the Classical series outlined above (Shape Studies, XI) and the abandonment in 146 B.C. While the evidence presented below is not conclusive, it is strong enough to make it necessary to draw these phialai to the reader's attention by discussing them with the Greek series.[32]

In addition to the 7 catalogued examples, 37 fragments (apparently representing as many vessels) of phialai in a thick, coarse fabric which is probably local were found in the sanctuary. These phialai are distinguished by a very large, hemispherical omphalos, a broad sloping floor separated from a very low, oblique wall by an angular carination, and a wide horizontal rim, usually with traces of a groove at its outer edge. They are relatively shallower and much broader than the normal Corinthian phialai, with diameters ranging from *ca.* 0.20 to 0.30 m. Only one or two fragments bear any trace of a slip; the remainder appear to have been only wet smoothed.

Most of the fragments of these phialai were found in destruction contexts and surface levels of the second half of the 4th century after Christ on the Upper Terrace around Building S–T:16–17,[33] on the central part of the Upper Terrace (Q–S:17–23)[34] extending down over Building O–P:19–20,[35] and one fragment farther east in Q:24–25;[36] the largest concentration of fragments (**678**, **680**, and 24 sherds) was on the central part of the Upper Terrace in the Theatral Area (lot 2107) and in the upper dumped filling of well 61-11 (lot 1945). In three other instances the Roman pottery with which the phialai were associated was no later than the 3rd or early 4th century.[37] The stratigraphic evidence so far presented points to a date in the 3rd or 4th century for this group of mesomphalic phialai, but the contexts of **676** and **677** (if the latter is a phiale) may complicate the picture: in both cases the associated finds were no later than late Hellenistic (figured moldmade relief bowls).[38] The phiale fragments must therefore either be late Hellenistic or provide a Roman

---

[32] The only phiale of Roman date which does not belong to this group is C-73-177, *Corinth* XVIII, ii, no. 141. Although of local manufacture it belongs to a completely different tradition.

[33] Lot 6638 (general debris over Building S–T:16–17): 8% Classical lamps and votives (figurines excluded), remainder Roman from 1st century after Christ to second half of 4th century.

[34] Lot 2107 (Q–S:17–20, surface to bedrock; pottery only): *ca.* 48% Archaic and Classical sherds and votives, remainder Roman, pottery and lamps from 1st century after Christ to second half of 4th century, one Byzantine (64-78) and one Turkish coin (64-87). Lot 2169 (R:17–18, pit D): 33 Greek votives, **675**, two Attic lamp sherds of the 4th century after Christ. Lot 4380 (R:16–17, southern pocket in bedrock/west end of wall 46 cutting): 20% Greek, remainder Roman from 1st century after Christ to second half of 4th century. Lot 6501 (R–S:21–22, stepped terrace, layer 4): 86% burned Greek votives, Roman: one wheel-ridged coarse sherd, three cooking including two late Roman rims, one phiale rim. Lot 1945 (well 61-11, upper dumped filling): *ca.* 40% Archaic to Hellenistic, remainder of pottery Roman, little 1st century after Christ, mostly 3rd and 4th centuries.

[35] Lot 2151 (Building O–P:19–20, south of south wall, from top of wall to − 0.10 m.): 620 Greek to Hellenistic, 22 Roman including at least one 1st century after Christ but mostly 3rd and 4th century. Lot 2240 (Building O–P:19–20, fill overlying floor, from top of south wall): *ca.* 7% Roman from pie-crust thymiateria to C-65-638, a Phocaean Red Slip Ware dish (*Corinth* XVIII, ii, no. 120). Lot 2247 (N–O:19–20, surface to − 0.15/ − 0.20 m.): 7.5% Roman, probably all 4th century, no Hellenistic.

[36] Lot 882 (Q:24–25, surface layer): *ca.* 18% Greek sherds, remainder Roman from mid-1st century after Christ to second half of 4th century.

[37] Lot 2164 (Q:23, cutting in bedrock): *ca.* 75% Greek, remainder Roman from 1st century after Christ to 3rd century. Lot 2239 (Building O–P:19–20, robbing trench over west wall; may also include part of foundation fill): *ca.* 83% Greek to Hellenistic, remainder Roman from 1st century after Christ to at least 3rd century. Lot 6642 (Building S–T:16–17, robbing trench of wall 205): 67% Greek, remainder Roman of 2nd or 3rd century.

[38] Lot 3215 (Building O–P:19–20, south of eastern end of north wall, stratum II): 221 Archaic to Hellenistic sherds and **677**. Lot 6191 (Building O–P:19–20, foundation trench of west wall): 11 Classical and Hellenistic (latest: rolled-rim plate, figured moldmade relief bowl) and **676** (two non-joining fragments).

date for the contexts, but it is not clear which of these interpretations is correct. One should note, however, that four other strata which abut the west end of the north wall and the west wall of Building O–P:19–20 contain among a handful of sherds one or two of Roman date.[39]

On the whole, the stratigraphic evidence suggests that this group of phialai is Roman in date, probably of the 4th century after Christ, but arguments in favor of a late Hellenistic date may be advanced. The strongest evidence is that of parallels. From elsewhere in the Corinth excavations a single possible parallel has been found. C-1981-160 with oblique wall and broad rim may be a phiale; it is a thin-walled vessel of fine orange Corinthian fabric, and the thin lime slip with which it is covered suggests a ritual use. The fabric can only be paralleled among Corinthian pottery of Greek times, but its context was disturbed: a late 3rd- to first half of 2nd-century B.C. fill which contained a few sherds of 1st-, 3rd-, and 12th-century date. More convincing parallels are two mesomphalic phialai of closely related form and of a size comparable to **680**, from Morgantina in Sicily.[40] Unfortunately their contexts (2nd century B.C. to third quarter of the 1st century B.C.) fall primarily in the period when Corinth itself was abandoned after the Mummian destruction of 146 B.C., but a date before 146 B.C. or after 44 B.C. should be considered for the Corinthian phialai. Of the two, a date before 146 B.C. seems more likely because the well-documented series of Classical phialai from the sanctuary stops abruptly in the 3rd century B.C., as shown above.

It is possible on the basis of the phialai from Roman contexts in the Sanctuary of Demeter to construct a typological development originating with the 3rd-century B.C. phialai, which are the latest of the documented Classical series. There is no question that **675** is the direct successor of the earlier phialai. It has a slightly gritty buff fabric and a vertical wall with a narrow rim, which are continuations of features already observed in the early 3rd-century phialai. **678**, of slightly gritty orange fabric, is a larger example with more evenly curving wall and wider rim. **679** is a thicker version of the same fabric as **678**; here the continuous curve of the interior profile is retained, but the exterior profile has acquired a slight break in its upper part. **680** shows that the same profile exists in the coarse fabric which is normal for the group, but the profile with a slight carination in the upper wall on both interior and exterior (like **681**) is more common.

Such a typological development may seem somewhat forced. The best alternative would be to accept the stratigraphic evidence and assign these phialai to the 3rd and 4th centuries after Christ. The single example of a phiale intervening between the 3rd century B.C. and the 3rd century after Christ would then be C-73-177 (*Corinth* XVIII, ii, no. 141) of the middle of the 1st century after Christ.[41]

675.   Phiale rim   Fig. 38

Lot 2169:1. R:17–18, pit D (second half of the 4th century after Christ). Corinthian, buff to orange, with a few large bits of lime.

676.   Phiale, rim and omphalos fragments   Fig. 38

Lot 6191:1 a, b. Building O–P:19–20, foundation trench of west wall (late 3rd or 2nd century B.C., this piece possibly Roman). Mended rim and non-joining omphalos. Est. D. rim 0.240 m. Coarse Corinthian, orange; very worn.

677.   Phiale rim?   Fig. 38

Lot 3215:1. Building O–P:19–20, south of eastern end of north wall, stratum II (late 3rd or 2nd century B.C., this sherd possibly Roman). Corinthian coarse or cooking, red.

---

[39] Lots 3209–3211, 5618; lot 3211 contains a pedestal-krater rim of 3rd-century (after Christ) type; lot 5618 has several pieces of the first half of the 1st century after Christ.

[40] I thank Shelley C. Stone, III for providing a photograph and drawing of 80-629, for information on the contexts of 80-629 and 80-630, and for permission to refer to them here.

[41] The possibility of an early Roman date for the phialai was raised in connection with the parallels from Morgantina. In this case the stratigraphic evidence remains as unhelpful as for a late Hellenistic date (except that one might give more emphasis to the evidence of lot 2247 in footnote 35 above, p. 191.) The putative typological development will not stand because the evidence is not sufficient to argue continuity of tradition across the period of abandonment. The gap in use of phialai in the sanctuary would still remain, unless one arbitrarily assigned **675** (and **678**?) to it. Furthermore it is difficult to place the phialai in the 75-year period after 44 B.C. because so little ceramic material which is certainly of this time is found in the sanctuary. But the Morgantina parallels lose their force if the Corinthian phialai belong to the second or third quarter of the 1st century after Christ, when there is an upsurge in the amount of Roman pottery in the sanctuary.

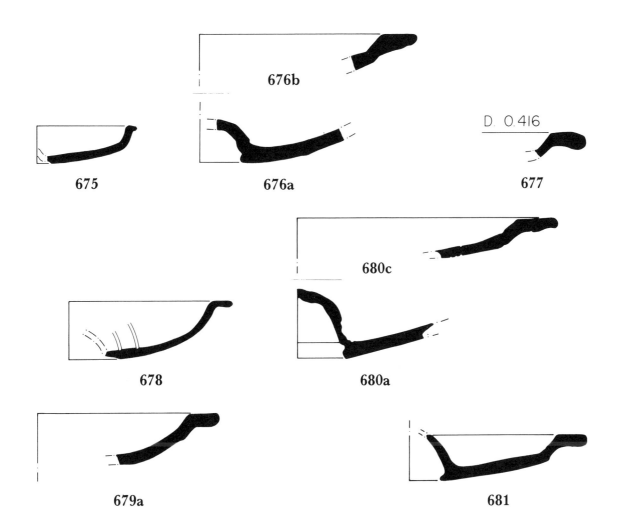

Fig. 38. Phialai

678. Probable phiale Fig. 38

C-64-468. Q–S:17–20, surface to bedrock; lot 2107. Single fragment with profile from base to rim. H. 0.030, est. D. base 0.050, est. D. rim 0.180 m. Corinthian, pale orange; self-slip.

Phiale with flat base and flaring wall, which is nearly vertical below a wide everted rim. Edge of omphalos possibly preserved in central interior; possibly two concentric grooves on floor.

Comparison with **680** and **681** suggests that this phiale had a hemispherical omphalos.

679. Phiale rim Fig. 38

Lot 6642:1 a, b. Building S–T:16–17, robbing trench of wall 205, destruction debris (latest piece early 3rd century after Christ). Probably Corinthian coarse with very fine inclusions: very pale brown (10YR 7/3) with light-red core (2.5YR 6/6).

680. Phiale Fig. 38

C-61-485a–c. a, c) Q:19, well 61-11, upper dumped filling; lot 1945 (second half of 4th century after Christ with a few later Roman to modern). b) Q–S:17–20, surface to bedrock; lot 2107. Three non-joining fragments allow reconstruction of profile. Est. H. 0.049, D. edge of base 0.052, est. D. rim 0.290 m. Not Corinthian(?): hard fabric with tiny calcareous, white, orange and black inclusions; fired reddish yellow (5YR 6/6) at core and surface and reddish brown between (5YR 5/4). Single drop of red glaze on interior.

Phiale with sloping floor, angular carination on exterior to low upper wall and broad everted rim; large hollow omphalos in center of floor strongly marked off by a groove at its base. Traces of a groove on the outer edge of the rim. Finish of exterior and of omphalos rough.

681. Phiale Fig. 38

C-65-639. Building O–P:19–20, fill overlying floor, from top of south wall; lot 2240 (second half of the 4th century after Christ). Single fragment preserves almost complete profile. H. 0.024, est. D. edge of base 0.036, est. D. rim 0.199 m. Coarse Corinthian, light orange; buff self-slip.

Shape as **680**, but the edge of the wall projects slightly into the hollow center of the omphalos and is slightly flattened to form a base, and the angular carination appears in both interior and exterior profiles.

CONCORDANCE AND INDEXES

CONCORDANCE OF POTTERY

Numbers in roman type are from the Demeter Sanctuary. Numbers in italic type are from elsewhere in Corinth. KN, KP, and KT numbers are from the Potters' Quarter. T numbers are from the North Cemetery. Lotted sherds from the Demeter Sanctuary are listed last. Bold numbers in parentheses indicate references to catalogue entries.

Inv. No.	Text Reference	Findspot
C-28-70	(497)	
C-28-104	12[15], 25[63]	
C-28-105	12[15], 25[63]	
C-28-106	12[15], 25[63]	
C-28-107	12[15], 25[63]	
C-28-108	12[15], 25[63]	
C-28-109	12[15], 25[63]	
C-28-110	24[62]	
C-30-47	(382)	
C-31-41	1[4]	
C-31-129	18[30], (78)	Well 1931-7
C-31-136	(5)	Well 1931-7
C-31-186	76	Well 1931-7
C-31-201	42[127]	Well 1931-8
C-31-206	(434)	Well 1931-8
C-31-235	(388)	Well 1931-8
C-31-446	76[254], (661)	Well 1931-14
C-31-479	(461)	
C-33-102	(461)	
C-34-21	42[128]	Fill 1934-1
C-34-25	75	Well 1934-3
C-34-36	58[194], (178)	Fill 1934-1
C-34-37	(187)	Fill 1934-1
C-34-362	129[8, 11], (292)	Well 1934-10
C-34-928	(382)	Well 1934-10
C-34-929	68, (639)	Well 1934-10
C-34-931	77	Well 1934-10
C-34-935	18[36]	Well 1934-10
C-34-1159	33[83]	Well 1934-10
C-34-1162	33[83]	Well 1934-10
C-34-1173	23[52]	Well 1934-10
C-34-1613	74	Well 1934-5
C-34-1645	(388)	Well 1934-5
C-34-2516	33[81]	Grave 1934-11

Inv. No.	Text Reference	Findspot
C-35-27	(211)	
C-35-114	44[145]	Well 1935-4
C-35-335	76	
C-35-557	(647)	
C-35-640	72	Well 1935-7
C-35-645	44[145]	Well 1935-4
C-35-962	44[145]	Well 1935-4
C-35-978	(459)	
C-35-984	44[145]	Well 1935-4
C-36-743	(413)	
C-36-836	129[8], 134[14]	Well 1936-1?
C-36-986	(659)	Well 1936-3
C-37-167	17[29]	Drain 1937-1
C-37-188	37[99]	Drain 1937-1
C-37-196	23[54]	Drain 1937-1
C-37-257	(298)	Drain 1937-1
C-37-422	38[103]	Well 1937-1
C-37-439	(301)	Well 1937-1
C-37-525	(61)	Well 1937-1
C-37-547	73	Well 1937-1
C-37-550	73	Well 1937-1
C-37-558	72	Drain 1937-1
C-37-567	72	Drain 1937-1
C-37-569	72	Drain 1937-1
C-37-582	30[79], (80)	Drain 1937-1
C-37-590	(3)	Well 1937-2
C-37-981	10[11]	Well 1937-3
C-37-1037	(292)	Well 1937-3
C-37-1059	10[11]	Well 1937-3
C-37-1569	(461)	
C-37-2058	72	Well 1937-3
C-37-2059	72	Well 1937-3
C-37-2076	76	Well 1937-3
C-37-2493	3[17]	Pit 1937-1
C-37-2502	18[30], (78)	Pit 1937-1
C-37-2508	73	Pit 1937-1
C-37-2517	18	Pit 1937-1

C-37-2536	42^{123}	Pit 1937-1	C-47-813	49^{160}	Well 1947-3
C-37-2537	42^{123}	Pit 1937-1	C-47-822	41	Well 1947-3
C-37-2546	44^{143}	Pit 1937-1	C-47-826	74	Well 1947-3
C-37-2548	38^{104}	Pit 1937-1	C-47-853	63^{206}, (**479**)	Well 1947-3
C-37-2549	38^{104}	Pit 1937-1	C-47-858 a, b	30^{79}	Well 1947-2
C-37-2550	38^{104}	Pit 1937-1	C-47-859	30^{79}	Well 1947-2
C-37-2551	38^{104}	Pit 1937-1	C-47-870	75, (**153**)	Well 1947-2
C-37-2553	38^{104}	Pit 1937-1	C-47-871	17^{29}	Well 1947-2
C-37-2554	38^{104}	Pit 1937-1	C-47-889	(**112**)	Well 1947-2
C-37-2584	47^{158}	Pit 1937-1	C-47-899	55^{183}, (**199**)	Well 1933-3
C-37-2589	(**449**)	Pit 1937-1			
C-37-2648	24	Pit 1937-1	C-48-12	56	Well 1948-4
			C-48-35	(**647**)	Well 1948-4
C-38-699	(**461**)		C-48-53	50^{164}, (**177**)	Well1948-2
			C-48-101	49^{160}	Well 1948-3
C-39-2	(**1**)		C-48-119	66^{217}	Well 1948-3
C-39-23	(**22**)	Well 1939-1	C-48-177	(**676**)	
C-39-56–					
C-39-79	37^{100}	Well 1939-1	C-50-17	76, (**664**)	
C-39-193	(**414**)	Well 1939-1	C-50-67	(**323**)	
C-39-226	33^{83}	Well 1939-1			
C-39-227	33^{83}	Well 1939-1	C-53-134	74^{241}	Well 1953-1
C-39-275	73	Well 1939-1	C-53-137	(**23**)	Well 1953-1
			C-53-156	(**24**)	Well 1953-1
C-40-36	(**664**)		C-53-157	(**414**)	Well 1953-1
C-40-67	18^{36}	Well 1940-6	C-53-160	(**24**)	Well 1953-1
C-40-128	(**4**)	Well 1940-2	C-53-209	33^{81}	Well 1953-1
C-40-390	(**77**)	Well 1940-1	C-53-225	(**414**)	Well 1953-1
C-40-415	18	Well 1940-1	C-53-248	(**136**)	Well 1953-2
C-40-433	52, (**188**)	Well 1940-1	C-53-268	(**658**)	Well 1953-2
			C-53-269	68, (**640**)	Well 1953-2
C-46-15	44^{145}	Well 1946-1	C-53-273	(**378**)	Well 1953-2
C-46-38	(**657**)	Well 1946-1			
			C-60-60	74	Well 1960-4
C-47-62	(**435**)	Well 1938-1	C-60-65	42^{122}	Well 1960-4
C-47-88	(**436**)	Well 1933-2	C-60-68	55^{182}, (**98, 200**)	Well 1960-4
C-47-107	(**187**)	Well 1933-1	C-60-125–		
C-47-130	18–19	Well 1938-1	C-60-127	57^{190}	Grave 1960-11
C-47-131	18	Well 1938-1	C-60-227	35^{92}	Grave 1960-7
C-47-228	54	Well 1934-5	C-60-228	55	Grave 1960-7
C-47-235	42^{128}	Well 1934-5	C-60-264	63^{209}	Well 1960-6
C-47-242	(**641**)	Well 1934-5	C-60-288	72	Well 1960-6
C-47-256	(**645**)	Well 1934-5			
C-47-264	41^{121}		C-61-154	**388**	
C-47-272	(**435**)	Well 1935-3	C-61-156	**543**	
C-47-357	(**437**)	Well 1936-13	C-61-162	**538**	
C-47-399	(**641**)	Well 1936-13	C-61-165	**550**	
C-47-443	42^{122}	Well 1947-5	C-61-166	**55**; 25	
C-47-750	18^{32}	Well 1947-5	C-61-167	**271**	
C-47-786	(**663**)	Well 1947-4	C-61-168	**475**; 17, 53	

C-61-175	**203**	C-61-286	**516**; 17
C-61-176	**257**	C-61-287	**590**; 65
C-61-180	**551**; 25	C-61-298	**544**
C-61-183	**562**	C-61-299	**549**
C-61-186	**(615)**	C-61-300	**534**
C-61-189	**578**; 65	C-61-304	**527**
C-61-190	**627**; 10[6]	C-61-305	**553**; 25
C-61-191	**579**; 65	C-61-308	**(419)**
C-61-193	**508**; 65	C-61-309	**418**; 33
C-61-202	**278**; 12	C-61-310	**(419)**
C-61-203	**501**; 12	C-61-311	**419**; 33
C-61-204	**(139)**	C-61-312	**(419)**
C-61-206	**116**	C-61-313	**(419)**
C-61-207	**150**	C-61-374	**119**; 34, **(175)**
C-61-208	**122**; 38	C-61-376	**(142)**
C-61-209	**114**; 26, 41	C-61-377	**143**; 24
C-61-210	**139**	C-61-378	**(145)**
C-61-211	**137**; 39	C-61-379	**141**; 24
C-61-213	**124**; 41–42	C-61-381	**129**; 47
C-61-214	**135**; 55	C-61-382	**133**; 48
C-61-215	**128**; 45	C-61-383	**130**; 48
C-61-219	**548**	C-61-384	**126**; 42
C-61-220	**(502)**	C-61-385	**151**; 67, 72
C-61-226	**63**	C-61-386	**153**; 75
C-61-227	**61**; 30, 143	C-61-387	**71**
C-61-228	**334**; 14[19]	C-61-388	**62**; 39, 41, 65, **(575)**
C-61-229	**554**; 25	C-61-389	**72**
C-61-235	**243**	C-61-390	**64**
C-61-236 a	**365c**	C-61-391	**65**
C-61-236 b	**365b**	C-61-392	**66**
C-61-236 c	**365d**	C-61-393	**67**
C-61-236 d	**365e**	C-61-394	**68**
C-61-236 e	**365f**	C-61-395	**69**
C-61-238	**518**	C-61-396	**70**
C-61-240	**254**	C-61-397	**305**
C-61-241	**283**; 50	C-61-399	**504**; 12
C-61-242	**524**	C-61-400	**476**; 17, 53, 54
C-61-245	**536**	C-61-401	**546**; 24
C-61-246	**535**; 23, **(115)**	C-61-403	**547**; 24
C-61-247	**522**	C-61-404	**470**; 50
C-61-256	**500**; 12	C-61-405	**577**; 65
C-61-259	**566**	C-61-406	**410**
C-61-260	**565**	C-61-407	**563**
C-61-262	**273**	C-61-408	**484**
C-61-273	**264**	C-61-412	**580**; 65
C-61-277	**517**	C-61-414	**205**; 13
C-61-279	**217**; 22	C-61-415	**381**; 14, 67
C-61-280	**(611)**	C-61-416	**426**; 33
C-61-281	**545**	C-61-417	**118**; 34
C-61-284	**632**; 14[18]	C-61-418	**117**; 33, 34, **(173)**

C-61-421	**123**; 38	C-61-480 a	**330d**
C-61-422	**140**	C-61-480 b	**330e**
C-61-423	**125**; 41–42	C-61-480 c	**330c**
C-61-424	**132**; 48, 49	C-61-480 d	**330a**
C-61-425	**131**; 48, 49	C-61-480 e	**330b**
C-61-426	**115**	C-61-485	**680**; 2, 34
C-61-427	**113**; 26, **(403)**	C-61-488	**630**
C-61-428	**389**; 18	C-61-489	**637**
C-61-429	**385**; 17, 18[31], **(78)**	C-61-490	**634**; 14[18]
C-61-430	**586**; 65	C-61-491	**648**; 65, 72
C-61-432	**649**; 73	C-61-492	**152**
C-61-433	**146**; 24		
C-61-434	**(143)**	C-62-254	**588**; 65
C-61-435	**(145)**	C-62-255	**539**
C-61-436	**147**; 24	C-62-256	**525**
C-61-437	**(143)**	C-62-257	**605**; 22
C-61-438	**(149)**	C-62-258	**623**
C-61-439	**(149)**	C-62-259	**569**; 65
C-61-440	**148**; 24	C-62-260	**596**
C-61-441	**142**; 24	C-62-261	**595**
C-61-442	**145**; 24	C-62-262	**559**; 25
C-61-443	**(149)**	C-62-264	**591**; 65
C-61-444	**(144)**	C-62-265	**568**
C-61-445	**144**; 24	C-62-271	**626**
C-61-446	**149**; 24	C-62-272	**27**; **(255)**
C-61-447	**138**; 12, **(504)**	C-62-275	**(664)**
C-61-450	**127**; 45	C-62-277	**672**; 75, 77
C-61-451	**136**; 39	C-62-278	**378**; 10
C-61-459	**341**; 17, 18	C-62-279	**669**
C-61-460	**279**; 17	C-62-283	**(626)**
C-61-461	**380**; 14	C-62-284	**(620)**
C-61-462	**354a, b**	C-62-293	**587**; 65
C-61-463	**226**	C-62-294	**583**
C-61-464	**312**	C-62-295	**585**; 65
C-61-465	**542**; 23	C-62-296	**581**
C-61-467	**121**; 37, 38	C-62-301	**317**
C-61-468	**(121)**	C-62-304	**223**
C-61-469	**134**; 55	C-62-305	**635**
C-61-470	**120**; 34, 36	C-62-306	**552**; 25
C-61-471	**373**; 9	C-62-307	**256**
C-61-472	**(410)**	C-62-317	**505**; 12
C-61-473	**394**; 26	C-62-321	**365a**
C-61-474	**331b**	C-62-322	**344**; 30
C-61-475 a	**298c**	C-62-325	**593**
C-61-475 b	**298e**	C-62-337	**81**; (410)
C-61-475 c	**298b**	C-62-338	**105**; 24
C-61-475 d	**298a**	C-62-339	**103**; 24
C-61-475 e	**298d**	C-62-340	**102**; 24
C-61-476	**369**	C-62-342	**88**; 41
C-61-478	**74**; 143	C-62-344	**101**; 24

C-62-345	17^{24}	
C-62-346	17^{24}	
C-62-347	**107**	
C-62-348	**520**	
C-62-350	**556**; 24	
C-62-351	**584**; 65	
C-62-352	**589**; 65	
C-62-353	**416**; 33	
C-62-354	**628**	
C-62-356	**417**; 33	
C-62-357	**(415)**	
C-62-358	**(415)**	
C-62-362	**663**; 76	
C-62-363	**322**	
C-62-364	**230**	
C-62-365	**234**; 31	
C-62-367	**221a**	
C-62-368	**221b**	
C-62-370	**262**	
C-62-371	**225**	
C-62-372	**247**	
C-62-373	**662**; 76	
C-62-374	**414**; 31	
C-62-505	**(413)**	Well 1962-5
C-62-582	10^5	Well 1962-5
C-62-618	22^{48}	Well 1962-5
C-62-645	10^5	Well 1962-5
C-62-651	68^{221}	Well 1962-5
C-62-652	68^{221}	Well 1962-5
C-62-653	68^{221}	Well 1962-5
C-62-654	68^{221}	Well 1962-5
C-62-655	68^{221}	Well 1962-5
C-62-673	10^5	Well 1962-5
C-62-674	10^5	Well 1962-5
C-62-675	10^5	Well 1962-5
C-62-685	**560**; 25	
C-62-692	**233**	
C-62-696	**486**	
C-62-699	**555**; 25	
C-62-700	**558**; 25	
C-62-706	**529**	
C-62-713	**530**	
C-62-716	**415**; 33	
C-62-720	**490**; 58	
C-62-722	**272**	
C-62-723	**528**	
C-62-730	**235**; 33	
C-62-731	**216**; 22	
C-62-733	**222**	
C-62-738	**420**; 33	

C-62-743	**540**
C-62-755	**661a, b**; 76
C-62-756	**249**
C-62-758	**519**
C-62-760	**270**
C-62-761	**210**; 17
C-62-762	**239**; 50
C-62-763	**23**
C-62-764	**22**
C-62-765	**31**
C-62-766	**28**
C-62-767	**32**; **(532)**
C-62-768	**29**
C-62-769	**25**; 33
C-62-770	**26a**; 50, 111, **(241)**
C-62-771	**30**
C-62-772	**443**; 39
C-62-773	**401**
C-62-774	**533**; 22
C-62-778	**515**; 17
C-62-779	**488**
C-62-780	**487**; 57
C-62-781	**421**; 33
C-62-782	**482**
C-62-783	**445**
C-62-784	**611**; 22
C-62-786	**629**
C-62-788	**509**; 65
C-62-789	**510**; 65
C-62-790	**513**
C-62-793	**265**
C-62-795	**567**
C-62-799	**575**; 65
C-62-804	**268**
C-62-805	**523**
C-62-813	**526**
C-62-817	**564**
C-62-820	**592**
C-62-821	**573**; 65
C-62-826	**604**; 22
C-62-827	**537**; 22
C-62-828	**618**; 22
C-62-830	**532**; **(32)**
C-62-831	**531**
C-62-832	**541**; 24
C-62-836	**643**; 68
C-62-841	**221c**
C-62-843	**320**
C-62-849	**574**; 65
C-62-851	**511**; 65

C-62-852	**315**; 28	
C-62-854	**(596)**	
C-62-864	**561**	
C-62-872	**229**	
C-62-874	**391**	
C-62-880	**616**; 22	
C-62-938	**213**; 17	
C-62-939	**236**; 39	
C-62-940	**220**	
C-62-943	**302**	
C-62-944	**331a**	
C-62-945	**601**	
C-62-946	**206**; 13	
C-62-947	**228**	
C-62-948	**24**	
C-63-654	66[217]	Grave 1963-9
C-63-662	66[217]	Grave 1963-8
C-63-737	**(198)**	
C-63-742	**(437)**	
C-64-35	**316**	
C-64-37	**458**; 46	
C-64-44	**424**; 33	
C-64-45	**576**; 65	
C-64-47	**512**; 65	
C-64-48	**582**	
C-64-59	**258**	
C-64-60	**664**; 76	
C-64-61	**250**	
C-64-65	**374**; 10	
C-64-66	**(596)**	
C-64-69	**364**; 31	
C-64-75	**309**	
C-64-76	**514**	
C-64-77	**571**	
C-64-91	**600**	
C-64-145	12[13]	Water-channel 1964-1
C-64-146	12[13]	Water-channel 1964-1
C-64-162	126	Water-channel 1964-1
C-64-176	126, **(283)**	Water-channel 1964-1
C-64-177	**(277)**	Water-channel 1964-1
C-64-186	**617**; 22	
C-64-188	**290**	
C-64-191	**570**; 65	
C-64-192	**358**	
C-64-196	**269**	
C-64-197	**308**	
C-64-199	**614**; 22	
C-64-200	**612**; 22	

C-64-201	**613**; 22	
C-64-207	**356**	
C-64-208	**296**; 50	
C-64-213	**370**; 178	
C-64-216	**211**; 17	
C-64-217	**483**	
C-64-219	**295**; 50	
C-64-221	**671**; 77	
C-64-222	**631**; 68	
C-64-223	**215**	
C-64-224	**333**; 61	
C-64-225	**297**; 50	
C-64-226 a	**287h**; 13–14, 30[78]	
C-64-226 b+l	**287b**; 13–14, 30[78]	
C-64-226 c	**287m**; 13–14, 30[78]	
C-64-226 d	**287i**; 13–14, 30[78]	
C-64-226 e	**287e**; 13–14, 30[78]	
C-64-226 f	**287f**; 13–14, 30[78]	
C-64-226 g	**287l**; 13–14, 30[78]	
C-64-226 h	**287j**; 13–14, 30[78]	
C-64-226 j	**287d**; 13–14, 30[78]	
C-64-225 k	**287g**; 13–14, 30[78]	
C-64-226 m	**287k**; 13–14, 30[78]	
C-64-226 n	**287c**; 13–14, 30[78]	
C-64-259	30[78]	Water-channel 1964-1
C-64-278	23[51]	Water-channel 1964-1
C-64-312	**329**	
C-64-396	**285**; 57, 58	
C-64-397	**395**; 26	
C-64-399	**340**	
C-64-398	136	
C-64-400	129[8]	
C-64-401	**313**; 28	
C-64-402	**423**; 33	
C-64-404	**242**	
C-64-405	**503**; 12	
C-64-407	**280**; 33	
C-64-408	**259**; 179	
C-64-409	**366a, c**; 53	
C-64-410	**379**; 13	
C-64-411	**209**; 13	
C-64-414	**246**	
C-64-417	129[8]	
C-64-418	**366b**; 53	
C-64-420	**95**; 47	
C-64-421	**83**; 34, 36	
C-64-422	**624**; **(261)**	
C-64-423	**82**; 31	
C-64-424	**251**	
C-64-429	**489**	

C-64-430	**207**	
C-64-431	**639**; 68	
C-64-432	**674**	
C-64-433	**109**; 74	
C-64-434	**110**; 75	
C-64-435	**112**	
C-64-436	**108**; 68	
C-64-437	**98**; 17, 55, (**200**)	
C-64-438	**325**	
C-64-439	**347**; 30	
C-64-440	**357**	
C-64-442	**307**	
C-64-446	**377**; 10	
C-64-447	**491**; 60, 61	
C-64-467	**375**; 10	
C-64-468	**678**; 2, 34	
C-64-470	(**267**)	
C-64-471	**661c**	
C-64-472	**661h**	
C-64-473	**670**; 76	
C-64-474	**668**; 77	
C-64-475	**642**; 68	
C-64-476	**275**; 17	
C-64-477	**359**	
C-64-478	**339**	
C-65-30	**599**	
C-65-31	(**615**)	
C-65-32 a	**608**; 22	
C-65-32 b	(**608**)	
C-65-33	**615**; 22	
C-65-34	**620**	
C-65-36	**610**; 22	
C-65-38	**261**; (**297**), 179, (**625**)	
C-65-41	**46**; 52	
C-65-42	**45**; 138	
C-65-117	**43**; 30	
C-65-118	(**43**)	
C-65-119	**40**	
C-65-120	**42**	
C-65-121	**41**	
C-65-122	**37**; 22, 23, 24	
C-65-123	**36**; 22, 23, 24	
C-65-124	**35**; 22, 23, 24	
C-65-125	**44**; (**51**)	
C-65-126	**33**; 17	
C-65-127	**34**; 17	
C-65-128	**48**; 65	
C-65-167	129[8]	
C-65-168	**603**; 22	
C-65-169	**390**; 18	
C-65-170	**607**; 22	
C-65-171	**413**; 31	
C-65-172	**52**; 65	
C-65-173	**54**; 39, 41, 65, (**575**)	
C-65-174	**50**	
C-65-175	**625**	
C-65-291 a	**292b**; 26	
C-65-291 c	**292c**; 26	
C-65-292	**437**; 36	
C-65-293	**497**	
C-65-294	**159**	
C-65-297	**644**; 68	
C-65-303	**462**; 4, 46	
C-65-307	**521**; 22, 179	
C-65-309	**478**; 17, 53, 54	
C-65-312	**327**	
C-65-313	**371**	
C-65-314	107[27]	
C-65-315	**397**; 26	
C-65-316	107[27]	
C-65-318	107[27]	
C-65-319	**472**; 4, 50	
C-65-320	**199**	
C-65-321	107[27]	
C-65-322	107	
C-65-323	107	
C-65-324	**667**; 77	
C-65-377	63[209], (**454**)	Well 1965-3
C-65-387	34[87]	Well 1965-3
C-65-400	(**645**)	Well 1965-3
C-65-410	**474**; 54	
C-65-412	**351**	
C-65-414	**324**	
C-65-417	**360b**; 30	
C-65-419	**314**; 28	
C-65-421	**440**	
C-65-422	**425**; 33	
C-65-423	**346**; 30	
C-65-424	**362**	
C-65-427	**284**	
C-65-429	**289b**	
C-65-432	**289a**	
C-65-434	**291**	
C-65-438	**655**; 74	
C-65-439	**363a**; 31	
C-65-440	**294a**	
C-65-441	**282**	
C-65-442	**237**; 39, 183[31]	

C-65-444	**319**; 31	
C-65-445	**204**; 13	
C-65-446	**218**; 22	
C-65-447	**219**; 22	
C-65-448	**306**; 77	
C-65-449	**241**; 50	
C-65-450	**293**	
C-65-451	**208**	
C-65-452	**321**	
C-65-453	**318**; 31	
C-65-457	**232**	
C-65-458	**266**	
C-65-459	**224**	
C-65-460	**267**	
C-65-465	**496**	
C-65-469	**609**; 22	
C-65-472	**244**; 50	
C-65-473	**469**	
C-65-474	**652**; 73	
C-65-475	**647**; 67, 72	
C-65-476	**386**; 17	
C-65-477	**248**	
C-65-481	**80**; 13[17], 30	
C-65-486	**191**; 4, 9	
C-65-487	**452**; 43	
C-65-488	**447**; 41	
C-65-489	**202**; 41, 58	
C-65-490	**197**; 52	
C-65-491	**287a**; 13–14, 30[78]	
C-65-492	**263**	
C-65-493	**572**	
C-65-494	**126**[2]	
C-65-496	**360a**; 30	
C-65-498	**435**; 36	
C-65-499	**276**; 17	
C-65-500	**47**; 12, (**501**)	
C-65-501	**274**	
C-65-506	**294b**	
C-65-507	**281**; 33, 134	
C-65-509	**26b**; 50, 111, (**241**)	
C-65-511	**499**	
C-65-512	**252**	
C-65-514	**196**	
C-65-516	**96**; 53	
C-65-517	**78**; 17, 18[31], (**385**)	
C-65-518	**346b**; 30	
C-65-519	**260**	
C-65-520	**227**	
C-65-521	136	
C-65-522 a	**300a**	
C-65-522 b	**300c**	
C-65-522 c	**300b**	
C-65-523	**299**	
C-65-525	**454**; 43	
C-65-526	**231**	
C-65-529	**393**; 19	cistern 1965-1
C-65-530	**657**; 74	
C-65-531	**656**; 74	
C-65-532	**645**	
C-65-533	**646**; 67, 72	
C-65-535	**84**; 34, 36	
C-65-537	**97**; 17, 53, 54	
C-65-538	**92**; 45	
C-65-539	**87**; 38	
C-65-540	**94**; 47	
C-65-541	136	
C-65-543	**598**	
C-65-545	**328a**; 58	
C-65-546	**99**; 12, (**138, 163**)	
C-65-547	**111**; 75	
C-65-548	**602**	
C-65-549	**79**	
C-65-550	**85**; 38	
C-65-551	**86**; 38	
C-65-552	**89**; 41	
C-65-554	**93**; 45	
C-65-555	**90**; 43	
C-65-556	**91**; 43	
C-65-557	**76**	
C-65-558	**77**;(**387**)	
C-65-559	**104**; 24	
C-65-560	**106**; 24	
C-65-563	**192**; 13, 111	
C-65-564	**200**; 17, (**90**)	
C-65-565	**194**; 46	
C-65-566	**198**; 52	
C-65-567	**201**; 56	
C-65-568	**195**; 49	
C-65-569	**606**; 22	
C-65-576	**641**; 68	
C-65-577	**506**; 12	
C-65-579	**507**; 12, 25	
C-65-580	**38**	
C-65-581	**39**	
C-65-582	**51**	
C-65-583	**55**	
C-65-584	**56**	
C-65-585	**58**	
C-65-586	**57**	
C-65-587	**59**	

C-65-588	**60**	
C-65-589	**53**; 65	
C-65-590	**100**; 24, (**545**)	
C-65-591	**162**; 48–49	
C-65-592	**157**; 26, 41	
C-65-593	**166**; (**140**)	
C-65-594	**167**; (**140**)	
C-65-595	**168**; 24	
C-65-596	**169**; 24	
C-65-597	**171**; 24	
C-65-598	**170**; 24	
C-65-599	**163**; 12	
C-65-600	**164**; 12	
C-65-601	**165**; 12	
C-65-602	**154**; 18	
C-65-603	**155**; 18	
C-65-604	**161**; 45	
C-65-606	**158**; 30	
C-65-607	**160**; 42	
C-65-608	**156**; 18, 19	
C-65-609	**473**; 4, 50, 52	
C-65-610	**492**; 60	
C-65-611	**348**; 30	
C-65-612	**349**; 30	
C-65-613	**363b**; 31	
C-65-614	**343**	
C-65-615	**352**	
C-65-621	**399**; 26, (**454**)	
C-65-622	**398**; 26	
C-65-623	**400**; 26, (**454**)	
C-65-624	**453**; 43	
C-65-625	**436**; 36	
C-65-626	**494**; 60	
C-65-627	**434**; 36, 65	
C-65-628	**404**; 26, 28, 41	
C-65-629	**448**; 42	
C-65-630	**479**	
C-65-631	**477**; 17, 53, 54	
C-65-638	191[35]	
C-65-639	**681**; 2, 34	
C-65-642	**636**	
C-65-644	**459**	
C-65-645	**460**; 46	
C-65-646	**461**; 46	
C-65-647	**463**; 4, 46	
C-65-648	**498**; (**437**)	
C-65-649	**661d**	
C-65-650	**49**; 69, 73	
C-65-651	**172**; 73	
C-65-652	**75**; 14, 67	

C-65-653	(**495**)	
C-65-654	**345**; 30	
C-65-656	**495**; 60	
C-66-175	63[209]	Well 1965-3
C-66-222	56	Well 1965-3
C-67-136	(**674**)	
C-67-161	72[230]	
C-68-58	22[46]	
C-68-120	68	
C-68-159	**619**	
C-68-160	107[27]	
C-68-198	**253**	
C-68-200	**497**	
C-68-201	**342**; 26	
C-68-218	**245**	
C-68-244	**73**; 143	
C-68-280	**193**	
C-68-304	**658**; 75	
C-68-305	**597**	
C-68-331	129[8]	
C-68-339	**353**	
C-68-349	(**619**)	
C-68-350	**665**; 76	
C-69-79	**654**	
C-69-102	72	
C-69-103	**594**; 66	
C-69-180	**292**; 26	
C-69-182	**292**; 26	
C-69-184	**361**; 31	
C-69-185	**238**; 50	
C-69-186	**387**; 43[134], (**77**)	
C-69-253	**650**; 73	
C-69-262	**412**; 30	
C-69-263	**446**; 41	
C-69-264	**439**; 37	
C-69-265	**466**; 47, 48	
C-69-266	**455**; 43[134], 45	
C-69-267	(**441**), 43[134]	
C-69-268	**450**; 43	
C-69-269	**451**; 43	
C-69-270	**402**	
C-69-271	**441**; 38	
C-69-297	**464**; 37, 47, 48	
C-69-298	**651**; 73	
C-69-299 a	**288b**; 37	
C-69-299 b	**288a**; 37	

C-69-299 c	**288d**; 37	
C-69-299 d	**288c**; 37	
C-69-301	54[177]	
C-69-302	**311**	
C-69-313	**481**	
C-69-314	**382**; 14, 67	
C-69-315	**666**; 76, 77	
C-69-320	**493**; 60	
C-70-2	**(21)**	
C-70-3	**20**; 20, 25	
C-70-203	**277**; 17	
C-70-204 a	**304b**	
C-70-204 b	**304a**	
C-70-205	**471**; 50	
C-70-206	**396**; 26	
C-70-212	**182**; 12,(**378, 506**)	
C-70-213	**183**; 12, (**378, 506**)	
C-70-214	**184**; 12, (**378, 506**)	
C-70-237	**485**	
C-70-352	**372**	
C-70-366	**405**; 2, 28	
C-70-367	**350**	
C-70-368	**338**	
C-70-369	**337**	
C-70-392	**438**; 37	
C-70-393	**384**	
C-70-477	**(5)**	
C-70-478	**8**; 26	
C-70-479	**1**; 17	
C-70-480	**2**; 17	
C-70-481	**18**; 20, 22	
C-70-482	**19**; 20, 22	
C-70-483	**15**; 20	
C-70-484	**(10)**	
C-70-485	**9**; 20	
C-70-486	**10**; 20	
C-70-487	**(10)**	
C-70-488	**(12)**	
C-70-489	**14**; 20	
C-70-490	**11**; 20	
C-70-491	**(15)**	
C-70-492	**(11)**	
C-70-493	**(16)**	
C-70-494	**(13)**	
C-70-495	**(15)**	
C-70-496	**17**; 20	
C-70-497	**(12)**	
C-70-498	**(12)**	
C-70-499	**(16)**	
C-70-500	**16**; 20	
C-70-501	**12**; 20	
C-70-502	**13**; 20	
C-70-503	**(10)**	
C-70-504	**(14)**	
C-70-505	**(9)**	
C-70-506	**(14)**	
C-70-507	**(15)**	
C-70-508	**(15)**	
C-70-509	**(13)**	
C-70-510	**(13)**	
C-70-511	**(14)**	
C-70-512	**(12)**	
C-70-513	**(15)**	
C-70-514	**(14)**	
C-70-515	**(21)**	
C-70-516	**(21)**	
C-70-517	**21**; 20, 25	
C-70-518	**177**; 50	
C-70-519	**178**; 58	
C-70-520	**176**; 49	
C-70-521	**4**; 26	
C-70-522	**3**; 26	
C-70-523	**6**; 26	
C-70-524	**5**; 26	
C-70-525	**7**; 26	
C-70-526	**(7)**	
C-70-563	**173**; 34, (**117**)	
C-70-564	**174**; 34	
C-70-565	**175**; 33, 34, (**119**)	
C-70-566	**179**; 12[15], 41, 58	
C-70-567	**180**; 12[15], 41, 58	
C-70-568	**181**; 12[15], 41, 58	
C-70-596	**673**; 75	
C-70-597	**406**; 2, 28	
C-70-598	**407**; 2, 28	
C-70-599	**409**; 2, 28	
C-70-600	**408**; 2, 28	
C-71-3	44[142]	Well 1971-1
C-71-15	73	Well 1971-1
C-71-46	43, (**90**)	Drain 1971-1
C-71-48	(**659**)	Drain 1971-1
C-71-50	41	Drain 1971-1
C-71-51	42	Drain 1971-1
C-71-52	41	Drain 1971-1
C-71-53	41	Drain 1971-1
C-71-73	47[157]	Drain 1971-1
C-71-75	24[60]	Drain 1971-1
C-71-87	(**410**)	

C-71-88	**653**; 73	
C-71-89	37[102]	Drain 1971-1
C-71-92	37[99]	Drain 1971-1
C-71-95	38[104]	Drain 1971-1
C-71-97	44	Drain 1971-1
C-71-105	**(410)**	Drain 1971-1
C-71-108	38[104]	Drain 1971-1
C-71-115	74	Drain 1971-1
C-71-116	74	Drain 1971-1
C-71-136	**449**; 42	
C-71-137	**456**; 45, 73	
C-71-170	**480**	
C-71-171	**403**	
C-71-173	**660**	
C-71-174	**467**; 48	
C-71-175	**411**	
C-71-176	**185**; 41	
C-71-177	**188**; 52	
C-71-178	**189**; 52	
C-71-180	**190**; 73	
C-71-181	**186**; 42	
C-71-191	58[192], 126[5]	Drain 1971-1
C-71-194	3[17]	Drain 1971-1
C-71-201	**335**	
C-71-238	**368**	
C-71-259	**(339)**	
C-71-266	42	Drain 1971-1
C-71-273	44, 44[140, 144]	Drain 1971-1
C-71-357	53[175]	Drain 1971-1
C-71-521	18	Drain 1971-1
C-71-522	63[209], **(480)**	Drain 1971-1
C-71-525	75	Drain 1971-1
C-71-541	72	Drain 1971-1
C-71-569	**212**; 17	
C-71-570	129[8]	
C-71-581	**(339)**	
C-71-583	106	
C-71-585	**187**; 43	
C-72-53	**468**; 49	
C-72-56	**621**	
C-72-86	**428**; 33	
C-72-87	**429**; 33	
C-72-88	**427**; 33	
C-72-89	**430**; 33	
C-72-120	72, **(151)**	Pit 1972-1
C-72-121	**(75)**	Pit 1972-1
C-72-149	**(244)**	
C-72-195	**640**; 68	
C-72-196	**214**	
C-72-210	**431**; 33	
C-72-211	**432**; 33, **(117, 118)**	
C-72-212	129[8]	
C-72-215	**392**; 18	
C-72-216	**(441)**	
C-72-217	**(410)**	
C-72-218	**(410)**	
C-72-219	**442**; 38	
C-72-220	**457**; 45	
C-72-221	**(464)**	
C-72-222	**(457)**	
C-72-241 a+c	**328c**; 58	
C-72-241 b	**328d**; 58	
C-72-241 d	**328b**; 58	
C-72-241 e	**328e**; 58	
C-72-244	**240**; 50	
C-72-245	**433**; 35[92], 36	
C-72-246	136	
C-72-254	**289c**	
C-72-269	**355**	
C-72-282	76[254]	
C-73-25	**376**; 10	
C-73-28	**286**	
C-73-58	**633**; 14[18], 67	
C-73-59	**332**	
C-73-99	**301**; 30	
C-73-177	191[32], 192	
C-73-186	**(564)**	
C-73-191	**(458)**	
C-73-259	**326**; 53	
C-73-260	**310**	
C-73-301	34[88]	
C-73-302	**622**	
C-73-305	**383**; 14, 67	
C-73-306	**367**; 53	
C-73-307	**659**; 75	
C-73-316	**465**; 47, 48	
C-73-320	**502**; 12	
C-73-327	**303a**	
C-73-328	**303b**	
C-73-355	**354c**	
C-73-356	**336**	
C-73-357	**255**	
C-73-358	**638**	
C-73-359	**422**; 33	
C-73-360	**323**	
C-74-115	63[208]	

C-75-91	63[209]	Well 1975-4
C-75-156	24[61]	Well 1975-4
C-75-157	24[61]	Well 1975-4
C-75-161	33[84]	Well 1975-4
C-75-162	33[84, 85]	Well 1975-4
C-75-167	58[195]	Well 1975-4
C-75-168	26[69]	Well 1975-4
C-75-171	42	Well 1975-4
C-75-172	42	Well 1975-4
C-75-173	42[126]	Well 1975-4
C-75-175	44, 44[140]	Well 1975-4
C-75-177	58[195]	Well 1975-4
C-75-183	10[10]	Well 1975-4
C-75-222	63[210]	
C-75-281	**444**; 39	
C-75-285	28[73], (**157, 404**)	Well 1975-5
C-75-301	75	Well 1975-4
C-75-302	72, (**646**)	Well 1975-4
C-75-303	42[129]	Well 1975-1
C-75-306	76	Pit 1975-1
C-75-320	**661e–g**	
C-1976-114	18, 19, (**156**)	
C-1976-152	(**671**)	
C-1976-198	(**641**)	
C-1976-279 a	(**379**)	
C-1976-279 b	(**379**)	
C-1978-255	(**642**)	
C-1979-115	34[89]	Cistern 1979-1
C-1979-116	37[99], 38[104]	Cistern 1979-1
C-1979-117	37[99]	Cistern 1979-1
C-1979-140	73, (**654**)	Cistern 1979-1
C-1979-145	38[104]	Cistern 1979-1
C-1979-243	(**75**)	Cistern 1979-1
C-1980-137	(**193**)	
C-1981-160	192	
CP-989	134[20]	
CP-1930	(**461**)	
CP-2355	(**252**)	
KN 162	77[260], (**667**)	
KP 213	35[92]	
KP 237	63[209]	
KP 548	33[82]	

KP 549	33[82]
KP 671	63[209]
KP 700	63[209]
KP 703	33[86]
KP 1170	(**283**)
KP 1329	23
KP 2424	(**275**)
KP 2429	(**275**)
KP 2702	35[92]
KT 3-4	(**610**)
KT 9-7	(**622**)
KT 9-11	(**612**)
KT 9-25	(**618**)
KT 9-32	(**618**)
KT 9-64	(**620**)
KV 372	22
KV 373	22
KV 376	23
KV 379	23
KV 551	22
KV 555	22
KV 627	22
KV 628	22
KV 642	23
KV 694	(**293**)
KV 841	22
KV 914	63[208]
KV 1257	23

The following MF numbers are those either of pottery or of terracottas from the same or similar molds.

MF 2524	(**615**)
MF 3892	(**612**)
MF 8343	(**615**)
MF 9500	68[225], (**631**)
MF 12152	(**612**)
MF-69-65	(**616**)
MF-72-20	(**615**)

T 568	37[101]	Grave 321
T 569	37[101]	Grave 321
T 1138	(**487**)	Grave 258
T 1159	58[195]	Grave 491
T 1513	(**624**)	Grave 157
T 1557	57[190]	Grave 168
T 1559	57[190]	Grave 168

T 1586	57[190]	Grave 157
T 1640	**(62)**	Grave 344
T 1662	63[208]	Grave 336
T 1665	**(40)**	Grave 265
T 1673	57[189]	Grave 271
T 1713	**(43)**	Grave 296
T 1864	57[190]	Grave 225
T 2369	58[195]	Deposit 36
T 2371	58[195]	Deposit 36
T 2484	63[209]	Grave 457
T 2451	26[69]	Grave 444
T 2453	26[69]	Grave 444
T 2483	**(139)**	Grave 457
T 2484	63[209]	Grave 457
T 2637	37[101]	Grave 429
T 2638	37[101]	Grave 429
T 2701	55[186]	Grave 495

T 2716	55[185]	Grave 496
T 2804	**(44)**	Grave 297
T 2871	33[83]	Grave 388
T 2902	**(567)**	Grave 253
T 2951	**(565)**	Grave 200
T 2980	**(484)**	Grave 333
T 3025	36[98]	Grave 294
T 3055	57[190]	Grave 224
T 3201	**(561)**	Grave 160
T 3202	**(500)**	Grave 160
T 3241	57[190]	Grave 159

Lot 2169:1	**675**; 2, 34
Lot 3215:1	**677**; 2, 34
Lot 6191:1	**676**; 2, 34
Lot 6642:1	**679**; 2, 34

BIBLIOGRAPHY FOR FINDSPOTS AT CORINTH OUTSIDE THE SANCTUARY

NORTH CEMETERY: *Corinth* XIII

POTTERS' QUARTER: *Corinth* XV, iii

OTHER CORINTH EXCAVATIONS:

Well 1931-7	New Museum well X: *Corinth* VII, iii, deposit no. 41
Well 1931-8	New Museum well Z: *Corinth* VII, iii, deposit no. 42
Well 1931-14	Asklepieion, votive deposit V: *Corinth* VII, iii, deposit no. 20
Well 1933-1	South Stoa well II: *Corinth* VII, iii, deposit no. 95
Well 1933-2	South Stoa well V: *Corinth* VII, iii, deposit no. 98
Well 1933-3	South Stoa well VII: *Corinth* VII, iii, deposit no. 99
Well 1934-3	South Stoa well IV: *Corinth* VII, iii, deposit no. 97
Well 1934-5	South Stoa well X: *Corinth* VII, iii, deposit no. 102
Well 1934-10	Well at E–K:30–37: Pease, *Hesperia* 6, 1937, pp. 257–316; *Corinth* VII, iii, deposit no. 10
Grave 1934-11	Anaploga, East grave, aloni of Skliris: unpublished
Fill 1934-1	South Stoa, deposit in shop I: *Corinth* VII, iii, deposit no. 94
Well 1935-3	South Stoa well XVI: *Corinth* VII, iii, deposit no. 108
Well 1935-4	Well in South Stoa terrace: unpublished
Well 1935-7	St. John's well: *Corinth* VII, iii, deposit no. 14[1]
Well 1936-1	Well at S:26–27 (V:20): unpublished
Well 1936-3	South Basilica well at IV-15: *Corinth* VII, iii, deposit no. 15
Well 1936-13	South Stoa well XX: *Corinth* VII, iii, deposit no. 111
Well 1937-1	Well at b–c:18–19: *Corinth* VII, iii, deposit no. 79
Well 1937-2	Well at Q:18 (T:17–18): *AJA* 41, 1937, p. 547; Weinberg, *Corinth* VII, i, nos. 153–173
Well 1937-3	Well at I–J:24–25: Campbell, *Hesperia* 7, 1938, pp. 557–611; *Corinth* VII, iii, deposit no. 3
Drain 1937-1	Drain at b–f:19–20: *Corinth* VII, iii, deposit no. 80
Pit 1937-1	Pit at N–O:21–23: *Corinth* VII, iii, deposit no. 90
Well 1938-1	South Stoa well XXX: *Corinth* VII, iii, deposit no. 115
Well 1939-1	Museum West well at K:23: *Corinth* VII, iii, deposit no. 8; *Corinth* VII, i, nos. 367, 372
Well 1940-1	New Museum East well A: *Corinth* VII, iii, deposit no. 36; Weinberg, *Hesperia* 17, 1948, group E, pp. 229–235
Well 1946-2	New Museum East well F: Weinberg, group D, pp. 214–229
Well 1940-6	Tile Works well A: *Corinth* VII, iii, deposit no. 27
Well 1946-1	South Stoa well XV: *Corinth* VII, iii, deposit no. 107
Well 1947-2	Southeast Building well at P:27: *Corinth* VII, iii, deposit no. 81
Well 1947-3	Southeast Building well at N-20: *Corinth* VII, iii, deposit no. 46
Well 1947-4	Southeast Building well at I:23: *Corinth* VII, iii, deposit no. 2
Well 1947-5	South Stoa well XXVII: *Corinth* VII, iii, deposit no. 113
Well 1948-2	South Stoa well IX: *Corinth* VII, iii, deposit no. 101
Well 1948-3	South Stoa well XIX: *Corinth* VII, iii, deposit no. 110
Well 1948-4	South Stoa well XXII: *Corinth* VII, iii, deposit no. 112
Well 1953-1	Well at T–U:2: Brann, *Hesperia* 25, 1956, pp. 350–374; *Corinth* VII, iii, deposit no. 1
Well 1953-2	Well at NW corner of Temple E: *Corinth* VII, iii, deposit no. 43
Well 1960-4	Well by excavation dump: *Corinth* VII, iii, deposit no. 38
Well 1960-6	Baths of Aphrodite well II: *Corinth* VII, iii, deposit no. 34
Grave 1960-7	Grave on road to Acrocorinth: *Corinth* VII, iii, deposit no. 58

---

[1] The exact location of and pottery from well 1935-7 are unclear. See the discussion in *Corinth* VII, iii, pp. 201–202 (deposit 14).
C. K. Williams has suggested that C-35-637 to -644 ought to derive from this well.

Grave 1960-11   Grave at Hexamilia: Lawrence, *Hesperia* 33, 1964, grave E, pp. 94–101

Well 1962-5   Anaploga well: Lawrence, *Corinth* VII, ii, pp. 61–167

Grave 1963-8   Anaploga cistern area grave 1, upper burial: *Corinth* VII, iii, deposit no. 65B;
                 Pemberton, *Hesperia* 54, 1985, pp. 298–299

Grave 1963-9   Anaploga cistern area grave 2: Pemberton, *Hesperia* 54, 1985, pp. 296–297

Water channel   Vrysoula deposit: Pemberton, *Hesperia* 39, 1970, pp. 265–307
   1964-1

Well 1965-3   Katsoulis well, manhole 3: unpublished

Grave 1968-1   Grave west of Babbius monument: Williams, *Hesperia* 39, 1970, pp. 16–20

Well 1971-1   South Stoa terrace, under stylobate, north of pier 4: unpublished

Drain 1971-1   Drain between Buildings I–II: Williams, *Hesperia* 41, 1972, pp. 154–163

Pit 1972-1   Pit west of well room, Building III: Williams, *Hesperia* 42, 1973, pp. 23–25

Well 1974-1   Well at SE corner of grid 70:D: unpublished

Well 1974-4   Votive "pit": Williams, *Hesperia* 45, 1976, pp. 117–124

Well 1975-5   Well in Centaur Bath: *ibid.* p. 109, n. 7

Pit 1975-1   Amphora Pit: *ibid.* pp. 104–107

Cistern 1979-1   South Stoa, south of Suites XX and XXI: Williams, *Hesperia* 49, 1980, pp. 120–121

LOT LIST: PUBLISHED VASES AND CITED SHERDS

The Lot List is a listing by Demeter iot numbers of all the vases from each lot published in this volume. Page references are listed in parentheses for any discussion of date or contents of a Lot, not easily retrievable by a specific catalogue entry or in the shape study discussion of an entry. The inventory numbers are followed by numbered sherds left in the Lot. Bold numbers in parentheses indicate references to catalogue entries.

<table>
<tr><td colspan="2">Lot 869</td></tr>
<tr><td>C-64-69</td><td>364</td></tr>
<tr><td colspan="2">Lot 871</td></tr>
<tr><td>C-61-154</td><td>388</td></tr>
<tr><td>C-61-156</td><td>543</td></tr>
<tr><td>C-61-162</td><td>538</td></tr>
<tr><td>C-61-165</td><td>550</td></tr>
<tr><td>C-61-166</td><td>557</td></tr>
<tr><td>C-61-167</td><td>271</td></tr>
<tr><td colspan="2">Lot 872</td></tr>
<tr><td>C-61-168</td><td>475</td></tr>
<tr><td colspan="2">Lot 874</td></tr>
<tr><td>C-61-476</td><td>369</td></tr>
<tr><td colspan="2">Lot 875</td></tr>
<tr><td>C-61-175</td><td>203</td></tr>
<tr><td>C-61-176</td><td>257</td></tr>
<tr><td>C-65-496</td><td>360</td></tr>
<tr><td colspan="2">Lot 877 (pp. 18[31], 73[239], 74)</td></tr>
<tr><td>C-61-180</td><td>551</td></tr>
<tr><td>C-61-183</td><td>562</td></tr>
<tr><td>C-61-186</td><td>615</td></tr>
<tr><td>C-61-189</td><td>578</td></tr>
<tr><td>C-61-406</td><td>410</td></tr>
<tr><td>C-61-407</td><td>563</td></tr>
<tr><td>C-61-408</td><td>484</td></tr>
<tr><td>C-61-412</td><td>580</td></tr>
<tr><td>C-61-414</td><td>205</td></tr>
<tr><td>C-61-415</td><td>381</td></tr>
<tr><td>C-61-416</td><td>426</td></tr>
<tr><td>C-61-428</td><td>389</td></tr>
<tr><td>C-61-429</td><td>385</td></tr>
<tr><td>C-61-430</td><td>586</td></tr>
<tr><td>C-61-432</td><td>649</td></tr>
<tr><td>C-61-463</td><td>226</td></tr>
<tr><td>C-61-464</td><td>312</td></tr>
<tr><td>C-61-490</td><td>634</td></tr>
</table>

<table>
<tr><td>877:1</td><td>74</td></tr>
<tr><td>877:2–10</td><td>73[239]</td></tr>
<tr><td colspan="2">Lot 878 (p. 24)</td></tr>
<tr><td>C-61-190</td><td>627</td></tr>
<tr><td>C-61-191</td><td>579</td></tr>
<tr><td>C-61-193</td><td>508</td></tr>
<tr><td>C-61-202</td><td>278</td></tr>
<tr><td>C-61-203</td><td>501</td></tr>
<tr><td>C-61-399</td><td>504</td></tr>
<tr><td>C-61-400</td><td>476</td></tr>
<tr><td>C-61-401</td><td>546</td></tr>
<tr><td>C-61-403</td><td>547</td></tr>
<tr><td>C-61-404</td><td>470</td></tr>
<tr><td>C-61-405</td><td>577</td></tr>
<tr><td>C-61-406</td><td>410</td></tr>
<tr><td>C-61-471</td><td>373</td></tr>
<tr><td>C-61-472</td><td>410</td></tr>
<tr><td colspan="2">Lot 880 (p. 73[239])</td></tr>
<tr><td colspan="2">Group 7</td></tr>
<tr><td>880:1</td><td>73[239]</td></tr>
<tr><td>880:2</td><td>73[239]</td></tr>
<tr><td colspan="2">Lot 881</td></tr>
<tr><td>C-61-219</td><td>548</td></tr>
<tr><td>C-61-220</td><td>502</td></tr>
<tr><td>C-61-473</td><td>394</td></tr>
<tr><td>C-61-474</td><td>331</td></tr>
<tr><td>C-61-475</td><td>298</td></tr>
<tr><td colspan="2">Lot 882 (p. 191[36])</td></tr>
<tr><td>C-61-478</td><td>74</td></tr>
<tr><td colspan="2">Lot 885</td></tr>
<tr><td>C-61-473</td><td>394</td></tr>
<tr><td>C-61-474</td><td>331</td></tr>
<tr><td colspan="2">Lot 886</td></tr>
<tr><td>C-61-236</td><td>365</td></tr>
<tr><td>C-61-478</td><td>74</td></tr>
</table>

Lot 887 (pp. 26[72], 89)

Group 5

887:1	89
887:2	89
887:4	89
887:5	26[72], 89

Lot 889

C-61-228	334
C-61-229	554
C-61-236	365

Lot 890

C-61-228	334
C-61-235	243
C-61-462	354
C-61-480	330
C-64-475	642

Lot 892

C-61-236	365
C-61-238	518
C-61-240	254
C-65-496	360

Lot 893

C-61-241	283
C-61-242	524
C-61-245	536
C-61-246	535
C-61-247	522
C-61-256	500
C-61-259	566
C-61-260	565
C-61-262	273
C-61-273	264
C-61-488	630
C-62-367	221

Lot 896

C-61-277	517
C-61-279	217
C-61-280	611
C-61-397	305
C-61-459	341
C-61-461	380
C-62-872	229
C-64-69	364

Lot 897 (p. 78)

C-61-281	545
C-62-872	229
C-64-69	364

Lot 898 (p. 23)

C-61-284	632
C-61-286	516
C-61-287	590
C-61-300	534
C-61-304	527
C-61-305	553
C-61-308	419
C-61-309	418
C-61-310	419
C-61-311	419
C-61-312	419
C-61-313	419
C-61-465	542
C-61-489	637
C-61-491	648
C-62-307	256
C-62-872	229

Lot 899 (p. 78)

C-61-460	279

Lot 1945 (pp. 60, 61, 191)

C-61-485	680
1945:1–6	60

Lot 1950

part of Group 6
in addition:

C-61-240	254
C-62-275	664

Lot 1952

C-62-874	391

Lot 1953

C-61-475	298
C-61-478	74
C-62-254	588
C-62-277	672
C-62-278	378
C-62-279	669
C-62-283	626
C-62-284	620
C-62-293	587
C-62-294	583
C-62-295	585
C-62-943	302
C-62-944	331

Lot 1954

C-62-296	581

Lot 1955

C-62-258	**623**
C-62-301	**317**
C-62-304	**223**
C-62-305	**635**
C-62-306	**552**
C-62-307	**256**

Lot 1961

C-61-478	**74**

Lot 1962

C-62-317	**505**

Lot 1964

C-62-321	**365**
C-65-496	**360**

Lot 1965

C-61-462	**354**
C-62-322	**344**
C-62-325	**593**
C-64-69	**364**

Lot 1966

C-73-58	**633**

Lot 1969

C-62-257	**605**

Lot 1977

C-62-255	**539**

Lot 1982

part of Group 6
in addition:

C-62-345	**17**[24]
C-62-346	**17**[24]

Lot 1985 (pp. 23, 24, 33, 78, 82)

C-62-256	**525**
C-62-261	**595**
C-62-271	**626**
C-62-348	**520**
C-62-350	**556**
C-62-351	**584**
C-62-352	**589**
C-62-353	**416**
C-62-354	**628**
C-62-356	**417**
C-62-357	**415**
C-62-358	**415**
C-62-362	**663**
C-62-363	**322**

C-62-364	**230**
C-62-365	**234**
C-62-367	**221**
C-62-368	**221**
C-62-370	**262**
C-62-371	**225**
C-62-372	**247**
C-62-373	**662**
C-62-374	**414**
C-62-685	**560**
C-62-692	**233**
C-62-696	**486**
C-62-699	**555**
C-62-700	**558**
C-62-706	**529**
C-62-713	**530**
C-62-716	**415**
C-62-720	**490**
C-62-880	**616**
C-62-938	**213**
C-62-939	**236**
C-62-940	**220**
C-62-946	**206**

Lot 1988 (pp. 33, 78)

C-62-692	**233**
C-62-722	**272**
C-62-723	**528**
C-62-730	**235**
C-62-731	**216**
C-62-733	**222**
C-62-738	**420**
C-62-743	**540**
C-62-755	**661**
C-62-947	**228**

Lot 1989 (p. 82)

C-62-756	**249**
C-62-758	**519**
C-62-760	**270**
C-62-761	**210**
C-62-762	**239**

Lot 1990

Group 2

Lot 1991 (pp. 24, 33[82], 65, 82)

C-62-259	**569**
C-62-260	**596**
C-62-364	**230**
C-62-772	**443**
C-62-773	**401**

C-62-774	**533**
C-62-778	**515**
C-62-779	**488**
C-62-780	**487**
C-62-781	**421**
C-62-782	**482**
C-62-783	**445**
C-62-784	**611**
C-62-786	**629**
C-62-788	**509**
C-62-789	**510**
C-62-790	**513**
C-62-793	**265**
C-62-795	**567**
C-62-799	**575**
C-62-804	**268**
C-62-805	**523**
C-62-813	**526**
C-62-817	**564**
C-62-820	**592**
C-62-821	**573**
C-62-826	**604**
C-62-827	**537**
C-62-828	**618**
C-62-830	**532**
C-62-831	**531**
C-62-832	**541**
C-62-836	**643**

Lot 1993

C-62-264	**591**
C-62-265	**568**
C-62-841	**221**
C-62-843	**320**
C-62-849	**574**
C-62-851	**511**
C-62-852	**315**
C-62-854	**596**
C-62-945	**601**

Lot 2000

C-62-262	**559**
C-62-864	**561**

Lot 2003

C-62-872	**229**

Lot 2009

C-64-35	**316**
C-64-37	**458**
C-64-446	**377**

Lot 2010

C-61-228	**334**

Lot 2011

C-64-44	**424**
C-64-45	**576**

Lot 2012

C-64-47	**512**
C-64-48	**582**
C-64-59	**258**
C-64-60	**664**
C-64-61	**250**
C-64-402	**423**
C-65-442	**237**
C-65-444	**319**

Lot 2013

C-61-478	**74**
C-64-65	**374**
C-64-66	**596**

Lot 2021

C-61-228	**334**

Lot 2026

C-64-91	**600**
C-64-312	**329**

Lot 2035

C-64-69	**364**

Lot 2038

C-64-75	**309**
C-64-475	**642**
C-73-58	**633**

Lot 2040

C-75-281	**444**

Lot 2042

C-61-167	**271**
C-64-186	**617**
C-64-404	**242**
C-64-432	**674**

Lot 2044 (p. 1[4])

C-64-77	**571**

Lot 2046 (p. 84[5])

C-62-763	**23**
C-64-69	**364**
C-64-312	**329**
C-64-401	**313**

C-65-42	**45**
C-65-526	**231**

Lot 2048

C-64-65	**374**
C-64-69	**364**

Lot 2049

C-61-228	**334**
C-64-474	**668**

Lot 2050

C-61-228	**334**

Lot 2051

C-64-424	**251**
C-64-442	**307**

Lot 2052

C-64-207	**356**

Lot 2057

C-72-241	**328**

Lot 2060

C-64-76	**514**

Lot 2063 (p. 61)

C-64-224	**333**
2063:1	61

Lot 2066

C-64-477	**359**

Lot 2067

C-61-478	**74**
C-64-475	**642**

Lot 2074 (p. 78)

C-64-216	**211**
C-64-472	**661**

Lot 2075

C-64-429	**489**
C-64-431	**639**
C-72-241	**328**

Lot 2079

C-64-405	**503**

Lot 2083 (p. 78)

C-64-471	**661**

Lot 2087

C-64-207	**356**
C-64-447	**491**

Lot 2088

C-62-692	**233**

Lot 2089

C-64-473	**670**

Lot 2090

C-64-473	**670**

Lot 2091 (p. 78)

Lot 2092

C-62-762	**239**

Lot 2094

C-62-755	**661**
C-64-407	**280**
C-64-476	**275**
C-68-201	**342**

Lot 2106

C-62-762	**239**

Lot 2107 (p. 191)

C-61-485	**680**
C-64-439	**347**
C-64-468	**678**

Lot 2110 (pp. 26[72], 36, 78)

C-61-462	**354**
C-64-399	**340**
C-64-400	129[8]
C-64-407	**280**
C-64-476	**275**
C-72-245	**433**
2110:1	36[97]
2110:2	26[72], 36[97]
2110:3	26[72], 36[97]

Lot 2111
part of Group 6

Lot 2140

C-64-476	**275**

Lot 2141 (p. 78)

C-61-480	**330**
C-64-188	**290**
C-64-399	**340**
C-64-417	129[8]

Lot 2142

C-61-480	**330**
C-64-467	**375**
C-64-476	**275**

Lot 2143

C-61-480	**330**
C-64-208	**296**
C-73-58	**633**

Lot 2144

C-64-467	**375**
C-64-476	**275**

Lot 2145

C-61-462	**354**

Lot 2150

C-64-199	**614**
C-64-411	**209**
C-64-430	**207**

Lot 2151 (p. 191[35])

C-64-200	**612**
C-64-201	**613**
C-64-410	**379**

Lot 2152

C-61-480	**330**
C-64-213	**370**
C-64-217	**483**
C-64-219	**295**
C-64-221	**671**
C-64-222	**631**
C-64-225	**297**
C-64-226	**287**
C-64-396	**285**
C-64-398	136
C-64-399	**340**
C-64-440	**357**
C-65-499	**276**
C-65-523	**299**

Lot 2155

C-61-228	**334**

Lot 2156

C-61-228	**334**
C-61-463	**226**
C-61-464	**312**
C-64-196	**269**
C-64-223	**215**
C-64-408	**259**
C-65-481	**80**

Lot 2157

C-61-480	**330**

Lot 2161

C-64-422	**624**

Lot 2163

C-64-192	**358**

Lot 2164 (p. 191[37])

Lot 2165

C-64-478	**339**

Lot 2169 (p. 191[34])

2169:1	**675**

Lot 2170

C-64-226	**287**
C-64-409	**366**

Lot 2171

C-64-438	**325**

Lot 2172

C-71-238	**368**

Lot 2173

C-65-499	**276**

Lot 2177

C-64-197	**308**

Lot 2178

C-64-226	**287**
C-64-409	**366**

Lot 2183

C-65-499	**276**

Lot 2185

C-65-499	**276**

Lot 2186 (p. 78)

Lot 2188

C-64-191	**570**

Lot 2196

C-65-545	**328**

Lot 2198

C-65-545	**328**

Lot 2204

C-61-228	**334**

Lot 2210

C-61-480	**330**
C-65-491	**287**
C-65-615	**352**
C-70-596	**673**

Lot 2212

C-64-312	**329**

Lot 2216 (p. 78)

Lot 2217

C-62-730	**235**
C-65-38	**261**

Lot 2220

C-73-58	**633**

Lot 2225 (p. 78)

Lot 2230 (pp. 78, 84, 126[2])

C-62-364	**230**
C-64-440	**357**
C-65-492	**263**
C-65-493	**572**
C-65-494	126[2]

Lot 2235 (p. 1)

Lot 2236 (p. 1)

Lot 2238 (p. 1)

Lot 2239 (p. 191[37])

C-65-292	**437**
C-65-501	**274**

Lot 2240 (p. 191[35])

C-64-414	**246**
C-65-30	**599**
C-65-569	**606**
C-65-639	**681**

Lot 2242

2242:1	

Lot 2244

C-64-476	**275**

Lot 2245

C-65-36	**610**

Lot 2247 (p. 191[35])

C-61-228	**334**
C-65-31	**615**
C-65-32 a	**608**
C-65-33	**615**
C-65-34	**620**
C-65-501	**274**

Lot 2249 (p. 18[31])
part of Group 6
in addition:

C-64-440	**357**
C-65-291	**292**
C-65-548	**602**
C-73-360	**323**

Lot 2250
part of Group 6
in addition:

C-61-475	**298**
C-65-499	**276**
C-73-355	**354**

Lot 2253

C-72-241	**328**

Lot 2259

C-64-226	**287**

Lot 2260
Group 3

Lot 3206

C-65-291	**292**
C-65-481	**80**
C-65-646	**461**
C-68-201	**342**

Lot 3207

C-65-292	**437**
C-68-201	**342**

Lot 3209 (p. 192[39])

C-65-292	**437**

Lot 3210 (p. 192[39])

Lot 3211 (p. 192[39])

Lot 3215 (p. 191[38])

C-65-293	**497**
3215:1	**677**

Lot 3217
Group 8

3217:1	74

Lot 3220 (p. 108)

C-65-563	**192**

Lot 3222 (pp. 108[8], 46[150])

C-64-226	**287**
C-65-32 b	**608**
C-65-297	**644**
C-65-307	**521**
C-65-309	**478**
C-65-458	**266**
C-65-481	**80**
C-65-509	**26**
C-65-522	**300**
C-65-579	**507**
C-72-196	**214**

3222:1	46[150]
3222:2	10[8]

Lot 3223

C-65-303	**462**
C-65-645	**460**
C-65-647	**463**

Lot 3226 (p. 108)

C-65-563	**192**
C-72-196	**214**

Lot 3227 (p. 63)

C-65-313	**371**
C-65-525	**454**
C-65-653	**495**
3227:1	63

Lot 3228 (pp. 12[14], 26, 56, 108, **506**)

C-65-315	**397**
C-65-567	**201**
C-65-577	**506**
C-65-610	**492**
C-65-621	**399**
C-65-622	**398**
C-65-623	**400**
C-65-624	**453**
C-65-625	**436**
C-65-626	**494**
C-65-627	**434**
C-65-628	**404**
C-65-629	**448**
C-65-630	**479**
C-65-631	**477**
3228:1	55

Lot 3229

C-65-312	**327**

Lot 3230

Group 11

3230:1–14	**108**
3230:15	34[89]

Lot 3231 (pp. 55, 63)

C-65-488	**447**
3231:1	63
3231:2	55

Lot 3232

C-65-487	**452**

Lot 3233 (pp. 58, 108)

C-65-565	**194**

C-65-644	**459**
3233:1	58
3233:2	58

Lot 3410

C-65-319	**472**
C-65-609	**473**

Lot 3411

C-65-324	**667**

Lot 4344

C-75-320	**661**

Lot 4347 (**382**)

C-64-478	**339**
C-65-167	129[8]
C-65-417	**360**
C-65-511	**499**
C-65-521	136
C-65-613	**363**

Lot 4348

C-62-755	**661**
C-65-481	**80**
C-65-614	**343**

Lot 4349

C-65-169	**390**
C-65-450	**293**
C-65-451	**208**
C-65-452	**321**
C-65-453	**318**
C-65-648	**498**

Lot 4350

C-65-170	**607**
C-65-458	**266**

Lot 4351 (p. 26[71])

Group 4

4351:1	87[9]

Lot 4352

C-61-463	**226**
C-65-168	**603**
C-65-457	**232**
C-65-460	**267**
C-65-481	**80**

Lot 4355

part of Group 6

in addition:

C-65-171	**413**

Lot 4356	
part of Group 6	
in addition:	
C-65-519	**260**
C-65-520	**227**
Lot 4359 (p. 1)	
Lot 4362	
C-68-201	**342**
Lot 4363	
C-65-446	**218**
C-65-447	**219**
Lot 4367	
C-65-543	**598**
C-75-320	**661**
Lot 4369	
part of Group 6	
Lot 4370	
C-65-459	**224**
Lot 4372	
C-73-357	**255**
Lot 4377	
C-65-175	**625**
C-65-522	**300**
Lot 4380 (p. 191[34])	
Lot 4382 (**382**)	
Lot 4385	
C-64-226	**287**
C-65-512	**252**
C-65-541	136
Lot 4387	
C-65-465	**496**
Lot 4391	
C-64-226	**287**
C-65-414	**324**
C-65-419	**314**
C-65-424	**362**
Lot 4393	
C-65-642	**636**
Lot 4394	
C-65-412	**351**
Lot 4398 (p. 78)	

Lot 4403	
C-65-449	**241**
Lot 4404	
C-65-438	**655**
C-65-498	**435**
C-65-611	**348**
C-65-612	**349**
Lot 4405	
C-65-469	**609**
Lot 4408	
C-64-35	**316**
C-65-442	**237**
C-65-444	**319**
C-65-445	**204**
C-65-526	**231**
Lot 4409	
C-65-439	**363**
C-65-440	**294**
C-65-441	**282**
C-65-506	**294**
C-65-507	**281**
Lot 4411	
C-65-477	**248**
Lot 4417	
C-65-656	**495**
Lot 4421	
C-65-518	**346**
Lot 4434	
C-61-236	**365**
C-65-429	**289**
C-65-649	**661**
Lot 4435	
C-65-432	**289**
Lot 4440	
C-64-219	**295**
C-65-423	**346**
Lot 4450	
C-65-526	**231**
Lot 4458	
C-65-410	**474**
C-65-422	**425**
C-65-499	**276**

Lot 4460
C-65-472	**244**
C-65-473	**469**

Lot 4461
C-65-442	**237**
C-73-357	**255**

Lot 4473
C-65-417	**360**

Lot 4474
C-64-440	**357**
C-64-478	**339**
C-65-427	**284**
C-65-499	**276**
C-65-523	**299**
C-68-201	**342**

Lot 4475
C-64-226	**287**
C-65-167	**129**[8]
C-65-434	**291**
C-65-496	**360**

Lot 4476
C-65-421	**440**

Lot 4477
C-64-226	**287**
C-65-499	**276**
C-65-654	**345**

Lot 4478
C-65-448	**306**
C-65-576	**641**

Lot 4479
C-65-532	**645**

Lot 4480 (p. 77)
C-65-530	**657**
C-65-532	**645**

Lot 4481
C-65-529	**393**

Lot 4482 (p. 74)
C-65-474	**652**
C-65-475	**647**
C-65-476	**386**
C-65-529	**393**
C-65-531	**656**
C-65-533	**646**
4482:1	74

Lot 4483
C-64-397	**395**

Lot 4488
C-65-499	**276**

Lot 4491
C-64-418	**366**

Lot 5613
C-65-611	**348**
C-68-218	**245**
C-68-244	**73**
C-68-349	**619**

Lot 5615
C-68-200	**497**

Lot 5618 (p. 192[39])

Lot 5620 (p. 75)
C-68-304	**658**

Lot 5624
C-68-200	**497**

Lot 5625 (pp. 63, 75)
C-68-304	**658**
C-69-314	**382**
C-69-315	**666**
5625:3	63
5625:4–6	75

Lot 5635 (p. 47)
C-69-265	**466**
5635:1	47

Lot 5639
C-68-305	**597**

Lot 5640
C-69-253	**650**

Lot 5643
C-68-201	**342**

Lot 5648 (p. 63)
5648:3	63

Lot 5652
C-64-410	**379**

Lot 5658
C-68-198	**253**

Lot 5692
C-68-339	**353**

Lot 5693
   C-68-244   **73**

Lot 5695 (p. 72)
     5695:1   72

Lot 5719
   C-68-350   **665**

Lot 6181 (pp. 36, 63, 74[247])
   C-69-313   **481**
     6181:1   36
     6181:2 36[94], 74[247]
     6181:3 36[94], 55

Lot 6182
   C-69-264   **439**
   C-69-297   **464**
   C-69-298   **651**
   C-69-314   **382**

Lot 6189
   C-69-297   **464**
   C-69-314   **382**
   C-69-315   **666**

Lot 6191 (p. 191[38])
     6191:1   **676**

Lot 6193
   C-69-79   **654**

Lot 6198
   C-69-180   **292**

Lot 6199
   C-65-291   **292**
   C-65-614   **343**
   C-68-201   **342**
   C-69-182   **292**
   C-69-302   **311**

Lot 6205 (p. 63)
   C-69-262   **412**
   C-69-263   **446**
     6205:1   63
     6205:6   52[170]

Lot 6206 (pp. 46, 74[243])
     6206:1   52[170]
     6206:2   55
     6206:3   74[243]
     6206:5   46

Lot 6208 (p. 43[134])
   C-69-186   **387**

   C-69-266   **455**
   C-69-267   **441**
   C-69-268   **450**

Lot 6214
   C-64-440   **357**
   C-65-522   **300**

Lot 6215
   C-61-236   **365**
   C-61-474   **331**
   C-69-185   **238**
   C-69-299   **288**

Lot 6217
   C-69-270   **402**
   C-69-271   **441**

Lot 6219
   C-64-440   **357**
   C-69-320   **493**

Lot 6231
   Group 1

Lot 6232 (p. 79[1])

Lot 6501 (p. 191[34])

Lot 6503
   Group 9

Lot 6508
   C-70-203   **277**
   C-70-204   **304**

Lot 6511
   C-70-237   **485**

Lot 6516
   C-70-392   **438**
   C-70-393   **384**

Lot 6638 (p. 191[33])

Lot 6640 (p. 28)
   C-70-366   **405**
   C-70-597   **406**
   C-70-598   **407**
   C-70-599   **409**
   C-70-600   **408**

Lot 6642 (p. 191[37])
     6642:1   **679**

Lot 6643
     6643:1   52

Lot 6656

C-70-352	**372**
C-70-367	**350**
C-70-368	**338**
C-70-369	**337**

Lot 6712

Group 10

Lot 6713 (p. 105[22])

C-71-176	**185**

Lot 6715 (p. 105[22])

C-71-176	**185**
C-71-177	**188**

Lot 6716 (pp. 56, 105[22])

C-71-181	**186**

Lot 6719 (p. 105[22])

C-71-181	**186**

Lot 6720 (p. 61)

6720:1	61

Lot 6722 (pp. 19[42], 105[22])

C-71-181	**186**
6722:2	19[42]

Lot 6723 (pp. 63, 74[245])

C-71-170	**480**
C-71-171	**403**
C-71-173	**660**
C-71-174	**467**
C-71-175	**411**
6723:4	74
6723:5	74[245]
6723:6	63

Lot 6826 (p. 91)

C-71-87	**410**
C-71-88	**653**
C-71-137	**456**

Lot 6827 (p. 91)

C-64-226	**287**
C-71-87	**410**
C-71-137	**456**

Lot 6828

C-62-722	**272**

Lot 6829

C-71-569	**212**

Lot 6830 (p. 78)

Lot 6832 (p. 78)

Lot 6838 (pp. 26[72], 43[132])

C-69-299	**288**
C-71-136	**449**
6838:1	43[132]
6838:2	26[72]

Lot 6839 (p. 78)

Lot 6840 (p. 78)

Lot 6841

C-69-299	**288**

Lot 6842

C-64-69	**364**

Lot 6845

C-71-570	129[8]

Lot 6847

C-61-241	**283**

Lot 6941 (p. 1[4])

Lot 72-111

C-72-195	**640**

Lot 72-121

C-65-429	**289**

Lot 72-122

C-73-58	**633**

Lot 72-128 (pp. 63, 91)

C-61-228	**334**
C-72-222	**457**
72-128:1	63

Lot 72-129 (pp. 78, 91)

C-72-216	**441**
C-72-217	**410**
C-72-254	**289**

Lot 72-134 (pp. 78, 91)

C-72-215	**392**
C-72-221	**464**

Lot 72-139 (pp. 78, 91)

C-72-218	**410**
C-72-219	**442**
C-72-220	**457**

Lot 72-140 (p. 91)

Lot 72-207

C-64-476	**275**

Lot 72-208

C-72-241	**328**
72-208:1	**(623)**

Lot 72-209

C-72-244	**240**

Lot 73-96

C-73-28	**286**

Lot 73-99

C-73-28	**286**

Lot 73-100

C-73-99	**301**

Lot 73-101

73-101:1	**(667)**

Lot 73-102

C-64-404	**242**
C-72-241	**328**
C-73-260	**310**
C-73-359	**422**

Lot 73-107

C-65-444	**319**

Lot 73-115

C-73-316	**465**

Lot 73-116

C-73-305	**383**
C-73-307	**659**
C-73-316	**465**

Lot 73-118

C-73-302	**622**

Lot 73-121 (p. 78)

Lot 73-130

C-61-279	**217**
C-73-357	**255**

Lot 73-134

C-73-306	**367**
C-73-356	**336**

Lot 73-137

C-62-692	**233**
C-65-442	**237**
C-73-360	**323**

Lot 73-138

C-64-69	**364**
C-73-358	**638**

Lot 73-139

C-61-475	**298**
C-73-58	**633**
C-73-59	**332**
C-73-358	**638**

Lot 73-141

C-62-947	**228**
C-70-596	**673**

Lot 75-248 (p. 78)

C-64-431	**639**
C-65-38	**261**
C-72-241	**328**
C-75-320	**661**

Lot 75-249

75-249:1	**(609)**

Lot 1980-129

1980-129:1	45[148]
1980-129:2	58[196]
1980-129:3	45[148]
1980-129:4	72
1980-129:5	72

INDEX I: GENERAL INDEX

SACRIFICE 87, 96, 129[10], **354**
satyr **82, 120, 159, 191, 308, 312, 316, 321, 326, 334**
scarab 87
siren **206, 212, 213, 228, 230, 251, 256, 262, 267,**
  269, 126, **280, 320, 377, 595**
snake **213, 245, 297**
sphinx 10, 53, **26, 27, 212, 213, 215, 218, 232, 233,**
  239, 240, 246, 259, 262, 263, 265, 268, 269, 282,
  135[22], **315, 367, 377, 627**
steer **22.** *See also* bull; cow
Sthenoi 129[9], **287l, 287m**
strainer 66, 68, **644**

TEMPLE, REPRESENTATION OF **290**
Thapsos class 2[10]

thorn decoration 36, **497**
thymiaterion 24, 61
tile 84, 87, 89, 96[15], 101
torch 129[8], **292, 293, 295**
tray 66, 68, **330, 642**
tripod **220, 287d**
triskeles **461**

WARPING 72
warrior 53, 111, **257, 274, 322, 328, 364**
wheat **295, 399, 400, 454**
winged boot, shoe **335**
winged bust **279**
women (see female figures)

INDEX II: DECORATIVE SCHEMES, GRAFFITI, AND DIPINTI

INDEX III: FINDSPOTS AND PROVENIENCES

CORINTH, SANCTUARY OF DEMETER AND KORE (see also Lot List)

altar 82
boundaries 1
buildings and rooms
  B. *See* P–Q:24
  Ca. *See* L–M: 28
  D. *See* R:23–24
  D (Pit). *See* R:17–18
  Da. *See* M–N:20–26
  E. *See* P–Q:26
  Ga. *See* M–N:20–26
  Ha. *See* L:26–27
  J. *See* N–O:25–26
  Ja. *See* K–L:25–26
  K:23 (Ra) 78
  K–L:23–24 (Ma) 47^{159}
  K–L:24–25 (Ka) 33, 38, 78, **431, 432**
  K–L:25–26 (Ja) 78
  Ka. *See* K–L:24–25
  L. *See* N–O:24–25
  L:26–27 (Ha) 78
  L–M:28 (Ca) 19^{42}, 48, 61, 74, 74^{245}, 105
  M:16–17 (Northwest Stucco Building or Northwest Building) 12, 46^{150}, 47, 61, 107–108
  M:21–22 (U–V) 43, 78
  M–N:19 (P), 36, 37, 47, 47^{159}, 74^{247}
  M–N:20–26 (Da, Ga) 43^{132}, 73, 78
  M–N:25–26 (Cistern Building) 19, 68, 72, 77
  Ma. *See* K–L:23–24
  N:21–22 38, 78
  N–O:17–18 101
  N–O:22–23 17^{25}, 78
  N–O:24–25 (L) 17^{25}, 78
  N–O:25–26 (J) 58^{193}, 78
  N–P:20–25 (Trapezoidal Stoa) 18^{31}, 91, 96, 136
  O–P:19–20 191, 191^{38}
  P. *See* M–N:19
  P–Q:24 (B) 23, 78
  P–Q:26 (E) 78, 84–85, 126^2
  R:17–18 (Pit D) 191^{34}
  R:23–24 (D) 17, 22, 23, 24, 33, 64, 65, 78, 81–82, 111
  R–S:21–22 191^{34}

S–T:16–17 191, 191^{37}
S–T:21–22 (Theater) 1, 103–104
T–U:19 (Mosaic Building) 136
U–V. *See* M:21–22
cisterns
  N:26 (cistern 1965-1) 3^{19}, 19
  cistern 1971-1 105^{22}
Groups 5–6
  Pit A (pit 1961:2), Q:25 (Group 5) 23, 26^{72}, 67, 89–90, 96, 101
  Pit B (pit 1961:1), P:24–25 (Group 7) 24, 34, 36^{97}, 38, 63, 67, 68, 96–100, 101, **175**
  Pit E (pit 1965:3), O–P:22 (Group 4) 2, 23, 24, 26^{71}, 67, 85, 87–88, 89, 96, 101
  pottery deposits
    N–O:17–18 (Group 8) 24, 38, 61, 63, 67, 68, 74, 101–103
    Q:26 (Group 3) 17, 23, 24, 36^{98}, 68, 73, 84–87, 89
    R:21 (Group 1) 1, 17, 67, 79–81, 104, 111
    S–T:21 (Group 9) 12, 24, 25^{64}, 34, 38, 50, 58, 59, 61, 63, 101, 103–105
  pottery fills
    L–M:28 (Group 10) 2, 34, 49, 63, 105–106, 107
    M:16–17 (Group 11) 2, 34, 58, 63, 67, 68, 107–109
    N–P:20–25 (Group 6) 18^{31}, 24, 34, 36^{97}, 63, 67, 68, 74, 91–96
    R:23–24 (Group 2) 2, 23, 68, 81–84, 111
road 1
terrace
  Lower 1, 2, 14^{19}, 20, 36, 45, 49, 69, 77, 101, 105, 136
  Middle 1, 61, 64, 77, 84^5, 136
  Upper 1, 79, 104, 136, 191
wall 1 **544, 549**
wall 13 84^5
wall 36 foundation trench 17^{25}
wall 46 191^{34}
wall 205, robbing trench 191^{37}
wall 245, foundation trench 33, **427–430**
well 1961-11 191

CORINTH, BUILDINGS AND AREAS OUTSIDE THE SANCTUARY OF DEMETER AND KORE

NON-CORINTHIAN PROVENIENCES

INDEX IV: PAINTERS, POTTERS, AND WORKSHOPS

PLATES

PLATE 1

a. Group 1

b. Group 7

c. Group 3

d. Group 3, detail

PLATE 2

a. Group 4, pit covered

b. Group 4, pit uncovered

c. Group 4, detail

PLATE 3

b. Group 8

c. Group 9

a. Group 5

PLATE 4

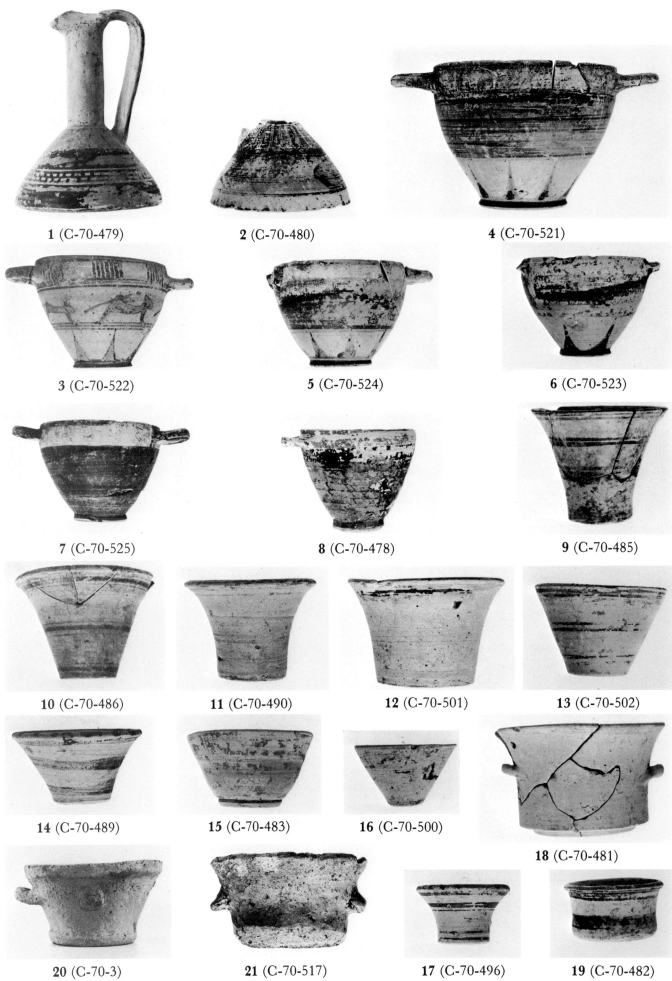

1 (C-70-479) 2 (C-70-480) 4 (C-70-521)

3 (C-70-522) 5 (C-70-524) 6 (C-70-523)

7 (C-70-525) 8 (C-70-478) 9 (C-70-485)

10 (C-70-486) 11 (C-70-490) 12 (C-70-501) 13 (C-70-502)

14 (C-70-489) 15 (C-70-483) 16 (C-70-500)

18 (C-70-481)

20 (C-70-3) 21 (C-70-517) 17 (C-70-496) 19 (C-70-482)

1:2

PLATE 5

22 (C-62-764)

23 (C-62-763)

24 (C-62-948)

25 (C-62-769)

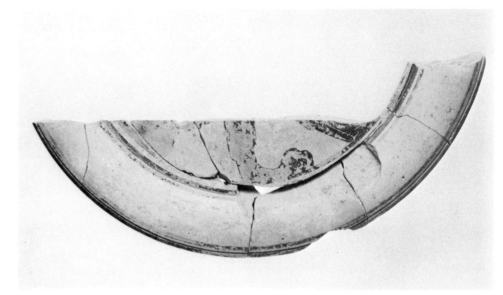

26a (C-62-770)

29 (C-62-768)

27 (C-62-272)

28, side A (C-62-766)

28, side B (C-62-766)

30 (C-62-771)

32 (C-62-767)

1:2

PLATE 6

GROUP 3

33 (C-65-126)

34 (C-65-127)

35 (C-65-124)

36 (C-65-123)

37 (C-65-122)

38 (C-65-580)

39 (C-65-581)

40 (C-65-119)

1:2

41 (C-65-121)

42 (C-65-120)

43 (C-65-117)

44 (C-65-125)

45 (C-65-42)   46 (C-65-41)

47 (C-65-500)

48 (C-65-128)

49 (C-65-650)

1:2

PLATE 8

GROUP 4

50 (C-65-174)

50, top view

52 (C-65-172)

54 (C-65-173)

55 (C-65-583)

56 (C-65-584)

57 (C-65-586)

58 (C-65-585)

59 (C-65-587)

60 (C-65-588)

1:2

62 (C-61-388)

61 (C-61-227)

63 (C-61-226)

64 (C-61-390)

66 (C-61-392)

67 (C-61-393)

68 (C-61-394)

70 (C-61-396)

71 (C-61-387)

1:2

PLATE 10

GROUP 6

73b (C-68-244 b)

73a (C-68-244 a)

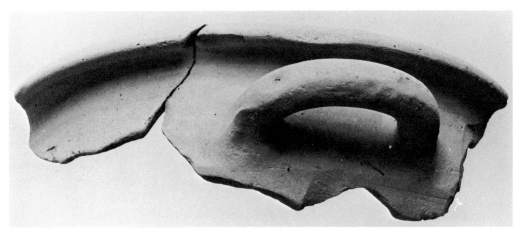

75 (C-65-652)

76 (C-65-557)

77 (C-65-558)

78 (C-65-517)

79 (C-65-549)

1:2

74b (C-61-478 b)

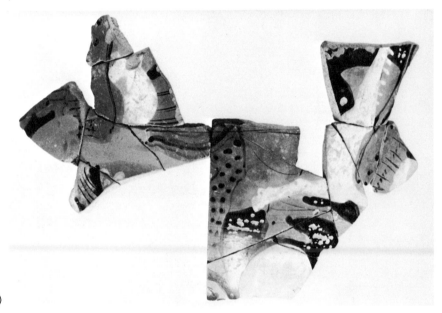

74c (C-61-478 c)

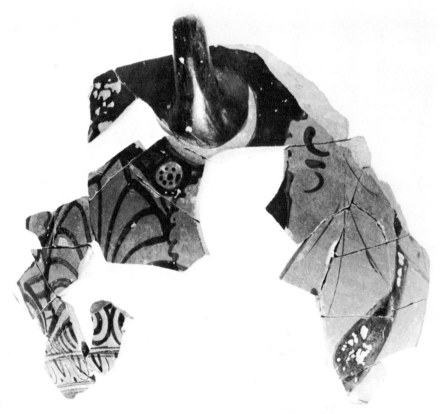

74d (C-61-478 d)

1:2

PLATE 12   GROUP 6

80 (C-65-481)

83 (C-64-421)

82 (C-64-423)

81 (C-62-337)

84 (C-65-535)

85 (C-65-550)   **86** (C-65-551)   **87** (C-65-539)

1:2

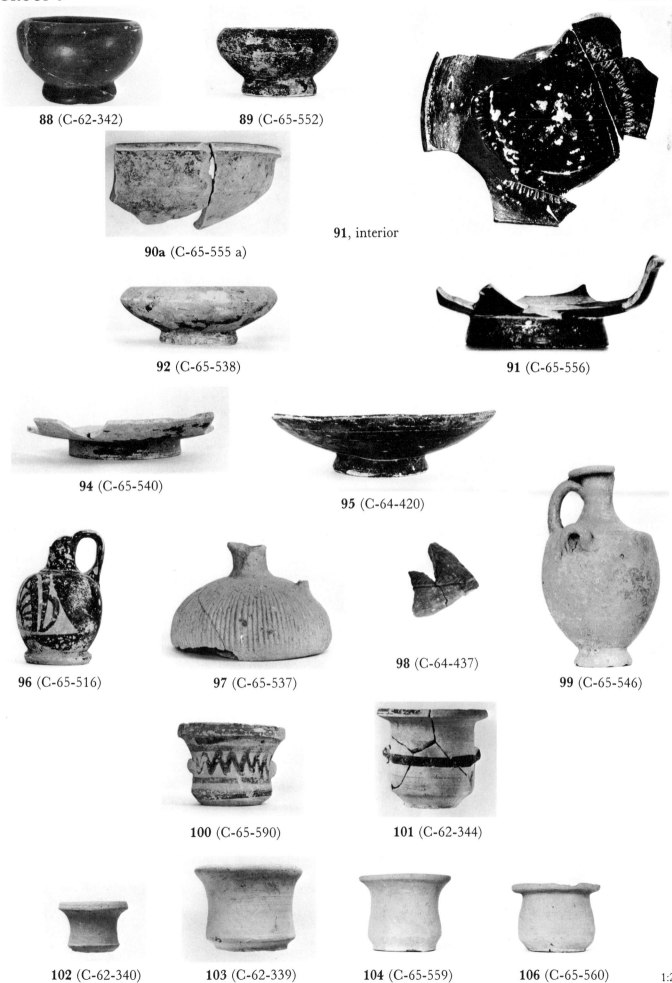

88 (C-62-342)   **89** (C-65-552)

90a (C-65-555 a)

91, interior

92 (C-65-538)   **91** (C-65-556)

94 (C-65-540)

95 (C-64-420)

98 (C-64-437)

96 (C-65-516)   **97** (C-65-537)   **99** (C-65-546)

100 (C-65-590)   **101** (C-62-344)

102 (C-62-340)   **103** (C-62-339)   **104** (C-65-559)   **106** (C-65-560)   1:2

PLATE 14

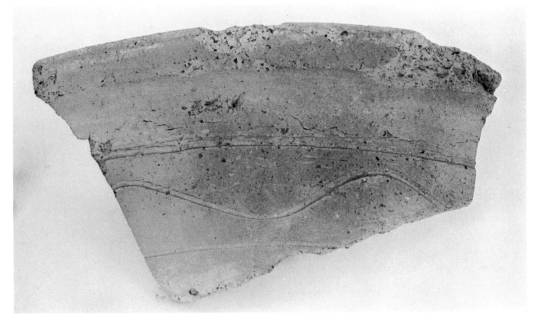

107 (C-62-347)

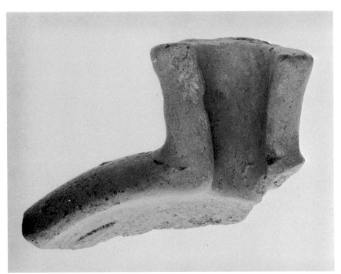

108 (C-64-436)

109 (C-64-433)

111 (C-65-547)

110 (C-64-434)

112 (C-64-435)

1:2 (**107** 1:3)

113 (C-61-427)

114 (C-61-209)

115 (C-61-426)

116 (C-61-206)

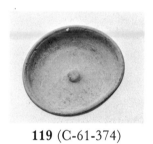

119 (C-61-374)

117 (C-61-418)

118 (C-61-417)

121 (C-61-467)

122 (C-61-208)

120 (C-61-470)

123 (C-61-421)

1:2

PLATE 16

124 (C-61-213)

125 (C-61-423)

126 (C-61-384)

127 (C-61-450)

128 (C-61-215)

129 (C-61-381)

130 (C-61-383)

131 (C-61-425)

132 (C-61-424)

133 (C-61-382)

134 (C-61-469)

135 (C-61-214)

136 (C-61-451)

137 (C-61-211)

1:2

138 (C-61-447)

139 (C-61-210)

140 (C-61-422)

141 (C-61-379)

143 (C-61-377)

144 (C-61-445)

146 (C-61-433)

148 (C-61-440)

149 (C-61-446)

150 (C-61-207)

152 (C-61-492)

153 (C-61-386)

1:2

PLATE 18   GROUP 8

154 (C-65-602)

155 (C-65-603)

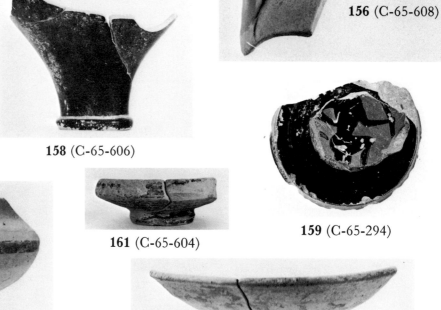

156 (C-65-608)

157 (C-65-592)

158 (C-65-606)

161 (C-65-604)

159 (C-65-294)

160 (C-65-607)

162 (C-65-591)

163 (C-65-599)   **164** (C-65-600)   **165** (C-65-601)

166 (C-65-593)

167 (C-65-594)

168 (C-65-595)   **169** (C-65-596)   **170** (C-65-598)   **171** (C-65-597)

1:2

GROUP 8

172 (C-65-651)

173 (C-70-563)

174 (C-70-564)

175 (C-70-565)

176 (C-70-520)

GROUP 9

177 (C-70-518)

178 (C-70-519)

179 (C-70-566)

180 (C-70-567)

181 (C-70-568)

182 (C-70-212)

183 (C-70-213)

184 (C-70-214)

1:2

PLATE 20

GROUP 10

186 (C-71-181)

187 (C-71-585)

188 (C-71-177)

190 (C-71-180)

1:2

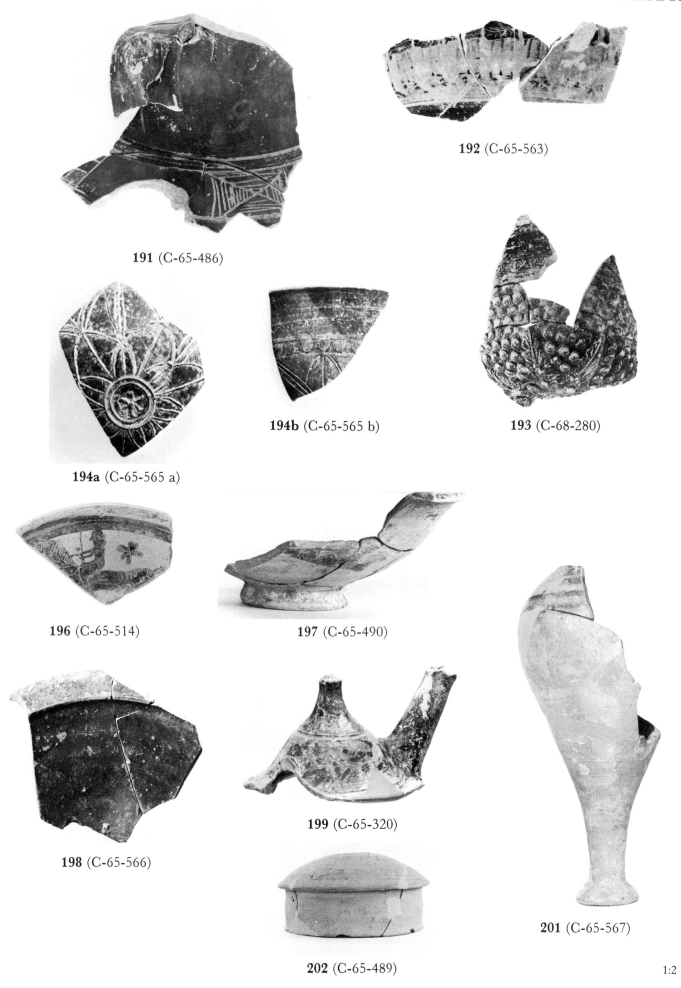

191 (C-65-486)

192 (C-65-563)

194a (C-65-565 a)

194b (C-65-565 b)

193 (C-68-280)

196 (C-65-514)

197 (C-65-490)

198 (C-65-566)

199 (C-65-320)

201 (C-65-567)

202 (C-65-489)

1:2

PLATE 22

203 (C-61-175)

204 (C-65-445)

205 (C-61-414)

206a (C-62-946 a)

206b (C-62-946 b)

207 (C-64-430)

208 (C-65-451)

209 (C-64-411)

210 (C-62-761)

211 (C-64-216)

212 (C-71-569)

213 (C-62-938)

214c (C-72-196 c)

214a (C-72-196 a)

214b (C-72-196 b)

1:2

216 (C-62-731)

215 (C-64-223)

218 (C-65-446)

217 (C-61-279)

221b (C-62-368)

219 (C-65-447)

221a (C-62-367)

221c (C-62-841)

220 (C-62-940)

221 (1:1)

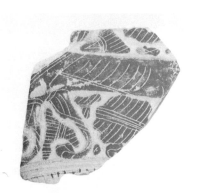

223 (C-62-304)

222 (C-62-733)

224 (C-65-459)

225 (C-62-371)

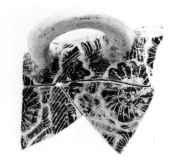

226 (C-61-463)

227 (C-65-520)

228 (C-62-947)

1:2

PLATE 24

CORINTHIAN BLACK FIGURE

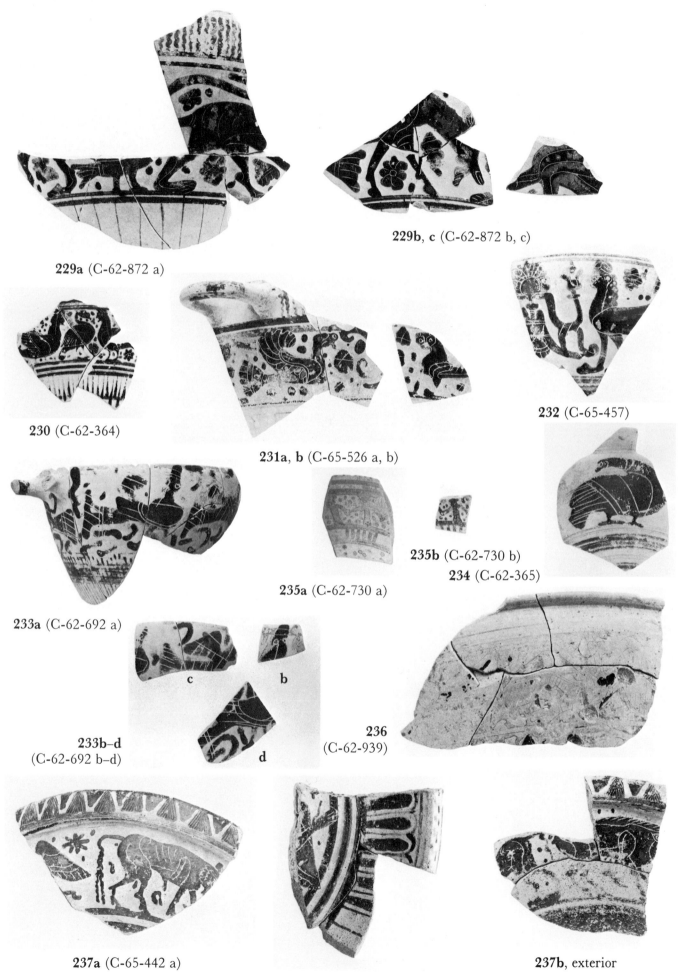

229a (C-62-872 a)

229b, c (C-62-872 b, c)

230 (C-62-364)

231a, b (C-65-526 a, b)

232 (C-65-457)

233a (C-62-692 a)

235a (C-62-730 a)

235b (C-62-730 b)

234 (C-62-365)

233b–d
(C-62-692 b–d)

c

b

d

236
(C-62-939)

237a (C-65-442 a)

237b, interior (C-65-442 b)

237b, exterior

1:2

238 (C-69-185)

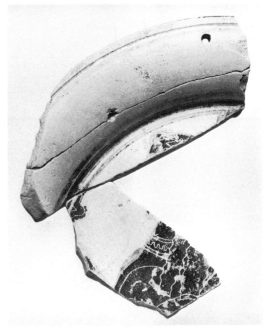

239a (C-62-762 a)

240 (C-72-244)

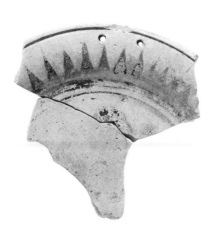

242, floor (C-64-404)

242, undersurface

241 (C-65-449)

243 (C-61-235)

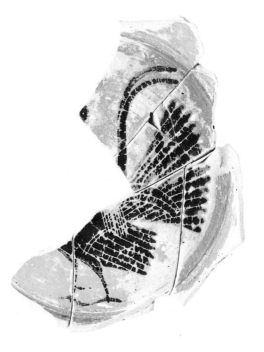

244 (C-65-472)

1:2

PLATE 26

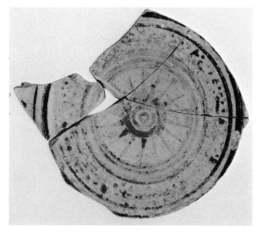

247, floor (C-62-372)

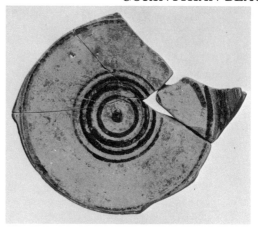

247, undersurface

246 (C-64-414)

245, floor (C-68-218)

248 (C-65-477)

245, undersurface

249 (C-62-756)

250 (C-64-61)

251 (C-64-424)

252, top view
(C-65-512)

252, handle

253 (C-68-198)

1:2 (**249**, **250** 1:1)

254 (C-61-240)

255 (C-73-357)

256a (C-62-307 a)

256b (C-62-307 b)

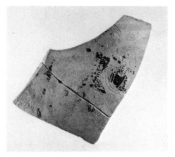

257 (C-61-176)

258 (C-64-59)

259 (C-64-408)

261, shoulder (C-65-38)

260 (C-65-519)

261, lower wall

1:2 (260 1:1)

PLATE 28   CORINTHIAN BLACK FIGURE

262 (C-62-370)

263 (C-65-492)

264 (C-61-273)

266 (C-65-458)

267 (C-65-460)

270 (C-62-760)

265 (C-62-793)

268 (C-62-804)

269 (C-64-196)

271 (C-61-167)

272b (C-62-722 b)

273 (C-61-262)

272a (C-62-722 a)

274 (C-65-501)

1:2 (**265**, **270**, **274** 1:1)

275a (C-64-476 a)

275c (C-64-476 c)

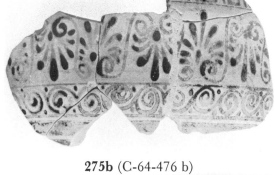

275b (C-64-476 b)

277 (C-70-203)

278 (C-61-202)

276c
(C-65-499 c)

276b (C-65-499 b)

276a (C-65-499 a)

1:2

PLATE 30

279 (C-61-460)

279, detail

280a (C-64-407 a)

281 (C-65-507)

282 (C-65-441)

284 (C-65-427)

283a (C-61-241 a)

285 (C-64-396)

1:2

PLATE 31

286b (C-73-28 b)

286a (C-73-28 a)

287m (C-64-226 c)

287k (C-64-226 m)

287l
(C-64-226 g)

287j (C-64-226 h)

287i
(C-64-226 d)

287h (C-64-226 a)

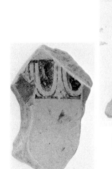

287d (C-64-226 j)

287e (C-64-226 e)

287c (C-64-226 n)

287b (C-64-226 b+l)

287f (C-64-226 f)

287a (C-65-491)

288d (C-69-299 c)

288c (C-69-299 d)

288b (C-69-299 a)

288a (C-69-299 b)

1:2

PLATE 32 CORINTHIAN OUTLINE STYLE. SAM WIDE GROUP

289b (C-65-429)

289a (C-65-432)

290 (C-64-188)

291 (C-65-434)

292a, interior

292a (C-69-182)

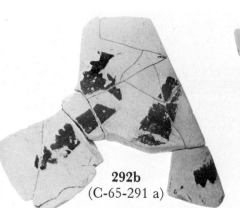

292b
(C-65-291 a)

292d (C-69-180)

292c (C-65-291 c)

CORINTHIAN OUTLINE STYLE

293 (C-65-450)

294a (C-65-440)
294b (C-65-506)

295 (C-64-219)

296 (C-64-208)

297 (C-64-225)

SAM WIDE GROUP

1:2

298e
(C-61-475 b)

298d (C-61-475 e)   **298c** (C-61-475 a)

298b (C-61-475 c)

298a (C-61-475 d)

299 (C-65-523)

300c (C-65-522 b)

300b (C-65-522 c)

300a (C-65-522 a)

301 (C-73-99)

302 (C-62-943)

304a, b (C-70-204 b, a)

303a (C-73-327)

303b (C-73-328)

1:2

PLATE 34

NON-CORINTHIAN BLACK FIGURE

305a (C-61-397 a)

306 (C-65-448)

305b (C-61-397 b)

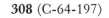

307 (C-64-442)

308 (C-64-197)

309 (C-64-75)

310 (C-73-260)

311 (C-69-302)

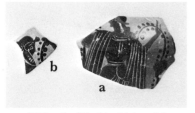

312a, b (C-61-464 a, b)

313b (C-64-401 b)

313c (C-64-401 c)

313a (C-64-401 a)

1:2

314 (C-65-419)

315 (C-62-852)

316 (C-64-35)

317 (C-62-301)

318, interior (C-65-453)

318, inner foot

319, interior (C-65-444)

319, exterior

320 (C-62-843)

321 (C-65-452)

322 (C-62-363)

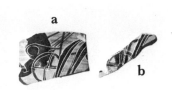

323a, b (C-73-360 a, b)

324 (C-65-414)

325 (C-64-438)

1:2 (**320–322** 1:1)

PLATE 36   NON-CORINTHIAN BLACK FIGURE

326 (C-73-259)

327 (C-65-312)

328d (C-72-241 b)

328c, detail (C-72-241 c)

328a (C-65-545)

328b (C-72-241 d)

328c, additional joins (C-72-241 a+c)

329 (C-64-312)

1:2 (**327** 1:1)

331b (C-61-474)

331a (C-62-944)

332 (C-73-59)

1:2

330a (C-61-480 d)

333 (C-64-224)

330c (C-61-480 c)

330b (C-61-480 e)

330d (C-61-480 a)

View D

View C

View B

View A

PLATE 38

NON-CORINTHIAN RED FIGURE

e

f

334d (C-61-228 d)

334c (C-61-228 c)

334e, **f** (C-61-228 e, f)

334b (C-61-228 b)

335 (C-71-201)

334a (C-61-228 a)

336 (C-73-356)

337 (C-70-369)

338 (C-70-368)

341b, a top view (C-61-459 b, a)

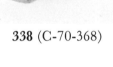

339c (C-64-478 c)

339b (C-64-478 b)   **340** (C-64-399)

341a, side view

339a (C-64-478 a)

1:2 (**337** 1:1)

342b (C-68-201 b)

343 (C-65-614)

344 (C-62-322)

342a (C-68-201 a)

345 (C-65-654)

347 (C-64-439)

346b (C-65-518)

346a (C-65-423)

349 (C-65-612)

350 (C-70-367)

348 (C-65-611)

351 (C-65-412)

352 (C-65-615)

353 (C-68-339)

1:1 (**342a, b, 343** 1:2)

PLATE 40											NON-CORINTHIAN RED FIGURE

354c, side A (C-73-355)

354a, sides A–B (C-61-462 a)

354b, side B (C-61-462 b)

354, side B, detail

354, side A, detail

355 (C-72-269)

356 (C-64-207)

354a–c, 356 1:2; **355** 1:1

357a (C-64-440 a)

357b (C-64-440 b)

357c (C-64-440 c)

360b, side A (C-65-417)

360a, side A (C-65-496)

360a, side B

358 (C-64-192)

359 (C-64-477)

361 (C-69-184)

362 (C-65-424)

1:2 (361, 362 1:1)

PLATE 42

363b, floor (C-65-613)

363a, floor (C-65-439)

363a, exterior

364a, exterior (C-64-69 a)

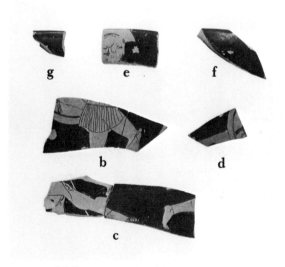

364b–g, exterior (C-64-69 b–g)

364a, interior

363 1:1; 364 1:2

365b, exterior (C-61-236 b)

365d–f, exterior (C-61-236 c–e)

365c, exterior (C-61-236 a)

365a, exterior (C-62-321)   **365a**, interior

366a (C-64-409 a)

367 (C-73-306)

368 (C-71-238)

369 (C-61-476)   **370** (C-64-213)

1:2 (**370** 1:1)

PLATE 44

372 (C-70-352)

373 (C-61-471)

376 (C-73-25)

379 (C-64-410)

380 (C-61-461)

380, top view

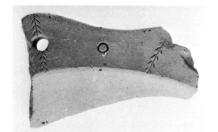

382 (C-69-314)

385 (C-61-429)

386 (C-65-476)

387 (C-69-186)

388 (C-61-154)

384 (C-70-393)

383 (C-73-305)

1:3 (**373**, **384**, **385** 1:2)

PLATE 45

389 (C-61-428)

391 (C-62-874)

392 (C-72-215)

393 (C-65-529)

394 (C-61-473)

395 (C-64-397)

396 (C-70-206)

398 (C-65-622)

399 (C-65-621)

401 (C-62-773)

403 (C-71-171)

404 (C-65-628)

405 (C-70-366)

406 (C-70-597)

407 (C-70-598)

1:3

PLATE 46   NON-FIGURED FINE WARES

408 (C-70-600)

409 (C-70-599)

410 (C-61-406)

412 (C-69-262)

411 (C-71-175)

413 (C-65-171)

414 (C-62-374)

415 (C-62-716)

417 (C-62-356)

419 (C-61-311)

421 (C-62-781)

423 (C-64-402)

424 (C-64-44)

425 (C-65-422)

427 (C-72-88)

430 (C-72-89)

432 (C-72-211)

433a (C-72-245 a)

435 (C-65-498)

436 (C-65-625)

434 (C-65-627)

1:3 (**413, 415, 417, 419, 423–425, 432** 1:2)

437a (C-65-292 a)

438 (C-70-392)

439 (C-69-264)

442 (C-72-219)

443 (C-62-772)

445 (C-62-783)

446 (C-69-263)

446, floor

447 (C-65-488)

448 (C-65-629)

450 (C-69-268)

451 (C-69-269)

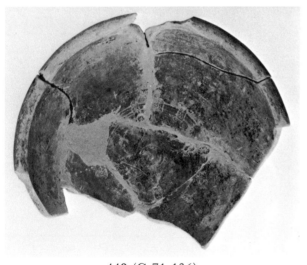

449 (C-71-136)

453 (C-65-624)

454 (C-65-525)

455 (C-69-266)

456 (C-71-137)

457 (C-72-220)

1:3 (**445, 449, 453, 455–457** 1:2)

PLATE 48   NON-FIGURED FINE WARES

458 (C-64-37)

459b (C-65-644 b)

460 (C-65-645)

b

a

461a, b (C-65-646 a, b)

463 (C-65-647)

459a (C-65-644 a)

462 (C-65-303)

465 (C-73-316)

466 (C-69-265)

467 (C-71-174)

469 (C-65-473)

472 (C-65-319)

474 (C-65-410)

475 (C-61-168)

476 (C-61-400)

480 (C-71-170)

481 (C-69-313)

477 (C-65-631)

478 (C-65-309)

1:3 (**458–463** 1:2)

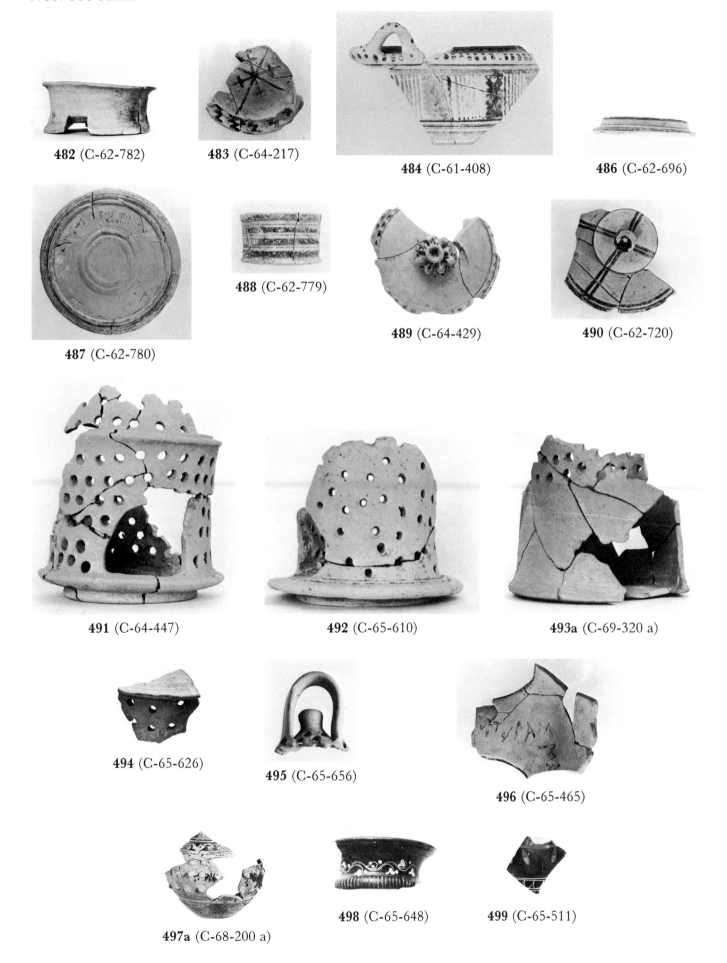

482 (C-62-782)

483 (C-64-217)

484 (C-61-408)

486 (C-62-696)

487 (C-62-780)

488 (C-62-779)

489 (C-64-429)

490 (C-62-720)

491 (C-64-447)

492 (C-65-610)

493a (C-69-320 a)

494 (C-65-626)

495 (C-65-656)

496 (C-65-465)

497a (C-68-200 a)

498 (C-65-648)

499 (C-65-511)

1:3 (**482**, **499** 1:2)

PLATE 50   MINIATURES

500 (C-61-256)

501 (C-61-203)

502 (C-73-320)

503 (C-64-405)

505 (C-62-317)

506 (C-65-577)

507 (C-65-579)

508 (C-61-193)

509 (C-62-788)

511 (C-62-851)

513 (C-62-790)

514 (C-64-76)

515 (C-62-778)

517 (C-61-277)

518 (C-61-238)

519 (C-62-758)

1:2

521 (C-65-307)

521, detail (1:1)

524 (C-61-242)

526 (C-62-813)

529 (C-62-706)

530 (C-62-713)

531 (C-62-831)

533 (C-62-774)

536 (C-61-245)

537 (C-62-827)

541 (C-62-832)

542 (C-61-465)

543 (C-61-156)

544 (C-61-298)

545 (C-61-281)

547 (C-61-403)

539 (C-62-255)

548 (C-61-219)

550 (C-61-165)

553 (C-61-305)

554 (C-61-229)

556 (C-62-350)

558 (C-62-700)

1:2

PLATE 52

MINIATURES

561 (C-62-864) **563** (C-61-407) **564** (C-62-817) **566** (C-61-259)

567 (C-62-795) **568** (C-62-265) **570** (C-64-191) **571** (C-64-77)

572 (C-65-493) **573** (C-62-821) **575** (C-62-799) **576** (C-64-45)

577 (C-61-405) **579** (C-61-191) **581** (C-62-296) **582** (C-64-48)

585 (C-62-295) **587** (C-62-293) **588** (C-62-254) **589** (C-62-352)

590 (C-61-287) **592** (C-62-820) **593** (C-62-325) **594** (C-69-103)

1:2

595 (C-62-261)

596 (C-62-260)

597 (C-68-305)

598 (C-65-543)

599 (C-65-30)   **600** (C-64-91)   **601** (C-62-945)   **602** (C-65-548)

612, back view (C-64-200)   **621**, back view (C-72-56)

604 (C-62-826)

603 (C-65-168)

605 (C-62-257)

1:2 (**603–605** 1:1)

PLATE 54

606 (C-65-569)

607 (C-65-170)

609 (C-65-469)

608 (C-65-32 a)

610 (C-65-36)

611 (C-62-784)

612 (C-64-200)

613 (C-64-201)

614 (C-64-199)

1:1

615 (C-65-33)

616 (C-62-880)

617 (C-64-186)

618 (C-62-828)

619 (C-68-159)

621 (C-72-56)

622 (C-73-302)

620 (C-65-34)

623 (C-62-258)

1:1 (618 1:2)

PLATE 56   HEADS

624 (C-64-422)

625b (C-65-175 b)

c   b   a

625a–c (C-65-175 a–c)

628 (C-62-354)

626 (C-62-271)

627 (C-61-190)

1:1 (**625a–c** 1:2)

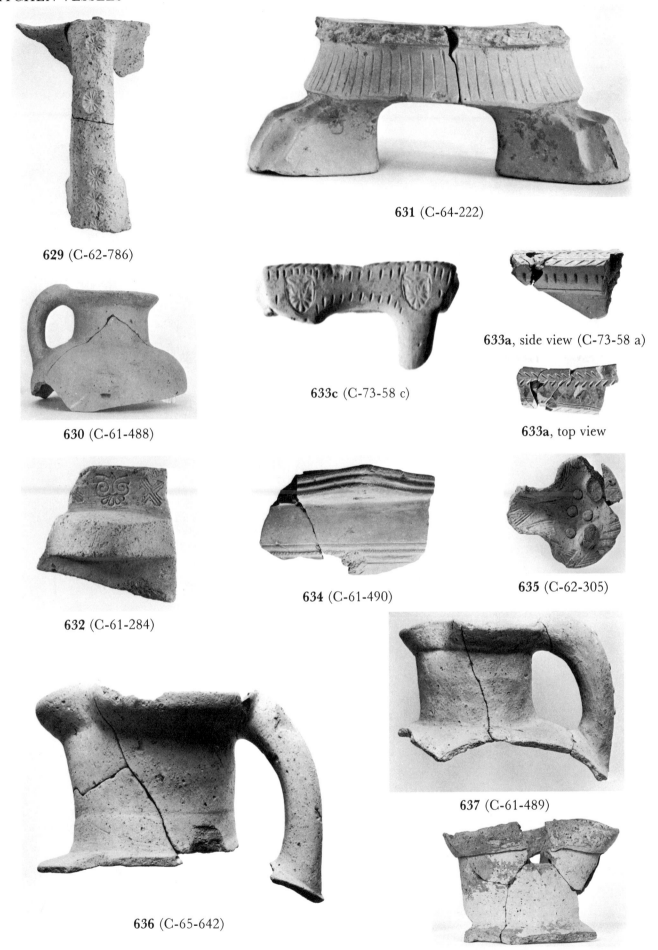

629 (C-62-786)

631 (C-64-222)

630 (C-61-488)

633c (C-73-58 c)

633a, side view (C-73-58 a)

633a, top view

632 (C-61-284)

634 (C-61-490)

635 (C-62-305)

636 (C-65-642)

637 (C-61-489)

638 (C-73-358)   1:3 (**632** 1:2)

PLATE 58

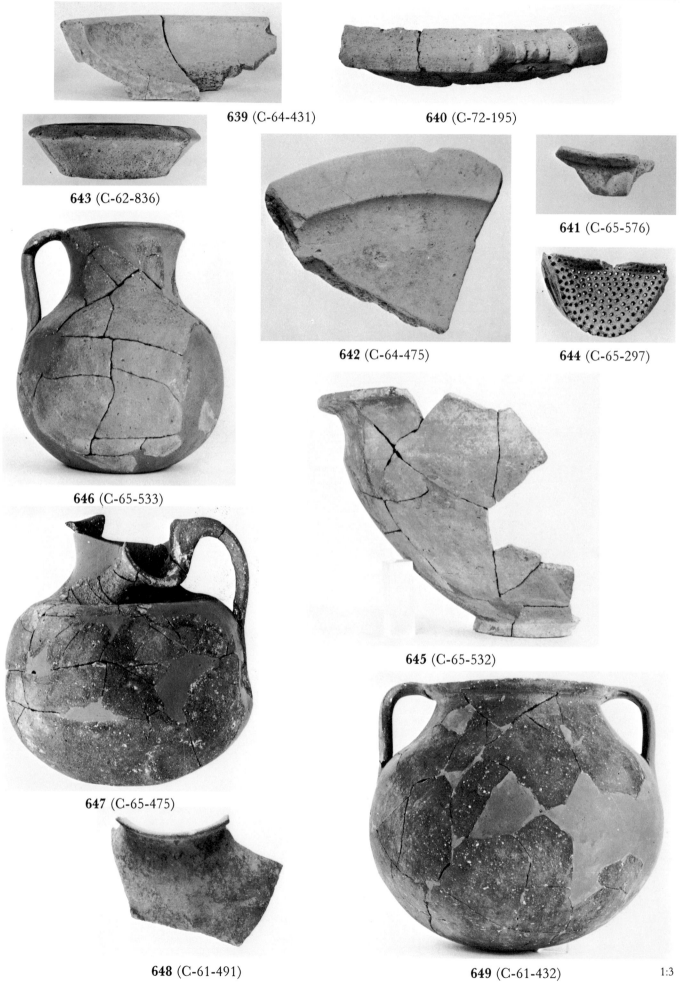

639 (C-64-431)

640 (C-72-195)

643 (C-62-836)

641 (C-65-576)

642 (C-64-475)

644 (C-65-297)

646 (C-65-533)

645 (C-65-532)

647 (C-65-475)

648 (C-61-491)

649 (C-61-432)

1:3

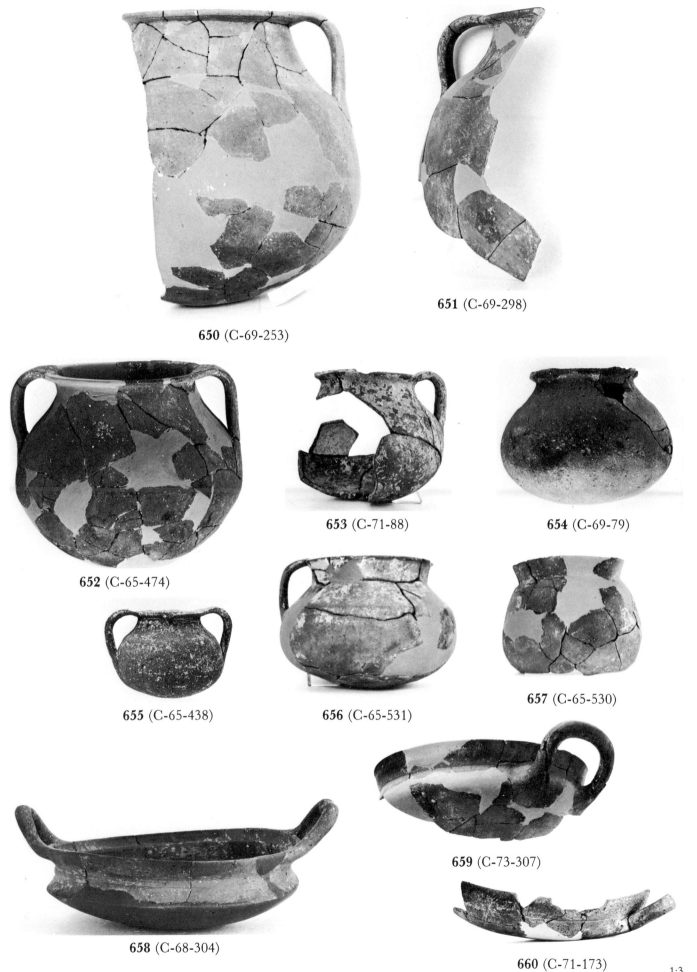

650 (C-69-253)

651 (C-69-298)

652 (C-65-474)

653 (C-71-88)

654 (C-69-79)

655 (C-65-438)

656 (C-65-531)

657 (C-65-530)

658 (C-68-304)

659 (C-73-307)

660 (C-71-173)

1:3

PLATE 60

661h, rim (C-64-472)

661e–g, shaft (C-75-320)

661d, shaft (C-65-649)

661c, shaft (C-64-471)

661a, base (C-62-755)

662 (C-62-373)

663 (C-62-362)

664 (C-64-60)

665 (C-68-350)

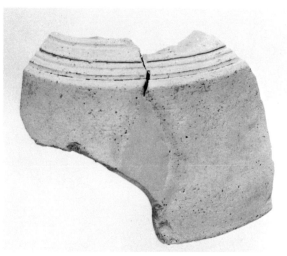

666 (C-69-315)

1:3 (**662** 1:2)

667 (C-65-324)

668 (C-64-474)

669 (C-62-279)

670 (C-64-473)

671 (C-64-221)

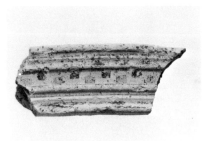

672 (C-62-277)

673 (C-70-596)

674 (C-64-432)

1:3

PLAN A

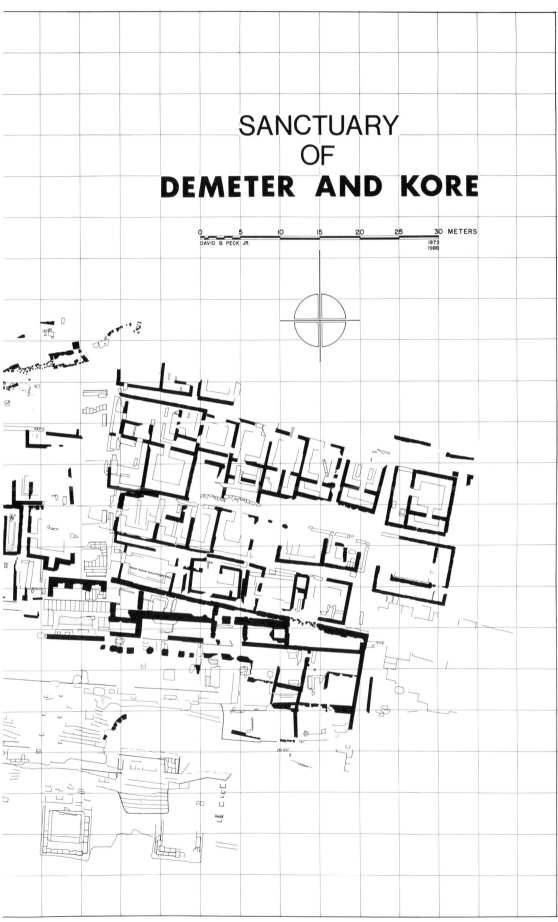

SANCTUARY
OF
DEMETER AND KORE

0   5   10   15   20   25   30 METERS

DAVID B. PECK JR.   1973
1988

18 19 20 21 22 23 24 25 26 27 28 29 30 31

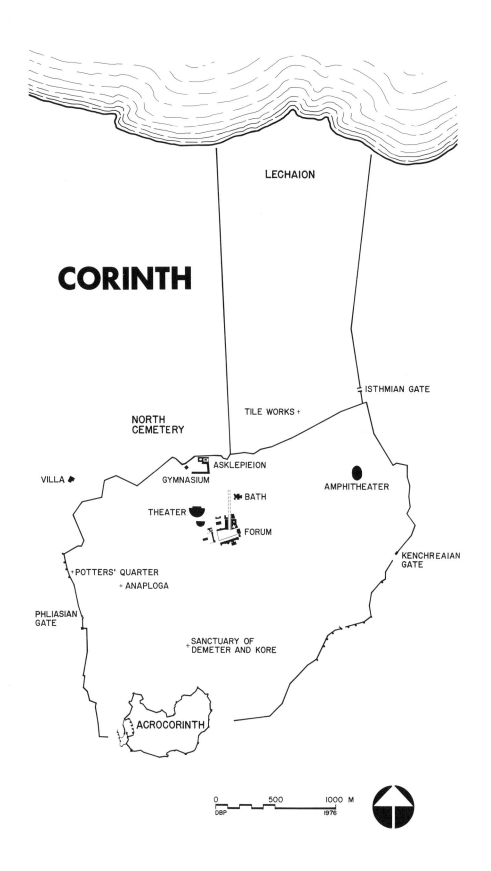

LECHAION

CORINTH

ISTHMIAN GATE

TILE WORKS +

NORTH
CEMETERY

ASKLEPIEION

VILLA

GYMNASIUM

AMPHITHEATER

BATH

THEATER

FORUM

KENCHREAIAN
GATE

+ POTTERS' QUARTER
+ ANAPLOGA

PHLIASIAN
GATE

+ SANCTUARY OF
DEMETER AND KORE

ACROCORINTH

0   500   1000 M
DBP   1976